Cardiovascul[illegible] 2000

Millennium Edition
(5th Edition)

Edited by:

Robert A. Kloner, MD, PhD
Yochai Birnbaum, MD

Studies Compiled by:

Robert A. Kloner, MD, PhD
Yochai Birnbaum, MD

Robert A. Kloner, MD, PhD
Director of Research
Heart Institute
Good Samaritan Hospital
Professor of Medicine
University of Southern California
Los Angeles, CA

Yochai Birnbaum, MD
Associate Director
Cardiac Intensive Care Unit
Department of Cardiology
Rabin Medical Center
Beilinson Campus
Petah-Tikva, Israel
Assistant Professor of Cardiology
Sackler Faculty of Medicine
Tel Aviv University
Tel Aviv, Israel

Dedicated to the memory of Philip Kloner

1925–1997

Cardiovascular Trials Review 2000, Millennium Edition, (5th Edition)

Editorial Director: Nancy Sharp, MA
Production Editor: Jennifer Duro
Graphic Designer: Susan Moore-Stevenson
President/Publishing Director: Sarah Howell
VP Group Publisher: Joanne Kalaka Adams
Founder: Louis Le Jacq

ISBN 1-929660-02-2

Printed in the United States of America.

Table of Contents

1. Acute Myocardial Infarction
a. Thrombolytic Therapy

b. PTCA vs Stenting vs Thrombolytic Therapy

c. Anticoagulation/Antiplatelet

d. Early vs Late Intervention After Acute Myocardial Infarction

g. Acute Treatment of Stroke

2. Unstable Angina/Non Q Wave Infarction

3. Stable Angina Pectoris and Silent Ischemia—Medical Therapy

4. Interventional Cardiology

a. PTCA or CABG vs Medical Therapy

b. PTCA vs CABG

c. PTCA vs Stenting vs Other Percutaneous Devices, IVUS Guided Stenting

d. Medical Therapy and Brachytherapy to Prevent Restenosis and/or Complications After Intracoronary Interventions or Occlusion After Coronary Artery Bypass Grafting

e. Other Therapy (Transmyocardial Laser Revascularization)

5. Hypertension

6. Congestive Heart Failure

7. Lipid Lowering Studies

8. Arrhythmia

9. Anticoagulation for Atrial Fibrillation

10. Deep Vein Thrombosis/Pulmonary Embolism

11. Coronary Artery Disease, Atherosclerosis, Prevention of Progression

12. Valvular Heart Disease

13. Preliminary Reports
a. Acute Myocardial Infarction

b. Unstable Angina, Non Q Wave Myocardial Infarction

c. Hypertension

d. Congestive Heart Failure

Page	Name	Acronym
1084	Outcomes of a Prospective Trial of IV Milrinone for Exacerbations of Chronic Heart Failure	OPTIME-CHF
1086	Prospective Randomized Amlodipine Survival Evaluation-2	PRAISE-2
1088	Warfarin/Aspirin Study of Heart Failure	WASH
1090	Levosimendan Infusion vs Dobutamine in Severe Congestive Heart Failure	LIDO
1092	CarvedilOL ProspEctive RaNdomIzed Cumulative Survival Trial	COPERNICUS
1093	SR MOXonidine for CONgestive Heart Failure	MOXON
1094	The Valsartan Heart Failure Trial	VAL-HeFT
1095	Intervention with Myocarditis and Acute Cardiomyopathy with IV Immunoglobulin	IMAC
1096	Beta blocker Evaluation of Survival Trial	BEST
1098	Inhibition of MetalloProteinase BMS-186716, Omipatrilat, in a Randomized Exercise and Symptom Study with Heart Failure	IMPRESS

e. Prevention of Progression of Coronary Artery Disease

Page	Name	Acronym
1102	Brachial Artery Ultrasound Normalization of Forearm Flow	BANFF
1103	Prospective, Randomized, Evaluation of Vascular Effects of Norvasc Trial	PREVENT
1105	The Simvastin/Enalapril Coronary Atherosclerosis Trial	SCAT
1107	Effects of Quinapril On Vascular ACE and Determinants of Ischemia	QUO VADIS
1108	Comparison of Amlodipine vs Enalapril to Limit Occurrences of Thrombosis	CAMELOT
	Norvasc for Regression of Manifest Atherosclerotic Lesions by Intravascular Sonagraphic Evaluation	NORMALISE
1110	Estrogen Replacement and Atherosclerosis trial	ERA
1112	Intracoronary Stenting and Antibiotic Regimen	ISAR
1114	Study to Evaluate Carotid Ultrasound Changes in Patients Treated with Ramipril and Vitamin E	SECURE
1116	Monotherapy Assessment of Ranolazine in Stable Angina	MARISA

f. Arrhythmia

g. Interventional Cardiology

h. Lipid Lowering Studies

i. Valvular Heart Disease

Introduction

The purpose of *Cardiovascular Trials Review 2000, The Millennium Edition* is to review those trials which have made a major impact on the practice of clinical cardiology within the last 10 years. We have included only studies that were published in English and concentrated mainly on publications that have appeared since 1990 and have studied either pharmacological or device therapy. The text is divided into major headings of diseases such as myocardial infarction and unstable angina. In general, we gave priority to prospective randomized trials with preference to multicenter studies and those that included several hundred patients. In this fourth edition, we have added over 190 new entries and concentrated on trials from 1998–2000.

The front section of the book concentrates on articles already in print. The preliminary reports section refers to studies that have been presented or discussed in abstract or other form at major cardiology meetings. Some of these studies are ongoing clinical trials. The Table of Contents lists studies by disease category. The Index at the back of the book lists acronyms alphabetically and the pages on which they can be found.

We truly have been amazed by the increasing number of new, large clinical trials in the literature. Since the early 90s there has been a virtual explosive growth in the number of these trials. A recent article by Cheng (*Am Heart J* 1999;137:726–765) listed over 2250 cardiology trials with acronyms. There were nearly 1000 new acronyms added since 1996!

Unfortunately, we were not able to include all studies in this text. There are many excellent studies, which may not appear in this book. However, a review of the trials included in this book should give the reader a flavor of the types and designs of major clinical trials that have influenced the practice of clinical cardiology.

We have tried to use only a minimal amount of abbreviations in the text: ACE-angiotensin converting enzyme; BP-blood pressure; CI-confidence interval; ECG-electrocardiogram; RR-relative risk; PCI-percutaneous coronary intervention; PTCA-percutaneous transluminal coronary angioplasty; CABG-coronary artery bypass graft; CHF-congestive heart failure; MI-myocardial infarction; LV-left ventricle; LVEF-left ventrcular ejection fraction; LDL-low density lipoprotein (cholesterol); HDL-high density lipoprotein (cholesterol); U-unit; hr-hour; min-minute; OR-odds ratio.

The drugs, indications for drugs, and drug dosages may or may not be approved for general use by the Food and Drug Administration (FDA). Physicians should consult the package inserts and/or Physicians' Desk Reference for drug indications, contraindications, side effects, and dosages as recommended.

Robert A. Kloner, MD, PhD — Los Angeles, June 2000
Yochai Birnbaum, MD

1. Acute Myocardial Infarction

a. Thrombolytic Therapy

GISSI

Gruppo Italiano per lo Studio della Streptochinasi nell'Infarto miocardico

Title	a. Effectiveness of intravenous thrombolytic treatment in acute myocardial infarction. b. Long term effects of intravenous thrombolysis in acute myocardial infarction: Final report of the GISSI study.
Authors	GISSI.
Reference	a. Lancet 1986;I:397-401. b. Lancet 1987;II:871-874.
Disease	Acute myocardial infarction.
Purpose	To evaluate the efficacy of intravenous streptokinase to reduce in-hospital and 1 year mortality in patients with acute myocardial infarction, and to define the time interval from onset of symptoms to therapy and that therapy is still effective.
Design	Randomized, open label, multicenter.
Patients	11,712 patients with suspected acute myocardial infarction ≤12 h of onset of symptoms, with ≥1 mm ST elevation or depression in any limb lead or ≥2 mm in any precordial lead. No age restriction.
Follow-up	1 year.
Treatment regimen	Streptokinase 1.5 million U IV over 1 h, or no treatment.
Additional therapy	According to normal practice. No restrictions.

GISSI

Gruppo Italiano per lo Studio della Streptochinasi nell'Infarto miocardico

(continued)

Results	a. 21 day course: Overall mortality was 13.0% in the control and 10.7% in the treated group (relative risk 0.81, 95% CI 0.72-0.90, p=0.0002). In patients treated within 3 h from onset of symptoms mortality was 12.0% and 9.2% for the control and streptokinase groups (RR 0.74, 95% CI 0.63-0.87, p=0.0005), while for those treated 3-6 h the mortality was 14.1% and 11.7%, respectively (RR 0.80, 95% CI 0.66-0.98, p=0.03). Treatment beyond 6 h did not result in a significant difference in mortality between the groups (14.1% vs 12.6%, p=NS, RR 0.87 for those treated 6-9 h; and 13.6% vs 15.8%, p=NS, RR 1.19 for those treated 9-12 h after onset of symptoms). Subgroup analysis revealed beneficial effects for streptokinase in patients with anterior and multisite infarction. However, patients with lateral infarctions or ST depression had a trend towards worse outcome with streptokinase than without (although without statistical significance). The incidence of anaphylactic shock and bleeding attributed to streptokinase were low. b. After 1 year, mortality was 17.2% in the streptokinase and 19.0% in the control group (RR 0.90, 95% CI 0.84-0.97, p=0.008). The difference in mortality was seen only in those treated within 6 h of onset of symptoms.
Conclusions	a. Streptokinase is a safe and effective therapy for patients with acute myocardial infarction treated within 6 h of onset of symptoms. b. The beneficial effects of streptokinase were still apparent after 1 year.

GISSI (10 year follow-up)

Gruppo Italiano per lo Studio della Sopravvivenza nell Infarto 1 Study

Title	Ten year follow-up of the first megatrial testing thrombolytic therapy in patients with acute myocardial infarction. Results of GISSI-1 study.
Authors	Franzosi MG, Santoro E, DeVita C, et al.
Reference	Circulation 1998; 98:2659-2665.
Disease	Acute myocardial infarction.
Purpose	To determine the outcome of single IV infusion of 1.5 million units of streptokinase in acute MI patients at 1 year.
Design	As per GISSI.
Patients	As per GISSI.
Follow-up	10 years.
Treatment regimen	As per GISSI.

GISSI (10 year follow-up)

Gruppo Italiano per lo Studio della Sopravvivenza nell Infarto 1 Study

(continued)

Results	Of 11,712 patients who originally entered the trial 5111 died by 10 years, with overall cumulative survival of 54%. Difference on survival produced by streptokinase was still significant at 10 years (by log rank test; p=0.02). The absolute benefit of streptokinase was 19 lives saved per 1000 patients treated; the estimated 10 year mortality rate was 45% in the streptokinase group and 46.9% in patients that received conventional therapy. Benefit was primarily obtained before hospital discharge. Patients receiving therapy within 1 and 3 hours had reduction of total mortality at hospital discharge, 1 year, and still present at 10 years. Patients receiving therapy within 1 hour showed slight although nonsignificant divergence of survival curves compared to controls following hospital discharge (90 lives saved per 1000 at 10 years vs 72 lives saved at hospital discharge).
Conclusions	IV streptokinase resulted in prolonged survival in acute myocardial infarct patients that was sustained for up to 10 years.

GISSI-Prevenzione Trial

Gruppo Italiano per lo Studio della Sopravvivenza nell'infarto miocardio

Title	Dietary supplementation with n-3 polyunsaturated fatty acids and vitamin E after myocardial infarction: Results of the GISSI-Prevenzione trial.
Authors	GISSI-Prevenzione Investigators.
Reference	Lancet 1999;354:447–455.
Disease	Acute myocardial infarction.
Purpose	To evaluate the effects of n-3 polyunsaturated fatty acids (n-3 PUFA), vitamin E, and their combination on mortality and morbidity after acute myocardial infarction.
Design	Randomized, two-by-two factorial, open label, multicenter.
Patients	11,324 patients, ≤3 months after myocardial infarction, with no contraindications to dietary supplements, overt heart failure, severe systemic disease, and congenital coagulation disorder.
Follow-up	42 months.
Treatment regimen	Randomization to n-3 PUFA (850 to 882 mg/d of eicosapentaenoic acid and docasahexenoic acid as ethyl esters) and to vitamin E 300 mg/d.
Additional therapy	Aspirin, ß-blockers, and ACE inhibitors were recommended.

GISSI-Prevenzione Trial

Gruppo Italiano per lo Studio della Sopravvivenza nell'infarto miocardio

(continued)

Results

2836 patients were randomized to n-3 PUFA alone, 2830 patients to vitamin E alone, 2830 to 3-n PUFA, and vitamin E, and 2828 patients to no supplement. The primary end point of death, nonfatal myocardial infarction or nonfatal stroke was reached by 12.6% of the patients assigned to 3-n PUFA vs 13.9% of the patients not receiving n-3 PUFA (relative risk [RR] 0.90; 95% CI 0.82–0.99; p=0.048). The combined end point of cardiovascular death, nonfatal myocardial infarction, and nonfatal stroke was reached by 9.7% and 10.8% of the patients receiving and not receiving n-3 PUFA, respectively (RR 0.89; 95% CI 0.80–1.01; p=0.053). Total mortality was 5.1% and 6.2% in patients receiving and not receiving n-3 PUFA (RR 0.86; 95% CI 0.76–0.97). Vitamin E was not effective. The primary end point of death, nonfatal myocardial infarction, and nonfatal stroke occurred in 12.9% and 13.6% of the patients receiving and not receiving vitamin E, respectively (RR 0.95; 95% CI 0.86–1.05), whereas the combined end point of cardiovascular death, nonfatal myocardial infarction, and nonfatal stroke occurred in 10.1% vs 10.3%, respectively (RR 0.98; 95% CI 0.87–1.10). However, using four way analysis, it was found that vitamin E was associated with lower cardiac death rate (RR 0.77; 95% CI 0.61–0.97), coronary death (RR 0.75; 95% CI 0.59–0.96), and sudden death (RR 0.65; 95% CI 0.48–0.89). Vitamin E did not have an additional benefit in patients receiving n-3 PUFA. At the end of the study 28.5% of the patients assigned to n-3 PUFA and 26.2% of the patients assigned to vitamin E had permanently stopped taking the study medication.

Conclusions

N-3 PUFA treatment for 3.5 years decreased the rates of death, nonfatal myocardial infarction, and nonfatal stroke in patients with recent myocardial infarction. In contrast, vitamin E was not effective in either patients not receiving or receiving n-3 PUFA. The effects of vitamin E on fatal cardiovascular events should be further investigated.

TIMI-1

Thrombolysis in Myocardial Infarction Trial (phase 1)

Title	Thrombolysis in Myocardial Infarction (TIMI) Trial, phase I: A comparison between intravenous tissue plasminogen activator and intravenous streptokinase. Clinical findings through hospital discharge.
Authors	Chesbero JH, Knatterud G, Roberts R, et al.
Reference	Circulation 1987;76:142-154.
Disease	Acute myocardial infarction.
Purpose	To compare two regimens of intravenous thrombolytic therapy: rt-PA and streptokinase.
Design	Randomized, double blind, multicenter.
Patients	290 patients with acute myocardial infarction <75 years old <7 hours from onset of symptoms with chest pain >30 min and ST elevation ≥0.1 mV in ≥2 contiguous leads. Patients with cardiogenic shock were excluded.
Follow-up	Coronary angiography before and 10, 20, 30, 45, 60, 75, 90 min, after onset of thrombolytic therapy and predischarge. Clinical visits at 6 weeks and 6 months.
Treatment regimen	Streptokinase 1.5 million units or placebo IV over 1 h, and rt-PA or placebo over 3 h (40, 20, and 20 mg in the 1st, 2nd and 3rd hours).
Additional therapy	Lidocaine (1–1.5 mg/kg bolus + infusion 2–4 μg/min) for >24 h; intracoronary nitroglycerin 200 μg; heparin 5000 U bolus and infusion 1000 U/h for 8–10 days. Aspirin 325 mg X3/d and dipyridamole 75 mg X3/d after heparin was stopped.

TIMI-1

Thrombolysis in Myocardial Infarction Trial (phase 1)

(continued)

Results

At 30 min after initiation of therapy 24% and 8% of the rt-PA and streptokinase treated patients achieved TIMI grade flow of 2 or 3 ($p<0.001$). At 90 min after initiation of therapy, 62% of the rt-PA and 31% of the streptokinase treated patients achieved TIMI grade flow of 2 or 3 ($p<0.001$). 44% and 22% of the rt-PA and streptokinase treated patients had patent arteries upon discharge ($p<0.001$). There was no difference in global or regional left ventricular function either in the pretreatment or predischarge study. Fever or chills occurred in 4% and 15% of the rt-PA and streptokinase groups ($p<0.01$). Death within 21 days occurred in 4% and 5% of the rt-PA and streptokinase groups. The reduction in circulating fibrinogen and plasminogen and the increase in plasma fibrin split products at 3 and 24 h were significantly more pronounced in the streptokinase treated patients ($p<0.001$). The occurrence of bleeding was comparable in the 2 groups (66% and 67% of the rt-PA and streptokinase, respectively).

Conclusions

Treatment with rt-PA resulted in more rapid reperfusion than streptokinase. However, there was no difference in either mortality, bleeding complications, or left ventricular function between the groups.

ISIS-2

International Study of Infarct Survival 2

Title	Randomized trial of intravenous streptokinase, oral aspirin, both, or neither among 17,187 cases of suspected acute myocardial infarction: ISIS-2.
Authors	ISIS-2 Collaborative Group.
Reference	Lancet 1988;II:349–360.
Disease	Acute myocardial infarction.
Purpose	To assess the efficacy of oral aspirin, streptokinase infusion, and their combination in the treatment of acute myocardial infarction.
Design	Randomized, double blind, 2X2 factorial, placebo controlled, multicenter.
Patients	17,187 patients with suspected acute myocardial infarction <24 h of onset of symptoms.
Follow-up	Maximum 34 months, median 15 months.
Treatment regimen	1. Streptokinase 1.5 million U over 1 h IV. 2. Aspirin 162.5 mg/d for 1 month. 3. Streptokinase 1.5 million U over 1 h IV + Aspirin 162.5 mg/d for 1 month. 4. Neither.
Additional therapy	No restrictions.

ISIS-2

International Study of Infarct Survival 2

(continued)

Results

5 week vascular mortality among the streptokinase and placebo treated patients was 9.2% and 12.0%, respectively (odds reduction: 25%, 95% CI 18-32%, p<0.00001). 5 week vascular mortality among the aspirin treated was 9.4% and for the placebo 11.8% (odds reduction: 23%, 95% CI 15-30%, p<0.00001). The combination of aspirin and streptokinase was better than either agent alone. 5 week vascular mortality among the streptokinase and aspirin treated patients was 8.0%, while it was 13.2% among those allocated to neither treatment (odds reduction: 42%, 95% CI: 34-50%). The odds reductions at treatment 0-4, 5-12, and 13-24 h after onset of symptoms were 35%, 16%, and 21% for streptokinase alone; 25%, 21%, and 21% for aspirin alone; and 53%, 32%, and 38% for the combination. Streptokinase was associated with excess bleeding requiring transfusion (0.5% vs 0.2%, p<0.001) and of cerebral hemorrhage (0.1% vs 0.0%, p<0.02). However, total strokes were similar (0.7% vs 0.8%). Aspirin reduced the rates of nonfatal reinfarction (1.0% vs 2.0%, p<0.00001) and nonfatal stroke (0.3% vs 0.6%, p<0.01) and was not associated with increased risk of cerebral or noncranial hemorrhages. Patients allocated to the combination therapy had fewer reinfarctions (1.8% vs 2.9%), strokes (0.6% vs 1.1%), and deaths (8.0% vs 13.2%) than those allocated to neither therapy. The difference in mortality produced by either aspirin, streptokinase, or their combination remained significant after 15 months of follow-up.

Conclusions

Aspirin and streptokinase independently reduced mortality in patients with acute myocardial infarction. The combination of the 2 drugs has a synergistic effect on mortality without increasing the rates of stroke.

AIMS

APSAC Intervention Mortality Study

Title	a. Effect of intravenous APSAC on mortality after acute myocardial infarction: Preliminary report of a placebo controlled clinical trial. b. Long term effects of intravenous anistreplase in acute myocardial infarction: Final report of the AIMS study.
Authors	AIMS Trial Study Group.
Reference	a. Lancet 1988;I;545-549. b. Lancet 1990;335:427-431.
Disease	Acute myocardial infarction.
Purpose	To compare survival up to 1 year in patients with acute myocardial infarction randomized to APSAC (anisoylated plasminogen streptokinase activator complex) or placebo.
Design	Randomized, double blind, placebo controlled, multicenter.
Patients	a. 1004 patients, age ≤70 years with acute myocardial infarction, ≥30 min pain, <6 h of onset of symptoms, ≥1 mm ST elevation in ≥2 limb leads or >2 mm in >2 precordial leads. b. 1258 patients, same criteria, including the first 1004 patients.
Follow-up	1 year.
Treatment regimen	APSAC 30 U or placebo IV over 5 min.

AIMS

APSAC Intervention Mortality Study

(continued)

Additional therapy	IV heparin started 6 h after initiation of therapy, warfarin for ≥3 months. Other medications according to common practice.Timolol 10 mg/d for 1 year if not contraindicated.
Results	a. 30 day mortality was 12.2% on placebo and 6.4% on APSAC (47% reduction of mortality, 95% CI 21-65%, p=0.0016). Percentage reduction of mortality with APSAC was similar whether therapy was started 0-4 or 4-6 h after onset of symptoms. b. 30 day mortality was 12.1% on placebo and 6.4% on APSAC (50.5% reduction of mortality, 95% CI 26-67%, p=0.0006). 1 year mortality was 17.8% on placebo and 11.1% on APSAC (42.7% reduction of mortality, 95% CI 21-59%, p=0.0007). Major cardiovascular complications (shock, cardiac arrest, rupture, ventricular septal defect, and ventricular fibrillation) occurred in 12.3% and 16.7% of the APSAC and placebo groups, respectively (p=0.03).
Conclusions	Intravenous APSAC within 6 h of onset of symptoms reduced mortality in acute myocardial infarction.

ASSET

Anglo-Scandinavian Study of Early Thrombolysis

Title	a. Trial of tissue plasminogen activator for mortality reduction in acute myocardial infarction. Anglo-Scandinavian Study of early Thrombolysis (ASSET). b. Effects of alteplase in acute myocardial infarction: 6 month results from the ASSET study.
Authors	Wilcox RG, von der Lippe G, Olsson CG, et al.
Reference	a. Lancet 1988;II:525–530. b. Lancet 1990;335:1175–1178.
Disease	Acute myocardial infarction.
Purpose	To evaluate the efficacy of tissue plasminogen activator versus placebo in reduction of mortality in acute myocardial infarction.
Design	Randomized, double blind, placebo controlled, multicenter.
Patients	a. 5009 patients. b. 5013 patients, age 18–75 years, with suspected acute myocardial infarction within 5 h of onset of symptoms. No ECG criteria were required.
Follow-up	6 months.
Treatment regimen	Tissue plasminogen activator (t-PA) or placebo 10 mg IV bolus, 50 mg infusion over 1 h, and then 40 mg over 2 h.
Additional therapy	IV heparin 5000 U bolus, and infusion of 1000 U/h for 21 h.

ASSET

Anglo-Scandinavian Study of Early Thrombolysis

(continued)

Results	a. One month mortality was 7.2% and 9.8%, in the t-PA and placebo groups (a relative reduction of 26%, 95% CI 11-39%, p=0.0011). Bleeding (major+minor) and major bleeding occurred in 6.3% and 1.4% of the t-PA, and 0.8% and 0.4% of the placebo groups, respectively. The incidence of stroke was similar (1.1% and 1.0%). There was no difference in recurrent infarction or development of heart failure rates. In those with abnormal ECG on entry, t-PA was associated with 24.5% relative reduction in 1 month mortality (8.5% vs 11.2%, 95% CI 9-37%). b. 6 month mortality rate was 10.4% in the t-PA and 13.1% in the placebo group (relative reduction of risk 21%, 95% CI 8-32%, p=0.0026). 6 month mortality for patients with proven infarction was 12.6% and 17.1%, respectively (relative reduction of risk 26.3%, 95% CI 14-38%). The effect was similar for anterior and inferior infarctions. However, t-PA did not reduce cardiac readmissions, reinfarctions, development of heart failure, angina, or death beyond 1 month. 12 month mortality (for 4230 patients) was 13.2% and 15.1% for t-PA and placebo group (p<0.05).
Conclusions	t-PA therapy within 5 h of onset of symptoms, compared to placebo, reduced mortality sustained to 1 year, but not the rates of recurrent infarction, angina, or development of heart failure.

GISSI-2

Gruppo Italiano per lo Studio della Streptochinasi nell'Infarto miocardico 2

Title	a. GISSI-2:A factorial randomized trial of alteplase vs streptokinase and heparin vs no heparin among 12,490 patients with acute myocardial infarction. b. In-hospital mortality and clinical course of 20,891 patients with suspected acute myocardial infarction randomized between alteplase and streptokinase with or without heparin.
Authors	a. GISSI b. The International Study Group.
Reference	a. Lancet 1990;336:65-71. b. Lancet 1990;336:71-75.
Disease	Acute myocardial infarction.
Purpose	To compare the efficacy of intravenous streptokinase and tissue plasminogen activator (t-PA) for the treatment of acute myocardial infarction, and to evaluate the effects of adding heparin therapy to aspirin on the incidence of recurrent ischemia.
Design	Randomized, open label, 2X2 factorial, multicenter.
Patients	a. 12,381 patients. b. 20,768 patients (including 12,490 from the GISSI-2). All patients had chest pain + ST elevation ≥ 1mm in any limb lead and/or ST ≥2 mm in any precordial lead, within 6 h of onset of symptoms. No age limit.
Follow-up	In-hospital course, predischarge echocardiography.

GISSI-2

Gruppo Italiano per lo Studio della Streptochinasi nell'Infarto miocardico 2
(continued)

Treatment regimen	a. Streptokinase 1.5 million U over 30–60 min + heparin SC 12,500 UX2/d, starting 12 h after initiation of thrombolytic infusion and continued until discharge. b. t-PA 10 mg bolus, 50 mg over 1 h, and 40 mg over 2 h + heparin SC 12,500 UX2/d, starting 12 h after initiation of thrombolytic infusion and continued until discharge. c. Streptokinase 1.5 million U over 30–60 min without heparin. d. t-PA 10 mg bolus, 50 mg over 1 h, and 40 mg over 2 h without heparin.
Additional therapy	Oral aspirin 300–325 mg/d. Atenolol 5–10 mg IV.
Results	a. The t-PA and streptokinase groups did not differ in mortality (9.0% and 8.6%), clinical heart failure (7.7% and 8.1%), or occurrence of left ventricular ejection fraction ≤35% (2.5% and 2.2%). Combined end points occurred in 23.1% and 22.5%, respectively. The rates of recurrent infarction, post infarction angina, stroke, and bleeding were not different between the t-PA and streptokinase groups. Allergic reactions and hypotension were more common in the streptokinase than t-PA treated patients. There was no differences regarding mortality (8.3% vs 9.3%), heart failure (8.0% vs 7.8%), or ejection fraction ≤35% (2.3% vs 2.4%) between the heparin and no heparin groups. There was no difference in reinfarction, post infarction angina, and stroke between the 2 groups. Major bleeding was more common in the heparin treated patients (1.0% vs 0.6%, RR 1.64, 95% CI 1.09–2.45). b. In-hospital mortality was 8.9% for t-PA, 8.5% for streptokinase (RR 1.05, 95% CI 0.96–1.16), and 8.5% for heparin vs 8.9% without heparin. More strokes occurred with t-PA (1.3%) than with streptokinase (0.9%), while major bleeding occurred in 0.6% and 0.9% of the t-PA and streptokinase treated patients.
Conclusions	Streptokinase and t-PA appear equally effective and safe. Adding heparin subcutaneously to thrombolysis and aspirin did not alter prognosis, except for an increase in major bleeding.

MITI-1

Myocardial Infarction Triage and Intervention

Title	a. Myocardial infarction triage and intervention project-phase I: Patient characteristics and feasibility of prehospital initiation of thrombolytic therapy. b. Prehospital initiated vs hospital initiated thrombolytic therapy. The myocardial infarction triage and intervention trial.
Authors	a. Weaver WD, Eisenberg MS, Martin JS, et al. b. Weaver WD, Cerqueira M, Hallstrom AD.
Reference	a. J Am Coll Cardiol 1990;15:925–931. b. JAMA 1993; 270:1211–1216.
Disease	Acute myocardial infarction.
Purpose	a. To assess the feasibility and the time saving, of the strategy of prehospital initiation of thrombolytic therapy by paramedics. b. To determine the effect of prehospital initiated treatment of acute myocardial infarction vs hospital initiated therapy.
Design	a. Patients with chest pain were evaluated by paramedics by obtaining history, physical examination, and electrocardiogram that was transmitted to a base station physician. The physician determined whether the patient met the criteria for prehospital thrombolysis. b. Randomized, controlled trial.
Patients	a. 2472 patients, <75 years old, with chest pain ≥15 min and <6 h, who called 911. b. 360 patients with symptoms of acute myocardial infarction for 6 or fewer hours. Patients had to have ST segment elevation and no risk factors for serious bleeding.

MITI-1

Myocardial Infarction Triage and Intervention

(continued)

Follow-up	a. 9 months. b. In-hospital:30 days.
Treatment regimen	b. Patients received aspirin and alteplase either before or after hospital arrival. Once in the hospital, both groups received heparin.
Results	a. 677 patients (27%) had suitable clinical findings consistent with possible acute myocardial infarction and no apparent risk for thrombolytic therapy. Electrocardiograms of 522 of the 677 patients were transmitted to the base station. Only 107 (21%) of these tracings demonstrated ST elevation. 453 patients developed acute myocardial infarction in hospital. 163 (36%) of the 453 patients met the screening history and examination criteria and 105 (23.9%) had ST elevation. The average time from onset of symptoms to prehospital diagnosis was 72±52 min (median 52 min). This was 73±44 min (median 62 min) earlier than the actual time when thrombolytic therapy was started in hospital. b. More patients whose therapy was started before hospital arrival had resolution of pain by admission, 23% vs 7%, ($p<0.001$). There was no difference in composite score of combined death, stroke, serious bleeding, and infarct size between groups. Secondary analysis of time to treatment and outcomes showed that treating within 70 min of symptoms resulted in better outcome, that is lower composite score, $p=0.009$. Early therapy was associated with lower mortality (1.2%) compared to late mortality (8.7%, $p=0.04$) and infarct size and ejection fraction were improved with early therapy.
Conclusions	a. Paramedic selection of patients for potential prehospital initiation of thrombolytic therapy is feasible and may shorten the time to initiation of thrombolytic therapy. b. Initiating treatment before hospital arrival did not improve outcome. However, therapy started within 70 min of symptom onset, whether in the hospital or outside of the hospital, was associated with the better outcome.

TEAM-2

The Second Thrombolytic Trial of Eminase in Acute Myocardial Infarction

Title	Multicenter patency trial of intravenous anistreplase compared with streptokinase in acute myocardial infarction.
Authors	Anderson JL, Sorensen SG, Moreno FL, et al.
Reference	Circulation 1991;83;126–140.
Disease	Acute myocardial infarction.
Purpose	To compare the efficacy of anistreplase (APSAC) and streptokinase on early patency and reocclusion rates.
Design	Randomized, double blind, multicenter.
Patients	370 patients, aged <76 years, with chest pain of >30 min, ≤4 h of onset of symptoms, and ST elevation of ≥1 mm in ≥1 limb lead or ≥2 mm in ≥1 precordial lead. Patients in cardiogenic shock, previous coronary artery bypass grafting, balloon angioplasty within 1 month, blood pressure >200/120 mm Hg, or contraindications to thrombolytic therapy were excluded.
Follow-up	90–240 min coronary angiography. Patients with TIMI flow 0 or 1 were allowed to undergo angioplasty. Patients with initial TIMI flow 2–3, who did not undergo mechanical intervention, were catheterized again 18–48 h after initiation of protocol.
Treatment regimen	1. Anistreplase 30 U over 2–5 min IV and streptokinase placebo. 2. Placebo and streptokinase 1.5 million U over 60 min.

TEAM-2

The Second Thrombolytic Trial of Eminase in Acute Myocardial Infarction (continued)

Additional therapy	Heparin 5000–10,000 U bolus at the start of catheterization. IV infusion 1000 U/h was commenced after the angiography for >24 h. Diphenhydramine 25–50 mg IV was recommended.
Results	Early (mean 140 min) patency rate (TIMI flow 2–3) was 72% with APSAC and 73% with streptokinase. However, TIMI flow 3 was seen in 83% and 72%, respectively (p=0.03). Mean residual coronary artery stenosis was 74% vs 77.2%, respectively (p=0.02), in those who achieved TIMI flow 2–3. Reocclusion risk within 1–2 days was found in 1.0% and 2.1% of the APSAC and streptokinase patients. Enzymatic and electrocardiographic evolution was similar. In-hospital mortality was 5.9% vs 7.1% (p=0.61). Bleeding complications, stroke, allergic reactions, and cardiovascular complications were similar.
Conclusions	Streptokinase and APSAC were equally effective and safe as thrombolytic therapy within 4 h of onset of acute myocardial infarction.

TAMI-5

Thrombolysis and Angioplasty in Myocardial Infarction-5

Title	a. Evaluation of combination thrombolytic therapy and timing of cardiac catheterization in acute myocardial infarction. Results of Thrombolysis and Angioplasty in Myocardial Infarction-Phase 5 randomized trial. b. Effects of thrombolytic regimen, early catheterization, and predischarge angiographic variables on 6 week left ventricular function.
Authors	a. Califf RM, Topol EJ, Stack RS, et al. b. Ward SR, Sutton JM, Pieper KS, et al.
Reference	a. Circulation 1991;83:1543-1556. b. Am J Cardiol 1997;79:539-544.
Disease	Acute myocardial infarction.
Purpose	To evaluate 3 thrombolytic regimens (tissue type plasminogen activator (t-PA), urokinase, or both) and 2 strategies (immediate vs predischarge catheterization).
Design	Randomized, open label, 3X2 factorial, multicenter.
Patients	575 patients, age <76 years, with suspected acute myocardial infarction (chest pain ≤6 h; ST elevation ≥1 mm in ≥2 leads).
Follow-up	a. 5-10 days (contrast ventriculogram and clinical evaluation). b. Predischarge and 6 week radionuclide ventriculography (MUGA).
Treatment regimen	1. Urokinase 1.5 million U bolus +1.5 million U infusion over 90 min. 2. t-PA 6 mg bolus, 54 mg over the first h, and 40 mg over 2 h. 3. Urokinase 1.5 million U over 60 min with 1mg/kg t-PA over 60 min (10% given as a bolus, maximal dose 90 mg). The early invasive strategy consisted of coronary angiography after 90 min of initiation of therapy with rescue angioplasty when indicated. The deferred strategy required coronary angiography 5-10 days after admission.
Additional therapy	Aspirin 325 mg/d. Heparin was started at the end of thrombolytic infusion at a dose of 1000 IU/h for >48 h. In the aggressive strategy additional 5000 IU heparin was given. Additional heparin was given during rescue angioplasty. Prophylactic lidocaine was used in most patients. Diltiazem 30-60 mgX3/d.

Results

a. Early patency rates were greater with the combination regimen (76%) vs 62% and 71% in the urokinase and t-PA arms (p=0.14). However, predischarge patency rates were similar. 5-10 days left ventricular ejection fraction was comparable among the three regimens and between the two strategies. Combination thrombolytic therapy was associated with less complicated clinical course and lower rate of reocclusion (2%) vs 7% and 11%, in the urokinase and t-PA regimens (p=0.04), and a lower rate of recurrent ischemia (25% vs 35% and 31%, respectively). Combination therapy was associated with the lower rates of the combined end point of death, stroke, reinfarction, reocclusion, heart failure, or recurrent ischemia (32% vs 45% and 40% for urokinase, and t-PA, respectively, p=0.04). Bleeding complications were comparable among the groups. Predischarge patency rates were 94% and 90% in the early invasive and early conservative strategies (p=0.065). Predischarge regional wall motion in the infarct zone was improved more with the early aggressive approach (-2.16 SDs/chord vs -2.49 SDs/chord, p=0.004). More patients in the early invasive strategy were free from adverse outcomes (67% vs 55%, p=0.004).

b. 219 patients underwent paired MUGA scan before discharge and at 6 weeks. Predischarge median left ventricular ejection fraction (25th, 75th percentile) was 58 (51, 63), 55 (46, 65), and 57 (48, 63) in the t-PA, urokinase, and combination groups, respectively (p=0.29). Predischarge ejection fraction was unaffected by the early catheterization strategy (p=0.75). The type of thrombolytic regimen (p=0.331, p=0.645) and the catheterization strategy (p=0.60, p=0.256)) had no effect on either rest or exercise global left ventricular ejection fraction 6 weeks after enrollment. The type of thrombolytic regimen (p=0.59) and the catheterization strategy (p=0.36) had no effect on regional wall motion score at the infarct zone. Rescue PTCA was associated with worse 6 week regional wall motion (p=0.002) in the early catheterization group (univariate analysis). After adjustment for predischarge infarct-zone wall motion score, rescue PTCA was still predictive of worse regional function at 6 weeks (p=0.007).

TAMI-5

Thrombolysis and Angioplasty in Myocardial Infarction-5

(continued)

Conclusions	Combination thrombolytic therapy is more effective than single agent therapy for achievement of early and sustained reperfusion and for reducing the incidence of in-hospital complications. The early intervention strategy may result in better clinical outcome. The early beneficial effect of early catheterization on regional function was not sustained, and both global and regional function was comparable among the 3 thrombolytic regimens and between the early and deferred coronary angiography groups.

TAMI-7

Thrombolysis and Angioplasty in Myocardial Infarction VII

Title	Accelerated plasminogen activator dose regimens for coronary thrombolysis.
Authors	Wall TC, Califf RM, George BS, et al.
Reference	J Am Coll Cardiol 1992;19:482–489.
Disease	Acute myocardial infarction.
Purpose	To evaluate the efficacy of 5 different regimens of tissue plasminogen activator (t-PA) administration in acute myocardial infarction.
Design	Randomized, multicenter.
Patients	219 patients, >18 and <76 years old, with suspected acute myocardial infarction >30 min pain unresponsive to sublingual nitrate, ≤6 h from onset of symptoms, ≥1 mm ST elevation in ≥2 leads or ST depression in V1–V4.
Follow-up	In-hospital events, pretreatment, and 5–10 days coronary angiography.
Treatment regimen	1. t-PA 1 mg/kg over 30 min (10% bolus), 0.25 mg/kg over 30 min. Max dose 120 mg. 2. t-PA 1.25 mg/kg over 90 min (20 mg bolus). Max dose 120 mg. 3. t-PA 0.75 mg/kg over 30 min (10% bolus), 0.50 mg/kg over 60 min. Max dose 120 mg. 4. t-PA 20 mg bolus, 30 min wait, 80 mg over 120 min. Max dose 100 mg. 5. t-PA 1 mg/kg over 30 min + urokinase 1.5 million U over 1 h. Max dose 90 mg.

TAMI-7

Thrombolysis and Angioplasty in Myocardial Infarction VII (continued)

Additional therapy	Standard care including lidocaine, oxygen, morphine, and nitrates. Aspirin 325 mg/d. Heparin infusion 1,000 U/h started at the end of thrombolytic infusion and continued for 5–10 days. Metoprolol IV 15 mg if no contraindication existed.
Results	90 min patency rates were 63%, 61%, 83%, 67%, and 72% for protocols 1–5, respectively. Reocclusion occurred in 11%, 3%, 4%, 14%, and 3%, respectively. Protocol 3 achieved the highest rate of reperfusion and a low rate of reocclusion. Predischarge left ventricular ejection fraction was not statistically different among the groups. There was no difference in bleeding complications among the groups. Death, reocclusion, restenosis, and reinfarction tended to be less frequent in protocol 3, however, without statistical significance.
Conclusions	Accelerated t-PA administration according to protocol 3 is a relatively safe strategy achieving high 90 min patency rate and low reocclusion and complication rates.

ISIS-3

International Study of Infarct Survival 3

Title	ISIS-3: A randomized comparison of streptokinase vs tissue plasminogen activator vs anistreplase and of aspirin plus heparin vs aspirin alone among 41,299 cases of suspected acute myocardial infarction.
Authors	ISIS-3 Collaborative Group.
Reference	Lancet 1992;339:753–770.
Disease	Acute myocardial infarction.
Purpose	1. To compare 3 thrombolytic agents: tissue plasminogen activator (t-PA), streptokinase, and anisoylated plasminogen streptokinase activator complex (APSAC). 2. To compare treatment with heparin + aspirin with aspirin.
Design	Randomized, double blind (for thrombolytic agents) and open label (for heparin), 3X2 factorial, multicenter.
Patients	41,299 patients with suspected acute myocardial infarction within 24 h of onset of symptoms. No ECG criteria were used.
Follow-up	6 months.
Treatment regimen	1. Streptokinase 1.5 million U over 1 h. 2. t-PA 0.04 MU/kg as a bolus, and 0.36 MU/kg over 1 h, and then 0.067 MU/kg/h for 3 h. 3. APSAC 30 U over 3 min. Half of the patients received heparin subcutaneous 12,500 U X2/d for 1 week started 4 h after initiation of thrombolytic therapy.
Additional therapy	162 mg chewed aspirin on admission and then 162 mg/d.

ISIS-3

International Study of Infarct Survival 3

(continued)

Results

Addition of heparin SC to aspirin resulted in excess of major noncerebral hemorrhages (1.0% vs 0.8%, $p<0.01$) and of cerebral hemorrhages (0.56% vs 0.40%, $p<0.05$). However, total stroke occurred equally (1.28% vs 1.18%). Recurrent infarction occurred less in the heparin treated patients (3.16% vs 3.47%, $p=0.09$), especially during the scheduled heparin treatment. During the scheduled heparin treatment (0–7 days) mortality was 7.4% and 7.9% in the heparin and no heparin groups ($p=0.06$). However, 35 day and 6 months mortality were comparable.
APSAC was associated with more allergic reaction and noncerebral bleeding and a trend towards more strokes than streptokinase. Reinfarction and 35 day mortality were comparable (3.47% and 10.6% vs 3.55% and 10.5% in the streptokinase and APSAC groups, respectively). There was no difference in 6 month survival between the groups. t-PA was associated with less allergic reactions than streptokinase, but with higher rates of noncerebral bleeding. Stroke occurred in 1.04% of the streptokinase and 1.39% of the t-PA groups ($p<0.01$). t-PA was associated with less reinfarction (2.93% vs 3.47% in the t-PA and streptokinase groups, $p<0.02$). However, 35 day mortality was comparable (10.3% vs 10.6%, respectively). 6 month survival was similar.

Conclusions

It might be that heparin may produce at least a small improvement in survival and will reduce reinfarction, especially during the treatment period. There was no advantage of APSAC over streptokinase. The excess strokes observed with t-PA overshadows the reduction in reinfarction rate. t-PA is not better than streptokinase.

LATE

Late Assessment of Thrombolytic Efficacy

Title	Late assessment of thrombolytic efficacy (LATE) study with alteplase 6–24 h after onset of acute myocardial infarction.
Authors	LATE Study Group.
Reference	Lancet 1993;342:759–766.
Disease	Acute myocardial infarction.
Purpose	To assess the efficacy of intravenous thrombolytic therapy beginning more than 6 h after the onset of symptoms.
Design	Randomized, double blind, placebo controlled, multicenter.
Patients	5711 patients with acute myocardial infarction >18 years old, 6–24 h from onset of symptoms.
Follow-up	Clinical follow-up for 6 months (73% were followed up for 1 year).
Treatment regimen	Intravenous alteplase (r-tPA) 10 mg bolus, 50 mg infusion over 1 h, and 20 mg/hour for 2 h or matching placebo.
Additional therapy	Aspirin 75–360 mg/d. IV heparin for 48 h was recommended.

Late Assessment of Thrombolytic Efficacy

(continued)

Results	35 day mortality for patients treated 6–12 h after onset of symptoms was 8.9% vs 12.0% in the alteplase and placebo groups, respectively (95% CI 6.3–45.0%, p=0.02). 35 day mortality for patients treated >12 h after onset of symptoms was 8.7% vs 9.2% in the alteplase and placebo groups, respectively (p=0.14).
Conclusions	Thrombolytic therapy reduces 35 day mortality even if given up to 12 h after onset of symptoms.

EMERAS

Estudio Multicèntrico Estreptoquinasa Reùblicas de Amèrica del Sur

Title	Randomized trial of late thrombolysis in patients with suspected acute myocardial infarction.
Authors	EMERAS Collaborative Group.
Reference	Lancet 1993;342:767–772.
Disease	Acute myocardial infarction.
Purpose	To evaluate the efficacy of late treatment (6–24 h) with intravenous streptokinase for acute myocardial infarction.
Design	Randomized, double blind, placebo control, multicenter.
Patients	4534 patients with acute myocardial infarction >6 h and ≤24 h of onset of symptoms. ECG criteria were not required.
Follow-up	1 year.
Treatment regimen	Streptokinase 1.5 million U or placebo infused over 1 h.
Additional therapy	Aspirin 160 mg/d.

EMERAS

Estudio Multicèntrico Estreptoquinasa Reùblicas de Amèrica del Sur (continued)

Results	Side effects such as hypotension, allergic reactions, and bleeding were more common with streptokinase therapy. There was no difference between in-hospital mortality, the streptokinase (11.9%), and placebo (12.4%) groups. Among the 2080 patients presenting 7–12 h from onset of symptoms there was a nonsignificant trend towards less mortality with streptokinase (11.7% vs 13.2%), whereas the mortality difference among the 1791 patients presenting 13–24 h after onset of symptoms was small (11.4% vs 10.7%). One year mortality was comparable between the streptokinase and placebo group.
Conclusions	Streptokinase therapy 7–24 h after onset of symptoms did not show clear benefit. A modest reduction in mortality among patients treated 6–12 h after onset of symptoms is possible.

GUSTO-1

Global Utilization of Streptokinase and Tissue Plasminogen Activator for Occluded Coronary Arteries

Title	a. An international randomized trial comparing 4 thrombolytic strategies for acute myocardial infarction. b. Risk factors for in-hospital nonhemorrhagic stroke in patients with acute myocardial infarction treated with thrombolysis. Results from GUSTO-1. c. Impact of an aggressive invasive catheterization and revascularization strategy on mortality on patients with cardiogenic shock in the global utilization of streptokinase and tissue plasminogen activator for occluded coronary arteries. (GUSTO-1) Trial. An observational study.
Authors	a. The GUSTO Investigators. b. Mahaffey KW, Granger CB, Sloan MA, et al. c. Berger PB, Holmes DR, Stebbins AL, et al.
Reference	a. N Engl J Med 1993;329:673-682. b. Circulation 1998; 97:757-764. c. Circulation 1997; 96:122-127.
Disease	a. + b. Acute myocardial infarction. c. Coronary artery disease, acute myocardial infarction, cardiogenic shock.
Purpose	a. To compare the effects of 4 thrombolytic strategies on outcome. b. To determine the risk factors that result in nonhemorrhagic stroke in patients with acute myocardial infarction. c. To determine the influence of an aggressive interventional strategy of early percutaneous transluminal coronary angioplasty and coronary bypass surgery on survival in patients with acute myocardial infarction with cardiogenic shock who survived ≥ h after shock from the GUSTO-1 study.
Design	a. Randomized, open label, multicenter. b. Assessment of univariable and multivariable risk factors for nonhemorrhagic stroke and creating a scoring normogram. c. Observational study. In GUSTO-1 angiography and revascularization were not protocol - mandated but were selected by some physicians.

GUSTO-1

Global Utilization of Streptokinase and Tissue Plasminogen Activator for Occluded Coronary Arteries

(continued)

Patients	a. 41,021 patients with acute myocardial infarction < 6 h from onset of symptoms with chest pain >20 min and ST segment elevation ≥0.1 mV in ≥2 limb leads , or ≥0.2 mV in ≥2 precordial leads. b. 247 patients with nonhemorrhagic stroke from the GUSTO 1 trial. c. 2200 patients with cardiogenic shock defined as systolic blood pressure <90 mm Hg for ≥1 h not responsive to fluids or the need for positive inotropic agents to maintain systolic blood pressure >90 mm Hg. Of these, 406 patients received early coronary angiography and 1794 did not.
Follow-up	a. 30 days clinical follow-up. b. Focuses on in-hospital: 30 day. c. 30 days.
Treatment regimen	a. 1) intravenous streptokinase 1.5 million U over 60 min with subcutaneous heparin 12,500 U bid; 2) streptokinase 1.5 million U over 60 min with intravenous heparin (5000 U bolus and 1000 U/h); 3) accelerated t-PA (15 mg bolus, 0.75 mg/kg over 30 min, and 0.5 mg/kg over 60 min) with intravenous heparin (5000 U bolus and 1000U/h); and 4) the combination of intravenous t-PA (1.0 mg/kg over 60 min, with 10% given as a bolus) and streptokinase (1.0 million U over 60 min) with intravenous heparin (5000 U bolus and 1000 U/h). b.As per GUSTO 1. c. Early coronary angiography within 24 h of shock onset and coronary angioplasty or bypass surgery vs no early angiography and interventional procedure.
Additional therapy	a. Chewable aspirin 160 mg on admission and 160-325 mg/d thereafter. IV 5 mg atenolol in 2 divided doses, followed by 50-100 mg/d PO was recommended if no contraindications existed.

GUSTO-1

Global Utilization of Streptokinase and Tissue Plasminogen Activator for Occluded Coronary Arteries

(continued)

Results	a. 30 day mortality was 7.2% for the streptokinase with SC heparin group; 7.4% for the streptokinase and IV heparin group, 6.3% for the accelerated t-PA and IV heparin group; and 7.0% for the combination group. Thus, 14% reduction (95% CI 5.9–21.3%) in 30 day mortality for accelerated t-PA as compared with the two groups of streptokinase therapy. Hemorrhagic stroke occurred in 0.49%, 0.54%, 0.72%, and 0.94% in the 4 groups, respectively (p=0.03 for the difference between t-PA and streptokinase; p<0.001 for the combination therapy compared to streptokinase-only). A combined end point of death or disabling stroke was lower in the t-PA treated patients (6.9%) than in patients receiving the streptokinase-only regimens (7.8%) (p=0.006). b. 42 (17%) died and 98 (40%) of the 247 nonhemorrhagic stroke patients were disabled at 30 day follow-up. Baseline clinical predictors of nonhemorrhagic stroke included older age, higher heart rate, history of stroke or transient ischemic attack, diabetes, prior angina, hypertension. Other factors included worse killip class, coronary angiography, coronary artery bypass surgery, and atrial fibrillation/flutter. c. 30 day mortality was 38% in patients with early angiography and revascularization where appropriate vs 62% in patients who did not receive this strategy (p=0.0001). There were important differences in baseline characteristics: the aggressive strategy group tended to be younger, had less prior infarction and a shorter time to thrombolytic therapy. After adjusting for baseline differences the aggressive strategy still was associated with reduced 30 day mortality (odds ratio 0.43, CI =0.34–0.54, p=0.0001).
Conclusions	a. The mortality of patients with acute myocardial infarction treated with accelerated t-PA and intravenous heparin is lower than those receiving streptokinase with either subcutaneous or intravenous heparin. b. A normogram can predict the risk of nonhemorrhagic stroke based on clinical characteristics. c. Early angiography and revascularization when appropriate is associated with lower 30 day mortality in patients with acute myocardial infarction and cardiogenic shock.

GUSTO-1 (Substudy)

Global Utilization of Streptokinase and Tissue Plasminogen Activator For Occluded Coronary Arteries

Title	Sustained ventricular arrhythmias in patients receiving thrombolytic therapy. Incidence and outcomes.
Authors	Newby KH, Thompson T, Stebbins A, et al.
Reference	Circulation 1998; 98:2567-2573.
Disease	Acute myocardial infarction.
Purpose	To determine the relationship among the type of ventricular arrhythmia (VT vs VF or both), time of arrhythmia occurrence, use of thrombolytic therapy, and outcome.
Design	As per GUSTO-1.
Patients	Of 40,895 patients with ventricular arrhythmia data, study of 4188 who had sustained VT, VF, or both.
Follow-up	Primary end point was 30 day mortality.
Treatment regimen	As per GUSTO-1.
Additional therapy	As per GUSTO-1.

GUSTO-1 (Substudy)

Global Utilization of Streptokinase and Tissue Plasminogen Activator For Occluded Coronary Arteries

(continued)

Results	Sustained VT was defined as "a regular wide complex tachycardia of ventricular origin lasting ≥30 secs or accompanied by hemodynamic compromise requiring electrical cardioversion." Of the 40,985 patients with arrhythmia data 3.5% had sustained VT only; 4.1% had VF only; and 2.7% had both. Higher incidence of sustained VT and/or VF were associated with "older age, previous infarct, hypertension, heart rate, anterior wall infarct, history of coronary bypass, and higher Killip class." Mean ejection fraction was lower at 46% in patients with sustained ventricular arrhythmias vs patients without VT (52%, $p<0.001$). 30 day mortality was higher in patients with sustained VT (18.3%), VF only (23.9%) or both (44.5%) vs patients with neither (4.6%; $p<0.001$). The same general trends were observed for in-hospital mortality, 1 year mortality, AV block, CHF, shock, atrial fibrillation, and stroke. Early (<2 days) and late (>2 days) episodes of sustained VT and VF were associated with higher mortality ($p<0.001$); patients with both VT and VF had worse outcomes than patients with either VT or VF alone. For patients who survived hospital discharge, mortality rates at one year were higher in VT alone and VT/VF patients.
Conclusions	VT, VF, or both were associated with higher 30 day mortality than in patients with neither.

GUSTO-1 (Substudy)

Global Utilization of Streptokinase and Tissue Plasminogen Activator For Occluded Coronary Arteries

Title	1 year survival among patients with acute myocardial infarction complicated by cardiogenic shock and its relation to early revascularization from GUSTO-1 Trial.
Authors	Berger PB, Tuttle RH, Holmes DR, et al.
Reference	Circulation 1999; 99:873-878.
Disease	Acute myocardial infarction.
Purpose	To determine the 1 year outcome of patients who survived cardiogenic shock from acute myocardial infarction at 30 days.
Design	As per GUSTO-1.
Patients	1321 patients who had cardiogenic shock (systolic blood pressure <90 mm Hg for ≥1 hour) with myocardial infarction and survived 30 days vs 36,333 who did not have shock as part of the GUSTO-1 study.
Follow-up	1 year.
Treatment regimen	As per GUSTO-1.

GUSTO-1 (Substudy)

Global Utilization of Streptokinase and Tissue Plasminogen Activator For Occluded Coronary Arteries

(continued)

Results	97.4% of patients without shock were alive at 1 year vs 88.0% of patients with shock (p=0.0001). Patients who had shock with acute myocardial infarction were older, were more likely to have had an anterior MI, have a history of prior MI, hypertension, cerebrovascular disease, and CABG. 44% of shock patients had undergone revascularization within 30 days and 56% had not. At 1 year 91.7% of patients in the shock group that had undergone revascularization were alive vs 85.3% of the shock patients that did not undergo revascularization.
Conclusions	88% of patients that had cardiogenic shock due to myocardial infarction and were alive at 30 days, survived to one year. Shock patients that underwent revascularization within 30 days were more likely to survive at 1 year than those that did not undergo revascularization.

GUSTO-1 (angiographic substudy)

Global Utilization of Streptokinase and Tissue Plasminogen Activator for Occluded Coronary Arteries

Title	a. The effects of tissue plasminogen activator, streptokinase, or both on coronary artery patency, ventricular function, and survival after acute myocardial infarction. b. Non Q wave vs Q wave myocardial infarction after thrombolytic therapy. Angiographic and prognostic insights from the Global Utilization of Streptokinase and Tissue Plasminogen Activator for Occluded Coronary Arteries-I Angiographic Substudy. c. Extended mortality benefit of early postinfarction reperfusion.
Authors	a. The GUSTO Angiographic Investigators. b. Goodman SG, Langer A, Ross AM, et al. c. Ross AM, Coyne KD, Moregra E, et al.
Reference	a. N Engl J Med 1993;329:1615-1622. b. Circulation 1998;97:444-450. c. Circulation 1998;97:1549-1556.
Disease	a. Acute myocardial infarction. b. Coronary artery disease, myocardial infarction. c. Coronary artery disease, myocardial infarction.
Purpose	a. To compare the speed of reperfusion and the effect on left ventricular function and outcome of tissue plasminogen activator and streptokinase. b. To obtain further insight into the pathophysiology and prognosis of non Q wave infarctions in the thrombolytic era and compare their outcomes to Q wave infarction. c. To describe the effect of early and complete reperfusion on left ventricular function and long term (2-year) mortality.

GUSTO-1 (angiographic substudy)

Global Utilization of Streptokinase and Tissue Plasminogen Activator for Occluded Coronary Arteries (continued)

Design	a. Randomized, open label, multicenter. b. Examination of ECG, coronary anatomy, LV function, mortality among patients with ST elevation infarction in GUSTO-1 angiographic subset in non Q wave vs Q wave infarcts. c. As per GUSTO-1. Follow-up extended to 2 years.
Patients	a. 2431 patients with acute myocardial infarction < 6 hours from onset of symptoms with chest pain >20 min and ST segment elevation ≥0.1 mV in ≥2 limb leads, or ≥0.2 mV in ≥2 precordial leads. b. 2046 patients with acute myocardial infarction. 409 non Q wave patients; 1637 Q wave patients. c. 2375 patients that were part of the angiography substudy.
Follow-up	a. Patients were randomized to cardiac catheterization at 90 min, 180 min, 24 h or 5–7 days. The group that underwent coronary angiography at 90 min underwent it again after 5–7 days. 30 days clinical follow-up. b. 2 years. c. 2 years.
Treatment regimen	a. 1) intravenous streptokinase 1.5 million U over 60 min with subcutaneous heparin 12,500 U bid; 2) streptokinase 1.5 million U over 60 min with intravenous heparin (5000 U bolus and 1000 U/hour); 3) accelerated t-PA (15 mg bolus, 0.75 mg/kg over 30 min, and 0.5 mg/kg over 60 min) with intravenous heparin (5000 U bolus and 1000 U/hour); and 4) the combination of intravenous t-PA (1.0 mg/kg over 60 min, with 10% given as a bolus) and streptokinase (1.0 million U over 60 min) with intravenous heparin (5000 U bolus and 1000 U/hour). b. As per GUSTO 1. c. As per GUSTO 1.

GUSTO-1 (angiographic substudy)

Global Utilization of Streptokinase and Tissue Plasminogen Activator for Occluded Coronary Arteries (continued)

Additional therapy	a. Chewable aspirin 160 mg on admission and 160–325 mg/d thereafter. IV 5 mg atenolol in 2 divided doses, followed by 50–100 mg/d PO was recommended if no contraindications existed.
Results	a. 90 min patency rate was 54% in the streptokinase+heparin SC, 60% in the streptokinase+heparin IV, 81% in the t-PA, and 73% in the combination therapy (p<0.001 for t-PA vs the 2 streptokinase groups). However, at 180 min the difference disappeared. TIMI flow III at 90 min was achieved by 29%, 32%, 54%, and 38%, respectively (p<0.001 for t-PA vs the 2 streptokinase groups). There was no significant differences among the groups in the rate of reocclusion. Regional wall motion was better in the t-PA than the other 3 groups. 30 day mortality was 6.5%, 7.5%, 5.3%, and 7.8%, respectively. Mortality was correlated with lack of patency at 90 min (8.9% in patients with TIMI flow grade 0–1 at 90 min vs 4.4% in patients with TIMI flow grade 3, p=0.009). b. Non Q wave patients were more likely to have an infarct-related artery that was nonanterior 67% vs 58% for Q wave patients (p=0.012). Non Q wave infarcts were less likely to have a proximal occlusion (33%) compared to patients with a Q wave infarct (39%; p=0.021). Non Q wave patients had a lesser degree of ST elevation in a nonanterior location. Infarct related patency occurred earlier and was more complete in non Q wave infarcts. Global ejection fraction was 66% in non Q wave vs 57% in Q wave infarcts (p<0.0001) and regional left ventricular function was also better. 2 year mortality was 6.3% in non Q waves vs 10.1% in Q Wave infarcts (p=0.02). Rates of in-hospital coronary revascularization procedures were similar in non Q (42%) and Q wave patients (44%). c. There was a significant survival benefit and preservation of left ventricular ejection fraction for early complete reperfusion assessed by angiography, that occurred beyond 30 days. Early TIMI 3 flow resulted in a 3 patient per 100 mortality reduction during the first 30 days; and an additional 5 lives per 100 from 30 days to 2 years.

GUSTO-1 (angiographic substudy)

Global Utilization of Streptokinase and Tissue Plasminogen Activator for Occluded Coronary Arteries (continued)

Conclusions	a. Accelerated t-PA regimen achieved faster and more complete reperfusion and was associated with better regional wall motion and outcome. b. Patients who developed non Q wave infarcts after thrombolysis had a better prognosis than Q wave patients probably related to earlier and more complete infarct related artery patency with better left ventricular function. c. Early and successful reperfusion provide mortality benefits that are amplified beyond the first month after reperfusion and extend into at least 2 years.
Update	A one year follow-up study [Califf RM, et al. Circulation 1996;94:1233-1238] showed that one year mortality rates remained in favor of t-PA (9.1%) vs streptokinase with subcutaneous heparin (10.1%, p=0.01), vs steptokinase with IV heparin (10.1%, p=0.009). Combination of IV t- PA and streptokinase had an intermediate outcome (9.9%).

GUSTO IIa

The Global Use of Strategies to Open Occluded Coronary Arteries (GUSTO) IIa

Title	Intravenous heparin vs recombinant hirudin for acute coronary syndromes.
Reference	Circulation 1994;90:1631–1637.
Disease	Acute myocardial infarction, unstable angina pectoris.
Purpose	To compare the efficacy and safety of recombinant hirudin with heparin in acute coronary syndromes.
Design	Randomized, double blind, multicenter.
Patients	Adult patients, with chest discomfort and ECG changes, within 12 h of onset of symptoms, and no contraindications to thrombolytic therapy or heparin.
Follow-up	30 day clinical follow-up.
Treatment regimen	Thrombolytic therapy with either tissue plasminogen activator or streptokinase for patients with ST segment elevation. Patients were randomized to heparin or hirudin infusion for 72–120 h.
Remarks	GUSTO-2A was terminated prematurely after 2564 patients were enrolled due to higher rates of hemorrhagic stroke in the hirudin treated patients. GUSTO 2B was continued with lower doses of hirudin. Preliminary data presented at the American College of Cardiology meeting 1996 suggested that hirudin had no major treatment benefit over heparin on 30 day mortality but a small reduction in recurrent myocardial infarction rate.

GUSTO IIb

The Global Use of Strategies to Open Occluded Coronary Arteries (GUSTO) IIb

Title	A comparison of recombinant hirudin with heparin for the treatment of acute coronary syndromes.
Author	GUSTO IIb Investigators.
Reference	N Engl J Med 1996;335:775-782.
Disease	Acute myocardial infarction.
Purpose	To compare the direct thrombin inhibitor, recombinant hirudin, to heparin in patients with unstable angina or acute myocardial infarction.
Design	Randomized, multicenter.
Patients	12,142 patients with unstable angina or non Q wave myocardial infarction.
Follow-up	30 days.
Treatment regimen	Infusion of hirudin or heparin for 3-5 days. Hirudin initially given in a bolus dose of 0.1 mg /kg IV followed by a continuous infusion of 0.1 mg/kg/hr. Heparin was given as a bolus of 5000 U followed by a continuous infusion of 1000 U per h.

GUSTO IIb

The Global Use of Strategies to Open Occluded Coronary Arteries (GUSTO) IIb (continued)

Results	At 24 h, death or myocardial infarction was lower in hirudin group compared to heparin group (1.3% vs 2.1%, p=0.001). At 30 days the primary end point of death or nonfatal myocardial infarction or reinfarction occurred in 8.9% in the hirudin group vs 9.8% in the heparin group (p=0.06). Hirudin's benefits mainly were related to reducing myocardial infarction or reinfarction. The incidence of serious or life threatening bleeding was similar in the 2 groups; hirudin was associated with higher incidence of moderate bleeding.
Conclusions	Hirudin had a small advantage over heparin, primarily related to reducing the risk of nonfatal myocardial infarction. The benefit was most pronounced at 24 h but dissipated over time.

GUSTO IIb (Substudy)

The Global Use of Strategies to Open Occluded Arteries

Title	Acute coronary syndromes in the GUSTO IIb Trial. Prognostic insights and impact of recurrent ischemia.
Authors	Armstrong PW, Fu Y, Chang WE, et al.
Reference	Circulation 1998; 98: 1860–1868.
Disease	Unstable angina or acute MI.
Purpose	To determine outcomes based on presence or absence of ST segment elevations and incidence of recurrent ischemia.
Design	As per GUSTO IIb.
Patients	4125 patients with ST segment elevation and 8001 patients without ST elevation. 3513 patients had myocardial infarction and 4488 had unstable angina.
Follow-up	As per GUSTO IIb.
Treatment regimen	As per GUSTO IIb.
Additional therapy	As per GUSTO IIb.

GUSTO IIb (Substudy)

The Global Use of Strategies to Open Occluded Arteries

(continued)

Results

Recurrent nonrefractory ischemia was defined as "symptoms of ischemia, with ST segment deviation or definite T wave inversion, and/or new hypotension, pulmonary edema, or cardiac murmur" thought to represent ischemia. Refractory recurrent ischemia was defined as symptom of ischemia plus ECG changes ≥10 minutes despite medical therapy. Recurrent ischemia was more common in patients presenting without ST elevation (35%) compared to those with ST elevation (23%; $p<0.001$). Rate of recurrent ischemia in patients without ST elevation was similar whether they had MI or unstable angina at admission. At 30 days mortality was greater in patients with ST elevation (6.1% vs 3.8%, $p<0.001$), but this difference was not present at 1 year. Higher reinfarction and death rates occurred in patients without ST elevation that had MI vs unstable angina on admission. Recurrent ischemia, especially the refractory variety, was associated with higher rates of reinfarction at 30 days and 6 months. Refractory ischemia nearly doubled mortality in patients with ST segment elevation and nearly tripled mortality in patients without ST segment elevation. Nonrefractory ischemia had a negative but less prominent effect on survival in both ST categories.

Conclusions

Recurrent refractory ischemia worsened outcome especially in patients without ST elevation on admission.

GUSTO IIb (Substudy)

The Global Use of Strategies to Open Occluded Arteries

Title	Randomized comparison of direct thrombin inhibitor vs heparin in conjunction with fibrinolytic therapy for acute myocardial infarction: Results from the GUSTO IIb Trial.
Authors	Metz BK, White HD, Granger CB, et al.
Reference	J Am Coll Cardiol 1998; 31:1493-1498.
Disease	As per GUSTO IIb.
Purpose	To determine whether there was a difference in interaction between hirudin and streptokinase vs hirudin and t-PA.
Design	As per GUSTO IIb.
Patients	3289 patients that received thrombolytic therapy for an acute coronary syndrome; 2274 received t-PA, 1015 received streptokinase.
Follow-up	30 days.
Treatment regimen	As per GUSTO IIb.

GUSTO IIb (Substudy)

The Global Use of Strategies to Open Occluded Arteries

(continued)

Results	In the streptokinase treated patients, hirudin resulted in a 34% decrease in 30 day mortality vs heparin (p=0.92). There was a 40% decrease in the incidence of the composite 30 day end point of death or nonfatal reinfarction (p=0.004). Within the t-PA group hirudin did not have a benefit over heparin. With adjustment for baseline differences between thrombolytics, rates of death or reinfarction at 30 days were 9.1% (streptokinase plus hirudin); 10.3% (t-PA plus hirudin); 10.5% (t-PA plus heparin); and 14.9% for streptokinase plus heparin ($\chi^2 = 4.5$, p=0.03).
Conclusions	Hirudin had a beneficial interaction with streptokinase but not with t-PA.

GUSTO IIb (angiographic substudy)

The Global Use of Strategies to Open Occluded Coronary Arteries in Acute Coronary Arteries (GUSTO IIb) Angiographic Substudy

Title	A clinical trial comparing primary coronary angioplasty with tissue plasminogen activator for acute myocardial infarction.
Author	The Global Use of Strategies to Open Occluded Coronary Arteries in Acute Coronary Syndromes (GUSTO IIb) Angioplasty Substudy Investigators.
Reference	N Engl J Med 1997; 336:1621-1628.
Disease	Acute myocardial infarction.
Purpose	To compare primary percutaneous transluminal coronary angioplasty to thrombolytic therapy for acute myocardial infarction.
Design	Randomized, multicenter.
Patients	1138 patients with acute myocardial infarction.
Follow-up	30 days-6 mon.
Treatment regimen	Primary angioplasty or accelerated thrombolytic therapy with recombinant tissue plasminogen activator.
Results	At 30 days the primary composite end point of death, nonfatal reinfarction, and nonfatal disabling stroke occurred in 9.6% of the angioplasty patients and 13.7% of the t-PA patients (odds ratio 0.67; 95% CI=0.47-0.97, p=0.033). At 6 mon the incidence of the composite end point was not significantly different between the 2 groups (14.1% for angioplasty vs 16.1% for t-PA, p = NS).
Conclusions	Primary angioplasty for acute myocardial infarction is an "excellent alternative" for myocardial reperfusion and has a "small to moderate short term clinical advantage over thrombolytic therapy with t-PA."

GUSTO III

The Global Use of Strategies to Open Occluded Coronary Arteries (GUSTO III)

Title	A comparison of reteplase with alteplase for acute myocardial infarction.
Author	The Global Use of Strategies to Open Occluded Coronary Arteries (GUSTO III) Investigators.
Reference	N Engl J Med 1997;337:1118-1123.
Disease	Acute myocardial infarction.
Purpose	To compare the efficacy and safety of reteplase, which is a mutant of alteplase that has a longer half life than alteplase, to alteplase in patients with acute myocardial infarction.
Design	Randomized, multicenter, open label.
Patients	15,059 patients with acute myocardial infarction. Patients had to present within 6 h after onset of symptoms with ST elevation or bundle branch block.
Follow-up	30 days.
Treatment regimen	Patients randomly assigned on a 2:1 ratio to receive a 10 MU reteplase bolus followed by a second bolus 30 min later or an accelerated infusion of alteplase, up to 100 mg over 90 min. Alteplase was given as a 15mg bolus followed by infusion of 0.75 mg/kg of body weight over 30 min (not to exceed 50 mg) and then 0.5 mg/kg (up to 35 mg) over the next 60 minutes. Aspirin and heparin were given to all patients.

GUSTO III

The Global Use of Strategies to Open Occluded Coronary Arteries (GUSTO III)

(continued)

Results	30 day mortality was 7.47% for reteplase and 7.24% for alteplase (p=NS). Stroke occurred in 1.64% of patients on reteplase and 1.79% of patients on alteplase (p=NS). Combined end point of death or nonfatal, disabling stroke were similar at 7.89% and 7.91% for reteplase and alteplase, respectively.
Conclusions	Although reteplase is easier to administer than alteplase it did not provide improved survival benefit and had the same rate of stroke.

GUSTO III (Substudy)

The Global Use of Strategies to Open Occluded Coronary Arteries

Title	Effects of reteplase and alteplase on platelet aggregation and major receptor expression during the first 24 hours of acute myocardial infarction treatment.
Authors	Gurbel PA, Serebruany VL, Shustov AR, et al.
Reference	J Am Coll Cardiol 1998; 31:1466–1473.
Disease	Acute myocardial infarction.
Purpose	To determine the effects of reteplase and alteplase on platelet function in acute myocardial infarction patients.
Design	As per GUSTO-III.
Patients	23 patients that were part of GUSTO-III.
Follow-up	As per GUSTO-III; platelet studies up to 24 hours.
Treatment regimen	As per GUSTO-III.

GUSTO III (Substudy)

The Global Use of Strategies to Open Occluded Coronary Arteries

(continued)

Result	Blood was drawn before thrombolytic therapy and at 3, 6, 12, and 24 hours after thrombolytic therapy. Platelet aggregation was induced with ADP, collagen, thrombin, ristocetin; surface antigen expression was assessed for a number of factors. At 24 hours platelet aggregation was higher for reteplase than alteplase when assessed by ADP, collagen, and thrombin. Increases with reteplase were especially prominent between 6–24 hours post thrombolysis. There was an increase in GP IIb/IIIa expression at 24 hours for both reteplase and alteplase, but it was greater for reteplase. Reteplase also exhibited greater very late antigen-2 and platelet/endothelial cell adhesion molecule-1 at 24 hours.
Conclusions	Thrombolytic therapy, especially with reteplase increased platelet aggregation and expression of GP IIb/IIIa.

EMIP

The European Myocardial Infarction Project Group

Authors	The European Myocardial Infarction Project Group.
Title	Prehospital thrombolytic therapy in patients with suspected acute myocardial infarction.
Reference	N Engl J Med 1993;329:383-389.
Disease	Acute myocardial infarction.
Purpose	To compare the efficacy and safety of prehospital vs in-hospital administration of thrombolytic therapy for patients with suspected acute myocardial infarction.
Study Design	Randomized, double blind, multicenter.
Follow-up	30 day clinical follow-up.
Treatment regimen	Patients were randomized to 30 U of anistreplase IV over 4-5 min given by the emergency medical personnel outside the hospital, followed by placebo after hospitalization, or to placebo outside the hospital followed by 30 units of anistreplase after admission.
Concomitant therapy	No limitations, except for anticoagulant therapy.
Patients	5469 patients with chest pain of ≥30 min, or pain unresponsive to nitrates, ≤6 h of onset of symptoms. Patients on oral anticoagulants, with a history of stroke, major trauma, or bleeding diathesis were excluded. Patients were stratified according to the presence of ST segment elevation on the qualifying ECG.

Results	The patients in the prehospital therapy group received thrombolytic therapy 55 min earlier than those in the hospital therapy group. 30 day mortality was 9.7% vs 11.1% in the prehospital and hospital groups (risk reduction 13%, 95% CI -1 to 26%, p=0.08). Cardiac mortality was 8.3% vs 9.8%, respectively (risk reduction 16%, 95% CI 0 to 29%, p=0.049). There was no obvious correlation between the reduction in 30 day mortality and the time interval between the onset of symptoms and the first injection. During the preadmission period there were more patients with ventricular fibrillation (2.5% vs 1.6%, p=0.02), shock (6.3% vs 3.9%, p<0.001), and stroke (0.1% vs 0, p=0.09) in the prehospital therapy than the in-hospital group. However, there was no differences between the groups in the incidence of bleeding, the overall incidence of stroke, ventricular fibrillation, and shock during the hospital period.
Conclusions	Prehospital administration of thrombolytic therapy for patients with suspected acute myocardial infarction is feasible and safe. Although overall mortality was not reduced, cardiac mortality was significantly reduced.

MITI-2

The Myocardial Infarction Triage and Intervention Trial

Title	Prehospital initiated vs hospital initiated thrombolytic therapy. The myocardial infarction triage and intervention trial.
Authors	Weaver DW, Cerqueira M, Hallstrom AP, et al.
Reference	JAMA 1993;270:1211–1216.
Disease	Acute myocardial infarction.
Purpose	To evaluate the effect of prehospital vs in-hospital administration of thrombolytic therapy for suspected acute myocardial infarction.
Study Design	Randomized, controlled, multicenter.
Follow-up	In-hospital clinical events. Estimation of final infarct size by thallium single photon emission tomography and left ventricular function by radionuclide ventriculography at 30 days.
Treatment regimen	Patients were randomized to either prehospital or in-hospital initiation of IV aspirin 325 mg and alteplase 100 mg infusion over 3 h. No placebo was given in the field to the hospital treated group.
Concomitant therapy	Standard care: oxygen, morphine, lidocaine, atropine, vasopressors or diuretics when indicated. IV heparin 5000 U bolus followed by continuous infusion for ≥48 h was started upon admission.
Patients	360 patients, ≤75 years old, with suspected acute myocardial infarction, within 6 h of onset of symptoms. Patients with risk factors for bleeding were excluded.

The Myocardial Infarction Triage and Intervention Trial

(continued)

Results

98% of the patients had subsequent evidence of acute myocardial infarction. Initiation of therapy before admission shortened the time interval from onset of symptoms to therapy from 110 to 77 min ($p<0.001$). 23% of the prehospital group vs 7% of the in-hospital group had resolution of pain upon admission ($p<0.001$). However, there was no difference between the groups in the composite score of death, stroke, serious bleeding, infarct size (406.4 vs 400.4 for the prehospital vs in-hospital groups, $p=0.64$), total mortality (5.7% vs 8.1%, $p=0.49$), infarct size (6.1% vs 6.5%, $p=0.72$), or ejection fraction (53% vs 54%, $p=0.34$). A secondary analysis of the time to therapy and outcome demonstrated that treatment initiated within 70 min of onset of symptoms was associated with better outcome (composite score, $p=0.009$; mortality 1.2% vs 8.7%, $p=0.04$; infarct size 4.9% vs 11.2%, $p<0.001$; and ejection fraction 53% vs 49%, $p=0.03$) than later treatment. Identification of patients eligible for thrombolytic therapy by paramedics reduced the time interval from hospitalization to therapy from 60 min (for nonrandomized patients) to 20 min (for the in-hospital therapy allocated group).

Conclusions

There was no improvement in outcome associated with prehospital administration of thrombolytic therapy. However, treatment within 70 min of onset of symptoms was associated with better outcome. Prehospital identification of patients eligible for thrombolytic therapy was associated with shortening of the time interval to therapy.

TIMI-4

Thrombolysis in Myocardial Infarction 4 Trial

Title	a. Comparison of front loaded recombinant tissue type plasminogen activator, anistreplase, and combination thrombolytic therapy for acute myocardial infarction: Results of the Thrombolysis in Myocardial Infarction (TIMI) 4 trial. b. Rescue angioplasty in the thrombolysis in myocardial infarction (TIMI) 4 trial.
Authors	a. Cannon CP, McCabe CH, Diver DJ, et al. b. Gibson CM, Cannon CP, Greene RM et al.
Reference	a. J Am Coll Cardiol 1994;24:1602-1610. b. Am J Cardiol 1997; 8:21-26.
Disease	a. Acute myocardial infarction.
Purpose	a. To compare 3 regimens of thrombolytic therapy: anistreplase (APSAC), front loaded recombinant tissue type plasminogen activator (rt-PA), or combination of the 2 agents. b. To determine the angiographic and clinical outcomes of patients with a patent coronary artery 90 min after thrombolysis compared to those that had an occluded infarct artery at this time treated with either rescue or no-rescue angioplasty.
Design	a. Randomized, double blind, multicenter study.
Patients	a. 382 patients with acute myocardial infarction <80 years old < 6 h from onset of symptoms with chest pain>30 min and ST segment elevation ≥0.1 mV in ≥2 contiguous leads or with new left bundle branch block.
Follow-up	a. 90 min and 18-36 h coronary angiography. Predischarge technetium-99m sestamibi scan. 6 week and 1 year follow-up.

TIMI-4

Thrombolysis in Myocardial Infarction 4 Trial

(continued)

Treatment regimen	a. Front loaded rt-PA; APSAC (Eminase); or a combination of rt-PA and APSAC.
Additional therapy	a. Heparin (5000 U bolus and infusion) and aspirin 325 mg/d. Intravenous and oral metoprolol.
Results	a. At 90 min, the incidence of TIMI grade 3 flow was 60.2%, 42.9%, and 44.8% of the rt-PA, APSAC, and combination-treated patients (rt-PA vs APSAC, p<0.01; rt-PA vs combination, p=0.02). The incidence of unsatisfactory outcome (death, severe heart failure, LVEF<40%, reinfarction, TIMI grade flow<2 at 90 min or 18–36 h, reocclusion, major hemorrhage, or severe anaphylaxis) was 41.3%, 49%, and 53.6% for the rt-PA, APSAC, and combination therapy (rt-PA vs APSAC, p=0.19; rt-PA vs combination, p=0.06). 6 week mortality was 2.2%, 8.8%, and 7.2%, respectively (rt-PA vs APSAC, p=0.02; rt-PA vs combination, p=0.06). b. The incidence of TIMI 3 flow was higher after successful rescue angioplasty (87%) than after successful thrombolysis (65%; p = 0.002) and the number of frames needed to opacify standard landmarks was lower (that is flow was faster) with PTCA compared to thrombolysis. In-hospital adverse events occurred in 29% of successful rescue PTCA patients and 83% of failed rescue PTCAs (p=0.01). Among patients in whom rescue PTCA was performed (including successes and failures) 35% experienced an adverse event, which was the same as 35% incidence in patients not undergoing rescue PTCA. These values tended to be higher than 23% incidence of adverse events in patients with patent arteries following thrombolysis (p=0.07).
Conclusions	a. Front loaded rt-PA is associated with higher rates of early reperfusion and trends toward better clinical outcome and survival than either APSAC or a combination of rt-PA and APSAC. b. While restoration of flow at 90 min with rescue PTCA was superior to successful thrombolysis, the incidence of adverse events for strategy of rescue PTCA was not improved over no rescue PTCA.

INJECT

International Joint Efficacy Comparison of Thrombolytics

Title	Randomized, double blind comparison of reteplase double bolus administration with streptokinase in acute myocardial infarction (INJECT): Trial to investigate equivalence.
Authors	International Joint Efficacy Comparison of Thrombolytics.
Reference	Lancet 1995;346:329-336.
Disease	Acute myocardial infarction.
Purpose	To compare the effect of reteplase and streptokinase in acute myocardial infarction.
Design	Randomized, double blind, multicenter.
Patients	6010 patients, ≥18 years old, with chest pain of ≥30 min, within 12 h of onset of symptoms, ST elevation ≥1 mm in ≥2 limb leads, or ≥2 mm in ≥2 precordial leads, or bundle branch block.
Follow-up	6 months clinical follow-up.
Treatment regimen	Two boluses of 10 MU reteplase given 30 min apart +1 h infusion of placebo streptokinase, or 2 retaplase placebo boluses and 1.5 MU IV streptokinase.
Additional therapy	Aspirin 250-320 mg initially, then 75-150 mg/d. IV heparin 5000 U before infusion of thrombolytics, and heparin infusion 1000 U/h 60 min after trial infusion for >24 h.

INJECT

International Joint Efficacy Comparison of Thrombolytics

(continued)

Results	35 day mortality was 9.02% vs 9.53% in the reteplase and streptokinase groups (a difference of -0.51%, 95% CI -1.98% to 0.96%). 6 month mortality was 11.02% vs 12.05%, respectively (a difference of -1.03%, 95% CI -2.65% to 0.59%, p=0.217). There was a nonsignificant excess of in-hospital strokes in the reteplase patients (1.23% vs 1.00%). Bleeding events were similar (total: 15.0% vs 15.3%, requiring transfusion: 0.7% vs 1.0%, respectively). Hypotension during hospitalization was more common with streptokinase (17.6% vs 15.5%, p<0.05). Allergic reactions occurred more often with streptokinase (1.8% vs 1.1%, p<0.05).
Conclusions	Reteplase is a safe and an effective thrombolytic agent.

RAPID

Reteplase vs Alteplase Infusion in Acute Myocardial Infarction

Title	More rapid, complete, and stable coronary thrombolysis with bolus administration of reteplase compared with alteplase infusion in acute myocardial infarction.
Authors	Smalling RW, Bode C, Kalbfleisch J, et al.
Reference	Circulation 1995;91:2725–2732.
Disease	Acute myocardial infarction.
Purpose	To compare the 90 min coronary patency rates of bolus administration of reteplase (r-PA) and standard-dose alteplase (tPA).
Design	Randomized, open label, multicenter.
Patients	606 patients, age 18–75 years, with ≥30 min chest pain and ST elevation of ≥1 mm in the limb leads and ≥2 mm in the precordial leads, within 6 h of onset of symptoms. Patients with left bundle branch block, prior coronary artery bypass surgery, previous Q wave infarction in the same territory, previous angioplasty within 2 weeks, previous cerebral vascular event, or severe hypertension were excluded.
Follow-up	30 min, 60 min, 90 min and 5–14 days coronary angiography.
Treatment regimen	1. 15 MU r-PA as a single bolus. 2. 10 MU r-PA bolus followed by 5 MU 30 min later. 3. 10 MU r-PA bolus followed by 10 MU 30 min later. 4. TPA 60 mg over 1 h (6–10 mg as an initial bolus) followed by 40 mg over 2 h.
Additional therapy	Soluble aspirin 200–325 mg/d. IV heparin 5000 U bolus before thrombolytic therapy, followed by 1000 U/h for ≥24 h.

RAPID

Reteplase vs Alteplase Infusion in Acute Myocardial Infarction

(continued)

Results	60 min patency (TIMI flow grade II and III) were 67.0%, 72.1%, 77.6%, and 66.3% in groups 1–4 (r-PA 10+10 vs TPA p=0.079). At 90 min, patency rates were 62.8%, 66.7%, 85.2%, and 77.2%, respectively (r-PA 10+10 vs TPA p=0.084). Late patency was 85.5%, 80.5%, 95.1%, and 87.8% (r-PA 10+10 vs TPA p=0.04). TIMI flow III was higher in the r-PA 10+10 than TPA at 60 min (51.0% vs 32.7%, p=0.009), at 90 min (62.7% vs 49.0%, p=0.019), and at discharge (87.8% vs 70.7%, p<0.001). Global left ventricular function at 90 min was similar in the TPA and r-PA 10+10 groups. However, at discharge ejection fraction was higher in the r-PA 10+10 (53±1.3% vs 49±1.3%, p=0.034). Regional wall motion improved in the r-PA 10+10 from 90 min to predischarge, while in the TPA group there was no improvement. There was a trend towards less rescue angioplasty in the r-PA 10+10 than TPA group (p=0.11). The need for blood transfusion was similar (4.5% in the TPA vs 3.9% in the r-PA 10+10), while intracranial bleeding occurred in 2.6% vs 0%, respectively. Reocclusion occurred in 7.8% of the TPA vs 2.9% in the r-PA 10+10 (p=NS). The 30 day mortality was 3.9% vs 1.9%, respectively. Reinfarction rate and the incidence of heart failure were similar between the groups.
Conclusions	r-PA given as a double bolus of 10 MU+ 10 MU 30 min apart resulted in more rapid and complete reperfusion than standard dose TPA and was associated with improved global and regional left ventricular function at discharge.

RAPID II

Reteplase vs Alteplase Infusion in Acute Myocardial Infarction II

Title	Randomized comparison of coronary thrombolysis achieved with double bolus reteplase (recombinant plasminogen activator) and front loaded, accelerated alteplase (recombinant tissue plasminogen activator) in patients with acute myocardial infarction.
Authors	Bode C, Smalling RW, Berg G, et al.
Reference	Circulation 1996;94:891-898.
Disease	Acute myocardial infarction.
Purpose	To assess whether a double bolus regimen of reteplase, a deletion mutant of wild type tissue plasminogen activator, results in better 90 min coronary artery patency rates compared with accelerated front loaded infusion of alteplase (tissue plasminogen activator).
Design	Randomized, open label, parallel group, multicenter.
Patients	324 patients, >18 years old with ≥30 min of chest pain that was not relieved by nitroglycerin, ≤12 h from onset of pain, and ST segment elevation of ≥0.1 mV in limb leads or ≥0.2 mV in precordial leads, or left bundle branch block. Patients with prior coronary artery bypass surgery, previous stroke or known intracranial structural abnormalities, PTCA within 2 weeks, previous Q wave myocardial infarction in the same territory, severe hypertension, use of oral anticoagulants, recent (<3 months) major surgery or active or potential internal bleeding were excluded.
Follow-up	Coronary angiography at 30, 60, 90 min, and 5-14 days after initiation of therapy, clinical follow-up for 35 days.

RAPID II

Reteplase vs Alteplase Infusion in Acute Myocardial Infarction II (continued)

Treatment regimen	Randomization to a bolus of reteplase (10 MU given over 2-3 min) at the start of therapy and after 30 min, or to alteplase 15 mg bolus, 0.75 mg/kg over 30 min (maximum 50 mg), 0.5 mg/kg over 60 min (maximum 35 mg).
Additional Therapy	Aspirin 160 to 350 mg/d. Intravenous heparin, 5000 IU bolus followed by 1000 IU/h for ≥24 h. Target aPTT 2.0 times the control value.
Results	90 min following initiation of therapy, infarct related coronary artery patency (TIMI flow grade 2 or 3) was higher in the reteplase group (83.4% vs 73.3%, p=0.031). TIMI flow grade 3 was achieved in 59.9% vs 45.2%, respectively (p=0.011). At 60 min, TIMI flow grade 2 or 3 was found in 81.8% of the reteplase group vs 66.1% in the alteplase group (p=0.032), and TIMI flow grade 3 was found in 51.2% vs 37.4%, respectively (p=0.006). Follow-up angiograms were available in 75.7% and 72.9% of the reteplase and alteplase treated patients. Late overall and TIMI flow grade 3 patency were comparable between the groups. Patients treated with reteplase had better patency in all time-to-treatment categories. Additional interventions to restore flow in the infarct related artery during the first 6 h was lower in the reteplase group (13.6% vs 26.5%; p=0.004). The incidence of reocclusion during hospitalization was comparable (9.0% vs 7.0% for reteplase and alteplase, respectively, p=0.61). 35 day mortality was 4.1% vs 8.4%, respectively (p=0.11). The incidence of stroke (1.8% vs 2.6%) was similar. The composite end point of unsatisfactory outcome at 35 days (death, reinfarction, congestive heart failure or shock, or an ejection fraction of <40%) was comparable (21.3% vs 22.6% in the reteplase and alteplase groups). 12.4% vs 9.7% of the patients, respectively, required transfusion (p=0.43). There was no difference in global or infarct zone left ventricular function between the groups.
Conclusions	Double bolus dose of reteplase was associated with higher rates of reperfusion at 60 and 90 min after initiation of therapy than front loaded alteplase infusion, without an increase in the risk of complications.

COBALT

The Continuous Infusion vs Double Bolus Administration of Alteplase (COBALT) Investigators

Title	A comparison of continuous infusion alteplase with double bolus administration for acute myocardial infarction.
Author	The Continuous Infusion vs Double Bolus Administration of Alteplase (COBALT) Investigators.
Reference	N Engl J Med 1997;337:1124–1130.
Disease	Acute myocardial infarction.
Purpose	To determine whether there are advantages of double bolus alteplase over accelerated infusion of alteplase.
Design	Randomized, multicenter, open design.
Patients	7169 patients with acute myocardial infarction.
Follow-up	30 days.
Treatment regimen	Weight adjusted, accelerated infusion of 100 mg alteplase or a bolus of 50 mg alteplase over a period of 1–3 min followed by a second bolus 30 min later of 50 mg (or 40 mg for patients weighing less than 60 kg).
Results	The study was stopped early because of concern about the safety of double bolus therapy. 30 day mortality was higher in the double bolus group at 7.98% vs the accelerated infusion group at 7.53%. Stroke incidence was 1.92% with double bolus alteplase vs 1.53% with accelerated infusion of alteplase (p=0.24) and hemorrhagic stroke was 1.12% and .81% respectively (p=0.23).

COBALT

The Continuous Infusion vs Double-Bolus Administration of Alteplase (COBALT) Investigators

(continued)

Conclusions	Double bolus alteplase was not equivalent to accelerated infusion alteplase, according to prespecified criteria. Accelerated infusion of alteplase over a period of 90 min remains the preferred regimen.

COMPASS

The Comparison Trial of Saruplase and Streptokinase

Title	Randomized, double blind study comparing saruplase with streptokinase therapy in acute myocardial infarction: the COMPASS equivalence trial.
Authors	Tebbe U, Michels R, Adgey J, et al.
Reference	J Am Coll Cardiol 1998;31:487-493.
Disease	Acute myocardial infarction.
Purpose	To compare the efficacy and safety of saruplase, a recombinant unglycosylated human single chain urokinase-type plasminogen activator, and streptokinase in patients with acute myocardial infarction.
Design	Randomized, double blind, multicenter.
Patients	3089 patients, >20 years old, with chest pain and ECG changes compatible with acute myocardial infarction, within 6 h of onset of symptoms. Patients with severe hypertension, high risk of bleeding, major trauma or surgery within 1 month, hypersensitivity to streptokinase or previous exposure to streptokinase within 1 year were excluded.
Follow-up	30 days and 1 year clinical follow-up.
Treatment regimen	Patients were randomized to: 1) heparin 5000 IU bolus, saruplase 20 mg bolus, and saruplase 60 mg infusion over 1 hour and streptokinase placebo infusion over 1 hour; or 2) placebo heparin, streptokinase 1.5 MU infusion over 60 min, and saruplase placebo infusion.

COMPASS

The Comparison Trial of Saruplase and Streptokinase

(continued)

Additional therapy	Oral or intravenous aspirin 200–400 mg on admission followed by ≥75 mg/d. Heparin infusion, started 30 min after the end of the thrombolytic infusion and continued for ≥24 hours. The use of intravenous nitrates was recommended.
Results	Total mortality at 30 days was 5.7% in the saruplase group vs 6.7% in the streptokinase group (odds ratio 0.84; p=0.242). One year mortality was 8.2% and 9.6%, respectively (p=0.193). Death from ventricular rupture/tamponade (21.6% vs 6.7%, of all mortality cases respectively; p=0.003) and fatal stroke (11.4% vs 4.8%; p=0.092) were more common in the saruplase group. In contrast, hypotension (31.4% vs 38.1%; p=0.001) and cardiogenic shock (3.3% vs 4.6%; p=0.067) occurred less frequently in the saruplase group. The incidence of arrhythmia and angina was similar in the 2 groups. Bleeding rates were comparable between the groups (mild in 10.4% of the saruplase group and 10.9% in the streptokinase group; moderate in 6.9% and 7.0%; and severe in 2.1% and 2.5%, respectively). The incidence of stroke was 1.4% in both groups. Hemorrhagic strokes occurred more frequently in the saruplase group (0.9%) than the streptokinase group (0.3%)(p=0.038), whereas thromboembolic strokes were more common in the streptokinase group (1.0% vs 0.5%; p=0.145). Allergic reactions were noted in 1.6% of the saruplase group and in 4.1% of the streptokinase group (p<0.001).
Conclusions	Saruplase was comparable to streptokinase in terms of total mortality. Saruplase was associated with more hemorrhagic strokes, but less thromboembolic strokes and less allergic reactions.

SESAM

Study in Europe with Saruplase and Alteplase in Myocardial Infarction

Title	Comparison of saruplase and alteplase in acute myocardial infarction.
Authors	Bar FW, Meyer J, Vermeer F, et al.
Reference	Am J Cardiol 1997;79:727-732.
Disease	Acute myocardial infarction.
Purpose	To compare the speed of reperfusion, 60 min and 90 min patency rates, and coronary reocclusion rates following thrombolytic therapy with alteplase (tPA) and saruplase unglycosylated recombinant single chain urokinase-type plasminogen activator in acute myocardial infarction.
Design	Randomized, double blind multicenter.
Patients	473 patients, ≤70 years old, with suspected acute myocardial infarction, within 6 h of onset of symptoms. Patients with nondiagnostic ECG, cardiogenic shock, previous coronary artery bypass surgery, use of oral anticoagulants, chronic concomitant disease, or an increased risk of bleeding were excluded.
Follow-up	Coronary angiography 45 min and 60 min after initiation of the thrombolytic therapy. If coronary flow was <TIMI grade III 60 min after initiation of thrombolytic therapy, an angiography was repeated at 90 min. Coronary angiography was repeated at 24-40 hours.

SESAM

Study in Europe with Saruplase and Alteplase in Myocardial Infarction
(continued)

Treatment regimen	Randomization to: 1) intravenous saruplase 20 mg bolus, followed by an infusion of 60 mg over 1 h; or 2) intravenous alteplase 10 mg bolus, followed by an infusion of 50 mg over 1 h and then 40 mg over the next 2 h. Patients with TIMI grade flow 0 to 1 at 90 min could undergo balloon angioplasty.
Additional therapy	Intravenous bolus heparin 5000 U before the thrombolytic agent and another 5000 U bolus before coronary angiography. Heparin infusion, started after the first bolus and continued until the second coronary angiography. Intravenous aspirin 300 mg before the study medication. If coronary flow was <TIMI grade III 60 min after initiation of thrombolytic therapy, repeated angiography at 90 min.
Results	82% of the patients underwent angiography at 45 min, 94.7% at 60 min, and 91.8% at 24–40 hours. At 45 min, 74.6% of the saruplase group vs 68.9% of the alteplase group had TIMI grade flow II or III (p=0.22). At 60 min 79.9% vs 75.3% of the saruplase and alteplase groups had TIMI grade II or III (p=0.26). Patency rates (excluding patients who underwent rescue angioplasty) were 79.9% vs 81.4% (p=0.72), respectively at 90 min and 99% vs 98% at 24–40 h. At 24–40 h, patency rates for all patients (including those who underwent intervention) were 94.0% vs 93.6%. Reocclusion within 24–40 h occurred in 1.2% of the saruplase group vs 2.4% of the alteplase group (p=0.68). Reocclusion after rescue angioplasty occurred in 22% of the saruplase vs 15% of the alteplase treated patients. In-hospital mortality was 4.7% in the saruplase group and 3.8% in the alteplase group. Reinfarction occurred in 4.2% in both groups, severe bleeding in 9.3% of the saruplase group and 8.4% of the alteplase group, hemorrhagic stroke in 0.8% in both groups, and embolic stroke in 0.8% and 1.3%, respectively.
Conclusions	Alteplase in a 3 h infusion regimen and saruplase had a similar safety profile. Early patency rates were high with both agents and reocclusion rates were similarly low.

TIMI 10A

Thrombolysis in Myocardial Infarction 10A

Title	TNK - Tissue plasminogen activator in acute myocardial infarction of the thrombolysis in myocardial infarction (TIMI) 10A dose ranging trial.
Author	Cannon CP, McCabe CH, Gibson M, et al.
Reference	Circulation 1997; 95:351-356.
Disease	Coronary artery disease, acute myocardial infarction.
Purpose	To evaluate the pharmacokinetics, safety, and efficacy of TNK-TPA (TNK-tissue plasminogen activator), a genetically engineered variant of TPA which has slower plasma clearance, greater fibrin specificity, and is more resistant to plasminogen activator inhibitor.
Design	Phase 1, dose ranging pilot trial.
Patients	113 patients with acute ST segment elevation myocardial infarction who presented within 12 h of chest pain.
Follow-up	360 min.
Treatment regimen	Single bolus of TNK-TPA over 5-10 sec with doses of 5 to 50 mg. All patients received aspirin and heparin.

TIMI 10A

Thrombolysis in Myocardial Infarction 10A

(continued)

Results	The plasma clearance of TNK-TPA was 125–216 mL/min across 5–50 mg doses, about one third of that previously reported for wild type TPA. Plasma half life ranged from 11–20 min (while previous reports with TPA report 3.5 min). There was a dose dependent increase in systemic plasmin generation but only a 3% reduction in fibrinogen and a 13% reduction in plasminogen. The frequency of TIMI grade 3 of the infarct vessel, documented by 90 min angiography was 59% at 30 mg and 64% at 50 mg (p=0.032). TIMI grade 2 or 3 flow (defined as patency) was 85% overall and did not differ by dose. Rescue angioplasty was performed in 16 of 17 patients with TIMI grade 0 or 1 flow. 6.2% of patients developed hemorrhage, which occurred mainly at vascular access sites.
Conclusions	TNK-TPA unlike the TPA has a long half life which allows it to be delivered as a single bolus. TNK-TPA is very fibrin specific and appears to have an encouraging initial patency rate.

TIMI 10B

Thrombolysis In Myocardial Infarction 10B

Title	TNK - Tissue plasminogen activator compared with front loaded alteplase in acute myocardial infarction. Results of the TIMI 10B Trial.
Authors	Cannon CP, Gibson CM, McCabe CH, et al.
Reference	Circulation 1998; 98:2805-2814.
Disease	Acute myocardial infarction.
Purpose	To compare efficacy of single bolus of 30 or 50 mg TNK-tPA (highly fibrin specific thrombolytic agent) to front loaded tPA.
Design	Randomized, multicenter.
Patients	886 patients with acute myocardial infarction (ischemic pain lasting ≥30 mins with ST segment elevation ≥0.1 mV in ≥2 contiguous leads and ability to randomize within 12 hours of symptoms.
Follow-up	30 days.
Treatment regimen	Single bolus of TNK-tPA (30 or 50 mg initially; 50 mg was discontinued because of increased intracranial hemorrhage and was replaced by a 40 mg dose and heparin dose was decreased) vs front loaded tPA (15 mg bolus; .75 mg/kg [up to 50 mg] infusion over 30 min, followed by 0.50 mg/kg [up to 35 mg] infusion over 60 min).
Additional therapy	Aspirin, heparin; ß-blockers at the discretion of the physician.

TIMI 10B

Thrombolysis In Myocardial Infarction 10B

(continued)

Results	TIMI grade 3 flow at 90 minute coronary angiogram was 62.8% in TNK-tPA 40 mg dose and similar with tPA (62.7%); and the rate for the 30 mg dose was significantly lower (54.3%, p=0.035). There was a TNK-tPA weight-based dose correlation with TIMI frame count such that the TIMI frame count was lower (representing faster flow) in patients with higher weight adjusted dose. Rates of intracranial hemorrhage were 1.0% at the 30 mg TNK-tPA dose; 1.9% for the 40 mg dose and 1.9% for the tPA group. Rates of serious bleeding and intracranial hemorrhage were lowered when the heparin dose was reduced and begun later in the protocol.
Conclusions	A 40 mg bolus of intravenous TNK-tPA achieved rates of TIMI grade 3 flow similar to those of front loaded tPA.

InTIME

Intravenous nPA for Treatment of Infarcting Myocardium Early

Title	Evaluation of a weight adjusted single bolus plasminogen activator in patients with myocardial infarction. A double blind, randomized angiographic trial of lanoteplase vs alteplase.
Authors	Heijer Pd, Vermeer F, Ambrosioni E, et al.
Reference	Circulation 1998; 98:2117-2125.
Disease	Acute myocardial infarction.
Purpose	To evaluate the dose response relationship and safety of single bolus, weight adjusted lanoteplase in patients presenting within 6 hours of acute myocardial infarction.
Design	Randomized, double blind, multicenter, double placebo angiographic trial.
Patients	602 patients.
Follow-up	30 days.
Treatment regimen	Single bolus injection of lanoteplase (15, 30, 60, or 120 KU/kg) or accelerated alteplase 15 mg IV bolus followed by 0.75 mg/kg (not to exceed 50 mg) over 30 minutes; then 0.5 mg/kg (not to exceed 35 mg) over 60 minutes.
Additional therapy	Aspirin, heparin, conventional antianginal therapy.

InTIME

Intravenous nPA for Treatment of Infarcting Myocardium Early

(continued)

Results	The primary end point was angiographic evaluation of TIMI grade flow in the infarct related artery at 60 minutes; the secondary end point was this analysis at 90 minutes after study medicine. Lanoteplase demonstrated a dose response in TIMI grade 3 flow at 60 minutes. The percent of patients who attained TIMI grade 3 at 15, 30, 60, and 120 KU/kg were 23.6%, 29.5%, 44%, and 47.1% respectively ($p<0.001$) vs 37.4% with alteplase. There was also a dose relationship for this end point at 90 minutes (26.1% to 57.1%; $p<0.001$). At 90 minutes, coronary patency defined as TIMI 2 or 3 increased at the 15, 30, 60, and 120 dose from 54.1%, 62.4%, 72.5%, and 83.0%, respectively ($p<0.001$). At the highest dose (120 KU/kg) lanoteplase had a higher patency rate (83%) compared to alteplase (71%) at 90 minutes (difference 11.6%, 95% CI= 0.7% to 22.5%). Safety of lanoteplase was comparable to alteplase.
Conclusions	Lanoteplase increased coronary patency at 60 and 90 minutes in a dose dependent fashion and at the highest dose (120 KU/kg) achieved greater coronary patency than alteplase.

Alteplase: Double bolus vs front loaded infusion

Title	An angiographic assessment of alteplase: Double bolus and front loaded infusion regimens in myocardial infarction.
Authors	Bleich SD, Adgey AAJ, McMechan SR, et al.
Reference	Am Heart J 1998;136:741-748.
Disease	Acute myocardial infarction.
Purpose	To compare the efficacy of two alteplase (tPA) regimens: Double bolus and front loaded.
Design	Randomized, open label, multicenter.
Patients	461 patients, 18-75 years old, with acute myocardial infarction, 30 min 6 hours of onset of symptoms, with ST segment elevation, who were able to undergo coronary angiography within 90 min of initiation of thrombolytic therapy. Patients with contraindication to thrombolytic therapy were excluded. Patients with previous CABG or in cardiogenic shock were not included.
Follow-up	Coronary angiography at 60 min, 90 min, and 24 hours. 30 days clinical follow-up.
Treatment regimen	Randomization to alteplase as two 50 mg boluses over 1-3 min upon enrollment and 30 min later (n=224); or 90 min front loaded regimen (15 mg bolus; 50 mg infusion over 30 min, and 35 mg infusion over 60 min) (n=237).
Additional therapy	All patients received ≥160 mg/d oral aspirin and IV heparin ≥5000 units as a bolus followed by IV infusion for ≥24 hours.

Alteplase: Double bolus vs front loaded infusion

(continued)

Results	97.3% of the double bolus group vs 93.7% of the front loaded group received treatment as assigned. 60 min TIMI 2-3 flow was observed in 76.8% of the double bolus vs 77.5% of the front loaded groups (p=0.89). However, TIMI 2-3 flow at 90 min was achieved by 74.5% of the double bolus patients vs 81.4% of the front loaded patients (p=0.08). TIMI-3 flow was achieved by 57.9% vs 66.1% of the double bolus and front loaded group, respectively (p=0.08). At 24 hours, TIMI 2-3 flow was seen in 95.5% vs 93.5% of the double bolus and front loaded groups, respectively (p=0.45). In-hospital mortality was 4.5% in the double bolus group vs 1.3% in the front loaded group (p=0.04). 30 day mortality was 4.5% and 1.7%, respectively (p=NS). Intracranial hemorrhages occurred in 0.9% and 0.4%, respectively, whereas stroke occurred in 2.7% of the double bolus group vs 0.84% in the front loaded group (p=NS). Severe bleeding events occurred in 6.3% in each group.
Conclusions	Double bolus alteplase administration tended to achieve less TIMI 3 flow at 90 min. In-hospital mortality was higher with the double bolus regimen.

ASSENT-2

Assessment of the Safety and Efficacy of a New Thrombolytic

Title	Single bolus tenecteplase compared with front loaded alteplase in acute myocardial infarction: The ASSENT-2 double blind randomized trial.
Authors	Assessment of the Safety and Efficacy of a New Thrombolytic (ASSENT-2) Investigators.
Reference	Lancet 1999;354:716-722.
Disease	Acute myocardial infarction.
Purpose	To assess whether body weight adjusted single bolus of tenecteplase would have comparable safety and efficacy as front loaded 90 minute infusion of alteplase in acute myocardial infarction.
Design	Randomized, placebo controlled, double blind, multicenter.
Patients	16,949 patients, ≥18 years old, with symptoms suggesting acute myocardial infarction started within 6 hours of randomization, ST elevation in ≥2 leads or left bundle branch block. Patients with blood pressure >180/110 mmHg, use of glycoprotein IIb/IIIa inhibitors within the preceding 12 hours, contraindications to thrombolytic therapy, and current therapy with oral anticoagulants were excluded.
Follow-up	30 days.

ASSENT-2

Assessment of the Safety and Efficacy of a New Thrombolytic

(continued)

Treatment regimen	Randomization to tenecteplase (30–50 mg) + placebo alteplase or placebo tenecteplase + front loaded alteplase. Tenecteplase or placebo was administered as a single bolus over 5–10 seconds, alteplase or placebo was administered as a 15 mg bolus followed by 0.75 mg/kg infusion over 30 minutes and than 0.50 mg/kg infusion over 60 minutes.
Additional therapy	All patients received oral aspirin 150–325 mg/d and IV heparin for 48–72 hours.
Results	8461 patients were assigned to receive tenecteplase and 8488 patients to receive alteplase. Covariate adjusted 30 day mortality rate was similar at 6.18% for tenecteplase vs 6.15% for alteplase (relative risk 1.004; 95% CI 0.914–1.104). Tenecteplase and alteplase were equally effective in all prespecified subgroups, except for a lower mortality in the tenecteplase assigned patients who were treated >4 hours after onset of symptoms (7.0% vs 9.2%; relative risk 0.766; 95% CI 0.617–0.952; p=0.018). Strokes occurred in 1.78% of the tenecteplase vs 1.66% of the alteplase assigned patients (p=0.555). Intracranial hemorrhages occurred in 0.93% vs 0.94%, respectively (p=1.00). Bleeding was noted in 26.4% in the tenecteplase group vs 28.9% in the alteplase group (p=0.0003). Major bleedings occurred in 4.66% vs 5.94%, respectively (p=0.0002).
Conclusions	The tenecteplase and alteplase assigned patients had similar 30 day mortality. Tenecteplase was safe and was associated with less bleedings than alteplase. Tenecteplase is easy to administer (a single bolus dose) and effective for acute myocardial infarction.

1. Acute Myocardial Infarction

b. PTCA vs Stenting vs Thrombolytic Therapy

PAMI-1

Primary Angioplasty in Myocardial Infarction 1

Title	a. A comparison of immediate angioplasty with thrombolytic therapy for acute myocardial infarction. b. Predictors of in-hospital and 6 month outcome after acute myocardial infarction in the reperfusion era: The primary angioplasty in myocardial infarction (PAMI) trial.
Authors	a. Grines CL, Browne KF, Marco J, et al. b. Stone GW, Grines CL, Browne KF, et al.
Reference	a. N Engl J Med 1993;328:673-679. b. J Am Coll Cardiol 1995;25:370-377.
Disease	Acute myocardial infarction.
Purpose	To compare the results of primary coronary angioplasty with intravenous tissue plasminogen activator for acute myocardial infarction.
Design	Randomized, open label, multicenter.
Patients	395 patients within 12 h of onset of chest pain with ≥1 mm ST elevation in ≥2 adjacent leads. No age limit.
Follow-up	a. Clinical follow-up at 6 months. Radionuclide ventriculography within 24 h and at 6 weeks. Exercise thallium scan predischarge. b. 6 month clinical follow-up.
Treatment regimen	1. Tissue plasminogen activator (t-PA) 100 mg over 3 h. 2. Immediate coronary angiography and angioplasty if suitable.

PAMI-1

Primary Angioplasty in Myocardial Infarction 1

(continued)

Additional therapy	Intravenous nitroglycerin for ≥24 h, chewed aspirin 325 mg and 325 mg/d thereafter and 10,000 U bolus heparin started before randomization. Intravenous heparin infusion was continued for 3–5 days. Diltiazem 30–60 mg X4/d.
Results	a. 90% of the patients assigned to angioplasty underwent the procedure. The success rate was 97%. In-hospital mortality was 6.5% and 2.6% in the t-PA and angioplasty groups, respectively (p=0.06). Reinfarction or death occurred in 12.0% and 5.1%, respectively (p=0.02). Intracranial hemorrhage occurred in 2.0% and 0, respectively (p=0.05). The mean length of the hospital stay was shorter in the angioplasty group (7.5±3.3 vs 8.4±4.6 days, p=0.03). The mean ejection fraction at rest and during exercise were similar at 6 weeks. By 6 months, death in 7.9% and 3.7% (p=0.08) and recurrent infarction or death had occurred in 16.8% and 8.5% (p=0.02) of the t-PA and angioplasty groups, respectively. b. By 6 months, cumulative mortality and reinfarction rate was 8.2% and 17.0% in the angioplasty and t-PA groups (p=0.02). By multiple logistic regression analysis only advanced age, prior heart failure, and treatment with t-PA vs angioplasty were independently associated with increased in-hospital mortality.
Conclusions	Primary angioplasty resulted in lower occurrence of nonfatal recurrent infarction or death and lower rates of intracranial hemorrhage than t-PA.

PAMI-1 (substudy)

Primary Angioplasty in Myocardial Infarction

Title	Long term outcome after primary angioplasty: Report from the Primary Angioplasty in Myocardial Infarction (PAMI-I) Trial.
Authors	Nunn CM, O'Neill WW, Rothbaum D, et al.
Reference	J Am Coll Cardiol 1999;33:640-646.
Disease	Acute myocardial infarction.
Purpose	To assess the 2 year outcome of primary PTCA vs thrombolytic therapy in acute MI.
Design	As per PAMI-I.
Patients	As per PAMI-I.
Follow-up	2 years.
Treatment regimen	As per PAMI-I.
Results	At 2 years the combined end point of death or reinfarction was significantly lower in patients who had received primary angioplasty (14.9%) vs those that received t-PA (23%; p=0.034). Recurrent ischemia was less common in the primary PTCA patients (36.4%) vs the t-PA patients (48%; p=0.026); reintervention and hospital readmission rates also were lower in the primary angioplasty vs thrombolytic group.

PAMI-1 (substudy)

Primary Angioplasty in Myocardial Infarction

(continued)

Conclusions The initial benefit of primary PTCA reported in PAMI-I persists at 2 year follow-up including decreased rate of reintervention and improved infarct free survival.

A Comparison of Immediate Coronary Angioplasty With Intravenous Streptokinase in Acute Myocardial Infarction

Title	A comparison of immediate coronary angioplasty with intravenous streptokinase in acute myocardial infarction.
Authors	Zijlstra F, de Boer MJ, Hoorntje JCA, et al.
Reference	N Engl J Med 1993;328:680-684.
Disease	Acute myocardial infarction.
Purpose	To compare the results of immediate coronary angioplasty with intravenous streptokinase infusion for acute myocardial infarction.
Design	Randomized, open labeled, one center.
Patients	142 patients, age <76 years, with acute myocardial infarction (symptoms ≥ 30 min; < 6 h from onset of symptoms, or 6–24 h if there was evidence of continuing ischemia; ST elevation >1 mm in ≥2 leads).
Follow-up	In-hospital recurrent ischemia, predischarge symptom-limited exercise test, radionuclide ventriculography, and coronary angiography.
Treatment regimen	1. Streptokinase 1.5 million U over 1 h. 2. Immediate coronary angiography and angioplasty.
Additional therapy	Aspirin 300 mg IV, and then 300 mg/d orally. Intravenous nitroglycerin and intravenous heparin for >48 h.

A Comparison of Immediate Coronary Angioplasty With Intravenous Streptokinase in Acute Myocardial Infarction

(continued)

Results	Death occurred in 4 (6%) of the 72 patients that received streptokinase, but in none of the 70 patients assigned to angioplasty ($p=0.13$). Recurrent infarction occurred in 9 (13%) patients that received streptokinase, but in none of the patients assigned to angioplasty ($p=0.003$). Post infarction angina developed in 14 (19%) and 4 (6%) patients in the streptokinase and angioplasty groups ($p=0.02$). Mean left ventricular ejection fraction before discharge was 45±12% in the streptokinase group, and 51±11% in the angioplasty group ($p=0.004$). The infarct related artery was patent in 68% and 91%, respectively ($p=0.001$). Residual stenosis was 76±19% and 36±20%, respectively ($p<0.001$). There was no difference in the complication rate between the groups. Ischemic ST segment depression during the exercise test developed in 41% and 21% of the streptokinase and angioplasty groups ($p=0.01$). Left ventricular ejection fraction during exercise was 46±15% and 52±14%, respectively ($p=0.02$).
Conclusions	Immediate angioplasty was associated with higher rates of patency, lower grade of residual stenosis, better left ventricular function, and less recurrent ischemia and infarction than intravenous streptokinase therapy.

Immediate Angioplasty Compared With the Administration of a Thrombolytic Agent

Title	Immediate angioplasty compared with the administration of a thrombolytic agent followed by conservative treatment for myocardial infarction.
Authors	Gibbons AJ, Holmes DR, Reeder GS, et al.
Reference	N Engl J Med 1993;328:685-691.
Disease	Acute myocardial infarction.
Purpose	To compare direct angioplasty with administration of thrombolytic agent followed by conservative approach in the management of acute myocardial infarction.
Design	Randomized, open labeled, one center.
Patients	103 patients, age <80 years, with acute myocardial infarction (pain ≥30 min, ≤12 h from onset of symptoms, ST elevation of ≥1 mm in ≥2 adjacent leads, or new ST depression of ≥2 mm in ≥2 precordial leads. Patients with contraindication to thrombolytic therapy or in cardiogenic shock were excluded.
Follow-up	Technetium 99m sestamibi scan before therapy, and 6-14 days later, radionuclide ventriculography at rest predischarge and at 6 weeks.
Treatment regimen	1. Double chain tissue plasminogen activator (duteplase) 0.6 million U/kg over 4 h. Heparin 5000 U bolus and infusion for 5 days, and then subcutaneous 12,500 U X2/d. 2. Heparin 5,000 +10,000 U bolus, coronary angioplasty. Intravenous heparin infusion for 5 days.
Additional therapy	162.5 mg of chewable aspirin, and 162.5 mg/d thereafter. ß-blockers if not contraindicated.

Results	56 patients received t-PA (time from onset of symptoms to start of infusion 232±174 min), and 47 underwent angioplasty (first balloon inflation 277±144 min after onset of symptoms). Mortality was similar (2 in each group). Myocardial salvage for anterior infarction, as assessed by the difference between the pretreatment to predischarge MIBI defect size, was 27±21% and 31±21% of the left ventricle, in the t-PA and angioplasty groups, respectively. For nonanterior infarctions salvage was 7±13% and 5±10%, respectively. There was no difference in ejection fraction between the groups at discharge or after 6 weeks.
Conclusions	There was no difference in myocardial salvage between immediate angioplasty and intravenous thrombolytic therapy followed by conservative therapy.

DANAMI

DANish Trial in Acute Myocardial Infarction

Title	Danish multicenter randomized study of invasive vs conservative treatment in patients with inducible ischemia after thrombolysis in acute myocardial infarction (DANAMI).
Author	Madsen JK, Grande P, Saunamaki K, et al.
Reference	Circulation 1997; 96:748-755.
Disease	Coronary artery disease, inducible myocardial ischemia post infarction.
Purpose	To compare invasive therapy (PTCA or CABG) with conservative therapy in patients with inducible myocardial ischemia after a first myocardial infarction treated with thrombolytic therapy.
Design	Randomized, multicenter.
Patients	1008 patients ≤69 years old with a definite acute myocardial infarction and thrombolytic therapy begun within 12 h of symptom onset. Patients had to have either symptomatic angina pectoris >36 hours after admission or a positive pre-discharge exercise tolerance test.
Follow-up	Median 2.4 years (range 1-4 years).
Treatment regimen	Patients were randomized to conservative therapy (nitrates, ß-blockers, calcium channel blockers) vs invasive therapy (PTCA or CABG) within 2-5 weeks of randomization. All patients received aspirin.

DANAMI

DANish Trial in Acute Myocardial Infarction

(continued)

Results	505 patients were randomized to conservative therapy; 503 to invasive. At 2.4 years mortality was 3.6% with invasive therapy vs 4.4% with conservative therapy (p=NS). The invasive strategy was associated with a lower incidence of recurrent acute myocardial infarction compared to conservative therapy (5.6% vs 10.5%; p=0.0038); and lower incidence of admission for unstable angina (17.9% vs 29.5%, p<0.00001). The primary end point was the composite of death, reinfarction, or unstable angina, and occurred at lower rates with invasive therapy at 1, 2, and 3 years (15.4%, 23.5%, 31.7%) than conservative therapy (29.5%, 36.6%, and 44.0% p≤0.00001).
Conclusions	Patients with inducible ischemia before discharge from acute myocardial infarction treated with thrombolysis should receive coronary arteriography and revascularization procedure.

Effects of coronary stenting on restenosis and occlusion after angioplasty of the culprit vessel in patients with recent myocardial infarction

Title	Effects of coronary stenting on restenosis and occlusion after angioplasty of the culprit vessel in patients with recent myocardial infarction.
Author	Bauters C, Lablanche J-M, Belle EV, et al.
Reference	Circulation 1997; 96:2854-2858.
Disease	Coronary artery disease, myocardial infarction.
Purpose	To determine the long term effect of coronary stenting of infarct-related coronary lesions vs percutaneous transluminal coronary angioplasty (PTCA) alone.
Design	Comparison of consecutive patients undergoing stent implanation of infarct artery to matched patients who underwent PTCA without stenting within 24 h to 30 days after an acute myocardial infarction. Patients were matched for a number of clinical variables. 6 month angiograms were analyzed by quantitiative angiography.
Patients	200 acute myocardial infraction patients average age 57±11 years; 89% men.
Follow-up	6 months.
Treatment regimen	Coronary stenting (including bailout implantation, implantation of stent for suboptimal result after PTCA, or elective stent implantation) compared to PTCA.

Effects of coronary stenting on restenosis and occlusion after angioplasty of the culprit vessel in patients with recent myocardial infarction

(continued)

Results	Immediately after the procedure there was a larger acute gain in the stent group ($p<0.0001$), with a mean minimal lumen diameter of 2.58±0.44 mm in the stent group vs the balloon group (1.97±0.43 mm, $p<0.0001$). At 6 months, patients in the stent group had a larger net gain (1.02±0.79 vs 0.56±0.68 mm, $p<0.0001$), and a larger minimal lumen diameter (1.72±0.69 vs 1.23±0.72 mm, $p<0.0001$). By categorical analysis 27% of the stent group had restenosis compared to 52% of the PTCA group ($p<0.005$). At 6 months, total occlusion at the dilated site occurred in 1% of the stent group and 14% of the PTCA group ($p<0.005$).
Conclusions	Coronary stenting of the infarct related artery was associated with less restenosis at 6 months compared to PTCA alone. Whether this translates to improvement in left ventricular function or clinical outcome remains to be determined.

PAMI-2

Primary Angioplasty in Myocardial Infarction-2

Title	a. A prospective, randomized trial evaluating early discharge (day 3) without noninvasive risk stratification in low risk patients with acute myocardial infarction: PAMI-2. b. A prospective, randomized evaluation of prophylactic intraaortic balloon counterpulsation in high risk patients with acute myocardial infarction treated with primary angioplasty.
Authors	a. Brodie B, Grines CL, Spain S, et al. b. Stone GW, Marsalese D, Brodie BR, et al.
Reference	a. J Am Coll Cardiol 1995;25 (Suppl A):430A. b. J Am Coll Cardiol 1997;29:1459-1467.
Disease	Acute myocardial infarction
Purpose	To evaluate the effectiveness of both early discharge (third day) in low risk patients and prophylactic intraaortic balloon pumping (IABP) in high risk patients with acute myocardial infarction undergoing primary angioplasty.
Design	Randomized, multicenter.
Patients	1100 patients with ongoing chest pain ≤12 h after symptom onset, with ST elevation ≥1 mm in ≥2 contiguous leads. Patients with ST depression, LBBB, or nondiagnostic ECG were included if acute catheterization demonstrated an occluded coronary artery with regional LV dysfunction. Patients with cardiogenic shock, bleeding diathesis, and those who had received thrombolytic therapy were excluded.
Treatment regimen	Chewable aspirin 324 mg and intravenous heparin 5000-10000 U, nitroglycerin and ß-blockers. Coronary angiography with left ventriculography, and then, primary PTCA or emergent CABG (for unprotected left main coronary artery stenosis >60%, severe 3 vessel disease with a patent infarct related artery, or features precluding PTCA). High risk patients (age >70 years, 3 vessel disease, LVEF ≤45%, vein graft occlusion, persistent malignant ventricular arrhythmias or suboptimal PTCA result) were randomized to prophylactic IABP for 36-48 h unless an IABP was contraindicated or conservative treatment (no IABP). Low risk patients were randomized into accelerated discharge (day 3) and traditional care (discharge at 5-7 days) groups.

PAMI-2

Primary Angioplasty in Myocardial Infarction-2 (continued)

Additional therapy	Stenting and atherectomy were rarely used during the study. Intravenous heparin for ≥72 h, nitroglycerin infusion for 24 h, and oral aspirin 325 mg/d were used.
Results	After PTCA 437 patients were considered high risk and 471 patients as low risk. Among the low risk patients in-hospital and postdischarge outcomes were similar in the early discharge and traditional care groups. High risk patients were randomized to IABP (n=211) or conservative therapy (no IABP)(n=226). In only 182 patients (86.3%) of the 211 patients IABP was successfully inserted. IABP was inserted in 26 (11.5%) of patients assigned to no IABP. In an intention to treat analysis, in-hospital death occurred in 4.3% of the IABP and 3.1% of the non IABP (p=0.52). IABP did not prevent reinfarction (6.2% vs 8.0%, in the IABP and no IABP, respectively (p=0.46)); reocclusion of the infarct related artery (6.7% vs 5.5% (p=0.64)); heart failure or hypotension (19.9% vs 23.0% (p=0.43)); or the combined end point of death, reinfarction, reocclusion, stroke, hypotension, or new onset heart failure (28.9% vs 29.2% (p=0.95)). IABP was associated with increased risk of stroke (2.4% vs 0.0% (p=0.03)). The findings were similar when only the 382 randomized patients who received their assigned therapy were included. However, IABP was associated with modest reduction of recurrent ischemia (13.3% vs 19.6% (p=0.08)) and need for repeated catheterization (7.6% vs 13.3% (p=0.05)), but an increased bleeding complications (36.0% vs 27.4% (p=0.05)). Paired pre PTCA and predischarge left ventriculography, performed in 217 patients, showed that there was no difference in improvement in global LVEF and infarct zone regional wall motion between the IABP and no IABP groups.
Conclusions	A prophylactic insertion of IABP in high risk hemodynamically stable acute myocardial infarction after primary angioplasty did not decrease mortality, reocclusion of the infarct related artery, or reinfarction, and was associated with an increased rate of stroke. Among the low risk patients in-hospital and postdischarge outcomes were similar in the early discharge and traditional care groups.

PAMI Stent Pilot Trial

Title	Prospective, multicenter study of the safety and feasibility of primary stenting in acute myocardial infarction: In-hospital and 30 day results of the PAMI stent pilot trial.
Authors	Stone GW, Brodie BR, Griffin JJ, et al.
Reference	J Am Coll Cardiol 1998;31:23-30.
Disease	Acute myocardial infarction.
Purpose	To evaluate the feasibility and safety of a primary stenting strategy in patients with acute myocardial infarction.
Design	Multicenter.
Patients	312 patients with chest pain ≤12 h in duration with ECG changes compatible with acute myocardial infarction. Patients in cardiogenic shock and those with contraindications to heparin, aspirin or ticlopidine, increased risk for bleeding, and recent thrombolytic therapy were excluded. Only patients that actually underwent primary PTCA were included in the study.
Follow-up	6 months clinical follow-up.
Treatment regimen	Percutaneous transluminal coronary angioplasty (PTCA), unless TIMI grade flow 3 was present with an infarct related artery stenosis <70%, or if a very small vessel was occluded, or if the infarct related lesion could not be identified. Patients treated medically or surgically were excluded from the study. After PTCA, an attempt was made to insert a Johnson & Johnson Palmaz-Schatz stent.

PAMI Stent Pilot Trial

(continued)

Additional therapy	Upon enrollment, oral aspirin 324–500 mg, 250–500 mg ticlopidine, and 5000–10,000 U bolus intravenous heparin. Intravenous ß-blockers were given unless contraindicated. 6 h after sheath removal, heparin infusion was given for 12 h. All patients received oral aspirin 325 mg/d, ticlopidine 250 mg bid, and ß-blockers. Angiotensin converting enzyme inhibitors were administered if hypertension, heart failure, or LV dysfunction was present.
Results	Primary angioplasty was performed in 312 patients; in 240 of them (77%) stenting was attempted. In 72 patients, stenting was not considered feasible. Stenting was performed more frequently in patients with 1 vessel disease, whereas it was attempted less often in patients with 3 vessel disease. In 236 (98%) of the 240 patients, stenting was successful. TIMI grade 3 flow was achieved in 94.4% of the stent group vs 87.3% of the PTCA only group (p=0.04). The mean residual stenosis was 12.1±16.2% in the stent group vs 33.3±14.3% in the PTCA only group (p<0.0001). A <50% residual stenosis was obtained in 93.7% of the stent group vs 77.3% of the PTCA only group (p<0.0001). In-hospital death occurred in 2 patients (0.8%), reinfarction in 4 patients (1.7%), and recurrent ischemia in 9 patients (3.8%) of the stent group. Only 3 patients (1.3%) needed target vessel revascularization for recurrent ischemia. None of the patients died or had reinfarction within 30 days after hospital discharge. Only 1 patient (0.4%) needed target vessel revascularization within 30 days after discharge.
Conclusions	Primary stenting is safe and feasible in most of the patients with acute myocardial infarction and is associated with good short term results.

Randomized comparison of coronary stenting with balloon angioplasty in selected patients with acute myocardial infarction

Title	Randomized comparison of coronary stenting with balloon angioplasty in selected patients with acute myocardial infarction.
Authors	Suryapranata H, Van't Hof AWJ, Hoorntje JCA, et al.
Reference	Circulation 1998; 97:2502-2505.
Disease	Acute myocardial infarction.
Purpose	To compare outcomes in patients with acute myocardial infarction receiving primary stenting with percutaneous transluminal coronary angioplasty (PTCA).
Design	Prospective, randomized.
Patients	Patients with acute myocardial infarction randomized to stenting (n=112) or PTCA (n=115). Average age 58; 83-85% male. Patients had to have a culprit lesion in a native coronary artery that was deemed suitable for stenting.
Follow-up	6 months.
Treatment regimen	Palmaz-Schultz stents vs PTCA.
Additional therapy	In stent patients initially heparin followed by warfarin and aspirin. Protocol then modified for stent patients to receive ticlopidine plus aspirin.

Randomized comparison of coronary stenting with balloon angioplasty in selected patients with acute myocardial infarction

(continued)

Results	Clinical end points included death, recurrent MI, subsequent CABG, repeat angioplasty of the infarct related vessel. Cardiac event free survival was 95% in stent group and 80% in PTCA group (p=0.0012). Recurrent MI occurred in 7% of patients after PTCA and 1% after stenting (p=0.036). Revascularization of target vessel was performed in 17% of PTCA and 4% of stent patients (p=0.0016).
Conclusions	In selected acute MI patients, primary stenting was effective, safe and resulted in lower incidence of recurrent infarction and need for subsequent target vessel revascularization vs PTCA.

Title	A randomized comparison of intra-aortic balloon pumping after primary coronary angioplasty in high risk patients with acute myocardial infarction.
Authors	Van't Hof AWJ, Liem AL, de Boer MJ, et al.
Reference	Eur Heart J 1999;20:659-665.
Disease	Acute myocardial infarction.
Purpose	To assess the effects of intra-aortic balloon pump (IABP) in high risk patients with acute myocardial infarction.
Design	Randomized, single center.
Patients	238 patients with acute myocardial infarction, with >20 mm sum of ST elevation, <70 years old, who were admitted within 3 hours of onset of symptoms and were candidates for primary PTCA.
Follow-up	6 months.
Treatment regimen	Randomization to IABP or not. The IABP was inserted via the femoral route immediately after the PTCA. Aortic counterpulsation was continued for 48 hours.
Additional therapy	Patients who were assigned to standard therapy group and had signs of cardiogenic shock, cross over to IABP was prespecified. All patients received intravenous acetylsalicylic acid, nitroglycerin infusion, and heparin infusion. All patients underwent coronary angiography and angioplasty.

Results	118 patients were randomized to IABP and 120 to no IABP. In the no IABP group, 37 (31%) patients received IABP, whereas 30 (25%) patients, assigned to IABP did not receive IABP. The primary end point (death, recurrent myocardial infarction, stroke, or a LVEF <30% at 6 months) occurred in 26% of the IABP group vs 26% of the no IABP group (p=0.94). Death occurred in 10% and 8% of the IABP and no IABP groups, respectively (p=0.47), heart failure in 8% and 12% (p=0.41), and recurrent myocardial infarction in 6% and 3%, respectively (p=0.16). There was no difference in enzymatic infarct size (LDHQ72) (1616±1148 vs 1608±1163, respectively, p=0.96), pre-discharge LVEF (39±12 vs 36±13; p=0.21), and LVEF at 6 month follow-up (42±13 vs 40±14; p=0.51) between the IABP and no IABP groups. Serious complications occurred in 8% of patients treated with an IABP.
Conclusions	Routine use of IABP after primary PTCA for acute myocardial infarction was not associated with better outcome. IABP after primary PTCA should probably be used only for patients with severe hemodynamic impairment.

Primary angioplasty vs systemic thrombolysis in anterior myocardial infarction

Title	Primary angioplasty vs systemic thrombolysis in anterior myocardial infarction.
Authors	Garcia E, Elizaga J, Perez-Castellano N, et al.
Reference	J Am Coll Cardiol 1999; 33:605-611.
Disease	Acute myocardial infarction.
Purpose	To compare primary PTCA vs t-PA for reducing in-hospital mortality in anterior wall MI patients.
Design	Prospective, randomized.
Patients	220 patients with anterior wall MI. 109 receive primary PTCA, 111 received t-PA.
Follow-up	6 months.
Treatment regimen	Primary PTCA vs standard dose t-PA.
Additional therapy	Aspirin, heparin.

Primary angioplasty vs systemic thrombolysis in anterior myocardial infarction

(continued)

Results	In-hospital mortality was reduced in the primary PTCA group (2.8%) vs t-PA group (10.8%; p=0.02). In-hospital post infarct angina or positive stress test were reduced in the PTCA group (11.9%) vs the t-PA group (25.2%, p=0.01). The primary PCTA group was less likely to require repeat PTCA or CABG (22.0%) vs the t-PA group (47.7%; p<0.001). The primary PTCA group had a lower cumulative rate of death at 6 months (4.6%) vs the t-PA group (11.7%, p=0.05) and also required less follow-up revascularization procedures.
Conclusions	Primary PTCA is superior to t-PA (obviously in interventional centers that are set up to perform acute PTCA).

Comparison of thrombolytic therapy and primary coronary angioplasty with liberal stenting for inferior myocardial infarction with precordial ST segment depression. Immediate and long term results of a randomized study.

Title	Comparison of thrombolytic therapy and primary coronary angioplasty with liberal stenting for inferior myocardial infarction with precordial ST segment depression. Immediate and long term results of a randomized study.
Authors	Ribichini F, Steffenino G, Dellavalle A, et al.
Reference	J Am Coll Cardiol. 1998; 32:1687-1694.
Disease	Acute myocardial infarction.
Purpose	To compare the effects of primary PTCA vs recombinant tissue plasminogen activator (rt-PA) in patients with inferior wall MIs.
Design	Randomized, single center.
Patients	110 patients with acute inferior wall MI presenting within 6 hours of symptoms with ST segment elevation in at least 2 inferior leads and ST depression in at least 3 precordial leads.
Follow-up	1 year.
Treatment regimen	rt-PA standard regimen vs PTCA. Stents as needed as part of PTCA protocol.
Additional therapy	Aspirin, heparin, others.

Comparison of thrombolytic therapy and primary coronary angioplasty with liberal stenting for inferior myocardial infarction with precordial ST segment depression. Immediate and long term results of a randomized study.

(continued)

Results	Coronary stents were implanted in 58% of patients in the PTCA group. The rate of in-hospital mortality and reinfarction did not differ significantly between the 2 groups (3.6% for PTCA and 9.1% for the rt-PA group, p=0.4). Primary PTCA was associated with lower rates of recurrent angina (1.8%) vs rt-PA (20%; p=0.002). Repeat target vessel revascularization was more common in rt-PA group (29.1%) vs PTCA group (3.6%; p=0.0003). Left ventricular ejection fraction at discharge was greater in the PTCA group (55.2%) vs the rt-PA group (48.2%, p=0.0001). At 1 year outcome, death, reinfarction or repeat revascularization was 11% in the PTCA group and 52.7% in the rt-PA group (p<0.0001).
Conclusions	Primary PTCA was superior to rt-PA for in-hospital reduction in recurrent angina, repeat revascularization and preservation of LV function. At 1 year PTCA was associated with better event free survival.

SHOCK

Should We Emergently Revascularize Occluded Coronaries for Cardiogenic Shock

Title	Early revascularization in acute myocardial infarction complicated by cardiogenic shock.
Authors	Hochman JS, Sleeper LA, Webb JG, et al.
Reference	N Engl J Med 1999;341:625-634.
Disease	Acute myocardial infarction complicated by cardiogenic shock.
Purpose	To evaluate the effect of early revascularization in patients with acute myocardial infarction complicated by shock.
Design	Randomized, multicenter.
Patients	302 patients with acute myocardial infarction and cardiogenic shock (confirmed by both clinical and hemodynamic criteria). Mean age 66 years; 32% were women; 55% were transferred from other hospitals.
Follow-up	6 months.
Treatment regimen	Patients were randomized to emergency revascularization (n=152) or intensive medical therapy and thrombolysis (n=150). Angioplasty or coronary bypass surgery had to be performed as soon as possible within 6 hours of randomization. 150 patients were randomized to medical stabilization-intensive medical therapy and thrombolytic therapy. Intraaortic balloon counterpulsation was recommended in both groups.
Additional therapy	As needed.

Should We Emergently Revascularize Occluded Coronaries for Cardiogenic Shock

(continued)

Results	The primary end point was death from all causes at 30 days and the secondary end point was survival at 6 months. Time from onset of myocardial infarction to shock was 5.6 hours (median value). Among patients randomized to early revascularization, 64% received angioplasty and 36% received surgery. At 30 days, 46.7% of the revascularization group died and 56.0% of the medical treatment group died (p=0.11). At 6 months, mortality was significantly lower among patients who received early revascularization (50.3%) vs those that received medical treatment (63.1%, p=0.027). Success rate for early revascularization of the culprit vessel was 77% for the group assigned to early revascularization. Successful angioplasty in the group assigned to early revascularization was associated with a lower 30 day mortality (38%) vs those that had an unsuccessful angioplasty (79%, p=0.003). Acute renal failure occurred in 13% assigned to revascularization and 24% to those assigned to medical therapy (p=0.03).
Conclusions	In patients with acute myocardial infarction and cardiogenic shock, emergency revascularization did not significantly decrease overall mortality at 30 days but did reduce overall mortality at 6 months. "Early revascularization should be strongly considered for patients with acute myocardial infarction complicated by cardiogenic shock."

Stent-PAMI

Stent Primary Angioplasty in Myocardial Infarction Study

Title	Coronary angioplasty with or without stent implantation for acute myocardial infarction.
Authors	Grines CL, Cox DA, Stone GW, et al.
Reference	N Engl J Med 1999;341:1949-1956.
Disease	Acute myocardial infarction.
Purpose	To compare outcomes in patients with acute myocardial infarction undergoing primary angioplasty to angioplasty with implantation of a heparin-coated Palmaz-Schatz stent.
Design	Randomized, multicenter.
Patients	900 patients with acute myocardial infarction undergoing emergency catheterization and angioplasty.
Follow-up	6-6.5 months.
Treatment regimen	Patients with vessels appropriate for stenting were randomized to angioplasty alone (n=448) or angioplasty with stenting (n=452).
Additional therapy	Aspirin, ticlopidine, heparin and, if no contraindications, ß-blockers.

Stent-PAMI

Stent Primary Angioplasty in Myocardial Infarction Study

(continued)

Results	Based on angiograms performed immediately after the procedure, stenting was associated with a larger mean minimal luminal diameter (2.56±0.44 mm) compared to angioplasty alone (2.12±0.45 mm, $p<0.001$). There was a trend toward slightly lower incidence of TIMI 3 grade flow in stented (89.4%) vs angioplasty alone group (92.7%) but this was not statistically significant ($p = 0.10$). The combined primary end point at 6 months of death, reinfarction, disabling stroke, or target vessel revascularization because of ischemia occurred in fewer patients that received stents (12.6%) compared to the angioplasty alone group (20.1%, $p < 0.01$). At 6 months mortality rates were 4.2% in the stent groups and 2.7% in the angioplasty group ($p=0.27$). Decrease in composite end point was secondary to decreased need for target vessel revascularization. The incidence of angina at 6 months was lower in the stent group (11.3%) compared to the angioplasty alone group (16.9%, $p=0.02$). Late angiograms at 6.5 months showed that patients who received stents had a larger minimal diameter, less residual stenosis, and a lower rate of restenosis (20.3% vs 33.5%, $p<0.001$).
Conclusions	Implantation of a stent for acute myocardial infarction "has clinical benefits beyond those of primary coronary angioplasty alone."

Long term benefit of primary angioplasty as compared with thrombolytic therapy for acute myocardial infarction

Title	Long term benefit of primary angioplasty as compared with thrombolytic therapy for acute myocardial infarction.
Authors	Zijlstra F, Hoorntje JCA, DeBoer M-J, et al.
Reference	N Engl J Med 1999;341:1413–1419.
Disease	Acute myocardial infarction.
Purpose	To compare the long term efficacy of primary angioplasty vs thrombolytic therapy for acute myocardial infarction.
Design	Prospective, randomized, multicenter.
Patients	395 patients with acute myocardial infarction. 194 were assigned to primary angioplasty; 201 to streptokinase.
Follow-up	5±2 years.
Treatment regimen	Primary coronary angioplasty or streptokinase (1.5 million units IV over one hour).
Additional therapy	All patients received aspirin and heparin.

Long term benefit of primary angioplasty as compared with thrombolytic therapy for acute myocardial infarction

(continued)

Results

The infarct related coronary artery was patent in 90% of the angioplasty group vs the streptokinase group (65%; $p<0.001$). Prior to discharge 26% of the streptokinase group vs 14% of the angioplasty group had LV ejection fraction <40% ($p=0.006$). Over ~5 years, 24% of the streptokinase group died vs 13% of the angioplasty patients (RR=0.54; 95 % CI=0.36-0.87). 22% of the streptokinase patients and 6% of the angioplasty patients experienced nonfatal reinfarction (RR=0.27, 95% CI=0.15-0.52). The incidence of death due to cardiac causes correlated with a lower LV ejection fraction. Reinfarctions were more common in the streptokinase group both within the first 30 days of enrollment and after 30 days of enrollment. The combined outcomes of death and nonfatal reinfarction were lower in the angioplasty compared to the streptokinase group during the first 30 days (RR=0.13, 95% CI=0.05-0.37 and after 30 days of randomizations (RR=0.62; 95% CI=0.43-0.91). There were fewer readmissions for ischemia in the angioplasty group compared to the streptokinase group.

Conclusions

Primary coronary angioplasty for acute myocardial infarction was associated with lower incidence of death and nonfatal reinfarction compared to streptokinase, over 5 years of study.

PACT

The Plasminogen activator Angioplasty Compatibility Trial

Title	A randomized trial comparing primary angioplasty with a strategy of short acting thrombolysis and immediate planned rescue angioplasty in acute myocardial infarction: The PACT Trial.
Authors	Ross AM, Coyne KS, Reiner JS, et al.
Reference	J Am Coll Cardiol 1999;34:1954–1962.
Disease	Acute myocardial infarction.
Purpose	To determine the efficacy and safety of a short acting and reduced dose fibrinolytic regimen rt-PA coupled with PTCA as the primary recanalization modality.
Design	Randomized, double blind , placebo controlled, multicenter.
Patients	606 patients with acute myocardial infarction.
Follow-up	1 year.
Treatment regimen	IV bolus of rt-PA (50 mg) given over 3 minutes or an IV placebo bolus and then angiography. If infarct artery was TIMI grade 0, 1, 2, immediate angioplasty; if it was TIMI grade 3, a second bolus of assigned study drug could be given.
Additional therapy	Heparin, aspirin.

PACT

The Plasminogen activator Angioplasty Compatibility Trial

(continued)

Results

The primary end points were patency at the time of initial angiography, technical results of the PTCA, complication rates, LV function (LV angiogram), and time to restored patency after angioplasty. The patency rates (TIMI flow grade 2 or 3) at the time of arrival in the catheterization laboratory were 34% with placebo vs 61% with rt-PA (p=0.001). Both rescue and primary PTCA restored TIMI 3 levels of flow in closed arteries at 77% and 79%, respectively. Stenting was done in 26% of patients in each group. The LV ejection fraction (EF) obtained at the first angiogram (following angioplasty if angioplasty was done) was 57.7±14.1% in the placebo group and 59.4±13.8% in the rt-PA group (p=NS). Follow-up LV function assessed on repeat or convalescent angiogram (at day 5-7) revealed an LVEF of 58.4±12.5% in the placebo group and 58.2±13.0% in the rt-PA group (p=NS). Patients arriving in the catheterization laboratory with TIMI flow grade 3 had convalescent LVEF of 62.4% vs those with later mechanical restoration (primary or planned rescue PTCA) of 57.9% (p=0.004). Lowest convalescent LVEF was seen in patients who never achieved TIMI flow grade 3 (EF=54.7%). No difference in adverse events occurred between placebo vs rt-PA patients, including the incidence of major hemorrhage (13.5 vs 12.9%, respectively).

Conclusions

A tailored thrombolytic regimen with subsequent PTCA if needed leads to better early recanalization prior to arrival to the cath lab, that facilitates better LV function and no adverse events.

CCP

The Cooperative Cardiovascular Project

Title	Primary coronary angioplasty vs thrombolysis for the management of acute myocardial infarction in elderly patients.
Authors	Berger AK, Schulman KA, Gersh BJ, et al.
Reference	JAMA 1999;282:341-348.
Disease	Acute myocardial infarction.
Purpose	To compare the efficacy of primary PTCA and thrombolysis in elderly patients with acute myocardial infarction.
Design	Observational.
Patients	80,356 patients, ≥65 years old with acute myocardial infarction, ≤12 hours of onset of symptoms and without contraindications to thrombolytic therapy. Patients with cardiogenic shock were excluded.
Follow-up	1 year.
Treatment regimen	Primary PTCA or thrombolytic therapy.

Results

28,955 patients presented within 6 hours of onset of symptoms and with ST segment elevation or LBBB.Among those, only 44.7% received reperfusion therapy within 6 hours of hospitalization. 18,645 patients (23.2%) received thrombolytic therapy and 2038 patients (2.5%) underwent primary PTCA within 6 hours after hospital arrival. The remaining 59,673 patients (74.2%) did not receive reperfusion therapy within the first 6 hours after hospital arrival, and 54,989 patients (68.4%) did not receive reperfusion therapy at all. Mean time to treatment after admission was 68.3±54.4 minutes in the thrombolysis group vs 142.6±68. 1 minute in the primary PTCA group ($p<0.001$). 30 day mortality was 8.7% in the primary PTCA group vs 11.9% in the thrombolysis group ($p=0.001$). 1 year mortality was 14.4% vs 17.6%, respectively ($p=0.001$).After adjusting for baseline cardiac risk factors the hazard ratio of death at 30 days was 0.74 (95% CI 0.63-0.88), and at one year it was 0.83 (95% CI 0.73-0.94). Patients undergoing primary PTCA had less cerebral hemorrhages (0.2% vs 1.4%; $p=0.001$), stroke (2.1% vs 3.0%; $p=0.03$), post infarction angina (24.0% vs 29.6%; $p=0.001$) and reinfarction (4.0% vs 5.3%; $p=0.009$) than the patients receiving thrombolytic therapy. However, among patients who presented within 6 hours of onset of symptoms and were eligible for thrombolytic therapy, 30 day mortality was insignificantly smaller with primary PTCA (10.1% vs 12.0%; $p=0.06$). Eventually, 39.2% of the patients receiving thrombolytic therapy underwent coronary angioplasty, 12.4% underwent PTCA and 6.3% CABG. After stratification of the patients by age, gender, hypertension, prior heart failure and the location of myocardial infarction, the benefit of primary PTCA persisted. The benefit of primary PTCA was still apparent when patients were stratified by hospital's volume of acute myocardial infarction patients (<150 per year vs ≥150 per year) and the presence of onsite catheterization laboratory.

CCP

The Cooperative Cardiovascular Project

(continued)

Conclusions	In patients, ≥65 years old, with acute myocardial infarction, primary PTCA was associated with a modest decrease in 30 day and 1 year mortality. In the subgroup analysis of patients eligible for thrombolytic therapy, the benefit of primary PTCA was not statistically significant.

PRAGUE

Primary Angioplasty in patients transferred from General community hospitals to specialized PTCA Units with or without Emergency thrombolysis

Title	Multicenter randomized trial comparing transport to primary angioplasty vs immediate thrombolysis vs combined strategy for patients with acute myocardial infarction presenting to a community hospital without a catheterization laboratory.
Authors	Widimsky P, Groch L, Zelizko M, et al.
Reference	Eur Heart J 2000;21:823-831.
Disease	Acute myocardial infarction.
Purpose	To compare three reperfusion strategies for patients with acute myocardial infarction presenting initially to hospitals without catheterization facility: 1) IV streptokinase; 2) transport to primary angioplasty; or 3) thrombolysis with streptokinase during transfer to immediate coronary angioplasty.
Design	Randomized, open label, multicenter.
Patients	300 patients with acute myocardial infarction and ST elevation or bundle branch block who presented to 17 participating hospitals without catheterization facility within 6 hours of onset of symptoms.
Follow-up	30 days.

Primary Angioplasty in patients transferred from General community hospitals to specialized PTCA Units with or without Emergency thrombolysis

(continued)

Treatment regimen	Randomization to 1) IV streptokinase (n=99); 2) thrombolytic therapy during transportation for immediate angioplasty (n=100); or 3) immediate transportation for primary angioplasty without thrombolytic therapy (n=101).
Additional therapy	Angioplasty was performed in all patients with TIMI flow 0-2 in the infarct related artery. In case of TIMI flow 3, angioplasty was performed at the discretion of the operator. Stents were implanted whenever anatomically suitable or when suboptimal results were achieved by balloon angioplasty.
Results	Two patients from the thrombolytic therapy + PTCA had ventricular fibrillation during transportation. No complications occurred during transportation in the PTCA without thrombolysis group. Median time from admission to reperfusion was 106 minutes and 96 minutes in the groups transferred for PTCA with and without thrombolysis, respectively. TIMI flow before angioplasty was 2 and 3 in 17% and 30% of the patients transferred with thrombolytic therapy and 15% and 12%, respectively, of the patients transferred without thrombolysis. PTCA was performed acutely in 82 and 91 of the patients transferred with and without thrombolysis. After PTCA, 91% and 92% of the patients transferred with and without thrombolysis had TIMI flow 3 and 5% and 3%, respectively, TIMI flow 2. 30 day mortality was 14% in the thrombolysis without PTCA, 12% in the PTCA + thrombolysis, and 7% in the PTCA without thrombolysis. Reinfarction occurred in 10%, 7%, and 1% ($p<0.03$), respectively, whereas stroke occurred in 1%, 3%, and 0 of the patients, respectively. The combined end point of death/ reinfarction/ stroke at 30 days occurred in 23%, 15%, and 8%, respectively ($p<0.02$).

Primary Angioplasty in patients transferred from General community hospitals to specialized PTCA Units with or without Emergency thrombolysis

(continued)

Conclusions	Transferring patients with acute myocardial infarction from community hospitals to a tertiary center for primary angioplasty is feasible and safe. Compared with the strategy of thrombolytic therapy, transfer for primary angioplasty was associated with less reinfarction and the combined end point of death/reinfarction/stroke at 30 days. The combined strategy of thrombolysis + PTCA was not associated with better outcome than thrombolytic therapy alone.

1. Acute Myocardial Infarction

c. Anticoagulation/ Antiplatelet

HART

Heparin-Aspirin Reperfusion Trial

Title	A comparison between heparin and low dose aspirin as adjunctive therapy with tissue plasminogen activator for acute myocardial infarction.
Authors	Hsia J, Hamilton WP, Kleiman N, et al.
Reference	N Engl J Med 1990;323:1433–1437.
Disease	Acute myocardial infarction.
Purpose	To compare early intravenous heparin with oral aspirin as adjunctive therapy to tissue plasminogen activator for acute myocardial infarction.
Design	Randomized, open label, multicenter.
Patients	193 patients, age <76 years, with chest pain and ST elevation ≥1 mm in ≥2 contiguous leads, within 6 h from onset of symptoms.
Follow-up	7–24 h and 7 day cardiac catheterization. 7 day clinical course.
Treatment regimen	1. Oral aspirin 80 mg/d, started with the t-PA for 7 days. 2. IV heparin 5000 U bolus, followed by 1000 U/h, started with the t-PA for 7 days.
Additional therapy	Intravenous tissue plasminogen activator (t-PA) 6 mg bolus, 54 mg over the first h, 20 mg over the second h, and 20 mg over 4 h.

HART

Heparin-Aspirin Reperfusion Trial

(continued)

Results	At the time of the first angiogram, 82% and 52% of the infarct related arteries of the patients assigned to heparin and aspirin were patent ($p<0.0001$). Of the arteries that were initially patent, 88% and 95% in the heparin and aspirin groups remained patent after 7.4±2.4 days ($p=0.17$). The number of bleeding events and recurrent ischemia were similar between the groups. The mortality rate was 1.9% vs 4.0% in the heparin and aspirin groups, respectively (p=NS).
Conclusions	Coronary patency rate improved when heparin was added to t-PA compare to when aspirin was added.

TIMI-5

Thrombolysis in Myocardial Infarction 5 Trial

Title	A pilot trial of recombinant desulfatohirudin compared with heparin in conjunction with tissue type plasminogen activator and aspirin for acute myocardial infarction: Results of the Thrombolysis in Myocardial Infarction (TIMI) 5 trial.
Authors	Cannon CP, McCabe CH, Henry TD, et al.
Reference	J Am Coll Cardiol 1994;23:993–1003.
Disease	Acute myocardial infarction.
Purpose	To compare the efficacy of recombinant desulfatohirudin (hirudin) to heparin as adjunctive therapy to thrombolysis in acute myocardial infarction.
Design	Randomized, multicenter, dose escalation trial.
Patients	246 patients with acute myocardial infarction < 6 hours from onset of symptoms with chest pain >30 min and ST segment elevation ≥0.1 mV in ≥2 contiguous leads or with new left bundle branch block.
Follow-up	90 min and 18–36 h coronary angiography. In-hospital clinical events.
Treatment regimen	Intravenous heparin or hirudin at 1 of 4 escalating doses (Bolus (mg/kg) and intravenous infusion mg/kg per h) of 0.15 and 0.05; 0.1 and 0.1; 0.3 and 0.1; and 0.6 and 0.2, respectively) for 5 days.
Additional therapy	Front loaded tissue type plasminogen activator and aspirin 160 mg/d. Intravenous and oral metoprolol.

TIMI-5

Thrombolysis in Myocardial Infarction 5 Trial

(continued)

Results	The primary efficacy end point (achievement of TIMI 3 flow at 90 min and 18–36 h without death or reinfarction before the second angiography) was achieved in 61.8% and 49.4% of the hirudin and heparin treated patients, respectively (p=0.07). While 90 min patency of the infarct related artery was similar at 18–36 h, 97.8% and 89.2 % of the hirudin and heparin-treated patients had an open artery, respectively (p=0.01). In-hospital death or reinfarction occurred in 6.8% and 16.7% of the hirudin and heparin groups, respectively (p=0.02). Major hemorrhage occurred in 1.2% and 4.7% of the patients, respectively (p=0.09).
Conclusions	Hirudin is a relatively safe drug and has a several advantages over heparin, as an adjunctive to front loaded tissue plasminogen activator therapy.

Title	Beneficial effects of RheothRx injection in patients receiving thrombolytic therapy for acute myocardial infarction. Results of a randomized, double blind, placebo controlled trial.
Authors	Schaer GL, Spaccavento LJ, Browne KF, et al.
Reference	Circulation 1996;94:298-307.
Disease	Acute myocardial infarction.
Purpose	To evaluate the safety and efficacy of adjunctive therapy with RheothRx (poloxamer 188, a surfactanct with hemorheological and antithrombotic properties) in patients with acute myocardial infarction undergoing thrombolytic therapy.
Design	Randomized, double blind, placebo controlled, multicenter.
Patients	114 patients, ≥18 years old, with suspected acute myocardial infarction (chest pain ≥30 min, ST elevation in ≥2 leads. All patients received thrombolytic therapy within 6 h of onset of symptoms. Patients with serum creatinine ≥3.0 mg/dL were excluded.
Follow-up	Clinical follow-up and 99mTc sestamibi tomographic imaging with radionuclide ventriculography before reperfusion and 5-7 days after infarction.
Treatment regimen	RheothRx (150 or 300 mg/kg over 1 h and then 15 or 30 mg/kg/h for 47 h) or placebo infusion was initiated immediately after initiation of thrombolytic therapy.
Additional therapy	Thrombolytic therapy (tPA or streptokinase). Chewable aspirin, nitrates, IV followed by oral ß-blocker, and heparin for ≥48 h.

Results	75 patients were randomized to RheothRx and 39 to placebo. Baseline characteristics were not significantly different between the groups. RheothRx treated patients had a 38% reduction in median infarct size (25th and 75th percentile) compared with placebo (16% (7,30) vs 26% (9,43); p=0.031), greater median myocardial salvage (13% (7,20) vs 4% (1,15); p=0.033), and higher ejection fraction (52% (43,60) vs 46% (35,60); p=0.02). RheothRx treated patients had lower rate of reinfarction (1% vs 13%, p=0.016). Therapy was well tolerated without adverse hemodynamic effects or bleeding.
Conclusions	Therapy with RheothRx was effective in reduction of infarct size and preservation of left ventricular function in patients undergoing thrombolytic therapy for acute myocardial infarction.

TIMI 9B

Thrombolysis and Thrombin Inhibition in Myocardial Infarction 9B

Title	a. Hirudin in acute myocardial infarction. Thrombolysis and thrombin inhibition in myocardial infarction (TIMI) 9B trial. b. Prospective temporal analysis of the outcome of preinfarction angina vs outcome. An ancillary study in TIMI-9B.
Authors	a. Antman EM, for the TIMI 9B Investigators. b. Kloner RA, Shook T, Antman E, et al.
Reference	a. Circulation 1996;94:911-921. b. Circulation 1998; 97:1042-1045.
Disease	Acute myocardial infarction.
Purpose	a. To compare the efficacy and safety of recombinant desulfatohirudin (Hirudin) with heparin as adjunctive therapy to thrombolysis and aspirin in acute myocardial infarction. b. To determine the importance of the time of onset of preinfarction angina in relationship to 30 day outcome in TIMI-9B.
Design	a. Randomized, double blind, multicenter. b. Standardized forms questioned patients regarding time of onset of angina in relationship to myocardial infarction.
Patients	a. 3002 patients, ≥21 years old, with acute myocardial infarction with ≥1 mm ST segment elevation in ≥2 leads or new LBBB, within 12 h of onset of symptoms, and no contraindications to thrombolytic therapy. Patients with serum creatinine >2.0 mg/dL, cardiogenic shock, or receiving therapeutic doses of anticoagulants were excluded. b. 3002 patients with myocardial infarction.
Follow-up	a. 30 day clinical follow-up. b. 30 days.
Treatment regimen	a. Randomization to heparin or hirudin. Therapy started within 60 min after thrombolysis and continued for 96 h. Hirudin: bolus of 0.1 mg/kg (maximum 15 mg), followed by a continuous infusion of 0.1 mg/kg/h (maximum 15 mg/h). Heparin: a bolus of 5000 U, followed by continuous infusion of 1000 U/h. Target aPTT 55 to 85 sec. b. As per TIMI 9B.

TIMI 9B

Thrombolysis and Thrombin Inhibition in Myocardial Infarction 9B (continued)

Additional therapy	a. Intravenous thrombolytic therapy by the treating physician front loaded tPA (maximum 100 mg) over 90 min or streptokinase, 1.5 million U over 1 h. Aspirin 150 to 325 mg/d, ß-blockers, nitrates, calcium channel blockers, and other medications were permitted.
Results	a. The hirudin-treated patients were more likely to have an aPTT within the target range (p<0.0001). Only 15% of the hirudin group vs 34% of the heparin group had aPTT values <55 sec within the first 24 h of therapy. The primary end point of death, recurrent myocardial infarction, severe heart failure, or cardiogenic shock by 30 days occurred in 11.9% of the heparin treated group vs 12.9% of the hirudin-treated patients (p=NS). After adjustment for age, time to therapy, and type of thrombolytic therapy administered, there was no significant difference between the groups concerning occurrence of the primary end point or in the occurrence of the individual elements of the composite end point. Kaplan-Meier plots of the time to development of the composite end point and to the occurrence of death or reinfarction were comparable between the groups. Subgroup analyses could not identify a subgroup that clearly benefited from hirudin compared with heparin therapy. Major hemorrhage occurred in 5.3% of the heparin and 4.6% of the hirudin groups (p=NS), whereas intracranial hemorrhage in 0.9% vs 0.4%, respectively. b. Of 3002 patients, 425 reported angina before their myocardial infarction. Those patients with angina onset within 24 h of infarct onset had a lower 30 day cardiac event rate (mortality, recurrent myocardial infarction, heart failure, or shock) at 4% compared to those with onset of angina >24 h (17%, p=0.03). Peak creatine kinase levels also were lower in patients with angina within 24 h of the infarction. Differences in baseline characteristics and use of antianginal drugs could not explain the difference.
Conclusions	a. Hirudin had no treatment benefit over heparin in patients with acute myocardial infarction that received intravenous thrombolytic therapy. b. Preinfarct angina was protective, only when it occurred within 24 h of the acute myocardial infarction. These temporal findings are consistent with the concept of preconditioning but do not rule out other mechanisms.

TIMI 9 Substudy

Thrombolysis and Thrombin Inhibition in Myocardial Infarction 9A and 9B

Title	Fatal cardiac rupture among patients treated with thrombolytic agents and adjunctive thrombin antagonists.
Authors	Becker RC, Hochman JS, Cannon CR, et al.
Reference	J Am Coll Cardiol 1999;33:479-487.
Disease	Acute myocardial infarction.
Purpose	To determine incidence and demographic characteristics of patients with cardiac rupture and determine if there are associations with thrombin inhibition.
Design	As per TIMI 9.
Patients	Analysis of 65 rupture events (1.7%) out of 3759 patients in the TIMI 9A & B trial.
Follow-up	As per TIMI 9.
Treatment regimen	As per TIMI 9.

TIMI 9 Substudy

Thrombolysis and Thrombin Inhibition in Myocardial Infarction 9A and 9B

(continued)

Results	Cardiac rupture was diagnosed clinically "in patients with sudden electromechanical dissociation in the absence of preceding congestive heart failure, slowly progressive hemodynamic compromise or malignant ventricular arrhythmias." The 65 rupture cases were fatal and most occurred within 48 hours of therapy. Patients that ruptured were older, had lower body weight and stature and were more likely to be female. Multivariate analysis showed that age > 70 years, female gender, and prior angina independently were associated with cardiac rupture. The most frequent ruptures were in anterior MI's. Of note about one in three ruptures occurred in non Q wave MI's. There was no difference in incidence of rupture between heparin vs hirudin treated patients and the intensity of anticoagulation (determined by a PTT) did not correlate with rupture.
Conclusions	Cardiac rupture following thrombolysis for acute MI occurs more commonly in older patients and women. Intensity of anticoagulation with heparin or hirudin does not influence the development of cardiac rupture.

IMPACT-AMI

Integrelin to Manage Platelet Aggregation to Combat Thrombosis

Title	Combined accelerated tissue-plasminogen activator and platelet glycoprotein IIb/IIIa integrin receptor blockade with integrilin in acute myocardial infarction. Results of a randomized, placebo controlled, dose ranging trial.
Authors	Ohman EM, Kleiman NS, Gacioch G, et al.
Reference	Circulation 1997;95:846-854.
Disease	Acute myocardial infarction.
Purpose	To evaluate the effects of platelet inhibition by integrilin on reperfusion, bleeding, and clinical outcome of patients with acute myocardial infarction treated with accelerated alteplase (tPA), heparin, and aspirin.
Design	Placebo controlled, dose ranging, multicenter.
Patients	180 patients, 18-75 years old, within 6 h of onset of acute myocardial infarction. Patients >125 kg, bleeding diathesis, severe hypertension, prior stroke, current warfarin therapy, anemia, thrombocytopenia, renal failure, recent noncompressible vascular puncture, ≥10 min cardiopulmonary resuscitation within 2 weeks, severe trauma within 6 months, or vasculitis were excluded.
Follow-up	Continuous 12 lead digital ECG for the first 24 h. Coronary angiography at 90 min after initiation of thrombolytic therapy. Clinical follow-up for in-hospital events.
Treatment regimen	Patients were enrolled in 1 of 7 treatment groups of integrilin or placebo. Integrilin or placebo was administered within 10 min of initiation of alteplase.

IMPACT-AMI

Integrelin to Manage Platelet Aggregation to Combat Thrombosis (continued)

Additional therapy	All patients received accelerated dose of alteplase IV (maximum dose 100 mg), and aspirin 325 mg/d. All but 2 groups received intravenous heparin. Target aPTT 2–2.5 times the control value.
Results	55 patients received placebo and 125 patients received integrilin. Of the 170 patients with adequate 90 min angiograms, patients allocated to the highest integrilin dose more often had complete reperfusion (TIMI flow grade III) than the placebo group (66% vs 39%, p=0.006). The rate of TIMI flow grade II or III was 87% vs 69%, respectively (p=0.01). The median time from initiation of thrombolytic therapy to steady state recovery of ST segment deviation was 95 min for all integrilin treated patients vs 116 min for the placebo treated patients (p=0.5). The duration was 65 min for the highest integrilin dose (p=0.05). 5.6% of the integrilin-treated patients vs 3.6% of the placebo treated patients died (p=0.57). Death or reinfarction occured in 8.0% vs 7.3%, respectively (p=0.87). The composite end point of death, reinfarction, stroke, revascularization, or new in-hospital heart failure of pulmonary edema occurred in 45% of the integrilin (43% of the patients at the highest integrillin dose) vs 42% of the placebo treated patients (p=0.71). Sustained hypotension occurred in 13% vs 16% respectively (p=0.53). Severe bleeding complications occurred in 2% of the integrilin-treated patients vs 5% of the placebo treated patients, whereas moderate bleeding occurred in 14% vs 9% and mild bleeding in 63% vs 67% respectively.
Conclusions	Integrilin, when combined with alteplase, aspirin, and heparin, accelerated the speed of reperfusion. However, integrilin therapy was not associated with improved in-hospital outcome.

CARS

Coumadin Aspirin Reinfarction Study

Title	Randomized double blind trial of fixed low dose warfarin with aspirin after myocardial infarction.
Authors	Coumadin Aspirin Reinfarction Study (CARS) Investigators.
Reference	Lancet 1997;350:389-396.
Disease	Acute myocardial infarction.
Purpose	To compare the efficacy and safety of low dose (80 mg/d) aspirin with low dose warfarin (1 or 3 mg/d) to that of aspirin (160 mg/d) in patients after acute myocardial infarction.
Design	Randomized, double blind, multicenter.
Patients	8803 men and postmenopausal women, 21-85 years of age, 3-21 days after an acute myocardial infarction. Patients with congestive heart failure, circulatory shock, rest angina unresponsive to medications, serious ventricular arrhythmias, history of bleeding or stroke, liver or renal disease, severe systemic disease, anemia, acute pericarditis during the index infarction, thyroid disorders, uncontrolled hypertension, hypersensitivity to warfarin, need for long term anticoagulation, or patients scheduled for CABG were excluded.
Follow-up	Maximum 33 months (median 14 months).
Treatment regimen	Randomization to: 1) aspirin 160 mg/d; 2) warfarin 1 mg/d with aspirin 80 mg/d; and 3) warfarin 3 mg/d with aspirin 80 mg/d.

Results

The study was terminated prematurely by the data and safety monitoring committee based on similar efficacy of all 3 treatment arms. 3393 patients were randomized to aspirin 160 mg/d; 2028 to warfarin 1mg/d +aspirin; and 3382 to warfarin 3 mg/d + aspirin. 1 year life table estimates for the primary event were 8.6% (95% CI 7.6-9.6%) for the aspirin 160 mg/d; 8.8% (95% CI 7.6-10.0%) for the warfarin 1mg/d + aspirin; and 8.4% (95% CI 7.4-9.4%) for the warfarin 3 mg/d + aspirin. The relative risk of primary event (first occurrence of reinfarction, nonfatal ischemic stroke or cardiovascular mortality) in the aspirin 160 mg/d vs warfarin 3 mg/d + aspirin was 0.95 (95% CI 0.81-1.12; p=0.57). The relative risk of primary event in the aspirin 160 mg/d vs warfarin 1mg/d + aspirin was 1.03 (95% CI 0.87-1.22; p=0.74). The relative risk of primary event in the warfarin 1 mg/d + aspirin vs warfarin 3 mg/d + aspirin was 0.93 (95% CI 0.78-1.11; p=0.41). Life table estimates for ischemic strokes in 1 year were the lowest in the aspirin 160 mg/d (0.58% [95% CI 0.29-0.87%]) than in the warfarin 1 mg/d + aspirin (1.1% [95% CI 0.64-1.5%; p vs aspirin alone = 0.05]) and in the warfarin 3 mg/d + aspirin (0.80% [95% CI 0.47-1.1%; p vs aspirin alone = 0.16]). 1 year life table estimates for spontaneous major hemorrhage was higher in the warfarin 3 mg/d + aspirin (1.4% [95% CI 0.94-1.8%]) than in the aspirin 160 mg/d (0.74% [95% CI 0.43-1.1%; p=0.014]). Among patients assigned to warfarin 3 mg/d + aspirin, the median INR values were 1.51 at week 1, 1.27 at week 4, and 1.19 at month 6.

Conclusions

The combination therapy of warfarin at a dose of 1 or 3 mg/d and low dose aspirin (80 mg/d) had similar efficacy to that of aspirin 160 mg/d alone in patients after acute myocardial infarction.

FRAMI

The Fragmin in Acute Myocardial Infarction Study

Title	Randomized trial of low molecular weight heparin (dalteparin) in prevention of left ventricular thrombus formation and arterial embolism after anterior myocardial infarction: the fragmin in acute myocardial infarction (FRAMI) study.
Authors	Kontny F, Dale J, Abildgaard U, et al, on the behalf of the FRAMI study group.
Reference	J Am Coll Cardiol 1997;30:962-969.
Disease	Acute myocardial infarction.
Purpose	To assess the role of dalteparin in prevention of left ventricular mural thrombus formation and arterial thromboembolism after an anterior wall acute myocardial infarction.
Design	Randomized, double blind, placebo controlled, multicenter.
Patients	776 patients with a first anterior acute myocardial infarction. Patients with previous myocardial infarction, non anterior myocardial infarction, time from onset of symptoms to randomization >15 h, ongoing treatment with or indication for heparin or oral anticoagulants, blood pressure over 210/115 mm Hg, cerebrovascular event within 2 months, known allergy to trial medication, peptic ulcer, bleeding disorder, serious renal or liver failure, concomitant life threatening disease, alcohol abuse, or pregnancy were excluded.
Follow-up	Echocardiography on day 9±2, and clinical follow-up for 3 months (the present study reports only in-hospital course).

Treatment regimen	Subcutaneous dalteparin 150 IU/kg body weight bid or placebo for 9±2 days.
Additional therapy	Intravenous streptokinase, if no contraindications existed and symptoms ≤6 h. Aspirin 300 mg on admission and 160 mg/d thereafter. No other antithrombotic agents were permitted. High risk patients of thromboembolic events received warfarin at discharge.
Results	There were 388 patients in each treatment group. Thrombolytic therapy was administered to 91.5% of the patients and aspirin to 97.6%. After randomization, 137 patients were excluded from further participation in the study. Echocardiography was available for 517 patients (270 placebo, 247 dalteparin). LV thrombus was detected by echocardiography in 59 patients (21.9%) of the placebo group vs 34 patients (13.8%) in the dalteparin group (p=0.022). LV thrombus formation or arterial embolism occurred in 59 patients (21.9%) of the placebo vs only 35 patients (14.2%) of the dalteparin group (p=0.03). Mortality and reinfarction rates were comparable between the 2 groups. Major bleeding occurred more commonly in the dalteparin group (2.9%) than in the placebo (0.3%)(p=0.006). Minor bleeding occurred in 2.1% of the placebo and 13.4% of the dalteparin group. No allergic reactions were reported. Thrombocytopenia was detected in one dalteparin-treated patient.
Conclusions	Dalteparin was effective in preventing LV thrombus formation in patients with first anterior acute myocardial infarction, but was associated with increased risk for bleeding.

Effect of glycoprotein IIb/IIIa receptor blockade on recovery of coronary flow and left ventricular function after the placement of coronary artery stents in acute myocardial infarction

Title	Effect of glycoprotein IIb/IIIa receptor blockade on recovery of coronary flow and left ventricular function after the placement of coronary artery stents in acute myocardial infarction.
Authors	Neumann F-J, Blasini R, Schmitt C, et al.
Reference	Circulation 1998; 98:2695-2701.
Disease	Acute myocardial infarction.
Purpose	To determine the effects of abciximab vs standard dose heparin in patients undergoing stenting for acute MI within 48 hours of symptoms.
Design	Randomized.
Patients	200 consecutive patients. 98 randomized to usual care; 102 to abciximab.
Follow-up	14 day angiographic follow-up; 30 day clinical outcome.
Treatment regimen	Abciximab bolus, 0.25 mg/kg body weight, followed by infusion of 10 μg/min for 12 hours, plus additional dose of heparin 25,000 U intraarterially. Usual care group received heparin 10,000 U intraarterially followed by IV heparin infusion 1000 U/hr for the first 12 hours.
Additional therapy	Prior to catheterization 5000 U heparin and 500 mg aspirin IV, ticlopidine 250 mg bid for 4 weeks, and aspirin 100 mg bid.

Effect of glycoprotein IIb/IIIa receptor blockade on recovery of coronary flow and left ventricular function after the placement of coronary artery stents in acute myocardial infarction

(continued)

Results	End points were changes in papaverine induced peak flow velocities and wall motion index assessed by angiography at initial study vs 14 day follow-up. There was no difference in the amount of residual stenoses of treated lesions between the two groups. Patients assigned to abciximab had a greater improvement in peak flow velocity 18.1 cm/s compared to standard therapy patients, 10.4 cm/s, p=0.024. Wall motion index was greater in abciximab patients (0.44SD/chord) compared to standard therapy (0.15 SD/chord p=0.007). Global LV ejection fraction was greater in abciximab patients (62%) compared to heparin alone patients (56%, p=0.003). At 30 day follow-up, 2 patients in abciximab and 9 in the standard therapy group had adverse cardiac events (p=0.031) including death, non-lethal reinfarction, and target lesion reintervention.
Conclusions	Abciximab improved microvascular perfusion and regional wall motion in patients that received stents for acute myocardial infarction.

RAPPORT

ReoPro and Primary PTCA Organization and Randomized Trial

Title	Randomized, placebo controlled trial of platelet glycoprotein IIb/IIIa blockade with primary angioplasty for acute myocardial infarction.
Authors	Brener SJ, Barr LA, Burchenal JFB, et al.
Reference	Circulation 1998; 98:734-741.
Disease	Acute myocardial infarction.
Purpose	To determine the effect of inhibition of platelet aggregation with a glycoprotein IIb/IIIa inhibitor in the setting of myocardial infarct/patients undergoing PTCA.
Design	Randomized, double blind, placebo controlled, multicenter.
Patients	483 patients with acute MI <12 hours duration who were candidates for PTCA.
Follow-up	Six months.
Treatment regimen	Abciximab, 0.25 mg/kg bolus followed by 12 hour infusion of 0.125 μg/kg/min (to a maximum of 10 μg/min) or placebo.
Additional therapy	Heparin, aspirin.

RAPPORT

ReoPro and Primary PTCA Organization and Randomized Trial

(continued)

Results	The primary end point was the composite of death, nonfatal reinfarction, any repeat target vessel revascularization (percutaneous or surgical) within 6 months. Seven and 30 day death, reinfarction and urgent target vessel revascularization were other end points. Incidence of major bleeding (intracerebral hemorrhage or >5g% decrease in hemoglobin) was recorded. The incidence of primary end point at 6 months was 28.1% in the placebo group and 28.2% in abciximab patients (p=NS), by intention to treat analysis. However the incidence of death/MI/urgent target vessel revascularization was lower with abciximab vs placebo at 7 days, 30 days and 6 months: at 7 days (9.9% vs 3.3%, p=0.003; at 30 days 11.2% vs 5.8%; at 6 months 17.8% vs 11.6%, p=0.048 in placebo vs abciximab groups, respectively). Major bleeding was more common with abciximab (16.6%) vs placebo (9.5%, p=0.02) and this was mostly at arterial access sites. Neither group had intracranial hemorrhages.
Conclusions	While abciximab given during primary PTCA for MI did not alter the primary end point at 6 months which included elective revascularization procedures it did decrease death/reinfarction/urgent revascularization; however bleeding rates were high.

BIOMACS II

Biochemical Markers in Acute Coronary Syndromes

Title	Low molecular weight heparin (dalteparin) as adjuvant treatment to thrombolysis in acute myocardial infarction: A pilot study. Biochemical markers in acute coronary syndromes (BIOMACS II).
Authors	Frostfeldt G, Ahlberg G, Gustafasson G, et al.
Reference	J Am Coll Cardiol 1999;33:627-633.
Disease	Acute myocardial infarction.
Purpose	To determine the affect of dalteparin as adjunctive therapy to streptokinase in patients with acute myocardial infarction.
Design	Randomized, double blind, placebo, controlled trial.
Patients	101 patients with acute myocardial infarction.
Follow-up	14-21 days.
Treatment regimen	100 IU/kg of dalteparin just prior to streptokinase and a second injection of 120 IU/kg after 12 hours.
Additional therapy	Aspirin, nitroglycerin.

BIOMACS II

Biochemical Markers in Acute Coronary Syndromes

(continued)

Results	Patients receiving dalteparin plus streptokinase did not show enhancement of early reperfusion as assessed by noninvasive indicators: rise of myoglobin during 90 minutes or regression of ST elevation by vector ECG at 120 minutes. There was a nonsignificant trend toward a higher rate of TIMI grade 3 flow at 24 hour angiography in dalteparin treated infarct related arteries (68%) vs placebo (51%, p=0.10). In patients who had signs of early reperfusion by myoglobin and vector ECG there was a trend toward higher rates of TIMI grade 3 flow of the infarct related arteries in the dalteparin group. There were fewer ischemic episodes on ECG at 6–24 hours in the dalteparin group (16%) vs the placebo group (38%; p=0.04).
Conclusions	Dalteparin plus streptokinase resulted in less ECG monitored episodes of recurrent ischemia during the first day of thrombolysis, and a trend toward better TIMI 3 flow at 24 hours.

PARADIGM

Platelet Aggregation Receptor Antagonist Dose Investigation and Reperfusion Gain in Myocardial Infarction

Title	Combining thrombolysis with the platelet glycoprotein IIb/IIIa inhibitor lamifiban: Results of the platelet aggregation receptor antagonist dose investigation and reperfusion gain in myocardial infarction (PARADIGM) trial.
Authors	The PARADIGM Investigators.
Reference	J Am Coll Cardiol 1998; 32:2003-2010.
Disease	Acute myocardial infarction.
Purpose	To determine the safety, pharmacodynamics and effects on reperfusion of lamifiban when given as adjunctive therapy to thrombolysis (t-PA or streptokinase) for acute MI's with ST elevation on the ECG.
Design	Part A: open label; Part B: randomized, double blind, comparison; Part C: randomized, double blind.
Patients	353 patients with acute MI with ST elevation.
Follow-up	In-hospital.
Treatment regimen	Part A: open label study in which all patients received lamifiban. Purpose was to identify a dose that resulted in 85%-95% adenosine diphosphate (ADP) inhibition of platelet aggregation. Part B: comparison of bolus followed by 24 hour infusion to placebo. Part C: infusion duration increased to 48 hours.

PARADIGM

Platelet Aggregation Receptor Antagonist Dose Investigation and Reperfusion Gain in Myocardial Infarction

(continued)

Results	Lamifiban inhibited platelet aggregation in a dose dependent manner. Bleeding was more common in patients receiving lamifiban (16.1% of lamifiban treated patients required transfusions; 10.3% of placebo treated patients required transfusions). Speed and stability of reperfusion were better in lamifiban group vs placebo as determined by continuous electrocardiographic monitoring. There were no differences in angiographic TIMI 3 flow rates, death, reinfarction rates, or refractory ischemic events between groups (although the authors point out that sample size was small).
Conclusions	Lamifiban given as adjunctive therapy to thrombolytics hastened ECG evidence of reperfusion but did not result in clear clinical benefits. Lamifiban median inhibition of platelet aggregation to ADP was greater than 85%.

TIMI-14

Thrombolysis in Myocardial Infarction-14

Title	Abciximab facilitates the rate and extent of thrombolysis. Results of the thrombolysis in myocardial infarction (TIMI) 14 trial.
Authors	Antman EM, Giugliano RP, Gibson M, et al.
Reference	Circulation 1999;99:2720-2732.
Disease	ST elevation acute myocardial infarction.
Purpose	To assess the efficacy of a combination of thrombolytic therapy and abciximab on achieving TIMI-3 flow at 90 minutes in the infarct related artery.
Design	Randomized open label, "dose finding and dose confirmation phases."
Patients	888 patients, 18-75 years old, presenting within 12 hours of ischemic symptoms that lasted for ≥30 min and was accompanied by ≥1 mm ST elevation in 2 contiguous leads. Patients with prior CABG, cardiogenic shock, excess bleeding risk, thrombolytic therapy in the preceding 7 days were excluded.
Follow-up	30 days.

TIMI-14

Thrombolysis in Myocardial Infarction-14

(continued)

Treatment regimen

Dose finding phase included 14 different treatment regimens including alteplase alone, abciximab alone and reduced dose lytic regimens (alteplase or streptokinase) combined with abciximab.

During dose confirmation phase patients were randomized to accelerated - dose alteplase control group (100 mg alteplase with standard front loaded regimen), 50 mg alteplase plus abciximab (0.25 mg/kg bolus + 12 hour infusion of 0.125 μg $\cdot kg^{-1} \cdot min^{-1}$) and either a low dose (60 U/kg bolus and infusion of 7 U $\cdot kg^{-1} \cdot hr^{-1}$) or very low dose (30 U/kg bolus and infusion of 4 U $\cdot kg^{-1} \cdot hr^{-1}$) heparin.

Additional therapy

All patients received aspirin; ß-blockers, nitrates, calcium blockers were at the discretion of the physician.

Results

90 minute TIMI-3 flow was achieved by 57% of the patients assigned to alteplase alone (100 mg) and 32% for abciximab alone. Patients that received streptokinase at doses between 500,000 U and 1.25 million U had TIMI 3 flow in 34% -46% of cases.

TIMI 3 flow rates were higher with the 50 mg alteplase plus abciximab vs alteplase alone group at 90 minutes (77% vs 62%, p = 0.02) and also at 60 minutes (72% vs 43%; p=0.0009). The rates of major hemorrhage were only 1% with the 50 mg alteplase plus abciximab patients that received very low dose heparin, vs 7% with 50 mg alteplase plus abciximab and low dose heparin; it was 6% in patients with alteplase alone, 3% with abciximab alone, and 10% with streptokinase plus abciximab.

Conclusions

The combination of half the usual dose of alteplase plus abciximab was associated with enhanced thrombolysis compared to usual dose alteplase. Combining this with very low dose heparin decreased the risk of intracerebral hemorrhage.

TIMI 14 (Substudy)

Thrombolysis in Myocardial Infarction 14 (Substudy)

Title	Abciximab improves both epicardial flow and myocardial reperfusion in ST elevation myocardial infarction: Observations from the TIMI 14 trial.
Authors	DeLemos JA, Antman EM, Gibson CM, et al for the TIMI 14 investigators.
Reference	Circulation 2000; 101:239-243.
Disease	Acute myocardial infarction.
Purpose	To determine the effect of abciximab and reduced dose tPA to full-dose tPA on resolution of ST segment elevation.
Design	As per TIMI 14.
Patients	125 patients with acute myocardial infarction that received full dose alteplase (tPA [tissue plasminogen activator]) vs 221 patients that received a combination of abciximab and reduced dose alteplase.
Follow-up	30 day.
Treatment regimen	As per TIMI 14.
Additional therapy	As per TIMI 14.

TIMI 14 (Substudy)

Thrombolysis in Myocardial Infarction 14 (Substudy)

(continued)

Results	ST segment resolution (of at least 70%) was observed in 59% of patients receiving abciximab plus low dose alteplase vs 37% of patients receiving full dose alteplase ($p<0.001$). In patients with TIMI grade 3 epicardial coronary flow at 90 minutes, complete ST segment resolution was observed in 69% of combination therapy patients vs 44% of alteplase alone patients. 30 day mortality was lower in patients with more complete ST segment resolution at 1.1% (complete resolution), 4.7% (partial resolution), and 7.1% (no resolution).
Conclusions	Combination of abciximab and reduced dose alteplase resulted in better resolution of ST segment elevation than full dose alteplase alone, suggesting that combination therapy may improve not only epicardial flow but microvascular perfusion as well.

MINT

Myocardial Infarction with Novastan and tPA

Title	A multicenter, randomized study of argatroban vs heparin as adjunct to tissue plasminogen activator (tPA) in acute myocardial infarction: MINT Study.
Authors	Jang I-K, Brown DFM, Giugliano RP, et al.
Reference	J Am Coll Cardiol 1999;33:1879-1885.
Disease	Acute myocardial infarction.
Purpose	To compare the small molecule, direct thrombin inhibitor, argatroban to heparin in patients with acute myocardial infarction who were reperfused with tPA.
Design	Randomized, multicenter, angiographic trial (tPA), single blind.
Patients	125 patients with acute myocardial infarction who presented within 6 hours.
Follow-up	90 minute angiography; 30 days.
Treatment regimen	Front loaded tPA and aspirin. Patients then randomized to either low dose argatroban (100 μg/kg bolus plus infusion of 1.0 μg/kg/min), high dose argatroban (100 μg/kg bolus plus 3.0 μg/kg/min. infusion) or heparin as 70 U/kg bolus and 15 U/kg/hr infusion up to 1500 U/hr. Patients then underwent a 90 minute angiogram. In patients not requiring PTCA, infusion continued for 48-72 hours.
Additional therapy	IV nitroglycerin prior to angiography; other meds as per physician.

MINT

Myocardial Infarction with Novastan and tPA

(continued)

Results	The primary end point was percentage of patients with TIMI grade 3 flow; secondary end point was corrected TIMI frame count at 90 minutes. TIMI grade 3 occurred in 56.8% of low dose argatroban (p=0.2 vs heparin), 58.7% of high dose argatroban patients, (p=0.13 vs heparin) and 42.1% of heparin patients. In those patients that presented after 3 hours, high dose argatroban resulted in more frequent TIMI 3 flow (57.1%) compared to heparin (20%; p=0.03). Corrected TIMI flow rates did not differ significantly among the 3 groups (30.4±3.4 in low dose argatroban, 28.0±2.4 in high dose argatroban, and 39.0±4.6 in the heparin group; p=0.19). Major bleeding occurred in 2.6% of low dose, 4.3% of high dose argatroban, and 10% of heparin patients (p=NS). At 30 days the composite end point of death, recurrent MI, cardiogenic shock, congestive heart failure, revascularization and recurrent ischemia was 32.0% with low dose, 25.5% of high dose, and 37.5% with heparin (p=NS).
Conclusions	In patients with delayed presentation of MI, argatroban enhanced reperfusion with tPA vs heparin. There was a trend (although not significantly different) toward lower rates of major bleeding and other adverse events with argatroban vs heparin.

ESCALAT

Title	Efegatran sulfate as an adjunct to streptokinase vs heparin as an adjunct to tissue plasminogen activator in patients with acute myocardial infarction.
Authors	Fung AY, Lorch G, Cambier PA, et al.
Reference	Am Heart J 1999;138:696-704.
Disease	Acute myocardial infarction.
Purpose	To determine the optimal dose of efegatran (a direct antithrombin agent) to be used as an adjunct to streptokinase, and to compare the safety and efficacy of 2 regimes of thrombolytic therapy: streptokinase + the optimal dose of efegatran vs accelerated t-PA + heparin in patients with acute myocardial infarction.
Design	Randomized, phase II, dose ranging study, multicenter.
Patients	245 patients, 21-75 years old, with ST elevation acute myocardial infarction, within 12 hours of onset of symptoms. Only patients who were eligible for thrombolytic therapy were included.
Follow-up	Coronary angiography at 90 minutes. Technetium-99m sestamibi single photon emission computed tomography at day 5-10.

Treatment regimen	Patients were randomized to either streptokinase 1.5 million U/60 minutes with 4 doses of efegatran: a) 0.05 mg/kg bolus and 0.3 mg/kg/h infusion; b) 0.075 mg/kg bolus and 0.5 mg/kg/h infusion; c) 0.1 mg/kg bolus and 0.7 mg/kg/h infusion; and d) 0.2 mg/kg bolus and 1.0 mg/kg/h, or to accelerated weight adjusted tPA infusion (up to 100 mg) and heparin therapy (5000 U bolus and 1000 U/h).The efegatran or heparin infusion was continued for 72-96 hours, unless the patients had major bleeding, reinfarction, or severe recurrent ischemia.
Additional therapy	All patients received aspirin 325 mg on admission, followed by 75-325 mg/d. Nitrates, calcium channel antagonists and other medications were permitted, ß-blockers usage was encouraged.
Results	At 90 minutes,TIMI flow grade 2-3 was found in 75%, 73%, 52%, and 58% of the patients in groups a to d of the streptokinase and efegatran groups, respectively. TIMI flow grade 3 was found in 56%, 40%, 16%, and 29%, respectively. The Safety and Monitoring Committee considered group b (streptokinase and efegatran [0.075 mg/kg bolus and 0.5 mg/kg/h infusion]) to be the "optimal" dose for comparing with the standard therapy of heparin and tPA combination. A total of 116 patients were randomized to receive the "optimal" dose of efegatran with streptokinase and 62 patients to tPA and heparin. A total of 100 patients in the streptokinase + efegatran group and 58 patients in the tPA+ heparin group underwent a 90 minute coronary angiography. 73% and 79% of the patients in the streptokinase +efegatran and the tPA+ heparin groups achieved TIMI flow grade 2-3, respectively (p=0.38), and 40% and 53% achieved TIMI flow grade 3 (p=0.10). Reocclusion (TIMI flow grade 2 or 3 at 90 minutes and TIMI flow grade 0-1 at 24 hours) was seen in 7% of patients in the streptokinase and efegatran group vs 0% in the tPA and heparin group (p=0.34). 15% and 17% of the patients in the streptokinase and the tPA groups

underwent rescue PTCA (p=0.82). Mortality was 5% and 0% in the streptokinase and tPA groups, respectively (p=0.09). The composite end point of death, reinfarction, or TIMI flow grade <3 occurred in 47% of patients in the streptokinase group vs 32% in the tPA group (p=0.07), and the composite end point of death, myocardial reinfarction, stroke, or refractory angina occurred in 15% vs 7% of the patients, respectively (p=0.14). Major bleeding occurred in 23% and 11% of the patients, respectively (p=0.07). No intracranial hemorrhages occurred. There was no significant difference in predischarge infarct size between the groups.

Conclusions

The regimen of streptokinase and efegatran was not more effective than the standard regimen of tPA and heparin in achieving early patency of the infarct related artery and was associated with a trend towards worse clinical outcome than tPA and heparin.

ISAR-2

The Intracoronary Stenting and Antithrombotic Regimen-2 Trial

Title	Effect of glycoprotein IIb/IIIa receptor blockade with abciximab on clinical and angiographic restenosis rate after the placement of coronary stents following acute myocardial infarction.
Author	Neumann F-J, Kastrati A, Schmitt C, et al.
Reference	J Am Coll Cardiol 2000;35:915-921.
Disease	Coronary artery disease, acute myocardial infarction.
Purpose	To evaluate the effects of abciximab on restenosis after stent implantation following acute myocardial infarction.
Design	Prospective, randomized, single blinded.
Patients	401 patients with ST segment elevation acute myocardial infarction undergoing coronary angiography and stent implantation within 48 hours after onset of symptoms.
Follow-up	Angiographic follow-up at 6 months, clinical follow-up for 12 months.
Treatment regimen	Before stent placement patients were randomized to abciximab (n=201) (0.25 mg/kg bolus, followed by a 10 μg/min continuous infusion for 12 hours) + heparin (2500 U intra-arterially), or to heparin alone (n=200) (10,000 U intra-arterially), followed by 1000 U/hour for 12 hours after sheath removal.

ISAR-2

The Intracoronary Stenting and Antithrombotic Regimen-2 Trial (continued)

Additional therapy	Before angiography, all patients received 5000 U heparin and 500 mg aspirin intravenously. Different types of slotted tube stents were used. All patients received ticlopidine 250 mg X2/d for 4 weeks and aspirin 100 mg/d throughout the study.
Results	In 14 patients of the heparin alone group, the operators administered nonstudy abciximab. At 30 days any cardiac event (death, reinfarction, and target lesion revascularization) occurred in 5.0% of the abciximab group vs 10.5% of the heparin alone group (relative risk [RR] 0.47; 95% CI 0.25-0.88; p=0.038). Death occurred in 2.0% vs 4.5%, respectively (RR 0.44; 95% CI 0.17-1.18; p=0.16), and myocardial infarction occurred in 0.5% vs 1.5%, respectively (RR 0.33; 95% CI 0.01-4.09; p=0.62). 3% vs 5.0% of the patients in the abciximab and heparin treated patients underwent target lesion revascularization (p=0.30), whereas 3.5% vs 4.5% needed blood transfusion (p=0.79). At 1 year abciximab was associated with 5.7% absolute reduction in cardiac events (death, reinfarction, or target lesion revascularization; p=NS). Among the 397 patients with successful revascularization, 292 patients underwent repeated angiography at 6 months. There were no differences in minimal luminal diameter, % diameter stenosis, and restenosis rate between the 2 groups both immediately after stenting and at 6 months. Restenosis occurred in 31.1% of the abciximab group vs 30.6% of the heparin group. Late luminal loss was 1.26±0.85 mm with abciximab and 1.21±0.74 mm with heparin (p=0.61).
Conclusions	Abciximab reduced the rates of death, reinfarction, and target lesion revascularization within the first 30 days following coronary stent insertion after acute myocardial infarction. However, abciximab did not reduce angiographic restenosis rates and was not associated with additional clinical benefits beyond the first 30 days.

HEAP

The Heparin in Early Patency

Title	High dose heparin as pretreatment for primary angioplasty in acute myocardial infarction: The Heparin in Early Patency (HEAP) randomized trial.
Authors	Liem A, Zijlstra F, Ottervanger JP, et al.
Reference	J Am Coll Cardiol 2000;35:600-604.
Disease	Coronary artery disease, acute myocardial infarction.
Purpose	To assess the efficacy of high dose heparin + aspirin on coronary artery patency in patients with acute myocardial infarction.
Design	Randomized.
Patients	584 patients, ≤75 years old, with ST segment elevation acute myocardial infarction, ≤6 hours of onset of symptoms, or ≤24 hours if there was evidence of ongoing ischemia.
Follow-up	In hospital; ~ 4 days.
Treatment regimen	All patients received oral or IV aspirin and IV nitroglycerin. Randomization to low dose heparin (n=285) or high dose heparin (n=299). Low dose: 5000 U heparin (in patients referred from other centers) or no heparin (for patients admitted directly to the angioplasty center). High dose: 300 IU/kg.

HEAP

The Heparin in Early Patency

(continued)

Additional therapy	Thrombolytics or glycoprotein IIb/IIIa inhibitors were prohibited. Patients underwent coronary angiography and primary PTCA when necessary, after administration of 5000 U heparin IV. Patients did not undergo primary PTCA if there was an indication for urgent CABG (if extensive coronary artery disease or left main coronary artery disease was found). Heparin infusion was continued for 24–48 hours after PTCA. All patients received aspirin 80 mg/d, ß-blockers, ACE inhibitors, and lipid lowering therapy on indication.
Results	3% of the patients in the high dose and 4% of the patients in the low dose heparin group died during hospitalization. Recurrent myocardial infarction occurred in 1% of the patients in both groups. Bleeding occurred in 10% and 6% of the patients in the high dose and low dose groups, respectively ($p=0.07$). TIMI flow grade 2–3 before angioplasty was observed in 22% of the patients in the high dose group vs 21% in the low dose group, whereas TIMI flow grade 3 was observed in 13% vs 8%, respectively ($p=0.11$). Among patients treated within 200 minutes of onset of symptoms, TIMI flow grade 3 before angioplasty was found in 11% of the high dose vs 6% in the low dose group ($p=0.09$). Outcome of primary PTCA was comparable between the groups. Mean LVEF at day 4 was 45±11% in both groups. Mean enzymatic infarct size (LDH$_{q72}$) was 1201±1091 U in the high dose vs 1285±1082 U in the low dose group (p=NS). High dose heparin was safe and was not associated with hemorrhagic stroke.
Conclusions	High dose heparin was not better than low dose heparin or no heparin achieving reperfusion of the infarct related artery before primary PTCA.

HIT 4

Hirudin for the Improvement of Thrombolysis

Title	Recombinant hirudin (lepirudin) for the improvement of thrombolysis with streptokinase in patients with acute myocardial infarction. Results of the HIT-4 Trial.
Authors	Neuhaus K-L, Molhoek GP, Zeymer U, et al.
Reference	J Am Coll Cardiol 1999;34:966-973.
Disease	Acute myocardial infarction.
Purpose	To compare hirudin vs heparin as adjunctive therapy to thrombolysis with streptokinase in patients with acute myocardial infarction.
Design	Randomized, double blind, multicenter.
Patients	1205 patients with acute myocardial infarction presenting within 6 hours of chest pain. ST segment elevation had to be present on the ECG.
Follow-up	90 minute angiography in substudy; 30 day clinical outcomes, 1 year mortality.
Treatment regimen	IV bolus of lepirudin (0.2 mg/kg body weight) or placebo given before streptokinase (1.5 million U IV over 60 minutes) followed by subcutaneous lepirudin (0.5 mg/kg) or unfractionated heparin 12,500 IU twice daily over 5-7 days beginning within 30 minutes of streptokinase. Dose adjustments by aPTT if needed.
Additional therapy	Aspirin 300 mg loading dose and then 100-200 mg per day.

HIT 4

Hirudin for the Improvement of Thrombolysis

(continued)

Results	Primary end point of early and complete patency of infarct artery at 90 minutes after start of drug in angiographic substudy. Secondary end points were composite and individual incidences of death, nonfatal stroke, nonfatal reinfarction, rescue PTCA, or refractory angina, within 30 days; individual incidences of strokes, resolution of ST elevation, and one year mortality. Angiographic substudy included 447 patients. Complete patency, defined as TIMI grade 3 flow, occurred in 40.7% (85/209) of lepirudin patients and 33.5% (70/209) of heparin treated patients (p=0.16). There was a nonsignificant trend toward higher TIMI 3 patency rates in lepirudin patients (43.2%) and heparin patients (36.8%) when treatment started within 180 minutes of symptoms vs when it occurred after more than 180 minutes (37.4% lepirudin and 27.6% heparin). Complete ST resolution tended to be higher with lepirudin (28%) than heparin (22%, p=0.05) at 90 minutes but this was not significantly different at 180 minutes (52% vs 48%; p=0.18). There was no difference in combined or individual clinical events between groups. Combined end point occurred in 22.7% of lepirudin and 24.3% of heparin groups (p=NS). One year mortality was 9.8% with lepirudin and 8.9% with heparin (p=NS). Total stroke occurred in 1.2% of lepirudin and 1.5% of heparin patients. Hemorrhagic stroke occurred in 0.2% of lepirudin and 0.3% of heparin patients. Major bleeding occurred in 3.3% and 3.5% of lepirudin and heparin groups, respectively.
Conclusions	Lepirudin did not significantly improve restoration of blood flow of the infarct artery vessel by angiography but did improve ST segment resolution at 90 minutes.

TIM

Triflusal in Myocardial Infarction

Title	Randomized comparative trial of triflusal and aspirin following acute myocardial infarction.
Authors	Cruz-Fernandez JM, Lopez-Bescos L, Garcia-Dorado D, et al.
Reference	Eur Heart J 2000;21:457-465.
Disease	Acute myocardial infarction.
Purpose	To assess the efficacy and tolerability of triflusal, a selective platelet cyclooxygenase blocker, in the prevention of cardiovascular events following acute myocardial infarction.
Design	A randomized, double blind, sequential, parallel group, multicenter.
Patients	2275 patients, 18-80 years old, <24 hours after onset of acute myocardial infarction were included. Patients who were taking antiplatelet drugs in the 15 days prior to enrollment, peptic disease, hepatic or renal disease, history of cerebrovascular hemorrhage, uncontrolled hypertension, AIDS or other severe illness were excluded.
Follow-up	35 days.
Treatment regimen	Randomization to triflusal 600 mg/d or aspirin 300 mg/d.
Additional therapy	Thrombolytic agents, and all other agents routinely administered for patients following acute myocardial infarction were permitted. Use of antiplatelet agents or nonsteroidal anti-inflammatory drugs was prohibited.

TIM

Triflusal in Myocardial Infarction

(continued)

Results

Of 6615 patients screened, 2275 patients were included. 1140 patients were randomized to aspirin and 1135 to triflusal. 2124 patients were included in the final analysis of primary and secondary end points.A total of 441 patients did not complete the 35 day treatment phase for reasons other than death (44.4 % due to revascularization, 14.3% due to use of prohibited medications, 13.2% due to adverse events, 11.8% due to non-compliance and 16.3% due to other reasons).The primary end point of death, nonfatal myocardial infarction, or nonfatal cerebrovascular events within 35 days occurred in 105 of the 1068 patients receiving aspirin and in 99 of the 1056 patients receiving triflusal (OR 0.882; 95% CI 0.634-1.227; p=0.582). Death occurred in 79 vs 69 patients in the aspirin and triflusal groups, respectively (OR 0.816; 95% CI 0.564 to 1.179; p=0.278). Nonfatal myocardial infarction occurred in 18 and 30 patients, respectively, (OR 1.577; 95% CI 0.873-2.848; p=0.131) and nonfatal cerebrovascular event in 14 and 5 patients, respectively, (OR 0.364; 95% CI 0.146-0.908; p=0.030). Adverse events occurred in 33.9% of the aspirin group vs 34.0% of the triflusal group. Triflusal was associated with a significantly less central nervous system associated bleeding (0.27% vs 0.97%; p=0.03) and a trend towards less overall bleeding (2.4% vs 3.6%; p=NS).

Conclusions

Patients treated with triflusal had similar event rates as those treated with aspirin.Triflusal and aspirin have comparable efficacy in secondary prevention of cardiovascular events after acute myocardial infarction.Triflusal had better safety profile than aspirin and was associated with reduced rate of nonfatal cerebrovascular events.

1. Acute Myocardial Infarction

d. Early vs Late Intervention After Acute Myocardial Infarction

TAMI

Thrombolysis and Angioplasty in Myocardial Infarction

Title	A randomized trial of immediate vs delayed elective angioplasty after intravenous tissue plasminogen activator in acute myocardial infarction.
Authors	Topol EJ, Califf RM, George BS, et al.
Reference	N Engl J Med 1987;317:581-588.
Disease	Acute myocardial infarction.
Purpose	To compare the efficacy of immediate vs delayed (7-10 days) coronary angioplasty in patients with acute myocardial infarction treated with intravenous tissue plasminogen activator.
Design	Randomized, open label, multicenter.
Patients	386 patients, age ≤75 years, with acute myocardial infarction < 4 h from onset of symptoms (<6 h if severe ongoing pain was present) with ST ≥1 mm in ≥2 leads. Only patients with TIMI grade 2-3 and ≥50% residual stenosis suitable to angioplasty 90 min after initiation of thrombolytic therapy, without ≥50% left main stenosis or left main equivalent stenosis were included (n=197).
Follow-up	7 days.
Treatment regimen	Immediate angioplasty or deferred elective angioplasty 5-10 days later.
Additional therapy	Tissue plasminogen activator (t-PA) 150 mg over 6-8 h, 60-90 mg over the first h (10% of this as a bolus), heparin 5000 U IV and 500-1000 U/h ≥24 h, aspirin 325 mg/d, dipyridamole 75 mg X3/d, and diltiazem 30-60 mg X4/d.

TAMI

Thrombolysis and Angioplasty in Myocardial Infarction

(continued)

Results	Bleeding complications were common (18% of patients needed transfusion). The incidence of reocclusion was similar in the immediate (11%) and delayed (13%) angioplasty. Global and regional left ventricular function were comparable. The mortality was higher in the immediate (4.0%) than delayed (1.0%) angioplasty (p=0.37). 7% and 2% of the immediate and elective angioplasty groups needed emergency CABG (p=0.17), while 5% and 16% needed emergency angioplasty, respectively (p=0.01).
Conclusions	In patients with acute myocardial infarction and initially successful thrombolysis, immediate angioplasty offers no advantage over delayed elective angioplasty.

TIMI-2A

Thrombolysis in Myocardial Infarction Trial (phase 2A)

Title	a. Immediate vs delayed catheterization and angioplasty following thrombolytic therapy for acute myocardial infarction. TIMI II-A results. b. Comparison of immediate invasive, delayed invasive, and conservative strategies after tissue type plasminogen activator. Results of the Thrombolysis in Myocardial Infarction (TIMI) phase II-A Trial.
Authors	a. The TIMI research group. b. Rogers WJ, Baim DS, Gore JM, et al.
Reference	JAMA 1988;260:2849-2858. Circulation 1990;81:1457-1476.
Disease	Acute myocardial infarction.
Purpose	To compare the results of 3 strategies of coronary angiography and angioplasty following intravenous thrombolytic therapy for acute myocardial infarction: immediate invasive, delayed invasive (18-48 h), and a conservative strategy.
Design	Randomized, open label, multicenter.
Patients	586 patients with acute myocardial infarction <76 years old < 4 hours from onset of symptoms with chest pain >30 min and ST elevation ≥0.1 mV in ≥2 contiguous leads.
Follow-up	Predischarge contrast ventriculography and coronary angiography. 1 year follow-up.

TIMI-2A

Thrombolysis in Myocardial Infarction Trial (phase 2A)

(continued)

Treatment regimen	1. Coronary angiography within 2 h of rt-PA initiation. PTCA was attempted if coronary anatomy was suitable. 2. Coronary angiography within 18–48 h of rt-PA initiation. PTCA was attempted if coronary anatomy was suitable. 3. Conservative strategy: coronary angiography and intervention only in those who had either spontaneous recurrent ischemia or a positive exercise test.
Additional therapy	Intravenous rt-PA (150 mg over 6 h for the first 520 patients, and 100 mg in the remaining 2742 patients). Lidocaine (1–1.5 mg/kg bolus + infusion 2–4 mg/min) for >24 h; heparin 5000 U bolus and infusion 1000 U/h for 5 days, and then subcutaneous until discharge. Aspirin 81 mg/d for 6 days and then 325 mg/d. Nifedipine 10–20 mg X3/d was administrated for 96 h. Metoprolol was started before discharge for 1 year.
Results	Predischarge contrast left ventricular ejection fraction was similar among the 3 groups. The rates of patency of the infarct related artery at the time of predischarge were similar among groups. However, the mean residual stenosis was greater in the conservative therapy arm (67.2%) than in the immediate invasive (50.6%) and delayed invasive (47.8%) arms (p<0.001). Immediate invasive strategy led to a higher rate of coronary artery bypass graft surgery after angioplasty (7.7%) than in the delayed invasive (2.1%) and conservative (2.5%) arms (p<0.01). The need for blood transfusion was greater in the immediate invasive (13.8%) than in the delayed invasive (3.1%) and conservative (2.0%) groups (p<0.001). 1 year mortality and reinfarction rates were similar among the 3 groups.
Conclusions	Conservative strategy achieves equally good results with less morbidity compared to invasive strategies.

TIMI-2

Thrombolysis in Myocardial Infarction Trial (phase 2)

Title	a. Comparison of invasive and conservative strategies after treatment with intravenous tissue plasminogen activator in acute myocardial infarction. Results of the Thrombolysis in Myocardial Infarction (TIMI) Phase II Trial. b. 1-year results of the Thrombolysis in Myocardial Infarction investigation (TIMI) phase II trial.
Authors	a. The TIMI Study Group. b. Williams DO, Braunwald E, Knatterud G, et al.
Reference	a. N Engl J Med 1989;320:618–627. b. Circulation 1992;85:533–542.
Disease	Acute myocardial infarction.
Purpose	To compare an invasive strategy consisting of coronary angiography and angioplasty within 18–48 h of infarction and a conservative approach in which angiography was performed only in patients with spontaneous or exercise induced ischemia in patients with acute myocardial infarction treated with rt-PA.
Design	Randomized, open label, multicenter.
Patients	3262 patients with acute myocardial infarction <76 years old <4 hours from onset of symptoms with chest pain >30 min and ST elevation ≥0.1 mV in ≥2 contiguous leads.
Follow-up	a. Predischarge radionuclide ventriculography at rest and during exercise. At 6 weeks clinical evaluation and maximal exercise test + radionuclide ventriculography. b. 1 year.

TIMI-2

Thrombolysis in Myocardial Infarction Trial (phase 2)

(continued)

Treatment regimen	Coronary angiography and angioplasty (if arteriography demonstrated suitable anatomy) within 18–48 h of thrombolytic therapy vs coronary angiography only for patients who had either spontaneous recurrent ischemia or a positive exercise test (the conservative arm).
Additional therapy	Intravenous rt-PA (150 mg over 6 h for the first 520 patients, and 100 mg in the remaining 2742 patients). Lidocaine (1–1.5 mg/kg bolus + infusion 2–4 mg/min) for >24 h; heparin 5000 U bolus and infusion 1000 U/h for 5 days, and then subcutaneous until discharge. Aspirin 80 mg/d for 6 days and then 325 mg/d.
Results	a. 53.7% and 13.3% of the invasive strategy and conservative groups underwent angioplasty within 14 days of admission. Reinfarction or death within 6 weeks occurred in 10.9% and 9.7% of the invasive and conservative group, respectively (p=0.25). Predischarge and 6 week left ventricular ejection fraction at either rest or during exercise were comparable. b. Death or nonfatal reinfarction within 1 year occurred in 14.7% and 15.2% of the invasive and conservative groups, respectively. There was no difference in death or recurrent infarction rates between the 2 groups. Anginal status at 1 year was comparable. Cardiac catheterization and angioplasty were performed more often in the invasive group (98% and 61.2%) vs the conservative group (45.2% and 20.5%). In patients with prior infarction, 6 weeks and 1 year mortality was lower in the invasive group (6.0% and 10.3%) than in the conservative group (11.5% and 17.0%), p= 0.04 and p=0.03, respectively.
Conclusions	In patients with acute myocardial infarction who are treated with rt-PA, heparin, and aspirin, the results of an invasive and conservative strategies are comparable.

SWIFT

Should We Intervene Following Thrombolysis?

Title	SWIFT trial of delayed elective intervention vs conservative treatment after thrombolysis with anistreplase in acute myocardial infarction.
Authors	SWIFT Trial Study Group.
Reference	BMJ 1991;302:555-560.
Disease	Acute myocardial infarction.
Purpose	To compare a strategy of conservative management to early elective angiography and intervention following thrombolytic therapy for acute myocardial infarction.
Design	Randomized, open label, multicenter.
Patients	800 patients, <70 years of age, with clinical features of first acute myocardial infarction, ≤3 h from onset of symptoms, and ST elevation >1 mm in ≥2 limb leads or >2 mm in ≥2 precordial leads. Patients with cardiogenic shock, severe hypertension, or contraindication to thrombolytic therapy were excluded.
Follow-up	12 month clinical follow-up. Radionuclide left ventriculography 2-3 months (523 patients) and 12 months (492 patients) after randomization.
Treatment regimen	1. Coronary angiography within 48 h. Angioplasty was attempted for >50% residual stenosis. 2. Conservative management. Angiography was permitted for persisting or recurrent ischemia or after a positive exercise test.

SWIFT

Should We Intervene Following Thrombolysis?

(continued)

Additional therapy	Anistreplase 30 U IV over 5 min. Heparin infusion 1000 U/h was started 4–6 h later. Oral anticoagulation was optional. Oral ß-blocker (timolol).
Results	43% of the early angiography group underwent angioplasty and 15% had coronary artery bypass grafting during the initial hospitalization. 3% of the conservative group had angioplasty and 2% bypass surgery. The median length of hospitalization was 11 and 10 days in the intervention and conservative groups (p<0.0001). 27% of the intervention group and 14% of the conservative group were in the hospital for >14 days. More patients in the conservative group underwent interventions during the 1 year follow-up. In-hospital mortality was 2.7% vs 3.3% in the conservative and intervention groups. 1 year mortality was 5.0% vs 5.8%, respectively (OR 1.18, 95% CI 0.64–2.10, p=0.64). In-hospital reinfarction occurred in 8.2% vs 12.1%, respectively, while reinfarction by 11 months was 15.1% vs 12.9% (OR 1.16, 95% CI 0.77–1.75, p=0.42). Angina at rest after 12 months occurred in 6.3% vs 3.4%, respectively (p=NS). The left ventricular ejection fraction at 2–3 and 12 months were comparable between the 2 groups.
Conclusions	There is no advantage for early routine intervention over a conservative approach following intravenous thrombolytic therapy for acute myocardial infarction.

MATE

Medicine vs Angiography in Thrombolytic Exclusion

Title	A prospective randomized trial of triage angiography in acute coronary syndromes ineligible for thrombolytic therapy: Results of the MATE trial.
Authors	McCullough PA, O'Neill WW, Graham M et al.
Reference	J Am Coll Cardiol 1998; 32:596-605.
Disease	Acute myocardial infarction.
Purpose	To determine whether early triage angiography with revascularization where indicated improves outcomes in patients with suspected acute MI who are not candidates for thrombolytic therapy.
Design	Prospective, randomized, multicenter.
Patients	201 patients who presented with ≤24 hours of acute chest pain consistent with acute MI but who were not eligible for thrombolysis due to lack of diagnostic ECG changes, symptoms longer than 6 hours, increased risk of bleeding or stroke.
Follow-up	Median of 21 months.
Treatment regimen	Patients randomized to either conservative arm—continued medical therapy or to triage angiography—patients taken acutely to catheterization and in those with suitable lesions PTCA, atherectomy or stenting as decided by the operator; CABG if needed.
Additional therapy	All patients were to be treated with aspirin, heparin, nitroglycerin, IV metoprolol, or propranolol.

MATE

Medicine vs Angiography in Thrombolytic Exclusion

(continued)

Results	Of the 109 patients in the triage angiography group, 58% received revascularization. In the conservative group 60% subsequently underwent nonprotocol angiography due to recurrent ischemia and 37% received revascularization. Time to revascularization was shorter in the triage angiography group (27 vs 88 hours, p=0.0001). The primary end point of recurrent ischemic events or in-hospital death occurred in 13% of the triage angiography group vs 34% in the conservative group (45% risk reduction, 95% CI=27%-59%, p=0.0002). At a median of 21 months there was no significant differences between groups in repeat hospitalization, subsequent angiography, late PTCA, or late CABG. There was no difference in cumulative incidence of PTCA, CABG, recurrent nonfatal MI, or all cause death at 21 months between groups.
Conclusions	Early triage angiography applied to patients with acute coronary syndromes who are ineligible for thrombolysis reduced recurrent ischemic events and in-hospital death, decreased the waiting time for revascularization, but was not associated with benefits in long term outcome.

1. Acute Myocardial Infarction

e. Remodeling After Infarction

SAVE

Survival And Ventricular Enlargement

Title	a. Rationale, design, and baseline characteristics of the Survival And Ventricular Enlargement trial. b. Effect of captopril on mortality and morbidity in patients with left ventricular dysfunction after myocardial infarction. Results of the Survival And Ventricular Enlargement trial. c. Cardiovascular death and left ventricular remodeling 2 years after myocardial infarction. Baseline predictors and impact of long term use of captopril: Information from the Survival And Ventricular Enlargement (SAVE) trial.
Authors	a. Moyé LA, Pfeffer MA, Braunwald E, et al. b. Pfeffer MA, Braunwald E, Moyé LA, et al. c. St. John Sutton M, Pfeffer MA, Moye L, et al.
Reference	a. Am J Cardiol 1991;68:70D-79D. b. N Engl J Med 1992;327:669-677. c. Circulation 1997; 96:3294-3299.
Disease	Acute myocardial infarction.
Purpose	To investigate whether captopril could reduce mortality and morbidity in patients with left ventricular dysfunction following myocardial infarction.
Design	Randomized, double blind, placebo controlled, multicenter.
Patients	2231 patients, 21-80 years of age, 3-16 days after myocardial infarction with left ventricular ejection fraction ≤40%, but without active ischemia or overt heart failure.
Follow-up	Clinical follow-up for 24-60 months (average 42 months). Radionuclide ventriculogram at baseline and an average of 36 months later.

SAVE

Survival And Ventricular Enlargement

(continued)

Treatment regimen	Captopril (initial dose 12.5 mg, dose was increased gradually to 50 mg X3/d), or placebo.
Results	Total mortality was lower in the captopril group (20% vs 25%, risk reduction 19%, 95% CI 3-32%, p=0.019). The reduction of risk for cardiovascular mortality was 21% (95% CI 5-35%, p=0.014). The reduction in the risk of death from progressive heart failure was 36% (95% CI 4-58%, p=0.032). Progressive heart failure unresponsive to digitalis and diuretics developed in 11% of the captopril and 16% of the placebo patients (risk reduction 37%, 95% CI 20-50%, p<0.001). Recurrent myocardial infarction was experienced by 15.2% of the placebo and 11.9% of the captopril group (risk reduction 25%, 95% CI 5-40%, p=0.015). Deterioration of ≥9 U in left ventricular ejection fraction was detected in 16% of the placebo and 13% of the captopril group (p=0.17). c. A recent analysis obtained 2-D echocardiograms at 11 days and 1 and 2 years postinfarction. In 373 patients who had serial echocardiograms LV end-diastolic and end-systolic sizes increased from baseline to 2 years. While captopril reduced diastolic dilatation at 2 years (p=0.048) this effect was carried over from the first year of therapy. Increase in left ventricular size after 1 year were similar in captopril and placebo groups.
Conclusions	Long term captopril therapy in patients with asymptomatic left ventricular dysfunction following acute myocardial infarction was associated with lower mortality and morbidity. These benefits were observed in patients who received thrombolytic therapy, aspirin, or ß-blockers, as well as those who did not.

CONSENSUS II

Cooperative New Scandinavian Enalapril Survival Study II

Title	Effects of the early administration of enalapril on mortality in patients with acute myocardial infarction. Results of the Cooperative New Scandinavian Enalapril Survival Study II (CONSENSUS II).
Authors	Swedberg K, Held P, Kjekhus J, et al.
Reference	N Engl J Med 1992;327:678-684.
Disease	Acute myocardial infarction.
Purpose	To evaluate whether early administration of enalapril after acute myocardial infarction would reduce mortality during the 6 months follow-up.
Design	Randomized, double blind, placebo controlled, multicenter.
Patients	6090 patients within 24 h of onset of pain, with ST elevation in ≥2 leads, or new Q waves, or elevated levels of enzymes. Patients with supine blood pressure less than 105/65 mm Hg were excluded.
Follow-up	41-180 days of follow-up.
Treatment regimen	IV infusion of 1mg enalapril at or placebo over 2h. If blood pressure declined <90/60 mm Hg, the infusion was stopped temporarily. 6 h later, oral enalapril or placebo was started. The recommended starting dose was 2.5 mg X2/d with gradual increase up to 20 mg/d.
Additional therapy	Standard therapy including nitrates, ß-blockers, calcium channel blockers, thrombolytic therapy, aspirin, anticoagulants, and diuretics, as indicated. If a patient needed angiotensin converting enzyme for heart failure, the patient was withdrawn from the study.

CONSENSUS II

Cooperative New Scandinavian Enalapril Survival Study II

(continued)

Results	The trial was terminated prematurely by the safety committee. By the end of the trial the mortality was 9.4% vs 10.2% in the placebo and enalapril groups (p=0.26). The mortality rates according to life table analysis at 10 days and at 1, 3, and 6 months were 4.3% vs 4.6%, 6.3% vs 7.2%, 8.2% vs 9.1%, and 10.2% vs 11.0%, respectively (p=0.26). The relative risk associated with enalapril therapy was 1.10 (95% CI 0.93–1.29). Death due to progressive heart failure occurred in 3.4% and 4.3% of the placebo and enalapril groups, whereas there was no difference in sudden death; death due to myocardial rupture, or stroke. 30% of the placebo and 27% of the enalapril treated patients needed change of therapy due to heart failure (p<0.006). Reinfarction occurred in 9% of the patients in each group. Early hypotension (systolic blood pressure <90 mm Hg, or diastolic blood pressure <50 mm Hg) occurred in 3% of the control and 12% of the enalapril patients (p<0.001).
Conclusions	Enalapril therapy, started within 24 h of the onset of acute myocardial infarction, did not improve survival during the 180 days of follow-up.

AIRE

The Acute Infarction Ramipril Efficacy

Title	a. The acute infarction ramipril efficacy (AIRE) study: Rationale, design, organization, and outcome definitions. b. Effect of ramipril on mortality and morbidity of survivors of acute myocardial infarction with clinical evidence of heart failure.
Authors	a. Hall AS, Winter C, Bogie SM, et al. b. The AIRE Study Investigators.
Reference	a. J Cardiovasc Pharmacol 1991;18(Suppl 2):S105-S109. b. Lancet 1993;342:821-828.
Disease	Acute myocardial infarction, heart failure.
Purpose	To determine whether early oral treatment with ramipril will reduce mortality in patients with heart failure complicating acute myocardial infarction.
Design	Randomized, double blind, placebo controlled, multicenter.
Patients	1986 patients, aged ≥18 years, with a definite myocardial infarction and signs of heart failure (even transient) in some period after the infarction. Patients with heart failure due to valvular heart disease, unstable angina, severe and resistant heart failure, or contraindications to angiotensin converting enzyme inhibition were excluded.
Follow-up	Clinical follow-up for >6 months (average 15 months).
Treatment regimen	3-10 days following infarction patients were randomized to receive ramipril 2.5 mg or placebo. The dose was increased to 5 mg X2/d (or 2.5 mg X2/d in case of intolerance).
Additional therapy	Patients could continue or begin any other medication except an ACE inhibitor.

Results	Total mortality was 17% in the ramipril and 23% in the placebo group (27% risk reduction, 95% CI 11%–40%, p=0.002). Separation of the survival curves occurred very early (within 30 days) and continued to diverge throughout the study. Severe heart failure developed in 14% vs 18%, respectively. There was no difference in the rates of stroke and reinfarction between the groups. Death, severe heart failure, myocardial infarction, or stroke developed in 28% vs 34% of the ramipril and placebo group (risk reduction 19%, 95% CI 5%–31%, p=0.008). Reported serious adverse events occurred in 58% of the ramipril vs 64% of the placebo. There was no difference in the occurrence of renal failure, angina, or syncope.
Conclusions	Ramipril therapy, started 3–10 days after infarction in patients with persistent or transient heart failure following infarction, resulted in reduction of mortality.

GISSI-3

Gruppo Italiano per lo Studio della Sopravvivenza nell'Infarto Miocardico III

Title	a. GISSI-3: Effect of lisinopril and transdermal glyceryl trinitrate singly and together on 6 week mortality and ventricular function after acute myocardial infarction. b. 6 month effects of early treatment with lisinopril and transdermal glyceryl trinitrate singly and together withdrawn 6 weeks after acute myocardial infarction: The GISSI-3 trial. c. Effect of the ACE inhibitor lisinopril on mortality in diabetic patients with acute myocardial infarction. Data from the GISSI 3 study.
Authors	a. + b. GISSI. c. Zuanetti G, Latini R, Maggioni AP, et al.
Reference	a. Lancet 1994;343:1115-1122. b. J Am Coll Cardiol 1996;27:337-344. c. Circulation 1997; 96:4239-4245.
Disease	Acute myocardial infarction.
Purpose	To evaluate the efficacy of lisinopril, transdermal glyceryl trinitrate, and their combination on survival and left ventricular function following acute myocardial infarction.
Design	Randomized, open label, 2X2 factorial, multicenter.
Patients	18,895 patients with chest pain, 24 h of onset of symptoms, and ST elevation or depression of ≥1 mm in ≥1 limb lead, or ≥2 mm in ≥1 precordial lead. Patients with severe heart failure, or contraindication to medications were excluded.
Follow-up	6 month clinical follow-up. Echocardiography at 6 weeks (14,209 patients).

GISSI-3

Gruppo Italiano per lo Studio della Sopravvivenza nell'Infarto Miocardico III (continued)

Treatment regimen	1. Oral lisinopril 5 mg at randomization and 10 mg/d for 6 weeks, or open control. 2. Glyceryl trinitrate (GTN) IV for 24 h, started at a rate of 5 μg/min and increased until systolic blood pressure fell by 10% or below 90 mm Hg. >24 h transdermal GTN 10 mg/d for 14 h each day for 6 weeks, or placebo.
Additional therapy	Recommended therapy included thrombolysis (72% of the patients), oral aspirin (84%), and IV ß-blockers (31%).
Results	a. + b. 13.3% of the control patients received non-study ACE inhibitors. The 6 week mortality was 6.3% and 7.1% in the lisinopril and control groups (OR 0.88, 95% CI 0.79–0.99, p=0.03). The survival curve separated on the first day and continued to diverge throughout the 6 weeks. The combined end point of mortality, heart failure beyond day 4 of infarction, left ventricular ejection fraction ≤35%, or ≥45% myocardial segments with abnormal motion occurred in 15.6% and 17.0% (OR 0.90, 95% CI 0.84–0.98, p=0.009). Rates of recurrent infarction, post infarction angina, cardiogenic shock, and stroke were similar between the lisinopril and control groups. 57.1% of the patients that were not assigned to GTN received nitrates (11.3% for >5 days). GTN did not alter total mortality (6.5% vs 6.9%, p=0.28) or the combined end point (15.9% vs 16.7%, p=0.12). The GTN group had lower rate of post infarction angina (20.0% vs 21.2%, OR 0.93, 95% CI 0.86–0.99, p=0.033), and cardiogenic shock (2.1.% vs 2.6%, OR 0.78, 95% CI 0.64–0.94, p=0.009). However, the rate of stroke was higher with GTN (0.9% vs 0.6%, p=0.027). After 6 months 18.1% vs 19.3% of the lisinopril and control groups developed severe left ventricular dysfunction or died (p=0.03), while 5.4% vs 5.8% developed clinical heart failure. No differences were found between patients with and without GTN, after 6 months. c. A recent retrospective analysis showed that in a subgroup of 2790 patients with diabetes that treatment with lisinopril decreased 6 week mortality (8.7% vs 12.4%) an effect that was greater (p=0.025) than in nondiabetic patients. The effect was maintained at 6 months despite withdrawal from therapy at 6 weeks.

GISSI-3

Gruppo Italiano per lo Studio della Sopravvivenza nell'Infarto Miocardico III

(continued)

Conclusions	6 week lisinopril therapy reduced mortality and improved outcome after myocardial infarction. There is no evidence that GTN altered these outcomes significantly. c. Early therapy with lisinopril in diabetic patients with acute myocardial infarction reduced 6 week mortality.

GISSI-3: 4 year follow-up

Title	GISSI-3: 4 year follow-up.
Authors	Tavazzi L, et al.
Reference	Presented at the 20th Congress of the European Society of Cardiology, August 22–26, 1998, in Vienna, Austria. Also Circulation 1999; 99:1127–1131.
Disease	Acute myocardial infarction.
Purpose	To determine long term outcome of early lisinopril therapy on survival and left ventricular function, over 4 years.
Design	As per GISSI-3.
Patients	95% of the original 19,394 cohort of the GISSI-3 trial.
Follow-up	4 years.
Treatment regimen	As per GISSI-3.
Results	At 6 weeks there was a reduction in mortality of 11% in the lisinopril group. At 6 months lisinopril patients had a nonsignificant trend toward lower mortality (9.1% vs 9.6%). At 4 years the lisinopril patients had a mortality of 20.9% and the placebo patients had a mortality of 21.7% (p=NS). The survival curves tracked in parallel after the initial benefit during the early phase of the study. Subgroups that benefited the most were patients with anterior myocardial infarctions and diabetes. Echocardiographic analysis suggested that late but not early ventricular remodeling was favorably affected by lisinopril.

(continued)

Conclusions	The benefit of lisinopril upon mortality in acute myocardial infarction is manifested primarily during the early phase (6 weeks); while its beneficial on LV remodeling is affected in the last phase.

ISIS-4

International Study of Infarct Survival

Title	ISIS-4: A randomized factorial trial assessing early oral captopril, oral mononitrate, and intravenous magnesium sulphate in 58050 patients with suspected acute myocardial infarction.
Authors	ISIS-4 (4th International Study of Infarct Survival) Collaborative Group.
Reference	Lancet 1995;345:669-685.
Disease	Acute myocardial infarction.
Purpose	To assess the effects on major morbidity and 5 week mortality in patients with suspected acute myocardial infarction of early initiation of oral captopril, oral controlled-release mononitrate, and intravenous magnesium sulphate.
Design	Randomized double blind, placebo controlled (captopril and mononitrate); randomized (magnesium vs open control), multicenter.
Patients	58,050 patients with suspected infarction admitted within 24 h of onset of symptoms with no clear indications for, or contraindications to, the study medications. Patients that received nitrates for only a few days were included.
Follow-up	Clinical follow-up for 5 weeks (97% of the patients); 1 year (68% of the patients).

ISIS-4

International Study of Infarct Survival

(continued)

Treatment regimen	1. Patients were randomized to oral captopril or placebo (6.25 mg initially; 12.5 mg 2 h later; 25 mg 10-12 h later; and thereafter 50 mg bid for 28 days). 2. Patients received either oral mononitrate or placebo (30 mg upon randomization and after 10-12 h; 60 mg/d for 28 days). 3. Half the patients receive intravenous magnesium sulfate (8 mmol as a bolus over 15 min and then 72 mmol over 24 h).
Additional therapy	Antiplatelet therapy was recommended (received by 94% of patients). 70% of the patients received thrombolytic therapy.
Results	Analysis was by intention to treat. Captopril reduced 5 week mortality by 7% (95% CI of 13%-1% reduction; p=0.02) (7.19% vs 7.69%, in the captopril and placebo groups, respectively). Mononitrate therapy did not alter 5 week mortality (7.34% vs 7.54% in the treated and control groups, respectively). Intravenous magnesium therapy did not reduce 5 week mortality (7.64% vs 7.24% in the magnesium and control groups, respectively).
Conclusions	Oral captopril , started early upon admission, reduces 5 week mortality in patients with suspected acute myocardial infarction. Oral mononitrate or intravenous magnesium sulfate did not reduce mortality.

SMILE

Survival of Myocardial Infarction Long Term Evaluation

Title	The effect of the ACE inhibitor zofenopril on mortality and morbidity after anterior myocardial infarction.
Authors	Ambrosioni E, Borghi C, Magnani B, for the Survival of Myocardial Infarction Long Term Evaluation (SMILE) Study Investigators.
Reference	N Engl J Med 1995;332:80-85.
Disease	Anterior wall acute myocardial infarction.
Purpose	To evaluate whether 6 weeks of therapy with ACE inhibitor zofenopril, started within 24 h after onset of infarction will improve short and long term outcome.
Design	Randomized, placebo controlled, multicenter.
Patients	1556 patients with anterior wall acute myocardial infarction who did not receive reperfusion therapy (772 and 784 patients received zofenopril and placebo, respectively).
Follow-up	Clinical follow-up for 1 year.
Treatment regimen	Oral zofenopril 7.5 mg initially, and 12 h later. The dose was increased gradually to 30 mg bid if SBP>100 mm Hg and there were no signs or symptoms of hypotension. Patients unable to tolerate the first dose were withdrawn from the study but included in the intention to treat analysis. Treatment was continued for 6 weeks.

SMILE

Survival of Myocardial Infarction Long Term Evaluation

(continued)

Results	6 weeks after randomization, the zofenopril treated patients had a 46% reduction in the risk of severe congestive heart failure (95% CI 11-71%; p=0.018) and a 25% reduction in mortality rate (95% CI -11-60%; p=0.19). The incidence of severe heart failure and death were 4.1% and 6.5% for the placebo group and 2.2% and 4.9% for the zofenopril group, respectively. The 1 year mortality was lower in the zofenopril treated group (10.0%) than in the control (14.1%) (29% risk reduction; 95% CI 6-51%; p=0.011)
Conclusions	6 weeks of therapy with zofenopril, started within 24 h after onset of myocardial infarction, reduced 6 week and 1 year mortality and reduced the incidence of severe heart failure in patients with anterior wall acute myocardial infarction not receiving reperfusion therapy.

TRACE

Trandolapril Cardiac Evaluation

Title	A clinical trial of the ACE inhibitor trandolapril in patients with left ventricular dysfunction after myocardial infarction.
Authors	Køber L, Torp-Pedersen C, Clarsen JE, et al.
Reference	N Engl J Med 1995;333:1670–1676.
Disease	Congestive heart failure, myocardial infarction.
Purpose	To determine whether patients with left ventricular dysfunction soon after myocardial infarction benefit from long-term oral ACE inhibition.
Design	Randomized, double blind, placebo controlled, multicenter.
Patients	1749 patients, >18 years old, who survived acute myocardial infarction 2–6 days earlier. Only patients with echocardiographic proof of left ventricular dysfunction (wall motion index ≤1.2) without contraindication or definite need for ACE inhibition were included.
Follow-up	24–50 months.
Treatment regimen	3–7 days after infarction patients were randomized to trandolapril 1 mg/d or placebo. The dose was gradually increased to 1–4 mg/d.
Additional therapy	Aspirin, ß-blockers, calcium antagonists, diuretics, nitrates, and digoxin, as clinically indicated.

TRACE

Trandolapril Cardiac Evaluation

(continued)

Results	Total mortality after 4 years was 34.7% in the trandolapril group and 42.3% in the placebo group. The relative risk of death from any cause for the treated vs placebo groups was 0.78 (95% CI 0.67-0.91, p=0.001). The mortality curves diverged early and continued to diverge throughout the follow-up period. Cardiovascular death occurred in 25.8% and 33.0% of the trandolapril and placebo groups (RR 0.75, 95% CI 0.63-0.89, p=0.001). Trandolapril also reduced the rate of sudden death (RR 0.76, 95% CI 0.59-0.98, p=0.03) and the progression to severe heart failure (RR 0.71, 95% CI 0.56-0.89, p=0.003). There was a trend towards reduction of recurrent infarction with trandolapril (RR 0.86, 95% CI 0.66-1.13, p=0.29).
Conclusions	Long term treatment with trandolapril in patients with left ventricular dysfunction soon after myocardial infarction reduces the rates of death, cardiovascular mortality, sudden death, and progression to severe heart failure.

TRACE

Trandolapril Cardiac Evaluation (update)

Title	Effect of ACE inhibitor trandolapril on life expectancy of patients with reduced left ventricular function after acute myocardial infarction.
Authors	Torp-Pedersen C, Kober L, for the TRACE Study Group.
Reference	Lancet 1999;354:9-12.
Disease	Congestive heart failure, left ventricular dysfunction, myocardial infarction.
Purpose	To calculate the long term effect of trandolapril on life expectancy in patients with left ventricular dysfunction after myocardial infarction.
Design	Randomized, double blind, placebo controlled, multicenter.
Patients	Same as above.
Follow-up	Up to 7 years.
Treatment regimen	3-7 days after myocardial infarction patients were randomized to placebo or trandolapril up to 4 mg/d. Therapy was continued for 2 years.
Additional therapy	After termination of the study, ACE inhibitors were prescribed to patients who would be expected to benefit from the therapy.

TRACE

Trandolapril Cardiac Evaluation (update)

(continued)

Results	The life expectancy of patients was significantly longer with trandolapril than placebo (6.2 years vs 4.6 years). The 50% mortality was reached after 55.2 months in the placebo group vs after 70.5 months in the trandolapril group. Therefore, the median lifetime was increased by 15.3 months or 27% increase in median lifetime (95% CI 7-51%). After 1, 2, 3, 4, 5, and 6 years, 32, 55, 87, 66, 64, and 64 lives, respectively, were saved per 1000 patients treated after each year.
Conclusions	In patients with left ventricular dysfunction after acute myocardial infarction, long term treatment with trandolapril for 2 years after myocardial infarction was associated with a significant prolongation of life expectancy.

TRACE (Diabetic Substudy)

Trandolapril Cardiac Evaluation Study

Title	Effect of the ACE inhibitor trandolapril on mortality and morbidity in diabetic patients with left ventricular dysfunction after acute myocardial infarction.
Authors	Gustafsson I, Torp-Pedersen C, Kober L, et al.
Reference	J Am Coll Cardiol 1999;34:83-89.
Disease	Myocardial infarction, left ventricular dysfunction.
Purpose	To determine the long term efficacy of treatment with the ACE inhibitor trandolapril in post myocardial infarction diabetic patients with left ventricular dysfunction.
Design	Retrospective analysis of a randomized, double blind, placebo controlled trial.
Patients	237 (14%) diabetic patients that were among the 1749 patients that participated in the TRACE study (original reference: N Engl J Med 1995;333:1670-1676). Patients had myocardial infarcts and LVEF ≤35%.
Follow-up	26 months.
Treatment regimen	As per TRACE study. Study medicine started 3-7 days post infarction.
Additional therapy	As per TRACE study.

TRACE (Diabetic Substudy)

Trandolapril Cardiac Evaluation Study

(continued)

Results	126 patients (53%) in the diabetic group died, vs 547 (36%) in the nondiabetic group. Death occurred in 51 (45%) of diabetic patients randomized to trandolapril vs 75 (61%) of diabetics randomized to placebo (RR=0.64; 95% CI=0.45-0.91).Among nondiabetics, death occurred in 253 (33%) of patients on trandolapril vs 294 (39%) of patients on placebo (RR=0.82; 95% CI=0.69-0.97). Trandolapril decreased the risk of progression to severe heart failure (RR=0.38; 95% CI=0.21-0.67), but this end point was not significantly reduced by trandolapril in nondiabetic patients. In diabetic patients trandolapril also decreased the incidence of cardiovascular death, sudden death, and reinfarction. In nondiabetic patients trandolapril significantly decreased the incidence of cardiovascular death, but not sudden death or reinfarction.
Conclusions	Trandolapril reduced death and other major cardiovascular complications in diabetics with post infarction LV dysfunction.

CATS

Captopril And Thrombolysis Study

Title	a. Acute intervention with captopril during thrombolysis in patients with first anterior myocardial infarction. Results from the captopril and thrombolysis study (CATS). b. Which patient benefits from early ACE inhibition after myocardial infarction? Results of 1 year serial echocardiographic follow-up from the captopril and thrombolysis study (CATS). c. Long term anti-ischemic effects of ACE inhibition in patients after myocardial infarction.
Authors	a. Kingma JH, van Gilst WH, Peels KH, et al. b. Van Gilst WH, Kingma H, Peels KH, et al. c. van den Heuvel, van Gilst, van Veldhuisen, et al.
Reference	a. Eur Heart J 1994;15:898-907. b. J Am Coll Cardiol 1996;28:114-121. c. J Am Coll Cardiol 1997;30:400-405.
Disease	Acute myocardial infarction.
Purpose	To evaluate the effects of early captopril therapy (within 6 h of onset of first anterior myocardial infarction) on left ventricular volume and clinical symptoms.
Design	Multicenter, randomized, double blind, placebo controlled.
Patients	298 patients with first anterior acute myocardial infarction treated with streptokinase <6 h of onset of symptoms. Patients with systolic blood pressure >200 or <100 mm Hg or diastolic blood pressure >120 or <55 mm Hg were excluded. Patients with renal insufficiency or intolerance to ACE inhibitors, severe valvular heart disease, arrhythmias requiring antiarrhythmic therapy, serious systemic disease, AV conduction disturbances, or left bundle branch block were excluded.

Follow-up	12 months, clinical 24h ambulatory ECG monitoring, exercise test, and echocardiographic follow-up.
Treatment regimen	Immediately upon completion of streptokinase, captopril (6.25 mg) or placebo was given PO. The dose was repeated after 4 and 8 h. Captopril 12.5 mg and 25 mg were given at 16 h and 24 h, respectively. If systolic blood pressure was <95 mm Hg, the study medication was withheld until the next dosing time. The target dose was 25 mgX3/d.
Additional therapy	IV Streptokinase 1.5 million IU over 30 min. Aspirin, calcium antagonists and β-blockers were at the discretion of the local investigators.
Results	a+b. In the captopril group the number of patients with paired ventricular premature beats, accelerated idioventricular rhythm (AIVR) and nonsustained ventricular tachycardia (NSVT) were lower than in the placebo group. During the acute phase AIVR occurred in 33.8% vs 44.5%, in the captopril and placebo group ($p<0.05$), and NSVT in 31.7% vs 40.9%, respectively ($p<0.05$). Peak creatine kinase and cumulative α-hydroxybutyrate dehydrogenase release over 72 h tended to be lower, and peak α-hydroxybutyrate dehydrogenase was lower in the captopril group than in the placebo group. A complete clinical follow-up over 1 year was obtained in 245 patients (82.2%). Analysis with the random coefficient model revealed no significant effect of captopril on changes in left ventricular volume over 12 months when compared with placebo. However, the occurrence of dilatation was lower in the captopril-treated group ($p=0.018$). Captopril was effective in reducing the occurrence of dilatation in medium size infarcts, tended to be effective in small infarcts, but was ineffective in large infarcts. The incidence of heart failure was lower in the captopril group ($p<0.04$). This effect was confined to patients with medium size infarctions.

Results c. 244 patients underwent predischarge exercise test. After 3 months of therapy, exercise time increased equally in the placebo (86±13 s) and captopril group (69±12 s)(p=0.8). At 1 year exercise time increased further (by 13±11 s, and 33±13 s, respectively; p=0.7). Mean ST segment depression was comparable between the groups at 3 months and 12 months. During the 12 month treatment phase, 82 ischemic events were reported in the placebo group vs 52 in the captopril group (p=0.015). The number of ischemic events during the first 3 months of therapy were comparable, however, between 3 to 12 months 45 vs 21 events were detected in the placebo and captopril groups, respectively (p=0.009). Between 3-12 months 32% of the placebo vs 18% of the captopril treated patients experienced ischemic events (p=0.018). After 12 months, medications were withdrawn and both groups continued on single blind placebo for a month. During this month, 9 ischemic episodes were detected in the previous captopril treated group vs only 1 in the previous placebo group (p=0.006). 11 patients in the captopril vs only 1 in the placebo group needed antianginal medication after termination of the treatment phase (p=0.005).

Conclusions Very early treatment with captopril reduces the occurrence of early dilatation and progression to heart failure, especially in patients with medium size infarction. Captopril reduced the incidence of ischemia related events after myocardial infarction. The effect became apparent only after 3 months of therapy. However, captopril did not alter exercise performance. After withdrawal from captopril therapy, a high incidence of ischemic events occurred.

AIREX

The Acute Infarction Ramipril Efficacy Extension Study

Title	Follow-up study of patients randomly allocated ramipril or placebo for heart failure after acute myocardial infarction: AIRE Extension (AIREX) Study.
Authors	Hall AS, Murray GD, Ball SG, on behalf of the AIREX Study Investigators.
Reference	Lancet 1997;349:1493-1497.
Disease	Acute myocardial infarction.
Purpose	To evaluate the long term effects of ramipril therapy started early after acute myocardial infarction.
Design	Randomized, double blind, placebo controlled, multicenter.
Patients	603 patients who participated in the AIRE study, aged ≥18 years, with a definite myocardial infarction and signs of heart failure (even transient) in some period after the infarction. Patients with heart failure due to valvular heart disease, unstable angina, severe and resistant heart failure, or contraindications to ACE inhibition were excluded.
Follow-up	Follow-up for a minimum of 42 months and a mean of 59 months.

AIREX

The Acute Infarction Ramipril Efficacy Extension Study

(continued)

Treatment regimen	2-9 days following myocardial infarction patients were randomized to receive ramipril (n=302) 1.25 or 2.5 mg bid or placebo (n=301). The dose was increased to 5 mg bid (or 2.5 mg bid in case of intolerance). Randomized trial medications were given for an average of 13.4 months in the placebo group and 12.4 months in the ramipril group. Thereafter, trial medication was stopped in both groups and therapy with ACE inhibitors was continued at the discretion of the attending physician.
Results	The average time from onset of myocardial infarction to therapy was 5 days in both groups. At hospital discharge 13.7% of the ramipril vs 5.3% of the placebo assigned patients were not receiving study medication. Withdrawal due to intolerance and refusal by the patients were more common in the ramipril group, whereas withdrawal because of severe heart failure was more common in the placebo group. All causes mortality was 38.9% in the placebo group and 27.5% in the ramipril group. The Kaplan-Meier survival curves separated early and continued to diverge over the first 2 years, and thereafter run parallel. The relative risk reduction 36% (95% CI 15-52%; p=0.002), and the absolute reduction in mortality was 11.4%.
Conclusions	The beneficial effects of ramipril started early after myocardial infarction in patients with heart failure were sustained over several years, despite discontinuation of the randomized study medication after approximately 1 year of therapy.

CCS-1

Chinese Cardiac Study

Title	Oral captopril vs placebo among 13,634 patients with suspected acute myocardial infarction: Interim report from the Chinese cardiac study (CCS-1).
Authors	Chinese Cardiac Study Collaborative Group.
Reference	Lancet 1995;345:686-687.
Disease	Acute myocardial infarction.
Purpose	To evaluate the effect of captopril therapy, started within 36 h of the onset of suspected acute myocardial infarction, on 4-week mortality.
Design	Randomized, placebo controlled, multicenter.
Patients	13,634 patients with suspected acute myocardial infarction, within the first 36 h of onset of symptoms. Patients with hypotension or chronic use of large doses of diuretics were excluded.
Follow-up	4 weeks.
Treatment regimen	Randomization to captopril (n=6814) or placebo (n=6820). Captopril was given at an initial dose of 6.25 mg, then 12.5 mg 2 h later, and then 12.5 mg tid.
Additional therapy	Low dose aspirin was recommended.

CCS-1

Chinese Cardiac Study

(continued)

Results	88% of the captopril assigned and 91% of the placebo assigned patients completed the protocol or died earlier. Hypotension was the cause of discontinuation of treatment in 8.4% of the captopril and 4.9% of the placebo treated patients. Overall, 73% of the patients received aspirin, 27% thrombolytic therapy, 39% intravenous nitrates, and 20% diuretics. 4 week mortality was 9.05% in the captopril group vs 9.6% in the placebo group (p=NS). Persistent hypotension occurred in 16.3% and 10.8% of the captopril and placebo groups, respectively (p<0.0001). There was no difference in the rates of heart failure, ventricular fibrillation, other cardiac arrest, or advanced heart block. However, there was a nonsignificant excess of cardiogenic shock with captopril (4.8% vs 4.2%; p=NS). Among patients with admission systolic blood pressure <100 mm Hg, 4 week mortality was 11.0% in the captopril group vs 10.0% in the placebo group. Among patients with systolic blood pressure 100–104 mm Hg, mortality was 11.4% vs 12.4%, respectively.
Conclusions	Captopril therapy, initiated within 36 h of onset of acute myocardial infarction, was associated with a nonsignificant reduction in 4 week mortality and excess of hypotension. Among patients with entry systolic blood pressure <100 mm Hg captopril may be hazardous, but in those with mild hypotension and in normotensive patients early initiation of captopril may be relatively safe.

CEDIM

The L-Carnitine Echocardiografia Digitalizzata Infarto Miocardico

Title	Effects of L-carnitine administration on left ventricular remodeling after acute anterior myocardial infarction: The L-Carnitine Echocardiografia Digitalizzata Infarto Miocardico (CEDIM) trial.
Authors	Iliceto S, Scrutinio D, Bruzzi P, et al.
Reference	J Am Coll Cardiol 1995;26:380-387.
Disease	Acute myocardial infarction.
Purpose	To assess the effects of L-carnitine on left ventricular remodeling after anterior acute myocardial infarction.
Design	Randomized, double blind, placebo controlled, multicenter.
Patients	472 patients, ≤80 years old, with a first anterior acute myocardial infarction, within 24 h of onset of infarction, and high quality 2-D echocardiograms. Patients with valvular, congenital heart disease, or cardiomyopathy were excluded.
Follow-up	12 months with repeated 2-D echocardiograms.
Treatment regimen	Randomization to L-carnitine (n=233) or placebo (n=239) within 24 h of onset of symptoms. L-carnitine was administered by continuous intravenous infusion at a dose of 9 g/d for the first 5 days and then 2 g tid orally for 12 months.

CEDIM

The L-Carnitine Echocardiografia Digitalizzata Infarto Miocardico

(continued)

Addtional therapy	ACE inhibitors were not recommended at the time of the study and were used by only 8% of patients. 78% of patients received thrombolytic therapy.
Results	348 patients had paired echocardiograms and were entered into the final analysis. Left ventricular end systolic and end diastolic volumes were significantly smaller at 3, 6, and 12 months after myocardial infarction in the L-carnitine treated patients than in the placebo group. On discharge, left ventricular end diastolic volume (LVEDV) was 90.9±2.33 mL in the L-carnitine group and 91.7±2.03 mL in the placebo group (p=0.15). After 12 months LVEDV was 99.3±2.06 mL and 105.4±2.37 mL, respectively (adjusted difference -7.23 mL; p=0.01). Discharge left ventricular end systolic volume (LVESV) was 47.8±1.16 mL and 48.8±1.53 mL, respectively (p=0.13). After the first year LVESV was 55.0±1.63 mL and 58.9±1.75 mL in the L-carnitine and placebo groups, respectively (adjusted difference -4.49 mL; p=0.03). Left ventricular ejection fraction at discharge was 48.1±0.47% and 48.1±0.52%, respectively (p=0.83). After 12 months it was 45.8±0.57% and 45.2±0.52% (adjusted difference +0.52%; p=0.46). In-hospital mortality was 4.7% in the L-carnitine group vs 5.9% in the placebo group (p=NS), whereas 1 year mortality was 4.3% vs 5.4%, respectively (p=NS). Heart failure during the first year developed in 1.7% of the L-carnitine group vs 4.2% in the placebo group (p=NS). However, there was no difference in the rates of unstable angina, reinfarction, coronary artery bypass surgery, or coronary angioplasty. In none of the patients, therapy was discontinued because of adverse events.
Conclusions	L-carnitine therapy for 12 months attenuated left ventricular remodeling and prevented dilatation in patients with first anterior acute myocardial infarction, without apparent adverse effects or increasing mortality and morbidity. However, no effect on left ventricular ejection fraction was detected.

Healing and Early Afterload Reducing Therapy

Title	Early vs delayed ACE inhibition therapy in acute myocardial infarction. The Healing and Early Afterload Reducing Therapy Trial.
Author	Pfeffer MA, Greaves SC, Arnold JMO, et al.
Reference	Circulation 1997; 95:2643-2651.
Disease	Coronary artery disease, acute myocardial infarction.
Purpose	To determine the safety and efficacy of early (day 1) vs delayed (day 14) initiation of the ACE inhibitor ramipril on echocardiographic measures of left ventricular dilatation and ejection fraction.
Design	Double blind, randomized, multicenter.
Patients	352 patients with anterior myocardial infarction.
Follow-up	14, 90 days.
Treatment regimen	Group I - early placebo, late full dose 10 mg ramipril; Group II - early low dose, late low dose [0.625 mg]; and Group III - early full dose and late full dose [10 mg]. Early treatment represented day 1-14; late 14-90 days.

Healing and Early Afterload Reducing Therapy

(continued)

Results	Early low dose did not alter clinical events. The risk of a systolic arterial pressure less than or equal to 90 mm Hg during the first 14 days was greater in both ramipril groups. While LV ejection fraction increased in all groups during the early period, the full dose ramipril group had the greatest improvement in ejection fraction (+4.9% in full dose; 3.9% in low and, 2.4% in delayed, $p<0.05$ for trend). The early full dose ramipril group was the only group that did not show an increase in LV diastolic area. At 6 months, only the group that received ramipril for the first time during the later period (placebo to full dose) showed improvement in wall motion. When all groups were on active therapy during the late phase, there was no further increase in diastolic area. Patients who were on placebo and then received full dose ramipril showed a trend toward decrease in LV end systolic area and improvement in ejection fraction during the late phase.
Conclusions	In patients with acute anterior myocardial infarction early use of ramipril (titrated to 10 mg) attenuated LV remodeling and resulted in prompter recovery of LV ejection fraction.

Early captopril administration after thrombolysis.

Title	Effects of early captopril administration after thrombolysis on regional wall motion in relation to infarct artery blood flow.
Authors	French JK, Amos DJ, Williams BF, et al.
Reference	J Am Coll Cardiol 1999;33:139-145.
Disease	Acute myocardial infarction.
Purpose	To evaluate the effect of early intervention (within 2 hours after streptokinase administration) with ACE inhibitor on left ventricular function and blood flow in the infarct related artery in patients with acute myocardial infarction.
Design	Randomized, placebo controlled.
Patients	493 patients, ≤75 years old, with ST elevation acute myocardial infarction, <4 hours of onset of symptoms. Patients who were receiving an ACE inhibitor or those with hypotension after thrombolytic therapy were excluded.
Follow-up	Coronary angiography + ventriculography at 3 weeks after myocardial infarction. Clinical follow-up for a median of 4 years.
Treatment regimen	Randomization to captopril 6.25 mg or placebo 2 hours after streptokinase infusion. Dosing was increased gradually to 50 mg tid for 3 weeks. ß-blockers were continued or started on days 2-3.

Additional therapy	All patients received intravenous streptokinase (1.5 X 10^6 U over 30-60 min), oral aspirin (300 mg), and heparin (5000 U as a bolus followed by 1000 U/h for 48 hours).
Results	512 patients received intravenous streptokinase 3.1±1.4 hours after onset of symptoms. 19 patients were excluded. 243 patients received captopril and 250 placebo 2.1±0.4 hours after streptokinase infusion. Angiography was performed in 432 (88%) patients 22±6 days after infarction. 30 day mortality was 2% in the captopril group vs 4.8% in the placebo group (p=0.078). Reinfarction occurred within 30 days in 13 (5.3%) of the captopril group, vs 6.8% in the placebo group. During the clinical follow-up period there were 20 cardiac deaths in the captopril group and 35 in the placebo group (p=0.036). 32% of patients in both the captopril and placebo group received ACE inhibitors during the follow-up. 3 weeks captopril therapy did not alter left ventricular ejection fraction, left ventricular end systolic volume, and end diastolic volume, both in anterior and inferior wall myocardial infarction. Captopril had no effects on these indices when patients with patent and occluded infarct related arteries were studied separately. Among patients with anterior wall acute myocardial infarction, the captopril group had fewer hypokinetic chords (40±13 vs 44±13; p=0.028), and fewer chords with >1 SD below normal (34±17 vs 39±17; p=0.041) in the infarct region. Among patients with anterior wall myocardial infarction and TIMI flow 0-2, the captopril treated patients had less hypokinetic chords (44±12 vs 50±9; p=0.043) than the control patients. There were no differences in regional wall motion indices between the captopril and the control patients among anterior wall myocardial infarction patients with TIMI flow 3. Among anterior wall myocardial infarction patients and corrected TIMI frame counts of >27, the captopril treated patients had fewer hypokinetic chords (42±13 vs 46±12; p=0.015), and fewer chords with >2 SD below normal (27±17 vs 32±17; p=0.047) than the control

Early captopril administration after thrombolysis

(continued)

	patients. There were no differences in regional wall motion indices between the captopril and control patients among those with corrected TIMI frame counts <27. Captopril had no effects in patients with inferior wall myocardial infarction.
Conclusions	Captopril therapy, started within 2 hours after streptokinase infusion was associated with better regional wall motion at 3 weeks in patients with anterior wall myocardial infarction (but not inferior wall myocardial infarction). The greatest benefit was observed in anterior wall myocardial infarction patients with impared flow in the infarct related artery.

FAMIS

Fosinopril in Acute Myocardial Infarction Study

Title	Short and long term effects of early fosinopril administration in patients with acute anterior myocardial infarction undergoing intravenous thrombolysis: Results from the fosinopril in acute myocardial infarction study.
Authors	Borghi C, Marino P, Zardini P, et al.
Reference	Am Heart J 1998;136:213-225.
Disease	Acute myocardial infarction.
Purpose	To assess the effects of early fosinopril administration in patients with anterior acute myocardial infarction receiving thrombolytic therapy.
Design	Randomized, double blind, placebo controlled, multicenter.
Patients	285 patients, 18-75 years old, with anterior acute myocardial infarction who received intravenous tPA ≤9 hours of onset of symptoms. Patients in Killip class IV on admission, hypotension, serum creatinine >2.1 mg/dL, history of congestive heart failure, CABG in the 3 months prior to randomization, current treatment with angiotensin converting enzyme inhibitors or contraindications to angiotensin converting enzyme inhibitors were excluded.
Follow-up	An average of 24±5 months (range 2-35 months). 2-D transthoracic echocardiography 24-48 hours after onset of symptoms, at discharge, and at 3 months.
Treatment regimen	Randomization to placebo (n=143) or fosinopril 5 mg (n=142), started within 3 hours after the completion of thrombolytic therapy. Fosinopril dose was increased to 20 mg/d if tolerated. Study drug was stopped after 3 months.

FAMIS

Fosinopril in Acute Myocardial Infarction Study

(continued)

Additional therapy	ß-blockers, aspirin, nitrates, calcium antagonists, diuretics, and anticoagulants were permitted.
Results	12 patients with unconfirmed acute myocardial infarction were excluded from further evaluation. The target dose of 20 mg/d was achieved in 81% of the patients at day 4. At the end of the 3 month follow up, 83.8% of the placebo vs 79.7% of the fosinopril group were taking their study medication. 28.9% of the placebo vs 31.4% of the fosinopril group received open label ACE inhibitors. The 3 month mortality was 5.2% in the placebo and 8.4% in the fosinopril group (p=NS). 2 year cumulative mortality was 14.1% in the placebo vs 14.5% in the fosinopril group (p=NS). At 3 months, 29.1% of the placebo group vs 28.2% of the fosinopril group died or developed congestive heart failure (p=NS), whereas at 2 years the cumulative mortality and congestive heart failure rate was 51.5% vs 45.0%, respectively (p=NS). Death or NYHA class III-IV occurred in 26.8% of the placebo vs 17.5% of the fosinopril group (p=0.04). Among patients with Killip class I on admission, congestive heart failure occurred in 26.8% of the placebo vs 17.5% of the fosinopril group (p=0.05). Among patients with LVEF ≥40%, mortality rate was 10.6% in the placebo vs 6.4% in the fosinopril (p=NS), whereas death + severe heart failure occurred in 14.6% vs 8.6%, respectively (p=0.04). The fosinopril group had less ventricular rhythm disturbances at 3 months than the placebo group (0.8% vs 6.0%; p=0.02). Fosinopril was well tolerated and safe. Hypotension (<100 mm Hg) occurred in 17.4% of the placebo and 29.3% of the fosinopril group (p=0.004). Transitory hypotension (<90 mm Hg) during the titration phase occurred in 7.7% vs 19.5%, respectively (p=0.001), however, persistent hypotension, requiring specific therapy was noted in 9.8% and 9.7% of the patients, respectively. Over the 3 month treatment phase, there was an insignificant trend towards greater increase in left ventricular end diastolic and end systolic volume index in the placebo group. Infarct size index and LVEF were comparable between the groups at 3 months.

FAMIS

Fosinopril in Acute Myocardial Infarction Study

(continued)

Conclusions

Fosinopril administration, started early after completion of thrombolytic therapy and continued for 3 months, reduced the combined end point of death or severe congestive heart failure in patients with anterior myocardial infarction treated with thrombolytic therapy. The effect was more pronounced in patients without heart failure on admission or in those with initial LVEF ≥40%.

1. Acute Myocardial Infarction

f. Miscellaneous and Adjunctive Therapy

TIMI-2B

Thrombolysis in Myocardial Infarction Trial (phase 2B)

Title	a. Comparison of invasive and conservative strategies after treatment with intravenous tissue plasminogen activator in acute myocardial infarction. Results of the Thrombolysis in Myocardial Infarction (TIMI) Phase II Trial. b. Immediate vs deferred ß-blockade following thrombolytic therapy in patients with acute myocardial infarction. Results of the Thrombolysis in Myocardial Infarction (TIMI) II-B Study.
Authors	a. The TIMI Study Group. b. Roberts R, Rogers WJ, Mueller HS, et al.
Reference	a. N Engl J Med 1989;320:618-627. b. Circulation 1991;83:422-437.
Disease	Acute myocardial infarction.
Purpose	To compare the effects of immediate vs delayed (6 days) metoprolol therapy in patients with acute myocardial infarction treated with rt-PA (a substudy of the TIMI-2 Trial).
Design	Randomized, open label, multicenter study.
Patients	2948 patients with acute myocardial infarction <76 years old < 4 hours from onset of symptoms with chest pain>30 min and ST elevation ≥0.1 mV in ≥2 contiguous leads, of whom 1434 (49%) were eligible for ß-blocker therapy.
Follow-up	Predischarge radionuclide ventriculography at rest and during exercise. At 6 weeks clinical evaluation and maximal exercise test + radionuclide ventriculography. 1 year follow-up.

TIMI-2B

Thrombolysis in Myocardial Infarction Trial (phase 2B)

(continued)

Treatment regimen	Immediate therapy: 3 IV injections of 5 mg metoprolol, and then 50 mg X2/d PO for 1 day and 100 mg X2/d thereafter. Delayed therapy: on day 6, 50 mg X2/d PO for 1 day and then 100 mg X2/d.
Additional therapy	Intravenous rt-PA (150 mg over 6 h for the first 520 patients, and 100 mg in the remaining 2742 patients). Lidocaine (1-1.5 mg/kg bolus + infusion 2-4 mg/min) for >24 h; heparin 5000 U bolus and infusion 1000 U/h for 5 days, and then subcutaneous until discharge. Aspirin 80 mg/d for 6 days and then 325 mg/d.
Results	The systolic blood pressure in the immediate group decreased during the first hour by 9.8% compared with 7.1% in the deferred therapy group ($p<0.01$). Mean heart rate decreased by 6% in the immediate group and increased in the deferred group ($p<0.001$). There was no difference in the occurrence of arrhythmias between the groups. Left ventricular ejection fraction was similar in both groups at predischarge (51.0% vs 50.1%) and at 6 weeks (50.4% and 50.8%, respectively). Regional ventricular function was also comparable. Overall, there was no difference in mortality between the groups. However, in the low risk patients 6 weeks mortality was 0 and 2.8% in the immediate and deferred ß-blocker therapy groups ($p=0.007$). Reinfarction was less common at 6 days and 6 weeks in the immediate treated group. However, there was no difference at 1 year.
Conclusions	ß-blockers are safe when given early after thrombolytic therapy to a selected population with acute myocardial infarction and are associated with lower risk of recurrent ischemia and reinfarction in the first week. However, long term prognosis and left ventricular function are similar to those who receive ß-blockers only after 6 days.

DAVIT II

The Danish Verapamil Infarction Trial II

Title	Effect of verapamil on mortality and major events after acute myocardial infarction (the Danish Verapamil Infarction Trial II- DAVIT II).
Authors	The Danish Study Group on Verapamil in Myocardial Infarction.
Reference	Am J Cardiol 1990;66:779-785.
Disease	Acute myocardial infarction.
Purpose	To assess whether long term therapy with verapamil, started from the second week after acute myocardial infarction will reduce mortality and morbidity compared with placebo.
Design	Randomized, double blind, placebo controlled, multicenter.
Patients	1775 patients, <76 years old, 7-15 days after proven acute myocardial infarction. Patients with severe heart failure, hypotension, atrioventricular or sinoatrial blocks, or therapy with calcium channel or ß-blockers due to angina, arrhythmia, or hypertension were excluded.
Follow-up	Clinical follow-up up to 18 months (mean 16 months).
Treatment regimen	Verapamil 120 mg X3/d (in cases of adverse drug reactions 120 mg X1-2/d was allowed) or placebo.
Additional therapy	Therapy with calcium channel blockers or ß-blockers was not permitted. Nitrates were allowed.

DAVIT II

The Danish Verapamil Infarction Trial II

(continued)

Results	1 month after randomization 38.7% of the placebo and 33.2% of the verapamil group reported angina (p=0.02). However, after 12 months, the difference did not reach statistical significance (33.7% vs 28.6%). There was a trend towards reduction of total mortality (11.1% vs 13.8%, Hazard ratio (HR) 0.80, 95% CI 0.61-1.05, p=0.11), and a significant reduction of death or first reinfarction (18.0% vs 21.6%, HR 0.80, 95% CI 0.64-0.99, p=0.03) at 18 months with verapamil. In patients without heart failure during hospitalization, verapamil was associated with lower mortality (7.7% vs 11.8%, HR 0.64, 95% CI 0.44-0.94, p=0.02) and reinfarction (9.4% vs 12.7%, HR 0.67, 95% CI 0.46-0.97, p=0.02), while there was no difference in mortality (17.5% vs 17.9%) or reinfarction (14.3% vs 14.2%) between the groups in patients with heart failure during hospitalization.
Conclusions	Long term verapamil therapy after an acute myocardial infarction resulted in reduction of mortality and reinfarction, but only in patients without heart failure.

Cardiac event rates after acute myocardial infarction in patients treated with verapamil and trandolapril vs trandolapril alone

Title	Cardiac event rates after acute myocardial infarction in patients treated with verapamil and trandolapril vs trandolapril alone.
Author	Hansen JF, Hagerup L, Sigurd B, et al, for the Danish Verapamil Infarction Trial (DAVIT) Study Group.
Reference	Am J Cardiol 1997;79:738-741.
Disease	Acute myocardial infarction.
Purpose	To determine whether verapamil given to post-myocardial infarct patients with congestive heart failure, already on diuretics and ACE inhibitor, would further reduce cardiac event rates.
Design	Randomized, double blind, multicenter study.
Patients	100 patients with acute myocardial infarction, congestive heart failure, on a diuretic.
Follow-up	3 months.
Treatment regimen	Patients were consecutively randomized to trandolapril 1 mg/day for 1 month and 2 mg/day for the following 2 months; or to trandolapril as above plus verapamil 240 mg/day for 1 month and 360 mg/day for 2 months. Trial medicines were begun 3-10 days after myocardial infarction.

Cardiac event rates after acute myocardial infarction in patients treated with verapamil and trandolapril vs trandolapril alone

(continued)

Results	The primary combined end point was of death, reinfarction, unstable angina, and readmission due to worsening congestive heart failure. 3 month event rates were 35% in the trandolapril group vs 14% in the trandolapril verapamil group (hazard ratio 0.35; 95% CI=0.15-0.85, p=0.015). Event rates of combined death, reinfarction, or unstable angina were 29% in the trandolapril group vs 10% in the trandolapril verapamil group (hazard ratio 0.31; 95% CI -0.11-0.86, p=0.018).
Conclusions	Verapamil reduced combined cardiac event rates when added to an ACE inhibitor in post myocardial infarction patients with heart failure.

LIMIT-2

Leicester Intravenous Magnesium Intervention II Trial

Title	Intravenous magnesium sulphate in suspected acute myocardial infarction: Results of the second Leicester Intravenous Magnesium Intervention Trial (LIMIT-2).
Authors	Woods KL, Fletcher S, Roffe C, Haider Y.
Reference	Lancet 1992;339:1553-1558.
Disease	Acute myocardial infarction.
Purpose	To evaluate the efficacy of intravenous magnesium sulphate infusion in reduction of early mortality following acute myocardial infarction.
Design	Randomized, double blind, placebo controlled, unicenter.
Patients	2316 patients with suspected acute myocardial infarction (within 24 h of onset of symptoms). No electrocardiographic criteria were specified.
Follow-up	28 days clinical follow-up.
Treatment regimen	Saline or magnesium sulphate 8 mmol over 5 min followed by 65 mmol over 24 h.
Additional therapy	No restriction. Thrombolytic therapy was not required.

LIMIT-2

Leicester Intravenous Magnesium Intervention II Trial

(continued)

Results	Acute myocardial infarction was confirmed in 65% of the patients. 36% vs 35% of the magnesium and placebo patients received thrombolytic therapy, while 65% vs 66% received aspirin. 28 day mortality was 10.3% in the placebo and 7.8% in the magnesium group (odds ratio 0.74, 95% CI 0.55-1.00, p=0.04). Mortality odds ratios were 0.76 (95% CI 0.46-1.27) in the patients that received thrombolytic therapy and 0.72 (95% CI 0.49-0.99) for those who did not receive thrombolytic therapy. The incidence of clinical left ventricular failure was 11.2% in the magnesium and 14.9% in the placebo group (25% risk reduction, 95% CI 7%-39%, p=0.009). The prevalence of hypotension <100 mm Hg for ≥1 h was similar. Sinus bradycardia was more common with magnesium (10.8% vs 8.0%, p=0.02). However, the incidence of AV block and tachyarrhythmias were similar.
Conclusions	Intravenous magnesium sulphate is a simple and safe therapy for acute myocardial infarction and was associated with reduction of mortality.

ESPRIM

European Study of Prevention of Infarct with Molsidomine

Title	The ESPRIM trial: Short term treatment of acute myocardial infarction with molsidomine.
Authors	European Study of Prevention of Infarct with Molsidomine (ESPRIM) Group.
Reference	Lancet 1994;344:91-97.
Disease	Acute myocardial infarction.
Purpose	To compare the effects of molsidomine (a nitric oxide donor) with placebo in patients with acute myocardial infarction.
Design	Randomized, double blind, placebo controlled, multicenter.
Patients	4017 patients with suspected acute myocardial infarction (chest pain >30 min, with onset <24 h). Patients in Killip class III or IV were excluded.
Follow-up	An average of 13 months clinical follow-up.
Treatment regimen	Molsidomine (IV linsidomine (the active metabolite of molsidomine) 1 mg/h for 48 h, followed by oral molsidomine 4 mg X4/d for 12 days.The control group received matching placebo.
Additional therapy	Nonstudy vasodilator therapy could be added by the physician. No limitation on additional therapy.

ESPRIM

European Study of Prevention of Infarct with Molsidomine

(continued)

Results	48.5% of the molsidomine and 51.0% of the placebo received thrombolytic therapy before randomization, and 21.7% vs 20.0% after randomization. 35 day mortality was similar (8.4% vs 8.8% in the molsidomine and placebo groups, RR 0.96, 95% CI 0.78-1.17, p=0.66). There was no difference in long term mortality 14.7% vs 14.2% in the molsidomine and placebo groups, respectively (p=0.67). The rates of the major and minor adverse events were similar, except for headache which was more common with the molsidomine group.
Conclusions	Nitric oxide donor was not effective in reduction of mortality following acute myocardial infarction.

TAMI-9

Thrombolysis and Angioplasty in Myocardial Infarction 9 Trial

Title	Intravenous fluosol in the treatment of acute myocardial infarction. Results of the Thrombolysis and Angioplasty in Myocardial Infarction 9 trial.
Authors	Wall TC, Califf RM, Blankenship J, et al.
Reference	Circulation 1994;90:114–120.
Disease	Acute myocardial infarction.
Purpose	To assess the efficacy of fluosol as an adjunctive therapy to reperfusion for acute myocardial infarction.
Design	Randomized, open label, multicenter.
Patients	430 patients, age >18 and <75 years, with suspected acute myocardial infarction <6 h of onset of symptoms, with ≥1 mm ST elevation in ≥2 leads.
Follow-up	Cardiac angiography and symptom-limited stress thallium scan 5–14 days after infarction. In-hospital clinical follow-up.
Treatment regimen	IV fluosol 1 mL/min, the rate was increased gradually to 20 mL/min. Total dose 15 mL/kg.
Additional therapy	Chewable aspirin 324 mg, IV heparin, and 100 mg tissue plasminogen activator over 3 h, 100% oxygen for 8 h. IV atenolol if no contraindications existed.

TAMI-9

Thrombolysis and Angioplasty in Myocardial Infarction 9 Trial

(continued)

Results	There was no significant difference between the control and fluosol groups in left ventricular ejection fraction (52% vs 51%), regional wall motion analysis (-2.2 SD/chord vs -2.4 SD/chord), or infarct size as measured by thallium scan. The analysis of anterior wall infarction yielded similar results. Patency rates of the infarct related arteries were similar. Rates of death (3.7% vs 5.6%) and stroke (0.9% vs 4.3%) were similar in the control and fluosol groups. However, the fluosol group experienced less recurrent infarction (4.2% vs 2.4%), but more heart failure and pulmonary edema (31% vs 45%; p=0.004). There was no difference in hemorrhagic complications.
Conclusions	Fluosol, as an adjunctive therapy to thrombolysis did not result in reduction of infarct size or improvement of left ventricular function and clinical outcome.

DIGAMI

Diabetes Mellitus Insulin Glucose Infusion in Acute Myocardial Infarction

Title	a. Randomized trial of insulin glucose infusion followed by subcutaneous insulin treatment in diabetic patients with acute myocardial infarction (DIGAMI study): Effects on mortality at 1 year. b. Prospective randomized study of intensive insulin treatment on long term survival after acute myocardial infarction in patients with diabetes mellitus.
Authors	a. Malmberg K, Rydén L, Efendic S, et al. b. Malmberg K for the DIGAMI Study Group.
Reference	a. J Am Coll Cardiol 1995;26:57-65. b. BMJ 1997;314:1512-1515.
Disease	Acute myocardial infarction, diabetes mellitus.
Purpose	a. To evaluate whether insulin glucose infusion followed by multidose insulin therapy will decrease mortality in diabetic patients with acute myocardial infarction. b. To assess the long term outcome of intensive insulin therapy begun at the time of an acute myocardial infarction in patients with diabetes mellitus.
Design	Randomized, open label, multicenter.
Patients	a. 620 patients with diabetes mellitus and a blood glucose level>11 mmol/l and with suspected acute myocardial infarction (chest pain of ≥15 min, ≤24 h of onset of symptoms).
Follow-up	a. 1 year. b. 3.4 years.

DIGAMI

Diabetes Mellitus Insulin Glucose Infusion in Acute Myocardial Infarction

(continued)

Treatment regimen	Insulin glucose or placebo infusion over ≥24 h, then SC insulin X4/d for ≥3 months.
Additional therapy	Thrombolytic therapy, if no contraindications existed and patients were admitted within 6 h of onset of symptoms. IV followed by oral metoprolol, if not contraindicated.
Results	a. Blood glucose decreased from 15.4±4.1-9.6±3.3 mmol/l in the infusion group over the first 24 h, and from 15.7±4.2-11.7±4.1 mmol/l among the control patients (p<0.0001). In-hospital mortality was 9.1% in the insulin vs 11.1% in the control group (p=NS). 1 year mortality was 18.6% vs 26.1%, respectively (relative risk reduction 29%, 95% CI 4%-51%, p=0.0273). The reduction in mortality was particularly evident in low risk patients and with no previous insulin therapy (3 month mortality 6.5% in the insulin vs 13.5% in the control, relative risk reduction 52%, p=0.046; 1 year mortality 8.6% vs 18.0%, respectively, relative risk reduction 52%, p=0.020). b. At 1 year fewer deaths (19%) occurred in the intensive insulin group vs the standard treatment group (26%; p=0.027). At 3.4 years the difference between groups persisted (33% vs 44%, p =0.011).
Conclusions	a. Insulin glucose infusion followed by a multidose insulin therapy improved 1 year survival in diabetic patients after acute myocardial infarction. b. Insulin glucose infusion followed by 3 months of multiple dose insulin reduced mortality long term in acute myocardial infarction patients with diabetes.

CRIS

Calcium antagonist Reinfarction Italian Study

Title	A controlled trial of verapamil in patients after acute myocardial infarction: Results of the calcium antagonist reinfarction Italian study (CRIS).
Authors	Rengo F, Carbonin P, Pahor M, et al.
Reference	Am J Cardiol 1996;77:365-369.
Disease	Acute myocardial infarction.
Purpose	To evaluate the effects of verapamil on total mortality, cardiac mortality, reinfarction, and recurrent angina after an acute myocardial infarction.
Design	Randomized, double blind, placebo controlled, multicenter.
Patients	1073 patients, age 30-75 years, who survived 5 days following an acute myocardial infarction. Patients with severe heart failure, Wolf-Parkinson-White syndrome, cardiac surgery, implanted pacemaker, right ventricular failure with pulmonary hypertension, concomitant severe disease, contraindication to verapamil, heart rate <50 bpm, hypotension or hypertension, and chronic therapy with ß-blockers or calcium channel blockers were excluded.
Follow-up	Mean follow-up 23.5 months.
Treatment regimen	7-21 days (mean 13.8 days) after myocardial infarction patients were randomized to placebo or verapamil retard 120 mgX3/d.

CRIS

Calcium antagonist Reinfarction Italian Study

(continued)

Results	Study medication was discontinued before completion of follow-up in 36.9% of the placebo group and 35.6% of the verapamil group. Intention to treat analysis revealed no difference in mortality (5.4% vs 5.6%), cardiac mortality (4.1% vs 4.0%;), and sudden death (1.8% vs 2.1%), in the placebo and verapamil group, respectively. There was a trend toward less reinfarction in the verapamil group (7.3% vs 9.0%; relative risk (RR) 0.81; 95% CI 0.53-1.24). Verapamil therapy was also associated with a nonsignificant reduction in the rates of first major event (death or reinfarction,9.0% vs 10.3%; RR 0.87; 95% CI 0.59-1.29), and first cardiac event (cardiac death, reinfarction, or hospital admission for chest pain, 15.4% vs 19.2%; RR 0.79; 95% CI 0.59-1.05). Less patients in the verapamil group developed angina (18.8% vs 24.3%; RR 0.8; 95% CI 0.5 to 0.9; $p<0.05$).
Conclusions	Verapamil therapy following myocardial infarction was not associated with reduced mortality. However, it was associated with less angina and a trend toward less reinfarction.

EMIAT

The European Myocardial Infarct Amiodarone Trial

Title	Randomised trial of effect of amiodarone on mortality in patients with left-ventricular dysfunction after recent myocardial infarction: EMIAT
Author	Julian DG, Camm AJ, Frangin G, et al.
Reference	Lancet 1997;349:667-674.
Disease	Acute myocardial infarction.
Purpose	To assess the efficacy of amiodarone on reduction of mortality of patients with left ventricular dysfunction following myocardial infarction.
Design	Randomized, double blind, placebo controlled, multicenter.
Patients	1486 patients, 18-75 years old, 5-21 days (mean 15±3.9 days) after acute myocardial infarction with left ventricular ejection fraction <40%. Patients with contraindications to amiodarone, amiodarone therapy within 6 months, bradycardia <50 bpm, advanced atrioventricular block, hepatic disease, thyroid dysfunction, long QT syndrome, severe angina or heart failure, a likelihood of cardiac surgery, and those requiring active antiarrhythmic medications were excluded.
Follow-up	Clinical follow-up for 12 to 24 months (median 21 months). 24 h Holter ECG monitoring at baseline and after 2 weeks and 4 months.
Treatment regimen	Placebo or amiodarone (800 mg/d for 14 days, 400 mg/d for 14 weeks, and then 200 mg/d).
Additional therapy	ß-blockers and digoxin were permitted.

EMIAT

The European Myocardial Infarct Amiodarone Trial

(continued)

Results	743 patients were included in each group. All cause mortality was similar (103 patients in the amiodarone group vs 103 in the placebo patients; risk ratio (RR) 0.99; 95% CI 0.76-1.31; p=0.96). Cardiac mortality was comparable (85 vs 89 patients, respectively; RR 0.94; 95% CI 0.70-1.26; p=0.67). However, arrhythmic deaths (33 vs 50 patients; RR 0.65; 95% CI 0.42-1.00; p=0.05) and arrhythmic death and resuscitated cardiac arrest (42 vs 61 patients; RR 0.68; 95% CI 0.46-1.00; p=0.05) were less common in the amiodarone than the placebo group. However, death from reinfarction occurred in 10 amiodarone treated patients vs only 3 of the placebo treated patients. Noncardiac mortality occurred in 18 of the amiodarone vs 13% of the placebo patients (RR 1.37; 95% CI 0.67-2.79). In intention-to-treat analysis of the 548 patients with arrhythmias at baseline, there was no statistically significant difference between the amiodarone and placebo groups concerning arrhythmic death, but there was reduction in the occurrence of the combined end point of arrhythmic deaths and resuscitated cardiac deaths in the amiodarone group (p=0.048). During the trial, 38.5% of the amiodarone vs 21.4% of the placebo group discontinued the study medication. Clinical hypothyroidism occurred in 1.5% vs 0% of the amiodarone and placebo groups, whereas hyperthyroidism in 1.6% vs 0.5%, respectively. Pulmonary disorders occurred in 5.2% vs 4.0%, respectively.
Conclusions	Amiodarone therapy in survivors of myocardial infarction with left ventricular dysfunction was not associated with reduction of total mortality or cardiac mortality during a median follow-up of 21 months. However, the reduction in arrhythmic death and the apparent lack of proarrhythmic effect support the use of amiodarone in patients with ischemic heart disease and left ventricular dysfunction for whom antiarrhythmic therapy is indicated.

CAMIAT

Canadian Amiodarone Myocardial Infarction Arrhythmia Trial

Title	Randomized trial of outcome after myocardial infarction in patients with frequent or repetitive ventricular premature depolarisations: CAMIAT.
Authors	Cairns JA, Connolly SJ, Roberts R, et al.
Reference	Lancet 1997;349:675-682.
Disease	Acute myocardial infarction.
Purpose	To assess the efficacy of amiodarone on reduction of the risk of resuscitated ventricular fibrillation or arrhythmic death among patients with left ventricular dysfunction following myocardial infarction with frequent or repetitive ventricular premature depolarizations.
Design	Randomized, double blind, placebo controlled, multicenter.
Patients	1202 patients, >19 years old, 6–45 days after myocardial infarction, with a mean of 10 ventricular premature depolarizations per h or more by 24 h ambulatory ECG monitoring, or ≥1 run of ventricular tachycardia. Patients with contraindications to amiodarone; bradycardia (<50 bpm); atrioventricular block; QTc >480 ms; peripheral neuropathy; liver disease; pulmonary fibrosis; asthma; thyroid disease; need for antiarrhythmic therapy; therapy with tricyclic antidepressants, phenytoin, or sotalol; severe congestive heart failure; hypotension or angina; and patients with life expectancy of <2 years were excluded.
Follow-up	Repeated 24 h ambulatory ECG monitoring at baseline, 4, 8, 12 and 16 months. Clinical follow-up for 1 to 2 years (mean 1.79±0.44 years).
Treatment regimen	Placebo or amiodarone (a loading dose of 10 mg/kg in 2 divided daily doses for 2 weeks, then 400 mg/d. Patients older than 75 years and those who weighed <60 kg received 300 mg/d). If arrhythmia suppression was detected, the dose was reduced to 200–300 mg/d at month 4 and to 200 mg/d for 5–7 days/week at month 8.

Canadian Amiodarone Myocardial Infarction Arrhythmia Trial (continued)

Results

There were 606 patients in the amiodarone group and 596 in the placebo group. 24 h ambulatory ECG monitoring at month 4 revealed arrhythmia suppression in 84% of the amiodarone group vs 35% of the placebo group, and at month 8 in 86% vs 39%, respectively. The mean percentage of the study drug being taken at each follow-up visit was 75% and 78% in the amiodarone and placebo groups. Only 6% of the patients in each group took <50% of the study medication. 221 (36.4%) patients of the amiodarone group vs 152 (25.5%) of the placebo group discontinued taking study medication for reasons other than outcome events (p<0.0005). Adverse effects resulting in discontinuation of study medication occurred in 159 (26.2%) patients of the amiodarone vs 82 (13.7%) patients in the placebo group (p<0.0005). Hypothyroidism was found in 3.3% vs 0.2%, respectively (p<0.0005). Proarrhythmia (0.3% vs 3.0%; p=0.002) and ventricular tachyarrhythmia (0.7% vs 2.0%; p=0.004) occurred less often in the amiodarone treated patients. Efficacy analysis revealed that the estimated risk of resuscitated ventricular fibrillation or arrhythmic death at 24 months was 1.77% per year for the amiodarone vs 3.38% per year for the placebo groups (48.5% relative risk reduction; 95% CI 4.5 to 72.2%; p=0.018). 37 vs 50 patients of the amiodarone and placebo group died (rate per year for all cause mortality 4.36% vs 5.42%; relative risk reduction 21.2%; 95% CI -20.6% to 48.5%; p=0.136). 30 vs 44 patients of the amiodarone and placebo group died from cardiac causes (rate per year 3.53% vs 4.77%; relative risk reduction 27.4%; 95% CI -15.5% to 54.4%; p=0.087). Intention-to-treat analysis revealed reduction in the risk for resuscitated ventricular fibrillation or arrhythmic death (relative risk reduction 38.2%; 95% CI -2.1% to 62.6%; p=0.029); arrhythmic death (29.3%; 95% CI -19.6% to 58.2%; p=0.097); cardiac mortality (22.0%; 95% CI -15.9% to 47.6%; p=0.108); and total mortality (18.3%; 95% CI -16.1% to 42.6%; p=0.129). The cumulative rates of nonarrhythmic death were comparable (5.8% in the amiodarone group vs 6.2% in the placebo group; p=0.70).

Conclusions

Amiodarone therapy in survivors of myocardial infarction with frequent or repetitive ventricular premature depolarizations was associated with reduction of ventricular fibrillation or arrhythmic death. No proarrhythmic effect was observed. However, adverse effects mandating discontinuation of amiodarone were relatively common.

Beneficial effects of intravenous and oral carvedilol treatment in acute myocardial infarction. A placebo controlled, randomized trial.

Title	Beneficial effects of intravenous and oral carvedilol treatment in acute myocardial infarction. A placebo controlled, randomized trial.
Author	Basu, S. Senior R, Raval U, et al.
Reference	Circulation 1997; 96:183-191.
Disease	Coronary artery disease. Acute myocardial infarction.
Purpose	To determine the effects of acute and long term treatment of acute myocardial infarction with the ß-blocker carvedilol.
Design	Placebo controlled, randomized, double blind, single center.
Patients	151 consecutive patients with acute myocardial infarction. Exclusion criteria included Killip Class IV heart failure, cardiogenic shock, bradycardia, hypotension, heart block, and insulin dependent diabetes.
Follow-up	6 months.
Treatment regimen	Initial therapy was 2.5 mg of carvedilol IV or placebo over 15 minutes, within 24 hours of chest pain, followed by 6.25 mg oral carvedilol or placebo twice a day for 2 days; then 12.5 mg to 25 mg x2/d for the duration of the study.

Beneficial effects of intravenous and oral carvedilol treatment in acute myocardial infarction. A placebo controlled, randomized trial.

(continued)

Results

At 6 months carvedilol was associated with fewer cardiac events (cardiac death, reinfarction, unstable angina, heart failure, emergency revascularization, ventricular arrhythmia requiring therapy, stroke, additional cardiovascular therapy other than sublingual nitroglycerin, diuretics, hypertension, continuing ACE inhibitors, digitalis, or antiarrhythmics), at 18 compared to placebo at 31 ($p<0.02$). After excluding end points of revascularization and requirement for other cardiovascular medicine, there were 24 events in placebo vs 14 in carvedilol ($p<0.03$). Among 54 patients with heart failure at study entry, 34 received carvedilol but did not exhibit adverse effects of carvedilol. As expected, carvedilol caused decreases in heart rate and blood pressure. Left ventricular ejection fraction was not significantly altered by carvedilol. In a subgroup of patient with LV ejection fraction <45%, carvedilol reduced LV remodeling.

Conclusions

Carvedilol was well tolerated following myocardial infarction, even in those with heart failure, and improved composite outcomes at 6 months.

CORE

Collaborative Organization for RheothRx Evaluation

Title	Effects of RheothRx on mortality, morbidity, left ventricular function, and infarct size in patients with acute myocardial infarction.
Author	Collaborative Organization for RheothRx Evaluation (CORE) Investigators.
Reference	Circulation 1997;96:192–201.
Disease	Coronary artery disease, acute myocardial infarction.
Purpose	To determine the effect of various doses of RheothRx (poloxamer 188) on outcomes in patients with acute myocardial infarction.
Design	Randomized, multicenter. Several modifications of dosing regimens occurred throughout the initial phases of the study.
Patients	2948 patients with acute myocardial infarction.
Follow-up	6 months.
Treatment regimen	RheothRx vs control. Ultimately RheothRx was given as a hour loading bolus plus 11-h infusion at low dose. Several dose modifications were made previous to this because of safety issues.

CORE

Collaborative Organization for RheothRx Evaluation

(continued)

Results	Initial high dose regimens of RheothRx were discontinued secondary to renal dysfunction (in 8.8% of patients). Lower dose regimens including boluses and infusions also were associated with renal dysfunction (2.7%–4.1%) vs controls (1%). The composite end point of death, cardiogenic shock, and reinfarction at 35 days was 13.6% in all RheothRx patients vs 12.7% in controls. RheothRx was associated with a higher incidence of atrial arrhythmias and heart failure and a lower LV ejection fraction.
Conclusions	RheothRx had no effect on mortality, reinfarction, or cardiogenic shock in acute infarct patients. RheothRx had an adverse effect on renal function, heart failure, LV function, and atrial arrhythmias, and is not indicated in acute myocardial patients.

Elevated chlamydia pneumoniae antibodies, cardiovascular events, and azithromycin in male survivors of myocardial infarction

Title	Elevated chlamydia pneumoniae antibodies, cardiovascular events, and azithromycin in male survivors of myocardial infarction.
Author	Gupta S, Leatham EW, Carrington D, et al.
Reference	Circulation 1997; 96:404-407.
Disease	Coronary artery disease, myocardial infarction.
Purpose	To determine the relationship between antibodies against chlamydia pneumonia (CP) and future cardiovascular events in male survivors of myocardial infarction (MI), and to determine the effect of azithromycin antibiotic therapy.
Design	Screening of 220 consecutive male survivors of myocardial infarction for anti Cp antibodies. Patients with persisting seropositivity of ≥1/64 dilution were randomized to oral azithromycin or placebo. There was also a non-randomized untreated arm.
Patients	220 consecutive males survivors of myocardial infarction.
Follow-up	Mean follow up 18 months.
Treatment regimen	For patients with persistent seropositivity ≥1/64 received either oral azithromycin 500 mg/d for 3 days or 500 mg/d for 6 days or placebo.

Elevated chlamydia pneumoniae antibodies, cardiovascular events, and azithromycin in male survivors of myocardial infarction

(continued)

Results	The occurrence of adverse cardiovascular events increased with increasing anti-Cp titre. Anti Cp titres fell to ≤1/16 in 43% of patients receiving azithromycin vs only 10% taking placebo (p =0.02). The azithromycin treated group had a 5 fold reduction in cardiovascular events compared to combined placebo and untreated nonrandomized group (odds ratio = 0.2; 95% C.I. = 0.05 to 0.8 p = 0.03). However the event rate was not significantly different between the azithromycin group and randomized placebo group alone.
Conclusions	Increased anti Cp antibody titres may be a predictor for future cardiovascular events following myocardial infarctions. A short course of azithromyicn might lower this risk but larger studies are needed (and underway) to look at this issue.

Short acting nifedipine and diltiazem do not reduce the incidence of cardiac events in patients with healed myocardial infarctions

Title	Short acting nifedipine and diltiazem do not reduce the incidence of cardiac events in patients with healed myocardial infarctions.
Author	Ishikowa K, Nakai S, Takenaka T, et al.
Reference	Circulation 1997;95:2368-2373.
Disease	Coronary artery disease, healed myocardial infarction.
Purpose	To determine whether treatment with short acting nifedipine or diltiazem reduces the likelihood of cardiac events.
Design	Open trial, randomized (to control vs calcium channel antagonist).
Patients	1115 patients with "healed myocardial infarction." Inpatients began at 8 days after onset of infarction. Outpatients entered on first visit to the department. Average time interval from onset of myocardial infarction was 27 months.
Follow-up	Up to 100 months.
Treatment regimen	595: no calcium blocker; 520 with calcium blocker. 341 received short acting nifedipine 30 mg/d and 179 received short acting diltiazem (90 mg/d).

Short acting nifedipine and diltiazem do not reduce the incidence of cardiac events in patients with healed myocardial infarctions

(continued)

Results	Cardiac events (fatal or nonfatal recurrent myocardial infarction; death from congestive heart failure; sudden death; hospitalization because of worsening angina, congestive heart failure, or premature ventricular contraction) occurred in 51 patients (8.6%) not on calcium blockers and in 54 (10.4%) in the calcium blocker group (odds ratio, 1.24; 95% CI 0.8–1.85).
Conclusions	Short acting nifedipine and diltiazem conferred no protection in healed myocardial infarct patients.

SPRINT-2

The Secondary Prevention Reinfarction Israel Nifedipine Trial 2 Study

Title	Early administration of nifedipine in suspected acute myocardial infarction.
Authors	Goldbourt U, Behar S, Reicher-Reiss H, et al.
Reference	Arch Intern Med 1993;153:345–353.
Disease	Acute myocardial infarction.
Purpose	To assess the secondary prevention efficacy of nifidipine, administered early after admission for acute myocardial infarction.
Design	Randomized, double blind, placebo controlled, multicenter.
Patients	1358 patients, 50–79 years old, with suspected acute myocardial infarction. Patients with hypotension, intolerance to nifedipine, heart disease other than coronary disease, previous cardiac surgery, LBBB or Wolff-Parkinson-White syndrome, or concomitant severe disease were excluded.
Follow-up	6 months.
Treatment regimen	Randomization to nifedipine or placebo, started within 48 h of admission. The nifedipine dose was titrated to 10 mg X 6/d by day 6. Patients with previous myocardial infarction, anginal syndrome before the index infarction, hypertension, NYHA class II–IV before admission, anterior myocardial infarction, maximal LDL levels >X3 the upper limit of normal could enter the long term phase after discharge (nifedipine 15 mg qid or placebo for 6 months).

SPRINT-2

The Secondary Prevention Reinfarction Israel Nifedipine Trial 2 Study

(continued)

Results	The study was terminated prematurely by the Review Committee due to excess in early mortality in the nifedipine group. In 532 patients medication was discontinued during the titration phase. Therefore, 826 patients were included in the final group. Mortality during the first 6 days was higher in the nifedipine group (7.8%) than in the placebo group (5.5%)(adjusted odds ratio 1.60; 95% CI 0.86 to 3.00). Among the 826 patients who continued study medications during the long term phase, mortality was 9.3% in the nifedipine group vs 9.5% in the placebo group. By intention-to-treat analysis, 6 month mortality in the 1358 randomized patients was 15.4% in the nifedipine group vs 13.3% in the placebo group (adjusted relative risk 1.33; 95% CI 0.98–1.80). Analysis according to the time of death for all randomized patients showed that the difference in mortality was mainly due to early (within 6 days) excess mortality in the nifedipine group. Recurrent nonfatal myocardial infarction among patients who participated in the long term phase occurred in 5.1% of the nifedipine vs 4.2% of the placebo group. Chest pain was reported by 36.0% of the nifedipine group vs 34.8% of the placebo group. 7.5% of the nifedipine vs 7.0% of the placebo group needed rehospitalization because of unstable angina.
Conclusions	Nifedipine, started soon after admission, was associated with increased early mortality in patients with acute myocardial infarction. Long term prophylactic therapy with nifedipine did not reduce mortality, recurrent myocardial infarction, anginal pain, or need for rehospitalization because of unstable angina. It should be noted that short and not long acting nifedipine was used.

ECLA (Estudios Cardiólogicos Latinoamérica)

Glucose Insulin Potassium Pilot Trial

Title	Metabolic modulation of acute myocardial infarction.
Authors	Diaz R, Paolasso EA, Piegas LS, et al.
Reference	Circulation 1998; 98:2227-2234.
Disease	Acute myocardial infarction.
Purpose	To determine the effect of glucose, insulin, and potassium (GIK) infusion on the outcome of acute myocardial infarction.
Design	Randomized, multicenter.
Patients	407 patients with suspected MI, admitted within 24 hours of onset of symptoms.
Follow-up	1 year.
Treatment regimen	High dose GIK (25% glucose, 50 IU insulin per liter, 80 mmol KCl per liter at an infusion rate of 1.5 mL/kg/hr over 24 hours) vs low dose GIK (10% glucose, 20 IU insulin per liter and 40 mmol KCL/liter at a rate 1.0 mL/kg/hr over 24 hours) or control (usual care).
Additional therapy	Reperfusion therapy (lytic or angioplasty as indicated).

ECLA (Estudios Cardiólogicos Latinoamérica)

Glucose Insulin Potassium Pilot Trial

(continued)

Results	The incidence of electromechanical dissociation was lower in the GIK groups vs controls (1.5% vs 5.8%, 2p=0.016). There was a nonsignificant trend toward reduction in major and minor in-hospital events in patients receiving GIK. In patients treated with reperfusion therapy, GIK was associated with a significant reduction in in-hospital mortality (RR=0.34; 95% CI=0.5 to 0.78; 2p=0.008) and nonsignificant trends toward severe heart failure and ventricular fibrillation. At 1 year there was some attenuation of treatment effect, but mainly in the low dose GIK group. Mortality was still reduced in the high dose vs control group at 1 year in patients that were reperfused (RR=0.37; 95% CI=0.14-1.00, log rank test 0.046). GIK therapy was associated with more phlebitis and changes in concentration of glucose or potassium.
Conclusions	GIK appeared to be beneficial in acute myocardial infarction patients that received repefusion therapy.

DECREASE

Dutch Echocardiographic Cardiac Risk Evaluation Applying Stress Echocardiography Study Group

Title	The effect of biosoprolol on perioperative mortality and myocardial infarction in high risk patients undergoing vascular surgery.
Authors	Poldermans D, Boersma E, Bax JJ, et al.
Reference	N Engl J Med 1999;341:1789-1794.
Disease	Cardiac death and myocardial infarction in patients undergoing major vascular surgery.
Purpose	To determine the effects of perioperative ß-adrenergic receptor blockade on outcomes in patients at high risk who were undergoing major vascular surgery.
Design	Randomized, multicenter.
Patients	846 patients with one or more cardiac risk factors undergoing elective abdominal aortic or infrainguinal arterial reconstruction underwent dobutamine echocardiography. Of these patients, 173 had positive results for ischemia on dobutamine echo and were considered high risk.
Follow-up	30 days after surgery.
Treatment regimen	Standard perioperative care (n=53) or standard care plus bisoprolol (n=59). Bisoprolol was started at least one week before surgery. Initial dose of bisoprolol was 5 mg orally once-a-day and increased to 10 mg once-a-day if heart rate remained >60 bpm.

DECREASE

Dutch Echocardiographic Cardiac Risk Evaluation Applying Stress Echocardiography Study Group

(continued)

Additional therapy	Standard perioperative care.
Results	9 patients (17%) in the standard care group died of cardiac causes vs 2 in the bisoprolol group (3.4%, $p=0.02$). 9 patients (17%) in the standard care group and 0 in the bisoprolol group developed a nonfatal myocardial infarction ($p<0.001$). The primary end point of death from cardiac causes or nonfatal myocardial infarction was reached in 18 patients in the standard care group (34%) and 2 patients in the bisoprolol group (3.4%, $p<0.001$).
Conclusions	Bisoprolol reduced perioperative mortality and myocardial infarction in high risk patients who were undergoing vascular surgery.

NEHDP

The National Exercise and Heart Disease Project

Title	Results of multicenter randomized clinical trial of exercise and long term survival in myocardial infarction patients. The NEHDP.
Authors	Dorn J, Naughton J, Imamura D, et al.
Reference	Circulation 1999;100:1764-1769.
Disease	Myocardial infarction.
Purpose	To determine whether a supervised exercise program improved survival in male myocardial infarct patients.
Design	Randomized, multicenter.
Patients	651 men ages 30-64 with documented MI ≥8 weeks but <3 years before being enrolled. Had to be able to exercise ≥3 metabolic equivalents.
Follow-up	19 years.
Treatment regimen	Following completion of a low level exercise program of 6 weeks duration patients were assigned to exercise group (n=323) or nonexercise group (n=328). Exercise prescription based on patient's performance on ECG monitored treadmill testing. Included various forms of physical activity. Initially they exercised for 8 weeks in a laboratory. After this, they jogged, cycled, or swam guided by target heart rate.
Additional therapy	As per physician.

NEHDP

The National Exercise and Heart Disease Project

(continued)

Results	All cause mortality risk estimates in the exercise group vs controls was 0.69 (95% CI=0.39–1.25) after 3 years follow-up; 0.84 (0.55–1.28) at 5 years; 0.95 (0.71–1.29) at 10 years; 1.02 (0.79–1.32) at 15 years; and 1.09 (0.87–1.36) at 19 years. Thus, the nonsignificant lower mortality estimates in the exercise group continued for up to 10 years but the reduction in risk was attenuated over time, especially by 15–19 years. A trend toward reduction in death due to cardiovascular disease was only detected during the earliest years of the study (a benefit in favor of exercise RR=0.73; 95% CI=0.37–1.43 at 3 years) and by 5 years relative risk approached unity. Thereafter there was a nonsignificant increased risk for cardiovascular death associated with exercise (RR=1.21, 1.14, and 1.16 at 10, 15, and 19 years, respectively). Men who were younger, smoked cigarettes, and had a low initial physical work capacity, benefited more from exercise than men who were older, nonsmokers, or had a high initial physical work capacity. Each 1 metabolic equivalent increase in work capacity from baseline to end of the trial was associated with a decrease in all cause mortality risk of 8%–14%.
Conclusions	Exercise program resulted in a nonsignificant decrease in mortality during the first 5 years of follow-up that then diminished over time.

AMISTAD

The Acute Myocardial Infarction Study of Adenosine Trial

Title	Results of multicenter, randomized, placebo controlled trial: The acute myocardial infarction study of adenosine (AMISTAD) Trial.
Authors	Mahaffey KW, Puma JA, Barbagelata A, et al.
Reference	J Am Coll Cardiol 1999; 34:1711-1720.
Disease	Acute myocardial infarction.
Purpose	To determine whether adenosine administered as an adjuvant to thrombolytic therapy would further reduce myocardial infarct size.
Design	Prospective, randomized, placebo controlled, open label, multicenter.
Patients	236 patients with acute ST segment elevation myocardial infarction who presented within 6 hours of chest pain slated for thrombolytic therapy.
Follow-up	6-day infarct size determination, inhospital outcomes.
Treatment regimen	Adenosine IV at 70 μg/kg/min for 3 hours or placebo infusion (normal saline). Adenosine was to begin prior to thrombolytic therapy (accelerated alteplase or streptokinase).
Additional therapy	Lidocaine prior to thrombolytic therapy (one experimental study suggested adenosine only reduced infarct size given with lidocaine).

AMISTAD

The Acute Myocardial Infarction Study of Adenosine Trial

(continued)

Results

Primary end point was infarct size determined with Tc-99 m sestamibi SPECT (single photon emission computed tomography) myocardial perfusion imaging 5-7 days after enrollment. Secondary end points included a myocardial salvage index and composite inhospital clinical outcomes (death, reinfarction, shock, congestive heart failure, or stroke). Adenosine was associated with a 33% relative reduction in myocardial infarct size (p=0.03). Final infarct size for anterior infarcts was 45.5% of the LV in placebo patients, vs 15% for adenosine patients (p=0.014). For nonanterior myocardial infarcts, infarct size was 11.5% in both adenosine and placebo groups (p=NS). Myocardial salvage index (myocardium at risk minus final infarct size/myocardium at risk) in patients with anterior infarcts was 0.62 in adenosine patients and was 0.15 in placebo patients. There was no difference in this index between groups in the nonanterior infarcts. There were no significant differences in clinical outcomes between adenosine and placebo, and event rates were small. However, there was a nonsignificant increase in deaths (10 vs 6), reinfarctions (7 vs 3), CHF (13 vs 8) and cardiogenic shock (6 vs 4) in adenosine vs placebo patients. This excess of adverse events tended to occur in the nonanterior MI group.

Conclusions

Adenosine decreased myocardial infarct size in anterior wall MIs; there was a nonsignificant trend toward increased adverse events in patients with nonanterior wall MIs who received adenosine. A large clinical outcome trial is warranted.

INTERCEPT

INcomplete Infarction Trial of European Research Collaborators Evaluating Progress Post-Thrombolysis

Title	Diltiazem in acute myocardial infarction treated with thrombolytic agents: A randomized placebo controlled trial.
Authors	Boden WE, van Gilst WH, Scheldewaert RG, et al.
Reference	Lancet 2000;355:1751-1756.
Disease	Coronary artery disease, acute myocardial infarction.
Purpose	To assess the role of long acting diltiazem in the secondary prevention of recurrent events after acute myocardial infarction.
Design	Randomized, placebo controlled, double blind, multicenter.
Patients	874 patients, ≤75 years old, who had received thrombolytic therapy and aspirin within 12 hours of onset of symptoms of an ST elevation acute myocardial infarction. Only patients with cardiac enzyme elevation were included. Patients were randomized within 36-96 hours of onset of myocardial infarction. Patients with congestive heart failure, bradycardia, atrioventricular block, sick sinus syndrome, hypotension, severe hypertension, hemodynamic instability, ongoing myocardial ischemia, current therapy with calcium antagonists, or intolerance to diltiazem or aspirin were excluded.
Follow-up	6 months.
Treatment regimen	Randomization to diltiazem 300 mg once a day (n=430) or placebo (n=444). Therapy was continued for 6 months.

INTERCEPT

INcomplete Infarction Trial of European Research Collaborators Evaluating Progress Post-Thrombolysis

(continued)

Additional therapy	All patients received aspirin. ß-blockers and nitrates were administered to patients who developed recurrent ischemia after randomization. ACE inhibitors and diuretics were recommended for hypertension. However, routine prophylactic use of ACE inhibitors and ß-blockers was prohibited.
Results	The primary end point of the study (cardiac death, nonfatal myocardial reinfarction, or refractory angina) occurred in 30% in the placebo group vs 23% in the diltiazem group (hazard ratio [HR] 0.79; 95% CI 0.61-1.02; p=0.07). Cardiac mortality was 1.4% in the placebo group vs 1.6% in the diltiazem group (HR 1.26; 95% CI 0.42-3.76; p=0.67). Nonfatal reinfarction occurred in 5% and 4% in the placebo and diltiazem groups, respectively (HR 0.79; 95% CI 0.41-1.50; p=0.47). Refractory ischemia occurred in 23% and 17%, respectively (HR 0.76; 95% CI 0.56-1.02; p=0.07). Nonfatal myocardial reinfarction or refractory ischemia occurred in 28% in the placebo group vs 21% in the diltiazem group (HR 0.76; 95% CI 0.58-1.00; p=0.05). Nonfatal myocardial reinfarction or revascularization occurred in 17% vs 11% (HR 0.67; 95% CI 0.46-0.96; p=0.03). 12% vs 7% in the placebo and diltiazem groups underwent revascularization (HR 0.61; 95% CI 0.39-0.96; p=0.03). Diltiazem was not associated with an increase in cancer, bleeding, strokes, or congestive heart failure.
Conclusions	Diltiazem was not associated with a reduction in the cumulative occurrence of cardiac death, myocardial reinfarction, or refractory ischemia during 6 month follow-up. Diltiazem reduced the occurrence of nonfatal cardiac events, especially the rates of revascularization.

EMIT

The European Mivazerol Trial

Title	Effect of mivazerol on perioperative cardiac complications during noncardiac surgery in patients with coronary heart disease.
Authors	Oliver MF, Goldman L, Julian DG, et al.
Reference	Anesthesiology 1999; 99:951-961.
Disease	Coronary heart disease.
Purpose	To determine whether mivazerol (has α_2 agonist properties that decreases post ganglionic noradrenaline availability and sympathetic output) reduced cardiac events in patients with known coronary heart disease or patients at risk for coronary heart disease undergoing noncardiac surgery.
Design	Double blind, randomized, placebo controlled, multicenter.
Patients	1897 patients with known coronary artery disease undergoing vascular surgery (48%), nonvascular thoracic or abdominal surgery (32%), or orthopedic surgery (20%).
Follow-up	30 days.
Treatment regimen	Saline or mivazerol given as an infusion starting 20 minutes prior to induction of anesthesia and for 72 hours postoperatively.

Results

The primary end point was the incidence of acute myocardial infarction or death during the intra and post-operative hospitalization period (up to 30 days post surgery). In the total cohort of 1897 patients, myocardial infarction and/or death occurred in 100 (10.6%) of placebo patients and in 91 (9.5%) of mivazerol patients (p=NS). However, in a subgroup of 904 patients with known coronary heart disease who had vascular surgery there were fewer myocardial infarctions and/or deaths in the mivazerol group (44; 9.7%) vs the placebo group (64; 14.2%; risk ratio = 0.67; 95% CI=0.45-0.98; p=0.039). All cause death in coronary patients undergoing vascular surgery was also lower in the mivazerol group (8; 1.8%) vs the placebo group (20; 4.4%; risk ratio=0.37; 95% CI=0.16-0.82; p=0.014).

Conclusions

Mivazerol did not reduce overall rate of myocardial infarction and death in patients with coronary disease undergoing noncardiac surgery, but may protect those patients with coronary disease who have vascular surgery.

1. Acute Myocardial Infarction

g. Acute Treatment of Stroke

ASK

Australian Streptokinase Trial Study Group

Title	Streptokinase for acute ischemic stroke with relationship to time of administration.
Author	Donnan GA, Davis SM, Chamber BR, et al.
Reference	JAMA 1996; 276:961-966.
Disease	Stroke.
Purpose	To determine whether intravenous streptokinase given within 4 h of onset of acute ischemic stroke reduces morbidity and mortality at 3 months. To assess whether administration of drug within 3 h of onset results in better outcome than when given after 3 h of onset of stroke.
Design	Randomized, double blind, placebo controlled trial, multicenter.
Patients	340 patients, ages 18-85 years with moderate to severe stroke.
Follow-up	3 months.
Treatment regimen	1.5 million U of intravenous streptokinase or placebo in 100 mL of normal saline administered over 1 h.

Results	Main end point was combined death and disability score. There was a nonsignificant trend toward unfavorable outcomes for streptokinase vs placebo (RR = 1.08; 95% CI = 0.74–1.56) and excess of hematomas with therapy (13.2% vs 3 %, $p<0.01$). The poor outcomes were observed in patients who received streptokinase therapy more than 3 h after stroke. Among 70 patients who received therapy within 3 h of onset of stroke there was a trend toward improved outcomes for those receiving streptokinase (RR =0.66; 95% CI = 0.28–1.58) and this improvement was better than in patients who received therapy after 3 h ($p=0.04$). Outcome of death was greater in patients treated with streptokinase after 3 h; but not in those treated within 3 h. Hypotension occurred in 33% of treated vs 6% of the placebo group.
Conclusions	Thrombolytic therapy with streptokinase therapy within 4 h increased morbidity and mortality at 3 months. Treatment was safer when instituted within 3 h than when instituted later; however even early treatment was not significantly better than placebo.

TOAST

Trial of ORG 10172 in Acute Stroke Treatment

Title	Low molecular weight heparinoid, ORG 10172 (Danaparoid), and outcome after acute ischemic stroke: A randomized controlled trial.
Authors	The publications committee for the TOAST Investigators.
Reference	JAMA 1998; 279:1265–1272.
Disease	Stroke.
Purpose	To determine whether the low molecular weight heparinoid (ORG 10172-danaparoid sodium) improves outcome at 3 months after ischemic stroke.
Design	Randomized, double blind, placebo controlled, multicenter,
Patients	1281 patients with acute or progressing ischemic stroke with symptoms more than 1 hour but less than 24 hours. Patients were excluded if they had mass effect on CT scan, intracranial bleed on CT, evidence for nonvascular cause of symptoms, active bleeding and other exclusions.
Follow-up	7 days, 3 months.
Treatment regimen	ORG 10172 vs placebo. ORG 10172 was given as initial IV bolus within 24 hours of stroke followed by infusion for 7 days. Rates of infusion adjusted after 24 hours to maintain antifactor Xa at 0.6–0.8 antifactor Xa U/mL.
Additional therapy	Ancillary care to treat medical and neurologic complications permitted. Heparin, warfarin, aspirin, ticlopidine, nonsteroidal antiinflammatory agents prohibited.

TOAST

Trial of ORG 10172 in Acute Stroke Treatment

(continued)

Results	482 (75.2%) of 641 patients assigned to ORG 10172 and 467 (73.7%) of patients treated to placebo had favorable outcomes at 3 months determined by combination of Glasgow Outcome Scale and Barthel Index. At 3 months the percent of patients having very favorable outcomes was similar in the 2 groups (49.5% vs 47%, p=NS). At 7 days, 376 (59.2%) of 635 patients receiving ORG 10172 and 344 (54.3%) of 633 receiving placebo had favorable outcomes (p=0.07). At 7 days 215 (33.9%) of 635 patients receiving ORG 10172 and 176 (27.8%) of 633 patients receiving placebo had very favorable outcomes (p=0.01). At 10 days serious intracranial bleeding occurred in 14 patients given ORG and in 4 placebo treated patients (p=0.05).
Conclusions	ORG 10172 had a transient benefit at 7 days but not at 3 months and was associated with more serious intracranial bleeding events.

NINDS

Neurological disorders and stroke recombinant tissue plasminogen activator stroke study

Title	Effects of tissue plasminogen activator for acute ischemic stroke at one year.
Authors	Kwiatkowski TG, Libman RB, Frankel M, et al.
Reference	N Engl J Med 1999;340:1781-1787.
Disease	Ischemic stroke.
Purpose	Previously, this group showed that patients treated with t-PA within 3 hours of symptoms of acute ischemic stroke were at least 30% more likely than patients treated with placebo to have minimal or no disability at 3 months. This study analyzed data on outcomes from this study at 6 and 12 months.
Design	Randomized, multicenter.
Patients	624 patients with stroke who could be treated within 3 hours of onset of symptoms.
Follow-up	12 months.
Treatment regimen	t-PA vs placebo.

NINDS

Neurological disorders and stroke recombinant tissue plasminogen activator stroke study

(continued)

Results	Primary outcome was "favorable outcome" which was defined as minimal or no disability using various neurologic indices and scales (Barthel index, modified Rankin scale, Glasgow outcome scale), and using a global statistic. Favorable effects of t-PA on the global statistic were observed in the t-PA group. At 6 months, the odds ratios for a favorable outcome with t-PA vs placebo was 1.7 (95% CI=1.3-2.3) and at 12 months was 1.7 (95% CI=1.2-2.3). Patients that received t-PA were at least 30% more likely to have minimal or no disability at 12 months than placebo patients. Mortality at 12 months was similar between the t-PA group (24%) vs the placebo group (28%, p=0.29). There was no difference in rates of recurrent strokes between groups.
Conclusions	Patients with acute ischemic stroke who were treated with t-PA within 3 hours after symptom onset were more likely to have minimal or no disability than patients receiving placebo at 6 and 12 months.

STAT

The Stroke Treatment with Ancord Trial

Title	Intravenous ancord for treatment of acute ischemic stroke. The STAT study: A randomized controlled trial.
Authors	Sherman DG, Atkinson MP, Chippendale T, et al.
Reference	JAMA 2000;283:2395-2403.
Disease	Stroke.
Purpose	To assess the safety and efficacy of the defibrinogenating agent ancord in patients with acute ischemic stroke.
Design	Randomized, double blind, placebo controlled, multicenter.
Patients	500 patients, ≥18 years old, within 30 minutes to 3 hours after onset of symptoms of an acute or progressing ischemic neurological deficit. Patients with rapidly improving neurologic deficits were excluded. Patients with intracranial hemorrhage, neoplasm, very mild stroke, coma, prior stroke within 6 weeks, hypertension or hypotension, coagulation disorder or recent thrombolytic therapy were excluded.
Follow-up	3 months.
Treatment regimen	Randomization to placebo (n=252) or ancord (n=248) infusion for 72 hours, followed by infusions lasting 1 hour, given at 90-102 hours and 114-126 hours after the beginning of therapy. The target fibrinogen level in the ancord treated patients was 1.18 to 2.03 μmol/L.
Additional therapy	During the study drug infusion aspirin, anticoagulants, dextran, and thrombolytic agents were prohibited.

Results	102 patients in the ancord group (41.1%) achieved favorable functional status vs only 89 patients in the placebo group (35.3%; odds ratio 1.55; 95% CI 1.02–2.36). The covariate adjusted proportion of patients reaching favorable functional status was 42.2% vs 34.4%, respectively (p=0.04). Ancord therapy reduced the proportion of severely disabled patients. The covariate adjusted proportion of severely disabled patients was 11.8% in the ancord group vs 19.8% in the placebo group (40.4% relative risk reduction; p=0.01). The covariate adjusted proportion of patients with complete recovery was 36.1% in the ancord group vs 28.4% in the placebo group (27.1% relative increase; p=0.02). 7 day mortality was 8.9% in the ancord group vs 9.5% in the placebo group. 90 day mortality was 25.4% and 23.0%, respectively (p=0.62). Adverse events occurred in 98.4% in the ancord group vs 99.2% in the placebo group (p=NS). Symptomatic intracranial bleeding occurred in 5.2% in the ancord group vs 2% in the placebo group (odds ratio 2.58; 95% CI 0.95–8.21; p=0.06). Asymptomatic intracranial hemorrhage occurred in 19.0% in the ancord group vs 10.7% in the placebo group (odds ratio 1.92; 95% CI 1.14–3.27; p=0.01). The beneficial effect of ancord was observed in all predefined subgroups of age, stroke severity, gender, pre-stroke disability, and time to treatment (≤3 or >3 hours after onset of symptoms). Achievement of early defibrinogenation state was related to treatment success with ancord. Treatment success was noted in 45.8% of the patients with 6 hour fibrinogen levels of ≤3.82 μmol/L vs only 34.6% of the patients with >3.82 μmol/L at 6 hours of therapy.
Conclusions	Ancord infusion, started 30 minutes to 3 hours after onset of acute ischemic stroke was associated with better functional status at 3 months compared with placebo. However, ancord therapy resulted in an increase in the rate of asymptomatic intracranial hemorrhage and a trend towards an increase in the rate of symptomatic intracranial hemorrhage, without affecting total mortality. Patients who achieved early controlled defibrinogenation had greater benefit from therapy.

ATLANTIS

Alteplase ThromboLysis for Acute Noninterventional Therapy in Ischemic Stroke

Title	Recombinant tissue type plasminogen activator (alteplase) for ischemic stroke 3-5 hours after symptom onset. The ATLANTIS study: A randomized controlled trial.
Authors	Clark WM, Wissman S, Albers GW.
Reference	JAMA 1999;282:2019-2026.
Disease	Ischemic stroke.
Purpose	To assess whether rt-PA administration to patients with acute ischemic stroke, presenting 3-5 hours after onset of symptoms, is effective and safe.
Design	Randomized, double blind, placebo controlled, multicenter.
Patients	613 patients, 18-79 years old, who presented within 3-5 hours of onset of symptoms of ischemic stroke. All patients underwent CT scan to exclude intracerebral hemorrhage before enrollment. Patients with signs of cerebral ischemia in >1/3 of the territory of the middle cerebral artery were excluded.
Follow-up	90 days.
Treatment regimen	Randomization to placebo or to rt-PA 0.09 mg/kg as a bolus, followed by a 60 minute infusion of 0.81 mg/kg.
Additional therapy	Administration of heparin, oral anticoagulants, other hemorrheologic agents, and antiplatelet agents was not permitted during the initial 24 hours.

ATLANTIS

Alteplase ThromboLysis for Acute Noninterventional Therapy in Ischemic Stroke

(continued)

Results	547 patients received study medication between 3-5 hours of onset of symptoms. Mean time to treatment was 4.40 hours in the placebo group and 4.47 hours in the rt-PA group. 32% of the placebo group vs 34% of the rt-PA group had an excellent recovery at 90 days (p=0.65). All secondary functional outcome measures were comparable between the 2 groups. Infarct volume at 30 days was 47±74% in the placebo group vs 46±66% in the rt-PA group (p=0.95). Symptomatic intracerebral hemorrhage occurred in 1.1% of the placebo vs 7.0% of the rt-PA group (p<0.001), whereas asymptomatic intracerebral hemorrhage occurred in 4.7% vs 11.4%, respectively (p=0.004), and fatal intracerebral hemorrhage in 0.3% vs 3.0%, respectively (p<0.001). 30 day mortality was 4.4% in the placebo group vs 7.0% in the rt-PA group (p=0.18), whereas 90 day mortality was 6.9% vs 11.0%, respectively (p=0.09).
Conclusions	rt-PA was associated with increased risk of intracerebral hemorrhage but was not associated with clinical benefits when administered to patients within 3-5 hours after onset of symptoms of stroke.

PROCAT II

Prolyse in Acute Cerebral Thromboembolism II trial

Title	Intra-arterial prourokinase for acute ischemic stroke. The PROCAT II study: A randomized controlled trial.
Authors	Furlan A, Higashida R, Wechsler L, et al.
Reference	JAMA 1999;282:2003-2011.
Disease	Ischemic stroke.
Purpose	To evaluate the efficacy and safety of intra-arterial administration of recombinant prourokinase in patients with acute ischemic stroke of <6 hours, caused by middle cerebral artery occlusion.
Design	Randomized, open label with blinded follow-up, multicenter.
Patients	180 patients, 18-85 years old, with new focal neurological signs related to the middle cerebral artery territory that could have been treated within 6 hours of onset of symptoms. Patients with a National Institutes of Health Stroke Scale (NIHSS) >30, coma, rapid improving neurological signs, clinical suspicion of subarachnoid hemorrhage, seizures, history of intracerebral bleeding, uncontrolled hypertension, and contraindications to thrombolytic therapy were excluded. All patients underwent CT scan before enrollment to exclude intracranial tumors and hemorrhage. Patients with acute hypodense parenchymal lesion or effacement of cerebral sulci in >1/3 of the middle cerebral artery territory were excluded. Then patients underwent cerebral angiography and only patients with complete occlusion of the middle cerebral artery were further included.
Follow-up	90 days.

PROCAT II

Prolyse in Acute Cerebral Thromboembolism II trial

(continued)

Treatment regimen	After cerebral angiography patients were randomized to selective intra-arterial administration of r-prourokinase 9 mg over 2 hours through an infusion microcatheter placed in the proximal one-third of the middle cerebral artery thrombus + IV heparin (n=121) or to IV heparin alone (n=59).
Additional therapy	All patients received IV heparin (2000 U bolus followed by 500 U/h for 4 hours).
Results	12,323 patients with acute ischemic stroke were screened, 474 (4%) underwent cerebral angiography at a median of 4.5 hours after onset of symptoms. 180 patients were finally randomized. The median time to initiation of prourokinase infusion was 5.3 hours. 40% of the prourokinase and 25% of the control patients had slight or no neurological disability (a modified Rankin score of ≤2) at 90 days (odds ratio 2.13; 95% CI 1.02-4.42; p=0.04). NIHSS stratum adjusted 90 day mortality was 25% in the prourokinase group vs 27% in the control group (p=0.80). Systemic hemorrhage (mainly minor) occurred in 7% of the prourokinase group vs 17% of the control group, whereas worsening of neurological symptoms occurred in 1% vs 0%, and anaphylaxis in 1% vs 0%, respectively. Intracranial hemorrhage within the first 24 hours occurred in 35% of the prourokinase group vs 13% of the control group (p=0.003). However, after 10 days, the rates of intracerebral hemorrhage were 68% and 57%, respectively (p=0.23). Intracranial hemorrhage with neurological deterioration within 24 hours of treatment occurred in 10% and 2% of the prourokinase and control groups, respectively (p=0.06). All symptomatic intracranial hemorrhages occurred in patients with large baseline stroke (NIHSS >11). Recanalization of the occluded middle cerebral artery within 2 hours of therapy occurred in 66% of the prourokinase group and in 18% of the control group (p<0.001). Complete reperfusion (TIMI flow grade 3) was found in 19% of the prourokinase group vs 2% of the control group (p<0.003).

PROCAT II

Prolyse in Acute Cerebral Thromboembolism II trial

(continued)

Conclusions	Selective intra-arterial prourokinase infusion within 6 hours of onset of acute ischemic stroke caused by occlusion of the middle cerebral artery was associated with improved recovery of neurological function, and recanalization of the occluded middle cerebral artery, however, there was a slight increased risk of early intracerebral hemorrhage with neurological deterioration.

2. Unstable Angina/ Non Q Wave Infarction

RISC

Risk of Myocardial Infarction and Death During Treatment With Low Dose Aspirin and Intravenous Heparin in Men With Unstable Coronary Artery Disease

Title	Risk of myocardial infarction and death during treatment with low dose aspirin and intravenous heparin in men with unstable coronary artery disease.
Authors	The RISC Group.
Reference	Lancet 1990;336:827-830.
Disease	Unstable angina pectoris, non Q wave myocardial infarction.
Purpose	To evaluate the efficacy and safety of low dose aspirin and IV heparin therapy for patients with unstable angina or non Q wave infarction.
Design	Randomized, double blind, placebo controlled, 2X2 factorial, multicenter.
Patients	796 men, <70 years old, with unstable angina or non Q wave infarction. Patients with left ventricular dysfunction from previous infarction or valvular disease, previous coronary bypass grafting surgery, permanent pacemaker, left bundle branch block, or inability to complete exercise test were excluded.
Follow-up	>3 months.
Treatment regimen	Randomization within 72 h after admission to oral aspirin 75 mg/d or placebo for 1 year, and to IV placebo or heparin 10,000 U X4/d as a bolus for the first day and 7500 U X4/d for 4 more days.

RISC

Risk of Myocardial Infarction and Death During Treatment With Low Dose Aspirin and Intravenous Heparin in Men With Unstable Coronary Artery Disease

(continued)

Additional therapy	No drug containing aspirin, NSAID, or anticoagulant was permitted. If not contraindicated, metoprolol 100–200 mg/d. Nitrates and calcium channel blockers were permitted.
Results	Myocardial infarction or death occurred in 5.8% vs 2.5% of the oral placebo and aspirin groups respectively after 5 days (RR 0.43, 95% CI 0.21–0.91, p=0.033). After 30 days the incidence was 13.4% vs 4.3% (RR 0.31, 95% CI 0.18–0.53, p<0.0001), while after 90 days it was 17.1% vs 6.5% (RR 0.36, 95% CI 0.23–0.57, p<0.0001), respectively. Treatment with intermittent bolus injections of heparin did not alter the rates of myocardial infarction or death, although the group treated with aspirin and heparin had the lowest number of events during the initial 5 days. Treatment was associated with few side effects and was well tolerated.
Conclusions	Low dose aspirin, but not intermittent bolus injections of heparin, reduced mortality and myocardial infarction rates in patients with unstable angina or non Q wave infarction.

UNASEM

Unstable Angina Study using Eminase

Title	Thrombolysis in patients with unstable angina improves the angiographic but not the clinical outcome. Results of UNASEM, a multicenter, randomized, placebo controlled, clinical trial with anistreplase.
Authors	Bär FW, Verheugt FW, Col J, et al.
Reference	Circulation 1992;86:131-137.
Disease	Unstable angina.
Purpose	To evaluate the role of thrombolytic therapy in unstable angina.
Design	Randomized, double blind, placebo controlled, multicenter.
Patients	126 patients, age 30-70 years, with unstable angina with electrocardiographic evidence of ischemia. Patients with previous infarction, angioplasty, cardiac surgery, cardiac pacemaker, intraventricular conduction abnormalities, valvular heart disease, hypertension, cardiomyopathy, heart failure, renal failure, anticoagulant therapy, or contraindication to thrombolysis were excluded. Patients with left main stenosis ≥70% or <50% stenosis of the coronary arteries were excluded.
Follow-up	Coronary angiography before randomization and after 12-28 h.
Treatment regimen	IV injection of 30 U anistreplase (APSAC) or placebo over 5 min after the first cardiac catheterization.

UNASEM

Unstable Angina Study using Eminase

(continued)

Additional therapy	IV nitroglycerin started before angiography. IV heparin 5,000 U bolus followed by infusion at a rate of 1000 U/h. ß blockers or calcium blockers were given routinely. Aspirin was given after the second angiogram. Angioplasty was recommended only for recurrent angina in spite of medical therapy.
Results	Anistreplase compared to placebo was associated with decrease in diameter stenosis between the baseline to follow-up angiography (11% change (70% to 59%) vs 3% change (66% to 63%), p=0.008). However, clinical outcome was not different. Bleeding complications were higher in the anistreplase group (32% vs 11%, p=0.001).
Conclusions	Anistreplase infusion was associated with angiographic, but not clinical improvement. Moreover, it was associated with excess of bleeding.

TIMI IIIA

Thrombolysis in Myocardial Ischemia Trial IIIA

Title	Early effects of tissue type plasminogen activator added to conventional therapy on the culprit coronary lesion in patients presenting with ischemic cardiac pain at rest. Results of the Thrombolysis in Myocardial Ischemia (TIMI IIIA) Trial.
Authors	The TIMI IIIA Investigators.
Reference	Circulation 1993;87:38-52.
Disease	Unstable angina, non Q wave myocardial infarction.
Purpose	To assess the early effects of t-PA on the culprit coronary lesion in patients with unstable angina or non Q wave myocardial infarction.
Design	Randomized, placebo controlled, multicenter.
Patients	306 patients age 22-75 years with ≥5 min but ≤6 h of chest pain occurring at rest accompanied by ECG changes or documented coronary artery disease.
Follow-up	Coronary angiography at baseline and after 18-48 h.
Treatment regimen	Tissue plasminogen activator (t-PA) at a total dose of 0.8 mg/kg (maximum total dose 80 mg) or placebo infusion over 90 min (1/3 of the total dose was given as a bolus).
Additional therapy	Bed rest, oxygen, nitrates, calcium antagonists and/or ß-blockers, heparin 5000 U bolus, and infusion for 18-48 h.

TIMI IIIA

Thrombolysis in Myocardial Ischemia Trial IIIA

(continued)

Results

Reduction of stenosis by ≥20% or improvement of TIMI flow by 2 grades was seen in 15% and 5% of the culprit lesions in the t-PA and placebo treated patients ($p=0.003$). Substantial improvement was seen more often with t-PA (36%) than placebo (15%) among lesions containing thrombus ($p<0.01$), and among patients with non Q wave infarction (33% vs 8%, respectively, $p<0.005$). By multivariate analysis, the adjusted p value for substantial improvement of the culprit lesion by t-PA was 0.01.

Conclusions

Angiographic improvement of the severity of the culprit lesion after conventional therapy with and without additional t-PA was only modest. However, substantial improvement of the culprit lesions was seen more frequently with t-PA than placebo, especially in 2 subgroups: those with apparent thrombus and those with non Q wave infarction.

TIMI IIIB

Thrombolysis in Myocardial Ischemia Trial IIIB

Title	Effects of tissue plasminogen activator and a comparison of early invasive and conservative strategies in unstable angina and non Q wave myocardial infarction. Results of the TIMI IIIB Trial.
Authors	The TIMI IIIB Investigators.
Reference	Circulation 1994;89:1545-1556.
Disease	Unstable angina, non Q wave myocardial infarction.
Purpose	To assess the early effects of t-PA and of an early invasive strategy on clinical outcome of patients with unstable angina or non Q wave myocardial infarction.
Design	Randomized, placebo controlled, multicenter.
Patients	1473 patients age 22-79 years with ≥5 min but ≤6 h of chest pain occurring at rest accompanied by ECG changes or documented coronary artery disease.
Follow-up	24 h Holter monitoring that began 60-120 h after randomization. Predischarge thallium scintigraphy. Clinical evaluation and exercise tolerance test at 6 weeks.
Treatment regimen	Tissue plasminogen activator (t-PA) at a total dose of 0.8 mg/kg (maximum total dose 80 mg) or placebo infusion over 90 min (1/3 of the total dose was given as a bolus). Patients were also randomized to early invasive and early conservative strategies. In the early invasive group patients underwent coronary angiography 18-48 h after randomization and followed by revascularization if suitable. In the conservative arm patients were referred to coronary angiography only after failure of initial therapy.

TIMI IIIB

Thrombolysis in Myocardial Ischemia Trial IIIB

(continued)

Additional therapy	Bed rest, oxygen, a long acting nitrate, ß-blockers, calcium antagonists, and heparin 5000 U bolus and infusion for 18–48 h. Aspirin 325 mg/d was began on the second day and continued for 1 year.
Results	The primary end point of death, myocardial infarction, or failure of initial therapy at 6 weeks occurred in 54.2% and 55.5% of the t-PA and placebo treated groups. Acute myocardial infarction was more prevalent in the t-PA (7.4%) than placebo treated patients (4.9%, p=0.04). Intracranial hemorrhage occurred in 0.55% and 0 of the t-PA and placebo groups (p=0.06). The primary end point for comparison between the early invasive and conservative group (death, myocardial infarction, or an unsatisfactory symptom limited exercise test at 6 weeks) occurred in 18.1% and 16.2% of the early conservative and early invasive strategies, respectively (p=NS). However, the initial hospitalization was shorter and the incidence of rehospitalization was lower in the early invasive treated patients.
Conclusions	The addition of t-PA was not beneficial and may even be harmful. There was no difference in the primary end points between the early invasive and conservative strategies, although the former resulted in a shorter hospitalization and lower rate of readmission.

TAUSA

Thrombolysis and Angioplasty in Unstable Angina

Title	a. Adjunctive thrombolytic therapy during angioplasty for ischemic rest angina: Results of the TAUSA Trial. b. Angioplasty of complex lesions in ischemic rest angina: Results of the Thrombolysis and Angioplasty in Unstable Angina (TAUSA) Trial.
Authors	a. Ambrose JA, Almeida OD, Sharma S, et al. b. Mehran R, Ambrose JA, Bongu RM, et al.
Reference	a. Circulation 1994;90:69-77. b. J Am Coll Cardiol 1995;26:961-966.
Disease	Coronary artery disease, unstable angina.
Purpose	To assess the role of prophylactic intracoronary thrombolytic therapy during coronary angioplasty in unstable angina.
Design	Randomized, double blind, placebo controlled, multicenter.
Patients	469 patients with unstable angina with ischemic rest pain or non Q wave infarction <7 d before angioplasty, or recurrent rest pain within 7 days <30 d after myocardial infarction. All patients had ≥70 % stenosis of a native artery or vein graft that was suitable for angioplasty. Patients >80 years old, with severe hypertension, prior stroke or contraindications to thrombolytic therapy were excluded.
Follow-up	Angiography 15 min after angioplasty. In-hospital clinical follow-up.

Treatment regimen	Urokinase 150,000 U or placebo over 3 min (Phase I) or 250,000 U or placebo over 10–15 min (Phase II), before wire placement. Additional 100,000 U (Phase I) or 250,000 U (Phase II) or placebo 1 min post angioplasty.
Additional therapy	Aspirin 80–325 mg and IV heparin 10,000 U before procedure. 75 μg intracoronary nitroglycerin before wire placement. IV heparin infusion overnight.
Results	a. 257 and 212 patients were included in phase I and II, respectively. Angioplasty was successful in 97% and 94% of the placebo and urokinase groups (p=NS). Definite filling defects were present at 15 min in 18.0% vs 13.8% of the placebo and urokinase patients (p=NS). Acute closure was more common with urokinase (10.2%) than placebo (4.3%, p<0.02). These differences were more pronounced in phase II (8.7% vs 1.9%, p=0.031) than in phase I. There was no difference in detection of coronary dissection between the groups. Emergency bypass surgery (5.2% vs 2.1%, p=0.09) and post procedure ischemia (9.9% vs 3.4%, p=0.005) were more common in the urokinase group, however, there was no difference in the occurrence of myocardial infarction. Bleeding complications were reported in 12.9% and 8.9% of the urokinase and placebo groups (p=NS). b. Complex lesions were associated with higher abrupt closure than simple lesions (10.6% vs 3.3%, p<0.003), and higher recurrent angina. Abrupt closure of the complex lesions was more common in the urokinase group (15.0% vs 5.9%, p<0.03).
Conclusions	Prophylactic urokinase intracoronary administration was associated with adverse angiographic and clinical outcome in patients with unstable angina undergoing coronary angioplasty.

ATACS

Antithrombotic Therapy in Acute Coronary Syndromes

Title	Combination antithrombotic therapy in unstable rest angina and non Q wave infarction in nonprior aspirin users. Primary end points analysis from the ATACS trial.
Authors	Cohen M, Adams PC, Parry G, et al.
Reference	Circulation 1994;89:81-88.
Disease	Unstable angina, non Q wave myocardial infarction.
Purpose	To compare the efficacy of combination of aspirin + anticoagulation vs aspirin alone in patients with rest unstable angina or non Q wave infarction.
Design	Randomized, open label, multicenter.
Patients	214 patients, >21 years of age, with unstable rest angina or non Q wave infarction. Patients that received ≥150 mg aspirin within 3 days of randomization were excluded.
Follow-up	12 weeks.
Treatment regimen	Aspirin 162.5 mg/d or aspirin 162.5 mg/d +heparin 100 U/kg IV bolus and then continuous infusion of heparin for 3-4 days. Warfarin was started on the second and third day, if coronary angiography did not appear imminent. Heparin was discontinued after INR reached 2.0-3.0.
Additional therapy	Antianginal therapy: low risk patients received metoprolol and oral isosorbide dinitrate; high risk patients received additional nifedipine. If ß-blockers were contraindicated, diltiazem was given instead of metoprolol. Patients already on ß-blockers, received maximal dose of ß-blockers + nifedipine.

Results	Trial therapy was begun by 9.5±8.8 h of qualifying pain. By intention to treat analysis, after 14 days 27% of the aspirin vs 10% of the aspirin+anticoagulation experienced death, recurrent angina, or infarction (adjusted p=0.004). After 12 weeks 28% of the aspirin vs 19% of the aspirin+anticoagulation experienced death, recurrent angina, or infarction (adjusted p=0.09). Major bleeding complications occurred in 0 and 2.9%, respectively, while minor bleeding or medication intolerance was found in 2.8% and 6.7%, respectively. Withdrawal from the study or occurrence of a secondary end point (major bleeding or coronary revascularization) occurred in 31% and 45%, respectively.
Conclusions	Combination of anticoagulation therapy and aspirin, compared with aspirin alone, significantly reduced recurrent ischemic events in the early phase of unstable angina or non Q wave infarction.

Title	Recombinant hirudin for unstable angina pectoris. A multicenter, randomized angiographic trial.
Authors	Topol EJ, Fuster V, Harrington RA, et al.
Reference	Circulation 1994;89:1557-1566.
Disease	Unstable angina pectoris.
Purpose	To compare the efficacy of hirudin and heparin in preventing accumulation of coronary artery thrombus in patients with unstable angina.
Design	Randomized, open label, comparing 2 regimens of heparin and 4 regimens of hirudin in multifactorial fashion, multicenter.
Patients	166 patients, ≤75 years of age, with ≥5 min of rest ischemic pain within 48 h, and ≥60% stenosis of a major epicardial coronary artery or vein graft interpreted as having an intraluminal thrombus. Patients with renal failure, hemodynamic instability, previous stroke, or history of significant bleeding were excluded.
Follow-up	Coronary angiography at baseline and after 72-120 h. Clinical follow-up for 30 days.
Treatment regimen	1. Hirudin 0.15 mg/kg bolus, 0.05 mg/kg/h infusion. 2. Hirudin 0.30 mg/kg bolus, 0.1 mg/kg/h infusion. 3. Hirudin 0.60 mg/kg bolus, 0.2 mg/kg/h infusion. 4. Hirudin 0.90 mg/kg bolus, 0.3 mg/kg/h infusion. 5. Hirudin 0.60 mg/kg bolus, 0.3 mg/kg/h infusion. 6. Hirudin 0.60 mg/kg bolus, 0.3 mg/kg/h infusion. In all regimens: heparin 5000 U bolus, 1000 U/h infusion. PTT was adjusted to 65-90 s in regimens 1-5, and to 90-110 s in regimen 6. Infusion was continued for 3-5 days.

Additional therapy	Aspirin 160-325 mg/d. ß-blockers, calcium channel blockers, and long acting nitrate. Coronary revascularization was discouraged until completion of the second angiogram.
Results	Hirudin led to a dose-dependent prolongation of the PTT that appeared to plateau at the 0.2 mg/kg/h infusion rate. 16% of the heparin and 71% of the hirudin treated patients had their aPTT within the therapeutic range ($p<0.001$). The hirudin treated patients showed better improvement in minimal cross sectional area of the culprit lesion (0.29 vs 0.10 mm2 , $p=0.028$), minimal luminal diameter (0.18 vs 0.03 mm, $p=0.029$), and % diameter stenosis (-5.19% vs -2.11%, $p=0.071$). There was no difference in any of the clinical events at 30 days between heparin and hirudin. There was no major adverse effects associated with hirudin.
Conclusions	Recombinant hirudin in patients with unstable angina improved the angiographic results, but not the clinical outcome.

TIMI-7

Thrombin Inhibition in Myocardial Ischemia 7

Title	Hirulog in the treatment of unstable angina. Results of the Thrombin Inhibition in Myocardial Ischemia (TIMI) 7 trial.
Authors	Fuchs J, Cannon CP, and the TIMI 7 Investigators.
Reference	Circulation 1995;92:727-733.
Disease	Unstable angina.
Purpose	To assess whether a dose response existed in the efficacy of hirulog used in conjunction with aspirin in unstable angina.
Design	Randomized, double blind, multicenter.
Patients	401 patients, age 21-75 years, with unstable angina (ischemic rest pain of 5-60 min) within 24 h of randomization, >24 h after myocardial infarction (if present).
Follow-up	6 weeks.
Treatment regimen	One of 4 doses of hirulog infusion for 72 h: 0.02, 0.25, 0.50, and 1.0 mg/kg/h.
Additional therapy	Aspirin 325 mg/d. No restriction on conventional therapy, excluding heparin during hirulog infusion.

TIMI-7

Thrombin Inhibition in Myocardial Ischemia 7

(continued)

Results	There was no difference among the groups in the primary end point (death, myocardial infarction, rapid clinical deterioration, or recurrent ischemia with ECG changes) at 72 h (primary end point occurred in 8.1%, 6.2%, 11.4%, and 6.2% of the patients in the 4 groups, respectively, p=0.56). Primary end points occurred in 15.0%, 7.4%, 14.8%, and 12.3% of the patients respectively at discharge (p=0.38). However, death or recurrent infarction at discharge occurred in 10% of the 0.02 mg/kg/h group vs 3.2% of the patients assigned to the 3 other groups (p=0.008). After 6 weeks end point occurred in 12.5% of the lower dose vs 5.2% of the upper 3 doses (p=0.009). Only 0.5% (2 patients) experienced a major bleeding attributed to hirulog.
Conclusions	Hirulog in conjunction with aspirin is a safe and promising therapy for unstable angina.

A Comparison of Hirudin with Heparin in the Prevention of Restenosis after Coronary Angioplasty

Title	A comparison of hirudin with heparin in the prevention of restenosis after coronary angioplasty.
Authors	Serruys PW, Herrman JP, Simon R, et al.
Reference	N Engl J Med 1995;333:757-763.
Disease	Coronary artery disease, unstable angina.
Purpose	To compare the efficacy of 2 regimens of recombinant hirudin with heparin in preventing restenosis following coronary angioplasty.
Design	Randomized, double blind, multicenter.
Patients	1141 patients with unstable angina with ≥1 lesion suitable for coronary angioplasty.
Follow-up	30 week clinical follow-up, coronary angiography after 26 weeks.
Treatment regimen	1. Recombinant hirudin IV 40 mg bolus followed by infusion of 0.2 mg/kg/h for 24 h, and then placebo X2/d SC for 3 days. 2. Recombinant hirudin IV 40 mg bolus followed by infusion of 0.2 mg/kg/h for 24 h, and then 40 mg X2/d SC for 3 days. 3. Heparin 10,000 U bolus followed by infusion of 15 U/kg/h for 24 h, and then placebo X2/d SC for 3 days.
Additional therapy	Aspirin 100-500 mg/d for ≥14 days.

A Comparison of Hirudin with Heparin in the Prevention of Restenosis after Coronary Angioplasty

(continued)

Results	At 30 weeks, event-free survival was 67.3%, 63.5%, and 68.0% for the heparin, hirudin IV, and hirudin IV+SC (p=0.61). However, early cardiac events (within 96 h) were reduced by hirudin (occurrence in 11.0%, 7.9%, and 5.6%, respectively, combined relative risk with hirudin vs heparin 0.61, 95% CI 0.41–0.90, p=0.023). In patients with severe unstable angina (Braunwald class III) the 96 h event rates were 21.6%, 5.3%, and 12.3% (combined relative risk 0.41, 95% CI 0.21–0.78, p=0.006). The minimal luminal diameter on the follow-up angiography was 1.54, 1.47, and 1.56 mm, respectively (p=0.08).
Conclusions	Although hirudin reduced the occurrence of early complications, long term results were the same as with heparin.

FRISC

Fragmin During Instability in Coronary Artery Disease Study

Title	Low molecular weight heparin during instability in coronary artery disease.
Authors	Fragmin during Instability in Coronary Artery Disease (FRISC) Study Group.
Reference	Lancet 1996;347:561-568.
Disease	Unstable angina, non Q wave infarction.
Purpose	To assess the efficacy of subcutaneous low molecular weight heparin, in combination with aspirin and antianginal medications, to prevent new cardiac events in patients with unstable angina.
Design	Randomized, double blind, placebo controlled, multicenter.
Patients	1506 patients, >40 years old, with unstable angina (<72 h from the last episode of chest pain). Premenopausal women, patients with an increased risk of bleeding, current treatment with anticoagulants, or coronary revascularization within 3 months were excluded.
Follow-up	150 days clinical follow-up. Predischarge and 40-50 day exercise test.
Treatment regimen	Placebo or dalteparin sodium 120 U/kg (maximum 10,000 U)X2/d SC for 6 days, and then 7,500 U X1/d for the next 35-45 days.
Additional therapy	Aspirin 75 mg/d (initial dose 300 mg), ß-blockers, nitrates, and calcium channel blockers.

Results	6 day mortality or development of new myocardial infarction was 4.8% in the placebo and 1.8% in the dalteparin group (RR 0.37, 95% CI 0.20-0.68, p=0.001). 1.2% vs 0.4%, respectively needed revascularization (RR 0.33, 95% CI 0.10-1.10, p=0.07), while 7.7% vs 3.8% needed intravenous heparin (RR 0.49, 95% CI 0.32-0.75, p=0.001). After 40 days the rate of death, myocardial infarction, revascularization, or the need for IV heparin was 25.7% in the placebo vs 20.5% in the dalteparin group (RR 0.79, 95% CI 0.66-0.95, p=0.011). There was an increased event rate during the first few days after the change of the dose in the dalteparin group, especially in smokers. There was no difference in the rates of end points after 150 days. The regimen was relatively safe with rare side effects and compliance was good.
Conclusions	Long term dalteparin and aspirin therapy is safe and effective in patients with unstable angina.

Title	Platelet membrane receptor glycoprotein IIb/IIIa antagonism in unstable angina. The Canadian Lamifiban study.
Authors	Thèroux P, Kouz S, Roy L, et al.
Reference	Circulation 1996;94:899-905.
Disease	Coronary artery disease, unstable angina.
Purpose	To assess the clinical benefit of GP IIb/IIIa inhibition by Lamifiban in patients with unstable angina.
Design	Randomized, double blind, placebo controlled, dose ranging multicenter.
Patients	365 patients, <75 years old, with unstable angina or myocardial infarction without ST segment elevation. Patients with identifiable precipitating secondary factors, or <6 months after PTCA or <2 months after coronary artery bypass surgery were excluded. Additional exclusion criteria were previous stroke, high risk for bleeding, uncontrolled hypertension, congestive heart failure or shock, thrombocytopenia, use of oral anticoagulants, concomitant life threatening disease, and left bundle branch block.
Follow-up	1 month.
Treatment regimen	Patients were randomized to 1 of 5 parallel arms: placebo and 4 doses of lamifiban. All arms included an IV bolus followed by an infusion for 72-120 hours. The bolus plus infusion doses were 1. 150 μg + 1μg/min; 2. 300 μg + 2 μg/kg; 3. 600 μg + 4 μg/min; and 4. 750 μg + 5 μg/min. 3 patients were randomized to lamifiban 600 μg bolus + 4 μg/min or to placebo for 1 patient in each of the other 3 groups.

Additional therapy	Aspirin 325 mg/d. Heparin was permitted. The use of nitrates, ß-blockers, and/or calcium channel blockers was recommended.
Results	During the infusion period the lamifiban treated patients (all doses) had lower rate of primary end point (death, myocardial infarction, or the need for an urgent revascularization) from 8.1% in the placebo group to 3.3% (odds ratio 0.39; 95% CI 0.15 to 0.99; p=0.04). The rates were 2.5%, 4.9%, 3.3%, and 2.4%, respectively for the 4 lamifiban dosage groups. The highest dose (5 μg/min) had an additional benefit on recurrent ischemia over the 3 other lower doses (odds ratio compared with placebo 0.32; 95% CI 0.12 to 0.89; p=0.02). At 1 month, mortality was 4.1% in the placebo vs 1.2% in the lamifiban treated patients. Death or myocardial infarction occurred in 8.1% of the placebo, 6.2% of the 2 lower lamifiban doses, and 2.5% of the patients treated with the higher doses of lamifiban. The odds ratio with the 2 high doses compared with placebo was 0.29 (95% CI 0.09 to 0.94; p=0.03). Lamifiban inhibited platelet aggregation in a dose dependent fashion. Bleeding was more frequent with lamifiban than placebo (11.1% vs 1.6% of minor bleeding (p=0.002), and 2.9% vs 0.8% of minor bleeding (p=NS)). Concomitant heparin therapy increased significantly the bleeding risk.
Conclusions	3 to 5 days lamifiban therapy reduced the rate of mortality, myocardial infarction, or the need for revascularization during the infusion period and at 1 month in patients with unstable angina.

CAPTURE

C7E3 Fab AntiPlatelet Therapy in Unstable REfractory Angina

Title	Randomized placebo controlled trial of abciximab before and during coronary intervention in refractory unstable angina: The CAPTURE study.
Authors	The CAPTURE investigators.
Reference	Lancet 1997;349:1429-1435.
Disease	Unstable angina.
Purpose	To evaluate the efficacy of abciximab, a platelet glycoprotein IIb/IIIa receptor blocker, started 18-24 h before procedure and continued until 1 h after procedure, in improving outcome among patients with refractory unstable angina who are undergoing coronary balloon angioplasty.
Design	Randomized, placebo controlled, multicenter.
Patients	1265 patients with refractory unstable angina, that continued to be active despite therapy with intravenous heparin and nitrates. Therapy should have been started within 48 h of last episode of pain. All patients should have an angiographically proven culprit coronary artery lesion suitable for angioplasty. Patients with recent myocardial infarction, persistent ischemia that mandated immediate intervention, >50% stenosis of the left main coronary artery, a culprit lesion in a bypass graft, bleeding diathesis, cerebrovascular accident within 2 years, planned administration of anticoagulants, intravenous dextran, or a thrombolytic agent before or during angioplasty, thrombocytopenia, or serious other medical conditions were excluded.
Follow-up	6 months.
Treatment regimen	Randomization to abciximab (0.25 mg/kg bolus followed by continuous infusion of 10 μg/min) or placebo. Treatment was given for 18-24 h before angioplasty and continued for 1 h after completion of angioplasty.

CAPTURE

C7E3 Fab AntiPlatelet Therapy in Unstable REfractory Angina (continued)

Additional therapy	Aspirin ≥50 mg/d. Intravenous heparin from before randomization until >1 h after angioplasty. Intravenous glyceryl trinitrate. The use of stents was avoided when feasible.
Results	The study was terminated prematurely by the Clinical End point Committee. Angioplasty was attempted in 1241 patients (98%), and was successful in 88.8% of the placebo group vs 94.0% of the abciximab group (p=0.001). Death, myocardial infarction, or urgent intervention within the first 30 days of study occurred in 15.9% of the placebo vs 11.3% of the abciximab group (p=0.012). There was no difference in mortality (1.3% vs 1.0% in the placebo and abciximab groups, respectively; p>0.1). However, myocardial infarction occurred less frequently in the abciximab group than in the placebo group, both before intervention (0.6% vs 2.1%; p=0.029), and within the first 24 h of angioplasty (2.6% vs 5.5%; p=0.009), but not after the procedure (day 2–30)(1.0% vs 0.9%; p>0.1). The abciximab treated patients needed less urgent interventions (7.8%) than the placebo treated patients (10.9%)(p=0.054). Major bleeding episodes were more common in the abciximab group (3.8%) than in the placebo group (1.9%)(p=0.043), and more patients in the abciximab group needed transfusions (7.1% vs 3.4%, respectively; p=0.005). There were no excess strokes in the abciximab group. At 6 months, death or myocardial infarction occurred in 9.0% of the abciximab group vs 10.9% of the placebo group (p=0.19). 5.4% of the abciximab vs 7.1% of the placebo group needed coronary artery bypass surgery (p=0.20), and angioplasty in 21.4% vs 20.7%, respectively. Less events (death, myocardial infarction, or repeated intervention) per patients occurred in the abciximab treated patients during the 6 months follow-up (274 events were recorded in 193 placebo treated patients compared with 242 events in 193 abciximab treated patients; p=0.067).
Conclusions	Abciximab infusion, started 18–24 h before and continued for 1 h after coronary angioplasty, reduced the rates of peri procedure myocardial infarction and the need for reintervention among patients with unstable angina undergoing coronary balloon angioplasty. However abciximab did not alter the rate of myocardial infarction after the first few days after angioplasty or the need for subsequent reintervention.

CAPTURE (Substudy)

C7E3 Fab AntiPlatelet Therapy in Unstable Refractory Angina

Title	Reduction of recurrent ischemia with abciximab during continuous ECG ischemia monitoring in patients with unstable angina refractory to standard treatment.
Authors	Klootwijk P, Meij S, Melkert R, et al.
Reference	Circulation 1998; 98:1358-1364.
Disease	Unstable angina.
Purpose	To determine the incidence of recurrent ischemia in a subset of patients from the CAPTURE trial, using continuous 12 lead ECG monitoring.
Design	As per CAPTURE study. Vector derived 12 lead ECG monitoring performed before, during, and up to 6 hours after PTCA.
Patients	332 patients who were part of the CAPTURE study. 163 received placebo and 169 received abciximab.
Follow-up	As per CAPTURE trial.
Treatment regimen	Placebo vs abciximab as per CAPTURE trial.

CAPTURE (Substudy)

C7E3 Fab AntiPlatelet Therapy in Unstable Refractory Angina

(continued)

Results	Ischemic episodes assessed by ECG monitoring occurred in 18% of abciximab patients and 23% of placebo patients (p=NS). 5% of patients on abciximab vs 14% on placebo had ≥2 ST shifts on the ECG (p<0.01). Abciximab also reduced total ischemic burden (total duration of ST episodes per patient, area under the curve of the ST vector magnitude, or sum of the areas under the curves of 12 leads during ischemic episodes). The presence of ST shifts (asymptomatic and symptomatic) during the monitoring period prior to the coronary intervention was associated with increased relative risk of myocardial infarction (3.2) and death (4.1), within 5 days of treatments.
Conclusions	Abciximab reduced frequent ischemia and ischemic burden in patients with refractory angina. Recurrent ischemia assessed by continuous vector derived 12 lead ECG monitoring predicts death and MI within 5 days.

Effects of Integrelin, a platelet glycoprotein IIb/IIIa receptor antagonist, in unstable angina. A randomized multicenter trial.

Title	Effects of Integrelin, a platelet glycoprotein IIb/IIIa receptor antagonist, in unstable angina. A randomized multicenter trial.
Author	Schulman SP, Goldschmidt-Clermont PJ, Topol EJ, et al.
Reference	Circulation 1996; 94:2083-2089.
Disease	Coronary artery disease, unstable angina.
Purpose	To determine the effect of the GPIIb/IIIa antagonist, Integrelin on the frequency and duration of Holter monitored ischemic events in patients with unstable angina.
Design	Randomized, double blind, placebo controlled.
Patients	227 patients with unstable angina.
Follow-up	In-hospital.
Treatment regimen	Patients were randomized to oral aspirin and placebo Integrelin, placebo aspirin and low dose Integrelin (45 μg/kg bolus plus 0.5 μg/kg/min infusion); or placebo aspirin and high dose Integrelin (90 μg/kg bolus followed by 1.0 μg/kg/min constant infusion). Drug was continued for 29-72 h. Patients received aspirin.

Effects of Integrelin, a platelet glycoprotein IIb/IIIa receptor antagonist, in unstable angina. A randomized multicenter trial.

(continued)

Results	Patients randomized to high dose Integrelin experienced fewer ischemic episodes (0.24±0.11) compared to aspirin (1.0±0.33, $p<0.05$) and shorter ischemic episodes (8.41±5.29 min.) compared to aspirin (26.2±9.8 min, $p=0.01$). Platelet aggregation was rapidly inhibited by Integrelin in a dose-dependent fashion. There were no differences in bleeding among the 3 arms.
Conclusions	Intravenous integrelin reduces the number and duration of ischemic events on Holter monitoring in patients with unstable angina.

FRIC

Fragmin in Unstable Coronary Artery Disease Study (FRIC)

Title	Comparison of low molecular weight heparin with unfractionated heparin acutely and with placebo for 6 weeks in the management of unstable coronary artery disease. Fragmin in unstable coronary artery disease study (FRIC).
Author	Klein W, Buchwald A, Hillis SE.
Reference	Circulation 1997;96:61-68.
Disease	Coronary artery disease, unstable angina, non Q wave myocardial infarction.
Purpose	To compare the efficacy and safety of dalteparin with unfractionated heparin in the acute treatment of unstable angina or non Q wave myocardial infarction.
Design	Prospective, randomized, multicenter with 2 phases. During days 1-6 patients received either dalteparin given subcutaneously and weight adjusted or dose adjusted unfractionated heparin. Days 6-45 days was double blind prolonged treatment phase in which patients received either dalteparin or placebo.
Patients	1482 patients with unstable angina or non Q wave myocardial infarction.
Follow-up	45 days.

FRIC

Fragmin in Unstable Coronary Artery Disease Study (FRIC)

(continued)

Treatment regimen	In the acute phase dalteparin 120 IU/kg x2/d, subcutaneously. In the prolonged treatment phase dalteparin 7500 IU x1/d, subcutaneously. Those randomized to heparin received a bolus of 5000 IU followed within 2 h by a continuous infusion of 1000 IU/h, adjusted to maintain the aPTT at 1.5 times control values. Aspirin was given to all patients.
Results	There were no differences in mortality, myocardial infarction, and recurrent angina between the unfractionated heparin and dalteparin treated patients during the first 6 days. Between days 6 and 45 the rate of death, infarction, or recurrence of angina was 12.3% for placebo and dalteparin groups. Revascularization procedures were performed in 14% of patients in both of these groups.
Conclusions	Low molecular weight heparin dalteparin given twice daily may be an alternative to unfractionated heparin for patients with unstable angina or non Q wave myocardial infarction. Prolonged therapy with dalteparin at a lower once a day dose did not confer benefit over aspirin plus heparin.

HASI

Hirulog Angioplasty Study Investigators

Title	a. Treatment with bivalirudin (hirulog) as compared with heparin during coronary angioplasty for unstable or postinfarction angina. b. Bivalirudin compared with heparin during coronary angioplasty for thrombus containing lesions.
Authors	a. Bittl JA, Strony J, Brinker JA, et al. b. Shah PB, Ahmed WH, Ganz P, Bittl JA.
Reference	a. N Engl J Med 1995;333:764-769. b. J Am Coll Cardiol 1997;30:1264-1269.
Disease	Unstable angina.
Purpose	To compare the efficacy of hirulog and heparin as an adjunctive therapy after angioplasty for unstable or postinfarction angina.
Design	Randomized, double blind, multicenter.
Patients	4098 patients, >21 years old, with unstable or postinfarction angina <2 week after infarction.
Follow-up	In-hospital, 3 and 6 months clinical course
Treatment regimen	1. Hirulog: 1.0 mg/kg bolus before angioplasty, followed by 4 h infusion at a rate of 2.5 mg/kg/h, and a 14-20 h infusion at a rate of 0.2 mg/kg/h. 2. Heparin: IV bolus 175 U/kg followed by infusion at a rate of 15 U/kg/h for 18-24 h.
Additional therapy	Aspirin 300-325 mg/d.

HASI

Hirulog Angioplasty Study Investigators

(continued)

Results

a. In the total population the occurrence of the primary end point (death, myocardial infarction, abrupt closure, or rapid clinical deterioration requiring coronary bypass surgery, intra-aortic balloon counterpulsation, or repeated angioplasty) were similar between hirulog (11.4%) and heparin (12.2%). However, hirulog resulted in lower incidence of major bleeding (3.8% vs 9.8%, p<0.001). In the subpopulation of postinfarction angina, hirulog resulted in a lower incidence of the in-hospital primary end points (9.1% vs 14.2%, p=0.04), lower incidence of myocardial infarction (2.0% vs 5.1%, p=0.04), and a lower incidence of bleeding (3.0% vs 11.1%, p<0.001). However, the cumulative rate of death, myocardial infarction, and repeated revascularization in the postinfarction angina patients during the 6 months follow-up were similar (20.5% vs 25.1%, p=0.17).

b. In patients with thrombus containing lesions on angiography (n=567) myocardial infarction (5.1% vs 3.2%; p=0.03) and abrupt vessel closure (13.6% vs 8.3%; p<0.001) occurred more frequently than in patients without angiographic evidence of a thrombus. However, the incidence of primary end points was not reduced by hirulog compared with heparin in patients with thrombus containing lesions. The cumulative incidence of ischemic events at 6 months was comparable between the hirulog group (26.9%) and the heparin group (27.1%)(p=0.95).

Conclusions

Hirulog (bivalirudin) was as effective as high dose heparin in preventing the ischemic complications following angioplasty for unstable angina. It was better than heparin in reducing the immediate complications in patients with postinfarction angina, however, heparin and hirulog had comparable efficacy in thrombus containing lesions. Hirulog was associated with a lower incidence of bleeding.

OASIS

Organization to Assess Strategies for Ischemic Syndromes

Title	Comparison of the effects of 2 doses of recombinant hirudin compared with heparin in patients with acute myocardial ischemia without ST elevation. A pilot study.
Author	Organization to Assess Strategies for Ischemic Syndromes (OASIS) investigators.
Reference	Circulation 1997;96:769-777.
Disease	Coronary artery disease, unstable angina, suspected acute myocardial infarction.
Purpose	To compare the effects of 2 different doses of hirudin with heparin on composite primary end point of cardiovascular death, development of new myocardial infarction, or refractory angina, and on the above primary end point plus severe angina (secondary outcome).
Design	Randomized, multicenter.
Patients	909 patients with unstable angina or suspected acute myocardial infarction without ST segment elevation on the electrocardiogram.
Follow-up	7-180 days.

OASIS

Organization to Assess Strategies for Ischemic Syndromes

(continued)

Treatment regimen	Patients randomized to receive 72 h infusion of heparin or hirudin at varying doses: 1. heparin: bolus of 5000 U followed by an infusion of 1200 U/h, or 1000 U/h for patients with body weight <60 kg; 2. low dose hirudin: bolus of 0.2/mg/kg followed by infusion of 0.10 mg/kg/h; or 3. medium dose hirudin: initial bolus 0.4mg/kg followed by infusion of 0.15 mg/kg/h. Infusions lasted 72 h. APPT monitored every 6–8 h; heparin and hirudin adjusted to maintain a PTT between 60–100 seconds.
Results	At 7 days, 6.5%, 4.4%, and 3.0% of patients developed primary outcome (cardiovascular death, recurrent myocardial infarction, or refractory angina) in heparin, low dose hirudin and medium dose hirudin groups, respectively (p=0.047 heparin vs medium dose hirudin). The percentage of patients developing secondary outcome (primary plus severe angina) were 15.6%, 12.5%, and 9.4%, (p=0.02 for heparin vs medium dose hirudin). New myocardial infarctions developed in fewer patients on medium hirudin dose (1.9%) than heparin (4.9%; p=0.046). Fewer patients required CABG in the 2 hirudin groups (3.7% low dose, 1.1% medium dose) vs heparin (4.0%; p=0.028 for heparin vs medium dose hirudin). While there was an increase in ischemic events after study drugs were stopped, the difference between heparin and hirudin persisted for 180 days.
Conclusions	Hirudin, especially at medium dose was better than heparin in reducing ischemic outcomes in patients with unstable angina or acute myocardial infarction without ST segment elevation.

OASIS (Warfarin Substudy)

Organization to Assess Strategies for Ischemic Syndromes

Title	Long term oral anticoagulant therapy in patients with unstable angina or suspected non Q wave myocardial infarction.
Authors	Anand SS, Yusuf S, Pogue J, et al.
Reference	Circulation 1998; 98:1064-1070.
Disease	Unstable angina, non Q wave myocardial infarction.
Purpose	To determine the effects of warfarin at two intensities in patients with acute ischemic syndromes without ST elevation in two consecutive trials.
Design	Randomized, controlled, multicenter.
Patients	309 patients in phase 1; 197 patients in phase 2. Patients had to be admitted to hospital within 12 hours (phase 1) or 48 hours (phase 2) of chest pain suspected to be due to unstable angina or MI without ST elevation on their admission ECG.
Follow-up	Phase 1-6 months; Phase 2-3 months
Treatment regimen	Phase 1: Warfarin (started 5-7 days after initial 72 hours IV infusion of heparin or hirudin) at 3 mg per day to achieve low level of anticoagulation (target INR = 1.5) or standard therapy for 180 days. Phase 2: Warfarin adjusted to achieve an INR of 2.0-2.5.
Additional therapy	Aspirin.

OASIS (Warfarin Substudy)

Organization to Assess Strategies for Ischemic Syndromes

(continued)

Results	Phase 1: At 6 months the rates of cardiovascular death, new MI, refractory angina were 6.5% in the warfarin group and 3.9% in the standard therapy group (p=NS). Rates of death, new MI, and stroke were 6.5% in warfarin group and 2.6% in standard therapy group (p=NS). Major and minor bleeding were more common in the warfarin group. Phase 2: At 3 months, the rates of cardiovascular death, new MI, and refractory angina were 5.1% in warfarin group and 12.1% in standard group (p=0.08). Rates of death, new MI, and stroke were 5.1% in warfarin group and 13.1% in standard therapy group (p=0.05). Patients on warfarin had less rehospitalization for unstable angina (7.1% vs 17.2%, p=0.03). Minor bleeding was more common in the warfarin group.
Conclusions	Moderate intensity warfarin (INR 2.0–2.5) plus aspirin but not low dose warfarin plus aspirin decreased recurrent ischemic events in patients with acute ischemic syndromes without ST elevation.

PRISM

The Platelet Receptor Inhibition in Ischemic Syndrome Management (PRISM) Study

Title	A comparison of aspirin plus tirofiban with aspirin plus heparin for unstable angina.
Author	The PRISM Investigators.
Reference	N Engl J Med 1998; 378:1498–1505.
Disease	Coronary artery disease, unstable angina.
Purpose	To determine whether the glycoprotein IIb/IIIa receptor antagonist tirofiban would improve clinical outcome in patients with unstable angina.
Design	Randomized, double blind, multicenter.
Patients	3232 patients with unstable angina already receiving aspirin.
Follow-up	30 days.
Treatment regimen	All patients received aspirin. Patients randomized to tirofiban (loading dose of 0.6 μg per kilogram per minute for 30 minutes followed by 0.15 μg per kilogram per minute for 47.5 hours). Patients randomized to heparin group received 5000 units IV bolus followed by an infusion of 1000 Units per h for 48 h.

PRISM

The Platelet Receptor Inhibition in Ischemic Syndrome Management (PRISM) Study

(continued)

Results	The incidence of attaining the composite end point (death, myocardial infarction, or refractory ischemia at 48 h) was 3.8% with tirofiban vs 5.6% with heparin (risk ration, 0.67; 95% CI=0.48-0.92, p=0.01). At 30 days there was a trend toward a reduction in death or myocardial infarction with tirofiban (5.8% vs 7.1%, p=0.11). At 30 days, mortality was 2.3% in the tirofiban group vs 3.6% in the heparin group (p=0.02). The incidence of refractory ischemia and myocardial infarction was not reduced by tirofiban at 30 days. Major bleeding was present in 0.4% of both groups.
Conclusions	Platelet inhibition with tirofiban plus aspirin may play a role in the treatment of unstable angina.

PRISM-PLUS

The Platelet Receptor Inhibition in Ischemic Syndrome Management in Patients Limited by Unstable Signs and Symptoms (PRISM-PLUS)

Title	Inhibition of the platelet glycoprotein IIb/IIIa receptor with tirofiban in unstable angina and non Q wave myocardial infarction.
Author	PRISM-PLUS Investigators.
Reference	N Engl J Med 1998; 338:1488-1497.
Disease	Coronary artery disease, unstable angina, non Q wave myocardial infarction.
Purpose	To evaluate the effectiveness of tirofiban in treating unstable angina and non Q wave infarctions.
Design	Randomized, double blind, multicenter.
Patients	1915 patients with unstable angina or non Q wave infarcts.
Follow-up	6 months.
Treatment regimen	All patients received aspirin. They were randomized to tirofiban, heparin, or tirofiban plus heparin. Study drugs were infused for a mean of 71 h. Coronary angiography and angioplasty performed when indicated after 48 h.

PRISM-PLUS

The Platelet Receptor Inhibition in Ischemic Syndrome Management in Patients Limited by Unstable Signs and Symptoms (PRISM-PLUS)

(continued)

Results	Tirofiban alone was associated with an excess of mortality at 7 days (4.6%) compared with patients on heparin alone (1.1%). The incidence of the composite end point (death, myocardial infarction, or refractory ischemia) was lower among patients on tirofiban plus heparin (12.9%) compared to patients on heparin alone (17.9%, risk ratio, 0.68, 95% CI = 0.53-0.88, p=0.004). This benefit persisted at 30 days (18.5% vs 22.3%, p=0.03) and 6 months (27.7% vs 32.1%, p=0.02) Tirofiban plus heparin was also associated with a lower rate of death or myocardial infarction at 7, 30, and 60 days. Major bleeding was present in 3% of heparin group and 4% in combination group.
Conclusions	Tirofiban alone (without heparin) caused excess mortality early. However, when administered with heparin it was associated with a better clinical outcome than patients who received heparin.

PRISM-PLUS (Angiographic Results)

Platelet Receptor Inhibition for Ischemic Syndrome Management In Patients Limited by Unstable Signs and Symptoms

Title	Intracoronary thrombus and platelet glycoprotein IIb/IIIa receptor blockade with tirofiban in unstable angina or non Q wave myocardial infarction. Angiographic results from the PRISM-PLUS Trial.
Authors	Zhao X-Q, Theroux P, Snapinn SM, et al.
Reference	Circulation 1999;100:1609-1615.
Disease	Unstable angina, non Q wave myocardial infarction.
Purpose	To describe the angiographic substudy results of the PRISM-PLUS study. To assess the effects of tirofiban on the characteristics of the culprit lesion in patients with unstable angina and non Q wave MI.
Design	As per PRISM-PLUS.
Patients	1491 patients with readable coronary angiograms obtained at a median of 65 hours after randomization.
Follow-up	Angiograms done at about 65 hours following randomization.
Treatment regimen	As per PRISM-PLUS.
Additional therapy	As per PRISM-PLUS.

PRISM-PLUS (Angiographic Results)

Platelet Receptor Inhibition for Ischemic Syndrome Management In Patients Limited by Unstable Signs and Symptoms

(continued)

Results	Angiograms were analyzed by a core laboratory. The primary end point was the intracoronary thrombus burden and secondary end points were TIMI flow grade distribution and severity of the obstruction and underlying atherosclerotic lesion. Compared to heparin alone, tirofiban plus heparin reduced the frequency and severity of thrombus. Tirofiban plus heparin decreased the intracoronary thrombus burden compared to heparin alone (odds ratio [OR]=0.65, p=0.002) and reduced the severity of obstruction (p=0.037). Small thrombus, medium thrombus, and large thrombus were seen in 9.0%, 15.8%, and 3.0% of heparin alone patients, respectively, vs 11.4%, 11.4%, and 2.1% of tirofiban plus heparin patients, respectively. TIMI grade 3 was present in 74% of heparin alone patients vs 82% of patients on tirofiban plus heparin. As expected tirofiban plus heparin did not alter the severity of underlying atherosclerotic plaque. Persistence of thrombus increased the odds of death and myocardial infarction.
Conclusions	Tirofiban plus heparin decreased thrombus burden of the culprit lesion and improved coronary perfusion in patients with unstable angina and non Q wave myocardial infarction.

ROXIS PILOT STUDY

Randomization trial of roxithromycin in non Q wave coronary syndromes

Title	Randomized trial of roxithromycin in non Q wave coronary syndromes: ROXIS pilot study.
Author	Gurfinkel E, Bozovich A, Daroca A, et al.
Reference	Lancet 1997;350:404-407.
Disease	Coronary artery disease, unstable angina or non Q wave myocardial infarction.
Purpose	To determine the effectiveness of the antibiotic roxithromycin for reducing severe recurrent angina, acute myocardial infarction, and death in patients with unstable angina or non Q wave infarction.
Design	Randomized, double blind, placebo controlled study.
Patients	202 patients with unstable angina or non Q wave infarction.
Follow-up	31 days.
Treatment regimen	Oral roxithromycin, 150 mg x2/d for 30 days vs placebo. All patients received, aspirin, IV nitroglycerin, heparin.
Results	No difference between groups for individual outcomes of angina, myocardial infarction, or death. There was a trend (p=0.06) for reduced triple end point of angina plus infarction plus death.
Conclusions	Nonsignificant trend toward improvement with antibiotic when examined in an intention-to-treat analysis.

TIMI 11A

Thrombolysis in Myocardial Infarction 11A

Title	Dose ranging trial of enoxaparin for unstable angina: results of TIMI 11A.
Authors	The Thrombolysis In Myocardial Infarction (TIMI) 11A Trial Investigators.
Reference	J Am Coll Cardiol 1997;29:1474-1482.
Disease	Unstable angina, non Q wave myocardial infarction.
Purpose	To assess the tolerability and safety of 2 weight adjusted doses of subcutaneous injections of enoxaparin, a low molecular weight heparin, in unstable angina and non Q wave myocardial infarction.
Design	Open label, dose ranging trial, multicenter.
Patients	630 patients with unstable angina or non Q wave myocardial infarction. Patients with evolving Q wave myocardial infarction, patients who had received thrombolytic therapy within 24 h of enrollment, renal failure, CABG within 2 months, history of heparin induced thrombocytopenia, contraindications to anticoagulation or aspirin, on continuous unfractionated heparin infusion, or a need for continuous anticoagulation were excluded.
Follow-up	14 days.
Treatment regimen	Intravenous bolus 30 mg followed by subcutaneous injection of either 1.25 mg/kg body weight or 1.0 mg/kg bid during in-hospital phase, and a fixed dose of either 60 mg (body weight ≥65 kg) or 40 mg (body weight <65 kg) subcutaneously bid after discharge.

TIMI 11A

Thrombolysis in Myocardial Infarction 11A

(continued)

Results

In the initial cohort of patients a dose of 1.25 mg/kg bid was used during hospitalization. This regimen was terminated prematurely after enrollment of 321 patients due to high major bleeding rate (6.5%), mainly at instrumented sites. Additional 309 patients received a regimen of 1.0 mg/kg bid during hospitalization. The duration of the in-hospital phase was a median of 3 days. In this cohort 6% of the patients stopped treatment because of bleeding, 7% due to coronary artery bypass surgery, and 3% at their request. The duration of the outpatient phase was a median of 10 days. Enoxaparin was stopped by 17% of the patients in this phase. Major bleeding occurred in 6 patients (1.9%; 95% CI 0.8%–4.4%) of the 1.0 mg/kg bid regimen, in 5 of them (1.6%) bleeding was at a puncture site and occurred a median of 34.5 h after a procedure. In only 1 patient, a major bleeding occurred spontaneously. Thrombocytopenia was noted in 2 patients (0.7%). The incidence of death was 2.2% in the first regimen and 0.6% in the second regimen. Myocardial infarction occurred in 2.2% and 2.9%, respectively, and recurrent ischemia requiring intervention in 1.2% and 1.6%, respectively (p=NS for all comparisons).

Conclusions

Enoxaparin therapy at a dose of 1.0 mg/kg was associated with an acceptable rate of major bleeding during the in-hospital phase, whereas a dose of 1.25 mg/kg was associated with excess of major bleeding. Efficacy should be tested in phase III trial.

TIMI 11A Substudy

Thrombolysis in Myocardial Infarction 11A

Title	C reactive protein is a potent predictor of mortality independently of and in combination with tropinin T in acute coronary syndromes: A TIMI 11 A substudy.
Authors	Morrow DA, Rifai N, Antman EM, et al.
Reference	J Am Coll Cardiol 1998; 31:1460-1465.
Disease	Unstable angina, non Q wave MI.
Purpose	To evaluate the usefulness of elevated C reactive protein (CRP) and in conjunction with a rapid assay for cardiac-specific tropinin T (cTnT) for predicting 14 day outcome.
Design	As per TIMI 11 A.
Patients	437 patients had both a rapid cTnT and quantitative CRP within 6 hours of symptom onset.
Follow-up	14 days in this analysis.
Treatment regimen	As per TIMI 11 A.

TIMI 11A Substudy

Thrombolysis in Myocardial Infarction 11A

(continued)

Results	CRP elevation was a predictor of mortality. Mean CRP was higher at 7.2 mg/dL among patients who died compared to survivors (1.3 mg/dL, p=0.0038). Among patients who demonstrated a positive rapid cTnT assay mortality was 0% in patients with CRP <1.55 mg/dL vs 5.1% with CRP's >1.55. If cTnT was negative, mortality was still higher in patients with CRP ≥1.55 mg/dL. Highest mortality occurred in patients who had both an early positive rapid cTnT ≤10 min and CRP ≥1.55. Patients with either CRP ≥1.55 or early positive rapid cTnT were intermediate in their outcome. Patients, with both a negative rapid cTnT and CRP <1.55 were at lowest risk (9.10 vs 4.65% vs 0.36%, p=0.0003).
Conclusions	In patients with unstable angina or non Q wave MI an elevation in C reactive protein correlates with increased 14 day mortality.

TIMI 12

Thrombolysis in Myocardial Infarction 12

Title	Randomized trial of an oral platelet glycoprotein IIb/IIIa antagonist, sibrafiban, in patients after an acute coronary syndrome. Results of the TIMI 12 Trial.
Author	Cannon CP, McCabe CH, Borzak S, et al.
Reference	Circulation 1998; 97:340-349.
Disease	Coronary artery disease, acute coronary syndromes.
Purpose	To evaluate pharmacokinetics, pharmacodynamics, safety and tolerability of sibrafiban.
Design	Double blind, dose ranging trial.
Patients	106 patients - pharmacokinetics, pharmacodynamics, 223 safety cohort. Patients had acute coronary syndromes - unstable angina, non Q wave myocardial infarction, or Q wave myocardial infarction.
Follow-up	28 days.
Treatment regimen	In the pharmacokinetic/pharmacodynamic cohort, 106 patients received 1 of 7 doses of sibrafiban ranging from 5mg daily to 10 mg x2/d for 28 days. In the safety cohort patients were randomized to 1 of 4 dose regimens (5 mg twice daily to 15 mg once daily) or aspirin.

TIMI 12

Thrombolysis in Myocardial Infarction 12

(continued)

Results	Sibrafibran successfully inhibited platelets from 47–97% inhibition of ADP induced platelet aggregation across doses. There was a correlation between concentration of drug and degree of ADP induced placebo inhibition. Twice daily dosing obtained more sustained inhibition, as with once daily dosing inhibition returned to baseline values by 24 h. Major hemorrhage occurred in 1.5% of patients receiving sibrafiban and in 1.9% of those receiving aspirin. Minor bleeding (usually mucocutaneous) occurred in 0–32% of patients on various doses of sibrafiban and none of aspirin. Minor bleeding correlated with total daily dose, twice daily dosing, renal function, and presence of unstable angina.
Conclusions	Sibrafiban, an oral glycoprotein IIb/IIIa antagonist is an effective long term platelet antagonist with a dose response. There was a relatively high incidence of minor bleeding. Further studies are warranted to assess outcome in acute coronary syndromes.

TRIM

Thrombin Inhibition in Myocardial Ischaemia

Title	A low molecular weight, selective thrombin inhibitor, inogatran, vs heparin, in unstable coronary artery disease in 1209 patients.
Authors	Thrombin Inhibition in Myocardial Ischaemia (TRIM) study group.
Reference	Eur Heart J 1997;18:1416-1425.
Disease	Unstable angina and non Q wave myocardial infarction.
Purpose	To assess the effects of Inogatran, a novel low molecular weight selective thrombin inhibitor in unstable angina and in non Q wave myocardial infarction.
Design	Randomized, double blind, multicenter.
Patients	1209 patients with unstable angina or non Q wave myocardial infarction. Patients with increased risk of bleeding, uncontrolled hypertension, history of stroke, active peptic ulcer, recent anticoagulant or fibrinolytic therapy, recent CABG, and uncompensated congestive heart failure or arrhythmia were excluded.
Follow-up	Clinical follow-up for 30-40 days.
Treatment regimen	Randomization to: 1) low dose inogatran (1.1 mg bolus, 2 mg/h infusion); 2) medium dose inogatran (2.75 mg bolus, 5 mg/h infusion); 3) high dose inogatran (5.5 mg bolus, 5.5 mg/h infusion); and 4) heparin (5000 U bolus, 1200 U/h infusion).All treatment regimens were given for 72h, within 24 h of the end of the qualifying episode of pain. If the activated partial thromboplastin time (aPTT) was >3 times normal, infusion rate was reduced.

TRIM

Thrombin Inhibition in Myocardial Ischaemia

(continued)

Additional therapy	Aspirin was recommended. Ticlopidine and oral anticoagulants were prohibited.
Results	aPTTs were higher in the heparin treated group than in the 3 inogatran groups after 6 h. However, after 24 h and 48h aPTTs were comparable. 41.3% of the heparin treated patients vs only 1.3%-4.4% of the inogatran treated patients needed infusion rate reduction due to prolonged aPTT. At the end of the 72 h infusion, death or myocardial (re)infarction occurred in 3.6%, 2.0%, and 4.0% of the low medium, and high dose inogatran groups vs only 0.7% in the heparin group (odds ratio 5.02; 95% CI 1.19-21.17). The composite end point (death, myocardial (re)infarction, refractory angina or recurrence of angina after 7 days) at the end of treatment occurred in 39.4%, 37.6%, and 36.1% of the inogatran groups, respectively vs only 29.5% in the heparin group (odds ratio 1.48; 95% CI 1.12-1.96). However, the composite end point at 7 days was not significantly different among groups (45.7%, 45.9%, 45.5% in the inogatran groups, respectively and 41.0% in the heparin group; odds ratio 1.23; 95% CI 0.95-1.61). The composite event rates at 30 days were also comparable (51.7%, 52.2%, 53.2%, and 47.9%; odds ratio 1.21; 95% CI 0.93-1.57). Major bleeding within 7 days occurred in 1.1% of the patients, with similar rates among the groups. No intracerebral hemorrhages were noted.
Conclusions	During the 3 days of therapy, event rates were lower with heparin than with inogatran. However, after cessation of infusion there was an increase in event rates in all treatment arms. Since the high inogatran dose was not associated with increased bleeding, a higher dose may be more effective.

VANQWISH

Veterans Affairs Non Q Wave Infarction Strategies In-Hospital

Title	Outcome in patients with acute non Q wave myocardial infarction rendomly assigned to an invasive as compared with a conservative management.
Author	Boden WE, O'Rourke RA, Crawford MH, et al.
Reference	a. J Am Coll Cardiol 1998;31:312-320. b. J Am Coll Cardiol 1997;30:1-7. c. N Engl J Med 1998;338:1785-1792.
Disease	Non Q wave myocardial infarction.
Purpose	To compare outcomes in patients with non Q wave myocardial infarctions randomized to early invasive strategy vs conservative management.
Design	Randomized, multicenter.
Patients	920 patients, ≥18 years old, with suspected non Q wave myocardial infarction. Patients with unstable angina or refractory angina after the non Q wave infarction, persistent left bundle branch block, congestive heart failure, pericarditis, ventricular tachyarrhythmias, revascularization within 3 months prior randomization, or concomitant severe illness were excluded.
Follow-up	12-44 months (mean 23 months).

VANQWISH

Veterans Affairs Non Q Wave Infarction Strategies In-Hospital

(continued)

Treatment regimen	Randomization within 1-7 days of infarction to early (3-7 days) coronary angiography (invasive strategy) or to conservative strategy (radionuclide left ventriculography and symptom limited treadmill exercise test with thallium scintigraphy). In the invasive strategy, angioplasty was performed in patients with single vessel disease, whereas coronary bypass surgery was considered for patients with multivessel disease. Patients assigned to the conservative strategy were referred to angiography only if they had post infarction angina, ≥2 mm ST deviation during exercise test, or if the thallium scan showed ≥2 redistribution defects or one redistribution defect or increased lung uptake of thallium.
Additional thearpy	All patients received aspirin 325 mg/d and diltiazem 180-300 mg/d. Nitrates, ACE inhibitors, ß-blockers, heparin and thrombolytic thearpy were permitted.
Results	Overall 96% of the invasive-strategy vs only 48% of the conservative strategy arm underwent coronary angiography. 44% vs 33% respectively underwent revascularization procedures. During an average of 23 months there were 152 cardiac events (80 deaths and 72 nonfatal infarctions) in 138 patients among the invasive-strategy arm whereas in the conservative arm there were 139 events (59 deaths and 80 nonfatal infarctions) in 123 patients (p=0.35; hazard ratio for the conservative strategy vs the invasive-strategy 0.87; 95% CI 0.68-1.10). However, during the first 12 monthe death or nonfatal myocardial infarction were more common in the invasive-strategy arm (111 vs 85 events; p=0.05). Mortality rate among the invasive and conservative arms were 21 vs 6 before hospital discharge (p=0.007); 23 vs 9 at 1 month (p=0.21); and 58 vs 36 at 1 year (p=0.025), respectively. During long term follow-up, cumulative all cause mortality was comparable between the conservative and invasive strategy arms (hazard ratio 0.72; 95% CI 0.51-1.01).

VANQWISH

Veterans Affairs Non Q Wave Infarction Strategies In-Hospital

(continued)

Conclusions	This study shows that the strategy of routine, early invasive management of patients with non Q wave myocardial infarction, consisting of coronary angiography and revascularization, is not better than the strategy of conservative, ischemia guided approach.

ESSENCE

Efficacy and Safety of Subcutaneous Enoxaparin in Non Q Wave Coronary Events

Title	A comparison of low molecular weight heparin with unfractionated heparin for unstable coronary artery disease.
Author	Cohen M, Demers C, Gurfinkel EP, et al.
Reference	N Engl J Med 1997; 337:447-452.
Disease	Coronary artery disease.
Purpose	To determine the safety and efficacy of the low molecular weight heparin, enoxaparin vs intravenous unfractionated heparin in patients with unstable angina and non Q wave myocardial infarction.
Design	Double blind, placebo controlled, randomized, multicenter.
Patients	3171 patients with angina at rest or non Q wave infarction. Average ages 63-64; 66%-67% males.
Follow-up	30 days.
Treatment regimen	1 mg/kg enoxaparin given subcutaneously x2/d vs continuous IV unfractionated heparin. Therapy continued from 48 h-8 days. Aspirin was given to all patients.

ESSENCE

Efficacy and Safety of Subcutaneous Enoxaparin in Non Q Wave Coronary Events

(continued)

Results	The composite end point of death, myocardial infarction, or recurrent angina was significantly lower in the enoxaparin group compared to unfractionated heparin group at 14 days (16.6% vs 19.8%, p=0.019), and at 30 days (19.8% vs 23.3%, p=0.016). Mortality was 0.4% in the unfractionated heparin group vs 0.5% in the enoxaprin group (p=0.18) at 48 h, 2.3% vs 2.2% respectively at 14 days (p=0.92), and 3.6% vs 2.9%, respectively (p=0.25) at 30 days. Need for revascularization was lower in patients on enoxaparin vs unfractionated heparin (27.0% vs 32.2%, p = 0.001). The incidence of major bleeding was similar in the 2 groups (6.5% vs 7.0%), but overall incidence of bleeding was higher in enoxaparin group (18.4%) compared to unfractionated heparin (14.2%=0.001) mainly related to ecchymoses at sites of injection.
Conclusions	Enoxaparin plus aspirin was more effective than unfractionated heparin plus aspirin in reducing the incidence of death, myocardial infarction, or recurrent angina. Enoxaparin increased minor but not the incidence of major bleeding.

PARAGON

Platelet IIb/IIIa Antagonism for the Reduction of Acute Coronary Syndrome Events in a Global Organization Network

Title	International, randomized, controlled trial of lamifiban (a platelet glycoprotein IIb/IIIa inhibitor), heparin, or both in unstable angina.
Authors	The PARAGON Investigators.
Reference	Circulation 1998; 97:2386-2395.
Disease	Unstable angina and non Q wave myocardial infarction.
Purpose	To determine the effect of different doses of lamifiban (a platelet IIb/IIIa antagonist) alone and in combination with heparin in patients with unstable angina and non Q wave MI.
Design	Partial factorial design, randomized, double blinded, multicenter.
Patients	2282 patients with chest discomfort within the previous 12 hours with transient or persistent ST segment depression on the ECG or T wave inversion or transient ST segment elevation.
Follow-up	6 months.
Treatment regimen	Lamifiban low dose, 300 μg bolus followed by infusion (1 μg/min) with and without heparin; lamifiban high dose, 750 μg bolus followed by infusion (5 μg/min) with or without heparin; or to standard therapy (placebo and heparin). All patients received aspirin. Study drug given for minimum of 3 days and maximum of 5 or more days.

PARAGON

Platelet IIb/IIIa Antagonism for the Reduction of Acute Coronary Syndrome Events in a Global Organization Network

(continued)

Additional therapy	Coronary revascularization not to be performed during first 48 hours unless medically necessary.
Results	The composite primary end point was death or nonfatal myocardial infarction at 30 days and occurred in 10.6% of patients on low dose lamifiban; 12.0% receiving high dose; and 11.7% on standard therapy (p=NS). At 6 months the composite primary end point was 13.7% at low dose (p=0.027 vs standard therapy); 16.4% for high dose (p=NS); and 17.9% in standard therapy group. At 6 months death or nonfatal MI was 23% lower with lamifiban with or without heparin compared to standard therapy. High dose lamifiban plus heparin was associated with more intermediate or major bleeding (12.1% vs 5.5%, p=0.002) while low dose lamifiban plus heparin had a similar rate of bleeding to the control group.
Conclusions	Lamifiban (at the lower dose) reduced adverse ischemic events at 6 months in patients with unstable angina or non Q waves.

PURSUIT

Platelet Glycoprotein IIb/IIIa in Unstable Angina: Receptor Suppression Using Integrilin Therapy (Substudy)

Title	Inhibition of platelet glycoprotein IIb/IIIa with eptifibatide in patients with acute coronary syndromes.
Authors	The PURSUIT Trial Investigators
Reference	N Engl J Med 1998; 339:436-443.
Disease	Acute coronary syndromes.
Purpose	To test the hypothesis that inhibition of platelets with eptifibatide would have benefit beyond heparin in decreasing adverse outcomes in patients with acute coronary syndromes.
Design	Randomized, double blind, multicenter.
Patients	10,948 patients. Patients had to present with ischemic chest pain within 24 hours and transient ST T changes compatible with ischemia (but not persistent ST elevation) or high CK-MB.
Follow-up	30 days.
Treatment regimen	Eptifibatide (bolus of 180 μg per kg. body weight, followed by infusion of 1.3 μg per kg. per minute; or bolus of 180 μg per kg followed by an infusion of 2.0 μg per kg. per minute). Infusion lasted until hospital discharge or 72 hours, whichever came first.
Additional therapy	All patients could receive aspirin and IV or subcutaneous heparin. During infusion of eptifibatide, thrombolytic therapy was not allowed.

PURSUIT

Platelet Glycoprotein IIb/IIIa in Unstable Angina: Receptor Suppression Using Integrilin Therapy (Substudy)

(continued)

Results	45%-46% of patients were admitted with myocardial infarction. About 65% had angina at rest. Patient enrollment occurred at a median of 11 hours of symptoms. The frequency of the composite end point (death from any cause or nonfatal myocardial infarction at 30 days) was 7.6% in eptifibatide group and 9.1% in placebo group at 96 hours (p=0.01); 10.1% vs 11.6% at 7 days, (p=0.02); and 14.2% vs 15.7% at day 30 (p=0.04). Thus at 30 days there was a 1.5% absolute reduction of primary end points with treatment. The effect was less consistent in women. Bleeding was more common in the treatment group and tended to be mild involving vascular access sites. There was no increase in hemorrhagic stroke in the treatment group.
Conclusions	Eptifibatide reduced the composite end point of death from any cause and nonfatal myocardial infarction in patients with acute coronary syndromes without persistent ST segment elevation on the electrocardiogram.

PURSUIT (Substudy)

Platelet Glycoprotein IIb/IIIa in Unstable Angina: Receptor Suppression Using Integrilin Therapy (Substudy)

Title	Early, percutaneous coronary intervention, platelet inhibition with eptifibatide, and clinical outcomes in patients with acute coronary syndromes.
Authors	Kleiman NS, Lincoff M, Flaker GS, et al.
Reference	Circulation 2000;101:751-757.
Disease	Acute coronary syndromes.
Purpose	To determine the effects of GP IIb/IIIa platelet antagonist eptifibatide in patients with acute coronary syndromes in those with percutaneous coronary interventions vs those managed conservatively.
Design	As per PURSUIT Trial.
Patients	1228 patients had early (<72 hours) percutaneous coronary intervention; 8233 did not.
Follow-up	30 days.
Treatment regimen	As per PURSUIT trial.
Additional therapy	As per PURSUIT trial.

PURSUIT (Substudy)

Platelet Glycoprotein IIb/IIIa in Unstable Angina: Receptor Suppression Using Integrilin Therapy (Substudy)

(continued)

Results	Primary end point was composite of death or MI within first 30 days; secondary end point was death or MI among patients who had percutaneous coronary intervention within the first 72 hours. Myocardial infarction preceded early percutaneous coronary intervention in 34 placebo patients (5.5%) vs 10 eptifibatide patients (1.7%; p=0.001). There was a reduction in primary composite end point in eptifibatide patients (p=0.035) when patients were censored for percutaneous coronary intervention over a 30 day period. In patients with early percutaneous coronary intervention, eptifibatide decreased 30 day event rates (11.6% vs 16.7%, p=0.01), and there was a trend for this benefit in patients who did not undergo early intervention (14.6% vs 15.6%, p=0.23). Following adjustment for intervention propensity, eptifibatide treatment did not appear to differ between patients who had vs those that did not have early intervention.
Conclusions	"Eptifibatide reduced the composite rates of death or myocardial infarction in patients receiving percutaneous coronary interventions and those managed conservatively."

CESAR 2

The Clinical European Studies in Angina and Revascularization 2

Title	Cardioprotection by opening of the K_{ATP} channel in unstable angina. Is this a clinical manifestation of myocardial preconditioning? Results of a randomized study with nicorandil.
Authors	Patel DJ, Purcell HJ, Fox KM, on behalf of the CESAR 2 Investigation.
Reference	Eur Heart J 1999;20:51-57.
Disease	Unstable angina.
Purpose	To evaluate the efficacy and safety of nicorandil, an ATP sensitive K^+ channel opener, in unstable angina.
Design	Randomized, double blind, placebo controlled, multicenter.
Patients	245 patients, 30-80 years old with unstable angina. Patients with acute Q wave or non Q wave myocardial infarction, aborted myocardial infarction, post infarction (within 1 month) angina were excluded. Patients with LBBB, LVH, or electrocardiographic signs of digoxin effect, contraindications to nicorandil, secondary angina, revascularization in the preceding 3 months, known arrhythmia, valvular heart disease, and women of child bearing potential were not included.
Follow-up	48 hour continuous ST segment and arrhythmia monitoring, with repeated cardiac enzymes and troponin T level measurements.

CESAR 2

The Clinical European Studies in Angina and Revascularization 2

(continued)

Treatment regimen	Randomization to nicorandil 20 mg bid or a matching placebo for ≥48 hours.
Additional therapy	All patients received diltiazem 180–360 mg/d, atenolol 50–100 mg/d, or metoprolol 12.5–50 mg tid, aspirin 150 mg/d. Intravenous heparin and nitrates were permitted.
Results	243 patients received at least one dose of the study medication. 43 patients were excluded because they had acute myocardial infarction on admission. 200 patients were included in the intention-to-treat analysis, 188 patients had satisfactory Holter data. During a mean of 41 hours of continuous electrocardiographic monitoring, 12.4% of the nicorandil assigned patients had 37 episodes vs 21.2% of the placebo assigned patients had 74 episodes of transient ischemia (p=0.12 patients; p=0.0028 episodes). Most of the episodes were silent. Chest pain was reported by 16.5% of the nicorandil group vs 31.1% of the placebo group (p=0.008). However, severe chest pain was reported by 11.5% vs 13.5% of the nicorandil and placebo patients, respectively (p=NS). Arrhythmia was detected in 11.2% of the nicorandil group vs 22.8% of the placebo group (p=0.05). The nicorandil assigned patients had less nonsustained ventricular tachycardia (3 vs 10 patients, p<0.087; 3 vs 31 episodes, p<0.0001) and less supraventricular tachycardia (3 vs 9 patients, p=0.14; 4 vs 15 episodes, p=0.017) than the placebo treated patients. During active treatment none of the patients died. In the overall safety analysis there were no differences in the rates of adverse effects between nicorandil and placebo.
Conclusions	Nicorandil, added to antianginal therapy for unstable angina, reduced the number of episodes of transient myocardial ischemia, nonsustained ventricular tachycardia, and supraventricular tachycardia. The drug was safe.

OASIS-2

Organisation to Assess Strategies for Ischemic Syndromes 2

Title	Effects of recombinant hirudin (lepirudin) compared with heparin on death, myocardial infarction, refractory angina, and revascularization procedures in patients with acute myocardial ischaemia without ST elevation: A randomised trial.
Authors	Organisation to Assess Strategies for Ischemic Syndromes (OASIS 2) Investigators.
Reference	Lancet 1999;353:429–438.
Disease	Unstable angina, Non Q wave myocardial infarction.
Purpose	To assess whether recombinant hirudin (lepirudin) would be superior to heparin in patients with acute coronary syndromes.
Design	Randomized, double blind, double-dummy, multicenter.
Patients	10,141 patients, 21–85 years old, with suspected unstable angina or non ST elevation acute myocardial infarction, within 12 hours of last episode of symptoms. Patients had to have ECG evidence of ischemia or previous objective evidence of coronary artery disease. Patients with contraindications to anticoagulation, a history of stroke in the previous year, creatinine >2.0 mg/dL, need for long term oral anticoagulation, PTCA within 6 months, planned thrombolysis or direct PTCA, cardiogenic shock, other severe diseases that might limit life expectancy, or current participation in other clinical trials were excluded.
Follow-up	7 days.

OASIS-2

Organisation to Assess Strategies for Ischemic Syndromes 2

(continued)

Treatment regimen	72 hour intravenous infusion of heparin (5000 units bolus followed by an infusion of 15 units/kg/h) + placebo hirudin or hirudin (0.4 mg/kg bolus followed by 0.15 mg/kg/h) + placebo-heparin. Doses were adjusted to maintain aPTT 60-100 sec.
Additional therapy	Aspirin 80-325 mg/d.
Results	More patients in the hirudin group (2.8%) than the heparin group (1.3%) had early discontinuation of the drug due to bleeding or adverse events (p<0.001). 14.6% of the heparin group vs 18.6% of the hirudin group had permanent early discontinuation of the study drug. Major bleeding requiring transfusion occurred in 0.7% of the heparin vs 1.2% of the hirudin treated patients (p=0.01). However, rates of life-threatening bleeding episodes were the same (0.4% in both groups). 12.0% of the heparin group vs 47.4% of the hirudin group required no dose adjustment of the drug. Cardiovascular death or new myocardial infarction within 7 days occurred in 3.6% of the hirudin group vs 4.2% of the heparin group (RR 0.84; 95% CI 0.69-1.02; p=0.077). Cardiovascular death, myocardial infarction, or refractory angina occurred at 7 days in 5.6% of the hirudin vs 6.7% of the heparin group (RR 0.82; 95% CI 0.70-0.96; p=0.0125). However, there was no difference in cardiovascular mortality (1.5% vs 1.4% in the heparin and hirudin groups, respectively). Most of the beneficial effect of hirudin was noted during the 72 hour infusion period. Cardiovascular death or myocardial infarction within 72 hours occurred in 2.6% of the heparin vs 2.0% of the hirudin group (RR 0.76; 95% CI 0.59-0.99; p=0.039). Differences between the hirudin and heparin groups were noted especially in patients who underwent intervention or those readmitted for unstable angina with electrocardiographic changes. Less patients in the hirudin (6.9%) than in the heparin (8.1%) underwent cardiac

intervention (RR 0.84; 95% CI 0.74–0.97; p=0.016). Death or myocardial infarction within 35 days occurred in 7.7% of the heparin vs 6.8% of the hirudin groups (RR 0.87; 95% CI 0.75–1.01; p=0.06).

Conclusions	Hirudin was better than heparin in reducing the combined end point of cardiovascular death, myocardial infarction and refractory angina at day 7 in patients with unstable angina or non ST elevation myocardial infarction.

FRISC II

Fragmin and Fast Revascularisation during InStability in Coronary artery disease

Title	a. Long term low molecular mass heparin in unstable coronary artery disease: FRISC II prospective randomized multicenter study. b. Invasive compared with noninvasive treatment in unstable coronary artery disease: FRISC II prospective randomized multicenter study.
Authors	Fragmin and Fast Revascularisation during InStability in Coronary artery disease (FRISC II) Investigators.
Reference	a. Lancet 1999;354:701-707. b. Lancet 1999;354:708-715.
Disease	Unstable angina, non Q wave myocardial infarction.
Purpose	a. To evaluate whether long term dalteparin therapy will be associated with better outcome than placebo in patients with unstable acute coronary syndromes undergoing a noninvasive treatment strategy. b. To compare noninvasive to early invasive strategy.
Design	Randomized, multicenter (the comparison between dalteparin treatment and placebo was double blind, and the comparison between the invasive vs noninvasive strategies was open).

FRISC II

Fragmin and Fast Revascularisation during InStability in Coronary artery disease

(continued)

Patients	Patients, ≤75 years old, within 48 hours of episode of ischemia at rest or suspected acute myocardial infarction accompanied by ST depression or T wave inversion or by raised creatine kinase or troponin-T levels. Patients at high risk of bleeding, anemia, indication for a treatment within the preceding 24 hours with thrombolytic agents, angioplasty within the preceding 6 months, being on the waiting list for coronary revascularization, renal or hepatic failure, other severe cardiac disease, osteoporosis, previous open heart surgery, and with other severe illness were excluded. a. 2267 patients. b. 2457 patients.
Follow-up	6 months.
Treatment regimen	a. After randomization, all patients received dalteparin 120 IU/kg bid for ≥5 days. Than patients were randomized to double blind therapy with subcutaneous injections of dalteparin or placebo bid for 3 months. b. Within 72 hours of open label therapy, patients were randomized to one of the 4 groups: 1) long term dalteparin + noninvasive strategy; 2) long term placebo + noninvasive strategy; 3) long term dalteparin + invasive strategy; or 4) long term placebo + invasive strategy.
Additional therapy	All patients initially received subcutaneous dalteparin or IV standard heparin before randomization. a. All patients for this study were treated with a noninvasive strategy. Coronary angiography or intervention was recommended only in patients with recurrent or refractory angina or with severe ischemia on exercise test. All patients received oral aspirin 75–320 mg/d. ß-blockers were recommended.
Results	a. 2267 patients were randomized into the noninvasive arm of the trial, 2105 of them actually entered the double blind treatment period. At one month, death or acute

myocardial infarction occurred in 6.2% of the dalteparin group vs 8.4% of the placebo group (risk ratio [RR] 0.73; 95% CI 0.54-0.99; p=0.048). Death, myocardial infarction, or revascularization occurred in 19.5% vs 25.7% of the dalteparin and placebo group, respectively (RR 0.76; 95% CI 0.65-0.89; p=0.001). At three months, the difference between the groups in the rate of death or myocardial infarction was statistically insignificant (10.0% vs 11.2%, respectively (RR 0.89;95% CI 0.70-1.13; p=0.34). However, there was still a statistically significant difference in favor of the dalteparin group in the rates of death, myocardial infarction, or revascularization (29.1% vs 33.4% (RR 0.87; 95% CI 0.77-0.99; p=0.031)). At 6 months, there was no difference in the occurrence of either death or myocardial infarction (13.3% vs 13.1%; p=0.93) or death, myocardial infarction, or revascularization (38.4% vs 39.9%; p=0.50) between the groups. Patients with elevated troponin-T concentrations had a 30.0% relative decrease in the incidence of death or myocardial infarction at 3 months (2.7% absolute decrease; p=0.07). In contrast, patients without troponin-T elevation had no apparent benefit from dalteparin. Dalteparin had no beneficial effects on symptoms of angina. There were 3.3% major and 23.0% minor bleeding episodes in the dalteparin group vs 1.5% and 8.4% in the placebo group. The rate of strokes was 1.0% in the dalteparin group vs 0.8% in the placebo group. Long term therapy with dalteparin was not associated with higher rates of thrombocytopenia, allergic reactions, or fractures.

b. 1222 patients were randomized to the invasive regimen and 1235 to the noninvasive regimen. 96% vs 10% of the invasive and noninvasive group underwent coronary angiography within 7 days of enrollment. Overall, during follow-up 98% vs 47% of the patients, respectively, underwent coronary angiography. Revascularization procedures were done within 10 days of enrollment in 71% of the invasive group vs 9% in the noninvasive group.

FRISC II

Fragmin and Fast Revascularisation during InStability in Coronary artery disease

(continued)

Within 6 months, 77% vs 37%, respectively, underwent revascularization procedures. After follow-up of 6 months, death or myocardial infarction occurred in 9.4% of the invasive regimen vs 12.1% of the noninvasive regimen (risk ration [RR] 0.78; 95% CI 0.62-0.98; p=0.031). Myocardial infarction occurred in 7.8% vs 10.1% of the invasive and noninvasive groups (RR 0.77; 95% CI 0.60-0.99; p=0.045), whereas death occurred in 1.9% vs 2.9%, respectively (RR 0.65; 95% CI 0.39-1.09; p=0.10). The percentages of patients with angina and the Canadian Cardiovascular Society angina class were significantly lower in the invasive compared to the noninvasive group, at 6 week, 3 month and 6 month visits. Re-admissions during the 6 months of follow-up occurred in 31% of the patients in the invasive strategy vs 49% of the noninvasive strategy (RR 0.62; 95% CI 0.60-0.69; p<0.001). The event rates during the first months of follow-up were lower in the noninvasive dalteparin group. However, after 6 months, the event rates were lower in the invasive approach (both in the dalteparin and placebo groups) than in the noninvasive regimen. Invasive approach was effective especially at older age, in men, and in patients with longer duration of angina, symptoms at rest, and those with ST segment depression.

Conclusions

a. 3 month therapy with low molecular weight heparin (dalteparin) resulted in lower rates of death, myocardial infarction, and need for revascularization in patients with acute coronary syndrome treated conservatively. This effect lasted for at least one month and vanished over the next 2 months of therapy and after additional 3 months of follow-up. Initial therapy with dalteparin could be used to decrease the risk of cardiac events in patients waiting for revascularization procedures.

b. Early invasive approach is preferred over noninvasive strategy in most patients with acute coronary syndromes. Early invasive approach resulted in lower rates of myocardial infarction and a trend towards lower mortality rate over 6 months of follow-up and marked improvement in the prevalence and severity of angina and lower rates of readmission.

FRAX.I.S

FRAxiparine in Ischemic Syndrome

Title	Comparison of two treatment durations (6 days and 14 days) of a low molecular weight heparin with a 6 day treatment of unfractionated heparin in the initial management of unstable angina or non Q wave myocardial infarction: FRAX.I.S. (FRAxiparine in Ischaemic Syndrome).
Authors	The FRAX.I.S. Study Group.
Reference	Eur Heart J 1999;20:1553-1562.
Disease	Unstable angina, non Q wave myocardial infarction.
Purpose	To compare the efficacy of two regimens (6 days and 14 days) of low molecular weight heparin (nadroparin) with that of unfractionated heparin in non ST elevation acute coronary syndromes.
Design	Randomized, double blind, multicenter.
Patients	3468 patients, >18 years old, weighing 40-110 kg, with suspected unstable angina or non Q wave myocardial infarction (anginal pain within the preceding 48 hours + ST depression, T wave inversion, or ST elevation not justifying thrombolysis). Patients with renal or hepatic failure, bleeding diathesis, thrombocytopenia, those with a need for long term treatment with oral anticoagulants, and those who underwent PTCA, CABG, acute myocardial infarction, unstable angina, or stroke in the preceding 6 months were excluded.
Follow-up	3 months clinical follow-up.

Treatment regimen	After randomization, patients received either nadoparin (IV bolus 86 anti Xa IU/kg followed by SC injections of 86 anti Xa IU/kg bid) or unfractionated heparin (IV bolus of 5000 IU, followed by an infusion of 1250 IU/h). IV unfractionated heparin was administered for 6±2 days, and subcutaneous nadoparin for 6 or 14 days. The unfractionated heparin group received subcutaneous injections of placebo and the nadoparin groups received IV infusion of placebo.
Additional therapy	All patients received up to 325 mg/d aspirin for 3 months. Nonstudy unfractionated heparin and low molecular weight heparin, oral anticoagulants, antiplatelet agents, antithrombin agents, and fibrinolytic drugs were prohibited during the study period. In case of coronary angiography or PTCA during the study treatment phase, open label heparin could be administered.

FRAX.I.S

FRAxiparine in Ischemic Syndrome

(continued)

Results	1151 patients received unfractionated heparin, 1166 nadoparin for 6 days, and 1151 nadoparin for 14 days. The primary end point of the study (cardiac mortality, myocardial infarction, refractory angina, and recurrence of unstable angina at day 14) occurred in 18.1% of the unfractionated heparin group, 17.8% in the nadoparin 6 days group, and 20.0% in the nadoparin 14 days group (p=NS). The absolute differences between the 3 groups with respect to the occurrence of the primary end point were -0.3% (95% CI -3.5%–2.8%; p=0.85) for the nadoparin 6 days vs the unfractionated heparin groups and +1.9% (95% CI -1.3%-5.1%; p=0.24) for the nadoparin 14 days group vs unfractionated heparin group. There were no statistically significant differences among the groups in the occurrence of any of the secondary end points (total mortality, cardiac mortality, myocardial infarction, refractory angina, recurrent angina, or the rates of PTCA+CABG) either at day 6, day 14, or at 3 months. At 3 months, recurrent angina occurred more often in the nadoparin 14 days group (19.9%) than in the nadoparin 6 days group (16.9%) or unfractionated heparin group (17.7%) (adjusted p value=0.09). The risk of major hemorrhage at day 14 was 1.6% in the unfractionated heparin, 1.5% in the nadoparin 6 days group, and 3.5% in the nadoparin 14 days group.
Conclusions	Nadoparin therapy for 6±2 days was comparable to IV infusion of unfractionated heparin for the same period of time in patients with unstable angina or non Q wave myocardial infarction. A prolonged regimen of nadoparin for 14 days was not associated with additional benefit and was associated with an increased risk of major hemorrhage.

TIMI 11B

Thrombolysis in Myocardial Infarction 11B Trial

Title	Enoxaparin prevents death and cardiac ischemic events in unstable angina/non Q wave myocardial infarction. Results of the TIMI 11B Trial.
Authors	Antman EM, McCabe CH, Gurfinkel EP, et al.
Reference	Circulation 1999;100:1593-1601.
Disease	Unstable angina/non Q wave myocardial infarction.
Purpose	To test the benefits of an extended course of antithrombotic therapy with uninterrupted enoxaparin with standard unfractionated heparin treatment for preventing death and cardiac events in patients with unstable angina or non Q wave myocardial infarction.
Design	Randomized, double blind, multicenter. Study had two phases: an acute phase and an outpatient phase.
Patients	3910 patients with unstable angina or non Q wave myocardial infarction.
Follow-up	43 days.

Treatment regimen	All patients received both an IV infusion (unfractionated heparin or placebo) and subcutaneous injections (enoxaparin or matched placebo). Unfractionated heparin was given in a weight adjusted fashion for a minimum of 3 days starting as a bolus of 70 U/kg and infusion of 15 U/kg/hour. Target aPTT was 1.5-2.5 times control. Enoxaparin was given as an initial IV bolus of 30 mg followed by subcutaneous injection of 1 mg/kg (100 anti-factor Xa units per kg) every 12 hours. Injections were continued until hospital discharge or day 8. For the chronic phase those originally assigned to enoxaparin received enoxaparin given as 40 mg subcutaneously every 12 hours if patients weighed <65 kg and 60 mg if they weighed ≥65 kg for 43 days; patients that had been originally assigned to IV unfractionated heparin received placebo subcutaneous injections, twice daily.
Additional therapy	Aspirin.
Results	The primary end point was the composite of all cause mortality, recurrent myocardial infarction, or urgent revascularization. This end point was achieved by 8 days in 14.5% of patients in the unfractionated heparin group and 12.4% in the enoxaparin group (OR=0.83; 95% CI=0.69-1.00; p=0.048). By 43 days the composite end point was reached in 19.7% of the unfractionated heparin group and 17.3% in the enoxaparin group (OR=0.85; 95% CI=0.72-1.00; p=0.048). The event rates for each element of the composite end point were also lower in the enoxaparin group through 14 days and there was no evidence of a rebound after discontinuing the study drugs. Benefits of enoxaparin were most evident during the acute phase without further relative decrease in events during the outpatient phase. Rates of major hemorrhage during hospitalization did not differ between groups. During the outpatient phase, major hemorrhage was more common in the enoxaparin group (2.9%) vs the group receiving placebo (1.5%; p=0.021).

TIMI 11B

Thrombolysis in Myocardial Infarction 11B Trial

(continued)

Conclusions	Enoxaparin was superior to unfractionated heparin for decreasing the composite end point of death, myocardial infarction, and urgent revascularization in patients with unstable angina or non Q wave myocardial infarction.

Randomized trial comparing IV nitroglycerin and heparin for treatment of unstable angina secondary to restenosis after coronary artery angioplasty

Title	Randomized trial comparing IV nitroglycerin and heparin for treatment of unstable angina secondary to restenosis after coronary artery angioplasty.
Authors	Doucet S, Malekianpour M, Théroux P, et al.
Reference	Circulation 2000;101:955-961.
Disease	Unstable angina, coronary artery disease.
Purpose	To determine the efficacy of IV nitroglycerin vs heparin for the treatment of unstable angina pectoris secondary to restenosis.
Design	Double blind, placebo controlled, randomized, single center.
Patients	200 patients with unstable angina hospitalized within 2-6 months of coronary angioplasty.
Follow-up	48-96 hours after randomization at which time coronary angiography was performed.
Treatment regimen	1) IV nitroglycerin infusion plus placebo heparin; 2) IV heparin 5000 U bolus plus 1000-1200 U/hour infusion plus placebo nitroglycerin; 3) IV nitroglycerin plus heparin; 4) placebo.
Additional therapy	Aspirin, ß-blockers, or calcium blockers allowed.

Randomized trial comparing IV nitroglycerin and heparin for treatment of unstable angina secondary to restenosis after coronary artery angioplasty (continued)

Results	75% of patients in the placebo group and heparin alone group developed recurrent angina vs 42.6% of patients in the nitroglycerin alone and 41.7% in the nitroglycerin plus heparin group ($p<0.003$). Refractory angina requiring angiography occurred in 22.9% of the placebo patients, 29.2% of the heparin patients, 4.3% of the nitroglycerin patients, and 4.2% of the combined patients ($p<0.002$). There was no interaction detected between heparin and nitroglycerin. Multivariate logistic regression analysis, that took into account the severity of restenosis, showed that the use of nitroglycerin highly predicted the absence of angina.
Conclusions	Nitroglycerin but not heparin prevented recurrent angina in patients with unstable angina secondary to restenosis.

Efegatran in Unstable Angina

Title	Anticoagulant properties, clinical efficacy and safety of efegatran, a direct thrombin inhibitor, in patients with unstable angina.
Authors	Klootwijk P, Lenderink T, Meij S, et al.
Reference	Eur Heart J 1999;20:1101-1111.
Disease	Unstable angina, acute coronary syndrome.
Purpose	To assess the efficacy and safety of efegatran sulphate, a direct thrombin inhibitor, in patients with unstable angina.
Design	Randomized, single blinded, dose ranging, multicenter.
Patients	432 patients, 21-75 years old, with unstable angina. Patients with suspected acute myocardial infarction or recent myocardial infarction, baseline EKG abnormalities, heparin therapy, current use of anticoagulants, recent administration of thrombolytic therapy and high risk for bleeding were excluded.
Follow-up	48 hours continuous EKG monitoring, clinical follow-up for 30 days.

Treatment regimen	In the dose ranging phase, patients were randomized to five doses of efegatran: the first 4 groups received an IV bolus of 0.1 mg/kg over 15 minutes, followed by continuous infusion of 0.105, 0.32, 0.63, or 0.84 mg/kg/h. Patients in the 5th group received a bolus of 0.3 mg/kg over 1 minute, followed by continuous infusion of 1.2 mg/kg/h. The study drug infusion was continued for 48±10 hours. In the parallel phase of the study patients were randomized to 3 groups: 1) efegatran 0.1 mg/kg bolus and 0.63 mg/kg/h infusion; 2) efegatran 0.3 mg/kg bolus and 1.2 mg/kg/h infusion; and 3) IV unfractionated heparin (5000 U bolus followed by a continuous infusion of 1000 U/h for 48±10 hours).
Additional therapy	Heparin was prohibited during efegatran infusion. After termination of the study drug infusion, nonstudy heparin could be initiated. All patients received aspirin 80 mg/d.
Results	There were 132 patients in the dose ranging phase and 300 in the parallel phase. Efegatran induced a dose dependent prolongation of the activated partial thromboplastin time (aPTT), with the highest dose of 1.2 mg/kg/h resulting in a steady state mean aPTT comparable to that of heparin. The aPTT was more stable with efegatran than with heparin. Prothrombin time (PT) was mildly increased with efegatran. Thrombin time was prolonged with a dose dependent manner by efegatran, whereas heparin did not affect thrombin time. Fibrinogen levels decreased with efegatran but not with heparin. All coagulation tests rapidly returned to normal range after discontinuation of efegatran. With continuous EKG monitoring, there was no significant difference between the number of patients with recurrent ischemia or the number or duration of ischemic episodes between the heparin group and the various efegatran groups. However, there was a trend towards less ≥30 minute ischemia with the highest doses of efegatran (11% and 23% in the 0.84 and 1.2 mg/kg/h groups) than with heparin (33%; p=0.068). Kaplan-Meier estimates of the probability of remaining free of recurrent ischemia during EKG monitoring were comparable among groups. At 7 days, the primary end point of recurrent

	angina, myocardial infarction, death or coronary intervention occurred in 71% in the heparin group vs 52%-71% in the various efegatran groups (p=NS), although the need for percutaneous interventions was slightly higher in the efegatran groups (8%-9%) than in the heparin group (4%). At 30 days 73%-81% of the patients in the efegatran groups reached a primary end point vs 81% in the heparin group, and death or acute myocardial infarction occurred in 3.2% in the efegatran groups vs 2.1% in the heparin group. Minor bleeding (p=0.001) and thrombophlebitis (p=0.0001) occurred more often with efegatran than with heparin, although there was no significant difference in the incidence of major bleeding (0.8% with efegatran vs 1.6% with heparin). No strokes occurred in this study.
Conclusions	Efegatran sulphate infusion provided a more stable anticoagulation effect than heparin. However, efegatran was not associated with better clinical outcomes and was associated with more thrombophlebitis and minor bleeding episodes.

SYMPHONY

Sibrafiban vs aspirin to yield maximum protection from ischemic heart events post acute coronary syndromes

Title	Comparison of sibrafiban with aspirin for prevention of cardiovascular events after acute coronary syndromes: A randomized trial.
Authors	The SYMPHONY Investigators.
Reference	Lancet 2000;355:337-345.
Disease	Acute coronary syndrome.
Purpose	To investigate whether sibrafiban, an oral glycoprotein IIb/IIIa receptor antagonist, would be more effective than aspirin in preventing cardiovascular events in patients with acute coronary syndromes.
Design	Randomized, double blind, multicenter.
Patients	9233 patients within 7 days of an acute coronary syndrome. All patients had to be clinically stable for 12 hours before enrollment, with Killip class ≤2. Patients at high risk for bleeding, previous stroke or intracerebral hemorrhage, anemia, thrombocytopenia, treatment with oral anticoagulants, antiplatelet agents or nonsteroidal anti-inflammatory agents, or renal failure were excluded.
Follow-up	90 days.
Treatment regimen	Randomization to aspirin 80 mg bid (n=3089), high dose sibrafiban (n=3039) or low dose sibrafiban (n=3105). The sibrafiban dose was between 3-6 mg bid, adjusted to body weight and serum creatinine.

SYMPHONY

Sibrafiban vs aspirin to yield maximum protection from ischemic heart events post acute coronary syndromes (continued)

Additional therapy	Other oral antiplatelet agents were prohibited, except for open label aspirin on the day of and the day after PCI. In case of stent implantation patients received a stent kit containing either ticlopidine (for the aspirin group) or placebo (for the sibrafiban groups).
Results	Premature discontinuation of the study drug occurred in 19.2% in the aspirin group, 22.3% in the low dose sibrafiban group and 23.8% in the high dose sibrafiban group. The primary end point of the study (death, myocardial [re]infarction, or severe recurrent ischemia at 90 days) occurred in 9.8% in the aspirin group, 10.1% in the low dose sibrafiban group and 10.1% in the high dose sibrafiban group (odds ratio for aspirin vs both the low- and high dose sibrafiban 1.03; 95% CI 0.87-1.21). Death or myocardial (re)infarction occurred in 7.0%, 7.4%, and 7.9%, respectively. There were no differences among the three groups concerning the predefined secondary end points of either all cause mortality, myocardial (re)infarction, severe recurrent ischemia, readmission, reversible coronary ischemia, or any revascularization. Large myocardial infarctions (CKMB >X5 the upper limit of normal) occurred less often in the aspirin group (37.4%) than in the low (45.3%) or high dose (49.7%) sibrafiban groups. Treatment effects were comparable among the various subgroups. Bleedings occurred in 13.0% in the aspirin group vs 18.7% and 25.4% in the low and high dose sibrafiban groups. Major bleedings occurred in 3.9%, 5.2%, and 5.7%, respectively. Thrombocytopenia was infrequent and did not differ among the treatment groups.
Conclusions	Sibrafiban had no advantage over aspirin for prevention of major ischemic events in stable patients after an acute coronary syndrome and was associated with higher bleeding rates than aspirin.

3. Stable Angina Pectoris and Silent Ischemia—Medical Therapy

ASIST

Atenolol Silent Ischemia Study

Title	Effects of treatment on outcome in mildly symptomatic patients with ischemia during daily life: the Atenolol Silent Ischemia Study (ASIST).
Authors	Pepine CJ, Cohn PF, Deedwania PC, et al.
Reference	Circulation 1994;90:762-768.
Disease	Coronary artery disease, silent myocardial ischemia.
Purpose	To assess whether atenolol therapy will decrease adverse outcome events in mildly symptomatic patients with coronary artery disease.
Design	Randomized, double blind, placebo controlled, multicenter.
Patients	306 patients with >50% stenosis of a major coronary artery, or previous myocardial infarction and transient ischemia documented by exercise ECG. Only patients with Canadian Cardiovascular Society class I or II, and without an abnormal ECG that could interfere with ambulatory ECG ST segment monitoring were included. Patients with unstable angina, myocardial infarction, or coronary revascularization within 3 months were excluded. Patients with contraindications to ß-blockers or with a need for antianginal medications other than nitrates, and patients with heart failure were excluded. The atenolol group included 152 patients and the placebo 154 patients.
Follow-up	1 year.
Treatment regimen	Atenolol (100 mg/d, in cases where adverse effects occurred, the dose was lowered to 50 mg/d) or placebo.

ASIST

Atenolol Silent Ischemia Study

(continued)

Results	After 4 weeks of therapy, the number (3.6±4.2 vs 1.7±4.6 episodes, p<0.001) and mean duration (30.0±3.3 vs 16.4±6.7 min, p<0.001) of ischemic episodes detected by 48 h of ambulatory ECG monitoring were reduced in the atenolol treated patients, compared to baseline recording, but not in the placebo group. After 1 year less patients in the atenolol group experienced death, VT/VF, myocardial infarction, hospitalization, aggravation of angina, or revascularization (11% vs 25%; relative risk 44%; 95% CI 26-75%; p=0.001). The atenolol treated patients had a longer time to first event (120 vs 79 days; p<0.001). The most significant predictor of event free survival in univariate and multivariate analysis was absence of ischemia on ambulatory ECG monitoring at 4 weeks. Side effects were comparable in both groups.
Conclusions	Treatment of asymptomatic or mildly symptomatic patients with coronary artery disease with atenolol reduced number and duration of ischemic episodes at 4 weeks and the risk for adverse events at 1 year.

CAPE

Circadian Anti-Ischemia Program in Europe

Title	Amlodipine reduces transient myocardial ischemia in patients with coronary artery disease: Double blind circadian antiischemia program in Europe (CAPE trial).
Authors	Deanfield JE, Detry J-M RG, Lichtlen PR, et al.
Reference	J Am Coll Cardiol 1994;24:1460–1467.
Disease	Coronary artery disease, angina pectoris.
Purpose	To evaluate the effect of once daily amlodipine on the circadian pattern of myocardial ischemia in patients with stable angina pectoris.
Design	Randomized, double blind, placebo controlled, multicenter.
Patients	315 males, age 35–80 years, with stable angina with ≥3 attacks/week. Patients with heart failure, uncontrolled arrhythmias, bradycardia, hypertension or hypotension, chronic therapy with calcium channel blockers, and ECG features that interfere with interpretation of ST segment changes were excluded. All patients had ≥4 ischemic episodes or ≥20 min of ST depression over 48 h ambulatory ECG monitoring.
Follow-up	Clinical follow-up and 48 h ambulatory monitoring at 8 weeks of phase II.
Treatment regimen	Phase I: 2 weeks of single blind placebo run in period. Phase II: randomization to amlodipine (started at 5 mg/d and increased to 10 mg/d) or placebo treatment for 8 weeks.

CAPE

Circadian Anti-Ischemia Program in Europe

(continued)

Additional therapy	Patients were instructed to maintain on stable doses of all concomitant cardiovascular medications. Nitroglycerin tablets were provided.
Results	Only 250 patients were fully evaluated for ambulatory ECG analysis. Amlodipine therapy resulted in greater reduction of the frequency of ST depression episodes (median reduction 60.0% vs 43.8%, p=0.025), ST segment integral (mm-min of ST depression)(median reduction 61.6% vs 49.5%, p=0.042), and total duration of ST depression (56% vs 49.5%, p=0.066) than placebo. The intrinsic circadian pattern of ischemia was maintained in both groups. Patients' diaries showed a significant reduction of anginal pain (70% vs 44%, p=0.0001) and in nitroglycerin consumption (67% vs 22%, p=0.0006) with amlodipine vs placebo. Adverse effects occurred in 17.3% of the amlodipine vs 13.3% of the placebo (p=0.422), discontinuation due to adverse events were 2.0% vs 4.4%, respectively (p=0.291).
Conclusions	Once daily amlodipine, in addition to regular anti-anginal therapy, reduced both symptomatic and asymptomatic ischemic episodes in patients with chronic stable angina.

ACIP

Asymptomatic Cardiac Ischemia Pilot Study

Title	a. The asymptomatic cardiac ischemia pilot (ACIP) study: Design of a randomized clinical trial, baseline data, and implications for a long term outcome trial. b. Effects of treatment strategies to suppress ischemia in patients with coronary artery disease: 12 week results of the asymptomatic cardiac ischemia pilot (ACIP) study. c. Asymptomatic cardiac ischemia pilot (ACIP) study: impact of antiischemia therapy on 12 week rest electrocardiogram and exercise test outcomes. d. Asymptomatic cardiac ischemia pilot (ACIP) study. Improvement of cardiac ischemia at 1 year after PTCA and CABG. e. Prognostic significance of myocardial ischemia detected by ambulatory electrocardiography, exercise treadmill testing, and electrocardiogram at rest to predict cardiac events by one year (The Asymptomatic Cardiac Ischemia Pilot [ACIP] Study). f. Asymptomatic cardiac ischemia pilot (ACIP) study 2 year follow-up. Outcomes of patients randomized to initial strategies of medical therapy vs revascularization.
Authors	a. Pepine CJ, Geller NL, Knatterud GL, et al. b. Knatterud GL, Bourassa MG, Pepine CJ, et al. c. Chaitman BR, Stone PH, Knatterud GL, et al. d. Bourassa MG, Knatterud GL, Pepine CJ, et al. e. Stone PH, Chaitman BR, Forman S, et al. f. Davies RF, Goldberg D, Forman S, et al.
Reference	a. J Am Coll Cardiol 1994;24:1-10. b. J Am Coll Cardiol 1994;24:11-20. c. J Am Coll Cardiol 1995;26:585-593. d. Circulation 1995;92:II1-II7. e. Am J Cardiol 1997; 80:1395-1401. f. Circulation 1997; 95:2037-2043.
Disease	Coronary artery disease.

ACIP

Asymptomatic Cardiac Ischemia Pilot Study

(continued)

Purpose	To compare 3 strategies of therapy (angina-guided medical therapy, ischemia guided medical therapy, and coronary revascularization) in reduction of myocardial ischemia at exercise testing after 12 weeks of therapy. f. As above. Purpose of this study was to describe 2 year clinical outcome of angina guided drug therapy, angina plus ischemia guided drug therapy, or revascularization by angioplasty or coronary artery bypass surgery.
Design	Randomized, open label, multicenter.
Patients	a+b. 618 patients. c+d. 558 patients with obstructive coronary artery disease suitable for revascularization, ≥1 episode of ischemia on 48 h ambulatory ECG monitoring, or evidence of ischemia on exercise test. f. 558 patients with coronary anatomy suitable to revascularization, randomized to: angina guided drug therapy (n=183), angina plus ischemia guided drug therapy (n=183) or revascularization (n=192).
Follow-up	12 week repeated exercise test. 1 year clinical follow-up. f. 2 years.
Treatment regimen	1. Angina guided medical therapy. 2. Angina + ambulatory ECG monitoring guided medical therapy. 3. Coronary revascularization. The medical therapy included randomization to either atenolol or diltiazem as the first drug, and addition of nifedipine to atenolol and isosorbide dinitrate to diltiazem.
Results	a+b. Ambulatory ECG ischemia was no longer present at 12 weeks in 39%, 41%, and 55% of the angina guided, ischemia guided, and revascularization strategies. All strategies reduced the median number of episode and total duration of ST depression. Revascularization was the most effective strategy ($p<0.001$, and $p=0.01$ for the number of episodes and total duration, respectively). More

patients were ischemia free in the atenolol + nifedipine (47%) than diltiazem + nitrates (32%, p=0.03).
c. Peak exercise time was increased by 0.5, 0.7, and 1.6 min in the angina guided, ischemia guided, and revascularization strategies from baseline to 12 weeks (p<0.001). The sum of exercise induced ST depression was similar at baseline. However, at 12 weeks ST depression during exercise was 7.4±5.7, 6.8±5.3, and 5.6±5.6 mm, (p=0.02).
d. At 12 weeks, ischemia on the ambulatory ECG monitoring was suppressed in 70% of the 78 CABG patients and in 46% of the 92 PTCA patients (p=0.002). Myocardial infarction or repeated revascularization occurred in 1 vs 7 of the CABG and PTCA patients (p<0.001).
e. In the two groups treated medically, there was an association between number of ischemic episodes on ambulatory monitoring and combined cardiac events at 1 year (p=0.003). In the ambulatory ECG monitored group there was a trend toward an association between reduction in number of ambulatory ECG ischemic episodes and reduction in combined cardiac events (p=0.06). This association was absent in the revascularization group. In the medically treated groups, the exercise duration on baseline exercise treadmill test was inversely associated with poor prognosis. Medical therapy only slightly improved exercise time. Exercise duration remained a significant prognosticator of outcome in the medically treated but not revascularization treated patients.
f. After 2 years, total mortality was 6.6% with angina guided therapy; 4.4% with ischemia guided therapy; and 1.1% with revascularization (p<0.02). Rates of death or myocardial infarction were 12.1%, 8.8%, and 4.7%, respectively (p<0.04). Rates of death, myocardial infarction or recurrent hospitalization for cardiac disease were 41.8%, 38.5%, and 23.1%, respectively (p<0.001). p values were significant for comparisons between revascularization and angina guided strategies.

Conclusions

Coronary revascularization significantly reduced the duration of silent ischemia on ambulatory ECG monitoring and the extent and frequency of exercise induced ischemia compared to the medical strategies.
f. Initial revascularization improved prognosis in these coronary artery disease patients at 2 years, compared to angina guided medical therapy.

TIBBS

Total Ischemic Burden Bisoprolol Study

Title	1. Medical treatment to reduce total ischemic burden: total ischemic burden bisoprolol study (TIBBS), a multicenter trial comparing bisoprolol and nifedipine. 2. Prognostic significance of transient ischemic episodes: response to treatment shows improved prognosis. Results of the Total Ischemic Burden Bisoprolol Study (TIBBS) follow-up. 3. Heart rate variability and ischemia in patients with coronary heart disease and stable angina pectoris. Influence of drug therapy and prognostic value.
Authors	1. von Arnim T, for the TIBBS Investigators. 2. Von Armin T, for the TIBBS Investigators. 3. Weber F, Schneider H, von Armin T, et al.
Reference	1. J Am Coll Cardiol 1995;25:231-238. 2. J Am Coll Cardiol 1996;28:20-24. 3. Eur Heart J 1999;20:38-50.
Disease	Coronary artery disease, stable angina pectoris.
Purpose	1. To compare the effects of bisoprolol and nifedipine on transient myocardial ischemia in patients with stable angina. 2. To assess the prognostic significance of transient ischemia, detected by ambulatory ECG, on cardiovascular events. 3. To compare the effects of bisoprolol and nifedipine on heart rate variability.
Design	Randomized, double blind, multicenter.

Patients	1. 330 patients with stable angina pectoris, positive exercise test with ST depression, and ≥2 episodes of transient myocardial ischemia on 48 hour ambulatory ECG monitoring. Patients with unstable angina, myocardial infarction within 3 months, bradycardia <50 bpm, AV block, or hypotension were excluded. 2. 520 patients. 3. 422 patients.
Follow-up	1. Exercise test and ambulatory ECG monitoring during the placebo phase, after 4 weeks of the first dose period and after 8 weeks (double dose period). 2. One year follow-up. 3. 48 hour ambulatory ECG monitoring during the placebo phase and after 8 weeks of therapy.
Treatment regimen	10 day placebo phase, and then randomization to either bisoprolol 10 mg/d or nifedipine slow release 20 mg/x2d for 4 weeks, and then the doses were doubled for an additional 4 weeks.
Additional therapy	Long acting nitrates, ß-blockers, calcium channel blockers, vasodilators, tricyclic antidepressants, digoxin, antiarrhythmic agents, and ß-mimetic agents were not permitted during the study.
Results	1. 4 weeks of bisoprolol 10 mg/d reduced the mean number of transient ischemic episodes from 8.1±0.6 to 3.2±0.4 episodes/48 hours (mean change -4.9, 95% CI -5.8 to -4.0). Nifedipine 20 mg/x2d reduced the number of ischemic episodes from 8.3±0.5 to 5.9±0.4 episodes/48 hour (mean change -2.5, 95% CI -4.3 to -1.5). The effect of bisoprolol was almost twice that of nifedipine (bisoprolol vs nifedipine p=0.0001). Total duration of ischemic episodes were reduced from 99.3±10.1 to 31.9±5.5 min/48 hours by bisoprolol (mean change -67.4, 95% CI -84.0 to -50.7), and from

101.0±9.1 to 72.6±8.1 min/48 hours by nifedipine (mean change -28.4, 95% CI -45.9 to -10.9)(bisoprolol vs nifedipine p=0.0001). Doubling the dose of the medications resulted in only small additional effects that were significant only for bisoprolol. Bisoprolol reduced the heart rate at onset of ischemia by 13.7±1.4 bpm (p<0.001). Heart rate was not changed by nifedipine. 73.7% of the bisoprolol 10 mg/d vs 42.4% of the nifedipine 20 mg/x2d showed ≥50% reduction in the number of ischemic episodes (p<0.0001). The corresponding rates for the higher dose were 80.5% vs 49.2% (p<0.0001). Only bisoprolol showed a marked circadian effect by reducing the morning peak of ischemia.

2. 120 patients (23.1%) experienced a total of 145 events of transient ischemia, detected by ambulatory ECG recording. Patients with >6 episodes had an event rate of 32.5%, patients with 2-6 episodes had an event rate of 25.0%, and patients with <2 episodes had 13.2% event rate (p<0.001). The combined end point (death, myocardial infarction, hospitalization for unstable angina) occurred in 12.2% of the patients with ≥2 transient ischemic episodes vs in only 4.7% in those with ≤1 episode (p=0.0049). Patients in whom transient ischemic episodes were not detected at all after initiation of therapy had 17.5% events at one year compared with 32.3% in those without 100% response to therapy (p=0.008). One year event rate was 22.1% among the bisoprolol treated patients vs 33.1% among the nifedipine treated patients (p=0.033).

3. Nifedipine reduced the mean values of the heart rate variability parameters tested. Bisoprolol increased the r-MSSD (square root of the mean of the squared differences of successive corrected RR intervals) from 27±12 to 37±18 (p≤0.05). However, bisoprolol did not change the SDNN (standard deviation of the mean of all corrected RR intervals) and the SDANN (standard deviation of the means of all corrected RR intervals, calculated at 5 min intervals) values. The increase in heart rate variability with therapy was associated with a trend towards better outcome.

Conclusions	1. Both agents reduced the number and duration of ischemic episodes in patients with stable angina. Bisoprolol was more effective than nifedipine. 2. Frequent episodes of transient ischemia, detected by ambulatory ECG monitoring, are a marker for an adverse outcome in patients with stable angina pectoris. Bisoprolol was associated with better one year outcome than nifedipine. 3. An increase in heart rate variability was detected only with bisoprolol, but not with nifedipine. An increase in heart rate variability parameters, combined with complete suppression of transient ischemic episodes was associated with better outcome.

IMAGE

International Multicenter Angina Exercise Study

Title	Combination therapy with metoprolol and nifedipine vs monotherapy in patients with stable angina pectoris. Results of the International Multicenter Angina Exercise (IMAGE) Study.
Authors	Savonitto S, Ardissino D, Egstrup K, et al.
Reference	J Am Coll Cardiol 1996;27:311-316.
Disease	Angina pectoris.
Purpose	To compare the efficacy of combination therapy with metoprolol and nifedipine vs either drug alone in patients with stable angina pectoris.
Design	Randomized, double blind, placebo controlled (second stage), multicenter.
Patients	280 patients, age ≤75 years, with stable angina for ≥6 months and a positive exercise test. Patients with myocardial infarction within 6 months, heart failure, inability to perform ≥3 min exercise test, or those with severe angina that preclude temporary cessation of medications, were excluded.
Follow-up	Exercise test at baseline, after the 6 weeks of monotherapy and after 10 weeks.
Treatment regimen	After 2 week placebo run in period, patients were randomized to metoprolol 200 mg/d or nifedipine retard 20 mg X2/d for 6 weeks. Then, patients were randomized to addition of the second drug or placebo for 4 more weeks.

IMAGE

International Multicenter Angina Exercise Study (continued)

Results	249 patients completed the study. By the end of 6 weeks the nifedipine treated group increased the mean duration of exercise time until 1 mm ST depression by 43 sec compared with baseline (95% CI 16–69 sec, $p<0.01$), and the metoprolol group by 70 sec (95% CI 47–92 sec, $p<0.01$). The improvement was greater with metoprolol ($p<0.05$). At week 10, the exercise time did not increase further in the patients who received placebo in addition to the metoprolol or nifedipine. However, addition of nifedipine to metoprolol resulted in further increase of the time 108 sec more than in the baseline test (95% CI 71–145 sec), and addition of metoprolol to nifedipine in 107 sec (95% CI 64–151 sec) more than in the baseline test ($p<0.05$ vs placebo). Analysis of the results in individual patients revealed that the additive effect was seen mainly in those who respond poorly to monotherapy.
Conclusions	Both drugs were effective as monotherapy in prolongation the exercise time (metoprolol more than nifedipine). The prolongation of exercise time, observed in the combination therapy, is not the result of an additive effect, but probably due to the effect of the second class of drug in patients not responding to the first one.

TREND

Trial on Reversing ENdothelial Dysfunction

Title	ACE inhibition with quinapril improves endothelial vasomotor dysfunction in patients with coronary artery disease. The TREND (trial on reversing endothelial dusfunction) study.
Authors	Mancini GBJ, Henry GC, Macaya C, et al.
Reference	Circulation 1996;94:258–265.
Disease	Coronary artery disease.
Purpose	To evaluate whether quinapril, an ACE inhibitor, improves endothelial dysfunction in normotensive patients with coronary artery disease and no heart failure, cardiomyopathy, or major lipid abnormalities.
Design	Randomized, double blind, placebo controlled, multicenter.
Patients	129 patients, ≤75 years old, with documented coronary artery disease: single or double vessel disease (>50% diameter stenosis) that required a nonsurgical revascularization, and one adjacent coronary artery with <40% stenosis that had never been revascularized. This artery had to show endothelial dysfunction defined as either constriction or no response to acetylcholine. Patients with LDL cholesterol >165 mg/dL, hypertension (>160 mm Hg systolic or >90 mm Hg diastolic blood pressure), previous CABG, history of coronary spasm, coronary revascularization within 3 months, myocardial infarction within 7days, left ventricular ejection fraction <0.40, type I diabetes mellitus, valvular heart disease, hepatic or renal dysfunction, 2nd or 3rd degree AV block, or lipid lowering therapy within 6 months were excluded.

Follow-up	Cardiac catheterization with assessment of the response to intracoronary injection of acetylcholine 10^{-6} and 10^{-4} mol/L over 2 min before revascularization and after 6 months of therapy.
Treatment regimen	Quinapril 40 mg/d or placebo for 6 months.
Additional therapy	All vasoactive medications, except for ß-blockers and sublingual nitrates, were discontinued 12 h before angiography.
Results	105 patients underwent repeated angiography at 6 months. At baseline, before initiation of study medications, the constrictive response to acetylcholine was comparable between the placebo and quinapril groups (4.4% vs 6.1% after infusion of 10^{-6} mol/L and 9.4% vs 14.3% after infusion of 10^{-4} mol/L ($p=0.125$), respectively). After 6 months of therapy there was no change in the response to acetylcholine in the placebo group (4.5% and 10.5% after acetylcholine 10^{-6} mol/L and 10^{-4} mol/L, respectively), whereas the quinapril treated patients showed less constrictor response (1.6% and 2.3%, respectively) compared with the baseline study ($p<0.014$). Responses, expressed as net change from baseline, improved by 4.5±3.0% and 12.1±3.0% at each acetylcholine dose in the quinapril group, whereas the placebo group responses did not change (-0.1±2.8% and -0.8±2.9%, respectively, $p<0.002$). The analysis of the response to a nitroglycerin bolus (100–700 μg) revealed no difference between the groups at baseline ($p=0.349$) and after 6 months ($p=0.336$).
Conclusions	ACE inhibition with quinapril improved endothelial function in normotensive patients without severe hyperlipidemia or heart failure.

Efficacy of mibefradil compared with amlodipine in suppressing exercise induced and daily silent ischemia. Results of a multicenter, placebo controlled trial.

Title	Efficacy of mibefradil compared with amlodipine in suppressing exercise induced and daily silent ischemia. Results of a multicenter, placebo controlled trial.
Author	Tzivoni D, Kadr H, Braat S, et al.
Reference	Circulation 1997; 96: 2557-2564.
Disease	Coronary artery disease, stable angina pectoris.
Purpose	To determine the effects of mibefradil (a new calcium channel blocker which blocks the T type channel) on exercise induced and daily silent ischemia in patients with stable angina pectoris and compare its efficacy to amlodipine.
Design	Prospective, randomized, double blind, placebo controlled, parallel design trial, multicenter. 1 to 2 week washout period of long acting antianginals. 1 week placebo run in phase with exercise tests and 48 h ECG ambulatory monitoring. 2 week treatment phase with repeat exercise test and ambulatory monitoring.
Patients	309 patients with coronary artery disease, stable angina, and positive exercise tests.
Follow-up	3 weeks.
Treatment regimen	For initial treatment period patients were randomized to 1 of 5 groups: placebo; 25, 50, or 100 mg of mibefradil; amlodipine 5 mg. At one week mibefradil doses were increased to 50, 100, or 150 mg, and amlodipine to 10 mg.

Efficacy of mibefradil compared with amlodipine in suppressing exercise induced and daily silent ischemia. Results of a multicenter, placebo controlled trial.

(continued)

Results	At 100 mg and 150 mg (but not 50 mg) mibefradil increased exercise duration by 55.5 and 51.0 sec, respectively vs placebo, p<0.001. At 100 and 150 mg mibefradil increased time to onset of angina (by 98.3 and 82.7 sec, respectively; p<0.001) and increased time to 1 mm ST depression (by 81.7 and 94.3 sec, respectively, p<0.001). Amlodipine at 10 mg/day increased time to onset of angina (by 38.5 seconds; p=0.036). Mibefradil 100 mg and 150 mg decreased the number of episodes of silent ischemia on ambulatory monitoring as did 10 mg of amlodipine. There was a nonsignificant trend toward a greater reduction in number of silent ischemic episodes at higher doses of mibefradil than amlodipine. As expected, mibefradil but not amlodipine reduced heart rate.
Conclusions	Mibefradil 100 or 150 mg once daily was effective in improving exercise tolerance and reducing ischemic episodes during ambulatory electrocardiographic monitoring. Amlodipine 10 mg improved time to onset of angina during exercise and had somewhat less of an effect of reducing silent ischemic episodes. (Note: mibefradil was taken off the U.S. market in 1998, in part due to interactions with other drugs).

THE ESBY STUDY

Electrical Stimulation Bypass Surgery

Title	Electrical stimulation vs coronary artery bypass surgery in severe angina pectoris. The ESBY study.
Author	Mannheimer C, Eliasson T, Augustinsson L-E.
Reference	Circulation 1998; 97:1157–1163.
Disease	Coronary artery disease; angina pectoris.
Purpose	To determine whether spinal cord stimulation (SCS) can be used as an alternative to coronary artery bypass grafting (CABG) in selected patients with coronary artery disease.
Design	Randomized, prospective, open comparison between SCS and CABG.
Patients	104 patients with symptomatic coronary artery disease who were considered to have only symptomatic (not prognostic) benefit from CABG, to be at increased risk of surgery, and to be ineligible for percutaneous transluminal coronary angioplasty.
Follow-up	6 months.
Treatment regimen	53 patients were randomized to SCS and 51 to CABG.

THE ESBY STUDY

Electrical Stimulation Bypass Surgery

(continued)

Results	Both treatments reduced angina to a similar extent. CABG resulted in an increase in exercise capacity, less ST segment depression on exercise compared to SCS; rate pressure product on maximum and comparable workloads were higher for the CABG patients. 7 patients died in the CAGB group and 1 died in the SCS group. By intention-to-treat mortality was lower in the SCS group (p=0.02). There also was less cerebrovascular morbidity in the SCS group.
Conclusions	SCS may be a therapeutic alternative for this group of patients with coronary artery disease.

FEMINA

Felodipine ER and Metoprolol CR in Angina

Title	Addition of felodipine to metoprolol vs replacement of metoprolol by felodipine in patients with angina pectoris despite adequate ß-blockade. Results of the felodipine ER and metoprolol CR in angina (FEMINA) study.
Authors	Dunselman P, Liem AH, Verdel G, et al.
Reference	Eur Heart J 1997;18:1755-1764.
Disease	Angina pectoris-stable.
Purpose	To compare the effect of metoprolol alone, adding felodipine to metoprolol or replacement of metoprolol by felodipine in patients with angina pectoris despite metoprolol therapy.
Design	Randomized, double blind, parallel, multicenter.
Patients	356 patients, aged 18-75 years, with angina pectoris, who had been receiving metoprolol controlled release 100-200 mg/d before enrollment and who had positive exercise tests despite therapy.
Follow-up	Clinical follow-up and repeated exercise tests at baseline, 2 and 5 weeks.
Treatment regimen	Randomization to continuation of metoprolol, replacement of metoprolol by felodipine ER 5-10 mg/d or a combination of metoprolol and felodipine ER.

FEMINA

Felodipine ER and Metoprolol CR in Angina

(continued)

Results	A total of 324 patients completed the study. After 5 weeks of therapy there was no difference among groups in time until end of exercise and time until onset of pain. The felodipine/metoprolol treated patients had 43 sec increase in the time until 1 mm ST depression (95% CI 20–65 sec; p<0.05). Both ST depression at highest comparable workload (0.46 mm, 95% CI 0.19–0.72; p<0.05) and maximal ST depression (difference from baseline) decreased in the combination group (0.49 mm; 95% CI 0.23–0.74; p<0.05). Exercise results in the felodipine alone treated patients were comparable to that of patients who received metoprolol alone. However, felodipine resulted in an increase in heart rate and in rate pressure product. Adverse effects occurred in 19 of the metoprolol alone treated patients, 28 in the metoprolol/felodipine treated patients (p=0.15 vs metoprolol alone), and 50 in the felodipine treated patients (p<0.01 vs metoprolol alone).
Conclusions	Adding felodipine to metoprolol is preferred to replacement of metoprolol with felodipine in patients with angina pectoris despite ß-blocker therapy.

SAPAT

The Swedish Angina Pectoris Aspirin Trial

Title	Double blind trial of aspirin in primary prevention of myocardial infarction in patients with stable chronic angina pectoris.
Authors	Juul-Moller S, Edvardsson N, Jahmatz B, et al.
Reference	Lancet 1992;340:1421-1425.
Disease	Angina pectoris.
Purpose	To assess the efficacy of aspirin in stable angina.
Design	Randomized, double blind, placebo controlled, multicenter.
Patients	2035 patients, 30-80 years old with stable angina pectoris. Patients already on aspirin, anticoagulants, nonsteroidal anti-inflammatory drugs, class I antiarrhythmic drugs or verapamil, patients with resting heart rate <55/min, history of myocardial infarction, chronic obstructive lung disease, active peptic ulcer, type I or uncontrolled diabetes mellitus, or hypersensitivity to aspirin were excluded.
Follow-up	A median of 50 (range 23-76) months.
Treatment regimen	Randomization to aspirin 75 mg/d (n=1009) or placebo (n=1026).
Additional therapy	Sotalol in increasing dose until symptoms were controlled.

SAPAT

The Swedish Angina Pectoris Aspirin Trial

(continued)

Results

At the end of the follow-up period there were 81 primary events (myocardial infarction or sudden death) in the aspirin group vs 124 in the placebo group (34% reduction; p=0.003). Aspirin therapy decreased the occurrence of sudden death by 38% (p=0.097), and nonfatal myocardial infarction by 39% (p=0.006). However, the incidence of fatal myocardial infarction was not changed. Vascular events were reduced by 32% with aspirin (p<0.001), stroke by 25% (p=0.246), and all cause mortality by 22% (p=0.103). There was no difference in the number of coronary artery bypass procedures between the aspirin and placebo groups. Treatment withdrawal due to adverse effects occurred in 109 patients of the aspirin group vs 100 patients of the placebo group (p=NS), bleedings in 27 patients vs 16 patients (p=NS), and major bleeding in 20 patients and 13 patients (p=NS), respectively. In a multivariate regression model the only variables found to be independently associated with primary events were aspirin therapy, gender, diabetes mellitus type II, and serum cholesterol levels. The relative risk of aspirin therapy vs placebo was 0.68 (95% CI 0.49-0.93).

Conclusions

Low dose aspirin, added to sotalol therapy reduced the occurrence of cardiovascular events, especially nonfatal myocardial infarction and vascular events in patients with stable angina pectoris without prior myocardial infarction. However, the effect on total mortality, fatal myocardial infarction, sudden death, and stroke were not statistically significant.

TIBET

The Total Ischaemic Burden European Trial

Title	a. The Total Ischaemic Burden European Trial (TIBET). Effects of atenolol, nifedipine SR and their combination on the exercise test and total ischaemic burden in 608 patients with stable angina. b. The Total Ischaemic Burden European Trial (TIBET). Effects of atenolol, nifedipine SR, and their combination on outcome in patients with chronic stable angina.
Authors	a. Fox KM, Mulcahy D, Findlay I, et al. b. Dargie HJ, Ford I, Fox KM, on behalf of the TIBET study group.
Reference	a. Eur Heart J 1996;17:96-103. b. Eur Heart J 1996;17:104-112.
Disease	Angina pectoris.
Purpose	To compare the effects of atenolol, nifedipine and their combination on exercise parameters, ambulatory ischemic activity, and prognosis in patients with mild stable angina pectoris and to evaluate the relationship between presence of ischemic events on ambulatory 48 h Holter ECG monitoring and outcome.
Design	Randomized, double blind, parallel group, multicenter.
Patients	a. 608, b. 682 patients (86% men), 40-79 years old, with stable angina pectoris over the preceding 3 months who were not being considered for revascularization and who had positive exercise test after a 2 week washout phase. Patients with recent (<3 months) coronary revascularization or myocardial infarction, conduction disturbances, contraindications to either nifedipine or atenolol, or medications that might affect the interpretation of the ST segment shift during exercise test were excluded.

TIBET

The Total Ischaemic Burden European Trial

(continued)

Follow-up	a. 1 year. Exercise test (treadmill Bruce protocol or bicycle protocol) at baseline, 2 and 6 weeks after randomization. 48 h Holter ambulatory ECG monitoring at baseline and 6 weeks. b. An average of 2 years or until death had occurred (range 1 to 3 years).
Treatment regimen	a.+ b. After 2 single blind run in phases of 2 weeks active combination therapy (to confirm tolerance) followed by 2 weeks placebo treatment, patients were randomized to atenolol 50 mg bid (n=205), nifedipine slow release 20 mg bid (n=202), or their combination (n=201). b. At the 6 week visit, the nifedipine dose could be increased to 40 mg bid.
Results	a. Atenolol alone and in combination caused a significant fall in resting heart rate (sitting heart rate decreased by 15.4 and 13.5 BPM in the atenolol alone and atenolol+nifedipine group, respectively), whereas nifedipine alone caused a 2.9 BPM increase in sitting heart rate. All three regimens caused a significant fall in blood pressure ($p<0.01$), which was more pronounced in the combination group. All three treatment regimens caused significant improvements in total exercise time, time to pain, time to 1 mm ST depression and maximum ST depression during exercise. Changes from baseline were significant for all these variables in all groups, but there was no significant difference among the three groups. All three groups had a significant reduction in the incidence of ischemic episodes during therapy, without a significant difference between the groups. b. There was no evidence of a relationship between the presence, frequency or total duration of ischemic ECG changes during continuous ambulatory Holter monitoring, either at baseline or during therapy, and cardiac mortality, the occurrence of myocardial infarction, unstable angina, revascularization, and treatment failure. Cardiac mortality, myocardial infarction, or unstable angina occurred in 12.8% of the atenolol group, 11.2% of the nifedipine group, and 8.5% of the combination group (p=NS). Comparison of the time to these events among

the 3 groups, using the logrank test, was insignificant (p=0.32). However, there was a non-significant trend towards less events in the combination group. During follow-up 27% of the atenolol group, 40% of the nifedipine, and 29% of the combination group withdrew from the study (p=0.001).

Conclusions

a. Combination of nifedipine and atenolol provided no additional benefit over either drug alone in patients with mild chronic angina pectoris.
b. Ischemic ECG changes on ambulatory Holter monitoring failed to predict prognosis in patients with mild chronic stable angina. Compliance was poorest with the nifedipine alone group, but there was no significant difference in prognosis among the three treatment groups.

Carvedilol vs Metoprolol

Title	Comparison of safety and efficacy of carvedilol and metoprolol in stable angina pectoris.
Authors	Van der Does R, Hauf-Zachariou U, Pfarr E, et al.
Reference	Am J Cardiol 1999;83:643-649.
Disease	Angina pectoris.
Purpose	To compare the safety and efficacy of carvedilol and metoprolol in younger and elderly patients with stable angina pectoris.
Design	Randomized, double blind, multicenter.
Patients	368 patients, ≤80 years old, with chronic stable exertional angina pectoris, documented coronary artery disease. Patients should have positive exercise test limited by moderate anginal pain associated with ST depression at the end of the 7 day run in phase before enrollment. Patients with recent (<3 months) myocardial infarction or CABG, left main stenosis, marked left ventricular hypertrophy, significant valvular disease, decompensated heart failure, obstructive lung disease, insulin dependent diabetes mellitus, or use of other antianginal medications were excluded.
Follow-up	13 weeks. An exercise test at the end of period I, II, and III.
Treatment regimen	Randomization in a 2:1 ratio to carvedilol or metoprolol. After a 7 day washout/run in period, patients received either low dose carvedilol (25 mg bid) or low dose metoprolol (50 mg bid) for 4 weeks (period II), then the doses were titrated to carvedilol 50 mg bid or metoprolol 100 mg bid, if total exercise time did not increase by ≥ 1 min systolic blood pressure was ≥100 mm Hg and heart rate ≥50 bpm, for 8 weeks (period III).

(continued)

Additional therapy	α-blockers, other ß-blockers, calcium antagonists, long acting nitrates, digitalis, quinidine, tricyclic antidepressants, phenothiazines and monoamine oxidase inhibitors were prohibited.
Results	248 patients were randomized to carvedilol and 120 to metoprolol. 345 patients completed period II, and 332 period III. Adverse effects occurred in 25% of the carvedilol vs 30% in the metoprolol group (p=0.137). The percentages of patients ≥65 years old with adverse events was slightly lower in the carvedilol group. Dizziness, the most common adverse effect, occurred in 4.8% of the carvedilol group vs 5.0% of the metoprolol group. Postural hypotension occurred in 0.8% of the carvedilol group vs 0 of the metoprolol group. Both metoprolol and carvedilol were associated with improvement in exercise test variables (total exercise time, time to onset of anginal pain, and time to onset of 1 mm ST segment depression). The median and quartiles of the prolongation in total exercise time were +60 (0; +120) seconds both with carvedilol and metoprolol. Time to angina was prolonged by +77 (+20; +140) seconds in the carvedilol group vs +76 (+25; +155) seconds in the metoprolol group. In contrast, prolongation of the time to 1 mm ST depression was greater with carvedilol (+75.5 [+47; +154] seconds) than with metoprolol (+60 [+0; +146] seconds)(p<0.05). Heart rate, systolic blood pressure and rate pressure product at maximal exercise at the end of the fist and third periods were comparable between the 2 groups.
Conclusions	Both metoprolol and carvedilol at high doses were safe and well tolerated. Both agents improved exercise performance. The increment in time to 1 mm ST depression was greater with carvedilol than with metoprolol.

A new pharmacological treatment for intermittent claudication: Results of a randomized, multicenter trial.

Title	A new pharmacological treatment for intermittent claudication: Results of a randomized, multicenter trial.
Authors	Beebe HG, Dawson DL, Cutler BS, et al.
Reference	Arch Intern Med 1999;159:2041-2050.
Disease	Claudication, peripheral vascular disease.
Purpose	To evaluate safety and efficacy of cilostazol, an inhibitor of platelet aggregation with vasodilating effects in patients with intermittent claudication.
Design	Multicenter, randomized, double blind, placebo controlled.
Patients	516 men and women age ≥40 years with a history of at least 6 months of stable, intermittent claudication with reproducible walking distances on screening treadmill tests.
Follow-up	24 weeks.
Treatment regimen	Cilostazol 100 mg or 50 mg orally twice a day.

A new pharmacological treatment for intermittent claudication: Results of a randomized, multicenter trial.

(continued)

Results	End points included exercise treadmill pain free and maximal walking distances, Doppler measured peripheral limb pressures, quality of life, and functional status questionnaires. 93% of patients had a history of smoking; more than one-third were current smokers. At 24 weeks, improvement in pain free walking distance was 59% in the 100 mg cilostazol group and 48% in the 50 mg group vs 20% with placebo ($p<0.001$ vs 100 mg and 50 mg.) Maximal walking distance improved by 51% in the 100 mg cilostazol group, 38% in the 50 mg group, and 15% in the placebo group ($p<0.001$ vs both treatment groups). The arithmetic mean increase was from 129.7 m at baseline to 259 m at 24 weeks for cilostazol 100 mg and from 131.5 at baseline to 198.8 m with cilostazol 50 mg. Improvements in treadmill times were observed as early as 4 weeks. Cilostazol also was associated with improvements in quality of life and functional status (which asked various questions about pain and discomfort with physical activities). There were no differences among the 3 groups in combined cardiovascular morbidity or all cause mortality. The most common side effects were headache, loose or soft stools, diarrhea, dizziness, and palpitation.
Conclusions	Cilostazol improved walking distance (both maximal and pain free) in patients with intermittent claudication.

MUST-EECP

Multicenter Study of Enhanced External Counterpulsation

Title	The multicenter study of enhanced external counterpulsation (MUST-EECP): Effect of EECP on exercise induced myocardial ischemia and anginal episodes.
Authors	Arora RR, Chou TM, Jain D, et al.
Reference	J Am Coll Cardiol 1999;33:1833-1840.
Disease	Coronary artery disease; stable angina pectoris.
Purpose	To determine the safety and efficacy of enhanced external counterpulsation.
Design	Randomized, placebo (sham) controlled, multicenter.
Patients	139 patients with chronic stable angina. Patients of I-III Canadian Cardiovascular Society Classification of angina were eligible with documented CAD and positive exercise tolerance test.
Follow-up	4-7 weeks.
Treatment regimen	Enhanced external counterpulsation (35 hours) or sham over 4-7 weeks. Cuffs were wrapped around the patient's legs. The cuffs were inflated with compressed air in sequence synchronized with the cardiac cycle. The technique increases retrograde aortic blood flow during diastole and decreases vascular impedance.
Additional therapy	Nitrates, aspirin, other antianginal agents.

MUST-EECP

Multicenter Study of Enhanced External Counterpulsation

(continued)

Results	Primary end point was exercise duration and time to development of ≥1 mm ST segment depression. In the active counterpulsation group exercise duration increased from 426±20 seconds at baseline to 470±20 seconds post-treatment. In the sham group exercise duration was 432±22 seconds at baseline and increased to 464±22 seconds post treatment (p=NS between groups). Change in time to ≥1 mm ST segment depression increased in the active counterpulsation group by 37±11 seconds whereas it decreased in the sham group (-4±12 sec; p=0.01). In patients who finished ≥34 sessions of active counterpulsation, angina counts (self reported episodes of angina per 24 hours) were 0.72±0.14 at baseline and 0.57±0.38 post treatment; in the sham group, angina counts were 0.77±0.14 at baseline and 0.76±0.22 post treatment. Difference between groups in change in angina counts was significant (p<0.035). There was a nonsignificant trend toward a reduction in sublingual nitroglycerin use in treated patients.
Conclusions	Enchanced external counterpulsation decreased angina frequency and improved time to exercise induced ischemia.

4. Interventional Cardiology

a. PTCA or CABG vs Medical Therapy

CASS

Coronary Artery Surgery Study

Title	a. Coronary artery surgery study (CASS): A randomized trial of coronary artery bypass surgery. Survival data. b. Myocardial infarction and mortality in the coronary artery surgery study (CASS) randomized trial. c. 10 year follow-up of survival and myocardial infarction in the randomized coronary artery surgery study. d. 10 year follow-up of quality of life in patients randomized to receive medical therapy or coronary artery bypass graft surgery. The coronary artery surgery study (CASS).
Authors	a+b. CASS Principal Investigators and Their Associates. c. Alderman EL, Bourassa MG, Cohen LS, et al. d. Rogers WJ, Coggin CJ, Gersh BJ, et al.
Reference	a. Circulation 1983;68:939-950. b. N Engl J Med 1984;310:750-758. c. Circulation 1990;82:1629-1646. d. Circulation 1990;82:1647-1658.
Disease	Coronary artery disease, angina pectoris.
Purpose	To compare the effects of coronary artery bypass grafting surgery and medical therapy on mortality and morbidity in patients with mild angina or aymptomatic patients after myocardial infarction with coronary artery disease.
Design	Randomized, open label, multicenter.
Patients	780 patients, ≤65 years of age, with angina pectoris Canadian Cardiovascular Society Class I or II, or myocardial infarction >3 weeks before randomization. Patients with prior coronary bypass surgery, unstable angina, heart failure (NYHA class III or IV) were excluded.
Follow-up	10 years.

CASS

Coronary Artery Surgery Study (continued)

Treatment regimen	Coronary artery bypass surgery or medical therapy.
Additional therapy	Common medical care including medications.
Results	The average annual mortality rate was 1.1% in the surgical group vs 1.6% in the medical group (p=NS). Annual mortality rates in patients with single, double, and 3 vessel disease were 0.7% vs 1.4%, 1.0% vs 1.2%, and 1.5% vs 2.1%, in the surgical and medical groups respectively. The differences were not significant. The annual mortality rate for patients with ejection fraction <0.50 was 1.7% vs 3.3% in the surgical and medical groups. In these patients the probability of survival after 5 years was 83±4% in the medical vs 93±3% in the surgical groups (p=0.11). The annual rate of bypass surgery in the medical group was 4.7%. 6% had surgery within 6 months and 40% within 10 years. Nonfatal Q wave myocardial infarction occurred in 14% vs 11% in the surgical and medical group after 5 years (p=NS). The 5 year probability of remaining alive and free from infarction was 83% vs 82% (p=NS). There was no significant difference in survival or myocardial infarction curves between subgroups of patients assigned to medical vs surgical therapy. At 10 years 82% of the surgical vs 79% of the medical groups were alive (p=NS), and 66% vs 69%, respectively were free of death and myocardial infarction (p=NS). However, 79% vs 61% of the surgical and medical patients with initial ejection fraction <0.50 were alive after 10 years (p=0.01), while more patients with ejection fraction ≥0.50 on the medical therapy were free of death and infarction after 10 years (75% vs 68%, p=0.04). 66% vs 30%, 63% vs 38%, and 47% vs 42% of the surgical and medical groups were free from angina after 1, 5, and 10 years. By 5 years indexes of quality of life appeared superior in the surgery group. However, after 10 years the differences were less apparent.
Conclusions	Coronary bypass surgery did not prolong life or prevent myocardial infarction as compared with medical therapy in patients with mild angina or patients who are asymptomatic after myocardial infarction. However, long term survival was improved by surgical therapy in patients with initial ejection fraction <0.50.

ACME

Angioplasty Compared to Medicine

Title	A comparison of angioplasty with medical therapy in the treatment of single vessel coronary artery disease.
Authors	Parisi AF, Folland ED, Hartigan P, et al.
Reference	N Engl J Med 1992;326:10-16.
Disease	Coronary artery disease, stable angina pectoris.
Purpose	To compare the results after 6 months of angioplasty vs medical therapy in patients with stable angina pectoris and single vessel coronary artery disease.
Design	Randomized, multicenter.
Patients	212 patients with stable angina pectoris, positive exercise test, or myocardial infarction within the past 3 months, and 70-99% stenosis of the proximal 2/3 of a coronary artery.
Follow-up	Clinical evaluation every month. Exercise test and angiography after 6 months.
Treatment regimen	1. Medical therapy: A stepped care approach including nitrates, ß-blockers, and calcium blockers. 2. Coronary angioplasty + calcium blocker for 1 month, and nitroglycerin during and for 12 h after the angioplasty.
Additional therapy	Oral aspirin 325 mg/d.

ACME

Angioplasty Compared to Medicine

(continued)

Results	Angioplasty was successful in 80 of the 100 patients who actually underwent the procedure. 2 patients in the angioplasty group required emergency coronary artery bypass surgery. After 6 months, 16 of the angioplasty group had repeated angioplasty. Of the 107 patients assigned to medical therapy, 11 underwent angioplasty. Myocardial infarction occurred in 5 and 3 of the patients assigned to angioplasty and medical therapy. After 6 months, 64% and 46% of the angioplasty and medical groups were free of angina ($p<0.01$). The angioplasty group were able to increase their total duration of exercise by 2.1 min, while the medical group by only 0.5 min ($p<0.0001$). The maximal heart rate blood pressure product decreased by 2800 units in the medical group, while it increased by 1800 units in the angioplasty group ($p<0.0001$). The overall psychological-well-being score improved by 8.6 and 2.4 in the angioplasty and medical therapy groups ($p=0.03$).
Conclusions	Angioplasty offers earlier and better relief of angina than medical therapy and is associated with better performance on the exercise test in patients with single vessel disease. However, the initial costs and the complication rates are higher with angioplasty.

RITA-2

Coronary Angioplasty vs Medical Therapy for Angina

Title	Coronary angioplasty vs medical therapy for angina: the second randomized intervention treatment of angina (RITA-2).
Authors	RITA-2 trial participants.
Reference	Lancet 1997;350:461–468.
Disease	Coronary artery disease.
Purpose	To compare 2 initial strategies for patients with coronary artery disease: initial coronary angioplasty vs conservative medical therapy.
Design	Randomized, multicenter.
Patients	1018 patients, >18 years old, with angiographically proven coronary artery disease considered to be suitable for both medical therapy and coronary angioplasty. Patients in whom myocardial revascularization was mandatory, patients with previous myocardial revascularization, left main coronary artery disease, significant valvular disease, or concomitant life threatening non cardiac disease were excluded.
Follow-up	5 years (the present study summarized interim results after a minimum of 6 months and a median of 2.7 years)
Treatment regimen	Randomization to conservative medical therapy or balloon angioplasty (PTCA). Patients assigned to PTCA underwent the procedure within 3 months of randomization.
Additional therapy	Stents and atherectomy were permitted if the initial standard PTCA results were unsatisfactory. All patients received aspirin unless contraindicated. Lipid lowering medications were prescribed at the discretion of the treating physician.

Coronary Angioplasty vs Medical Therapy for Angina (continued)

Results

Of the 504 patients randomized to initial PTCA strategy, 471 (93%) underwent the intended procedure within a median time of 5 weeks from randomization. PTCA was successful in 93% of the 642 attempted coronary lesions. 7 patients (1.5%) randomized to PTCA underwent emergency CABG. During follow-up 2.2% of the PTCA vs 1.4% of the conservative therapy group died (p=0.32). Cardiac mortality was 0.99% vs 0.60%, respectively. Nonfatal myocardial infarction occurred in 4.2% of the PTCA group vs only 1.9% in the medical group.The difference was due to 7 randomized procedure related myocardial infarctions in the PTCA group. Death or definite myocardial infarction occurred in 6.3% of the PTCA group vs 3.3% of the medical group (relative risk 1.92; 95% CI 1.08–3.41; p=0.02).The absolute treatment difference was 3.0% (95% CI 0.4%–5.7%). During follow-up 7.9% of the PTCA group and 5.8% of the medical group underwent CABG. Additional nonrandomized PTCA was performed in 12.3% of the PTCA group vs 19.6% of the medical group. In this group, the risk of requiring CABG or PTCA within 1 year of randomization was 15.4%. Improvement in reported angina was greater in the PTCA group, with a 16.5% excess of grade 2+ angina in the medical group after 3 months of therapy (p<0.001). However, after 2 years of follow-up, the medical group had only 7.6% excess of grade 2+ angina (p=0.02). Bruce treadmill exercise test was performed by about 90% of the patients at each follow-up. After 3 months the PTCA group exercised longer than the medical group (mean difference 35 seconds; 95% CI 20–51 seconds; p<0.001). However, the difference was attenuated at 1 year to 25 sec (95% CI 7–42 sec; p=nonsignificant). The beneficial effects of PTCA over medical therapy were more pronounced in patients with more severe angina at baseline.

Conclusions

In patients with stable coronary artery disease suitable for either medical therapy or PTCA, initial strategy of PTCA was associated with greater symptomatic improvement, especially in patients with more severe baseline symptoms. However, the differences between the PTCA and medical therapy tended to decrease over time and the initial PTCA strategy was associated with a significant excess of mortality and nonfatal myocardial infarction.

4. Interventional Cardiology

b. PTCA vs CABG

RITA-1

Randomized Intervention Treatment of Angina (RITA) Trial

Title	a. The randomized intervention treatment of angina (RITA) trial protocol: A long term study of coronary angioplasty and coronary artery bypass surgery in patients with angina. b. Coronary angioplasty vs coronary artery bypass surgery: The Randomized Intervention Treatment of Angina (RITA) trial. c. Health service costs of coronary angioplasty and coronary artery bypass surgery: The Randomized intervention Treatment of Angina (RITA) trial. d. Long term results of RITA-1 trial: Clinical and cost comparisons of coronary angioplasty and coronary artery bypass grafting.
Authors	a. Henderson RA, for the RITA trial. b. RITA Trial Participants. c. Sculpher MJ, Henderson RA, Buxton MJ, et al. d. Henderson RA, Pocock SJ, Sharp SJ, et al.
Reference	a. Br Heart J 1989;62:411–414. b. Lancet 1993;341:573–580. c. Lancet 1994;344:927–930. d. Lancet 1998;352:1419–1425.
Disease	Coronary artery disease.
Purpose	To compare the long term effects of percutaneous transluminal coronary angioplasty (PTCA) vs coronary artery bypass surgery (CABG) in patients with 1, 2, and 3 vessel disease.
Design	Randomized, multicenter.
Patients	1011 patients with coronary artery disease with a need for revascularization. Patients with left main coronary artery disease, previous PTCA or CABG, and significant valvular disease were excluded.

RITA-1

Randomized Intervention Treatment of Angina (RITA) Trial

(continued)

Follow-up	b. > 6 months, median 2.5 years. d. median 6.5 years (range 5.0–8.7 years).
Treatment regimen	CABG vs PTCA.
Results	Angioplasty was successful in 87% of the lesions. Emergency CABG was required in 4.5% of the PTCA group. Additional 1.4% underwent CABG before hospital discharge due to unsuccessful PTCA. Among the CABG patients 0.6% had pulmonary embolism and 4.9% wound-related complications. Median hospital stay was 12 and 4 days for CABG and PTCA, respectively. Mortality was 3.6% in the CABG and 3.1% in the PTCA group. Definite myocardial infarction occurred in 4.0% vs 6.5% of the CABG and PTCA patients. However, there was no difference in the rate of the primary end point (myocardial infarction or mortality) between the groups (RR CABG vs PTCA 0.88, 95% CI 0.59–1.29, p=0.47). Within 2 years an estimated 38% of the PTCA vs 11% of the CABG patients had experienced further CABG, PTCA, myocardial infarction, or death (p<0.001). The prevalence of angina during follow-up was 32% in the PTCA vs 11% in the CABG group after 6 months (RR 0.35, 95% CI 0.26–0.47, p<0.001) and 31% vs 22% after 2 years (p=0.007). 5 year follow-up was completed in 97% of the patients. Long term mortality was 7.6% in the PTCA and 9.0% in the CABG patients (p=0.51). Nonfatal myocardial infarction occurred in 10.8% of the PTCA group vs 7.4% of the CABG group (p=0.08). Death or myocardial infarction occurred in 17.1% and 16.0% of the PTCA and CABG group, respectively (p=0.64). The cumulative rate of death or myocardial infarction at 5 years was 14.1% in the PTCA group vs 11.1% in the CABG group (p=NS). In both groups, the risk for death or myocardial infarction was higher in the first year (6.4%) after enrollment than in years 2-5 (1.0% per year). During follow-up 26% of the PTCA group underwent subsequent CABG and 27% underwent an additional PTCA. During the same time, 3% of the CABG group underwent second CABG and 9%

underwent PTCA. At 5 years there was 9.0% excess of angina ≥ grade 2 in the PTCA group ($p<0.001$). 66% of the CABG patients and 51% of the PTCA assigned patients were angina free at both 1 year and 5 years after randomization. 24% of the PTCA and 20% of the CABG group had worsening of their angina class, whereas 17% and 9% of the patients, respectively had improvement. After 5 years 47.7% of the CABG group vs 22.2% of the PTCA group remained alive, free of angina, disease events and reinterventions. Persistent angina ≥ grade 2 was noted in 17.6% of the PTCA and 10.5% of the CABG group. The mean total health service costs over 5 years were £426 higher in the CABG group than in the PTCA group (95% CI -£383 to +£1235; $p=0.30$). During the first 3 months, costs were ≥50% higher in the CABG group. Between 6 months and 2 years, the PTCA group had 3 times the costs of the CABG group, mainly because of reinterventions. Between 2 and 5 years, the PTCA group had 44% higher costs than the CABG group.

Conclusions

While there was no difference in mortality, CABG was associated with less recurrent angina and need for revascularization. The long term follow-up results are similar. There was no difference in mortality, myocardial infarction rate, and costs between the groups. Patients in the PTCA group had more often residual or recurrent angina and needed more re-interventions than in the CABG group.

ERACI

Argentine Randomized Trial of Percutaneous Transluminal Coronary Angioplasty vs Coronary Artery Bypass Surgery in Multivessel Disease

Title	Argentine randomized trial of percutaneous transluminal coronary angioplasty vs coronary artery bypass surgery in multivessel disease (ERACI): In-hospital results and 1 year follow-up.
Authors	Rodriguez A, Boullon F, Perez-Baliño N, et al.
Reference	J Am Coll Cardiol 1993;22:1060–1067.
Disease	Coronary artery disease.
Purpose	To compare outcome following coronary artery bypass surgery (CABG) vs percutaneous transluminal coronary angioplasty (PTCA) in patients with multivessel coronary artery disease.
Design	Randomized, 1 center.
Patients	127 patients, age 33–76 years, with stable angina and multivessel disease which was suitable to either PTCA or CABG.
Follow-up	1 year clinical follow-up.
Treatment regimen	CABG vs PTCA.

ERACI

Argentine Randomized Trial of Percutaneous Transluminal Coronary Angioplasty vs Coronary Artery Bypass Surgery in Multivessel Disease

(continued)

Results	The overall primary success rate of angioplasty was 91.7% per lesion. There was no significant difference with in-hospital mortality (4.6% vs 1.5%), myocardial infarction (6.2% vs 6.3%), stroke (3.1% vs 1.5%), or need for repeated emergency procedure (1.5% vs 1.5%) between the CABG and the PTCA groups. Complete revascularization was achieved in 88% vs 51% of the CABG and PTCA groups ($p<0.001$). Mortality after 1 year was 3.2% in the PTCA vs 0% in the CABG patients (p=NS). New Q wave infarction occurred in 3.2% of the PTCA and 1.8% of the CABG (p=NS). 32% of the PTCA group needed revascularization vs 3.2% of the CABG patients ($p<0.001$). However, freedom from angina (including patients with repeated procedure) after 1 year was similar.
Conclusions	No significant differences were found in major in-hospital complications and 1 year outcome between the groups. However, after 1 year more patients treated with PTCA needed repeated revascularization.

GABI

The German Angioplasty Bypass Surgery Investigation

Title	A randomized study of coronary angioplasty compared with bypass surgery in patients with symptomatic multi vessel coronary disease.
Authors	Hamm CW, Reimers J, Ischinger T, et al.
Reference	N Engl J Med 1994;331:1037–1043.
Disease	Coronary artery disease.
Purpose	To compare the outcomes of coronary revascularization with coronary artery bypass grafting (CABG) and percutaneous transluminal coronary angioplasty (PTCA) in patients with multivessel disease.
Design	Randomized, multicenter.
Patients	337 patients, <75 years old, with symptomatic multivessel disease (Canadian Cardiovascular Society class ≥II, and ≥70% stenosis) and a need for revascularization of ≥2 major coronary arteries. Patients with 100% occlusion or >30% stenosis of the left main coronary artery were excluded. Patients who underwent prior CABG or PTCA and patients with myocardial infarction within 4 weeks were excluded.
Follow-up	1 year.
Treatment regimen	CABG vs PTCA.

GABI

The German Angioplasty Bypass Surgery Investigation

(continued)

Results	Among the CABG patients an average of 2.2±0.6 vessels were grafted and among the PTCA patients 1.9±0.5 vessels were dilated. Complete revascularization was achieved in 86% of the PTCA patients. Hospitalization was longer after CABG (median days 19 vs 5) and Q wave infarction related to the procedure was more common (8.1% vs 2.3%, p=0.022). However, there was no significant difference in mortality (2.5% vs 1.1%, p=0.43). At discharge 93% vs 82% of the CABG and PTCA patients were angina free (p=0.005). During the following year 6% of the CABG patients vs 44% of the PTCA patients underwent repeated interventions (p<0.001). The cumulative risk of death or myocardial infarction was 13.6% in the CABG and 6.0% in the PTCA patients (p=0.017). 1 year after the procedure 74% vs 71%, respectively were angina free (p=NS). Exercise capacity was similar. However, 22% of the CABG vs only 12% of the PTCA patients did not require antianginal medication (p=0.041). 219 patients underwent coronary angiography after 6 months. The clinical course of these patients did not differ from that of those who refused to undergo repeated catheterization. 13% of the vein grafts were occluded and 7% of the internal thoracic artery anastomoses did not function, whereas 16% of the vessels dilated by angioplasty were ≥70% stenotic.
Conclusions	In selected patients with multivessel disease PTCA and CABG resulted in similar improvement after 1 year. However, the PTCA treated patients needed more additional interventions and antianginal medication, whereas CABG was more associated with procedure related myocardial infarction.

EAST

The Emory Angioplasty vs Surgery Trial

Title	a. A randomized trial comparing coronary angioplasty with coronary bypass surgery. b. A comparison of the costs of and quality of life after coronary angioplasty or coronary surgery for multivessel coronary artery disease: Results from the Emory Angioplasty vs Surgery Trial (EAST).
Authors	a. King SB III, Lembo NJ, Weintraub WS, et al. b. Weintraub WS, Mauldin PD, Becker E, et al.
Reference	a. N Engl J Med 1994;331:1044-1050. b. Circulation 1995;92:2831-2840.
Disease	Coronary artery disease.
Purpose	To compare the outcome following coronary artery bypass surgery (CABG) vs percutaneous transluminal coronary angioplasty (PTCA) in patients with multivessel coronary artery disease.
Design	Randomized, single center.
Patients	392 patients of any age with 2 to 3 vessel disease and had not previously undergone PTCA or CABG. Patients with old 100% occlusion of vessels serving viable myocardium, ≥2 total occlusions, >30% left main artery stenosis, ejection fraction ≤25%, or myocardial infarction <5 d, were excluded.
Follow-up	3 year clinical follow-up. Repeated angiography and thallium scan after 1 and 3 years.
Treatment regimen	PTCA vs CABG.

EAST

The Emory Angioplasty vs Surgery Trial

(continued)

Results	In hospital mortality was 1.0% in each group. Q wave infarction occurred in 10.3% of the CABG and 3.0% of the PTCA patients (p=0.004). Stroke occurred in 1.5% vs 0.5%, respectively (p=0.37). 0% and 10.1% of the patients, respectively underwent emergency CABG during hospitalization. 3 year mortality was 6.2% in the CABG and 7.1% in the PTCA groups (p=0.72). Q wave infarction within 3 years occurred in 19.6% vs 14.6%, respectively (p=0.21). Large ischemic defect on thallium scan were found in 5.7% vs 9.6%, respectively (p=0.17). There was no difference in the occurrence of the composite end point (death, Q wave infarction, or a large ischemic defect on thallium scan)(27.3% vs 28.8%, p=0.81). After 3 years 1% of the CABG vs 22% of the PTCA group underwent CABG (p<0.001), while PTCA was performed in 13% vs 41%, respectively (p<0.001). Initially, 99.1% vs 75.1% of the index segments per patients were revascularized in the CABG and PTCA, respectively. 1 year later, 88.1% vs 58.8% of the index segment per patients were revascularized (p<0.001). However, by 3 years the differences were narrowed (86.7% vs 69.9%, respectively, p<0.001). There was no difference in ejection fraction between the groups. However, angina was present in 12% and 20% of the patients after 3 years, respectively.
Conclusions	PTCA and CABG did not differ significantly with respect to the occurrence of the composite end points. However, PTCA was associated with more repeated procedures and residual angina.

EAST (8 year mortality data)

Emory Angioplasty vs Surgery Trial

Title	Eight year mortality in the Emory angioplasty vs surgery trial (EAST).
Authors	King SB, Kosinski AS, Guyton RA, et al.
Reference	J Am Coll Cardiol 2000; 35:1116–1121.
Disease	Coronary artery disease.
Purpose	To assess long term outcome of patients randomized to initial coronary angioplasty vs coronary artery bypass surgery.
Design	Randomized, single center.
Patients	392 patients with multivessel coronary artery disease as per EAST.
Follow-up	8 years.
Treatment regimen	Initial percutaneous transluminal coronary angioplasty (PTCA; n=198) or coronary artery bypass surgery (CABG; n=194).

EAST (8 year mortality data)

Emory Angioplasty vs Surgery Trial

(continued)

Results	Results of the primary EAST trial are reported elsewhere in this book. In brief, at 3 years follow up the primary composite end point of death, myocardial infarction, or large ischemic defect, did not differ between groups. Repeat revascularization procedures were more frequent in the angioplasty group. Late follow up was achieved by annual patient questionnaires, telephone contact, and examination of medical records. Survival at 8 years for the CABG group was 82.7% and for the angioplasty group was 79.3% (p=0.40). There was a small but not statistically significant survival advantage for 3 vessel disease with CABG (81.6%) vs PTCA (75.5%; p=0.35); but this benefit of surgery was not observed in patient with double vessel disease (83.4% with CABG vs 81.8% with PTCA). Patients with proximal left anterior descending coronary stenoses faired slightly but not significantly better with CABG (85.6% survival) vs PTCA (79.6%; p=0.16) as did diabetics (75.5% survival with CABG and 60.1% with PTCA, p=0.23). During the first 3 years after revascularization, additional procedures were more common in the PTCA group; after this time the curves of percent of patients having additional revascularization remained parallel.
Conclusions	8 year survival of patients with multivessel coronary artery disease did not differ between PTCA and CABG.

CABRI

Coronary Angioplasty vs Bypass Revascularization Investigation

Title	First year results of CABRI (Coronary Angioplasty vs Bypass Revascularization Investigation).
Authors	CABRI trial participants.
Reference	Lancet 1995;346:1179-1184.
Disease	Coronary artery disease.
Purpose	To compare the effects of percutaneous transluminal coronary angioplasty (PTCA) vs coronary artery bypass surgery (CABG) in patients with multivessel disease.
Design	Randomized, multicenter.
Patients	1054 patients, <76 years old, with >1 vessel disease with left ventricular ejection fraction >0.35. Patients with left main or severe triple vessel disease, overt cardiac failure, myocardial infarction within 10 days, a previous coronary revascularization, or a recent cerebrovascular event were excluded. At least 1 lesion had to be suitable for PTCA.
Follow-up	1 year.
Treatment regimen	CABG or PTCA (stents and atherectomy were permitted).
Additional therapy	Aspirin. The use of fish oil and lipid lowering agents were allowed.

CABRI

Coronary Angioplasty vs Bypass Revascularization Investigation

(continued)

Results	After 1 year 2.7% of the CABG and 3.9% of the PTCA allocated patients had died (RR 1.42, 95% CI 0.73–2.76, p=0.3). Kaplan-Meier survival curves did not demonstrate a difference in survival at 28 months. The PTCA allocated group required more repeated interventions. 20.8% vs 2.7% needed angioplasty, while 15.7% vs 0.8% needed CABG. 66.4% of the PTCA vs 93.5% of the CABG group had only a single procedure in the first year. The rate of reintervention was 5 times higher in the PTCA group (RR 5.23, 95% CI 3.90–7.03, p<0.001). The PTCA group needed more antianginal medications (RR 1.30, 95% CI 1.18–1.43, p<0.001). After 1 year 67 % of the PTCA vs 75% of the CABG were angina free . The presence of angina at 1 year was greater in the PTCA than in the CABG group (RR 1.54, 95% CI 1.09–2.16, p=0.012).
Conclusions	CABG as the initial revascularization strategy for multivessel disease was associated with decreased need for repeated procedure. However, 1 year survival was similar.

BARI

The Bypass Angioplasty Revascularization Investigation

Title	a. Comparison of coronary bypass surgery with angioplasty in patients with multivessel disease. b. 5 year clinical and functional outcome comparing bypass surgery and angioplasty in patients with multivessel coronary disease. A multicenter randomized trial. c. 5 year clinical and functional outcome comparing bypass surgery and angioplasty in patients with multivessel coronary disease. A multicenter randomized trial. d. Influence of diabetes on 5 year mortality and morbidity in a randomized trial comparing CABG and PTCA in patients with multivessel disease. The bypass angioplasty revascularization investigation (BARI). e. Medical care costs and quality of life after randomization to coronary angioplasty or coronary bypass surgery.
Authors	a + b. The Bypass Angioplasty Revascularization Investigation (BARI) Investigators. c. The writing group for the bypass angioplasty revascularization investigation (BARI) investigators. d. The BARI Investigators. e. Hlatky MA, Rogers WJ, Johnstone I, et al.
Reference	a. N Engl J Med 1996;335:217-225. b. JAMA 1997;277:715-721. c. JAMA 1997;277:715-721. d. Circulation 1997;96:1761-1679. e. N Engl J Med 1997;336:92-99.
Disease	Coronary artery disease. d. Coronary artery disease, diabetes mellitus.
Purpose	a + b. To compare the long term effects of percutaneous transluminal coronary balloon angioplasty (PTCA) and coronary artery bypass grafting surgery (CABG) in patients with multivessel coronary artery disease. c. To assess the clinical and functional status of patients with similar 5 year survival following coronary artery bypass grafting (CABG) vs percutaneous transluminal coronary angioplasty (PTCA).

	d. More details on original trial in regards to diabetes. Examination of course specific mortality, CABG efficacy by using internal mammary artery (IMA) grafts vs saphenous vein grafts (SVGs) only. e. To compare quality of life, employment, and costs of medical care in patients treated with PTCA vs CABG in the BARI study.
Design	Randomized, multicenter. c. Randomized trial. Symptoms, use of medications, quality of life questionnaire and exercise test, results obtained at 4–14 weeks, 1, 3, and 5 years after randomization. Multicenter. e. As per BARI study. Data on quality of life collected annually; economic data collected quarterly.
Patients	1829 patients with angiographically documented multivessel coronary artery disease, clinically severe angina, or evidence of ischemia requiring revascularization, and were suitable for both PTCA and CABG. c. 1829 patients with multivessel coronary artery disease with clinically severe angina or objective evidence for ischemia requiring either CABG or PTCA as suitable therapies. Average age 61.5 years; 73% male. d. 353 treated diabetic patients and 1476 patients classified as not having treated diabetes. e. 934 of the 1829 patients enrolled in the BARI study.
Follow-up	Mean follow-up 5.4 years (range 3.8–6.8 years). c. 5.4 years. d. Average 5.4 years. e. 3–5 years.

Treatment regimen	PTCA vs CABG. New interventional devices, such as stents and atherectomy devices were not used during the initial revascularization procedure. c. CABG or PTCA within 2 weeks of randomization. d. CABG vs PTCA e. Coronary angioplasty vs coronary artery bypass surgery.
Results	Of the 915 patients randomized to PTCA, 904 (99%) actually underwent the procedure, 9 underwent CABG, and 2 received medical therapy alone. Of the 914 patients randomized to CABG, 892 (98%) underwent the procedure, 15 underwent PTCA as the initial procedure, and 7 were treated medically. Among the 892 patients who underwent CABG as assigned, an average of 3.1 coronary arteries were bypassed with a mean of 2.8 grafts. In 91% of patients all intended vessels were revascularized. At least 1 internal thoracic artery was used in 82% of patients. Among the 904 patients who underwent PTCA as assigned, angioplasty was attempted on an average of 2.4 lesions. Multilesion angioplasty was attempted in 78% of patients and multivessel angioplasty in 70% of patients. Immediate angiographic success was achieved in 78% of the attempted angioplasties. Rates of in-hospital mortality were comparable between the CABG and PTCA groups (1.3% vs 1.1% in the CABG and PTCA group, respectively; p=NS). Q wave myocardial infarction during hospitalization occurred in 4.6% vs 2.1%, respectively ($p<0.01$). There was no statistically significant difference between the groups in the occurrence of stroke, congestive heart failure, cardiogenic shock, and nonfatal cardiac arrest. However, more of the CABG patients experienced respiratory failure (2.2% vs 1.0%, $p<0.05$), wound dehiscence or infection (4.1% vs 0.4%, $p<0.001$), and reoperation for bleeding (3.1% vs 0.4%, $p<0.001$). Emergency CABG (6.3% vs 0.1%; $p<0.001$) and PTCA (2.1% vs 0; $p<0.001$) following the initial procedure were performed more often in the PTCA group. Nonemergency CABG was also performed more often in the PTCA patients (3.9% vs 0; $p<0.001$). The median hospital stay was longer after CABG (7 days) than after PTCA (3 days). The cumulative survival rates at 5 years were 89.3% and 86.3% for the CABG and PTCA groups, respectively

(2.9% difference, 95% CI -0.2% to 6.0%; p=0.19). The cumulative rates of Q wave myocardial infarction at 5 years were 11.7% and 10.9%, respectively (p=0.45). At 5 years 80.4% and 78.7% of the CABG and PTCA patients were alive and free of Q wave myocardial infarction (1.6% difference, 95% confidence interval -2.2% to 5.4%, p=0.84). During the 5 year follow-up, 8% of the CABG patients underwent repeated revascularization procedures (1% underwent repeated CABG and 7% PTCA), while 54% of the PTCA group underwent at least 1 additional procedure (31% underwent CABG and 34% repeated PTCA, 11% underwent both CABG and PTCA). Multiple additional revascularization procedures were required for 19% of the PTCA patients vs 3% of the CABG patients. Patients undergoing PTCA had more frequent hospitalizations than the CABG patients (an average ofage of 2.5 per patient vs 1.9, p<0.001). At 4–14 weeks 95% of the CABG vs 73% of the PTCA patients reported no angina (p<0.001). At the 5 year visit 86% of the CABG vs 78% of the PTCA patients were angina free (p=0.003). At the 4–14 weeks visit, 20% of the CABG vs 31% of the PTCA group had abnormal exercise induced ST segment changes (p<0.001), however, at 5 years there was no difference (28% vs 31%). At 5 years there was no difference in the proportion of patients experiencing exercise induced angina. During follow-up, patients in the PTCA were more likely to receive anti-ischemic medications than the CABG group (89% vs 44% at 4–14 weeks (p<0.001), 76% vs 57% by the fifth year (p<0.001). At follow-up of 1 year and later, quality of life, return to work, modification of smoking and exercise behaviors, and cholesterol levels were similar for the 2 groups. Subgroup analysis did not reveal a difference in survival between CABG and PTCA in patients with unstable angina or non Q wave infarction, stable angina, severe ischemia, normal or reduced left ventricular function, double or triple vessel disease, and presence of type C coronary lesions (complicated lesions). However, a significant survival benefit was observed in patients with treated diabetes mellitus assigned to CABG. The 5 year survival in diabetic patients was 80.6% in the CABG compared to 65.5% in the PTCA group (15.1% difference, 99.5% confidence interval 1.4% to 28.9%, p=0.003).

c. At each follow-up period CABG patients were more likely to be angina free compared to PTCA group. At 4–14 weeks 95% of CABG patients had no angina vs 73% of PTCA patients ($p<0.001$). This difference narrowed by 5 years at which time 86% of CABG patients and 78% of PTCA patients were angina free ($p=0.003$). Among the asymptomatic CABG patients 94% did not require additional revascularization procedures. Among the asymptomatic PTCA patients 48% did not require additional revascularization procedures. Quality of life and return to work were similar at 1 year between groups. Antianginal medicines were more commonly used among PTCA patients. A larger percent of PTCA patients experienced angina pectoris on exercise and exercise induced ST segment changes than CABG patients except at 5 years when there was no difference between groups.

d. The improved 5.4 year survival with CABG over PTCA in the treated diabetics was due to a reduction in cardiac mortality (5.8% vs 20.6%, $p=0.0003$) and confined to patients receiving at least one internal mammary artery graft.

e. During the first 3 years, functional status scores that measure the ability to perform common activities of daily living improved to a greater extent in patients that received CABG compared to PTCA ($p=0.05$). Patients receiving PTCA returned to work 5 weeks sooner than patients in the surgery group ($p<0.001$). While the initial cost of PTCA was 65% of the surgical cost, after 5 years the total medical cost of angioplasty was 95% that of surgery. 5 year cost of PTCA was significantly lower than surgery in patients with 2 vessel disease ($p<0.05$), but not among patients with 3 vessel disease. CABG was especially cost-effective in diabetes because of their better survival.

Conclusions	The 5 year survival of patients assigned to initial strategy of PTCA was comparable to that of patients assigned to CABG. However, subsequent repeated revascularization was required more often in the PTCA group. In patients with diabetes mellitus, 5 year survival was significantly worse with PTCA than with CABG. c. There was a narrowing of treatment benefits of CABG over PTCA in these 5 year survivors. The narrowing of benefits in angina and exercise induced ischemia are related to return of symptoms among patents assigned to CABG and an increase in surgical procedures among patients originally assigned to PTCA. d. Patients with treated diabetes mellitus have a marked reduction in cardiac mortality when initially treated with CABG rather than PTCA which appears to be related to long term patency of the internal mammary artery. e. CABG resulted in a better quality of life than PTCA in patients with multivessel disease, after the initial morbidity associated with the procedure. In patients with double (but not triple) disease PTCA had a lower 5 year cost.

BARI (Substudy)

Bypass Angioplasty Revascularization Investigation

Title	Better outcome for women compared with men undergoing coronary revascularization. A Report from the Bypass Angioplasty Revascularization Investigation.
Authors	Jacobs AK, Kelsey SF, Brooks MM, et al.
Reference	Circulation 1998; 98:1279–1285.
Disease	Coronary artery disease.
Purpose	Assess outcome of women undergoing CABG or PTCA in BARI trial.
Design	As per BARI.
Patients	As per BARI.
Follow-up	As per BARI.
Treatment regimen	As per BARI.

BARI (Substudy)

Bypass Angioplasty Revascularization Investigation

(continued)

Results	27% of the 1829 patients in BARI were women. They were older (64 vs 60.5 years), and had more congestive heart failure, hypertension, treated diabetes, and unstable angina compared to men. The extent of multivessel disease and LV function was similar between women and men. At 5.4 years crude mortality rates were the same in women and men (12.8% vs 12.0%). Incidence of death in patients undergoing CABG was similar in women and men (1.3% vs 1.4%) as was the incidence of non Q wave myocardial infarction (4.7% vs 4.6%). In patients undergoing PTCA there was also a low incidence of death in women and men (0.8% vs 1.2%) and also Q wave MI (1.2% vs 2.4%). However, after adjusting for baseline differences, women had a lower risk of death (RR = 0.60; 95% CI = 0.43-0.84; p=0.003) than men.
Conclusions	After adjusting for risk, and contrary to previous beliefs, women had improved 5 year survival after coronary revascularization.

BARI (7 year outcome, diabetics)

Bypass Angioplasty Revascularization Investigation (BARI)

Title	7 year outcome in the bypass angioplasty revascularization investigation (BARI) by treatment and diabetic status.
Authors	The BARI Investigators.
Reference	J Am Coll Cardiol 2000; 35:1122-1129.
Disease	Coronary artery disease.
Purpose	To assess 7 year survival in coronary artery disease patients randomized to initial therapy with CABG or PTCA.
Design	As per BARI.
Patients	1829 symptomatic coronary artery patients with multi-vessel coronary artery disease, including diabetic patients.
Follow-up	Average of 7.8 years.
Treatment regimen	Initial PTCA vs CABG.
Additional therapy	As per BARI.

BARI (7 year outcome, diabetics)

Bypass Angioplasty Revascularization Investigation (BARI)

(continued)

Results	At 7 years, survival for total population was 84.4% for CABG patients vs 80.9% for PTCA (p=0.043). This treatment difference was secondary to differences in a subgroup of 353 patients who had treated diabetes. At 7 years, among these diabetics 76.4% that received CABG survived vs 55.7% assigned to PTCA (p=0.001). These differences in treatment between CABG and PTCA in treated diabetics were even greater than observed at 5 years. Among 1476 patients without treated diabetes, survival was 86.4% in CABG patients and 86.8% in PTCA patients (p=NS). Subsequent revascularization rates remained higher in the PTCA patients (59.7%) compared to the CABG patients (13.1%, p<0.001). Among diabetic patients who underwent CABG, those who received at least one internal mammary artery graft had improved survival (83.2%) compared to those diabetic patients that had only saphenous vein bypass grafts (54.5%—a rate that was actually similar to diabetic patients who received PTCA (55.5%). Among survivors with 7 year follow-up, incidence of angina was 15.1% in PTCA patients vs 11.4% in CABG patients (p=0.075).
Conclusions	At 7 years CABG had a significant survival benefit over PTCA which was due to improved survival in diabetic patients who received CABG, especially those that received an internal mammary implant.

4. Interventional Cardiology

c. PTCA vs Stenting vs Other Percutaneous Devices, IVUS Guided Stenting

CAVEAT-1

Coronary Angioplasty vs Excisional Atherectomy Trial

Title	a. A comparison of directional atherectomy with coronary angioplasty in patients with coronary artery disease. b. 1 year follow-up in the coronary angioplasty vs excisional atherectomy trial (CAVEAT I).
Authors	a. Topol EJ, Leya F, Pinkerton CA, et al. b. Elliott JM, Berdan LG, Holmes DR, et al.
Reference	a. N Engl J Med 1993;329:221-227. b. Circulation 1995;91:2158-2166.
Disease	Coronary artery disease, angina pectoris.
Purpose	To compare outcome of percutaneous transluminal coronary angioplasty (PTCA) with that of directional coronary atherectomy (DCA).
Design	Randomized, controlled trial.
Patients	1012 patients (median age 59 years, 73% men) with symptomatic coronary artery disease. Only patients with angiography proven native coronary artery lesions ≥60% stenosis, and <12 mm length, with no prior intracoronary interventions were included. Patients who had acute myocardial infarction within 5 days of procedure were excluded. 512 and 500 patients were assigned to DCA and PTCA, respectively.
Follow-up	1 year.
Treatment regimen	Percutaneous transluminal coronary angioplasty (PTCA) or directional coronary atherectomy (DCA).

CAVEAT-1

Coronary Angioplasty vs Excisional Atherectomy Trial

(continued)

Additional therapy	Before procedure, all patients received ≥160 mg aspirin, ≥1 dose of calcium channel blocker, and heparin as a bolus of 10000 U with additional boluses to maintain clotting time >350 sec during the procedure.
Results	Reduction of stenosis to ≤50% was more successful with DCA (89%) than PTCA (80%), p<0.001. The success rates (≤50% residual stenosis and no major complications) were higher in the DCA group (82%) than the PTCA group (76%, p=0.016). The immediate gain in luminal diameter was greater in the DCA (1.05 mm) than PTCA (0.86 mm, p<0.001) patients. However, early complications were more frequent in the DCA than PTCA patients (11% vs 5%, p<0.001). At 6 months 50% and 57% of the DCA and PTCA patients had restenosis, respectively (p=0.06). 1 year mortality was 2.2% and 0.6% in the DCA and PTCA groups, respectively (p=0.035). Myocardial infarction within 1 year occurred in 8.9% of the DCA and 4.4% of the PTCA patients (p=0.005). By multivariate analysis, DCA was the only variable predictive of the combined end point of death or myocardial infarction. Rates of repeated interventions at the target site were similar.
Conclusions	DCA, as compared with PTCA, was associated with an increase rates of restenosis at 6 months, and 1 year mortality and occurrence of myocardial infarction.

Directional Atherectomy vs Balloon Angioplasty for Lesions of the Left Anterior Descending Coronary Artery

Title	A comparison of directional atherectomy with balloon angioplasty for lesions of the left anterior descending coronary artery.
Authors	Adelman AG, Cohen EA, Kimball BP, et al.
Reference	N Engl J Med 1993;329:228–233.
Disease	Coronary artery disease, restenosis.
Purpose	To compare the rates of restenosis for directional atherectomy and balloon angioplasty in lesions of the proximal left anterior descending coronary artery.
Design	Randomized, open label, multicenter.
Patients	274 patients with de novo ≥60% stenosis of the proximal one-third of the left anterior descending coronary artery. Patients within 7 days of acute infarction or severe left ventricular dysfunction were excluded.
Follow-up	Clinical evaluation and repeated angiography at 4–7 months (median 5.9 months).
Treatment regimen	Directional atherectomy or balloon angioplasty.
Additional therapy	Aspirin, calcium channel blocker, and nitrates were started ≥12 h before procedure and continued for 24 h. Heparin was given during procedure. Antianginal medications were discontinued. The use of n-3 fatty acids was prohibited.

Directional Atherectomy vs Balloon Angioplasty for Lesions of the Left Anterior Descending Coronary Artery

(continued)

Results	The procedural success rate was 94% in the atherectomy and 88% in the angioplasty patients (p=0.06). Major in-hospital complications occurred in 5% and 6%, respectively. Repeated angiography was performed in 257 patients. After 6 months, the restenosis rate was 46% and 43% (p=0.7). Despite a greater initial gain in minimal luminal diameter (1.45±0.47 vs 1.16±0.44 mm, p<0.001), there was a larger loss (0.79±0.61 vs 0.47±0.64 mm, p<0.001) in the atherectomy group, resulting in a similar minimal luminal diameter at follow-up (1.55±0.60 vs 1.61±0.68 mm, p=0.44). The clinical outcome was similar in the 2 groups.
Conclusions	Despite better initial success rate and gain in minimal luminal diameter, atherectomy did not result in better clinical outcome or late angiographic results with lesions of the proximal third of the left anterior descending coronary artery.

BENESTENT

Belgium Netherlands Stent

Title	a. A comparison of balloon-expandable stent implantation with balloon angioplasty in patients with coronary artery disease. b. Continued benefit of coronary stenting vs balloon angioplasty: 1 year clinical follow-up of Benestent Trial.
Authors	a. Serruys PW, de Jaegere P, Kiemenij F, et al. b. Macay a C, Serruys PW, Ruygrok P, et al.
Reference	a. N Engl J Med 1994;331:489-495. b. J Am Coll Cardiol 1996;27:255-261.
Disease	Coronary artery disease, restenosis.
Purpose	To compare elective balloon angioplasty with Palmaz-Schatz stent implantation in patients with stable angina and de novo coronary artery lesions.
Design	Randomized, multicenter.
Patients	516 patients, age 30-75 years, with stable angina and a single new lesion of the native coronary circulation <15 mm, located in vessels >3 mm and supplying normally functioning myocardium.
Follow-up	12 months (0.3-34 months). Exercise test and repeated angiography at 6 months.
Treatment regimen	Balloon angioplasty or Palmaz-Schatz stent implantation.
Additional therapy	Aspirin 250-500 mg/d and dipyridamole 75 mg X3/d, started ≥1 day before procedure and continued for >6 months. IV heparin 10,000 U bolus before procedure. Calcium channel blockers until discharge. Patients undergoing stent implantation received dextran infusion (1000 mL over 6-8 h), heparin infusion (started after sheath removal and continued for ≥36 h), and warfarin for 3 months (target INR 2.5-3.5).

BENESTENT

Belgium Netherlands Stent *(continued)*

Results	The procedural success rate was 92.7% in the stent group and 91.1% in the angioplasty group, whereas the angiographic success was 96.9% vs 98.1%, respectively. There was no differences in the incidence of death, stroke, myocardial infarction, or the need for repeated procedures during the index hospitalization between the groups. There was no difference in the composite end point of all in-hospital clinical events (6.2% in the angioplasty vs 6.9% in the stent group (RR 1.12, 95% CI 0.58–2.14)). Subacute vessel closure occurred in 2.7% of the angioplasty and 3.5% of the stent group (p=NS). The incidence of bleeding and vascular complications was higher in the stent group 13.5% vs 3.1%, RR 4.34, 95% CI 2.05–9.18, p<0.001). Mean hospitalization was 8.5±6.8 days in the stent vs 3.1±3.3 days in the angioplasty group (p=0.001). After 7 months primary events occurred in 29.6% vs 20.1% of the angioplasty and stent groups (RR 0.68, 95% CI 0.50–0.92, p=0.02). The major difference was the need for repeated angioplasty in the angioplasty group (20.6% vs 10.0%, RR 0.49, 95% CI 0.31–0.75, p=0.001). The minimal luminal diameter after the procedure was 2.48±0.39 vs 2.05±0.33 mm (p<0.001), and at follow-up it was 1.82± 0.64 vs 1.73±0.55 mm (p=0.09), in the stent and angioplasty groups. The incidence of >50% restenosis was 22% vs 32%, respectively (p=0.02). After 1 year a primary end point occurred in 32% of the angioplasty vs 23% of the stent group (RR 0.74, 95% CI 0.55–0.98, p=0.04). However, the only significant difference was the rate of repeated interventions.
Conclusions	Implantation of stent is associated with better initial gain in luminal stenosis, a larger minimal diameter after 7 months and a significant reduction of the need for repeated interventions that was maintained to at least 1 year. However, stent implantation is associated with longer hospital stay and more bleeding and vascular complications.

BENESTENT II

Belgium Netherlands Stent II

Title	Randomized comparison of implantation of heparin-coated stents with balloon angioplasty in selected patients with coronary artery disease (Benestent II).
Authors	Serruys PW, van Hout B, Bonnier H, et al.
Reference	Lancet 1998;352:673–681.
Disease	Coronary artery disease.
Purpose	To evaluate whether a strategy of heparin coated Palmaz-Schatz stent implantation + antiplatelet agents is superior to standard PTCA in selected patients with stable or stabilized unstable angina.
Design	Randomized, multicenter.
Patients	827 patients scheduled to undergo coronary angioplasty, who had ≥1 de novo coronary lesions and stable or unstable angina. Patients with left ventricular ejection fraction <30%, recent myocardial infarction within a week, contraindications to aspirin or ticlopidine, left main artery disease, bifurcation lesion, and those who were suitable for CABG were excluded. The target lesion should be in a vessel larger than 3.0 mm and of <18 mm in length.
Follow-up	12 months clinical follow-up. A subset of patients underwent repeated coronary angiography at 6 months.
Treatment regimen	Randomization to heparin coated stent implantation or standard PTCA. The stent assigned patients received ticlopidine 250 mg/d for 1 month.

BENESTENT II

Belgium Netherlands Stent II

(continued)

Additional therapy	All patients received 10000–15000 U heparin during procedure, and oral aspirin >100 mg/d for 6 months.
Results	414 patients were assigned to stenting and 413 to PTCA. 4 patients did not undergo coronary revascularization and were excluded from analysis. 3.4% of the 413 stent-assigned patients did not receive heparin coated stent because the lesion could not be crossed with the delivery system. 13.4% of the 410 PTCA assigned patients received bailout stents. The angiographic success rate was 99% in both groups and the procedural success rate was 96% in the stent group and 95% in the PTCA group. Bleeding and vascular complications occurred in 1.2% of the stent and 1.0% of the PTCA group. The mean hospital stay was 2.8 and 2.3 days, respectively. The primary end point (death, myocardial infarction, CABG, and repeated target-lesion PTCA at 6 months) occurred in 12.8% of the stent group vs 19.3% of the PTCA group (relative risk 0.67; 95% CI 0.48 to 0.92; p=0.013). The difference in outcome was maintained at 12 months (event free survival 84.3% in the stent group vs 77.6% in the PTCA group, p=0.01). At 6 months 77% of the stent vs 70% of the PTCA group were asymptomatic. Angiographic follow-up was obtained for 92% of the 416 pre assigned to repeated angiography. Minimum lumen diameter at 6 months was larger in the stent group (1.89±0.65) than in the PTCA group (1.66±0.57)(p=0.0002). Mean diameter stenosis at 6 months was 35±17% vs 43±17%, in the stent and PTCA group, respectively (p<0.001). Restenosis rate was 16% in the stent group vs 31% in the PTCA group (p=0.0008). The initial costs were significantly higher for the stent strategy. The 12 month event free survival for patients without obligatory angiographic follow-up was 89.3% in the stent group vs 78.6% in the PTCA group (p=0.003) at an additional cost of $1020 per patient.

Conclusions	A strategy of elective heparin coated stenting with ticlopidine was better than standard PTCA alone.

STRESS

Stent Restenosis Study

Title	a. A randomized comparison of coronary-stent placement and balloon angioplasty in the treatment of coronary artery disease. b. 1 year follow-up of the Stent Restenosis (STRESS-1) Study.
Authors	a. Fischman DL, Leon MB, Baim DS, et al. b. George CJ, Baim DS, Brinker JA, et al.
Reference	a. N Engl J Med 1994;331:496-501. b. Am J Cardiol 1998; 81:860-865.
Disease	Coronary artery disease, restenosis.
Purpose	a. To compare the results of Palmaz-Schatz stent placement and conventional balloon angioplasty on restenosis and clinical outcome.
Design	Randomized, open label, multicenter.
Patients	a. 407 patients with new ≥70% stenotic lesions, ≤15 mm in length, in ≥3.0 mm of a native coronary artery. Patients with myocardial infarction within 7 days, ejection fraction <40%, diffuse coronary or left main artery disease, or angiographic evidence of thrombus were excluded.
Follow-up	a. Clinical follow-up for 6 months. Repeated angiography at 6 months.
Treatment regimen	Palmaz-Schatz stent placement or balloon angioplasty.

STRESS

Stent Restenosis Study

(continued)

Additional therapy	For the stent arm: aspirin 325 mg/d, dipyridamole 75 mg X3/d, and calcium channel blocker. IV low molecular weight dextran started 2 h before procedure at a dose of 100 mL/h for 2 h, and during and after procedure 50 mL/h. IV heparin 10,000–15,000 U before procedure, and IV infusion 4–6 h after removal of the sheath. Warfarin sodium started on the day of procedure. Dipyridamole and warfarin were administered for 1 month, and aspirin indefinitely. For the angioplasty arm: aspirin 325 mg/d, without warfarin sodium or dipyridamole.
Results	a. Clinical success was achieved in 96.1% and 89.6% of the stent and angioplasty groups (p=0.011). The stent group had a larger immediate gain in minimal diameter of the lumen (1.72±0.46 vs 1.23±0.48 mm, p<0.001), and a larger luminal diameter after the procedure (2.49±0.43 vs 1.99±0.47 mm, p<0.001). There was no statistical significant difference in the rate of any of the early clinical events (days 0–14) between the groups. At 6 months, the stent group had a larger luminal diameter (1.74±0.60 vs 1.56±0.65 mm, p=0.007), and a lower rate of ≥50% restenosis (31.6% vs 42.1%, p=0.046). 80.5% and 76.2% of the stent and angioplasty groups were event free after 6 months (p=0.16). Revascularization of the original lesion was performed in 10.2% and 15.4% of the stent and angioplasty patients (p=0.06). b. 1 year follow-up results: 75% of patients assigned to stent implantation were free of all clinical events (death, myocardial infarction, revascularization, procedures) compared to 70% of PTCA patients. 79% of stent patients were alive vs 74% of PTCA patients. These differences were not significantly different. There was no difference in freedom from angina at 1 year between groups (84%).
Conclusions	a. In selected patients, placement of Palmaz-Schatz stent was associated with better immediate results, lower rate of 6 months restenosis, and less revascularization procedures. b. Authors note that although there was no statistically significant improvement in outcome in stented group, the study had a relatively low statistical power.

CAVEAT-II

Coronary Angioplasty vs Directional Atherectomy-II

Title	A multicenter, randomized trial of coronary angioplasty vs directional atherectomy for patients with saphenous vein bypass graft lesions.
Authors	Holmes DR, Topol EJ, Califf RM, et al.
Reference	Circulation 1995;91:1966–1974.
Disease	Coronary artery disease, saphenous vein grafts.
Purpose	To compare outcome after directional coronary atherectomy vs angioplasty in patients with de novo venous bypass graft stenosis.
Design	Randomized, open label, multicenter.
Patients	305 patients with de novo saphenous vein graft lesions, ≥60% and <100% stenosis, who required revascularization and were suitable for either angioplasty or atherectomy.
Follow-up	Clinical evaluation and repeated coronary angiography at 6 months.
Treatment regimen	Balloon angioplasty or directional atherectomy.
Additional therapy	Aspirin ≥160 mg and a calcium blocker <24 h before procedure. A bolus of 10,000 U heparin before procedure. Aspirin 325 mg/d and a calcium channel blocker for 1 month.

CAVEAT-II

Coronary Angioplasty vs Directional Atherectomy-II

(continued)

Results	Initial angiographic success was 89.2% with atherectomy vs 79.0% with angioplasty (p=0.019), as was initial luminal gain (1.45 vs 1.12 mm, p<0.001). Distal embolization occurred in 13.4% and 5.1% of the patients, respectively (p=0.012), and non Q wave infarction in 16.1% and 9.6%, respectively (p=0.09). The restenosis rates (>50% stenosis) were similar at 6 months (45.6% vs 50.5%, p=0.49). 13.2% of the atherectomy and 22.4% of the angioplasty patients required repeated interventions (p=0.41).
Conclusions	Atherectomy of de novo vein graft lesion was associated with better initial angiographic success, but with increased distal embolization. There was no difference in restenosis rates, however, there was a trend towards less target vessel revascularization procedures.

AMRO

Amsterdam-Rotterdam Trial

Title	Randomised trial of excimer laser angioplasty vs balloon angioplasty for treatment of obstructive coronary artery disease.
Authors	Appelman YEA, Piek JJ, Strikwerda S, et al.
Reference	Lancet 1996;347:79-84.
Disease	Coronary artery disease, restenosis.
Purpose	To compare the initial and 6 month clinical and angiographic outcome of excimer laser coronary angioplasty vs balloon angioplasty.
Design	Randomized, multicenter.
Patients	308 patients with stable angina pectoris, coronary lesions >10 mm, or total or functional occlusions (TIMI flow grade 0 or 1), either with single or multivessel disease, who were suitable for coronary angioplasty. Patients with unstable angina; myocardial infarction within 2 weeks; a life expectancy of <1 year; intended angioplasty of a venous graft; unprotected left main disease angulated, highly eccentric, ostial or bifurcation lesions; lesions with a thrombus or dissection; and total occlusions with low likelihood of passage with a guide wire were excluded.
Follow-up	Clinical follow up and repeated coronary angiography at 6 months.
Treatment regimen	Excimer laser angioplasty (wave length 308 nm) or balloon angioplasty (PTCA).

AMRO

Amsterdam-Rotterdam Trial

(continued)

Additional therapy	Nifedipine 20 mgX3/d during hospitalization. Aspirin 250–500 mg/d, started a day before the procedure and continued for 6 months. Intravenous heparin for ≥12 h after procedure.
Results	155 patients (162 lesions) were randomized to excimer laser and 158 patients (162 lesions) to PTCA. In 5 patients, the randomized segment was not treated. Excimer laser could not be done in 25 patients. Of the remaining 133 lesions, 98% (130 lesions) were treated with additional PTCA. Of the 167 lesions (157 patients) assigned to PTCA, PTCA was not done in 24 patients due to inability to cross the lesion. The angiographic success rate was 80% after laser and 79% after PTCA. There were no deaths. Myocardial infarction occurred in 4.6% vs 5.7% of the excimer laser and PTCA groups, respectively (p=0.67). There was no difference in the rates of coronary artery bypass surgery (10.6% vs 10.8%, respectively; p=0.95), repeated angioplasty (21.2% in the laser vs 18.5% in the PTCA group; p=0.55), or in the occurrence of primary end point (death, myocardial infarction, or repeated revascularization; 33.1% vs 29.9%; p=0.55). The incidence of transient occlusions of the randomized segment was higher in the excimer laser (10 patients) than PTCA (1 patient) (relative risk 10.57; 95% CI 1.37 to 81.62; p=0.005). Arterial diameter stenosis was comparable between the groups before procedure, immediately after and at follow up. The restenosis (>50% diameter) rate was higher in the excimer laser group (51.6% vs 41.3%; difference 10.3%; 95% CI -2.0% to 22.6%; p=0.13). Minimal lumen diameter in the excimer laser and PTCA groups were 0.77±0.44 vs 0.77±0.47 mm before procedure, 1.69±0.41 vs 1.59±0.34 mm immediately after procedure (p=0.05), and 1.17±0.71 vs 1.25±0.68 mm at follow-up (p=0.34). Net gain in lumen minimal diameter (at follow-up minus before procedure) tended to be larger with PTCA (0.48±0.66 vs 0.40±0.69 mm; p=0.34). Late minimal lumen diameter loss (immediately after procedure minus at follow-up) was greater with excimer laser (0.52±0.70 vs 0.34±0.62 mm; 0.18 mm difference; 95% CI 0.15 to 0.35; p=0.04).
Conclusions	Excimer laser coronary angioplasty followed by PTCA was not better than conventional PTCA alone in the treatment of obstructive coronary lesions.

SICCO

Stenting In Chronic Coronary Occlusion

Title	Stenting in chronic coronary occlusion (SICCO): A randomized, controlled trial of adding stent implantation after successful angioplasty.
Authors	Sirnes PA, Golf S, Myreng Y, et al.
Reference	J Am Coll Cardiol 1996;28:1444–1451.
Disease	Coronary artery disease, restenosis.
Purpose	To investigate whether stent implantation improves long term results after recanalization by angioplasty of chronic coronary artery occlusions.
Design	Randomized, multicenter.
Patients	117 patients, >18 years old, who underwent conventional balloon angioplasty (PTCA) of an occluded native coronary artery (TIMI flow grade 0 or I). Patients with occlusion of <2 weeks old, inability to tolerate anticoagulant therapy, reference artery diameter <2.5 mm, major dissection following angioplasty, elastic recoil >50% after angioplasty, lesions with complex anatomy, poor distal runoff, or angiographically visible thrombus were excluded.
Follow-up	Repeated coronary angiography after 6 months.
Treatment regimen	After conventional successful PTCA, patients were randomized to either a control group with no additional intervention, or to Palmaz-Schatz stent implantation.

SICCO

Stenting In Chronic Coronary Occlusion

(continued)

Addtional therapy	Aspirin 75 to 160 mg/d, started before angioplasty, heparin 10,000 to 15,000 IU before PTCA and then heparin infusion for 12 to 24 h in the control group and for 2 to 5 days in the stented group. The patients in the stent group received an infusion of dextran (1000 mL, 50 mL/h). The stented patients received dipyridamole 75 mgX3/d and warfarin (INR 3.5 to 4.0) for 3 months.
Results	There were no deaths throughout the follow-up period. Stent delivery was unsuccessful in one patient. One patient with stent implantation had a myocardial infarction. Stent implantation resulted in an increase in minimal luminal diameter from 2.21±0.50 to 2.78±0.49 mm ($p<0.001$). Vessel closure within 14 days occurred in 6.9% and 5.1% of the stent and control groups (p=NS). Inguinal hematoma was more common in the stent group (11 vs 0 patients; $p=0.04$). At follow-up, 57% vs 24% of the stent and control groups had no angina ($p<0.001$). There was no difference in late target revascularization during the 6 month follow-up (3 patients in each group), however, at 300 days after the procedure more patients in the control than stent group underwent repeated revascularization (42.4% vs 22.4%). Follow-up angiography was performed in 114 patients. ≥50% diameter stenosis developed in 32% vs 74% of the stent and control group, respectively (Odds ratio 0.165; 95% CI 0.07 to 0.37; $p<0.001$); reocclusion occurred in 12% vs 26%, respectively ($p=0.058$). Minimal luminal diameter at follow-up was larger in the stent group (1.92±0.95 vs 1.11±0.78 mm; $p<0.001$).
Conclusions	Stent implantation after successful balloon angioplasty of chronic coronary artery occlusions improved long term angiographic results, and was associated with less recurrence of angina and less revascularization procedures.

SICCO-Late Follow-up

Stenting In Chronic Coronary Occlusion

Title	Sustained benefit of stenting chronic coronary occlusion: Long term clinical follow-up of the stenting in chronic coronary occlusion (SICCO) study.
Authors	Sirnes PA, Golf S, Myreng Y, et al.
Reference	J Am Coll Cardiol 1998; 32:305-310.
Disease	Coronary artery disease.
Purpose	To determine the long term outcome of stenting chronic coronary occlusions.
Design	As per SICCO.
Patients	As per SICCO.
Follow-up	33±6 months.
Treatment regimen	As per SICCO.
Results	Major adverse cardiac events (cardiac death, lesion related acute MI, repeat target lesion revascularization or angiographic evidence of reocclusion) occurred in 14 (24.1%) of stent patients vs 35 (59.3%) of patients in the PTCA group (p=0.0002). 24% of stent group required target vessel revascularization vs 53% of the PTCA group (p=0.002). After 8 months there were no further events in the patients that received stents, while events continued to occur in the patients that received PTCA. Major adverse cardiac events correlated with PTCA group, left anterior descending coronary artery lesion, and lesion length, as assessed by multivariate analysis.

SICCO-Late Follow-up

Stenting In Chronic Coronary Occlusion

(continued)

Conclusions	Stenting showed long term safety and clinical benefit in patients with chronic occlusions. Late clinical events were reduced in stented patients vs those who received PTCA alone.

A comparison of coronary artery stenting with angioplasty for isolated stenosis of the proximal left anterior descending coronary artery

Title	A comparison of coronary artery stenting with angioplasty for isolated stenosis of the proximal left anterior descending coronary artery.
Author	Versaci F, Gaspardone A, Tomai F, et al.
Reference	N Engl J Med 1997;336:817-822.
Disease	Coronary artery disease.
Purpose	To compare treatment of isolated coronary artery stenosis with percutaneous transluminal coronary angioplasty vs coronary artery stent deployment.
Design	Randomized, prospective.
Patients	120 patients with isolated stenosis of the proximal left anterior descending coronary artery.
Follow-up	12 months.
Treatment regimen	Stent implantation vs PTCA.
Results	The rates of procedural success (residual stenosis of less than 50%; absence of death, myocardial infarction, and need for coronary artery bypass surgery during hospital stay) were similar between the 2 groups (95% with stenting; 93% with angioplasty, p=NS). The 12 month rates of event free survival (freedom from death, myocardial infarction, and the recurrence of angina) were 87% for stenting and 70% for angioplasty (p=0.04). Rates of restenosis were 19% after stenting and 40% after PTCA (p=0.02).

A comparison of coronary artery stenting with angioplasty for isolated stenosis of the proximal left anterior descending coronary artery

(continued)

Conclusions	Stenting resulted in a lower rate of restenosis and better long term clinical outcome compared to PTCA in patients with asymptomatic isolated coronary artery stenosis.

BOAT

Balloon vs Optimal Atherectomy Trial (BOAT)

Title	Final results of the balloon vs optimal atherectomy trial (BOAT).
Author	Baim DS, Cutlip DE, Sharma SK, et al.
Reference	Circulation 1998; 97:322-331.
Disease	Coronary artery disease.
Purpose	To determine whether optimal directional coronary atherectomy provides short and long term benefits compared to percutaneous transluminal coronary angioplasty.
Design	Randomized, multicenter.
Patients	1000 patients with single de novo atherosclerotic narrowing in a coronary artery.
Follow-up	1 year.
Treatment regimen	Optimal atherectomy included use of 7F cutters as the final device, removal of as much tissue as safe, postdilation with balloon, obtaining a final residual stenosis <20%, and special training.

BOAT

Balloon vs Optimal Atherectomy Trial (BOAT)

(continued)

Results	Optimal directional atherectomy resulted in a lesion success rate of 99%, vs PTCA at 97% (p=0.02). Residual diameter stenosis was less with atherectomy at 15% vs 28% for PTCA (p<0.0001). Atherectomy was associated with more patients exhibiting an increase in creatine kinase -MB > 3x normal (16% vs 6%, p<0.0001). Major clinical complications (death, Q wave MI, or emergent CABG) were similar between groups. At 6.9 months angiographic restudy showed reduction of angiographic restenosis by atherectomy (31.4%) compared to angioplasty (39.8%, p=0.016). Clinical follow-up showed nonsignificant trends toward lower mortality rate, target vessel revascularization, and target vessel failure (21.1% vs 24.8%, p=0.17) with atherectomy compared to angioplasty.
Conclusions	Optimal directional coronary atherectomy improved short-term success compared to angioplasty, but did not significantly improve late clinical events.

ERBAC

Excimer Laser, Rotational Atherectomy, and Balloon Angioplasty Comparison (ERBAC) study

Title	Randomized comparison of angioplasty of complex coronary lesions at a single center. Excimer laser, rotational atherectomy, and balloon angioplasty comparison (ERBAC) study.
Author	Reifart N, Vandormael M, Krajcar M, et al.
Reference	Circulation 1997; 96:91-98.
Disease	Coronary artery disease.
Purpose	To test whether coronary revascularization with ablation of either excimer laser or rotational atherectomy improves initial angiographic and clinical outcomes vs percutaneous transluminal coronary angioplasty alone.
Design	Randomized, single center.
Patients	685 patients with symptomatic coronary artery disease warranting revascularization procedure.
Follow-up	6 months.
Treatment regimen	Patients randomized to balloon angioplasty, excimer laser angioplasty, or rotational atherectomy.

ERBAC

Excimer Laser, Rotational Atherectomy, and Balloon Angioplasty Comparison (ERBAC) study (continued)

Results	Procedural success was defined by diameter stenosis <50%, survival, no Q wave infarction, or coronary artery bypass surgery. Patients who received rotational atherectomy had higher rate of procedural success (89%) vs laser angioplasty (77%) or balloon angioplasty (80%; p=0.0019). There were no differences in major in-hospital complications (3.1-4.3%). At 6 months, revascularization of target lesion was more frequently required in the rotational atherectomy group (42.4%) and the excimer laser group (46.0%) than the angioplasty group (31.9%, p=0.013).
Conclusions	Although rotational atherectomy resulted in better early procedural success, it did not result in better late outcomes compared to laser atherectomy or balloon angioplasty.

SAVED

Saphenous Vein De Novo Trial

Title	Stent placement compared with balloon angioplasty for obstructed coronary bypass grafts.
Author	Savage MP, Douglas JS, Fischman DL, et al.
Reference	N Engl J Med 1997;337:740-747.
Disease	Coronary artery disease, obstructed coronary bypass grafts.
Purpose	To compare the effects of stent placement with those of balloon angioplasty in patients with obstruction of saphenous vein grafts.
Design	Multicenter, randomized.
Patients	270 patients with new lesions in aortocoronary-venous bypass grafts.
Follow-up	6 months.
Treatment regimen	Randomized to Palmaz-Schatz stents vs standard balloon angioplasty.

Results

Patients receiving stents had a higher initial procedural success with reduction in stenosis to less than 50% of vessel diameter (92% vs 69% with angioplasty, p=0.001), but more hemorrhagic complications (17% vs 5%, p<0.01). The stent group had a greater mean increase in luminal diameter immediately after the procedure and a greater mean net gain in luminal diameter as well (0.85 ± 0.96 with stents vs 0.54 ± 0.91 mm with angioplasty, p=0.002). At 6 months restenosis occurred in 37% of patients that received stents and 46% that received angioplasty (p=0.24). The stent group had a better clinical outcome at 73% (freedom from death, myocardial infarction, repeat coronary artery bypass grafting, or repeat revascularization) compared to the angioplasty group at (58%, p=0.03).

Conclusions

Stenting of venous bypass graft stenoses resulted in a better initial outcome, larger gain in luminal diameter, but no significant long term improvement in angiographic evidence of restenosis. Stents did reduce the frequency of major cardiac events.

Coronary artery stenting compared with balloon angioplasty for restenosis after initial balloon angioplasty

Authors	Erbel R, Haude M, Höpp HW, et al, for the Restenosis Stent Study Group.
Reference	N Engl J Med 1998; 339:1672–1678.
Disease	Coronary artery disease.
Purpose	To determine whether intracoronary stenting vs percutaneous transluminal coronary angioplasty reduces the recurrence of luminal narrowing in lesions with restenosis.
Design	Prospective, randomized, multicenter.
Patients	383 patients who previously had undergone balloon angioplasty and had clinical and angiographic evidence of restenosis.
Follow-up	6 months.
Treatment regimen	Angioplasty alone (192 patients) vs intracoronary stenting with a Palmaz-Schatz stent (191 patients).
Additional therapy	Aspirin, heparin during procedure. Following stenting heparin followed by coumadin for 3 months. After angioplasty, 300 mg aspirin.

Coronary artery stenting compared with balloon angioplasty for restenosis after initial balloon angioplasty

(continued)

Results	The rate of restenosis (defined as stenosis of more than 50% of the lumen) at 6 months was higher in the angioplasty group (32%) compared to the stent group (18%; p=0.03). Revascularization of the target vessel was necessary in 27% of angioplasty patients but in only 10% of stent patients (p=0.001). There was a smaller mean minimal luminal diameter in the angioplasty vs the stent group. Subacute thrombosis was more common in the stent group (3.9%) compared to the angioplasty group (0.6%). Event free survival (free of death, myocardial infarction, bypass surgery, revascularization of target vessel after randomization) was present in 72% of angioplasty patients and 84% of stent patients, at 250 days (p=0.04).
Conclusions	Coronary artery stenting reduced the rate of recurrent restenosis despite a higher incidence of subacute thrombosis.

MUSIC

Multicenter Ultrasound Stenting In Coronaries Study

Title	Intravascular ultrasound guided optimized stent deployment. Immediate and 6 months clinical and angiographic results from the Multicenter Ultrasound Stenting In Coronaries Study (MUSIC).
Authors	De Jaegere P, Mudra H, Figulla H, et al.
Reference	Eur Heart J 1998;19:1214–1223.
Disease	Coronary artery disease, stenting, restenosis.
Purpose	To assess the feasibility and safety of intravascular ultrasound (IVUS) guided stent deployment followed by aspirin alone, without subsequent anticoagulation.
Design	Observational, open label, multicenter.
Patients	161 patients with stable angina due to a single de novo coronary lesion, suitable for coronary angioplasty. Patients with intolerance to aspirin or anticoagulation were not included. The target lesion had to be <15 mm long, able to receive a 3.0 mm diameter Palmaz-Schatz stent. Only lesions in coronary arteries supplying normally functioning myocardium were included. Patients with angiographic evidence of thrombus, diffuse disease or multiple focal lesions, left main coronary artery stenosis, ostial and bifurcational lesions, and severely tortuous arteries were excluded.
Follow-up	Repeated coronary angiography at 6 months. Clinical follow-up for a mean of 198±38 days.

MUSIC

Multicenter Ultrasound Stenting In Coronaries Study (continued)

Treatment regimen	14 mm Palmaz-Schatz stents, after predilatation by PTCA. IVUS was then performed. If optimal deployment was not achieved, additional in-stent balloon dilatations were performed.
Additional therapy	All patients received aspirin before procedure. In patients without optimal stent deployment, aspirin 100 mg/d, intravenous heparin, and acenocoumarol for 3 months was given. In patients in whom IVUS showed optimal stent deployment, aspirin 100 mg/d was given.
Results	In 4 patients a stent could not be implanted. A total of 186 stents were deployed in 157 patients. In-hospital in-stent thrombosis occurred in 2 patients (1.3%). 5 patients (3.2%) had a non Q wave myocardial infarction. In 6 patients (3.7%) IVUS was not performed. IVUS was not associated with complications, except for a coronary dissection that induced a non Q wave myocardial infarction in one patient. Of the 155 patients who underwent IVUS, 123 (81%) had optimal results and were treated with aspirin alone. Of the remaining 38 patients, 22 patients were treated with aspirin and anticoagulation and 16 with aspirin alone. During the follow-up, one patient had Q wave myocardial infarction, one patient underwent CABG, 9 patients (5.7%) underwent repeated angioplasty, and 7 patients (4.5%) underwent target lesion revascularization). 6 month repeated angiography was performed in 144 patients (92%). ≥50% restenosis was documented in 12 patients (8.3%).
Conclusions	In selected patients with stable angina, stent deployment, guided by IVUS is feasible and safe. In patients with optimal stent deployment, as detected by IVUS, the 6 months clinical and angiographic results are excellent, and low dose (100 mg/d) aspirin without the use of anticoagulation may be sufficient.

Title	Treatment of calcified lesions with Palmaz-Schatz stents. An intravascular ultrasound study.
Authors	Hoffmann R, Mintz GS, Popma JJ, et al.
Reference	Eur Heart J 1998;19:1224-1231.
Disease	Coronary artery disease, stent.
Purpose	1.To study the results of coronary artery stent deployment in calcified lesions. 2. To evaluate whether rotational atherectomy before stenting will improve the results. 3. To define intravascular ultrasound characteristics for prediction of nonoptimal stent deployment.
Design	Open label, single center.
Patients	303 patients (197 men), 63.9±11.5 years old who underwent intravascular ultrasound (IVUS) as part of routine coronary angioplasty. Patients were divided into 4 groups based on the arc of circumferential lesion calcification (0-90° [n=120], 91-180° [n=58], 181-270° [n=71], and 271-360° [n=74]).
Treatment regimen	26 lesions were treated with "biliary" stents and 297 with coronary Palmaz-Schatz stents. IVUS was performed before and after stent deployment, after administration of 0.2 mg intracoronary nitroglycerin.
Additional therapy	In 117 lesions rotational atherectomy was used before stent deployment.

(continued)

Results	Mean age increased as the arc of calcium increased (61.2, 63.4, 65.7, and 66.9 years in the 0-90°, 91-180°, 181-270°, and 271-360° groups, respectively; p=0.0051). There were 3 non Q wave and one Q wave myocardial infarctions and 2 deaths among patients with arc of calcium >180°. Among patients with ≤180° arc of calcium, there were 3 non Q wave and one Q wave myocardial infarctions, and 2 urgent CABGs. Higher balloon inflation pressures were utilized in patients with greater arc of calcium (14.2±3.9, 14.8±3.7, 16.7±3.0, and 16.3±3.1 atm, respectively; p<0.0001). More patients with greater arc of calcium underwent rotational atherectomy before stenting (0%, 21%, 69%, and 76%, respectively; p<0.0001). Despite using higher inflation pressures, the post procedure IVUS minimal lumen diameter decreased with increasing arc of calcium (2.80±0.45, 2.81±0.44, 2.54±0.35, and 2.65±0.42 mm, respectively; p=0.0013). The differences in post procedure lesion cross sectional area were not statistically different (7.7, 7.7, 7.0, and 7.2 mm^2, respectively; p=0.16). However, acute cross sectional area gain decreased as the arc of calcium increased (5.4±2.0, 5.1±2.3, 4.4±1.9, and 4.8±2.0 mm^2, respectively; p=0.041). Final % diameter stenosis was 7±14, 9±12, 16±11, and 15±12, respectively (p<0.0001). Among lesions with >180° arc of calcium, acute diameter gain (1.94±0.48 mm vs 1.72±0.57 mm; p=0.024), and final acute gain in cross sectional area (5.41±1.99 mm^2 vs 4.57±1.97 mm^2; p=0.024) were greater in lesions treated than not treated with rotational atherectomy before stenting. Final angiographic diameter stenosis was 4±12% vs 9±11% among patients who underwent or did not undergo rotational atherectomy (p=0.0444). Final stent eccentricity was greater in heavily calcified lesions, especially in lesions with eccentric calcification pattern.
Conclusions	Implantation of stents in heavily calcified lesions (especially in eccentric calcified lesions) results in less optimal stent expansion, than in less calcified lesions. Use of rotational atherectomy before stent deployment may improve the procedural results.

GISSOC

Gruppo Italiano Di Studio Sullo Stent Nelle Occlusioni Coronariche

Title	Stent implantation vs balloon angioplasty in chronic coronary occlusions: Results from the GISSOC Trial.
Authors	Rubartelli P, Niccoli L, Verna E, et al.
Reference	J Am Coll Cardiol 1998; 32:90–96.
Disease	Coronary artery disease.
Purpos	To determine whether Palmaz-Schatz stent implantation after successful PTCA in chronic coronary occlusions would improve outcome.
Design	Randomized, multicenter.
Patients	110 patients with chronic total occlusion of a coronary artery who were symptomatic or had evidence of inducible ischemia in the territory supplied by the occluded coronary artery. Patients underwent successful PTCA and were randomized to stent or no stent.
Follow-up	9 months.
Treatment regimen	PTCA alone or stent.
Additional therapy	Aspirin, calcium channel blocker, heparin. In stented patients, warfarin for 1 month.

GISSOC

Gruppo Italiano Di Studio Sullo Stent Nelle Occlusioni Coronariche

(continued)

Results	Primary end point at repeat coronary angiography at 9 months was minimal lumen diameter (MLD) assessed by quantitative coronary angiography read at a core facility. At 9 months the MLD was 0.85±0.75 mm in PTCA alone patients vs 1.74±0.88 mm in stent patients ($p<0.001$). Fewer stent patients showed restenosis (32%) compared to PTCA patients (68%; $p<0.001$). Reocclusion of the target artery was less common in stented patients (8%) compared to PTCA alone patients (34%). Stent patients experienced less recurrent ischemia (14%) compared to PTCA alone patients (46%, $p=0.002$) and required less target coronary artery revascularization.
Conclusions	Stenting after successful PTCA of chronic total coronary artery occlusions improved coronary angiographic findings, reduced restenosis and improved clinical outcome.

TOSCA

The Total Occlusion Study of Canada

Title	Primary stenting vs balloon angioplasty in occluded coronary arteries.
Authors	Buller CE, Dzavik V, Carere RG, et al.
Reference	Circulation 1999;100:236–242.
Disease	Coronary artery disease.
Purpose	To determine whether routine stenting improves late complete patency of recanalized total coronary artery occlusions.
Design	Randomized, controlled, multicenter.
Patients	Patients undergoing coronary interventions with a total coronary occlusion defined as high grade native coronary stenosis with TIMI grade 0 or 1 antegrade flow.
Follow-up	6 months.
Treatment regimen	Percutaneous transluminal coronary angioplasty (PTCA) vs heparin coated 15 mm long PS-153 Palmaz-Schatz coronary stent.
Additional therapy	Aspirin, ticlopidine, as per investigator.

TOSCA

The Total Occlusion Study of Canada

(continued)

Results	The primary end point was failure of sustained complete target vessel patency with TIMI flow of <3. Secondary end points included repeat revascularization, adverse cardiovascular events, and restenosis (>50% diameter stenosis on angiography). Primary stenting was associated with a 10.9% failed patency rate vs PTCA at 19.5%, p=0.025 resulting in a 44% decrease in failed patency at 6 months. Target vessel revascularization was 8.4% with stenting vs 15.4% with PTCA (p=0.03), reflecting at 45% decrease in revascularization rates. Incidence of adverse cardiovascular events (defined as any revascularization, myocardial infarction or death) was 23.3% in the stent group and 23.6% in the PTCA group; p=NS. By angiography, stenting was associated with a larger minimum lumen dimension at 6 months (1.48 mm) vs PTCA (1.23 mm; p<0.01) and decreased binary restenosis rate (55% vs 70%; p<0.01).
Conclusions	Primary stenting is superior to PTCA for nonacute total coronary occlusions.

START (Stent vs Atherectomy)

Stent Vs Directional Coronary Atherectomy Randomized Trial

Title	Final Results of the STent Vs directional coronary Atherectomy Randomized Trial (START).
Authors	Tsuchikane E, Sumitsuji S, Awata N, et al.
Reference	J Am Coll Cardiol 1999;34:1050–1057.
Disease	Coronary artery disease.
Purpose	To compare primary stenting with optimal directional coronary atherectomy (DCA).
Design	Randomized clinical study.
Patients	Patients with coronary artery disease who had suitable coronary lesions for both stenting and DCA, by angiography and intravascular ultrasound (IVUS).
Follow-up	6 month angiography; 1 year clinical outcome.
Treatment regimen	Stenting (62 lesions) with high pressure adjunctive PTCA to achieve a minimal lumen cross sectional area of ≥7.5 mm^2 assessed by IVUS. In the DCA group (n=60 lesions) aggressive debulking using a Simpson Atherocath and increasing balloon pressures to 40 psi. Debulking was guided by IVUS with the goal of a residual percent plaque plus media cross sectional area of <50%. Low pressure adjunct balloon dilatation was performed.
Additional therapy	Ticlopidine and aspirin for stenting. Aspirin in DCA group. Glycoprotein IIb/IIIa antagonists or anticoagulants were not used.

START (Stent vs Atherectomy)

Stent Vs Directional Coronary Atherectomy Randomized Trial

(continued)

Results	Serial quantitative angiography and IVUS performed at pre and post procedure and 6 months. Primary end point was restenosis (≥50% diameter stenosis at 6 months) defined by angiography. Initial procedural success (<50% residual diameter stenosis); minimal luminal diameter and percent diameter stenosis at baseline, postprocedure and 6 months were also assessed. Clinical end points also were determined. Initial procedural success was achieved in all patients in both groups. Postprocedural minimal luminal diameter was 2.79±0.39 mm in the stent group vs 2.90±0.38 mm in the DCA group. Postprocedural percent diameter stenosis was 14.8±10% in the stent and 12.9±8.1% in the DCA group (p=NS). Luminal cross sectional area was 8.1±2.2 mm^2 in the stent and 8.5±1.8 mm^2 in the DCA group. Postprocedural percent plaque plus media cross sectional areas was higher for stent arm vs DCA arm (58.6±5.9% vs 52.4±8.2%, p=0.0001). At 6 months the minimal lumen diameter was smaller (1.89±0.73 mm) in the stent group vs the DCA group (2.18±0.62 mm; p=0.023) and diameter stenosis was higher in the stent group (40.1±19.2%) vs the DCA group (32.1±16.9%; p=0.018). The primary end point of angiographic restenosis was lower in the DCA group (15.8%) vs the stent group (15.8%; p=0.032). Follow-up IVUS showed larger area in the DCA group (7.0 mm^2) vs stent group (5.3 mm^2; p=0.03) and more intimal proliferation in the stent group (3.1 mm^2) vs the DCA group (1.1 mm^2; p<0.0001). There was a trend toward lower one year target vessel failure in the DCA arm (18.3%) vs stent group (33.9%; p=0.056). Death occurred in 1 stent and zero DCA patients. Target lesion revascularization was 29% in the stent group and 15% in the DCA group (p=0.062).
Conclusions	Aggressive DCA including IVUS directed debulking may provide better angiographic and clinical outcomes compared to primary stenting.

START (Stenting vs PTCA)

Stent Implantation and Balloon Angioplasty in the Treatment of De Novo Coronary Artery Lesions

Title	Randomized comparison of coronary stent implantation and balloon angioplasty in the treatment of de novo coronary artery lesions (START).
Authors	Betriu A, Masotti M, Serra A, et al.
Reference	J Am Coll Cardiol 1999;34:1498-1506.
Disease	Coronary artery disease.
Purpose	To determine whether stenting of de novo coronary artery lesions would decrease restenosis rates and lead to better long term clinical outcomes compared to PTCA.
Design	Randomized, multicenter.
Patients	452 patients with either stable (n=129) or unstable angina (n=229), with angiographic evidence of a coronary stenosis of at least 70% and had not undergone previous dilation.
Follow-up	6 month repeat angiography. 4 year clinical follow-up.
Treatment regimen	Stenting (n=229) vs angioplasty (n=223).
Additional therapy	For stenting aspirin, dipyridamole, dextran, calcium blocker, heparin, warfarin. After first 100 stents, oral ticlopidine replaced dextran, dipyridamole, and warfarin.

START (Stenting vs PTCA)

Stent Implantation and Balloon Angioplasty in the Treatment of De Novo Coronary Artery Lesions

(continued)

Results	84% of PTCA and 95% of stented patients achieved procedural success, defined as residual stenosis <50% in absence of death, acute MI, need for emergency CABG, or bail out stenting. Rate of vessel closure was 4% in the PTCA group and 2.6% in stent group. At 6 months, 397 patients underwent angiography. The stent group had demonstrated a greater increase in immediate minimal luminal diameter (2.02±0.6 mm) vs the PTCA group (1.43±0.6 mm; p<0.0001) and a greater increase in the 6 month minimal luminal diameter (1.98±0.7 mm vs 1.63±0.7 mm; p<0.001). Restenosis rates were 37% in the PTCA group and 22% in the stent group (RR=0.60; 95% CI=0.43-0.82; p=0.0013). Inhospital mortality was 1.3% in the PTCA group and 0.9% in the stenting group. At 4 years mortality rates were 2.4% and 2.7% in the stent vs angioplasty group; MI rates were 2.8% and 2.2% respectively (p=NS). The need for further revascularization procedures of the target lesions was reduced in the stent (12%) vs the PTCA group (25%; RR=0.49; CI=0.32-0.75, p=0.0006). Repeat procedures were most likely to be carried out within the first 6 months of the study.
Conclusions	Stenting reduced restenosis rates and resulted in better minimal luminal diameters compared to PTCA. Stenting also decreased the need for repeat revascularization compared to PTCA.

ABACAS

Adjunctive Balloon Angioplasty after Coronary Atherectomy Study

Title	Effects of adjunctive balloon angioplasty after intravascular ultrasound guided optimal directional coronary atherectomy. The results of ABACAS.
Authors	Suzuki T, Hosokawa H, Katoh O, et al.
Reference	J Am Coll Cardiol 1999;34:1028–1035.
Disease	Coronary artery disease.
Purpose	To determine the effect of adjunctive PTCA after directional coronary atherectomy vs stand alone atherectomy and to assess the outcome of intravascular ultrasound guided, aggressive atherectomy.
Design	Prospective, randomized, multicenter.
Patients	225 patients who had intravascular ultrasound guided directional coronary artherectomy. Optimal debulking was achieved in 214 patients who were than randomized to no further therapy or PTCA.
Follow-up	12 months.
Treatment regimen	Directional coronary atherectomy with a Simpson Coronary AtheroCath and guidance with intravascular ultrasound to obtain angiographic criteria of <30% or adequate debulking (estimated plaque area <50%). Patients randomized to adjunctive PTCA or no further therapy.
Additional therapy	IV nitroglycerin during procedure.

Results	Primary end point was angiographic restenosis rate at 6 months (>50% stenosis by angiography). Quantitative coronary angiography and quantitative coronary ultrasound also assessed. Secondary end point was clinical event rate (death, MI, target vessel revascularizaton) at 6 months. Acute postprocedure analysis revealed an improved minimum luminal diameter (2.88±0.48) in the adjunctive PTCA group vs the no further therapy group (2.6±0.51 mm; p=0.006). The adjunctive PTCA group had less residual stenosis (10.8% vs 15%; p=0.009). Acute quantitative ultrasound also showed a larger minimum luminal diameter (3.26±0.48 mm) in the adjunctive PTCA group vs the no further therapy group (3.04±0.5 mm; p<0.001). The adjunctive PTCA group also had a lower residual plaque mass (42.6%) vs the no therapy group (45.6%; p<0.001) on the ultrasound. However, at 6 months minimal luminal diameter was 33.4±19.9 mm in the adjunctive PTCA group vs 32.3±15.9 in the no further therapy group (p=NS); and restenosis rates were 23.6% for adjunctive PTCA vs 19.6% for the no further therapy group (p=NS). Cumulative clinical event rate at 6 months was 20.6% in the adjunctive PTCA group and 17.1% in the no further therapy group (p=NS). At 12 months there also was no difference between groups.
Conclusions	Adjunctive PTCA following aggressive directional atherectomy improved acute quantitative coronary angiographic and intravascular ultrasound outcomes. The benefit was not maintained at 6 months. Adjunctive PTCA also did not improve clinical outcomes over aggressive ultrasound guided directional atherectomy alone.

4. Interventional Cardiology

d. Medical Therapy and Brachytherapy to Prevent Restenosis and/or Complications After Intracoronary Interventions or Occlusion After Coronary Artery Bypass Grafting

CARPORT

Coronary Artery Restenosis Prevention on Repeated Thromboxane Antagonism Study

Title	Prevention of restenosis after percutaneous transluminal coronary angioplasty with thromboxane A2 receptor blockade. A randomized, double blind, placebo controlled trial.
Authors	Serruys PW, Rutsch W, Heyndrick GR, et al.
Reference	Circulation 1991;84:1568-1580.
Disease	Coronary artery disease, restenosis.
Purpose	To evaluate the efficacy of GR32191B, a thromboxane A2 receptor antagonist, to prevent restenosis following coronary angioplasty.
Design	Randomized, double blind, placebo controlled, multicenter.
Patients	697 patients, >21 years old, with coronary artery disease who were excluded for angioplasty for de novo lesions in native arteries. Patients with myocardial infarction within 2 weeks of procedure were excluded.
Follow-up	Clinical evaluation, exercise test, and repeated angiography at 6 months.
Treatment regimen	1. GR32191B 80 mg PO 1 h + saline infusion before procedure. 40 mg X2/d GR32191B thereafter. 2. Placebo PO + 250 mg aspirin IV before procedure. Placebo X2/d thereafter. Aspirin and NSAID were prohibited during the follow-up.
Additional therapy	Heparin IV 10,000 U bolus, 10 mg nifedipine every 2 h for 12 h, and then 20 mg of slow released nifedipine X3/d for 2 days.

CARPORT

Coronary Artery Restenosis Prevention on Repeated Thromboxane Antagonism Study (continued)

Results	522 compliant patients underwent repeated angiography. The mean minimal luminal diameter loss was 0.31±0.54 vs 0.31±0.55 mm in the control and treated group. A loss of ≥0.72 mm was found in 19% and 21% of the patients, respectively. 6 months after procedure 72% and 75% of the patients, respectively were symptom free. There was no difference in the rates of clinical events during the 6 months between the groups. There was no difference in exercise performance between the groups.
Conclusions	Long term blockade of the thromboxane A2 receptor with GR32191B did not prevent restenosis or reduced clinical events after coronary angioplasty.

MERCATOR

Multicenter European Research Trial With Cilazapril After Angioplasty to Prevent Transluminal Coronary Obstruction and Restenosis

Title	Does the new angiotensin converting enzyme inhibitor cilazapril prevent restenosis after percutaneous transluminal coronary angioplasty? Results of the MERCATOR study: A multicenter, randomized, double blind, placebo controlled trial.
Authors	The MERCATOR Study Group.
Reference	Circulation 1992;86:100–110.
Disease	Coronary artery disease, restenosis.
Purpose	To assess the effect of ACE inhibition with cilazapril on restenosis after coronary angioplasty.
Design	Randomized, double blind, placebo controlled, multicenter.
Patients	693 patients with successful angioplasty of a coronary artery.
Follow-up	Clinical evaluation, exercise test, and repeated angiography at 6 months.
Treatment regimen	Medications were started in the evening following the angioplasty. Cilazapril 2.5 mg PO initially, and then 5 mg X2/d or placebo for 6 months.
Additional therapy	Aspirin 150–250 mg/d, started before angioplasty. IV heparin 10,000 U bolus before angioplasty, and infusion. calcium channel blockers for 48 h were permitted.

MERCATOR

Multicenter European Research Trial With Cilazapril After Angioplasty to Prevent Transluminal Coronary Obstruction and Restenosis

(continued)

Results	The mean difference in minimal coronary luminal diameter between the baseline and follow-up angiography was -0.29±0.49 and -0.27±0.51 mm in the control and cilazapril treated patients, respectively. The occurrence of clinical events including death, myocardial infarction, coronary revascularization, or recurrent angina were similar in both groups. 63.6% and 62.2% of the control and cilazapril patients were event free after 6 months. No difference in exercise test results were found between the groups.
Conclusions	Long term ACE inhibition with cilazapril did not prevent restenosis and did not reduce clinical events.

PARK

Post Angioplasty Restenosis Ketanserin

Title	Evaluation of ketanserin in the prevention of restenosis after percutaneous transluminal coronary angioplasty. A multicenter randomized, double blind placebo controlled trial.
Authors	Serruys PW, Klein W, Tijssen JPG, et al.
Reference	Circulation 1993;88:1588-1601.
Disease	Coronary artery disease, restenosis.
Purpose	To evaluate the role of ketanserin in prevention of restenosis after coronary angioplasty.
Design	Randomized, double blind, placebo controlled, multicenter.
Patients	658 patients, >30 years old, with angina due to a single or multivessel coronary artery disease who underwent coronary angioplasty.
Follow-up	Clinical evaluation and repeated angiography at 6 months.
Treatment regimen	Oral ketanserin 40 mg X2/d or placebo started 1 h before balloon insertion and continued for 6 months (the first 79 patients received IV infusion of ketanserin or placebo).
Additional therapy	Aspirin 250-500 mg/d, started before angioplasty. Heparin 10,000 U bolus before procedure.

Post Angioplasty Restenosis Ketanserin

(continued)

Results	Clinical follow-up of 525 patients was reported.There was no difference in the occurrence of any of the clinical end points (death, myocardial infarction, coronary bypass surgery, or repeated angioplasty) between the 2 groups. Any of the end points occurred in 28% and 32% of the ketanserin and placebo patients (RR 0.89, 95% CI 0.70–1.13). 592 patients underwent serial angiographic studies. The mean loss of minimal luminal diameter between the post-angioplasty and follow-up angiogram was 0.27 ± 0.49 and 0.24±0.52 mm in the ketanserin and placebo groups (difference 0.03 mm, 95% CI -0.05–0.11, p=0.5). Restenosis (>50%) occurred in 32% and 32% of the patients, respectively.
Conclusions	Ketanserin at a dose of 80 mg/d failed to reduce restenosis rate and did not lower the incidence of adverse clinical events at 6 months.

CABADAS

Prevention of Coronary Artery Bypass Graft Occlusion by Aspirin, Dipyridamole, and Acenocoumarol/Phenoprocoumon Study

Title	a. Prevention of 1 year vein graft occlusion after aortocoronary bypass surgery: A comparison of low dose aspirin, low dose aspirin plus dipyridamole, and oral anticoagulants. b. Effects of low dose aspirin (50 mg/d), low dose aspirin plus dipyridamole, and oral anticoagulant agents after internal mammary artery bypass grafting: Patency and clinical outcome at 1 year.
Authors	a. van der Meer J, Hillege HL, Kootstra GJ, et al. b. van der Meer J, de la Rivière AB, van Gilst WH, et al.
Reference	a. Lancet 1993;342:257-264. b. J Am Coll Cardiol 1994;24:1181-1188.
Disease	Coronary artery disease, coronary artery bypass grafting.
Purpose	To assess the benefits of low dose aspirin, aspirin+dipyridamole, and anticoagulation on 1 year patency rate of: a. vein grafts b. internal thoracic artery bypass.
Design	Randomized, double blind (placebo controlled for dipyridamole, open label for anticoagulation), multicenter.
Patients	a. 948 patients, ≤70 years old, who underwent elective aortocoronary bypass surgery with saphenous vein grafts. Patients with unstable angina or myocardial infarction within 7 days were excluded. b. 494 patients of the previous group, who received both internal thoracic artery and vein grafts.
Follow-up	Clinical follow-up and coronary angiography after 1 year.

CABADAS

Prevention of Coronary Artery Bypass Graft Occlusion by Aspirin, Dipyridamole, and Acenocoumarol/Phenoprocoumon Study (continued)

Treatment regimen	1. Aspirin 50 mg/d started after surgery. 2. Aspirin 50 mg/d started after surgery + dipyridamole IV 5 mg/kg/d started before surgery and continued for 28 h, and then orally 200 mg X2/d. 3. Oral anticoagulation, started 1 d before surgery. Target INR 2.8–4.8.
Additional therapy	Coronary artery bypass grafting surgery. Paracetamol as an analgesic. Drugs that interfere with platelet aggregation were prohibited.
Results	a. After 1 year, occlusion rate of distal anastomosis was 11% in the aspirin+dipyridamole, 15% in the aspirin alone, and 13% in the oral anticoagulation (aspirin+dipyridamole vs aspirin RR 0.76, 95% CI 0.54–1.05, oral anticoagulants vs aspirin+dipyridamole RR 0.90, 95% CI 0.65–1.25). Clinical events (death, myocardial infarction, thrombosis, or major bleeding) occurred in 20.3%, 13.9% (RR 1.46, 95% CI 1.02–2.08), and 16.9% (RR 1.22, 95% CI 0.84–1.77), respectively. b. Occlusion rates were 4.6%, 5.3%, and 6.8% in the aspirin+dipyridamole, aspirin, and oral anticoagulants (p=NS). Overall clinical event rates were 23.3%, 13.3% (RR 1.75, 95% CI 1.09–2.81, p=0.025), and 17.1% (RR 1.29, 95% CI 0.77–2.15, p=0.42), respectively.
Conclusions	Addition of dipyridamole to low dose aspirin did not improve patency of either venous or internal thoracic artery grafts significantly. However, the overall clinical event rate was increased by adding dipyridamole.

EPIC

Evaluation of 7E3 for the Prevention of Ischemic Complications

(continued)

Title	a. Randomized trial of coronary intervention with antibody against platelet IIb/IIIa integrin for reduction of clinical restenosis: Results at 6 months. b. Use of monoclonal antibody directed against the platelet glycoprotein IIb/IIIa receptor in high risk coronary angioplasty. c. Effects of platelet glycoprotein IIb/IIIa receptor blockade by a chimeric monoclonal antibody (Abciximab) on acute and 6 month outcomes after percutaneous transluminal coronary angioplasty for acute myocardial infarction. d. Increased risk of non Q wave myocardial infarction after directional atherectomy is platelet dependent: Evidence from the EPIC Trial. e. Long term protection from myocardial ischemic events in a randomized trial of brief integrin (3 blockade with percutaneous coronary intervention. f. Role of platelet glycoprotein IIb/IIIa receptor inhibition on distal embolization during percutaneous revascularization of aortocoronary saphenous vein grafts.
Authors	a. Topol EJ, Califf RM, Weisman HF, et al. b. The EPIC Investigators. c. Lefkovits J, Ivanhoe RJ, Carliff RM, et al. d. Lefkovits J, Blankenship JC, Anderson KM, et al. e. Topol EJ, Ferguson JJ, Weisman HF, et al. f. Mak K-H, Challapalli R, Eisenberg MJ, et al.
Reference	a. Lancet 1994;343:881-886. b. N Engl J Med 1994;330:956-961. c. Am J Cardiol 1996; 77:1045-1051. d. J Am Coll Cardiol. 1996; 28:849-855. e. JAMA 1997, 278: 479-484. f. Am J Cardiol 1997; 80:985-988.
Disease	Coronary artery disease, restenosis.

EPIC

Evaluation of 7E3 for the Prevention of Ischemic Complications

(continued)

Purpose	To evaluate the effect of a monoclonal antibody Fab fragment (c7E3), directed against the IIb/IIIa integrin, to reduce restenosis following balloon angioplasty or directional atherectomy of coronary lesions in high risk coronary lesions. e. A previous study showed that abciximab improves outcomes for patients undergoing percutaneous transluminal coronary angioplasty (PTCA) at 30 days and 6 months. The purpose of this study was to determine if abciximab improves 3 year outcome following PTCA. f. 101 patients treated for narrowing of saphenous vein grafts in the EPIC study.
Design	Randomized, double blind, placebo controlled, multicenter. e. Double blind, placebo controlled, randomized trial, multicenter. Primary outcome was composite of death, myocardial infarction, or coronary revascularization. Secondary end points were death, myocardial infarction, coronary revascularization, separately.
Patients	2099 patients, age <80 years, who needed coronary angioplasty or directional atherectomy and had an evolving or recent myocardial infarction, unstable angina, or high risk angiographic or clinical characteristics. e. 2099 high risk coronary artery disease patients undergoing PTCA.
Follow-up	6 month clinical follow-up. e. 2.5 years among 2001 patients; 3 years among 1559 patients.

EPIC

Evaluation of 7E3 for the Prevention of Ischemic Complications (continued)

Treatment regimen	1. Placebo bolus and placebo infusion for 12 h; 2. c7E3 0.25 mg/kg bolus and placebo infusion for 12 h; and 3. c7E3 0.25 mg/kg bolus and 10 μg/min infusion for 12 h. The bolus was given at least 10 min before procedure. e. Abciximab bolus of 0.25 mg/kg followed by infusion of 10 μg/min for 12 h; abciximab bolus of 0.25 mg/kg followed by placebo infusion; placebo bolus followed by placebo infusion.
Additional therapy	Aspirin 325 mg/d, with the first dose at least 2 h before procedure. IV heparin bolus 10,000–12,000 U before procedure and for ≥12 h after the procedure.
Results	Bleeding complications that mandated transfusion occurred in 7%, 14%, and 17% of the 3 groups, respectively (p<0.001). There was no difference in the events rates during the first 48 h. At 30 days, the composite end point of death, infarction, and repeated revascularization occurred in 12.8%, 11.5%, and 8.3%, respectively (c7E3 bolus+infusion vs placebo p=0.008). >48 h–6 months, the composite end point occurred in 25.4%, 24.3%, and 19.2%, respectively (p=0.007). Total events rates within 6 months were 35.1%, 32.6%, and 27.0%, respectively (p=0.001). The favorable long term effect was mainly due to reduced need for repeated revascularization (22.3%, 21.0%, and 16.5%, respectively p=0.007). By regression analysis the c7E3 bolus+infusion was independently associated with fewer events during the 6 month follow-up (hazard ratio 0.75, p=0.025). c. 42 patients underwent direct PTCA for acute myocardial infarction and 22 patients had rescue PTCA after failed thrombolysis. Patients receiving abciximab (as bolus and as bolus plus infusion) had a reduced primary composite end point (death, reinfarction, repeat intervention, or bypass surgery) with 26.1% in the placebo group reaching the end point, vs 4.5% in the treated group (p=0.06). Major bleeding was more common with abciximab (24% vs 13%, p=0.28). At 6 months there was a significant reduction in ischemic events in patients that received abciximab (47.8% in placebo vs

4.5% in abciximab p=0.002) including reinfarction (p=0.05) and repeat revascularization (p=0.002).

d. Directional atherectomy was performed in 197 patients in the EPIC trial. These patients had a lower baseline risk for acute complications but had a higher rate of myocardial infarction, including non Q wave myocardial infarction than PTCA patients. Bolus and infusion of C7E3 decreased non Q wave myocardial infarctions after atherectomy (15.4% for placebo; 4.5% for treated, p=0.046). Bolus and infusion of C7E3 reduced incidence of development of Q waves infarctions in PTCA patients (2.6% with placebo vs 0.8% with C7E3, p=0.017).

e. At 3 years primary end point occurred in 41.1% on abciximab bolus plus infusion; 47.4% on abciximab bolus only; and 47.2% on placebo only (p=0.009 for abciximab bolus plus infusion vs placebo). There was no significant difference in death among these groups (6.8%, 8.0%, 8.6%). Myocardial infarction occurred in 10.7%, 12.2%, and 13.6% respectively (p=0.08 for abciximab bolus plus infusion vs placebo). Revascularization occurred in 34.8%, 38.6%, and 40.1%, respectively (p=0.02 for abciximab bolus plus infusion vs placebo). In the subgroup of patients with refractory angina or evolving myocardial infarction death occurred in 5.1%, 9.2% and 12.7%, respectively (p=0.01 for abciximab bolus plus infusion vs placebo). There was a correlation between the increase in periprocedural creatine kinase levels and mortality.

f. Bolus and infusion therapy of abciximab resulted in a significant reduction in distal embolization (2%) vs placebo (18%; p=0.017), and a trend towards reduction in early large non Q wave acute myocardial infarction (2% vs 12%). At 30 days and 6 months the occurrence of composite end point were not different among the groups, in these patients undergoing revascularization of aortocoronary saphenous vein grafts.

Conclusions	c7E3 bolus and infusion reduced the revascularization procedure rate during 6 month follow-up of high risk angioplasty patients. However, bleeding complications were increased. e. Abciximab bolus plus infusion administered at the time of PTCA improved outcomes for as long as 3 years. f. Adjunctive therapy with abciximab reduced the occurrence of distal embolization and possibly non Q wave myocardial infarction in patients undergoing percutaneous therapy for narrowed saphenous vein bypass grafts.

EPIC (Substudy)

Evaluation of c7E3 for the Prevention of Ischemic Complications (EPIC) Study Group

Title	Occurrence and clinical significance of thrombocytopenia in a population undergoing high risk percutaneous coronary revascularization.
Authors	Berkowitz SD, Sane DC, Sigmon KN.
Reference	J Am Coll Cardiol 1998; 32: 311-319.
Disease	Coronary artery disease.
Purpose	To determine the frequency of thrombocytopenia and its association with clinical outcome in the EPIC trial.
Design	As per EPIC.
Patients	As per EPIC.
Follow-up	As per EPIC.
Treatment regimen	As per EPIC.

EPIC (Substudy)

Evaluation of c7E3 for the Prevention of Ischemic Complications (EPIC) Study Group (continued)

Results	81 patients (3.9% of 2099 patients developed thrombocytopenia, nadir platelet count <100 x 10^9/L) during hospitalization. 19 (0.9%) developed severe thrombocytopenia (<50 x 10^9/L). Thrombocytopenia and severe thrombocytopenia were more common among patients receiving bolus plus infusion (5.2% and 1.6%, respectively) vs patients receiving bolus only (3.0% and 0.4%; p=0.02) or placebo (3.3% and 0.7%; p=0.025). Median time to developing thrombocytopenia was shorter in patients receiving abciximab (0.50) vs placebo (1.68 days). Two cases of acute, profound thrombocytopenia occurred in 2 patients receiving bolus plus infusion of abciximab. Thrombocytopenia was associated with more bleeding and unfavorable clinical outcome. However, patients with thrombocytopenia who received abciximab still had better outcomes at 30 days than patients not receiving abciximab.
Conclusions	Bolus plus infusion treatment of abciximab was a significant predictor of thrombocytopenia; however patients receiving abciximab had better clinical outcomes than patients receiving placebo.

ERA

Enoxaparin Restenosis Trial

Title	Low molecular weight heparin in prevention of restenosis after angioplasty. Results of enoxaparin restenosis (ERA) trial.
Authors	Faxon DP, Spiro TE, Minor S, et al.
Reference	Circulation 1994;90:908-914.
Disease	Coronary artery disease, restenosis.
Purpose	To evaluate whether enoxaparin given subcutaneously for 28 days will reduce the restenosis rates after coronary angioplasty.
Design	Randomized, double blind, placebo controlled, multicenter.
Patients	458 patients, >21 years old, with ≥50% stenosis of a coronary artery, reduced to <50% with ≥20% change in diameter by angioplasty. Patients with asthma, hypertension, acute myocardial infarction within 5 days, angioplasty of venous grafts, or restenosis after prior angioplasty were excluded.
Follow-up	Clinical evaluation, exercise test, and repeated angiography at 24 weeks.
Treatment regimen	Enoxaparin 40 mg/d SC or placebo, started <24 h after angioplasty and continued for 28 days.
Additional therapy	Aspirin 325 mg/d started 1 day before procedure. IV heparin was given during angioplasty. Calcium channel blockers were given before and after angioplasty.

ERA

Enoxaparin Restenosis Trial

(continued)

Results	Restenosis (loss of >50% of the initial gain in luminal diameter or death, reinfarction, need for bypass surgery, or worsening of angina in patients without follow-up angiography) occurred in 51% of the placebo and 52% of the enoxaparin patients (RR 1.07, p=0.63). Restenosis occurred in 49% and 50% of the patients with follow-up angiography, respectively.The late loss of minimal luminal diameter was 0.49 and 0.54 mm, in the control and enoxaparin, respectively (p=0.78). Adverse clinical events were infrequent and similar between the groups. Minor bleeding complications were more common with enoxaparin (48% vs 34%). In a subset of patients, there was no difference in performance in exercise test.
Conclusions	Enoxaparin 40 mg/d did not reduce the occurrence of restenosis or of adverse clinical events.

MARCATOR

Multicenter American Research Trial With Cilazapril After Angioplasty to Prevent Transluminal Coronary Obstruction and Restenosis

Title	Effect of high dose ACE inhibition on restenosis: Final results of the MARCATOR study, a multicenter, double blind, placebo controlled trial of cilazapril.
Authors	Faxon DP, MARCATOR Study Group.
Reference	J Am Coll Cardiol 1995;25:362-369.
Disease	Coronary artery disease, restenosis.
Purpose	To assess the effect of high and low dose ACE inhibition on restenosis after coronary angioplasty.
Design	Randomized, double blind, placebo controlled, multicenter.
Patients	1436 patients, age 25-80 years, without recent myocardial infarction (<5 days), prior revascularization, or severe hypertension or valvular disease.
Follow-up	Clinical evaluation and repeated angiography at 24 weeks.
Treatment regimen	Study medication were started <6 h after successful angioplasty and continued for 6 months. 1. Cilazapril 1mg X2/d. 2. Cilazapril 5 mg X2/d. 3. Cilazapril 10 mg X2/d. 4. Placebo.
Additional therapy	Aspirin 325 mg/d, started before angioplasty. IV heparin 10,000 U before procedure, and infusion thereafter. Calcium channel blockers were recommended.

MARCATOR

Multicenter American Research Trial With Cilazapril After Angioplasty to Prevent Transluminal Coronary Obstruction and Restenosis

(continued)

Results	The mean difference in minimal coronary lumen diameter between the baseline and follow-up angiography was -0.35±0.51, -0.37±0.52, -0.45±0.52, and -0.41±0.53 mm for the placebo, 2, 10, and 20 mg/d cilazapril, respectively (p=NS). Restenosis >50% at follow-up occurred in 33%, 40%, 36%, and 34%, respectively. Clinical events during follow-up did not differ among the 4 groups.
Conclusions	Long term ACE inhibition with cilazapril did not prevent restenosis and did not reduce clinical event rate after angioplasty.

SHARP

The Subcutaneous Heparin and Angioplasty Restenosis Prevention (SHARP) trial

Title	The Subcutaneous Heparin and Angioplasty Restenosis Prevention (SHARP) trial. Results of a multicenter randomized trial investigating the effects of high dose unfractionated heparin on angiographic restenosis and clinical outcome.
Authors	Brack MJ, Ray S, Chauhan A, et al.
Reference	J Am Coll Cardiol 1995;26:947-954.
Disease	Coronary artery disease.
Purpose	To investigate whether high dose subcutaneous heparin will improve outcome after coronary angioplasty.
Design	Randomized, open label with blinded analysis of data, 3 centers.
Patients	339 patients who had undergone successful coronary angioplasty. Patients with restenotic lesions, chronic total occlusions, or conduit lesions were not included.
Follow-up	4 month clinical evaluation and repeated angiography.
Treatment regimen	Subcutaneous heparin 12,500 U X2/d for 4 months, started 2 h after femoral sheath removal, or no therapy.
Additional therapy	Coronary angioplasty, aspirin 300 mg, and heparin IV bolus 10,000 U before the procedure. After angioplasty, heparin infusion 1,000 U/h for up to 24 h. Aspirin 75-300 mg/d. Other medications according to operator choice.

SHARP

The Subcutaneous Heparin and Angioplasty Restenosis Prevention (SHARP) trial (continued)

Results	Repeated angiography was performed in 90% of the patients. The difference in minimal luminal diameter between the post angioplasty and follow-up study was -0.55±0.58 mm for the control and -0.43±0.59 mm for the heparin group (p=NS). The occurrence of myocardial infarction, coronary artery bypass surgery, repeated angioplasty, and angina at 4 months was comparable. There was no difference between the groups in the number of patients with ischemia during follow-up exercise test.
Conclusions	Long term treatment with high dose subcutaneous heparin for 4 months failed to improve outcome and to prevent restenosis.

REDUCE

Reviparin in Percutaneous Transluminal Coronary Angioplasty

Title	Low molecular weight heparin (Reviparin) in percutaneous transluminal coronary angioplasty. Results of a randomized, double blind, unfractionated heparin and placebo controlled, multicenter trial (REDUCE trial).
Authors	Karsch KR, Preisack MB, Baildon R, et al.
Reference	J Am Coll Cardiol 1996;28:1437-1443.
Disease	Coronary artery disease.
Purpose	To evaluate the effect of low molecular weight heparin on the incidence of restenosis in patients with coronary artery disease undergoing percutaneous transluminal coronary angioplasty (PTCA).
Design	Randomized, double blind, multicenter.
Patients	612 patients with single lesion coronary artery obstruction scheduled to undergo coronary angioplasty. Patients with class 3C unstable angina or unstable angina requiring continuous heparin infusion, myocardial infarction within 14 days, bleeding disorders, active peptic ulcer, uncontrolled asthma or hypertension, left main coronary artery stenosis >50%, and angioplasty of saphenous vein graft or previous angioplasty at the same site were excluded.
Follow-up	Clinical follow-up for 30 weeks. Repeated coronary angiography at 26±2 weeks after angioplasty.

REDUCE

Reviparin in Percutaneous Transluminal Coronary Angioplasty

(continued)

Treatment regimen	At the time of arterial access, patients were randomized to either a bolus of unfractionated heparin (10,000 IU), followed by infusion of 24,000 IU heparin over 16±4h, or reviparin (7,000 IU anti Xa U), followed by infusion of reviparin 10,500 IU anti Xa U over 16±4h. Then, patients received either 3,500 IU anti Xa U of reviparin or placebo subcutaneously X2/d for 28 days.
Additional therapy	Standard balloon angioplasty. Aspirin 100 mg/d was started 1 day before angioplasty.
Results	By intention to treat analysis, treatment failure (death, myocardial infarction, bypass surgery, or emergency or elective repeat angioplasty) occurred in 33.3% of the reviparin and 32.0% of the controls (p=0.71). Angiographic restenosis was present in 33.0% of patients of the reviparin vs 34.4% of the control group. 16.4% of the reviparin vs 19.9% of the control group developed significant angina. Acute events within 24 hours after the procedure occurred less often in the reviparin-treated group (3.9% vs 8.2%, respectively; relative risk (RR) 0.49; 95% CI 0.26-0.92; p=0.027). Only 6 patients in the reviparin-treated group vs 21 patients in the control group needed emergency stent implantation (RR 0.29; 95% CI 0.13-0.66; p=0.003). Analysis of primary end points after 30 weeks revealed that the occurrence of clinical events was comparable between the groups (31.7% vs 30% in the reviparin and control, respectively). There was no difference in late loss of minimal lumen diameter between the 2 groups. Bleeding complications were comparable (2.3% in the reviparin vs 2.6% in the control group; p=0.8).
Conclusions	Reviparin use started immediately before coronary balloon angioplasty and continued for 28 days did not reduce the rate of major clinical events or the incidence of restenosis over 30 weeks follow-up.

ISAR

Intracoronary Stenting and Antithrombotic Regimen trial

Title	a. A randomized comparison of antiplatelets and anticoagulant therapy after the placement of coronary artery stents. b. Major benefit from antiplatelet therapy for patients at high risk for adverse cardiac events after coronary Palmaz-Schatz stent replacement. c. Restenosis after coronary stent placement and randomization to a 4 week combined antiplatelet or anticoagulant therapy. 6 month angiographic follow-up of the intracoronary stenting and antithrombotic regimen (ISAR) trial.
Authors	a. Schömig A, Neumann F-J, Kastrati A, et al. b. Schuhlen H, Hadamitzky M, Walter H, et al. c. Kastrati A, Schuhlen H, Hausleiter J, et al.
Reference	a. N Engl J Med 1996;334:1084-1089. b. Circulation 1997; 95:2015-2021. c. Circulation 1997; 96:462-467.
Disease	a. Coronary artery disease, restenosis. b. Coronary artery disease. c. Coronary artery disease.
Purpose	a. To compare the efficacy of 2 therapeutic regimens after placement of coronary artery stents: 1) combined antiplatelet therapy with ticlopidine plus aspirin, and 2) anticoagulation with intravenous heparin, phenprocoumon, and aspirin. b. Comparison of antiplatelet therapy to anticoagulant therapy after coronary artery stent deployment. This study was an analysis of prospective risk stratification. c. The ISAR Trial compared outcomes of patients randomized to either combined antiplatelet therapy-aspirin plus ticlopidine or phenprocoumon (anticoagulant) with initial aspirin and heparin after coronary stent deployment. Within the first 4 weeks of therapy, combined antiplatelet therapy resulted in fewer ischemic complications. The purpose of this study was to determine whether 4 weeks of antiplatelet therapy could reduce angiographic evidence of restenosis at 6 months.

ISAR

Intracoronary Stenting and Antithrombotic Regimen trial (continued)

Design	a. Randomized, 1 center. b + c. Prospective, randomized study.
Patients	a. 257 patients in whom intracoronary Palmaz-Schatz stents were successfully implanted after balloon angioplasty. The indications for stenting were extensive dissection after angioplasty, complete vessel closure, residual stenosis ≥30%, and lesions in venous bypass grafts. Patients with absolute indication for anticoagulation, or contraindications to 1 of the drugs, cardiogenic shock, or who had needed mechanical ventilation were excluded. b. 517 patients from original ISAR study [N Engl J Med 1996; 334:1084–1089]. Risk stratification performed based on clinical, procedural, and angiographic variables. 165 patients with 2 or fewer criteria = low risk; 148 patients with 3 criteria = intermediate risk; 204 with 4 or more criteria = high risk. c. 432 patients with 6 month follow-up angiograms.
Follow-up	a. Hospitalization for 10 days. Clinical follow-up for 30 days. b. 30 days. c. 6 months.
Treatment regimen	In patients assigned to antiplatelet therapy, heparin infusion was started after arterial sheath removal for 12 h. Ticlopidine 250 mgX2/d was administered for 4 weeks. In patients assigned to anticoagulation therapy, heparin infusion, started after sheath removal, was continued for 5 to 10 days. Phenoprocoumon was given for 4 weeks (target INR 3.5 to 4.5). Aspirin 100 mg bid given to both groups.
Additional therapy	a. Heparin and aspirin intravenously before PTCA. All patients received aspirin 100 mgX2/d throughout the study.

ISAR

Intracoronary Stenting and Antithrombotic Regimen trial (continued)

Results

a. 30 days after randomization, mortality was comparable (0.4% vs 0.8% in the antiplatelet and anticoagulant group, respectively). Myocardial infarction occurred in 0.8% vs 4.2% of the patients, respectively (relative risk (RR) 0.18; 95% CI 0.02 to 0.83; p=0.02) and the need for revascularization was 1.2% vs 5.4% (RR 0.22; 95% CI 0.04 to 0.77; p=0.01). A primary cardiac event (cardiac death, myocardial infarction, or revascularization) occurred in 1.6% of the antiplatelet vs 6.2% of the anticoagulant patients (RR 0.25; 95% CI 0.06 to 0.77; p=0.01). Occlusion of the stented vessel occurred less often in the antiplatelet group (0.8% vs 5.4%; RR 0.14; 95% CI 0.02 to 0.62; p=0.004). A primary noncardiac end point (noncardiac death, cerebrovascular accident, or severe peripheral vascular or hemorrhagic event) was reached by 1.2% vs 12.3% of the antiplatelet and anticoagulant groups, respectively (RR 0.09; 95% CI 0.02 to 0.31; p<0.001). Bleeding complications occurred only in the anticoagulant group (6.5%; p<0.001). Peripheral vascular events occurred in 0.8% of the antiplatelet group vs 6.2% of the anticoagulant group (RR 0.13; 95% CI 0.01 to 0.53; p=0.001).

b. At 30 day follow-up there was a decrease in risk for noncardiac and cardiac complications, especially occlusion of the stented vessel, in patients treated with antiplatelet vs anticoagulation therapy. Cardiac event rate (death, myocardial infarction, repeat intervention) was 6.4%, 3.4% , and 0% for high, intermediate and low risk patients, respectively (p<0.01). Occlusion of the stented vessel occurred in 5.9%, 2.7%, and 0% respectively (p<0.01). In high risk patients the cardiac event rate was 12.6% with anticoagulation therapy vs 2.0% for antiplatelet therapy (p=0.007) and rate of stent vessel occlusion was 11.5% vs 0% (p<0.001). There were no significant differences between anticoagulant and antiplatelet in low and intermediate risk groups.

c. At 6 months there were no differences in minimal diameter, late lumen loss, or restenosis rates (26.8% in antiplatelet group and 28.9% in anticoagulation group, respectively p =0.20).

ISAR

Intracoronary Stenting and Antithrombotic Regimen trial

(continued)

Conclusions	a. After successful placement of coronary artery stents, the combination of aspirin and ticlopidine was associated with lower rate of cardiac events, fewer vascular, and hemorrhagic complications. b. Patients in the high risk group had the greatest benefit from anitplatelet therapy. c. Aspirin plus ticlopidine for 4 weeks after stent placement did not reduce restenosis rates compared to phenprocoumon with initial overlapping heparin plus aspirin treatment.

ACCORD

Angioplasie Coronaire Corvasal Diltiazem

Title	Effect of the direct nitric oxide donors linsidomine and molsidomine on angiographic restenosis after coronary balloon angioplasty. The ACCORD study.
Authors	Lablanche J-M, Grollier G, Lusson J-R, et al.
Reference	Circulation 1997;95:83-89
Disease	Coronary artery disease, restenosis.
Purpose	To evaluate the effect of molsidomine and linsidomine, direct nitric oxide donors, on restenosis after coronary balloon angioplasty.
Design	Randomized, multicenter.
Patients	700 patients, ≤70 years old, with angina and/or evidence of myocardial ischemia who were referred for balloon angioplasty. Patients with myocardial infarction within 3 months, recent unstable angina, ejection fraction <0.35, systolic blood pressure <100 mm Hg, contraindications to aspirin, restenotic graft or left main coronary artery lesions and totally occluded lesions were excluded.
Follow-up	Clinical follow-up with repeated coronary angiography at 6 months.
Treatment regimen	Randomization to active treatment group or controls. The active treatment consisted of continuous infusion of linsidomine (1 mg/h), started 3-18 h before the angioplasty, and continued for 24 h after the procedure, and then, molsidomine 4 mgX3/d PO for 6 months. The control group received diltiazem 60 mgX3/d.

ACCORD

Angioplasie Coronaire Corvasal Diltiazem

(continued)

Additional therapy	Aspirin 250 mg/d. Heparin 10,000 IU at the start of angio plasty, additional doses of heparin 5000 IU after each h of procedure. Long-acting nitrates, calcium channel blockers, oral anticoagulants, and ACE inhibitors were prohibited.
Results	3520 patients had 3 angiograms (at baseline, immediately after angioplasty, and at follow-up). Despite the intracoronary administration of isosorbide dinitrate before angiography, the mean reference luminal diameter was greater in the NO donor group than in the diltiazem group before angioplasty (2.94 vs 2.83 mm; p=0.014). The mean minimal luminal diameter (MLD) before angioplasty was comparable. However, immediately after angioplasty, MLD was 1.94 vs 1.81 mm, in the NO donor and the diltiazem group, respectively (p=0.001). Mean MLD remained larger in the NO donor group at follow-up (1.54 vs 1.38 mm; p=0.007). Late loss, loss index, and the slope of the regression between late loss and acute gain were comparable. At 6 months, restenosis (≥50%) occurred in 38.0% of the NO donor treated patients vs 46.5% of the diltiazem group (p=0.062). After adjustment for center and hypercholesterolemia the p value was 0.026. The combined rate of major clinical events (death, myocardial infarction, and coronary revascularization) were comparable (32.2% in the NO donor group vs 32.4% in the diltiazem group). The incidence of side effects and the number of dropouts due to adverse effects were similar (13 vs 10, respectively).
Conclusions	NO donor therapy was associated with larger MLD immediately after and at follow-up following coronary balloon angioplasty and lower rate of restenosis. However, late luminal loss did not differ between the groups and there was no difference in the occurrence of major clinical events.

EMPAR

Enoxaparin MaxEPA Prevention of Angioplasty Restenosis

Title	Fish oils and low molecular weight heparin for the reduction of restenosis after percutaneous transluminal coronary angioplasty. The EMPAR Study.
Author	Cairns JA, Gill J, Morton B, et al.
Reference	Circulation 1996; 94:1553-1560.
Disease	Coronary artery disease, restenosis post angioplasty.
Purpose	To determine whether fish oils reduce the incidence of restenosis following percutaneous transluminal coronary angioplasty.
Design	Randomized, placebo controlled, multicenter.
Patients	814 patients with coronary artery disease, undergoing PTCA.
Follow-up	16->28 weeks.
Treatment regimen	Starting 6 days before PTCA patients were randomized to fish oils (5.4 g n-3 fatty acids) or placebo and continued on this for 18 weeks post PTCA. At the time of sheath removal patients were randomized to low molecular weight heparin or control.
Results	Restenosis rates per patient were 46.5% in the fish oil group and 44.7% in the placebo group.Rates were 45.8% of patients receiving low molecular weight heparin and 45.4% in controls.
Conclusions	Fish oils did not reduce restenosis rates. Low molecular weight heparin did not reduce restenosis rates.

EPILOG

Evaluation in PTCA to Improve Long-Term Outcome with Abciximab GPIIb/IIIa Blockade

Title	Platelet glycoprotein IIb/IIIa receptor blockade and low dose heparin during percutaneous coronary revascularization.
Author	The EPILOG Investigators.
Reference	N Engl J Med 1997; 336:1689-1696.
Disease	Coronary artery disease, urgent or elective percutaneous coronary revascularization.
Purpose	To determine whether the clinical benefits of abciximab (known to diminish ischemic complications in patients undergoing high risk angioplasty and atherectomy procedures) could be extended to all patients undergoing coronary intervention, regardless of risk. To determine whether adjusting the heparin dose could limit the hemorrhagic complications associated with abciximab use.
Design	Prospective, double blind, randomized, multicenter.
Patients	2792 patients undergoing urgent or elective percutaneous coronary revascularization.
Follow-up	30 days.

EPILOG

Evaluation in PTCA to Improve Long-Term Outcome with Abciximab GPIIb/IIIa Blockade

(continued)

Treatment regimen	1. Abciximab (0.25 mg per kg 10–60 min before inflation, followed by an infusion of 0.125 μg/kg/min, maximum of 10 μg per min for 12 h) plus standard dose heparin (bolus of 100 U per kg (maximum 10,000 U) prior to intervention, with additional boluses to achieve an activated clotting time of at least 300 sec or 2. Abciximab plus low dose weight adjusted heparin (bolus of 70 U/kg, maximum 7000 U) with additional boluses to maintain activated clotting time of at least 200 sec) or 3. Placebo with standard dose, weight adjusted heparin.
Results	At 30 days the composite event rate of death, myocardial infarction, or urgent revascularization within 30 days was 5.4% in group assigned to abciximab plus standard dose heparin (hazard ratio 0.45, 95% CI = 0.32–0.63, p<0.001); 5.2% in group assigned to abciximab with low dose heparin (hazard ratio 0.43; 95% CI 0.30–0.60, p< 0.001) and 11.7% in group assigned to placebo with standard dose heparin. Major bleeding did not differ among groups. Minor bleeding was more frequent in patients receiving abciximab plus standard dose heparin.
Conclusions	Abciximab plus low dose, weight adjusted heparin reduced ischemic complications in patients undergoing percutaneous revascularization procedures and did not increase risk of hemorrhage.

EPILOG Substudy

Evaluation in PTCA to Improve Long-Term Outcome with Abciximab GP IIb/IIIa Blockade

Title	Abciximab therapy and unplanned coronary stent deployment. Favorable effects on stent use, clinical outcomes, and bleeding complications.
Author	Kereiakes DJ, Lincoff AM, Miller DP.
Reference	Circulation 1998; 97:857-864.
Disease	Coronary artery disease.
Purpose	To describe the effects of abciximab on clinical outcomes in patients in the EPILOG study who required unplanned coronary stent deployment.
Design	Randomized, double blind, placebo controlled trial.
Patients	326 patients that required unplanned coronary stent deployment.
Follow-up	6 months.
Treatment regimen	As per EPILOG protocol.

EPILOG Substudy

Evaluation in PTCA to Improve Long-Term Outcome with Abciximab GP IIb/IIIa Blockade

(continued)

Results	Patients requiring stents had greater coronary lesion complexity, longer lesion length, more lesion eccentricity, irregularity, and involvement of bifurcations, compared to nonstented patients. Patients that were treated with abciximab and low dose, weight adjusted heparin required unplanned stents less frequently (9.0%) than patients on placebo and standard dose heparin (13.7%, p=0.001). Patients with unplanned stents had a more complicated course-more death, myocardial infarction, or urgent intervention (14.4%) vs patients with no stents (6.3%, p=0.001). At 6 months abciximab reduced the incidence of death, infarction, or urgent revascularization compared to placebo in patients who had unplanned stents. Abciximab's benefit was somewhat greater in patients requiring compared to not requiring a stent. It did not cause an increase in bleeding in the stented patients.
Conclusions	Patients that required unplanned stenting had more complex coronary artery lesions and a more complicated clinical course. Abciximab reduced the need for unplanned stent deployment and improved clinical outcome in those patients requiring a stent.

EPILOG-One year Outcome

Evaluation in PTCA to Improve Long-Term Outcome with Abciximab GP IIb/IIIa Blockade

Title	Sustained suppression of ischemic complications of coronary intervention by platelet GP IIb/IIIa blockade with abciximab.One year outcome in the EPILOG Trial.
Authors	Lincoff AM,Tcheng JE, Califf RM, et al.
Reference	Circulation 1999; 99:1951-1958.
Disease	Coronary artery disease.
Purpose	To determine the long term outcome of patients receiving GP IIb/IIIa blockade with abciximab for percutaneous coronary interventions.
Design	As per EPILOG.
Patients	2792 patients in EPILOG followed for 1 year.
Follow-up	1 year.
Treatment regimen	As per EPILOG.

EPILOG-One year Outcome

Evaluation in PTCA to Improve Long-Term Outcome with Abciximab GP IIb/IIIa Blockade

(continued)

Results	At 1 year, the composite end point (death, myocardial infarction, urgent repeat revascularization) occurred in 16.1% of placebo patients, 9.6% in the abciximab plus low dose heparin (p<0.001), and 9.5% in abciximab plus standard dose heparin group (p<0.001). The components of the composite end points were also reduced in the abciximab groups. The composite end point of death, myocardial infarction, or any revascularization—whether urgent or elective—developed in 32.4% of placebo patients; 29.4% of abciximab plus low dose heparin (p=0.093), and 29.2% of abciximab plus standard dose heparin (p=0.077). The benefit of abciximab was most evident during the first 30 day period followed by no attenuation of benefit over the course of the year. CK-MB elevation during the periprocedural period or first 30 days was associated with an increased risk of death at one year.
Conclusions	Abciximab reduced acute ischemic events with PTCA and the benefits were sustained over a year.

THE FACT STUDY

Fraxiparine Angioplastie Coronaire Transluminale

Title	Effect of nadroparin (Fraxiparine), a low molecular weight heparin, on clinical and angiographic restenosis after coronary balloon angioplasty. The FACT study.
Author	Lablanche J-M, McFadden EP, Meneveau N, et al.
Reference	Circulation 1997;96:3396-3402.
Disease	Coronary artery disease.
Purpose	To determine whether nadroparin, a low molecular-weight heparin, begun 3 days prior to percutaneous transluminal coronary angioplasty (PTCA) improved clinical outcome following the procedure.
Design	Prospective, multicenter, double blind, randomized.
Patients	354 patients with angina or objective evidence of myocardial ischemia, > 50% stenosis of a coronary artery, and scheduled for PTCA.
Follow-up	6 months.
Treatment regimen	Subcutaneous nadroparin (0.6 mL of 10 250 antiXa IU/mL) or placebo from 3 days prior to angioplasty until 3 months after the procedure.

THE FACT STUDY

Fraxiparine Angioplastie Coronaire Transluminale

(continued)

Results	The primary end point of angiographic restenosis, determined by quantitative coronary angiography at 3 months did not differ between treated and control groups. Combined major cardiac related events also did not differ between groups (30.3% in treated vs 29.6% in controls).
Conclusions	Pretreatment with the low molecular weight heparin nadroparin did not affect angiographic restenosis or clinical outcome.

IMPACT-II

Integrillin to Minimize Platelet Aggregation and Coronary Thrombosis-II

Title	Randomized, placebo controlled trial of effect of eptifibatide on complications of percutaneous coronary intervention: IMPACT-II.
Authors	The IMPACT-II Investigators.
Reference	Lancet 1997;349:1422–1428.
Disease	Coronary artery disease.
Purpose	To assess whether eptifibatide (integrillin), a platelet glycoprotein IIb/IIIa inhibitor, would prevent ischemic complications following percutaneous coronary interventions.
Design	Randomized, double blind, placebo controlled, multicenter.
Patients	4010 patients, scheduled for elective, urgent, or emergency transcutaneous coronary intervention (balloon angioplasty, directional atherectomy, rotational atherectomy, or excimer laser ablation). Patients with bleeding diathesis, severe hypertension, major surgery within 6 weeks, stroke, other major illness, or pregnancy were excluded.
Follow-up	6 months.
Treatment regimen	Randomization to: 1) eptifibatide 135 μg/kg bolus followed by an infusion of 0.5 μg/kg for 20–24 h (the 135/0.5 group); 2) eptifibatide 135 μg/kg bolus followed by an infusion of 0.75 μg/kg for 20–24 h (the 135/0.75 group); or 3) placebo bolus and placebo infusion. Therapy was started after vascular access had been established and heparin 100 U/kg was administered.

IMPACT-II

Integrillin to Minimize Platelet Aggregation and Coronary Thrombosis-II (continued)

Additional therapy	Aspirin 325 mg before the procedure. No further heparin was given after the coronary intervention and arterial sheath was removed within 4-6 h.
Results	By 30 days, mortality was 1.1% in the placebo group, 0.5% in the 135/0.5 group and 0.8% in the 135/0.75 group. The composite end point of death, myocardial infarction, urgent or emergency revascularization (PTCA or CABG), or index insertion of an intracoronary stent for abrupt closure in 30 days occurred in 11.4% of the placebo group, 9.2% in the 135/0.5 group (p=0.063 vs placebo; OR 0.79; 95% CI 0.61-1.01) and in 9.9% of the 135/0.75 group (p=0.22 vs placebo; OR 0.86; 95% CI 0.67-1.10). Death or myocardial infarction occurred in 8.4% of the placebo, compared with 6.9% in the 135/0.5 group (p=0.13; OR 0.80; 95% CI 0.60-1.07) and 7.3% in the 135/0.75 group (p=0.27; OR=0.85; 95% CI 0.64-1.13). Most events occurred within the first 6 h of procedure. By the end of infusion of eptifibatide/placebo, the composite event rate was 9.3% in the placebo vs 6.8% in the 135/0.5 group (p=0.017) and 7.0% in the 135/0.75 group (p=0.026). There was no clustering of events after the end of infusion, suggesting that there is no rebound phenomenon. During 6 months of follow-up, death or myocardial infarction occurred in 11.6% of the placebo group, 10.5% in the 135/0.5 group (p=0.33), and 10.1% in the 135/0.75 group (p=0.19). Revascularization rates were comparable among the groups. There was no differences in the rates of major bleeding among the groups (4.8%, 5.1%, and 5.2%, respectively), or the need for transfusion (5.2%, 5.6%, and 5.9%, respectively). The rates of stroke were comparable.
Conclusions	Eptifibatide infusion reduced early abrupt closure and reduced the rates of 30 day ischemic events, without increasing the risk of bleeding complications. However, the effect on 30 day mortality or occurrence of myocardial infarction, and on 6 month cumulative ischemic event rate were not statistically significant.

M-HEART II

Multi-Hospital Eastern Atlantic Restenosis Trialists

Title	Effect of thromboxane A2 blockade on clinical outcome and restenosis after successful coronary angioplasty. Multi-Hospital Eastern Atlantic Restenosis Trial (M-Heart II).
Author	Savage MP, Goldberg S, Bove AA, et al.
Reference	Circulation 1995;92:3194-3200.
Disease	Coronary artery disease.
Purpose	To determine the effects of aspirin (a nonselective inhibitor of thromboxane A2 synthesis) and sulotroban (a selective blocker of the thromboxane A2 receptor) on late clinical events and restenosis after coronary angioplasty.
Design	Prospective, randomized, multicenter.
Patients	752 patients with coronary artery disease.
Follow-up	6 months.
Treatment regimen	Aspirin (325 mg daily), sulotroban (800 mg 4 times a day) or placebo within 6 h before PTCA and for 6 months.
Results	Neither of the agents differed from placebo in the rate of angiographic restenosis. Aspirin significantly improved clinical outcome compared to placebo. Myocardial infarction was reduced by aspirin (1.2%), sulotroban (1.8%) compared to placebo (5.7%; p=0.03).
Conclusions	Thromboxane A2 blockade protects against late ischemic events after angioplasty but not angiographic restenosis. Overall clinical outcome was superior for aspirin compared with sulotroban.

MVP

Multivitamins and Probucol

Title	a. Probucol and multivitamins in the prevention of restenosis after coronary angioplasty. b. Prevention of restenosis after angioplasty in small coronary arteries with probucol.
Author	a. Tardif J-C, Cote G, Lesperance J, et al. b. Rodes J, Cote G, Lesperance J, et al.
Reference	a. N Engl J Med 1997; 337: 365–372. b. Circulation 1998; 97:429–436.
Disease	Coronary artery disease, patients undergoing angioplasty.
Purpose	a. To determine whether antioxidant drugs could decrease the incidence and severity of restenosis after angioplasty. b. To determine whether probucol therapy was successful in reducing restenosis in smaller coronary arteries (<3.0 mm).
Design	Double blind, placebo controlled trial with 4 study groups.
Patients	a. 317 patients undergoing angioplasty. b. Subset of 189 patients undergoing angioplasty with at least 1 coronary segment with a diameter of <3.0 mm.
Follow-up	6 months.

MVP

Multivitamins and Probucol

(continued)

Treatment regimen	1 month before angioplasty patients were randomized to placebo; probucol (500 mg); multivitamins (30,000 IU of beta carotene, 500 mg of vitamin C, and 700 IU of vitamin E) or both probucol and multivitamins taken twice-a-day. Patients were treated for 4 weeks prior to and 6 months after angioplasty. They received an extra 1000 mg of probucol, 2000 IU vitamin E, both probucol and vitamin E, or placebo 12 h prior to the procedure. Angiograms at baseline and at 6 months were read by blinded observer.
Results	a. Mean reduction in luminal diameter at 6 months was 0.12 ± 0.41, 0.22 ± 0.46, 0.33 ± 0.51 and 0.38 ± 0.50 mm in the probucol, combined treatment, multivitamin and placebo groups respectively ($p=0.006$ for probucol vs no probucol; $p = 0.70$ for multivitamins vs no multivitamins). Restenosis rates per coronary segment were 20.7, 28.9, 40.3, and 38.9 in the probucol, combined treatment, multivitamin, and placebo groups, respectively ($p=0.003$ for probucol vs no probucol). Patients receiving probucol also had lower rates of need for repeated angioplasty. b. In small coronary arteries restenosis rates were 20%, 29%, 45%, and 37% for probucol, combined therapy, vitamins and placebo ($p=0.006$ for probucol). Probucol also reduced absolute lumen loss.
Conclusions	a. Probucol was effective in reducing restenosis rates following coronary angioplasty. b. Probucol was effective in reducing restenosis in small coronary arteries.

MVP-Substudy

Multivitamins and Probucol Study

Title	Effects of probucol on vascular remodeling after coronary angioplasty.
Authors	Côtè G, Tardif J-C, Lesperance J, et al.
Reference	Circulation 1999;99:30-35.
Disease	Coronary artery disease, restenosis following PTCA.
Purpose	Previous study by this group showed that probucol reduces restenosis after PTCA. The purpose here was to determine whether it acted by preventing neointimal formation or vascular remodeling.
Design	Intravascular ultrasound substudy of MVP. Randomized, placebo controlled, multicenter.
Patients	94 patients that were part of MVP who underwent intravascular ultrasound.
Follow-up	5-7 months.
Treatment regimen	Probucol 500 mg twice a day, alone; multivitamins alone, probucol plus multivitamin, or placebo starting 30 days before scheduled angioplasty.

MVP-Substudy

Multivitamins and Probucol Study

(continued)

Results	In the overall MVP study probucol reduced angiographic lumen loss by 68%, restenosis rate by 47% and need for repeat PTCA by 58%. In this substudy, lumen area decreased by 1.21±1.88 mm^2 and wall area and external elastic membrane area increased by 1.50±2.50 and 0.29±2.93 mm^2, respectively, in the placebo group. Changes in lumen area correlated more closely with change in external elastic membrane area than changes in wall area. Lumen loss was -0.83±1.22 mm^2 for vitamins, -0.25±1.17mm^2 for combined therapy, and -0.15±1.70 mm^2 for probucol therapy (p=0.002 for probucol). External elastic membrane area increased by 1.74±1.80 mm^2 (p=0.005) for probucol, 0.29±2.93 mm2 for placebo, 0.09±2.33 mm^2 for vitamins, and 1.17±1.61 mm^2 for combined therapy.
Conclusions	Probucol antirestenotic properties occurred by improving vascular remodeling following PTCA.

RESTORE

Randomized Efficacy Study of Tirofiban for Outcomes and Restenosis

Title	Effects of platelet glycoprotein IIb/IIIa blockade with tirofiban on adverse cardiac events in patients with unstable angina or acute myocardial infarction undergoing coronary angioplasty.
Author	The RESTORE Investigators.
Reference	Circulation 1997; 96: 1445–1453.
Disease	Coronary artery disease, myocardial infarction, unstable angina.
Purpose	To determine effect of tirofiban, a platelet glycoprotein IIb/IIIa blocker, in patients undergoing balloon angioplasty or directional atherectomy within 72 h of presentation of unstable angina or acute myocardial infarction on the following end points: death, myocardial infarction, coronary bypass surgery secondary to angioplasty failure or recurrent ischemia, need for repeat angioplasty (PTCA), stent insertion due to actual or threatened closure, and the primary end point-a composite of the above.
Design	Randomized, double blind, placebo controlled trial, multicenter.
Patients	2139, mean age 60 years, > 70% males.
Follow-up	30 days.
Treatment regimen	Tirofiban bolus 10 μg/kg over a 3 min period followed by a 36 h infusion of 0.15 μg/kg/min or placebo. Patients were already receiving aspirin and heparin.

RESTORE

Randomized Efficacy Study of Tirofiban for Outcomes and Restenosis

(continued)

Results	The primary composite end point was 12.2% in the placebo group and 10.3% in the tirofiban group (p=0.16), at 30 days. At 2 days post angioplasty tirofiban had a 38% relative reduction in the composite end point (p ≤0.005); at 7 days there was a 27% relative reduction (p=0.022) mainly secondary to reduction in nonfatal myocardial infarction and need for repeat PTCA. If only urgent or emergent repeat angioplasty or coronary bypass surgery were included in the composite end point, the 30 day event rates were 10.5% for placebo and 8.0% for tirofiban (p=0.052). Major bleeding occurred in 3.7% of the placebo group and 5.3% in the tirofiban group (p=0.096).
Conclusions	Tirofiban protected against early adverse cardiac events related to thrombotic closure in patients undergoing PTCA for acute coronary syndromes; however at 30 days this reduction in adverse cardiac events was no longer statistically significant.

RESTORE (6 Month Follow-up)

Randomized Efficacy Study of Tirofiban for Outcomes and Restenosis

Title	6 month angiographic and clinical follow-up of patients prospectively randomized to receive either tirofiban or placebo during angioplasty in the RESTORE trial.
Authors	Gibson CM, Goel M, Cohen D, et al.
Reference	J Am Coll Cardiol 1998; 32:28-34.
Disease	Coronary artery disease.
Purpose	To determine 6 month follow-up of patients that received tirofiban vs placebo following coronary interventions.
Design	As per RESTORE.
Patients	Original patients in RESTORE as well as 619 patient cohort of the original RESTORE trial who were part of a 6 month angiographic restenosis substudy.
Follow-up	6 months.
Treatment regimen	As per RESTORE.

RESTORE (6 Month Follow-up)

Randomized Efficacy Study of Tirofiban for Outcomes and Restenosis

(continued)

Results	The composite end point at 6 months (death from any cause, new MI, CABG for PTCA failure or recurrent ischemia, repeat target vessel PTCA, stenting for actual or abrupt closure) developed in 1070 placebo patients (27.1%) vs 1071 tirofiban patients (24.1%, p=0.11). 6 month coronary angiography did not show a difference between groups in the incidence of ≥50% diameter stenosis (57% placebo vs 51% tirofiban, p=NS); loss of ≥50% lumen gained or loss of ≥0.72 mm of lumen diameter.
Conclusions	Tirofiban did not decrease the 6 month incidence of coronary artery restenosis.

Results of a consecutive series of patients receiving only antiplatelet therapy after optimized stent implantation. Comparison of aspirin alone vs combined ticlopidine and aspirin therapy.

Title	Results of a consecutive series of patients receiving only antiplatelet therapy after optimized stent implantation. Comparison of aspirin alone vs combined ticlopidine and aspirin therapy.
Author	Albiero R, Hall P, Itoh A, et al.
Reference	Circulation 1997; 95:1145-1156.
Disease	Coronary artery disease.
Purpose	To determine whether ticlopidine combined with aspirin is superior to aspirin alone in preventing stent thrombosis.
Design	Retrospective analysis of consecutive patients assigned to receive either aspirin alone or a combination of ticlopidine plus aspirin after a successful intracoronary stent insertion.
Patients	801 consecutive coronary artery disease patients, average age 57-58 years; 86-89% male.
Follow-up	1-4 months.
Treatment regimen	Aspirin before stent employment plus heparin. Then aspirin 325 mg x1/d or ticlopidine 250 mg x2/d for 1 month and long term aspirin.

Results of a consecutive series of patients receiving only antiplatelet therapy after optimized stent implantation. Comparison of aspirin alone vs combined ticlopidine and aspirin therapy.

(continued)

Results	At 1 month the rate of stent thrombosis was 1.9% in the aspirin group as well as the combined ticlopidine plus aspirin group. The rates of major adverse clinical events were 1.9% and 2.0% respectively.
Conclusions	There was no difference in rates of stent thrombosis or clinical outcomes at 1 month follow-up in patients receiving either aspirin alone or aspirin plus ticlopidine. There was no benefit to adding ticlopidine to aspirin in these coronary artery disease patients that received stents.

ORBIT

Oral glycoprotein IIb/IIIa Receptor Blockade to Inhibit Thrombosis

Title	Pharmacodynamic efficacy, clinical safety, and outcomes after prolonged platelet glycoprotein IIb/IIIa receptor blockade with oral xemilofiban. Results of a multicenter, placebo controlled, randomized trial.
Authors	Kereiakes DJ, Kleiman NS, Ferguson JJ, et al.
Reference	Circulation 1998; 98:1268-1278.
Disease	Coronary artery disease.
Purpose	To determine pharmacodynamic response of 2 doses of xemilofiban vs placebo on platelet aggregation and determine the drug's safety and effect on clinical outcome.
Design	Multicenter, placebo controlled, randomized.
Patients	549 patients who had undergone elective percutaneous coronary interventions.
Follow-up	3 months.
Treatment regimen	Placebo, xemilofiban 15 mg, xemilofiban 20 mg, orally 3 times a day for 2 weeks and then 2 times daily for 2 weeks. Patients receiving abciximab during acute coronary intervention received a lower dosage of xemilofiban for the first 2 weeks.
Additional therapy	Patients receiving stents also were administered ticlopidine. All patients received aspirin.

ORBIT

Oral glycoprotein IIb/IIIa Receptor Blockade to Inhibit Thrombosis

(continued)

Results	Platelet aggregation to both ADP and collagen was inhibited by xemilofiban in a dose dependent fashion. The degree of platelet inhibition was similar at 14 and 28 days after long term therapy. There were no intracranial hemorrhages. Use of red cell transfusion was infrequent (1.7% in placebo; 1.8% in xemilofiban treated patients). Overall incidence of moderate (3.4%) and severe (1.1%) bleeding rates were low with xemilofiban compared to placebo (1.3% and 0%). There was a trend toward a lower composite cardiovascular event rate (death, myocardial infarction, nonhemorrhagic stroke, urgent coronary revascularization) at 3 months in patients who were not treated with abciximab during coronary intervention, who received the 20 mg dose of xemilofiban.
Conclusions	Oral xemilofiban successfully inhibited platelet aggregation when administered chronically. There was a favorable trend in reduction of cardiac events that awaits larger trial results.

FANTASTIC

The Full Anticoagulation vs Aspirin and Ticlopidine Study

Title	Randomized multicenter comparison of conventional anticoagulation vs antiplatelet therapy in unplanned and elective coronary stenting.
Authors	Bertrand ME, Legrand V, Boland J, et al.
Reference	Circulation 1998; 98:1597-1603.
Disease	Coronary artery disease.
Purpose	To determine safety and efficacy of conventional anticoagulation or antiplatelet therapy alone in patients receiving stents.
Design	Randomized, multicenter.
Patients	485 patients: 249 randomized to antiplatelet therapy; 236 to conventional anticoagulation.
Follow-up	6 months.
Treatment regimen	Antiplatelet therapy: ticlopidine 500 mg then 250 mg bid for 6 weeks and aspirin 100-325 mg a day. Conventional anticoagulant therapy: heparin then oral anticoagulation to achieve INR between 2.5-3.0.

The Full Anticoagulation vs Aspirin and Ticlopidine Study

(continued)

Results	A primary end point (occurrence of bleeding or peripheral vascular complications) occurred in 13.5% in the antiplatelet group and 21% in the anticoagulation group (p=0.03). Major cardiac events (death, infarction, or stent occlusion) in electively stented patients were less common in the antiplatelet group (2.4%) compared to the anticoagulation group (9.9%) and hospital stay was shorter in the antiplatelet group (4.3±3.6 days) vs the anticoagulation group (6.4±3.7 days, p=0.0001).
Conclusions	Antiplatelet therapy was more successful than conventional anticoagulation in reducing subacute stent occlusion and reducing rates of bleeding.

MATTIS

The Multicenter Aspirin and Ticlopidine Trial after Intracoronary Stenting

Title	Randomized evaluation of anticoagulation vs antiplatelet therapy after coronary stent implantation in high risk patients.
Authors	Urban P, Macaya C, Rupprecht HJ, et al.
Reference	Circulation 1998; 98:2126-2132.
Disease	Coronary artery diseases.
Purpose	To compare outcomes in high risk patients that received stents and were randomized to aspirin plus ticlopidine vs aspirin plus oral anticoagulation.
Design	Randomized, controlled, open label, multicenter.
Patients	350 patients who received stents who were considered to be at high risk for subacute occlusion (stent implanted to treat abrupt closure after PTCA); suboptimal angiographic result post-stenting; a long segment was stented; or the largest balloon inflated in the stent had a diameter of ≤2.5 mm.
Follow-up	30 days.
Treatment regimen	Aspirin 250 mg and ticlopidine 500 mg/day vs aspirin 250 mg/day and oral anticoagulation targeted to an INR of 2.5-3.0.
Additional therapy	Heparin.

Results	The primary composite end point (cardiovascular death, myocardial infarction, repeat revascularization at 30 days) occurred in 5.6% of the patients in the aspirin plus ticlopidine group and 11% in the aspirin plus oral anticoagulation group (p=0.07). Major vascular access site and/or bleeding complications occurred in 1.7% of the aspirin plus ticlopidine group and 6.9% in the aspirin plus oral anticoagulation group (p=0.02).
Conclusions	Aspirin plus ticlopidine was superior to aspirin plus oral anticoagulation for high risk patients after coronary artery stenting.

STARS (3 Anti-thrombotics)

Stent Anticoagulation Regimen Study

Title	A clinical trial comparing three antithrombotic drug regimens after coronary artery stenting.
Authors	Leon MB, Baim DS, Popma JJ, et al.
Reference	N Engl J Med 1998; 339:1665-1671.
Disease	Coronary artery disease.
Purpose	To compare the efficacy and safety of aspirin, aspirin plus warfarin, and aspirin plus ticlopidine following coronary artery stenting.
Design	Randomized, multicenter.
Patients	1965 patients with coronary artery disease with one or two target lesions with more than 60% stenosis not involving the left main or a major coronary bifurcation, undergoing stenting.
Follow-up	30 days.
Treatment regimen	325 mg of nonenteric coated aspirin orally once a day; 325 mg aspirin plus IV heparin (10,000-15,000 units per day) to achieve an activated partial thromboplastin time of 40-60 seconds and discontinued once an INR of 2-3 was reached with oral warfarin (continued for 4 weeks); and 325 mg of aspirin and 250 mg of ticlopidine, orally twice a day. Ticlopidine was continued for 4 weeks.

STARS (3 Anti-thrombotics)

Stent Anticoagulation Regimen Study

(continued)

Results	The primary end point (death, revascularization of target lesion, angiographically proven thrombosis, or myocardial infarction) occurred in 20 (3.6%) of patients receiving aspirin alone; 15 (2.7%) receiving aspirin plus warfarin; and 3(0.5%) receiving aspirin plus ticlopidine (p=0.001 comparison of all 3 groups). Relative risk of primary end point in group assigned to aspirin plus ticlopidine was 0.15 vs aspirin alone (p<0.001); and 0.20 vs aspirin plus warfarin (p=0.01). Hemorrhagic complications occurred in 1.8% of patients on aspirin alone; 6.2% of patients on aspirin plus warfarin; and 5.5% on aspirin plus ticlopidine (p<0.001 for comparison among all 3 groups). Vascular surgical complications occurred in 0.4%, 2.0%, and 2.0%, respectively (p=0.02).
Conclusions	Treatment of patients receiving coronary stents with aspirin plus ticlopidine resulted in lower rates of stent thrombosis and outcomes associated with it, compared to patients receiving aspirin alone or aspirin plus warfarin; but was associated with more hemorrhagic complications than aspirin alone.

FLARE

Fluvastatin Angioplasty Restenosis

Title	A randomized placebo controlled trial of fluvastatin for prevention of restenosis after successful coronary balloon angioplasty. Final results of the fluvastatin angiographic restenosis (FLARE) trial.
Authors	Foley DP, Bonnier H, Jackson G, et al. Serruys PW, Foley DP, Jackson G, et al.
Reference	Am J Cardiol 1994;73:50D-61D. Eur Heart J 1999;20:58-69.
Disease	Coronary artery disease.
Purpose	To determine the effect of fluvastatin, a 3-hydroxy-3-methylglutaryl-coenzyme A reductase inhibitor, on restenosis after successful percutaneous transluminal coronary angioplasty.
Design	Randomized, double blind, placebo controlled, multicenter.
Patients	1054 patients with native primary coronary artery lesions, who were scheduled for elective coronary angioplasty, who had an LDL cholesterol <6.0 mmol/L. Patients with myocardial infarction within the previous 3 months, restenotic lesions, lesions in bypass graft, patients requiring urgent revascularization and those with a fasting triglycerides >4.5 mmol/L were excluded.
Follow-up	Coronary angiography at baseline and after 26±2 weeks. Clinical follow-up for 40 weeks.

FLARE

Fluvastatin Angioplasty Restenosis

(continued)

Treatment regimen	Randomization to fluvastatin 40 mg bid or placebo. Patients started study medication 2 weeks before scheduled procedure. Those who had successful PTCA without reaching a major adverse cardiac event continued therapy for 26±2 weeks after angioplasty.
Additional therapy	All patients received aspirin ≤325 mg/d. ß-blockers, calcium antagonists, and nitrates were permitted. Nonaspirin antiplatelet agents and oral anticoagulants were discouraged.
Results	526 patients were randomized to fluvastatin and 528 patients to placebo. A total of 409 and 425 patients in the fluvastatin and placebo group, respectively, completed the pre PTCA phase, underwent uneventful and successful PTCA and entered the intention to treat analysis. In the fluvastatin group, LDL cholesterol decreased by 37% within the first 2 weeks of therapy before angioplasty was performed, whereas in the placebo group no significant change occurred. At 6 months, serum LDL cholesterol was 33% lower than at baseline in the fluvastatin group, whereas in the placebo group there was no change in LDL cholesterol. There were no significant changes in HDL cholesterol, apolipoprotein A1 or lipoprotein (a) levels. An increase in serum ALAT >3 times the upper limit was observed in 1.7% and 0.7% of the fluvastatin and placebo group, respectively. Fluvastatin had no effect on minimum lumen diameter after 26 weeks (1.55±0.59 mm in the fluvastatin and 1.53±0.58 mm in the placebo group; p=0.77). Restenosis (>50% diameter stenosis) occurred in 28% of the fluvastatin group vs 31% in the placebo group (p=0.42). Major cardiac events (death, myocardial infarction, coronary artery bypass surgery, or repeated angioplasty) within 40 weeks occurred in 22.4% in the fluvastatin group vs 23.3% patients in the placebo group (log rank p=0.74). Mortality was 0.7% in the fluvastatin group vs 1.6% in the placebo group (p=0.37). However, the combined incidence of death and myocardial infarction was 1.4% in the fluvastatin group vs 4.0% in the placebo group (log rank p=0.025).

Conclusions	Fluvastatin 80 mg/d, started 2 weeks before elective coronary angioplasty and continued for 26 weeks did not reduce the rate of restenosis, however, it reduced the incidence of the combined end point of death and myocardial infarction.

EPISTENT

Evaluation of Platelet IIb/IIIa Inhibitor for Stenting

Title	Randomized placebo controlled and balloon angioplasty controlled trial to assess safety of coronary stenting with use of platelet glycoprotein-IIb/ IIIa blockade.
Authors	The EPISTENT Investigators.
Reference	Lancet 1998;352:87–92.
Disease	Coronary artery disease.
Purpose	To compare outcomes of stent + placebo; to stent + abciximab; to PTCA + abciximab.
Design	Randomized, controlled, multicenter.
Patients	2399 patients with coronary artery disease and ≥60% coronary artery stenosis eligible for PTCA or stenting. Patients with unprotected left main stenosis, bleeding diathesis, intracranial tumor, stroke within the preceding 2 years, uncontrolled hypertension, recent surgery or PTCA within 3 months, and those who received oral anticoagulants were excluded.
Follow-up	30 days.

EPISTENT

Evaluation of Platelet IIb/IIIa Inhibitor for Stenting

(continued)

Treatment regimen	Randomization to sent + placebo (n=809); stent+abciximab (n=794), or PTCA + abciximab (n=796). Abciximab or identical placebo was administered as a bolus 0.25 mg/kg up to 1 hour before intervention, followed by an infusion of 0.125 μg/kg/min for 12 hours. Patients assigned to abciximab received heparin 70 U/kg as a bolus with repeated boluses to maintain activated clotting time ≥200 s. Patients assigned to placebo received heparin 100 U/kg as a bolus followed by additional boluses to maintain activated clotting time ≥300 s.
Additional therapy	Aspirin 325 mg/d. Ticlopidine 250 mg bid before the start of the study agent.
Results	>98.5% of patients in each group received the study medications. 91.5% of the patients completed 12 hours of infusion. Abrupt closure occurred in 0.7% of the stent+placebo group vs 0% in the stent+abciximab and 0.5% in the PTCA+abciximab group (p=0.060). Side-branch closure occurred in 4.5%, 2.4%, and 1.7%, respectively (p=0.02). 19.3% of the patients assigned to PTCA+abciximab received stents because of suboptimal results. The primary end point (30 day mortality, myocardial infarction or severe myocardial ischemia requiring revascularization) occurred in 10.8% of the stent+placebo group, 5.3% of the stent+abciximab group (hazard ratio 0.48; 95% CI 0.33 to 0.69; p<0.001), and 6.9% of the PTCA+abciximab group (hazard ratio 0.63; 95% CI 0.45 to 0.88; p=0.007). 30-day mortality was 0.6% in the stent+placebo group, 0.3% in the stent+abciximab group, and 0.8% in the PTCA+abciximab group. Myocardial infarction occurred in 9.6%, 4.5%, and 5.3%, respectively. Death or large myocardial infarction occurred in 7.8%, 3.0% (p<0.001), and 4.7% (p=0.010), respectively. Major bleeding occurred in 2.2% of the stent+placebo, 1.5% of the stent+abciximab, and 1.4% of the PTCA+abciximab. Subgroup analysis revealed that abciximab was beneficial in patients younger and older than 65 years, patients with and without diabetes, and in patients with either unstable

	angina or stable angina pectoris. Women had better results with PTCA+abciximab (5.1% event rate) than with stent+abciximab (8.6% event rate). This may be explained by the smaller diameter of the coronary arteries in women.
Conclusions	GP IIb/IIIa blockade with abciximab significantly improved outcome of percutaneous coronary artery interventions. PTCA+abciximab was better and safer than stenting without abciximab administration.

EPISTENT (6 month outcome)

Evaluation of Platelet IIb/IIIa Inhibition in Stenting (EPISTENT)

Title	Complementary clinical benefits of coronary artery stenting and blockade of platelet glycoprotein IIb/IIIa receptors.
Authors	Lincoff AM, Califf RM, Moliterno DJ, et al.
Reference	N Engl J Med 1999;341:319-327.
Disease	Coronary artery disease.
Purpose	To determine the efficacy of abciximab and stent implantation in improving cardiac outcomes.
Design	Randomized, multicenter, blinding to abciximab vs placebo.
Patients	2399 patients undergoing elective or urgent percutaneous coronary revascularization.
Follow-up	6 months.
Treatment regimen	Patients were randomized to stenting plus placebo, stenting plus abciximab, and balloon angioplasty plus abciximab. Abciximab was given as a 0.25 mg per kg body weight bolus 10-60 minutes before balloon inflation, and then 0.125 μg/kg/min up to 10 μg per minute infusion for 12 hours.
Additional therapy	Aspirin, ticlopidine to all patients receiving stents. Low dose, weight adjusted heparin in abciximab patients; standard, weight adjusted heparin in placebo group.

EPISTENT (6 month outcome)

Evaluation of Platelet IIb/IIIa Inhibition in Stenting (EPISTENT) (continued)

Results	The primary end points were composite of death or myocardial infarction at 6 months and repeated revascularization of the target vessel. In the stent plus placebo group, 11.4% reached the end point of death or myocardial infarction; vs 5.6% in stent plus abciximab group (hazard ratio, 0.47; 95% CI=0.33-0.68; p<0.001); vs 7.8% in balloon angioplasty plus abciximab (hazard zone 0.67; 95% CI=0.49-0.92, p=0.01). Hazard ratio for stenting plus abciximab vs angioplasty plus abciximab was 0.7 (95% CI=0.48-1.04, p=0.07). 10.6%, 8.7%, and 15.4% required repeat revascularization in the stent plus placebo, stent plus abciximab, and angioplasty plus abciximab group, respectively (p=0.22 stent plus abciximab vs stent plus placebo; p=0.005 for angioplasty plus abciximab vs stent plus placebo, and p<0.001 for stent plus abciximab vs angioplasty plus abciximab group). In diabetes, rates of repeated revascularization after stenting were lower among patients receiving abciximab vs placebo; in patients without diabetes abciximab had no effect on need for repeated revascularization. Angiographic substudy showed better early angiographic outcomes with stenting and a trend toward greater minimal luminal diameters at 6 months with a lower loss index in stented patients who received abciximab vs placebo.
Conclusions	Abciximab plus stenting have long term complementary beneficial effects.

EPISTENT (Diabetic Substudy)

Evaluation of Platelet IIb/IIIa Inhibition for Stenting Trial

Title	Optimizing the percutaneous interventional outcomes for patients with diabetes mellitus. Results of the EPISTENT Diabetic Substudy.
Authors	Marso SP, Lincoff AM, Ellis SG, et al.
Reference	Circulation 1999; 100:2477-2484.
Disease	Coronary artery disease, diabetes.
Purpose	To determine whether abciximab plus stenting is better than stenting alone or PTCA-abciximab in diabetic patients who were part of the EPISTENT Trial.
Design	As per EPISTENT.
Patients	491 diabetic patients in the EPISTENT study. Patients eligible to undergo stenting or PTCA with an epicardial coronary stenosis ≥60%.
Follow-up	6 months-1 year.
Treatment regimen	As per EPISTENT. 173 diabetic patients randomized to stent-placebo; 162 to stent-abciximab; 156 to balloon angioplasty-abciximab.
Additional therapy	Diabetes was managed with insulin, oral hypoglycemics, diet, or combination of these treatments.

EPISTENT (Diabetic Substudy)

Evaluation of Platelet IIb/IIIa Inhibition for Stenting Trial

(continued)

Results	Main composite end point was 6 month rate of death, MI, or target vessel revascularization. This end point was achieved in 25.2% of stent-placebo diabetic patients, 23.4% of balloon-abciximab diabetic patients, and 13.0% of stent-abciximab diabetic patients (p=0.005). 6 month death or MI rates were reduced by abciximab whether patients received balloon angioplasty (7.8%) or stenting (6.2%) vs stent-placebo (12.7%; p=0.029). The 6 months target vessel revascularization rate was lowest for stent-abciximab (8.1%) compared to stent-placebo (16.6%) and balloon-abciximab (18.4%). By angiographic follow-up stent-abciximab demonstrated a significant increase in angiographic net gain and a decrease in the late loss index compared to stent-placebo. One year mortality rates were 4.1% for stent-placebo diabetic patients, vs 1.2% for stent-abciximab diabetic patients (p=0.11).
Conclusions	The composite end point of 6 month death, myocardial infarction, and target vessel revascularization in diabetics was lowest when abciximab was combined with stenting vs placebo plus stenting or PTCA plus abciximab.

EPISTENT (Substudy)

Evaluation of Platelet IIb/IIIa Inhibitor for Stenting

Title	Incidence and clinical course of thrombotic thrombocytopenic purpura due to ticlopidine following coronary stenting.
Authors	Steinhubl SR, Tan WA, Foody JM, et al.
Reference	JAMA 1999; 281:806-810.
Disease	Coronary artery disease.
Purpose	To assess the frequency and course of thrombotic thrombocytopenic purpura (TTP) due to the drug ticlopidine following coronary artery stenting.
Design	Retrospective analysis of patients undergoing stenting in the EPISTENT trial.
Patients	43,322 patients from EPISTENT trial plus collection of additional cases of ticlopidine associated with TTP.
Treatment regimen	As per EPISTENT trial. Ticlopidine 250 mg p.o. bid post stent given for 5-60 days; average duration was 22 days.
Results	From 1996-1997, 9 cases (out of 43,322 patients receiving stents) or 0.02% developed TTP. This is more common than the rate of TTP in the general population (0.0004%). An additional 10 patients were identified outside the main cohort. TTP was diagnosed on avenge 2.5 days after starting ticlopidine (with a range 8-67 days). 73% of patients had central nervous symptoms, 47% renal dysfunction, 32% recurrent cardiac symptoms. Overall mortality rate was 21% (4/19). 13 patients who had plasmapheresis survived; the mortality rate was 67% (4/6) in patients who did not receive plasmapheresis.

EPISTENT (Substudy)

Evaluation of Platelet IIb/IIIa Inhibitor for Stenting

(continued)

Conclusions	TTP incidence following ticlopidine for stenting is significantly greater than the incidence in the general population. Although the complication is rare following stenting (0.02%) the mortality rate is greater than 20%, limiting ticlopidine therapy to 2 weeks following stenting does not prevent the complication; plasmapheresis helps improve outcome.

RESIST

Restenosis After IVUS Guided Stenting

Title	Impact of intravascular ultrasound guidance in stent deployment 6 month restenosis rate: A multicenter, randomized study comparing two strategies with and without intravascular ultrasound guidance.
Authors	Schiele F, Meneveau N, Vuillemenot A, et al.
Reference	J Am Coll Cardiol 1998; 32:320-328.
Disease	Coronary artery disease.
Purpose	To determine the effect of using intravascular ultrasound (IVUS) guided stent deployment on rates of 6 month restenosis.
Design	Randomized, single blinded, multicenter.
Patients	155 patients with coronary lesions amenable to stenting and optimal angiographic result following stent deployment.
Follow-up	6 months.
Treatment regimen	Stent deployed and patients randomized to no further dilatation (Group A) or additional balloon dilatation within the stent until criteria for optimal stent deployment by IVUS reached (Group B).
Additional therapy	Heparin, aspirin, ticlopidine.

RESIST

Restenosis After IVUS Guided Stenting

(continued)

Results	There was no difference in minimal luminal diameter between groups. The cross-sectional area of the stent lumen was greater in Group B (7.95±2.21 mm^2) vs Group A (7.16±2.48 mm^2, p=0.04). At 6 months there was no significant difference in restenosis rates: 28.8% in Group A vs 22.5% in Group B, p=NS). At 6 months the minimal luminal diameter again was not significantly different between groups (1.60±0.65 mm in Group A vs 1.70±0.64 mm in Group B; p=NS), but the lumen cross sectional area was 20% larger in Group B patients (5.36±2.81 mm^2) compared to Group A patients (4.47±2.59 mm^2, p=0.03).
Conclusions	There was a nonsignificant 6.3% decrease in restenosis rate in patients receiving IVUS guided stenting. It did not significantly affect minimal luminal diameter, but did improve lumen cross sectional area.

CART

Coronary Angioplasty Restenosis Trial

Title	n-3 fatty acids do not prevent restenosis after coronary angioplasty. Results from the CART study.
Authors	Johansen O, Brekke M, Seljeflot I, et al.
Reference	J Am Coll Cardiol 1999; 33:1619–1626.
Disease	Coronary artery disease, restenosis.
Purpose	To determine whether omega-3 fatty acids (n-3FA) decrease restenosis following PTCA.
Design	Randomized, placebo controlled, double blind.
Patients	500 patients undergoing elective PTCA.
Follow-up	6 months.
Treatment regimen	n-3FA, 5.1 g/day vs corn oil (control) beginning at least 2 weeks prior to elective PTCA until 6 month angiographic assessment of restenosis.
Results	A mean of 1.4 stenoses were treated per patient. Quantitative coronary angiography was utilized to gauge restenosis. Restenosis was defined as ≥20% late loss of diameter and stenosis >50%, or increase in stenosis of ≥0.7 mm. There was no difference in restenosis rates between the two groups: 40.6% in the n-3FA group and 35.4% in the placebo group (p=NS). One or more restenoses occurred in 45.9% of patients in the n-3FA group vs 44.8% of the placebo group.
Conclusions	n-3FA did not reduce the incidence of restenosis following PTCA.

ERASER

The Evaluation of Reo Pro® And Stenting to Eliminate Restenosis

Title	Acute platelet inhibition with abciximab does not reduce in-stent restenosis (ERASER Study).
Authors	The ERASER Investigators.
Reference	Circulation 1999;100:799-806.
Disease	Coronary artery disease, restenosis.
Purpose	To determine whether IV abciximab would decrease neointimal hyperplasia following intracoronary stenting.
Design	Double blind, placebo controlled, randomized, multicenter.
Patients	215 patients with a de novo target coronary artery stenosis of ≥50% referred for intracoronary stent implantation.
Follow-up	6 months.
Treatment regimen	Intravascular ultrasound (IVUS) was used to guide optimal stenting. Patients undergoing stenting were randomized to 1 of 3 groups: 1) placebo bolus plus placebo infusion; 2) abciximab 0.25 mg/kg bolus plus 12 hours of 0.125 μg/kg/min (up to 10 μg/min) infusion; or 3) abciximab 0.25 mg/kg bolus plus two consecutive 12 hour 0.125 μg/kg/min (up to 10 μg/min) infusions.
Additional therapy	Aspirin, heparin, ticlopidine, nitroglycerin.

Results	Primary end point was percent in-stent volume obstruction of the target lesion, measured at 6 months with IVUS. Secondary end points were target lesion mean and minimum lumen diameter (MLD), late loss and loss index by quantitative coronary angiography at 6 months, and composite end point of death, myocardial infarction, and target lesion revascularization. Tissue volume as percentage of stent volume was similar in the placebo, 12 hour, and 24 hour abciximab groups at 25±15%, 27±15%, and 29±14%, respectively (p=NS). Dichotomous restenosis rates assessed by late quantitative coronary angiography were 11.6%, 18.9%, and 19.4%, respectively (p=NS). Late loss index assessed by coronary angiography were 0.33, 0.52, and 0.47, respectively (p=NS). The composite end point of death, myocardial infarction, or target lesion revascularization at 6 months was similar among groups at 25.4% in placebo and 21.4% of the combined abciximab groups (p=NS).
Conclusions	Platelet inhibition with abciximab did not decrease the rate of in-stent restenosis.

3 year clinical and angiographic follow-up after intracoronary radiation. Results of a randomized trial.

Title	3 year clinical and angiographic follow-up after intracoronary radiation. Results of a randomized trial.
Authors	Teirstein PS, Massullo V, Jani S, et al.
Reference	Circulation 2000;101:360-365.
Disease	Coronary artery disease, restenosis.
Purpose	To determine angiographic and clinical outcome 3 years following treatment of restenosis with catheter based intracoronary radiation.
Design	Double blind, randomized.
Patients	55 patients with previous restenosis following coronary angioplasty who either had a stent or were candidates for a stent.
Follow-up	3 years.
Treatment regimen	Patients received a 0.76 mm ribbon with sealed sources of ^{192}Ir (n=26) vs placebo (n=29) for 20-45 minutes.

3 year clinical and angiographic follow-up after intracoronary radiation. Results of a randomized trial.

(continued)

Results	Target lesion revascularization was lower in the ^{192}Ir group (15.4%) vs the placebo group (48.3%) by 3 years ($p<0.01$). Restenosis rates were lower in the group receiving intracoronary radiation (33%) vs placebo (64%; $p<0.05$). There was no difference in rates of death in the radiation group (11.5%) vs placebo group (10.3%) or rates of myocardial infarction (3.9% vs 10.3%, respectively). In patients with 3 year angiographic follow-up who did not undergo target lesion revascularization, mean minimal luminal diameter decreased between 6 months to 3 years (2.49 to 2.12 mm) in radiation treated patients, but was unchanged in the placebo patients.
Conclusions	At 3 year follow-up intracoronary radiotherapy was associated with lower rates of target lesion revascularization and restenosis in patients who had undergone stenting for restenosis.

VIP

Visipaque in Percutaneous Transluminal Coronary Angioplasty Trial

Title	Influence of a nonionic, iso-osmolar contrast medium (Iodixanol) vs an ionic, low osmolar contrast medium (Ioxaglute) on major adverse cardiac events in patients undergoing percutaneous transluminal coronary angioplasty (PTCA). A multicenter, randomized, double blind study.
Authors	Bertrand ME, Esplugas E, Piessens J, et al.
Reference	Circulation 2000;101:131-136.
Disease	Coronary artery disease.
Purpose	To determine the influence of both nonionic and ionic contrast media on major adverse cardiac events (MACE) in coronary artery disease patients undergoing PTCA.
Design	Randomized, parallel group, double blind , multicenter.
Patients	1141 patients undergoing PTCA. They had to have stable or unstable angina or silent ischemia. Recent MIs not included.
Follow-up	2 day, 1 month.
Treatment regimen	697 received iodixanol (nonionic) and 714 received ioxaglate (ionic) contrast medium.
Additional therapy	Heparin and aspirin, ticlopidine to patients with stents.

VIP

Visipaque in Percutaneous Transluminal Coronary Angioplasty Trial

(continued)

Results	Primary end point was a composite of MACE which included: death, stroke, myocardial infarction, coronary artery bypass grafting, and repeat PTCA at 2 days. MACE were similar in the iodixanol (4.7%) and ioxaglate group (3.9%; p=0.45). Between 2 days and 1 month follow-up there was again no difference in MACE between the 2 groups.The frequency of adverse events during the 2 day follow-up were similar in the iodixanol (27.5%) and ioxaglate group (27.6%). Hypersensitivity reactions were less common in the iodixanol (nonionic) group at 0.7% vs the ioxaglate (ionic) group at 2.5% (p<0.007). Contrast related adverse events were less common in the iodixanol group (1.0%) vs the ioxaglate group (3.5%; p<0.002). Rash, urticaria, or pruritis occurred in 5 iodixanol vs 12 ioxaglate patients. One patient in the ioxaglate group developed anaphylactic shock.
Conclusions	While there was no overall difference in major adverse cardiac events between the use of iodixanol vs ioxaglate, hypersensitivity reactions and adverse drug reactions were less frequent with the use of the nonionic contrast agent, iodixanol.

EXCITE

Evaluation of Oral Xemilofiban in Controlling Thrombotic Events

Title	Long term treatment with a platelet glycoprotein receptor antagonist after percutaneous coronary revascularization.
Authors	O'Neill WW, Serruys P, Knudtson M, et al.
Reference	N Engl J Med 2000;342:1316-1324.
Disease	Coronary artery disease.
Purpose	To determine whether long term oral glycoprotein IIb/IIIa receptor antagonist, xemilofiban, would reduce death, MI, and need for urgent revascularization.
Design	Double blind, randomized, placebo controlled, multicenter.
Patients	7232 patients with angiographic evidence of clinically significant CAD in need of percutaneous transluminal coronary revascularization.
Follow-up	182 days.
Treatment regimen	Single oral dose of 20 mg xemilofiban prior to percutaneous intervention and maintenance of 20 mg three times daily after procedure; 20 mg before and maintenance of 10 mg three times daily after; or placebo given before and after.
Additional therapy	Ticlopidine in stent patient on placebo or placebo ticlopidine in xemilofiban patients; all patients received aspirin.

EXCITE

Evaluation of Oral Xemilofiban in Controlling Thrombotic Events

(continued)

Results	One primary end point was death, nonfatal myocardial infarction, or urgent revascularization at 182 days. The other primary end point was death or nonfatal myocardial infarction at 182 days. At 182 days, death, nonfatal myocardial infarction, or urgent revascularization occurred in 324 (13.5%) placebo patients, 332 (13.9%) who received 10 mg of xemilofiban, and 306 (12.7%) who received 20 mg of xemilofiban (p=NS among groups). Death or nonfatal myocardial infarction developed in 215 (8.9%) patients in the placebo group, 220 (9.2%) in the 10 mg xemilofiban group, and 199 (8.2%) in the 20 mg xemilofiban group. There were no significant differences among the 3 groups. The percent of patients who withdrew for bleeding was 6.1% and 11.6% at the 10 mg and 20 mg dose of xemilofiban vs 1.5% in the placebo group (p<0.001 vs treatment groups). Myocardial infarcts occurring within one day after randomization were lower in the 10 and 20 mg xemilofiban groups (4.1% and 4.0%, respectively) compared to placebo (5.5%; p=0.02).
Conclusions	The glycoprotein IIb/IIIa antagonist xemilofiban given prior to percutaneous coronary intervention and then for up to 6 months did not decrease the incidence of death, myocardial infarction, or urgent revascularization.

Clopidogrel as adjunctive antiplatelet therapy during coronary stenting

Title	Clopidogrel as adjunctive antiplatelet therapy during coronary stenting.
Authors	Mishkel GJ, Aguirre FV, Ligon RW, et al.
Reference	J Am Coll Cardiol 1999;34:1884–1890.
Disease	Coronary artery disease.
Purpose	To determine procedural and 30 day clinical outcomes in patients receiving ticlopidine vs clopidogrel during coronary artery stenting.
Design	Prospective, single center analysis.
Patients	875 consecutive patients undergoing stenting who received aspirin plus either clopidogrel or ticlopidine.
Follow-up	30 days.
Treatment regimen	All patients received oral aspirin (325 mg) before the procedure and then daily. Therapy with oral ticlopidine (250 mg twice daily) or oral clopidogrel (75 mg once daily) was begun the night before or the day of the procedure and continued for 2–4 weeks after the procedure.
Additional therapy	Heparin; glycoprotein IIb/IIIa antagonists and intracoronary nitroglycerin could be used.

Clopidogrel as adjunctive antiplatelet therapy during coronary stenting

(continued)

Results	End points included procedural success (all lesions dilated and stented with angiographic residual stenosis of <10%).The presence of acute (≤24 hrs) and subacute (>24 hrs and ≤ month) stent thrombosis noted. Major adverse cardiac events were also assessed. 514 patients received clopidogrel and 316 received ticlopidine. Procedural success occurred in 99.6% of patients on clopidogrel and 99.4% of patients on ticlopidine. Subacute stent thrombosis occurred in one clopidogrel and one ticlopidine patient. Combined rates of death, nonfatal myocardial infarction, and need for target revascularization were 2.1% in the clopidogrel patients and 1.4% in the ticlopidine patients. Death occurred in 0.9% of clopidogrel and 0.6% of ticlopidine patients. Bleeding complications occurred in 5.4% of clopidogrel and 4.4% of ticlopidine patients (p=0.35).There was no difference in hemorrhagic stroke, need for transfusion, or need for vascular access surgical repair between the 2 groups.
Conclusions	Aspirin plus clopidogrel was as effective as aspirin plus ticlopidine in terms of the incidence of thrombotic complications and major adverse cardiovascular events in a broad spectrum of coronary artery disease patients undergoing stenting.

Title	Clopidogrel vs ticlopidine after intracoronary stent placement.
Authors	Berger PB, Bell MR, Rihal CS, et al.
Reference	J Am Coll Cardiol 1999;34:1891-1894.
Disease	Coronary artery disease.
Purpose	To compare efficacy and safety of ticlopidine with clopidogrel in intracoronary stent patients.
Design	Comparison of events in 500 consecutive coronary stent patients who received aspirin plus clopidogrel to 827 consecutive stent patients who received aspirin plus ticlopidine. Single center study.
Patients	1327 coronary artery disease patients receiving stents.
Follow-up	30 days.
Treatment regimen	All patients received aspirin. Clopidogrel was given as a 300 mg load in the catheterization lab before stent implantation and then 75 mg/day for 14 days. Ticlopidine was given as 500 mg load before stent implantation and 250 mg that evening and 250 mg twice daily for 14 days.
Additional therapy	Heparin; abciximab, enoxaparin could be given at the discretion of the cardiologist.

Results	Despite the fact that at baseline clopidogrel patients had more adverse clinical characteristics (older, more severe angina, more diabetes and hypertension, and lower LV ejection fraction), the frequency of death, nonfatal MI, stent thrombosis, and repeat angioplasty or bypass surgery was slightly, although not statistically significantly lower than patients treated with ticlopidine. The composite of death, MI, stent thrombosis, repeat revascularization was 0.8% in clopidogrel patients vs 1.6% in the ticlopidine group (p=NS). Death occurred in 0.4% vs 1.1% of clopidogrel vs ticlopidine patients, respectively. Nonfatal MI occurred in 0% vs 0.5%; stent thrombosis in 0.2% vs 0.7%, and repeat revascularization in 0.4% vs 0.5% of clopidogrel vs ticlopidine patients, respectively. Thrombotic thrombocytopenic purpura and neutropenia were not observed in any patient.
Conclusions	Clopidogrel can safely be substituted for ticlopidine in coronary artery disease patients receiving stents.

Title	Minimal heparinization in coronary angioplasty. How much heparin is really warranted?
Authors	Kaluski E, Krakover R, Cotter G, et al.
Reference	Am J Cardiol 2000;85:953-956.
Disease	Coronary artery disease, PTCA.
Purpose	To assess outcomes of nonemergency PCI, performed with a single low dose of heparin (2500 U).
Design	A cohort, single center.
Patients	300 patients undergoing nonemergency PCI.
Follow-up	6 months.
Treatment regimen	All patients received a bolus of 2500 U of unfractionated heparin before insertion of the guiding catheter. Additional heparin was at the discretion of the operator. Femoral arterial sheaths were removed within 2 hours of PCI.
Additional therapy	All patients received aspirin 250 mg/d and patients with stents received ticlopidine 250 mg bid for 30 days. IV platelet glycoprotein IIb/IIIa were permitted. Coumadin or hirudin were prohibited for 12 hours after PCI.

Results	Angiographic success was obtained in 96% of the patients, clinical success in 93.3% of the patients. Mean activated clotting time 5 minutes after heparin administration was 185±19 seconds. In 61% of the patients stents were deployed. 16% of the patients received IV glycoprotein IIb/IIIa inhibitors. Mean post PCI sheath dwelling time was 45±58 minutes. 77.6% of the patients stayed in the hospital <24 hours. Two patients (0.66%) had cardiac arrest and died during hospitalization. None of the patients needed emergency CABG or had a stroke. One patient had a Q wave myocardial infarction due to acute target vessel occlusion 6 hours after PTCA and stenting. Six patients (2%) had abrupt coronary artery occlusion within 14 days of PTCA. No bleeding or vascular complications were detected. At 6 months (184 patients) 4 patients died (2.1%) and one patient had Q wave myocardial infarction. 9.7% of the patients had repeated target vessel revascularization.
Conclusions	Very low dose heparin administration is safe in patients undergoing nonemergency PCI and may be associated with lower bleeding complications, hospitalization length, and probably costs.

TREAT

Tranilast Restenosis Following Angioplasty Trial

Title	Impact of tranilast on restenosis after coronary angioplasty: Tranilast restenosis following angioplasty trial (TREAT).
Authors	Tamai H, Katoh O, Suzuki S, et al.
Reference	Am Heart J 1999;138:968-975.
Disease	Coronary artery disease, PCI, restenosis.
Purpose	To assess whether tranilast, an antiallergic drug that suppresses the release of platelet derived growth factor and other cytokines, will prevent restenosis after percutaneous balloon angioplasty.
Design	Randomized, double blind, placebo controlled, multicenter.
Patients	255 patients, ≤75 years old, with angina pectoris or old myocardial infarction, >50% diameter stenosis in de novo native type A coronary artery lesions with TIMI flow grade 2-3. Before enrollment patients had to undergo successful PTCA.
Follow-up	Follow-up angiography at 3 months. Clinical follow-up for 12 months.
Treatment regimen	Randomization to tranilast 600 mg/d (86 patients, 100 lesions), tranilast 300 mg/d (84 patients, 94 lesions), or placebo (85 patients, 95 lesions) for 3 months after successful PTCA.

Tranilast Restenosis Following Angioplasty Trial

(continued)

Additional therapy	All patients received IV 10,000 IU heparin just before PTCA. It is unclear whether aspirin was mandatory, whether stents, other devices, and IV glycoprotein IIb/IIIa were permitted.
Results	The per-protocol population included 59 patients (68 lesions) in the tranilast 600 mg/d, 64 patients (71 lesions) in the tranilast 300 mg/d, and 65 patients (71 lesions) in the placebo group. ≥50% diameter stenosis occurred in 17.6% of the tranilast 600 mg/d (p=0.005 vs placebo), 38.6% in the tranilast 300 mg/d and 39.4% in the placebo group. ≥50% loss of the initial gain was found in 14.7%, 35.2%, and 46.5% of the patients, respectively (p=0.000065 for tranilast 600 mg vs placebo). Multivariable model showed that tranilast (odds ratio 0.275; 95% CI 0.116-0.612; p=0.002) and female gender (odds ratio 0.352; 95% CI 0.119-0.991; p=0.042) were independent predictors of restenosis. 23.1% of the patients in the placebo group, 32.8% in the tranilast 300 mg/d and 15.3% in the tranilast 600 mg/d underwent revascularization within the first year (p=NS). The overall incidence of side effects per patient was 7.2% for the placebo group, 16.3% for the tranilast 300 mg/d and 9.5% for the tranilast 600 mg/d.
Conclusions	Oral administration of tranilast 600 mg/d for 3 months was safe and effective in reducing restenosis rate after percutaneous transluminal coronary angioplasty.

CAPARES

Coronary AngioPlasty Amlodipine REStenosis Study

Title	Restenosis and clinical outcome in patients treated with amlodipine after angioplasty: Results from the coronary angioplasty amlodipine restenosis study (CAPARES).
Authors	Jorgensen B, Simonsen S, Endresen K, et al.
Reference	J Am Coll Cardiol 2000:35:592-599.
Disease	Coronary artery disease, coronary angioplasty.
Purpose	To assess the effect of amlodipine, a calcium channel blocker, on restenosis and clinical outcome after PTCA.
Design	Randomized, double blind, placebo controlled, multicenter.
Patients	635 patients, with stable angina, scheduled for elective PTCA of ≥1 major native coronary artery. Patients with totally occluded arteries and those with small (<2 mm) reference lumen diameter were excluded.
Follow-up	4 months.
Treatment regimen	Patients were randomized to placebo (n=317) or amlodipine (n=318), started 2 weeks before scheduled PTCA. The initial amlodipine dose was 5 mg/d and the dose was increased to 10 mg/d. Patients randomized to placebo received 20 mg of nifedipine twice before PTCA and once after the procedure.

CAPARES

Coronary AngioPlasty Amlodipine REStenosis Study

(continued)

Additional therapy	All patients received aspirin. Lipid lowering agents, ACE inhibitors, diuretics, and ß-blockers were permitted. Nonstudy calcium channel blockers were prohibited. Stents were implanted only in bail out situation or in cases with unsatisfactory post PTCA results. All patients received 10,000 U heparin before PTCA.
Results	10 patients in the amlodipine group and 7 in the placebo group stopped study medications. PTCA was performed in 585 patients (92.1%), and stents were implanted in 91 patients (15.6%). 236 patients of the amlodipine group and 215 patients of the placebo group underwent follow-up angiography at a median time of 132 and 131 days, respectively, after the initial PTCA. The minimal lumen diameter was comparable between the amlodipine and the placebo group both before angioplasty (0.92±0.35 mm vs 0.92±0.40 mm; p=0.95), immediately after PTCA (1.82±0.37 mm vs 1.79±0.34 mm; p=0.40), and at follow-up (1.52±0.57 mm vs 1.50±0.59 mm; p=0.71). The mean loss in minimal luminal diameter at follow-up was 0.30±0.45 mm in the amlodipine group vs 0.29±0.49 mm in the placebo group (p=0.84). Similarly, percent diameter stenosis at follow-up was comparable (41.3±17.5% in the amlodipine group vs 42.9±19.3% in the placebo group; p=0.34). Restenosis occurred in 29.7% in the amlodipine group vs 29.9% in the placebo group (p=0.97). In contrast to the angiographic results, fewer patients in the amlodipine group needed repeated PTCA (3.1% vs 7.3%; relative risk [RR] 0.45; 95% CI 0.22-0.91; p=0.02). Mortality was 0.3% in the amlodipine group vs 0.6% in the placebo group (p=0.62), whereas myocardial infarction occurred in 2.5% vs 3.5%, respectively (p=0.49). The composite end point of death, myocardial infarction or repeated revascularization occurred in 9.4% vs 14.5% in the amlodipine and placebo group, respectively (RR 0.65; 95% CI 0.43-0.99; p=0.049).

Conclusions	Amlodipine, started 2 weeks before elective PTCA and continued for 4 months after the procedure, did not prevent restenosis or late loss in minimal lumen diameter after 4 months. However, amlodipine was associated with a reduction in the rate of the composite end point of death, myocardial infarction, and repeated revascularization, mainly due to a reduction in the need for repeated PTCA.

WRIST

Washington Radiation for In-Stent Restenosis Trial (WRIST)

Title	Intracoronary γ-radiation therapy after angioplasty inhibits recurrence in patients with in-stent restenosis.
Authors	Waksman R, White L, Chan RC, et al.
Reference	Circulation 2000;101:2165–2171.
Disease	Coronary artery disease.
Purpose	To determine the effects of intracoronary γ-radiation on clinical and angiographic outcomes in patients with in-stent restenosis.
Design	Prospective, randomized, double- blind trial.
Patients	130 symptomatic patients with in-stent restenosis (≥50% diameter stenosis in the stent site) who underwent successful (<30% residual stenosis with no complications) with balloons, ablative devices, additional stents, or combinations of these techniques.
Follow-up	6 months, 12 months.
Treatment regimen	Patients randomized to receive a nylon ribbon containing either placebo or seed trains of ^{192}Ir at the lesion site.
Additional therapy	Routine postangioplasty care; ticlopidine for 1 month.

WRIST

Washington Radiation for In-Stent Restenosis Trial (WRIST)

(continued)

Results

Primary clinical end point was cumulative composite of death, MI, repeat target lesion revascularization at 6 months. At 6 months angiographic end points were restenosis (diameter stenosis ≥50%), magnitude of late loss, and late loss index. Restenosis (binary angiographic) was 19% in the irradiated group vs 58% in the placebo group (p=0.001). The main angiographic pattern of restenosis in the radiation group occurred at the edges of the stent. Late luminal loss was lower in the radiated vs placebo patients. Late loss index was 0.16±0.73 mm in the radiated patients vs 0.70±0.46 in placebo patients (p=0.0001). At 6 months 29.2% of radiated patients had a major cardiac event (death, Q wave MI, and target vessel revascularization) vs 67.6% in the placebo group (p<0.001). There was no difference in death at 6 months between radiated (4.6%) or nonradiated groups (6.2%) and no patients had Q wave infarcts. Hence the major clinical difference was a reduction in target vessel revascularization in the radiation group (26.1%) vs the placebo group (67.6%; p<0.001). Target lesion revascularization also was lower in the radiation group (13.8%) vs the placebo group (63.1%) and the same pattern was observed at 12 months.

Conclusions

Gamma radiation as adjunct therapy for patients with in-stent restenosis reduced angiographic evidence of restensois and reduced the need for target lesion and target vessel revascularization.

COURT

Contrast Media Utilization in High Risk PTCA

Title	Randomized trial of contrast media utilization in high risk PTCA (The COURT Trial).
Authors	Davidson, CJ, Laskey WK, Hermiller JB, et al.
Reference	Circulation 2000;101:2172-2177.
Disease	Coronary artery disease.
Purpose	To compare the isosmolar nonionic dimer iodixanol with the low osmolar ionic agent ioxaglate in patients undergoing PTCA.
Design	Prospective, multicenter, randomized trial.
Patients	865 high risk coronary artery disease patients undergoing coronary artery intervention. High risk defined as angina at rest within the previous 2 hours, evolving MI within 72 hours, including patients who failed thrombolysis, post MI ischemia within 2 weeks of a MI.
Follow-up	Inhospital, 30 days.
Treatment regimen	Patients randomly assigned to iodixanol (n=405) or ioxaglate (n=410).
Additional therapy	Aspirin, ticlopidine if stents used. Abciximab and heparin could be used.

COURT

Contrast Media Utilization in High Risk PTCA

(continued)

Results	Primary composite end point of inhospital major adverse clinical events (emergency recatheterization or repeat PTCA, abrupt closure of target vessel, stroke, systemic thromboembolic event, periprocedural nonfatal MI, unplanned CABG, or cardiac death). This composite end point occurred in 5.4% of those receiving iodixanol vs 9.5% in those patients receiving ioxaglate (p=0.027). Angiographic success was achieved in 92.2% of patients receiving iodixanol vs 13.2% of patients receiving ioxaglate (p=0.07). Events from hospital discharge to 30 days did not differ between groups. A multivariate analysis showed that significant predictors for inhospital major adverse clinical events were ioxaglate and treatment of de novo coronary artery lesions.
Conclusions	Although the incidence of inhospital clinical events was low in both groups, it was lower in the patients receiving nonionic contrast (iodixanol) vs ionic contrast (ioxaglate) in high risk patients undergoing PTCA.

4. Interventional Cardiology

e. Other Therapy (Transmyocardial Laser Revascularization)

The Transmyocardial Laser Revascularization International Registry

Title	The transmyocardial laser revascularization international registry report.
Authors	Burns SM, Sharples LD, Tait S, et al.
Reference	Eur Heart J 1999;20:31-37.
Disease	Coronary artery disease, intractable angina pectoris.
Purpose	To report the patient characteristics, operative details, and early complications after transmyocardial laser revascularization in Europe and Asia.
Design	Registry, multicenter.
Patients	932 patients (84% males), 62±9 years old (range 32-84), with refractory angina not amenable to conventional revascularization by PTCA or CABG. 70% of the patients had previous CABG, and 32% had previous PTCA.
Follow-up	12 months.
Treatment regimen	Transmyocardial laser revascularization using the PLC Medical Systems CO_2 laser.
Additional therapy	In 20% of the patients transmyocardial laser revascularization was combined with CABG, and in 1% with PTCA.

The Transmyocardial Laser Revascularization International Registry

(continued)

Results	On average, 28.6±12.2 channels were created in each patient. In-hospital mortality was 9.7%. Bleeding occurred in 7.6%, infections in 4.1%, myocardial infarctions in 3.5%, tamponade in 0.6%, and LV dysfunction in 8.2%. Complication rates were comparable to similar cardiothoracic surgical procedures. Improvement (≥2) of Canadian Cardiovascular Score classes was noted in 47.3%, 45.4%, and 34.0% of the survivors at 3, 6, and 12 months, respectively ($p=0.001$). NYHA score improved by ≥2 classes in 38.0%, 42.4%, 49.1% of the survivors at 3, 6, and 12 months, respectively ($p<0.001$). LVEF did not change significantly at 3 and 6 months, compared with baseline. However, at 12 months there was a 4.3% decrease in LVEF compared with baseline ($p<0.01$). Treadmill exercise time increased significantly by 42 seconds at 3 months compared with baseline ($p=0.008$). This effect was maintained over the 12 months follow-up (1 min 50 seconds increase at 12 months; $p<0.001$).
Conclusions	This uncontrolled registry shows that transmyocardial laser revascularization may cause amelioration of symptoms and improved exercise performance. However, the procedure is associated with high mortality (9.7%) rate.

Title	Results of transmyocardial laser revascularization in non-revascularizable coronary artery disease after 3 years follow-up.
Authors	Nagele H, Stubbe HM, Nienaber C, et al.
Reference	Eur Heart J 1998;19:1525-1530.
Disease	Coronary artery disease, angina pectoris.
Purpose	To describe the 3 year follow-up results of transmyocardial laser revascularization as a sole therapy in patients with nonrevascularizable coronary artery disease.
Design	Registry.
Patients	126 patients with severe coronary artery disease unsuitable for conventional revascularization (PTCA or CABG).
Follow-up	A mean follow-up of 1.94±0.8 years (0.3 to 3.4 years).
Treatment regimen	Patients received maximal drug therapy for 1-2 months. Therapy included nitrates, molsidomin, ß-blockers (75%), calcium antagonists (84%), and ACE inhibitors (64%). Only patients who remained refractory despite therapy (n=60) were referred to transmyocardial laser revascularization, using a 800 W CO_2 Heart-Laser (PLC system). A mean of 33 channels was created in each patient.

Results	68% of the 60 patients who underwent transmyocardial laser revascularization were men, 78.3% had previous CABG surgery. Perioperative 30-day mortality was 12%. One and 3 year mortality was 23% and 30%. The risk of the procedure was higher in patients with initial LVEF <40% than >40% (p<0.001). Canadian Cardiovascular Society class was 3.31±0.51 at baseline and improved to 1.84±0.77 3 months after the procedure (p<0.0001). However the Canadian Cardiovascular Society score increased to 2.02±0.92 after 6 months, and to 2.58±0.9 after 3 years. The angina class deteriorated over time. Nuclear studies (MIBI-SPECT and PET) in 22 patients before and after transmyocardial laser revascularization showed a small decrease in normally perfused segments, and a small increase in ischemic or nonviable segments (p<0.05).
Conclusions	Half the patients with nonrevascularizable coronary artery disease can be stabilized with medical therapy. Transmyocardial laser revascularization was associated with high perioperative mortality (12%), led to a rapid early amelioration of symptoms, but the beneficial effect decreased over time. Transmyocardial laser revascularization should be performed only after failure of maximal medical therapy and only in patients with LVEF >40%.

Title	Transmyocardial laser revascularization in patients with refractory angina: A randomized controlled trial.
Authors	Schofield PM, Sharples LD, Caine N, et al.
Reference	Lancet 1999; 353; 519-524.
Disease	Coronary artery disease.
Purpose	To compare the effects of transmyocardial laser revascularization (TMLR) and medical therapy in patients with coronary artery disease.
Design	Randomized, single center.
Patients	188 patients with refractory angina due to diffuse and distal coronary artery disease. Patients had to have reversible ischemia seen on radionuclide perfusion scan. Patients with a disease amenable for conventional revascularization, left ventricular ejection fraction <30%, or those unable to do exercise testing were excluded. Patients who received intravenous therapy to control the anginal symptoms and those with a life expectancy of <12 months were not included.
Follow-up	At least one year. A modified Bruce treadmill exercise test and 12 min walk test at 3, 6, and 12 months.
Treatment regimen	Randomization to transmyocardial laser revascularization (TMLR) + normal medical therapy or medical therapy alone. TMLR was done through a small anterolateral thoracotomay, using a 1000W carbon dioxide laser device (PLC Medical Systems, MA, USA). The channels were about 1 mm in diameter and were performed at about 1/cm^2. 6-75 (median 30) channels were performed in each patients.

Results	312 patients were considered for the study. 188 were included and randomized (94 patients to each group). Morbidity associated with the TMLR procedure (including infections) was seen in 68% of the TMLR group. Perioperative mortality was 5%. The mean hospitalization was 10.5 days. 12 month survival was 96% for the medically treated group vs 89% for the TMLR group (p=0.14). Autopsy reports on 3 patients who died after discharge showed dense fibrous scarring. There was no evidence that the channels were functioning. Mean treadmill exercise time at 12 months, adjusted for baseline values, was 40 seconds (95% CI 15 to 94) longer in the TMLR group (p=0.152). The exercise test was stopped because of angina less frequently in the TMLR group (43%) than in the medically treated group (70%, p<0.001). The TMLR patients walked for a longer distance during the 12 min walk test at 3 (p=0.005) and 6 months (p=0.005), but not at 12 months (p=0.108). A reduction of ≥2 Canadian cardiovascular Society score classes was seen in 34%, 22%, and 25% of the TMLR patients at 3, 6, and 12 months, respectively, but in only 3%, 4%, and 4% of the medically treated patients, respectively. Angina scores, reported by the patients, were lower in the TMLR group at 3 (p=0.002), 6 (p=0.046), and 12 months (p=0.053). TMLR did not change the resting left ventricular ejection fraction at 12 months. In both groups, the number of segments with reversible ischemia on radionuclide perfusion scans decreased and the number of segments with irreversible ischemia increased over time. The overall number of segments with reversible ischemia was not statistically different between the 2 groups.
Conclusions	TMLR resulted in mild subjective improvement in symptoms. However, objective evidence of amelioration of ischemia was not observed. The procedure was associated with relatively high mortality and morbidity. TMLR should not be adopted for patients with angina unsuitable for conventional revascularization.

PRINCE

The Prevention of Radiocontrast Induced Nephropathy Clinical Evaluation (PRINCE)

Title	A prospective randomized trial of prevention measures in patients at high risk for contrast nephropathy. Results of PRINCE study.
Authors	Stevens MA, McCullough PA, Tobin KJ, et al.
Reference	J Am Coll Cardiol 1999; 33:403-411.
Disease	Coronary artery disease.
Purpose	To determine whether forced diuresis and maintenance of intravascular volume after contrast exposure could decrease contrast induced renal injury.
Design	Prospective, randomized, controlled, single blind.
Patients	98 patients scheduled for elective coronary angiography with or without intervention; serum creatinine greater than 1.8 mg/dL.
Follow-up	48 hours.
Treatment regimen	Controls received 0.45 normal saline alone at a rate of 150 mL/hr upon arrival to cath lab and this was continued through the procedure. Experimental group received same crystalloid, plus furosemide (1 mg/kg up 100 mg) and IV dopamine (3 mcg/kg/min). If pulmonary capillary wedge pressure was <20 mm Hg, then mannitol (12.5g in 250 mL of 5% dextrose) was infused over 2 hours. 43 patients received forced diuretic; 55 received placebo.

The Prevention of Radiocontrast Induced Nephropathy Clinical Evaluation (PRINCE)

(continued)

Results	The experimental (forced diuresis group) had higher urine flow rates (163 mL/hr) vs control group (123 mL/hr) over 24 hours (p=0.001). Five patients in the control group required dialysis vs 2 in the experimental group. At 48 hours, mean change in serum creatinine was 0.48 in the experimental group and 0.51 in the control group (p = NS). While there was no difference in rates of renal failure between groups the rise in serum creatinine related inversely to the degree of induced diuresis when baseline renal function was factored in (r=-0.036, p=0.005). Urine flow rates of >150 mL/hour during the post procedure period were associated with lower rates of renal failure.
Conclusions	Forced diuresis provided a modest benefit against contrast induced renal injury if high urine flow rates are achieved.

LARS

Laser Angioplasty of Restenosed Stents

Title	Laser angioplasty of restenosed coronary stents. Results of a multicenter surveillance trial.
Authors	Köster R, Hamm CW, Seabra-Gomes R, et al.
Reference	J Am Coll Cardiol 1999;34:25-32.
Disease	Coronary artery disease. Restenosis or occluded stents.
Purpose	Determine the feasibility, safety, and efficacy of excimer laser angioplasty, with saline flush and adjunctive balloon angioplasty for in-stent restenosis.
Design	Prospective, nonrandomized, multicenter, surveillance trial.
Patients	440 patients with restenosis or occlusions in 527 coronary artery stents.
Follow-up	Inhospital.
Treatment regimen	Xenon chloride excimer laser unit used to debulk as much tissue in the in-stent restenosis as possible.
Additional therapy	Aspirin, heparin, IV nitroglycerin; abciximab if necessary.

Results	Laser angioplasty success was defined as ≤50% residual stenosis or successful pass with a 2.0 mm or an eccentric 1.7 mm laser catheter. Success was attained in 92% of patients. Adjunctive PTCA was carried out in 99% of patients. Procedural success was defined as laser angioplasty success followed by ≤30% residual stenosis with or without PTCA and occurred in 91% of cases. Success was not dependent upon length of the lesion, size of vessel, or procedure in native vessels vs vein grafts. Death occurred in 1.6%, Q wave infarct in 0.5%, and non Q wave infarct in 2.7% of patients. Laser treatment caused perforation of the coronary artery in 0.2% cases. Dissections occurred in 4.8% of patients following laser treatment and 9.3% after PTCA. Cardiac tamponade occurred in 0.5%.
Conclusions	Excimer laser angioplasty with adjunctive PTCA was safe and effective for treating in-stent coronary artery restenoses and a randomized comparison to PTCA alone is justified.

ATLANTIC

Angina Treatments-Lasers And Normal Therapies in Comparison

Title	Transmyocardial laser revascularization compared with continued medical therapy for treatment of refractory angina pectoris: A prospective randomised trial.
Authors	Burkhoff D, Schmidt S, Schulman SP, et al.
Reference	Lancet 1999;354:885-890.
Disease	Angina pectoris, coronary artery disease.
Purpose	To compare transmyocardial laser revascularization (TMR) with standard medical therapy in patients with medically refractory angina pectoris.
Design	Randomized, open label, multicenter.
Patients	182 patients with Canadian Cardiovascular Society Angina (CCSA) Class III (38%) or IV (62%), despite maximum medical therapy, LVEF ≥30%, and reversible perfusion defects on dipyridamole thallium stress test. Patients with symptomatic heart failure, a history of significant ventricular arrhythmias, or who had cardiac transplantation were excluded. In addition, those patients who had been hospitalized for acute coronary syndromes or changes in antianginal medications were not included within 21 days of the last event or within 3 months for acute myocardial infarction.
Follow-up	12 months with repeated anginal class assessment, exercise test, dipyridamole thallium stress test, and angina questionnaire.

ATLANTIC

Angina Treatments-Lasers And Normal Therapies in Comparison

(continued)

Treatment regimen	Patients were randomized to TMR with continued medical therapy (n=92) or medical therapy alone (n=90). TMR was applied under general anesthesia through a limited muscle sparing left thoracotomy with a holmium:YAG laser (CardioGenesis Corp, Sunnyvale, CA, USA).
Results	5% of the TMR patients and 10% of the medical therapy patients died during the study. Unstable angina requiring hospitalization occurred in 37 patients of the TMR group vs 69 patients in the medical therapy group. Heart failure or left ventricular dysfunction occurred in 25 patients of the TMR group vs 10 patients in the medical therapy group, and myocardial infarction was noted in 14 and 8 patients of the TMR and medical therapy group, respectively. Exercise duration increased in the TMR group at all time points, with median improvement of >60 seconds. Over 50% of the medical therapy group had a decrease in their exercise time. At 12 months, total exercise time increased by a median of 65 seconds in the TMR group and decreased by 46 seconds in the medical therapy group ($p<0.0001$). Only 26% of the TMR patients had angina during the final exercise test, compared with 58% of the medical therapy group. After 12 months, CCSA score had decreased by ≥2 scores in 61% of the TMR group vs only 11% in the medical therapy group. Patients with more severe angina at baseline were more likely to have greater improvement with TMR. At 12 months 48% of the TMR group vs only 14% of the medical therapy group were in CCSA Class ≤2 ($p<0.001$). The quality of life index score increased significantly more in the TMR group than in the medical treatment group. However, the change in the percentage of myocardium with fixed and reversible perfusion defects at 3, 6, and 12 months was comparable between the TMR and medical therapy group. LVEF did not change in the medical therapy group from baseline to 3 months, whereas it decreased by 3% in the TMR group ($p<0.0001$).

ATLANTIC

Angina Treatments-Lasers And Normal Therapies in Comparison

(continued)

Conclusions	TMR was more effective than medical therapy alone in alleviating symptoms of angina and increasing exercise performance. However, it was not associated with improvement in myocardial perfusion, as assessed by dipyridamole thallium scan. TMR may provide benefits in patients with no other therapeutic options.

Transmyocardial revascularization with CO_2 laser in patients with refractory angina pectoris. Clinical results from the Norwegian Randomized Trial.

Title	Transmyocardial revascularization with CO_2 laser in patients with refractory angina pectoris. Clinical results from the Norwegian Randomized Trial.
Authors	Aaberge L, Nordstrand K, Dragsund M, et al.
Reference	J Am Coll Cardiol 2000;35:1170–1177.
Disease	Coronary artery disease, angina pectoris.
Purpose	To determine the effects of CO_2 laser transmyocardial revascularization (TMR) plus maximal medical therapy vs maximal medical therapy alone on anginal symptoms, exercise performance, and maximal oxygen consumption.
Design	Open, randomized, prospective, single center study.
Patients	100 patients with refractory angina pectoris (Class III or IV despite optimal medical therapy).
Follow-up	3 months and 12 months.
Treatment regimen	800 W CO_2 laser, 30–50 J, pulse duration of 30–50 msec. Approximately one channel/cm^2 of myocardium, confirmed by transesophageal ultrasound probe (average of 48±7 channels).
Additional therapy	Included ß-blockers, calcium blockers, long acting nitrates, aspirin, warfarin, ACE inhibitors, statins, diuretics, and others as per physician.

Transmyocardial revascularization with CO_2 laser in patients with refractory angina pectoris. Clinical results from the Norwegian Randomized Trial.

(continued)

Results	Primary end points were time to 1 mm ST segment depression on exercise testing and MVO_2 (maximal oxygen consumption). Secondary end points included time to chest pain, total exercise time and accumulated work. 63% of TMR patients experienced an improvement in one or more functional classes at 3 months; 71% at 12 months. While mean functional class in TMR patients was 3.3 at baseline, it decreased to 2.3 at 3 months and 2.0 at 1 year. In contrast, only 14% of patients on maximal medical therapy improved by 1 or more classes at 3 months and only 22% improved at 12 months. While baseline class in the maximal medical therapy group was 3.2, it remained 3.1 at both 3 and 12 months in contrast to TMR (p<0.01). TMR increased time to angina during exercise from baseline by 78 seconds after 3 months (p=NS) and 66 seconds (p<0.01) after 12 months, whereas maximal medical therapy failed to improve this parameter. TMR did not improve total exercise time or MVO_2. One year mortality was 12% vs 8% in the TMR group vs maximal medical therapy group, respectively (p=NS). Postoperative mortality with TMR was 4%.
Conclusions	TMR with CO_2 laser improved symptoms and time to chest pain during exercise in coronary artery disease patients with refractory angina, who were not candidates for CABG or PTCA. In this study, overall exercise capacity was not improved.

5. Hypertension

SHEP

Systolic Hypertension in the Elderly Program

Title	a. Prevention of stroke by antihypertensive drug treatment in older persons with isolated systolic hypertension. Final results of the Systolic Hypertension in the Elderly Program (SHEP). b. Prevention of heart failure by antihypertensive drug treatment in older persons with isolated systolic hypertension. c. Effect of treatment of isolated systolic hypertension on left ventricular mass. d. Effect of diuretic based antihypertensive treatment on cardiovascular disease risk in older diabetic patients with isolated systolic hypertension. e. Influence of long term, low dose, diuretic based antihypertensive therapy on glucose, lipid, uric acid, and potassium levels in older men and women with isolated systolic hypertension.
Authors	a. SHEP Cooperative Research Group. b. Kostis JB, Davis BR, Cutler J, et al. c. Ofili EO, Cohen JD, St.Vrain J, et al. d. Curb JD, Pressel SL, Cutler JA, et al. e. Savage PL, Precsel SL, Curb JD, et al.
Reference	a. JAMA 1991;265:3255-3264. b. JAMA 1997; 278:212-216. c. JAMA 1998; 279: 778-780. d. JAMA 1996; 276:1886-1892 e. Arch Intern Med 1998;158:741-751.
Disease	Hypertension.
Purpose	a. To evaluate the efficacy of antihypertensive drug therapy to reduce the risk of stroke in patients with isolated systolic hypertension. b. To determine the effect of diuretic based stepped care antihypertensive therapy on the development of heart failure in older patients with isolated systolic hypertension.

SHEP

Systolic Hypertension in the Elderly Program

(continued)

	c. To determine the ability of antihypertensive drugs to reduce left ventricular mass in older patients with isolated systolic hypertension. d. To determine the effect of diuretic based antihypertensive treatment on major cardiovascular disease event rates in older patients with isolated systolic hypertension with noninsulin treated diabetic patients vs nondiabetic patients. e. Retrospective analysis to determine development of diabetes in SHEP participants, including changes in serum chemistries over 3 years.
Design	a. Randomized, double blind, placebo controlled, multicenter. b. Further analysis of data from multicenter randomized, double blind placebo controlled clinical trial. c. Echocardiographic substudy of SHEP trial. d. Additional analysis from SHEP trial.
Patients	a. 4736 patients, ≥60 years old, with systolic blood pressure 160–219 and diastolic blood pressure <90 mm Hg. Patients with major cardiovascular diseases or other serious illnesses were excluded. b. 4736 patients aged 60 years and older with systolic blood pressure between 160–219 mmHg and diastolic pressure below 90 mm Hg. c. 104 patients at St. Louis SHEP site who had echocardiograms; 94 had 3 year follow-up. d. 583 noninsulin dependent diabetic patients and 4149 nondiabetic patients.
Follow-up	a. Average 4.5 years. b. Average 4.5 years. c. Minimum follow-up was 3 years. d. 5 years.

Treatment regimen	a. The goal of blood pressure reduction was <160 mm Hg systolic blood pressure for those with initial pressure >180 mm Hg, and by at least 20 mm Hg for those with initial pressure 160–179 mm Hg. Patients were randomized to placebo or chlorthalidone 12.5 mg/d. Dose was doubled if the pressure goal was not reached and then atenolol 25 mg/d or placebo was added. If contraindications existed, reserpine 0.05 mg/d was given. b. As described in SHEP. c. As described in SHEP. d. As per SHEP protocol.
Additional therapy	a. Potassium supplements to all patients with serum K <3.5 mmol/l.
Results	a. After 5 years 44% of the placebo group received active antihypertensive therapy. During the trial, the goal blood pressure was reached by 65%–72% of the active drug therapy vs 32%–40% of the placebo group. Mean systolic blood pressure was lower in the active treatment than the placebo group throughout the protocol. By life table analysis, 5 year cumulative stroke rates were 5.2% vs 8.2% for the active therapy and placebo groups, respectively (RR 0.64, 95% CI 0.50–0.82, p=0.0003). After a mean of 4.5 years follow-up the mortality was 9.0% vs 10.2% (RR 0.87 [0.73–1.05]), myocardial infarction occurred in 2.1% vs 3.1% (RR 0.67 [0.47–0.96]), left ventricular failure in 2.0% vs 4.3% (RR 0.46 [0.33–0.65]), and total major cardiovascular events in 12.2% vs 17.5% (RR 0.68 [0.58–0.79]). b. Fatal or nonfatal heart failure occurred in 55 of 2365 patients randomized to therapy and 105 of 2371 patients that received placebo [relative risk (RR) .51; 95% CI 0.37–0.71, p<0.001]. Heart failure was more likely to develop in older patients, in men, those with higher systolic blood pressures and history or ECG evidence of myocardial infarction. Among patients with history or ECG evidence of myocardial infarction treatment reduced the relative risk of developing heart failure substantially (RR = 0.19; 95% CI 0.06–0.13; p=0.002). c. LV mass index was 93 g/m^2 in active therapy group and 100g/m^2 in placebo group (p<0.001). LV mass index

declined by 13% with therapy and increased by 6% in the placebo group over 3 years (p=0.01). 8% of subjects were receiving chlorthalidone alone by the end of year 3.
d. The 5 year rate of all outcomes and major cardiovascular disease events, [nonfatal or fatal myocardial infarction, sudden or rapid cardiac death, CABG , PTCA, stroke, transient ischemic attack, aortic aneurysm, endarterectomy] was 34% lower with active therapy vs placebo for both diabetics (95% C.I. 6%-54%) and nondiabetics (95% C.I. 21%-45%). Absolute reduction in risk with active therapy was twice as great in diabetics (101/1000) vs nondiabetics (51/1000) which reflects the higher risk of developing vascular events in diabetic patients.
e. New cases of diabetes occurred in 8.6% of patients receiving active treatment and 7.5% of patients on placebo (p=NS). Active treatment was associated with small increases in fasting blood glucose levels (+3.6 mg/dL, p<0.01) and total cholesterol (+3.5 mg/dL, p<0.01); small decreases in HDL cholesterol (-0.77 mg/dL); and small increases in creatinine (+0.03 mg/dL, p<0.001). Active therapy was associated with larger increases in fasting triglyceride levels (+17 mg/dL; p<0.001) and a decrease in potassium (-0.3 mmol/L, p<0.001). Active therapy was associated with an increase in uric acid, +.06 mg/dL, p<.001).

Conclusions

a. Stepped care drug therapy for isolated systolic hypertension in patients ≥60 years old reduced the incidence of major cardiovascular events and stroke.
b. In older patients with isolated systolic hypertension, stepped care therapy based on low dose chlorthalidone reduced the incidence of heart failure. Treatment was especially dramatic among patients with prior myocardial infarctions.
c. Treatment of isolated systolic hypertension in older patients with chlorthalidone-based regimen reduces LV mass.
d. Treating older diabetic patients with isolated systolic hypertension with diuretic based therapy (chlorthalidone) is effective in prevention of major cardiovascular and cerebrovascular events.
e. Low dose chlorthalidone lowered isolated systolic hypertension and had relatively mild effects on other cardiovascular risk factors.

TOMHS

Treatment of Mild Hypertension Study

Title	a. Characteristics of participants in the treatment of mild hypertension study (TOMHS). b. The treatment of mild hypertension study. A randomized, placebo controlled trial of a nutritional hygienic regimen along with various drug monotherapies. c. Treatment of mild hypertension study. Final results. d. Comparison of 5 antihypertensive monotherapies and placebo for change in left ventricular mass in patients receiving nutritional hygienic therapy in the treatment of mild hypertension study (TOMHS). e. Long-term effects on plasma lipids of diet and drugs to treat hypertension. f. Comparison of 5 antihypertensive monotherapies and placebo for change in left ventricular mass in patients receiving nutritional hygienic therapy in the treatment of mild hypertension study (TOMHS).
Authors	a. Masciolo SR, Grimm RH, Neaton JD, et al. b. TOMHS Research Group. c. Neaton JD, Grimm RH Jr, Prineas RJ, et al. d. Liebson PR, Grandits GA, Dianzumba S, et al. e. Grimm RH, Flack JM, Grandits GA, et al. f. Liebson, PR, Grandits GA, Dianzumba S, et al.
Reference	a. Am J Cardiol 1990;66:32C–35C. b. Arch Intern Med 1991;151:1413–1423. c. JAMA 1993;270:713–724. d. Circulation 1995;91:698–706. e. JAMA 1996;275:1549–1556. f. Circulation 1995; 91:698–706.
Disease	Hypertension.
Purpose	To assess the relative efficacy and safety of a combination of nonpharmacological therapy alone with those of nonpharmacological therapy and 5 pharmacological monotherapy regimens.
Design	Randomized, double blind, multicenter.

TOMHS

Treatment of Mild Hypertension Study (continued)

Patients	902 patients, age 45–69 years, with mild hypertension (diastolic blood pressure 90–99 mm Hg, or if they were previously treated with antihypertensive drugs, 85–99 mm Hg). Patients with cardiovascular disease or life threatening illness were excluded.
Follow-up	>4 years (mean 4.4 years).
Treatment regimen	Randomization to: 1) Acebutalol 400 mg/d; 2) amlodipine 5 mg/d; 3) chlorthalidone 15 mg/d; 4) Doxazosin 1 mg/d for 1 month and then 2 mg/d; 5) enalapril 5 mg/d; 6) placebo. For a participant with diastolic blood pressure ≥95 mm Hg on 3 visits, or ≥105 mm Hg at a single visit, medication dose was doubled. If blood pressure remained high, a second drug was added. For all groups, except the diuretic group, chlorothalidone 15 mg/d was added. In the chlorthalidone group, enalapril 2.5 mg was given.
Additional therapy	Behavior change, 10% weight loss, lowering sodium intake to ≤70 mmol/d, lowering alcohol intake, and increasing activity.

TOMHS

Treatment of Mild Hypertension Study (continued)

Results

a–e. After 12 months, weight loss averaged 4.5 kg, urinary sodium excretion declined by 23%, and physical activity was almost doubled. After 12 months blood pressure was decreased by 20.1±1.4/13.7±0.7, 17.5±1.1/12.9±0.7, 21.8±1.3/13.1±0.7, 16.1±1.2/ 12.0±0.7, 17.6±1.2/12.2± 0.7, and 10.6±1.0/8.1±0.5 mm Hg in groups 1–6, respectively (p<0.01 for each drug compared to placebo). Overall the compliance and tolerance were good for all groups and side effects were acceptable. After 4 years, 59% of the placebo and 72% of the active drug groups continued their initial drug as monotherapy. Major clinical events occurred in 7.3% of the placebo vs 5.1% of the active drug groups (p=0.21), and major cardiovascular event in 5.1% vs 3.9%, respectively (p=0.42). 844 patients underwent serial echocardiographic assessment of left ventricular mass. Average decrease in LV mass was 24, 25, 34, 24, 23, and 27 grams for groups 1–6 (p=0.53 for the difference among groups). The only significant difference vs placebo for reduction in LV mass was with chlorthalidone (p=0.03). In all treatment groups, there was a favorable change in the serum lipid profile. After 4 years total cholesterol decreased by 11.7±2.0 mg/dL in the acebutolol; 3.9±2.9 mg/dL in the amlodipine; 5.9±2.5 mg/dL in the chlorthalidone; 16.1±2.7 mg/dL in the doxazosin; 11.2±2.4 mg/dL in the enalapril; and 6.0±1.9 mg/dL in the placebo group (p=0.002 for the difference among groups). LDL cholesterol decreased by 11.5±2.4 mg/dL in the acebutolol; 2.9±2.7 mg/dL in the amlodipine; 4.9±2.4 mg/dL in the chlorthalidone; 13.0±2.5 mg/dL in the doxazosin; 9.5±2.4 mg/dL in the enalapril; and 5.1±1.5 mg/dL in the placebo group (p=0.002 for the difference among groups). HDL cholesterol decreased by 0.6±0.7 mg/dL in the acebutolol; increased by 0.2±0.7 mg/dL in the amlodipine; increased by 0.6±0.8 mg/dL in the chlorthalidone; increased by 0.9±0.7 mg/dL in the doxazosin; increased by 0.8±0.7 mg/dL in the enalapril; and decreased by 0.3±0.5 mg/dL in the placebo group (p=0.57 for the difference among groups). Triglycerides increased by 1.3±5.0 mg/dL in the acebutolol; decreased by 5.4±5.0 mg/dL in the amlodipine; decreased by 7.3±5.6 mg/dL in the chlorthalidone; decreased by 20.0±5.2 mg/dL in the doxazosin; decreased by 12.6±7.1 mg/dL in the enalapril; and decreased by 2.8±4.6 mg/dL in the placebo group (p=0.03 for the difference among groups). Decreases in plasma total cholesterol, LDL cholesterol, and triglycerides were greater with doxazosin

f. Echocardiographic assessment revealed that all groups showed significant decreases (10–15%) in left ventricular mass from baseline, that appeared by 3 months continuing for 48 months. The greatest reduction was in the chlorthalidone group. Reduction even occurred in the placebo group. Change in weight, urinary sodium restriction, and systolic blood pressure moderately correlated with changes in left ventricular mass.

Conclusions

Adding 1 of the 5 different classes of drugs resulted in significant additional decrease of blood pressure with minimal side effects. Differences among the 5 drug groups did not consistently favor one over the others concerning clinical outcomes. However, these drugs affect serum lipid profile and left ventricular mass differently, with doxazosin having the greater reduction in total cholesterol, LDL cholesterol and triglycerides, and chlorthalidone having the greater effect on reducing left ventricular hypertrophy.

STOP-Hypertension

Swedish Trial in Old Patients With Hypertension

Title	a. Morbidity and mortality in the Swedish Trial in Old Patients with Hypertension (STOP-Hypertension). b. Swedish trial in old patients with hypertension (STOP-Hypertension). Analyses performed up to 1992.
Authors	Dahlöf B, Lindholm LH, Hansson L, et al.
Reference	a. Lancet 1991;338:1281-1285. b. Clin Exper Hypertension 1993;15:925-939.
Disease	Hypertension.
Purpose	To evaluate the efficacy of pharmacological treatment of hypertension in patients 70-84 years old.
Design	Randomized, double blind, placebo controlled, multicenter.
Patients	1627 patients, age 70-84 years, with blood pressure ≥180/90 mm Hg, or diastolic blood pressure >105 mm Hg. Patients with blood pressure above 230/120 mm Hg, orthostatic hypotension, myocardial infarction, or stroke within the previous 12 months were excluded.
Follow-up	1-4 years (average of 25 months).
Treatment regimen	Patients were randomized to either active therapy or placebo. The centers were free to chose 1 of the 4 following agents: atenolol 50 mg/d, hydrochlorothiazide 25 mg/d + amiloride 2.5 mg/d, metoprolol 100 mg/d, or pindolol 5 mg/d. If blood pressure was >160/95 mm Hg after 2 months of therapy, diuretic therapy was added to the ß blocker, and vice versa. If blood pressure exceeded 230/120 mm Hg on 2 subsequent visits, open antihypertensive therapy was given.

STOP-Hypertension

Swedish Trial in Old Patients With Hypertension

(continued)

Results	a. Compared with placebo, active therapy reduced the number of myocardial infarctions (16.5 vs 14.4 per 1000 patient-years, RR 0.87, 95% CI 0.49–1.56), stroke (31.3 vs 16.8 per 1000 patient years, RR 0.53, 95% CI 0.33–0.86, p=0.0081), total mortality (35.4 vs 20.2 per 1000 patient years, RR 0.57, 95% CI 0.37–0.87, p=0.0079), and the occurrence of the primary endpoints (stroke, myocardial infarction or cardiovascular death) (55.5 vs 33.5 per 1000 patient years, RR 0.60, 95% CI 0.43–0.85, p=0.0031). b. A majority of the patients needed combined treatment to reach the goal blood pressure (160/95 mm Hg). The impact on mortality and morbidity was greater than previously seen in middle aged patients. Women benefited from treatment at least as much as men.
Conclusions	Antihypertensive therapy in hypertensive patients aged 70–84 reduced cardiovascular morbidity and mortality.

STOP Hypertension 2 (update)

Title	Randomised trial of old and new antihypertensive drugs in elderly patients: Cardiovascular mortality and morbidity The Swedish Trial in Old Patients with Hypertension-2 study.
Authors	Hansson L, Lindholm LH, Ekbom T, et al.
Reference	Lancet 1999;354:1751-1756.
Disease	Hypertension.
Purpose	To compare the effects of older antihypertensive drugs (ß-blockers and diuretics) to the newer agents (calcium channel blockers [isradipine and felodipine] and ACE inhibitors [enalapril and lisinopril]) on cardiovascular mortality in elderly patients with hypertension.
Design	Prospective, randomized, open label, blinded end point evaluation, multicenter.
Patients	6614 patients, aged 70-84 years, with hypertension (≥180/105 mm Hg).
Follow-up	54 months. 33,249 patient-years.
Treatment regimen	Randomization to conventional treatment (diuretics, ß-blockers), ACE inhibitors (enalapril 10 mg/d or lisinopril 10 mg/d) or calcium antagonists (felodipine 2.5 mg/d or isradipine 2.5 mg/d).
Additional therapy	If target blood pressure (<160/95 mm Hg) had not been achieved, diuretics were added to patients on ß-blockers or on ACE inhibitors, and ß-blockers to those on calcium antagonists or diuretics.

(continued)

Results	The blood pressure lowering effects were comparable among the three groups. Total mortality was 33.1 per 1000 patient-years in the conventional therapy group, 34.4 per 1000 patient-years in the ACE inhibitors group and 32.8 per 1000 patient-years in the calcium antagonist group. Cardiovascular mortality was 19.8, 20.5, and 19.2 per 1000 patient-years, respectively. Sudden death occurred in 4.8 per 1000 patient-years of the conventional therapy group, 5.3 per 1000 patient-years of the ACE inhibitors group, and 4.7 per 1000 patient-years of the calcium antagonists group. Myocardial infarction occurred in 14.1, 12.8, and 16.7 per 1000 patient-years, respectively, whereas stroke occurred in 22.2, 20.2, and 19.5 per 1000 patient-years, respectively. Congestive heart failure occurred in 16.4, 13.9, and 17.5 per 1000 patient-years, respectively. The relative risk of congestive heart failure for ACE inhibitors vs calcium antagonists was 0.78 (95% CI 0.63–0.97; $p=0.025$), whereas the relative risk for acute myocardial infarction was 0.77 (95% CI 0.61–0.96; $p=0.018$). Otherwise, none of the comparisons in secondary end points of cardiovascular mortality and morbidity among the three treatment groups were statistically significant.
Conclusions	ACE inhibitors and calcium antagonists have similar efficacy in prevention of cardiovascular mortality to the old antihypertensive agents (diuretics and ß-blockers) in elderly patients with hypertension. ACE inhibitors were associated with less myocardial infarction and congestive heart failure than calcium antagonists, but not compared with conventional therapy.

TAIM

Trial of Antihypertensive Interventions and Management

Title	a. Effect of drug and diet treatment of mild hypertension on diastolic blood pressure. b. The Trial of Antihypertensive Interventions and Management (TAIM) study. Adequate weight loss, alone and combined with drug therapy in the treatment of mild hypertension. c. Effect of antihypertensives on sexual function and quality of life: The TAIM study.
Authors	a. Langford HG, Davis BR, Blaufox D, et al. b. Wassertheil-Smoller S, Blaufox MD, Oberman AS, et al. c. Wassertheil-Smoller S, Blaufox D, Oberman A, et al.
Reference	a. Hypertension 1991;17:210-217. b. Arch Intern Med 1992;152:131-136. c. Ann Intern Med 1991;114:613-620.
Disease	Hypertension.
Purpose	To evaluate the relative efficacy of various combinations of the commonly used approaches to drug and diet therapy for hypertension.
Design	Randomized, double blind (drug therapy), placebo controlled, 3X3 factorial, 3 centers.
Patients	787 patients, age 21-65 years, with diastolic blood pressure 90-100 mm Hg without medications, and body weight of 110-160% of the ideal body weight. Patients with prior stroke, myocardial infarction, asthma, insulin treated diabetes mellitus, and renal failure were excluded.
Follow-up	6 months.
Treatment regimen	9 groups of treatment combinations of 1 out of 3 drug regimens with 1 out of 3 diet interventions. The drugs were: placebo, chlorthalidone 25 mg, or atenolol 50 mg. The diet interventions were: usual, a weight reduction (goal 10% of basal body weight or 4.54 kg), or low in sodium (52-100 mmol/d) and high in potassium (62-115 mmol/d) diets. Patients who failed to

	achieve blood pressure control were given additional therapy in a double blind fashion (chlorthalidone or atenolol for the placebo and combination of atenolol and chlorthalidone to the other 2 drug groups.) If diastolic blood pressure remained ≥100 mm Hg, the doses were increased, and if it did not help open label therapy was added.
Results	a. Among the placebo drug assigned patients 20.0%, 10.0%, and 16.5% of the usual, weight loss, and low sodium diet received additional medications to control blood pressure over the 6 months of follow-up. Only 2.7% and 3.0% of the chlorthalidone and atenolol treated patients needed an additional medication. The mean weight reduction in the weight loss diet group was 4.7 kg. The low Na/high K group had an average decrease in urinary sodium of 27.4 mmol/d and increase of potassium excretion of 10.9 mmol/d. The mean reduction of diastolic blood pressure in patients on usual diet was 7.96, 10.78, and 12.43 mm Hg for placebo, chlorthalidone and atenolol groups. For patients in the weight loss diet it was 8.78, 15.06 and 14.81 mm Hg, respectively, and for the low Na/high K diet it was 7.91, 12.18 and 12.76 mm Hg, respectively. Atenolol as a single therapy achieved the greatest reduction of blood pressure ($p=0.001$ vs low Na/high K diet alone, and $p=0.006$ vs weight loss alone. Adding weight loss diet to chlorthalidone enhanced the blood pressure lowering response significantly ($p=0.002$). b. Among the patients assigned to placebo drug and weight loss diet, diastolic blood pressure reduction after 6 months was greater among patients who lost ≥4.5 kg than among those who achieved only <2.25 kg reduction (11.6 vs 7.0 mm Hg; $p<0.046$). The effect of ≥4.5 kg body weight reduction was comparable to that of chlorthalidone or atenolol. The weight loss diet benefited quality of life most, reducing total physical complaints ($p<0.001$) and increasing satisfaction with health ($p<0.001$). Low dose chlorthalidone and atenolol produced few side effects, except in men. Sexual problems developed in 29%, 13% and 3% of men receiving usual diet and chlorthalidone, atenolol and placebo, respectively ($p=0.006$ for the difference among groups). The low Na/high K diet was associated with increased fatigue.
Conclusions	Drug therapy was more efficient than diet intervention in reducing diastolic blood pressure. Weight loss of ≥4.5 kg is beneficial, especially in combination with diuretics.

TOHP-1

Trial of Hypertension Prevention (Phase I)

Title	a. The effects of nonpharmacologic interventions on blood pressure of persons with high normal levels. Results of the trials of hypertension prevention, phase I. b. The effect of potassium supplementation in persons with a high normal blood pressure. Results from phase I of the Trials of Hypertension Prevention (TOHP). c. Lack of blood pressure effect with calcium and magnesium supplementation in adults with high normal blood pressure. Results from phase I of the Trials of Hypertension Prevention (TOHP).
Authors	a. The Trials of Hypertension Prevention Collaborative Research Group. b. Whelton PK, Buring J, Borhani NO, et al. c. Yamamoto ME, Applegate WB, Klag MJ, et al.
Reference	a. JAMA 1992;267:1213–1220. b. Ann Epidemiol 1995;5:85–95. c. Ann Epidemiol 1995;5:96–107.
Disease	Hypertension.
Purpose	To evaluate the short term feasibility and efficacy of 7 nonpharmacologic interventions to reduce diastolic blood pressure.
Design	3 randomized, parallel group trials, multicenter.
Patients	2182 patients, 30–54 years old, with diastolic blood pressure of 80–89 mm Hg, who were not taking medications in the prior 2 months.
Follow-up	18 months.

TOHP-1

Trial of Hypertension Prevention (Phase I)

(continued)

Treatment regimen	3 lifestyle change groups (weight reduction, sodium intake reduction, and stress management) were each compared with unmasked nonintervention control over 18 months. 4 nutritional supplement groups (calcium, magnesium, potassium, and fish oil) were each compared in a double blind fashion with placebo controls over 6 months.
Results	Weight reduction intervention resulted in 3.9 kg weight loss ($p<0.01$, compared to baseline), diastolic blood pressure reduction of 2.3 mm Hg ($p<0.01$), and systolic blood pressure reduction of 2.9 mm Hg ($p<0.01$). Sodium restriction intervention resulted in 44 mmol/24 h decrease of urinary sodium excretion ($p<0.01$), diastolic and systolic blood pressure reduction of 0.9 ($p<0.05$) and 1.7 mm Hg ($p<0.01$). Potassium supplementation resulted in 1.8 mm Hg ($p=0.04$) reduction in diastolic blood pressure after 3 months. However, the effect disappeared after 6 months (mean reduction 0.3 mm Hg). Neither stress management nor nutritional supplements reduced blood pressure significantly.
Conclusions	Weight reduction was the most effective of the strategies in reducing blood pressure in normotensive persons. Sodium restriction was also effective.

MRC

Medical Research Council Trial of Treatment of Hypertension in Older Adults

Title	Medical Research Council trial of treatment of hypertension in older adults: Principal results.
Authors	MRC Working Party.
Reference	Br Med J 1992;304:405-412.
Disease	Hypertension.
Purpose	To evaluate the efficacy of ß-blockers and diuretic therapy to reduce cardiovascular mortality and morbidity in hypertensive older adults.
Design	Randomized, single blind, placebo controlled, multicenter.
Patients	4396 patients, age 65-74 years, with systolic blood pressure 160-209 mm Hg, and diastolic blood pressure <115 mm Hg. Patients on antihypertensive medications, or with secondary hypertension, heart failure, angina pectoris, myocardial infarction or stroke within 3 months, impaired renal function, diabetes mellitus, asthma, or other serious intercurrent disease were excluded.
Follow-up	Mean follow-up 5.8 years (25,355 patients years of observation).
Treatment regimen	1. Amiloride 2.5 mg/d+ hydrochlorothiazide 25 mg/d or placebo. 2. Atenolol 50 mg/d or placebo. Drug doses were modified to reach the target blood pressure of 150-160 mm Hg.
Additional therapy	Additional therapy was started if mean blood pressure was >115 mm Hg or systolic blood pressure >210 mm Hg.

MRC

Medical Research Council Trial of Treatment of Hypertension in Older Adults (continued)

Results	Both treatment arms reduced systolic blood pressure compared with the placebo group. After 3 months, the diuretic therapy reduced blood pressure more than atenolol. However, after 2 years, systolic and diastolic blood pressures were similar in the diuretics and atenolol groups. More patients randomized to atenolol required supplementary drugs to control hypertension than the diuretic group (52% vs 38%). The atenolol group had significantly more withdrawals from the study compared to diuretics for both suspected major side effects and inadequate blood pressure control (345 vs 161 patients, respectively). In the placebo group 257 patients were withdrawn. The number of strokes was reduced with active therapy 7.3%, 9.0%, and 10.8% in the diuretics, atenolol, and placebo groups (25% reduction of risk (active therapy vs placebo), 95% CI 3-42%, p=0.04). Coronary events occurred in 7.7%, 12.8%, and 12.7%, respectively (19% reduction of risk (active therapy vs placebo), 95% CI -2% to 36%, p=0.08). Total mortality was not different among the groups (21.3%, 26.4%, and 24.7%, respectively). After adjusting for baseline characteristics the diuretic group had reduced risks of stroke (31%, 95% CI 3%-51%, p=0.04), coronary events (44%, 95% CI 21%-60%, p=0.0009), and all cardiovascular events (35%, 95% CI 17%-49%, p=0.0005), compared with placebo. The atenolol group showed no significant reduction in these end points. Reduction of stroke was mainly in nonsmokers taking diuretics.
Conclusions	Hydrochlorothiazide and amiloride are better than atenolol in reducing the incidence of stroke and coronary events in older hypertensive patients.

Metoprolol in the Treatment of Hypertension in the Elderly

Title	Safety and efficacy of metoprolol in the treatment of hypertension in the elderly.
Authors	LaPalio L, Schork A, Glasser S, et al.
Reference	J Am Geriatr Soc 1992;40:354-358.
Disease	Hypertension.
Purpose	To evaluate the short term efficacy and safety of metoprolol in the treatment of hypertension in patients 50-75 years old.
Design	Open label, surveillance, multicenter.
Patients	21,692 patients, 50-75 years old, with hypertension (systolic blood pressure ≤200 mm Hg and diastolic blood pressure 90-104 mm Hg for patients that had not been under therapy before and ≤95 mm Hg for those who were previously treated). Patients who needed ß-blockers for angina, patients with heart block or bradycardia <55 bpm, congestive heart failure, or intolerance to ß-blockers were excluded.
Follow-up	8 week clinical follow-up.
Treatment regimen	Metoprolol 100 mg/d. If diastolic blood pressure remained >90 mm Hg after 4 weeks, hydrochlorothiazide 25 mg/d was added.

Results	After 4 weeks mean systolic and diastolic blood pressure were reduced from 162/95 to 148/87 mm Hg ($p<0.001$). 58% of the patients had adequate blood pressure control with 100 mg/d metoprolol. After 8 weeks blood pressure decreased to 143/84 mm Hg. At the termination of the study 50% of the patients continued with metoprolol as monotherapy and 27% needed combined therapy. There was <5% incidence of medical problems. Excellent or good tolerability was noted for 94% of the patients.
Conclusions	Metoprolol administered either as monotherapy or in combination with diuretic was an effective and safe therapy for elderly hypertensive patients.

Veterans Affairs Cooperative Study Group on Antihypertensive Agents

Title	Single drug therapy for hypertension in men. A comparison of 6 antihypertensive agents with placebo.
Authors	Materson BJ, Reda DJ, Cushman WC, et al.
Reference	N Engl J Med 1993;328:914-921.
Disease	Hypertension.
Purpose	To compare the efficacy of different classes of antihypertensive agents as monotherapy for hypertension according to age and race.
Design	Randomized, double blind, placebo controlled, multicenter.
Patients	1292 men, age ≥21 years, and diastolic blood pressure 95-109 mm Hg on placebo.
Follow-up	For at least 1 year.
Treatment regimen	Randomization to: 1. placebo; 2. hydrochlorothiazide 12.5-50 mg/d; 3. atenolol 25-100 mg/d; 4. clonidine 0.2-0.6 mg/d; 5. captopril 25-100 mg/d; 6. prazosin 4-20 mg/d; and 7. sustained release diltiazem 120-360 mg/d. Patients who reached diastolic blood pressure <90 mm Hg on 2 visits entered a maintenance phase for ≥1 year.

Veterans Affairs Cooperative Study Group on Antihypertensive Agents

(continued)

Results	At the end of the titration phase 33%, 57%, 65%, 65%, 54%, 56%, and 75% of the patients in groups 1-7 reached diastolic blood pressure <90 mm Hg. 745 patients reached diastolic blood pressure <90 mm Hg without intolerable side effects during the titration phase and entered the maintenance phase. The percentage of patients with initial control of blood pressure in whom diastolic blood pressure remained <95 mm Hg over 1 year was similar among groups (p=0.93). However, by intention to treat analysis, 25%, 46%, 51%, 50%, 42%, 42%, and 59% of the patients in groups 1-7 had reached diastolic blood pressure <90 mm Hg during the titration phase and <95 mm Hg during the maintenance phase (p<0.001 for a difference among the groups). The most effective drug was diltiazem. Diltiazem was the most effective drug in young and old blacks, while captopril was the most effective in young whites and atenolol in old whites. The least effective drug in young and old blacks was captopril, while hydrochlorothiazide was the least effective in young whites and prazosin in old whites. Intolerance to medication during the titration phase was more common with clonidine and prazosin than the other drugs.
Conclusions	Among men, age, and race are important determinants of the response to monotherapy for hypertension.

Veterans Affairs Cooperative Study Group on Antihypertensive Agents (Substudy)

Title	Effect of single drug therapy on reduction of left atrial size in mild to moderate hypertension. Comparison of six antihypertensive agents.
Authors	Gottdiener JS, Reda DJ, Williams DW, et al, for the VA Cooperative Study Group on Antihypertensive Agents.
Reference	Circulation 1998; 98:140-148.
Disease	Hypertension.
Purpose	To determine the effects of antihypertension therapy on left atrial size.
Design	Randomized, double blind, placebo controlled.
Patients	1105 men at VA Centers; diastolic blood pressure 95-109 mm Hg.
Follow-up	2 years.
Treatment regimen	Atenolol, captopril, clonidine, diltiazem, hydrochlorothiazide, or prazosin (see description of main study for doses).

Results	Left atrial size was measured by echocardiography at baseline, 8 weeks, 1 and 2 years. Without adjusting for covariates only hydrochlorothiazide decreased left atrial size compared to baseline at -1.0, -2.0, and -4.6 mm at 8 weeks, 1 year, and 2 years respectively (p=0.052-0.002). For patients with normal left atrial size at baseline, hydrochlorothiazide had the greatest reduction in size (-3.3 mm) at 2 years after adjusting for covariates. For patients with enlarged left atrial size at baseline and adjusting for covariates, hydrochlorothiazide, atenolol, clonidine, and diltiazem reduced left atrial size at one year and at 2 years all drugs decreased left atrial size. At 2 years, the reduction in left atrial size with hydrochlorothiazide was greater than that of captopril or prazosin.
Conclusions	Hydrochlorothiazide had the overall greatest reduction of left atrial size in hypertensive patients.

BBB

Behandla Blodtryck Bättre (Treat Blood Pressure Better)

Title	The BBB study: The effect of intensified antihypertensive treatment on the level of blood pressure, side effects, morbidity, and mortality in "well treated" hypertensive patients.
Authors	Hansson L, for the BBB study group.
Reference	Blood Press 1994;3:248-254.
Disease	Hypertension.
Purpose	To investigate whether it is feasible to lower the diastolic blood pressure further through intensified therapy without an increase in side effects, and whether such intensified therapy will reduce morbidity and mortality.
Design	Randomized, open label, multicenter.
Patients	2127 patients, age 46-71 years, with essential hypertension (diastolic blood pressure 90-100 mm Hg).
Follow-up	>4 years.
Treatment regimen	Intensified therapy (use of pharmacologic and nonpharmacologic means to reduce diastolic blood pressure ≤80 mm Hg) or unchanged therapy (maintain diastolic blood pressure 90-100 mm Hg).
Additional therapy	No restriction on medications.

BBB

Behandla Blodtryck Bättre (Treat Blood Pressure Better)

(continued)

Results	With intensified therapy blood pressure fell from 155/95 to 141/83 mm Hg (a difference of 14/12 mm Hg, p<0.001/0.001). In the conventional therapy, blood pressure declined from 155/94 to 152/91 mm Hg (a difference of 3/3 mm Hg, p<0.05/0.05). A difference in diastolic blood pressure of 7–8.5 mm Hg between the groups persisted for more than 4 years. In both groups there was no difference in heart rate between baseline and at the end of the study. Fewer adverse effects were reported in the intensified than conventional therapy group. There was no significant difference between the intensified and conventional therapy groups in the rates of stroke (8 vs 11 patients), myocardial infarction (20 vs 18 patients). No data on mortality was provided.
Conclusions	Blood pressure can be further reduced in intensified therapy without increment of adverse effects. However, it was not associated with improved outcome.

ACCT

Amlodipine Cardiovascular Community Trial

Title	Sex and age related antihypertensive effects of amlodipine.
Authors	Kloner RA, Sowers JR, DiBona GF, et al.
Reference	Am J Cardiol 1996;77:713-722.
Disease	Hypertension.
Purpose	To assess whether there are age, sex, or racial differences in the response to amlodipine 5-10 mg/d in patients with mild to moderate hypertension.
Design	Open label, multicenter.
Patients	1084 patients, age 21-80 years, with mild to moderate hypertension (diastolic blood pressure 95-110 mm Hg on 2 visits). Patients with history of stroke or transient ischemic attack, myocardial infarction within 6 months, angina pectoris, ventricular ejection fraction <40%, NYHA class ≥II heart failure, arrhythmias, or other systemic diseases were excluded.
Follow-up	18 weeks.
Treatment regimen	A 2 week placebo run in phase, a 4 week titration/efficacy phase, amlodipine 5-10 mg/d was administered once daily, a 12 week maintenance phase, and an optional long term follow-up phase.
Additional therapy	All other antihypertensive medications were not permitted.

ACCT

Amlodipine Cardiovascular Community Trial

(continued)

Results

At the end of the titration/efficacy phase, mean decrease in blood pressure was 16.3±12.3/12.5±5.9 mm Hg ($p<0.0001$). 86% of the patients achieved diastolic blood pressure ≤90 mm Hg and/or a 10 mm Hg decrease in diastolic blood pressure. The blood pressure response was greater in women (91.4%) than men (83.0%, $p<0.001$), and in those ≥65 years (91.5%) than those <65 years old (84.1%, $p<0.01$). 86.0% and 85.9% of the whites and blacks responded (p=NS). Amlodipine was well tolerated. Mild to moderate edema was the most common adverse effect. 14.6% discontinued therapy during the titration phase. Discontinuation due to adverse effects related to the drug occurred in 2.4%. During the maintenance phase 5.9% discontinued medication due to adverse effects (5.1% due to adverse effects possibly related to amlodipine).

Conclusions

Amlodipine was effective and relatively safe as a once a day monotherapy for mild to moderate hypertension in a community based population. The response rate in women was greater than in men.

Enalapril/Diltiazem ER Dose Response Group

Title	Evaluation of blood pressure response to the combination of enalapril (single dose) and diltiazem ER (4 different doses) in systemic hypertension.
Authors	Applegate WB, Cohen JD, Wolfson P, et al.
Reference	Am J Cardiol 1996;78:51-55.
Disease	Hypertension.
Purpose	To assess the efficacy, safety, and dose response of a combination of enalapril with a new once daily formulation of diltiazem.
Design	Randomized, double blind, placebo controlled, multicenter.
Patients	336 patients, 21-75 years of age, with essential hypertension (diastolic blood pressure 95-115 mm Hg). Patients with myocardial infarction within 2 years, secondary hypertension, previous cerebrovascular event, congestive heart failure, serious cardiac arrhythmias, or angina pectoris were excluded.
Follow-up	6 weeks.
Treatment regimen	After 7 day washout period, patients underwent 4 week single blind placebo baseline phase. Then, patients entered the 6 week double blind treatment phase: randomization to 1 of 6 groups. 1. Placebo; 2. Enalapril 5 mg/d (E5); 3. Enalapril 5 mg/d and diltiazem ER 60 mg/d (E5/D60); 4. Enalapril 5 mg/d and diltiazem ER 120 mg/d (E5/D120); 5. Enalapril 5 mg/d and diltiazem ER 180 mg/d (E5/D180); 6. Enalapril 5 mg/d and diltiazem ER 240 mg/d (E5/D240).
Additional therapy	ß-blockers, digitalis, any medication that could lower blood pressure, psychotropic agents, and cimetidine were prohibited.

Enalapril/Diltiazem ER Dose Response Group (continued)

Results

By the end of the 6 week treatment period, diastolic blood pressure was reduced by 3.2 mm Hg in the placebo; 5.6 mm Hg in the E5; 6.8 mm Hg in the E5/D60; 8.3 mm Hg in the E5/D120; 10.1 mm Hg in the E5/D180; and 10.3 mm Hg in the E5/D240 group ($p<0.05$ for each group vs placebo). There was a significant linear dose response relation ($p<0.001$). Diastolic blood pressure <90 mm Hg was found in 25.5% of the E5/D60, 43.1% of the E5/D120, 40.0% of the E5/D180, and 49.1% of the E5/D240 groups. Only the enalapril alone (8.2 mm Hg) and the 3 higher diltiazem doses (7.9, 12.8, and 13.8 mm Hg in the E5/D120, E5/ D180, and E5/D240 groups) resulted in a significant reduction of systolic blood pressure ($p<0.05$), whereas systolic blood pressure was reduced by only 2.0 and 6.5 mm Hg in the placebo and E5/D60 groups, respectively. Drug related adverse effects were noted in 8.6% of the placebo group, 14.3% of the E5 group, and in 8.9% to 19.0% of the 4 combination groups.

Conclusions

A combination of low dose of enalapril and diltiazem ER was effective in lowering blood pressure in mild to moderately hypertensive patients. The combination of E5/D180 appeared to be the optimal dosage for reduction of blood pressure with acceptable rate of adverse events.

Enalapril Felodipine ER Factorial Study

Title	Combined enalapril and felodipine extended release (ER) for systemic hypertension.
Authors	Gradman AH, Cutler NR, Davis PJ, et al.
Reference	Am J Cardiol 1997;79:431-435.
Disease	Hypertension.
Purpose	To investigate the efficacy and safety of combination treatment with enalapril, an ACE inhibitor, and felodipine extended release, a vascular selective calcium antagonist, in patients with essential hypertension.
Design	Randomized, double blind, placebo controlled, multicenter.
Patients	707 patients (65% men), mean age 53.5 years, with essential hypertension and sitting diastolic blood pressure 95-115 mm Hg. Patients with creatinine clearance <60 mL/min, hepatic dysfunction, recent myocardial infarction, or congestive heart failure were not included.
Follow-up	8 weeks.
Treatment regimen	Randomization to 12 groups in a 3X4 factorial design: placebo, enalapril 5 or 20 mg/d, felodipine ER (2.5, 5, or 10 mg/d), and their combination.
Results	Data were available for 705 patients for efficacy analysis. After 8 weeks of therapy, trough sitting diastolic blood pressure decreased by 4.4 mm Hg in the placebo group, 7.3 mm Hg in the felodipine 5 mg/d, 11.7 mm Hg in the felodipine 10 mg/d, 6.0 mm Hg in the enalapril 5 mg/d, 8.9 mm Hg in the enalapril 5 mg/d+ felodipine 2.5 mg/d, 10.8 mm Hg in the enalapril 5 mg/d+ felodipine 5 mg/d, 13.3

mm Hg in the enalapril 5 mg/d+ felodipine 10 mg/d, 8.1 mm Hg in the enalapril 20 mg/d, 11.0 mm Hg in the enalapril 20 mg/d+ felodipine 2.5 mg/d, 12.9 mm Hg in the enalapril 20 mg/d+ felodipine 5 mg/d, and 15.4 mm Hg in the enalapril 20 mg/d+ felodipine 10 mg/d. Systolic blood pressure had the same trend. In both medications, dose increment resulted in greater reduction in trough sitting systolic blood pressure and the combination of the drugs had a synergistic effect. Trough systolic blood pressure decreased by 4.0 mm Hg in the placebo group, 15.0 mm Hg in the felodipine 10 mg/d, 10.0 mm Hg in the enalapril 20 mg/d, and 21.0 mm Hg in the combination of enalapril 20 mg/d+ felodipine 10 mg/d. The estimated trough to peak ratios for sitting diastolic blood pressure ranged from 0.63 to 0.79 in the different combination groups and were consistent with effective blood pressure reduction with a once a day dose. Heart rate did not significantly change with enalapril, felodipine, or their combinations. Excellent or good blood pressure reduction was achieved in 24.0% of the placebo group, 39.8%, 54.0%, and 66.3% of the felodipine 2.5, 5, and 10 mg/d, respectively; in 36.5%, 52.1%, 66.5%, and 79.8% in the enalapril 5 mg/d combined with felodipine 0, 2.5, 5, and 10 mg/d; and 44.4%, 60.0%, 74.4%, and 86.7% of the enalapril 20 mg/d combined with felodipine 0, 2.5, 5, and 10 mg/d. Thus the combination of enalapril 20 mg/d with felodipine 10 mg/d achieved excellent or good response in the majority of the patients. The average sitting diastolic blood pressure reduction was 9.3 mm Hg for patients <50 years (n=249), 9.6 mm Hg for patients 50–64 years old (n=337), and 11.7 mm Hg for patients older than 65 (n=119). No serious drug related adverse effects were reported. Patients receiving combination therapy had less peripheral edema (4.1%) than patients receiving felodipine alone (10.8%). 641 (91%) completed the 8 week study period. Only 3% dropped out because of a clinical adverse event.

Conclusions

The combination therapy of felodipine ER and enalapril was highly effective in diastolic and systolic blood pressure reduction and was well tolerated and safe.

Low Dose Reserpine-Thiazide Combination vs Nitrendipine Monotherapy

Title	Different concepts in first line treatment of essential hypertension. Comparison of a low dose reserpine-thiazide combination with nitrendipine monotherapy.
Authors	Krönig B, Pittrow DB, Kirch W, et al.
Reference	Hypertension 1997;29:651-658.
Disease	Hypertension.
Purpose	To compare the efficacy and tolerability of reserpine, clopamid, their combination, and nitrendipine.
Design	Randomized, double blind, parallel, multicenter.
Patients	273 patients, ≥18 years old, with essential hypertension (diastolic blood pressure 100-114 mm Hg). Patients with drug or alcohol abuse, history of allergy, contraindications to one of the study medications, mental impairment, secondary hypertension, cerebrovascular event within 6 weeks, unstable angina or myocardial infarction within 3 months, severe heart failure or valvular heart disease, colitis, severe gastroenteritis, hepatic or renal impairment, depression, electrolyte disorders, and hyperlipidemia were excluded.
Follow-up	12 weeks.
Treatment regimen	4 week wash out period followed by a 2 week single blind placebo run in phase and then, randomization to 1 of 4 groups: 1. Reserpine 0.1 to 0.2 mg/d; 2. Clopamid 5 to 10 mg/d; 3. Reserpine 0.1 mg/d + clopamid 5 mg/d; and 4. Nitrendipine 20 to 40 mg/d. If diastolic blood pressure remained ≥90 mm Hg after 6 weeks, the medication dose was doubled.

Additional therapy	The use of digitalis and nitroglycerin was permitted. Nonsteroidal antiinflammatory agents, steroids, psychotropic, or antidepressant drugs were prohibited.
Results	Compliance was not less than 95.4% in all study groups at any visit. After 6 weeks of therapy with 1 capsule daily, mean reductions in sitting systolic/diastolic blood pressure from baseline was 14.0/11.7 mm Hg in the reserpine, 13.6/11.9 mm Hg in the clopamid, 11.6/12.3 mm Hg in the nitrendipine, and 23.0/17.1 mm Hg in the reserpine-clopamid combination group ($p<0.01$). 39.7% of the reserpine, 36.2% of the clopamid, 33.3% of the nitrendipine, and 55.2% of the combination therapy group achieved diastolic blood pressure <90 mm Hg. Doubling of the respective medication dosage in the patients in whom diastolic blood pressure remained ≥90 mm Hg after the 6th week resulted in normalization of diastolic blood pressure in 35.3% of the reserpine, 39.1% of the clopamid, 44.9% of the nitrendipine, and 65.7% of the combination therapy group ($p<0.0001$). Linear regression modeling indicated that the combination of reserpine and clopamid acted more than additively. 28% of the reserpine, 29% of the clopamid, 48% of the nitrendipine, and 27% of the combination therapy group had one or more adverse effects ($p<0.05$). Serious adverse effects were found in 0, 1%, 1%, and 0, respectively. Withdrawal from the study because of adverse effects occurred in 3%, 7%, 13%, and 3%, respectively ($p=0.06$). The percentage of patients whose diastolic blood pressure was normalized and remained free of any adverse event was 40% in the combination therapy group, 19% in the reserpine group, 20% in the clopamid group, and 12% in the nitrendipine group ($p<0.0001$).
Conclusions	A low dose combination therapy with reserpine and clopamid was more effective than either drug alone or nitrendipine alone in lowering blood pressure. The combination therapy was well tolerated and safe. Reserpine, clopamid, and nitrendipine as monotherapy were associated with relatively low success rates.

Title	Fosinopril vs enalapril in the treatment of hypertension: a double blind study in 195 patients.
Authors	Hansson L, Forslund T, Höglund C, et al.
Reference	J Cardiovasc Pharmacol 1996;28:1-5.
Disease	Hypertension.
Purpose	To compare the efficacy of 2 ACE inhibitors, fosinopril, and enalapril, in reducing blood pressure in patients with essential hypertension.
Design	Randomized, double blind, multicenter.
Patients	195 patients, 18-80 years old, with mild to moderate essential hypertension (supine diastolic blood pressure 95-110 mm Hg). Patients with collagen vascular disease, significant cardiac, renal, hepatic, hematologic, or cerebrovascular disease were excluded.
Follow-up	24 weeks.
Treatment regimen	After 4 weeks of placebo period, patients were randomized to fosinopril 20 to 40 mg/d or enalapril 10 to 20 mg/d. If supine diastolic blood pressure remained >90 mm Hg, hydrochlorothiazide 12.5 mg was added.

Results	After 8 weeks of therapy diastolic blood pressure had decreased by 8.3 mm Hg ($p<0.01$) in the fosinopril group and by 7.3 mm Hg ($p<0.01$) in the enalapril group, whereas systolic blood pressures were reduced by 10.6 mm Hg in both groups. After 8 weeks, the medication dose was doubled in 42% of the fosinopril group and 49% of the enalapril group. At week 16, hydrochlorothiazide was added to 27% of the fosinopril vs 30% of the enalapril-treated patients. By the end of the 24th week, there was no difference in reduction of either diastolic (10.7 vs 10.5 mm Hg) or systolic blood pressure (14.7 vs 14.5 mm Hg) between the fosinopril and enalapril groups. 8 patients in the fosinopril group vs 14 in the enalapril group were withdrawn from the study due to adverse effects. Adverse effects were reported in 58% and 67%, respectively. Serum ACE activity was significantly lower during fosinopril therapy than during enalapril therapy.
Conclusions	Fosinopril was equally effective as enalapril in reducing blood pressure in mild to moderate essential hypertension. Fosinopril was associated with better inhibition of the serum ACE activity.

Title	Alpha-blockade and thiazide treatment of hypertension. A double blind randomized trial comparing doxazosin and hydrochlorothiazide.
Authors	Grimm RH Jr, Flack JM, Schoenberger JA, et al.
Reference	Am J Hypertens 1996;9:445–454.
Disease	Hypertension.
Purpose	To compare the effect of hydrochlorothiazide and the α_1 blocker doxazosin in patients with hypertension.
Design	Randomized, double blind, parallel.
Patients	107 patients with hypertension.
Follow-up	1 year.
Treatment regimen	Hydrochlorothiazide (25 to 50 mg/d) or doxazosin (2 to 16 mg/d).

Results	Both drugs were well tolerated. Only 4% of the doxazosin and 7% of the hydrochlorothiazide treated patients were withdrawn from the study. Both drugs were equally effective in controlling hypertension. After 1 year of treatment systolic/diastolic blood pressure was reduced, compared to baseline, by 19/16 mm Hg in the doxazosin and by 22/15 in the hydrochlorothiazide groups. Sitting heart rate was not affected by the drugs. There was no evidence of tolerance development to either drug. Average final doses were 7.8 mg for doxazosin and 36 mg for hydrochlorothiazide. Changes in quality of life scores were comparable between the groups.
Conclusions	Over 1 year of therapy, both hydrochlorothiazide and doxazosin were effective in treating hypertension.

Losartan vs Placebo and Enalapril

Title	An in-patient trial of the safety and efficacy of losartan compared with placebo and enalapril in patients with essential hypertension.
Authors	Byyny RL, Merrill DD, Bradstreet TE, et al.
Reference	Cardiovasc Drugs Ther 1996;10:313–319.
Disease	Hypertension.
Purpose	To compare the effects of losartan, a specific and selective angiotensin II (subtype 1) receptor antagonist, and enalapril, an ACE inhibitor, in patients with mild to moderate essential hypertension.
Design	Randomized, double blind, placebo controlled multicenter.
Patients	100 in-patients, 21–72 years old (mean age 54 years), within 30% of their ideal body weight, with mild to moderate hypertension (supine diastolic blood pressure 95–120 mm Hg). Black patients were not included. Patients with concomitant active medical problems that might have affected the antihypertensive therapy were excluded.
Follow-up	6 days.
Treatment regimen	After a 2 week outpatient single blind placebo phase, patients were hospitalized for 2 days to determine patient eligibility for randomization, then a 5 day in-patient double blind treatment phase, and a 1 day off drug phase. Patients were randomized to placebo, losartan 50, 100, or 150 mg/d or enalapril 10 mg/d.
Additional therapy	ß-blockers, digitalis, diuretics, ACE inhibitors, nitrates, and calcium channel blockers were prohibited.

Results	Diastolic and systolic blood pressure decreased in all 5 treatment groups, as compared with the placebo group ($p \le 0.05$). The magnitude of the blood pressure response to 50 mg/d losartan was comparable at 24 h to that achieved with enalapril 10 mg/d. There was an apparent plateauing of response with losartan, indicating no further decrease in mean diastolic blood pressure with doses >50 mg/d on the fifth day of therapy. The area under the 24 h blood pressure curve was comparable among the treatment groups on day 5. No rebound hypertension was observed after discontinuation of the study medications on day 6. Any adverse effects were noted in 48% of the placebo, 60% of the losartan 50 mg/d, 56% of the losartan 100 mg/d, 55% of the losartan 150 mg/d, and in 63% of the enalapril 10 mg/d group. Drug-related adverse effects were noted in 17%, 30%, 28%, 30%, and 42%, respectively. There were no serious clinical adverse effects.
Conclusions	Losartan was effective and safe in treating patients with mild to moderate essential hypertension.

ABCD Trial

The Appropriate Blood Pressure Control in Diabetes (ABCD)

Title	The effect of nisoldipine as compared with enalapril on cardiovascular outcomes in patients with noninsulin dependent diabetes and hypertension.
Author	Estacio RO, Jeffers BW, Hiatt WR, et al.
Reference	N Engl J Med 1998; 338:645-652.
Disease	Hypertension and noninsulin dependent diabetes.
Purpose	To compare the effects of moderate blood pressure control (target diastolic pressure of 80-89 mm Hg) to intensive control (75 mm Hg) on complications of diabetes.
Design	Prospective, randomized, double blind.
Patients	Patients 40-74 years with noninsulin dependent diabetes and diastolic pressures greater than 80 mm Hg. This study focuses on 470 patients who had hypertension (diastolic blood pressure (90 mm Hg) and diabetes.
Follow-up	5 years.
Treatment regimen	Nisoldipine (235 patients) 10-60 mg per day vs enalapril (235 patients) 5-40 mg per day. Could add metoprolol and hydrochlorothiazide.

ABCD Trial

The Appropriate Blood Pressure Control in Diabetes (ABCD)

(continued)

Results	There was similar control of blood pressure in both groups. There was no difference in blood glucose levels, glycosylated hemoglobin, or cholesterol between groups. The secondary end point of the incidence of myocardial infarction also was examined. There was a lower incidence of fatal and nonfatal myocardial infarction in patients on enalapril (5) compared to nisoldipine (25); risk ratio, 9.5; 95% C.I. = 2.3–21.4. There was no statistically significant difference in cardiovascular mortality, all cause mortality, occurrence of congestive heart failure, or stroke between the nisoldipine and enalapril treated groups.
Conclusions	In the population of patients with hypertension and non-insulin dependent diabetes both enalapril and nisoldipine were capable of controlling blood pressure to the same extent. Enalapril was associated with a lower incidence of fatal and nonfatal myocardial infarctions compared to nisoldipine. The authors pointed out that since the infarct findings were based on a secondary end point, confirmation will be required.

Title	Doxazosin in hypertension: Results of a general practice study in 4809 patients.
Authors	Langdon CG, Packard RS.
Reference	Br J Clin Pract 1994;48:293-298.
Disease	Hypertension.
Purpose	To evaluate the efficacy and safety of doxazosin, a selective α_1 adrenergic blocker, in hypertensive patients.
Design	Open, non comparative, multicenter.
Patients	4809 hypertensive patients, >18 years old, with a sitting diastolic blood pressure 95-114 mm Hg. Pregnant patients, patients with childbearing potential, secondary hypertension, unstable angina, a recent (<3 months) myocardial infarction or cerebrovascular accident, postural hypotension, or a history of intolerance to α receptor blocking agents were excluded.
Follow-up	10 weeks.
Treatment regimen	Doxazosin. The initial dose was 1 mg/d. Dose was increased up to 8 mg/d at 2 weekly intervals to achieve diastolic blood pressure ≤90 mm Hg.
Additional therapy	Patients were not consulted to change diet, lifestyle or smoking habits during the study. Patients that had received antihypertensive medications before entry continued their medications.

Results	4385 patients (91%) completed the study, including 89% of those 65 years or older. The average daily dose of doxazosin was 2.9 mg. 63% of all patients required 1–2 mg/d. The goal of diastolic blood pressure ≤90 mm Hg or a decrease of ≥10 mm Hg was reached by 81% of the patients. After 10 weeks of therapy, mean systolic and diastolic blood pressure decreased by 21 mm Hg and 15 mm Hg, respectively. There was no change in heart rate. Mean systolic and diastolic blood pressure reduction was 22.6 mm Hg and 15.0 mm Hg among patients ≥65 years old, and 20.7 mm Hg and 14.4 mm Hg among patients <65 years old. Adverse events related or possibly related to doxazosin were detected in 17% of the patients, were severe in 1.5% of the patients and led to withdrawal from the study in 5.7% of the patients. The most frequent adverse events were dizziness (6%, severe 1.1%), headache (3.8%), and fatigue (2.6%). Syncope or fainting occurred in 0.3% of the patients. Total cholesterol levels decreased by 4.1%, LDL cholesterol decreased by 5.1%, triglycerides decreased by 9.1%, and HDL cholesterol increased by 1.55%.
Conclusions	Doxazosin was effective in blood pressure control, well tolerated, and associated with modest but statistically significant effect on blood lipid profile.

The effect of an endothelin receptor antagonist, bosentan, on blood pressure in patients with essential hypertension

Title	The effect of an endothelin receptor antagonist, bosentan, on blood pressure in patients with essential hypertension.
Author	Krum H, Viskoper RJ, Lacourciere Y, et al.
Reference	N Engl J Med 1998; 338; 784-790.
Disease	Hypertension.
Purpose	To determine the contribution of endothelin to blood pressure elevation by studying the effects of an endothelin receptor antagonist, bosentan.
Design	Randomized, double blind to 1 of 6 treatments as below. There was a placebo run in phase period of 4-6 weeks followed by the randomization phase.
Patients	293 patients with mild to moderate essential hypertension.
Follow-up	4 weeks after therapy.
Treatment regimen	Randomization was to 1 of 4 oral dose of bosentan, (100, 500, or 1000 mg x1/d, or 1000mg x2/d, placebo), or enalapril (20 mg once daily).

The effect of an endothelin receptor antagonist, bosentan, on blood pressure in patients with essential hypertension

(continued)

Results	Compared to placebo the 500 or 2000 mg dose caused a significant reduction in diastolic blood pressure of 5.7 mm Hg which was comparable to the reduction observed with enalapril 5.8 mm Hg. Bosentan did not alter heart rate or activate the renin-angiotensin system or increase plasma norepinephrine levels.
Conclusions	Bosentan, an endothelial receptor antagonist, significantly lowered blood pressure in patients with essential hypertension suggesting that endothelin may contribute to hypertension.

HALT

Hypertension and Lipid Trial Study

Title	Principal results of the hypertension and lipid trial (HALT): A multicenter study of doxazosin in patients with hypertension.
Authors	Levy D, Walmsley P, Levenstein M, for the Hypertension and Lipid Trial Study Group.
Reference	Am Heart J 1996;131:966-973.
Disease	Hypertension.
Purpose	To evaluate the efficacy and safety of doxazosin, a selective α_1 adrenergic blocker, in hypertensive patients.
Design	Open, noncomparative, multicenter.
Patients	851 patients (60% men), >35 years old, with essential hypertension and a mean sitting diastolic blood pressure 96–110 mm Hg. Patients with malignant or secondary form of hypertension, pregnant or lactating, hypersensitivity to α-blockers, orthostatic hypotension, drug or alcohol abuse, or other medical conditions that might interfere with completion of the study were excluded. Patients on lipid lowering therapy and those who had donated blood within 30 days of the study were not included.
Follow-up	A 2 week baseline period without antihypertensive medications, a 6 week titration period, and 8 weeks of maintenance phase.
Treatment regimen	Doxazosin once daily.

Results

650 patients completed the study. 103 (12.1%) patients discontinued therapy because of side effects and 98 (11.5% of patients, because of other reasons). Final mean doxazosin dose was 7.8 mg/d. Doxazosin significantly did decreased mean sitting and standing systolic blood pressure by 15.2 and 16.1 mm Hg, respectively, and mean sitting and standing diastolic blood pressure by 12.5 and 12.7 mm Hg, respectively (p=0.0001 compared with baseline). Mean sitting systolic and diastolic blood pressure was reduced by 13.3 and 11.4 mm Hg in men and by 18.1 and 14.2 mm Hg in women (p=0.0001). Doxazosin was more effective in patients 65 years or older than in those younger than 65. Systolic and diastolic blood pressure were reduced by 14.4 and 11.9 mm Hg in the young patients (p=0.0001 compared with baseline) vs 18.3 and 14.6 mm Hg in patients 65 years or older (p=0.0001 compared with baseline). There was no significant difference in the magnitude of blood pressure reduction when patients were stratified by race. Doxazosin had no significant effect on heart rate. Doxazosin therapy resulted in 8.3 mg/dL reduction in total cholesterol (p<0.001 compared with baseline), 6.9 mg/dL reduction in LDL cholesterol (p<0.001 compared with baseline), 8.9 mg/dL reduction in triglycerides (p<0.05 compared with baseline), and 0.4 mg/dL increase in HDL cholesterol (p=NS). The drug was well tolerated and major side effects were infrequent.

Conclusions

Doxazosin is effective therapy for patients with essential hypertension, with good efficacy in young and elderly patients, in both women and men, and in all races. The drug was well tolerated and was associated with a favorable effects on plasma lipid levels.

MIDAS

Multicenter Isradipine Diuretic Atherosclerotic Study

Title	Final outcome results of the multicenter isradipine diuretic atherosclerosis study (MIDAS). A randomized controlled trial.
Author	Borhani NO, Mercuri M, Bohani PA.
Reference	JAMA 1996; 276:785-791.
Disease	Hypertension.
Purpose	To compare rate of medial thickening of the carotid arteries in hypertensive patients on isradipine vs hydrochlorothiazide.
Design	Randomized, double blind, control, multicenter.
Patients	883 patients, 40 years or older with diastolic pressure from 90-115 mm Hg and presence of intimalmedial thickness assessed by B mode ultrasound of between 1.3-3.5 mm.
Follow-up	3 years.
Treatment regimen	Isradipine 2.5-5.0 mg or hydrochlorothiazide 12.5-25mg PO x2/d.

MIDAS

Multicenter Isradipine Diuretic Atherosclerotic Study

(continued)

Results	There was no difference in rate of progression of mean maximum intimal medial thickness between isradipine and hydrochlorothiazide over 3 years. Mean diastolic blood pressure decreased to the same level with either treatment at 6 months (-13.0 mm Hg); mean systolic blood pressure decreased by 19.5 mm Hg with hydrochlorothiazide compared to 16.0 mm Hg with isradipine (p=0.002). Major vascular events (myocardial infarction, stroke, congestive heart failure, angina, sudden death) occurred more frequently in the isradipine group (5.65%) than hydrochlorothiazide group (3.17%, p=0.07). There was a significant (p=0.02) increase in nonmajor vascular events and procedures in the isradipine compared to the hydrochlorothiazide group. The increased incidence of vascular events in patients treated with isradipine could not be explained by the difference in systolic blood pressure alone.
Conclusions	There was no difference in progression of the mean maximum intimal medial thickness of the carotid arteries in isradipine vs hydrochlorothiazide treatment. The increased incidence of vascular events in the isradipine requires further study.

STONE

Shanghai Trial Of Nifedipine in the Elderly (STONE)

Title	Shanghai trial of nifedipine in the elderly (STONE).
Author	Gong L, Zhang W, Zhu Y, et al.
Reference	J Hypertens 1996; 14:1237-1245.
Disease	Hypertension.
Purpose	To determine whether there was a difference between nifedipine and placebo in development of cardiovascular events in elderly hypertensive patients.
Design	Single blind, randomized, multicenter. After 4 weeks physicians could reallocate some of the subjects.
Patients	1632 patients with hypertension, between ages 60-79 years. Blood pressure ≥160/90 mm Hg.
Follow-up	Mean of 30 months.
Treatment regimen	Placebo or slow release retard preparation of nifedipine 10 mg x 2/day, up to 60 mg. Captopril or dihydrochlorothiazide added if blood pressure remained above 159/90 mm Hg.

Shanghai Trial Of Nifedipine in the Elderly (STONE)

(continued)

Results	Clinical event end points determined prior to trial included stroke, congestive heart failure, myocardial infarction, severe arrhythmia, sudden death, and others. 77 events occurred in placebo vs 32 in the nifedipine group and this was highly significant. There was a significant decrease in risk of strokes and severe arrhythmias; relative risk decreased from 1.0-0.41 on therapy; 95% confidence interval 0.27-0.61.
Conclusions	Long acting nifedipine decreased the number of clinical events (including strokes and arrhythmias) in elderly hypertensive patients.

Syst-Eur

Systolic Hypertension-Europe

Title	Randomized double blind comparison of placebo and active treatment for older patients with isolated systolic hypertension.
Authors	Staessen JA, Fagard R, Thijs L, et al.
Reference	Lancet 1997;350:757-764.
Disease	Hypertension.
Purpose	To evaluate the effectiveness of antihypertensive therapy in prevention of cardiovascular complications in patients >60 years old with isolated systolic hypertension.
Design	Randomized, double blind, placebo controlled, multicenter.
Patients	4695 patients, ≥60 years old, with sitting systolic blood pressure 160-219 mm Hg, and diastolic blood pressure <95 mm Hg when treated with masked placebo. Standing systolic blood pressure should have been ≥140 mm Hg. Patients with secondary systolic hypertension that needed special medical or surgical correction, retinal hemorrhage or papilledema, congestive heart failure, aortic dissection, renal failure, stroke or myocardial infarction in the preceding year, dementia, substance abuse, or severe concomitant disease were excluded.
Follow-up	A median of 2 years (range 1-97 months).
Treatment regimen	Nitrendipine 10-40 mg/d (if necessary replaced or combined with enalapril 5-20 mg/d, hydrochlorothiazide 12.5-25 mg/d or both) or matching placebo. Goal of systolic blood pressure: <150 mm Hg, with a reduction of at least 20 mm Hg.

Results

After 2 years, 58.9% of the patients who had been assigned to nitrendipine and 39.6% of the patients assigned to placebo still received the study drug as the only treatment. Among the patients who withdrew from the study treatment, but continued to be followed, 36.5% of the patients assigned to active treatment and 58.1% of the patients in the placebo group were on antihypertensive medications. By intention-to-treat analysis, the sitting systolic and diastolic blood pressure decreased after 2 years by 13 and 17 mm Hg, respectively in the placebo group, and by 23 and 7 mm Hg in the active treatment group. Standing systolic and diastolic blood pressure decreased by 10 and 2 mm Hg in the placebo group, and by 21 and 7 mm Hg in the active treatment group. At median follow-up, more patients from the active treatment group (43.5%) than the placebo group (21.4%) had reached the target blood pressure (p<0.001). The between group differences in sitting blood pressure (the mean change from baseline in the active treatment group minus the mean change in the placebo group) were 10.1 mm Hg (95% CI 8.8–11.4) systolic and 4.5 mm Hg (95% CI 3.9–5.1) diastolic at 2 years, and 10.7 mm Hg (95% CI 8.8–12.5) and 4.7 mm Hg (95% CI 3.7–5.6) at 4 years. Heart rate was not changed with active treatment. Withdrawal from the study due to uncontrolled hypertension occurred in 5.5% of the placebo group vs 0.5% of the active treatment group (p<0.001). Total mortality per 1000 patient years was 24.0 in the placebo and 20.5 in the active treatment group (-14% difference; 95% CI -33-+9%; p=0.22). Cardiovascular mortality was 13.5 vs 9.8, respectively (-27% difference; 95% CI -48-+2%; p=0.07). Fatal myocardial infarction occurred at a rate of 2.6 and 1.2 per 1000 patient years in the placebo and active treatment, respectively (-56% difference; 95% CI -82–9%; p=0.08). Non cardiovascular and cancer mortality were comparable between the 2 groups. The cumulative stroke rates were 13.7 and 7.9 per 1000 patient years (-42% difference, 95% CI -60–17%; p=0.003). Non fatal cardiac end points (heart failure, fatal and non fatal myocardial infarction, and sudden death) occurred at a rate of 20.5 per 1000 patient years in the placebo group vs 15.1 in the active treatment group (-26% difference; 95% CI -44–3%; p=0.03). The rate of all cerebrovascular events was 18.0

and 11.8 per 1000 patient years in the placebo and active treatment group, respectively (-34% difference; 95% CI -51-11%; p=0.006). Angina pectoris occurred less frequently in the active treatment group (18.1 vs 23.9 per 1000 patient years; -24% difference; 95% CI -41-2%; p=0.04). The cumulative rate of all fatal and nonfatal cardiovascular end points was 33.9 per 1000 patient years in the placebo group and 23.3 in the active treatment group (-31% difference; 95% CI -45-14%; p<0.001).

Conclusions

Nitrendipine therapy reduced the rate of cardiovascular complications and cerebrovascular events in patients ≥60 years old with isolated systolic hypertension. However, the decrease in total mortality was not statistically significant.

Syst-Eur (Substudy)

Title	Effects of calcium channel blockade in older patients with diabetes and systolic hypertension.
Authors	Tuomilehto J, Rastenyte D, Birkenhäger WH, et al.
Reference	N Engl J Med 1999; 340:677–684.
Disease	Systolic hypertension and diabetes.
Purpose	To compare the outcome of treating patients with nitrendipine in diabetic vs nondiabetic patients.
Design	Randomized, double blind, multicenter.
Patients	492 patients (10.5%) of the randomized patients in Syst-Eur who had diabetes.
Follow-up	Median of 2 years.
Treatment regimen	As per Syst-Eur protocol.
Results	Hypertension therapy reduced systolic and diastolic blood pressures by 8.6 and 3.9 mm Hg compared to placebo in the diabetic patients. In these patients with diabetes and after adjusting for confounding variables, active therapy decreased mortality by 55%; mortality from cardiovascular disease by 76%, strokes by 73%, and cardiac events by 63%. Treatment reductions in overall mortality, mortality from cardiovascular disease, and all cardiovascular events were greater among diabetic patients compared to nondiabetic patients ($p=0.01-0.04$).

(continued)

Conclusions	Antihypertensive therapy based on the long acting dihydropyridine calcium channel blocker nitrendipine was beneficial in older patients with hypertension and diabetes and failed to support the notion that long acting calcium channel blockers are harmful in diabetics.

TONE

Trial Of Nonpharmacologic interventions in the Elderly

Title	Sodium reduction and weight loss in the treatment of hypertension in older persons. A randomized controlled trial of nonpharmacologic interventions in the elderly (TONE).
Author	Whelton PK, Appel LJ, Espeland MA, et al.
Reference	JAMA 1998; 279:839-846.
Disease	Hypertension.
Purpose	To determine the efficacy of weight loss and sodium restriction as therapy for hypertension in older patients.
Design	Randomized, controlled, multicenter.
Patients	875 men and women, 60–80 years old with systolic blood pressure lower than 145 mm Hg and diastolic blood pressure lower than 85 mm Hg on a single antihypertensive medication.
Follow-up	Median was 29 months; range 15–36 months.
Treatment regimen	585 obese patients randomized to reduced sodium intake, weight loss, both vs usual care. 390 nonobese patients randomized to reduced sodium intake or usual care. After 3 months of intervention withdrawal of antihypertensive medicines was attempted.

TONE

Trial Of Nonpharmacologic interventions in the Elderly

(continued)

Results	The combined outcome measures (occurrence of hypertension at 1 or more study visits following attempted withdrawal of antihypertensive medication, treatment with an antihypertensvie medicine, or occurrence of a clinical cardiovascular event (myocardial infarction, angina, congestive heart failure, stroke, coronary artery bypass grafting, or percutaneous transluminal coronary angioplasty) was less frequent among those assigned to reduced sodium intake vs not assigned to reduced sodium intake; relative hazard ratio 0.69; 95% CI 0.59–0.81, $p<0.001$). The combined outcome measures was less frequent in obese patients assigned to weight loss vs not assigned to weight loss; relative hazard ratio 0.70; 95% CI 0.57–0.87, $p<0.001$). For obese patients the hazard ratios were reduced compared to usual care for reduced sodium intake alone, weight loss and combined sodium intake, and weight loss. There were no differences in the frequency of cardiovascular events during follow-up among the groups.
Conclusions	Weight loss and reduction in sodium intake are feasible, effective, and safe non pharmacologic therapies of hypertension in the elderly.

CAPPP

The Captopril Prevention Project

Title	Effect of ACE inhibition compared with conventional therapy on cardiovascular morbidity and mortality in hypertension: The Captopril Prevention Project (CAPPP).
Authors	Hansson L, Lindholm LH, Niskanen L, et al.
Reference	J Hypertens 1990;8:985-990. Lancet 1999;353:611-616.
Disease	Hypertension.
Purpose	To compare the effectiveness of conventional therapy with diuretics and or ß-blockers vs captopril in patients with hypertension regarding cardiovascular morbidity and mortality.
Design	Randomized, open label, multicenter, with blinded end point evaluation.
Patients	10,985 men and women, 25-66 years old, with diastolic blood pressure ≥100 mm Hg. Patients with secondary hypertension, serum creatinine >150 μmol/L, or indications for ß-blockers were excluded.
Follow-up	An average of 6.1 years.
Treatment regimen	Randomization to captopril 50-100 mg/d (once or twice a day) or conventional therapy (diuretics and/or ß-blockers).
Additional therapy	If diastolic blood pressure was >90 mm Hg with maximal dose of captopril, a diuretic was added. A calcium antagonist could be added in both groups.

CAPPP

The Captopril Prevention Project (continued)

Results

5492 patients were randomized to captopril and 5493 to conventional therapy. Only 27 (0.25%) patients were lost to follow-up. Primary end point (myocardial infarction, stroke or cardiovascular death) occurred in similar rates in the two groups (11.1 per 1000 patient years in the captopril group and in 10.2 per 1000 patient years in the conventional therapy group, RR 1.05; 95% CI 0.90–1.22; [p=0.52]). Cardiovascular mortality tended to be lower in the captopril group (76 patients) than in the conventional therapy group (95 patients) (RR 0.77; 95% CI 0.57–1.04; p=0.092). In contrast, strokes were more common in the captopril group (RR 1.25; 95% CI 1.01–1.55; p=0.044), whereas the rates of myocardial infarction were comparable. Total mortality was also comparable between the groups (RR 0.93; 95% CI 0.76–1.14; p=0.49). Less captopril-assigned patients developed diabetes mellitus (RR 0.79; 95% CI 0.67–0.94; p=0.007). On-treatment analysis did not demonstrate a significant difference in the primary end point, cardiovascular mortality, total mortality, myocardial infarction rates, and cardiac event rates. Stroke remained more common in the captopril group (RR 1.43; p=0.004). Among patients with diabetes mellitus, captopril was associated with less primary end point event rate (RR 0.59; 95% CI 0.38–0.91; p=0.019), less myocardial infarction (RR 0.34; 95% CI 0.17–0.67; p=0.002), and less cardiac events (RR 0.67; 95% CI 0.46–0.96; p=0.030).

Conclusions

Captopril was not better than conventional hypertensive therapy with ß-blockers and diuretics in preventing cardiovascular morbidity and mortality in the whole study population. However, among diabetic patients, captopril was better than conventional therapy in reducing mortality and cardiovascular morbidity.

HOT

Hypertension Optimal Treatment

Title	a. The Hypertension Optimal Treatment study (the HOT study). b. The Hypertension Optimal Treatment (HOT) Study patient characteristics: Randomization, risk profiles, and early blood pressure results. c. Effects of intensive blood pressure lowering and low dose aspirin in patients with hypertension: Principal results of the hypertension optimal treatment (HOT) randomized trial.
Authors	a. Hansson L, Zanchetti A, for the HOT Study Group. b. Hansson L, Zanchetti A, Carruthers SG, et al. c. Hansson L, Zanchetti A, for the HOT Study Group.
Reference	a. Blood Press 1993; 2: 62-68. b. Blood Press 1994; 3: 322-327. c. Lancet 1998; 351: 1755-1762.
Disease	Hypertension.
Purpose	1) To evaluate the optimal target diastolic blood pressure in treated hypertensive patients. 2) To assess the potential benefit of adding low dose aspirin to the treatment of hypertension.
Design	Prospective, randomized, open with blinded end point evaluation (PROBE), multicenter.
Patients	19,193 patients, 50-80 years old (mean 61.5 years) with hypertension (diastolic blood pressure 100-115 mm Hg).
Follow-up	An average follow-up of 3.8 years (3.3-4.9 years).

HOT

Hypertension Optimal Treatment

(continued)

Treatment regimen	Randomization to 3 diastolic blood pressure targets: ≤90 mm Hg (n=6264), ≤85 mm Hg (n=6264), or ≤80 mm Hg (n=6262). All patients received felodipine 5 mg/d. Additional therapy was given to reach the target diastolic blood pressure. ACE inhibitors or ß-blockers as step two. At step three the felodipine dose was increased to 10 mg/d, and in step four, the dose of the ß-blocker or ACE inhibitor was doubled. At step five, a diuretic agent was added. In addition patients were randomized to aspirin 75 mg/d (n=9399) or placebo (n=9391).
Results	403 patients were excluded early in the trial. In addition, 491 (2.6%) patients were lost to follow-up. At the end of the study 78% of patients were still taking felodipine, usually with an ACE inhibitor (41%) or a ß-blocker (28%). The diastolic blood pressure was reduced from a mean of 105 mm Hg at baseline to 85.2 mm Hg in the ≤90 mm Hg group, 83.2 mm Hg in the ≤85 mm Hg group, and 81.1 mm Hg in the ≤80 mm Hg group. A diastolic blood pressure >90 mm Hg was found in 12%, 7%, and 6% of the ≤90 mm Hg, ≤85 mm Hg, and ≤80 mm Hg groups, respectively. Blood pressure achieved was no different between patients randomized to aspirin or to placebo. Major cardiovascular events (myocardial infarction, stroke, and cardiovascular deaths) occurred at a rate of 9.9, 10.0, and 9.3 events/1000 patient years in the ≤90 mm Hg, ≤85 mm Hg, and ≤80 mm Hg groups, respectively (p=0.50). Myocardial infarctions occurred at a rate of 3.6, 2.7, and 2.6 events/1000 patient years, respectively (p=0.05). Strokes occurred at a rate of 4.0, 4.7, and 3.8 events/1000 patient years, respectively (p=0.74), cardiovascular mortality at a rate of 3.7, 3.8, and 4.1 events/1000 patient years, respectively (p=0.49), and total mortality at a rate of 7.9, 8.2, and 8.8 events/1000 patient years, respectively (p=0.32). The lowest risk for major cardiovascular events occurred at a mean diastolic blood pressure of 82.6 mm Hg and a systolic blood pressure of 138.5 mm Hg. The lowest risk for cardiovascular mortality was at a mean diastolic blood pressure of 86.5 mm Hg and a systolic blood pressure of

138.8 mm Hg. In patients with diabetes mellitus major cardiovascular events occurred at a rate of 24.4, 18.6, and 11.9 events/1000 patient years, in the ≤90 mm Hg, ≤85 mm Hg, and ≤80 mm Hg groups, respectively ($p = 0.005$). In diabetic patients total mortality was 15.9, 15.5, and 9.0 per 1000 patient years, respectively ($p=0.068$), and cardiovascular mortality was 11.1, 11.2, and 3.7 per 1000 patient years, respectively ($p=0.016$). Low dose aspirin significantly reduced the rate of major cardiovascular events (8.9 vs 10.5 events/1000 patient years; $p=0.03$; relative risk 0.85; 95% CI 0.73–0.99), myocardial infarction (2.3 vs 3.6 events/1000 patient years; $p=0.002$; relative risk 0.64; 95% CI 0.49–0.85), but not cardiovascular mortality (3.7 vs 3.9 events/1000 patient years; $p=0.65$; relative risk 0.95; 95% CI 0.75–1.20) and total mortality (8.0 vs 8.6 events/1000 patient years; $p=0.36$; relative risk 0.93; 95% CI 0.79–1.09). Fatal bleeding occurred in similar rates in the aspirin and placebo group, however, non-fatal major bleeding was more common in the aspirin group (1.4% vs 0.7% (risk ratio 1.8; $p<0.001$).

Conclusions

Intensive lowering blood pressure to a target of 140 mm Hg systolic and 85 mm Hg diastolic pressure was associated with lowering the major cardiovascular event rates. Efforts to lower blood pressure further gave little further benefit. Intensive lowering of diastolic blood pressure was especially effective in patients with diabetes mellitus. Low dose aspirin significantly reduced major cardiovascular events, but had no effect on the incidence of stroke, cardiovascular mortality, or total mortality. On the other hand, aspirin was associated with a small increase in the risk for nonfatal major bleeding.

UKPDS 38 & 39

United Kingdom Prospective Diabetes Study

Title	1. Tight blood pressure control and risk of macrovascular and microvascular complications in type 2 diabetes mellitus: UKPDS 38. 2. Efficacy of atenolol and captopril in reducing risk of macrovascular and microvascular complications in type 2 diabetes: UKPDS 39.
Authors	UK Prospective Diabetes Study Group.
Reference	1. BMJ 1998;317:703–713. 2. BMJ 1998;317:713–720.
Disease	Diabetes mellitus, hypertension.
Purpose	1. To determine whether tight blood pressure control to a target of >150/85 mm Hg will reduce micro and macrovascular complications in patients with type 2 diabetes mellitus. 2. To compare the effect of intensive lowering of blood pressure with captopril and atenolol on prevention of micro- and macrovascular complications in patients with type 2 diabetes mellitus.
Design	Randomized, controlled, multicenter.
Patients	1. 1148 patients (637 men) with type 2 diabetes mellitus, 25–65 years old (mean age 56±8 years), with blood pressure ≥160/90 mm Hg or ≥150/85 mm Hg on antihypertensive therapy. 758 patients were randomized to tight blood pressure control and 390 to less tight blood pressure control. 2. 758 patients who were randomized to tight blood pressure control. Patients with ketonuria, myocardial infarction in the previous year, current angina or heart failure, >1 major vascular event, renal failure, retinopathy treated by laser, malignant hypertension, uncorrected endocrine disorder, inability to use insulin, and severe concomitant disease were excluded.

UKPDS 38 & 39

United Kingdom Prospective Diabetes Study

(continued)

Follow-up	1. Median 8.4 years. 2. Up to 9 years.
Treatment regimen	1. Randomization to tight blood pressure control (<150/85 mm Hg) with captopril or atenolol or to less tight control (<180/105 mm Hg), avoiding angiotensin converting enzyme inhibitors or ß-blockers. 2. Randomization to captopril (n=400) or atenolol (n=358). The initial atenolol dose was 50 mg/d, increasing to 100 mg/d if needed. Captopril was started at a dose of 25 mg bid. The dose was increased to 50 mg bid. Target blood pressure was <150/ <85 mm Hg.
Additional therapy	Patients were randomized to intensive blood glucose control (<6.0 mmol/L) with oral hypoglycemic agents or insulin or to conventional glycemic control, primarily by diet. If target blood pressure was not reached with the maximal dose of captopril or atenolol, frusemide, slow released nifedipine, methyldopa, and prazosin were added.
Results	1. Mean blood pressure was 154±16/87±7 mm Hg in the less-tight control and 144±14/82±7 mm Hg in the tight control group (p<0.0001). The absolute risk for any diabetes related end point was 50.9 and 67.4 events per 1000 patient years in the tight and less tight control groups (relative risk 0.76; 95% CI 0.62–0.92; p=0.0046). Diabetes related death occurred at a rate of 13.7 and 20.3 per 1000 patient years, respectively (relative risk 0.68; 95% CI 0.49–0.94; p=0.019). Total mortality occurred at a rate of 22.4 and 27.2 in the tight and less tight control group (relative risk 0.82; 95% CI 0.63–1.08; p=0.17). Tight blood pressure control reduced also the risk for stroke (relative risk 0.56; 95% CI 0.35–0.89; p=0.013), heart failure (relative risk 0.44; 95% CI 0.20–0.94; p=0.0043), and the risk of microvascular complications (relative risk 0.63; 95% CI 0.44–0.89; p=0.0092). The reduction in microvascular end points was predominantly due to a reduction in the risk of deterioration of retinopathy (p=0.004) and retinal photocoagulation.

2. Blood pressure was equally reduced to a mean of 144±14 /83±8 mm Hg in the captopril group and 143±14 /81±7 mm Hg in the atenolol group. Less patients in the atenolol group (65%) than in the captopril group (78%) took the assigned treatment at their last clinic visit (p<0.0001). Impaired peripheral circulation (4% vs 0%) and bronchospasm (6% vs 0%) were more common with atenolol, whereas cough (0% vs 4%) was less common with atenolol than with captopril. 27% of the captopril assigned patients and 31% of the atenolol-assigned patients needed ≥3 agents to reach target blood pressure. The incidence of any end point related to diabetes was similar in the 2 groups (53.3 vs 48.4 events/1000 patient years in the captopril and atenolol groups, respectively; relative risk for captopril 1.10; 95% CI 0.86–1.41; p=0.43). Death related to diabetes occurred at a rate of 15.2 and 12.0 per 1000 patient years, respectively; RR 1.27; 95% CI 0.82–1.97; p=0.28). Similarly, there were no differences in the rates of total mortality (p=0.44), myocardial infarction (p=0.35), stroke (p=0.74), peripheral vascular disease (p=0.59), and microvascular disease (p=0.30) between the captopril and atenolol groups. At 9 years, 37% of the captopril and 37% of the atenolol assigned patients had deterioration in retinopathy by 2 grades. 31% vs 26% of the captopril and atenolol group had urinary albumin concentration of ≥50 mg/L at 9 years (p=0.31), and 5% vs 10%, respectively had clinical proteinuria (≥300 mg/L (p=0.090). Plasma creatinine concentrations were comparable. Over the first 4 years mean hemoglobin A1c was higher in the atenolol group (7.5±1.4% vs 7.0±1.4%, p=0.0044). However, during the last years of follow-up levels were comparable. At 8 years 81% of the atenolol group vs only 71% of the captopril group were receiving an additional glucose lowering treatment (p=0.029). Hypoglycemia occurred in similar rates in the two groups. However, mean weight gain was greater in the atenolol group (3.4±8.0 kg vs 1.6±9.1 kg over 9 years, p=0.02). There were no significant differences between the groups in serum lipid concentrations.

Conclusions	1. Tight blood pressure control was associated with reduction in the risk of diabetes related mortality and morbidity in hypertensive patients with type 2 diabetes mellitus. 2. Captopril and atenolol were equaly effective in reducing blood pressure and the complications of diabetes mellitus in hypertensive patients. Blood pressure reduction in itself may be more important than the specific therapy used for prevention of diabetes complications.

UKPDS 33

United Kingdom Prospective Diabetes Study

Title	Intensive blood glucose control with sulphonylureas or insulin compared with conventional treatment and risk of complications in patients with type 2 diabetes (UKPDS 33).
Authors	UK Prospective Diabetes Study (UKPDS) group.
Reference	Lancet 1998; 352: 837-853.
Disease	Diabetes mellitus.
Purpose	To compare the effects of intensive blood glucose control with either sulphonylurea agents or insulin and conventional therapy on micro and macrovascular complications in patients with type 2 diabetes mellitus.
Design	Randomized, multicenter.
Patients	3867 patients, 25-65 years old, with newly diagnosed diabetes mellitus, who had a fasting plasma glucose >6 mmol/L on 2 mornings, 1-3 weeks apart. Patients with ketonuria >3 mmol/L, serum creatinine >175 μmol/L, myocardial infarction in the preceeding year, angina pectoris or congestive heart failure, >1 major vascular event, retinopathy treated by laser, malignant hypertension, uncorrected endocrine disorder, inability to use insulin, and severe concomitant disease were excluded.
Follow-up	Median follow-up 10.0 years (7.7-12.4 years).

UKPDS 33

United Kingdom Prospective Diabetes Study

(continued)

Treatment regimen	Patients had a 3 month run in period in which they were instructed to consume a low saturated fat, moderately high fiber diet. Thereafter, patients were randomized to intensive treatment with insulin (n=911), intensive therapy with sulphonylurea (chlorpropamide [n=619] or glibenclamide or glipizide [n=615]), or conventional therapy with diet (n=1138). Overweight patients were randomized also to metformin. The aim of the conventional regimen was to maintain fasting plasma glucose levels <15 mmol/L without symptoms of hyperglycemia. If marked hyperglycemia was detected patients were randomized to the above mentioned therapies. The aim of intensive therapy was fasting plasma glucose <6 mmol/L.
Results	The median hemoglobin A1c values was 7.0% (6.2–8.2%) in the intensive therapy groups, compared with 7.9% (6.9–8.8%) in the conventional group (p<0.0001). The median hemoglobin A1c values over 10 years was 6.7% in the chlorpropamide group, 7.2% in the glibenclamide group and 7.1% in the insulin group (p=0.008 for the difference between chlorpropamide and the glibenclamide groups, p=NS for the difference between chlorpropamide and insulin groups). Patients in the sulphonylurea groups gained more weight than the patients assigned to conventional therapy, whereas weight gain was the greatest among the insulin assigned patients. Systolic and diastolic blood pressure were significantly higher in the chlorpropamide assigned patients than in the other groups (p<0.001). The absolute risk for any diabetes related end point was 40.9 per 1000 patient years in the intensive groups vs 46.0 in the conventional group (RR 0.88; 95% CI 0.79–0.99; p=0.029). All cause mortality occurred at a rate of 17.9 and 18.9 per 1000 patient years, respectively (RR 0.94; 95% CI 0.80–1.10; p=0.44). Similarly, diabetes related mortality was not significantly reduced (RR 0.90; 95% CI 0.73–1.11; p=0.34). Myocardial infarction

occurred at a rate of 14.7 and 17.4 per 1000 patient years in the intensive and conventional therapy groups (RR 0.84; 95% CI 0.71-1.00; p=0.052). Most of the difference in event rate between the intensive and conventional groups was due to reduction in microvascular complications in the intensive group (RR 0.75; 95% 0.60-0.93; p=0.0099). There was no difference for any of the end points between chlorpropamide, glibenclamide and insulin intensive therapy groups. Hypoglycemic episodes were more common in the intensive groups (p<0.0001). Major hypoglycemic episodes occurred at a rate of 0.7%, 1.0%, 1.4%, and 1.8% in the conventional therapy, chlorpropamide, glibenclamide, and insulin groups, respectively.

Conclusions

Intensive control of plasma glucose leves in patients with type 2 diabetes by either insulin or sulphonylurea agents reduced the risk of microvascular complications, but not the risk of macrovascular complications. None of the drugs had an adverse effect on cardiovascular outcomes. Intensive therapy increased the risk of hypoglycemia.

CAB

Calcium Antagonists in Blacks

Title	Comparison of the efficacy of dihydropyridine calcium channel blockers in African American patients with hypertension.
Authors	Hall WD, Reed JW, Flack JM, et al.
Reference	Arch Intern Med 1998; 158:2029–2034.
Disease	Hypertension.
Purpose	To determine the efficacy of three antihypertensive calcium channel blockers: nifedipine coat core (Adalat CC), nifedipine gastrointestinal therapeutic system (GITS; Procardia XL) and amlodipine (Norvasc) in black hypertension patients.
Design	Randomized, double blind, multicenter.
Patients	192 African American hypertensive patients with Stage 1 or 2 hypertension.
Follow-up	8 weeks.
Treatment regimen	Monotherapy with nifedipine coat core, nifedipine gastrointestinal therapeutic system, or amlodipine.

Results	Average office systolic blood pressure was reduced by 19–22 mm Hg and average diastolic blood pressure was reduced by 12–14 mm Hg without significant differences among the three treatments. By ambulatory monitoring diastolic blood pressure was reduced by -8.5, -6.1, and -9.0 mm Hg in the nifedipine CC, nifedipine GITS, and amlodipine groups, respectively; systolic blood pressure was reduced by -14.3, -11.8, and -15.7 mm Hg, respectively. There were no significant differences among the groups. Overall response rates and adverse event rates were similar among the three groups.
Conclusions	Nifedipine coat core, nifedipine gastrointestinal therapeutic system, and amlodipine have comparable efficacy in controlling hypertension in African Americans.

ARIC

Atherosclerosis Risk In Communities

Title	Hypertension and antihypertensive therapy as risk factors for type II diabetes mellitus.
Authors	Gross TW, Nieto J, Shahar E, et al.
Reference	N Engl J Med 2000;342:905-912.
Disease	Hypertension.
Purpose	To determine whether there was a relationship between antihypertensive medications and the development of type II diabetes mellitus.
Design	Prospective, multicenter, cohort study.
Patients	12,550 adults, 45-64 years of age without diabetes at the start of the study.
Follow-up	6 years.
Treatment regimen	The categories for treatment of those with hypertension included ACE inhibitors, ß-blockers, calcium channel antagonists, and thiazide diuretics.

Results	3804 patients had hypertension and 8746 did not have hypertension at baseline. 569 new cases of diabetes occurred in subjects with hypertension and 577 occurred in patients without hypertension. Thus there were 29.1 new cases of diabetes per 1000 person years among patients with hypertension and 12.0 per 1000 person years in patients without hypertension (RR=2.43; 95% CI=2.16–2.73). Much of the risk of developing diabetes was due to hypertension (rather than to antihypertensive drugs alone). For patients not taking antihypertensive medicines, the risk of diabetes was higher among patients with hypertension vs those without hypertension. After adjusting for a number of variables, subjects on thiazide diuretics, ACE inhibitors, or calcium channel blockers were not at greater risk for developing diabetes than untreated hypertensives. However development of diabetes was 28% more likely to occur in subjects on ß-blockers vs those not taking medicines (relative hazard = 1.28; 95% CI=1.04–1.57).
Conclusions	Type II diabetes is about 2.5 times as likely to develop in subjects with hypertension vs those that are normotensive. After taking into account the increased risk of diabetes among hypertensives, ß-blockers but not thiazide diuretics, ACE inhibitors, or calcium blockers were associated with an increased risk of developing diabetes.

DRASTIC

Dutch Renal Artery Stenosis Intervention Cooperative Study

Title	The effect of balloon angioplasty on hypertension in atherosclerotic renal artery stenosis.
Authors	Van Jaarsveld BC, Krijnen P, Pieterman H, et al.
Reference	N Engl J Med 2000;342:1007–1014.
Disease	Hypertension, atherosclerotic renal artery stenosis.
Purpose	To determine the effect of balloon angioplasty vs antihypertensive therapy on hypertension associated with atherosclerotic renal artery stenosis in patients with mild or only mildly impaired renal function.
Design	Randomized, controlled, multicenter.
Patients	106 patients with hypertension and angiographically documented atherosclerotic renal artery stenosis and serum creatinine of ≤2.3 mg/dL. Diastolic blood pressure had to be at least 95 mm Hg despite therapy with 2 antihypertensive drugs or an increase of at least 0.2 mg/dL in serum creatinine with an ACE inhibitor.
Follow-up	12 months.
Treatment regimen	Antihypertensive drug therapy vs angioplasty. If after 3 months patients in the drug therapy group had a diastolic blood pressure that was 95 mm Hg or higher despite therapy with 3 or more drugs or if there was evidence of worsening renovascular disease, they underwent balloon angioplasty.
Additional therapy	Aspirin in the angioplasty group.

DRASTIC

Dutch Renal Artery Stenosis Intervention Cooperative Study (continued)

Results	Primary outcome was systolic and diastolic blood pressure at 3 and 12 months. Other outcome measures included numbers and defined daily doses of drugs, the serum creatinine concentration as well as others. Baseline blood pressures were elevated to similar levels in the angioplasty group (179/104 mm Hg) and the drug group (180/103 mm Hg). At 3 months, blood pressure was 169±28/99±12 mm Hg in the angioplasty group (n=56), and 176±31/101±14 mm Hg in the drug group (n=50; p=NS). The number of defined daily doses of medicines in the angioplasty group was 2.1±1.3 vs the drug group at 3.2±1.5 (p<0.001). 22 patients in the drug therapy group underwent angioplasty secondary to persistent hypertension despite therapy with 3 or more drugs or worsening renal function. At 12 months, by intention-to-treat analysis, there was no difference in systolic and diastolic blood pressure between the angioplasty group (160±26/93±13 mm Hg) vs the drug therapy group (163±25/96±10 mm Hg). The number of defined daily doses was no longer significantly lower in the angioplasty vs drug therapy group at 12 months. However, at 12 months blood pressure control did improve in 38 of 56 patients in the angioplasty group (68%) but in 18 of 48 patients (38%) in the drug therapy group. At 12 months there was no difference in serum creatinine or creatinine clearance between groups.
Conclusions	Angioplasty has little advantage over antihypertensive drug therapy for the treatment of hypertension in patients with atherosclerotic renal artery stenosis.

ALLHAT

The Antihypertensive and Lipid Lowering Treatment to Prevent Heart Attack Trial

Title	Major cardiovascular events in hypertensive patients randomized to doxazosin vs chlorthalidone.
Authors	The ALLHAT Officers and coordinators for the ALLHAT Collaborative Research Group.
Reference	JAMA 2000;283:1967–1975.
Disease	Hypertension.
Purpose	As part of the overall ALLHAT study which was to determine the incidence of fatal coronary heart disease and nonfatal MI in patients with hypertension randomized to 1 of 4 antihypertensives; this analysis compares the effect of the α-blocker doxazosin to the diuretic chlorthalidone.
Design	Randomized, double blind, active controlled, multicenter.
Patients	24,335 patients with hypertension plus at least one other coronary disease risk factor who received the α-blocker doxazosin or diuretic chlorthalidone.
Follow-up	Median follow-up was 3.3 years.

ALLHAT

The Antihypertensive and Lipid Lowering Treatment to Prevent Heart Attack Trial

(continued)

Treatment regimen	While the overall ALLHAT hypertensive protocol compares long term outcome of chlorthalidone, doxazosin, amlodipine, and lisinopril, an independent data review committee recommended terminating the doxazosin arm based on comparison to chlorthalidone. Data here reflect outcomes from February 1994 to December 1999 and shows comparison of doxazosin (2-8 mg per day (n=9067) to chlorthalidone, 12.5-25 mg per day (n=15,268). Other limbs of the study are continuing.
Additional therapy	There is also a lipid lowering protocol with pravastatin.
Results	365 patients in the doxazosin and 608 in chlorthalidone group achieved end point of fatal coronary heart disease or nonfatal MI and there was no difference between these 2 groups in this outcomes (RR=1.03; 95% CI=0.90-1.17, p=0.71). There was no difference in total mortality between groups (9.62%, 4 year rate for doxazosin vs 9.08% for chlorthalidone; RR=1.03; 95% CI=0.90-1.15; p=0.56). The secondary end point of combined cardiovascular disease (coronary heart disease death, nonfatal MI, stroke, revascularization, angina, congestive heart failure, and peripheral arterial disease) was higher in the doxazosin arm vs chlorthalidone arm (4 year rate of 25.45% vs 21.76%, respectively; RR=1.25; 95% CI=1.17-1.33, p<0.001); and stroke rate was higher in doxazosin vs chlorthalidone group (RR = 1.19; 95% CI = 1.01 - 1.40; p=0.04). Considering other elements of combined cardiovascular disease outcome, congestive heart failure was higher in the doxazosin vs chlorthalidone group (4 year rates, 8.13% vs 4.45%; RR=2.04; 95% CI=1.79-2.32; p<0.001). RRs for angina and coronary revascularization also were higher at 1.16 (p<0.001) and 1.15 (p=0.05), respectively.

ALLHAT

The Antihypertensive and Lipid Lowering Treatment to Prevent Heart Attack Trial

(continued)

Conclusions	Chlorthalidone and doxazosin resulted in comparable risks of coronary heart disease death and nonfatal MI, but chlorthalidone decreased the risk of combined cardiovascular events, notably congestive heart failure, compared to doxazosin, in high risk patients with hypertension.

Losartan and low dose hydrochlorothiazide in essential hypertension

Title	Losartan and low dose hydrochlorothiazide in patients with essential hypertension.A double blind , placebo controlled trial of concomitant administration compared with individual components.
Authors	MacKay JH,Arcuri KE, Goldberg AI, et al.
Reference	Arch Intern Med 1996;156:278-285.
Disease	Hypertension.
Purpose	To assess the effects of losartan + low dose hydrochlorothiazide as initial therapy in patients with essential hypertension.
Design	Randomized, double blind , placebo controlled, multicenter.
Patients	703 patients, ≥18 years old, with an untreated sitting diastolic blood pressure of 95-115 mm Hg. Patients with a significant hematological, renal, gastrointestinal, hepatic, immune, cerebrovascular or cardiovascular disorder were not included.
Follow-up	12 weeks of double blind therapy phase.
Treatment regimen	After 4 weeks of single blind, placebo run-in phase, patients were randomized to placebo (n=140), losartan (50 mg/d; n=139), hydrochlorothiazide (12.5 mg/d; n=142) and losartan (50 mg/d)+ hydrochlorothiazide (6.25 [n=144] or 12.5 mg/d [n=138]) for 12 weeks.

Losartan and low dose hydrochlorothiazide in essential hypertension

(continued)

Results	18.6% of the placebo, 14.1% of the hydrochlorothiazide, 14.4% of the losartan, 10.4% of the losartan +6.25 mg hydrochlorothiazide, and 13.0% of the losartan +12.5 mg hydrochlorothiazide treated patients discontinued their study medication, mainly because of ineffective therapy. The combination of losartan +12.5 mg hydrochlorothiazide caused the largest reduction in systolic and diastolic blood pressure. The mean reduction in peak sitting diastolic blood pressure at 12 week was 5.4±8.6 mm Hg with placebo, 7.4±8.0 mm Hg with hydrochlorothiazide, 10.9±9.5 mm Hg with losartan, 13.3±13.2 mm Hg with losartan +6.25 mg hydrochlorothiazide, and 15.3±8.9 mm Hg with losartan +12.5 mg hydrochlorothiazide ($p \leq 0.001$). After 12 weeks, 20.9%, 34.3%, 40.6%, 43.5%, and 57.8% of the patients treated with placebo, hydrochlorothiazide, losartan, losartan +6.25 mg hydrochlorothiazide and losartan +12.5 mg hydrochlorothiazide, respectively, had a sitting diastolic blood pressure <90 mm Hg.
Conclusions	Combination therapy with losartan 50 mg/d and hydrochlorothiazide 12.5 mg/d resulted in greater reduction in trough sitting systolic and diastolic blood pressure. The combination was well tolerated and was not associated with increased adverse effects.

A comparison of ACE inhibitors, calcium antagonists, ß-blockers, and diuretic agents on reactive hyperemia in patients with essential hypertension: A multicenter study

Title	A comparison of ACE inhibitors, calcium antagonists, ß-blockers, and diuretic agents on reactive hyperemia in patients with essential hypertension:A multicenter study.
Authors	Higashi Y, Sasaki S, Nakagawa K, et al.
Reference	J Am Coll Cardiol 2000;35:284-291.
Disease	Hypertension.
Purpose	To compare the effects of calcium antagonists, ACE inhibitors, ß-blockers, diuretics, on endothelial function in patients with essential hypertension.
Design	Multicenter study evaluating forearm blood flow (measured using a strain gauge plethysmograph) and reactive hyperemia (induced by inflating a blood pressure cuff to 280 mm Hg for 5 minutes and then releasing the cuff) and flow after sublingual nitroglycerin in patients on various antihypertensives; normotensive control group for comparison.
Patients	296 Japanese patients with essential hypertension (>160/>95 mm Hg). 47 normotensives as controls.
Follow-up	Acute study.
Treatment regimen	Patients on monotherapy for at least 24 weeks with calcium blockers, ACE inhibitors, ß-blockers, or diuretics were randomly recruited.

A comparison of ACE inhibitors, calcium antagonists, ß-blockers, and diuretic agents on reactive hyperemia in patients with essential hypertension: A multicenter study

(continued)

Additional therapy	Nitroglycerin, Intraarterial infusion of NO synthase inhibitor NG-monomethyl-L-arginine (L-NMMA), indomethacin.
Results	Forearm reactive blood flow was lower in hypertensive patients compared to normotensive patients. Sublingual nitroglycerin induced an increase in forearm blood flow that was similar in normotensive and hypertensive individuals. All 4 antihypertensive agents were associated with equal systolic-diastolic blood pressures, and forearm vascular resistance. Maximal forearm blood flow response from reactive hyperemia was greatest with the ACE inhibitors ($p<0.05$) (40.5±5.2 mL/min per 100 mL tissue) vs calcium blockers (32.9±5.8), ß-blockers (34.0±5.6), diuretics (32.1±5.9), or nothing (31.9±5.8 mL/min per 100 mL tissue). Changes in forearm blood flow after sublingual nitroglycerin were similar among all drug groups and untreated group. The nitric oxides synthase inhibitor, N^G-monomethyl-L-arginine abolished the effect of ACE inhibitors on enhancing reactive hyperemia.
Conclusions	ACE inhibitors augment reactive hyperemia, an index of endothelium dependent vasodilation, in hypertensive patients. An increase in NO may contribute to this effect by ACE inhibitors.

CANDLE

Candesartan vs Losartan Efficacy Study

Title	Comparative effects of candesartan cilexetil and losartan in patients with systemic hypertension.
Authors	Gradman A, Lewin A, Bowling BT, et al.
Reference	Heart Disease 1999;1:52-57.
Disease	Hypertension.
Purpose	To compare the efficacy of 2 angiotensin receptor blockers: candesartan cilexetil vs losartan in patients with hypertension.
Design	Multicenter, randomized, double blind, parallel group, titration to effect.
Patients	332 patients with hypertension. Diastolic sitting blood pressure of 95-114 mm Hg as entry criteria.
Follow-up	8 weeks.
Treatment regimen	Candesartan (16-32 mg) vs losartan (50-100 mg) daily.
Results	Candesartan was more effective than losartan in lowering blood pressure. Trough sitting diastolic blood pressure at 8 weeks was reduced by -11.0 mm Hg with candesartan vs -8.9 mm Hg with losartan. Responder rates (sitting diastolic blood pressure <90 mm Hg or reduction in blood pressure ≥10 mm Hg) were higher with candesartan (64%) vs losartan (54%). 1.9% of patients taking candesartan and 6.5% taking losartan discontinued the study prematurely because of lack of efficacy or adverse events.

CANDLE

Candesartan vs Losartan Efficacy Study

(continued)

Conclusions	Candesartan was more effective than losartan in reducing blood pressure in this hypertensive cohort.

Long term effects of weight loss and dietary sodium reduction on incidence of hypertension

Title	Long term effects of weight loss and dietary sodium reduction on incidence of hypertension.
Authors	He J, Whelton PK, Appel LJ, et al.
Reference	Hypertension 2000;35:544-549.
Disease	Hypertension.
Purpose	To determine if weight loss and sodium restriction could decrease the development of frank hypertension in a population with high-normal blood pressure.
Design	Randomized, multicenter.
Patients	208 participants, with high-normal blood pressure defined in this paper as diastolic blood pressure of 80-89 mm Hg and systolic blood pressure <160 mm Hg.
Follow-up	7 years.
Treatment regimen	Structured weight loss program vs sodium restriction vs control, for 18 months.

Long term effects of weight loss and dietary sodium reduction on incidence of hypertension

(continued)

Results	Body mass index was similar (overweight but not obese) in the weight loss group (29.0 body mass index) vs the control group (28.7) at baseline. Patients in the weight loss group lost 2.4 kg while those in the control group gained 1.1 kg. Sodium restriction was associated with a significant decrease in 24 hour urinary sodium excretion vs the control group. At 7 years among follow-up on 181 participants there was marked decrease in the incidence of frank hypertension in the weight loss group (19%) vs controls (41%) as well as the use of antihypertensive medicines (13% vs 29%). Sodium restriction led to a modest but not statistically significant decrease in the incidence of development of frank hypertension (22% vs 33% for controls). Use of antihypertensives also tended to be lower in the salt restricted participants (19% vs controls, 24%).
Conclusions	Reduction in weight may forestall the development of frank hypertension.

NORDIL

Nordic Diltiazem Study

Title	Randomized trial of effects of calcium antagonists compared with diuretics and ß-blockers on cardiovascular morbidity and mortality in hypertension. The Nordic Diltiazem Study.
Authors	Hansson L, Hedner T, Lund-Johansen P, et al.
Reference	Lancet 2000: 356:359-365.
Disease	Hypertension.
Purpose	To compare diltiazem with diuretics, ß-blockers, or both on cardiovascular morbidity and mortality in middle-aged hypertensive patients.
Design	Prospective, randomized, open trial with blinded end point evaluation (PROBE).
Patients	10,881 patients aged 56-74 years with diastolic blood pressure of 100 mm Hg or more.
Follow-up	Mean of 4.5 years.
Treatment regimen	Diltiazem (n=5410) given as 180-360 mg daily vs diuretics, ß-blockers, or both (n=5471).
Additional therapy	Additional antihypertensives could be added to lower diastolic blood pressure <90 mm Hg, including ACE inhibitor, diuretic, and/or α blocker.

NORDIL

Nordic Diltiazem Study

(continued)

Results

The primary combined end point was fatal and nonfatal stroke, fatal and nonfatal myocardial infarction, and other cardiovascular death. Mean blood pressure during the study was 154.9/88.6 mm Hg with diltiazem and 151.7/88.7 mm Hg with diuretic/ß-blocker. Decrease in diastolic pressure was the same between groups (-18.7 mm Hg) and the decrease in systolic pressure was greater in the diuretic and ß-blocker group (-23.3) vs the diltiazem group (-20.3; p<0.001). The primary end point occurred with equal frequency in both groups (403 patients in the diltiazem group; 16.6 events per 1000 patient-years; 400 patients in the diuretic and ß-blocker group (16.2 events per 1000 patient-years; RR=1.00; 95% CI=0.87-1.15; p=0.97). The incidence of fatal plus nonfatal stroke was lower in the diltiazem group (159) vs the diuretic and ß-blocker group (196); 6.4 vs 7.9 events per 1000 patient-years; RR=0.80; 95% CI=0.65-0.99; p=0.04. The incidence of fatal and nonfatal myocardial infarction did not differ significantly between groups (183 in diltiazem; 157 in diuretic and ß-blocker group; 7.4 vs 6.3 events per 1000 patient-years; RR=1.16; 95% CI=0.94-1.44; p=0.17).

Conclusions

Therapy based vs diltiazem vs diuretics, ß-blockers, or both was effective in lowering blood pressure; both were equally effective in preventing the combined end point of stroke, myocardial infarction, cardiovascular death.

INSIGHT

The International Nifedipine GITS Study: Intervention as a Goal in Hypertensive Treatment

Title	Morbidity and mortality in patients randomized to double blind treatment with long-acting calcium channel blocker or diuretic in the International Nifedipine GITS study: Intervention as a Goal in Hypertensive Treatment (INSIGHT).
Authors	Brown, MJ, Palmer CR, Castaigne A, et al.
Reference	Lancet 2000;356:366-372.
Disease	Hypertension.
Purpose	To compare the effects of the once daily long acting calcium channel blocker, nifedipine GITS (gastrointestinal-transport system) with the diuretic combination co-amilozide (hydrochlorothiazide plus amiloride) on cardiovascular morbidity and mortality in high risk hypertensive patients.
Design	Prospective, randomized, double blind, multicenter.
Patients	6321 patients, aged 55-80 years with blood pressure >150/95 mm Hg or >160 mm Hg systolic plus one additional cardiovascular risk factor beside hypertension.
Follow-up	>3 years.
Treatment regimen	Nifedipine GITS (30 mg initially); or co-amilozide (hydrochlorothiazide 25 mg plus amiloride 2.5 mg, initially) with dose titration by dose doubling and if needed addition of atenolol or enalapril.

INSIGHT

The International Nifedipine GITS Study: Intervention as a Goal in Hypertensive Treatment

(continued)

Results	Primary outcome was cardiovascular death, myocardial infarction, heart failure or stroke. 3/57 patients on nifedipine GITS completed 10,976 patient-years treatment; 3164 on co-amilozide completed 11,015 patient-years of treatment. 725 in the nifedipine group withdrew because of adverse events; 518 in the co-amilozide group withdrew because of adverse events. 255 patients in nifedipine group withdrew secondary to peripheral edema, but more patients on co-amilozide had metabolic disorders such as hypokalemia, hyponatremia, hyperglycemia, hyperuricemia, and renal impairment. Serious adverse events were more frequent in the co-amilozide group (880) vs the nifedipine group (796; p=0.02). Mean blood pressure fall was comparable between the 2 groups falling from 173/99 mm Hg to 138/82 mm Hg. The primary outcome did not differ between groups: 200 (6.3%) in the nifedipine group vs 182 (5.8%) in the co-amilozide group; with 18.2 events per 1000 patient-years in the nifedipine group vs 16.5 for co-amilozide; RR=1.10; 95% CI=0.91-1.34; p=0.35.
Conclusions	Long acting, once daily nifedipine and co-amilozide had similar efficacy on blood pressure lowering and the primary outcomes of cardiovascular death, myocardial infarction, heart failure, or stroke.

6. Congestive Heart Failure

Title	Xamoterol in severe heart failure.
Authors	The Xamoterol in Severe Heart Failure Study Group.
Reference	Lancet 1990;336:1-6.
Disease	Congestive heart failure.
Purpose	To evaluate the efficacy and safety of xamoterol therapy for heart failure.
Design	Randomized, double blind, placebo controlled, multicenter.
Patients	516 patients, >18 years old, with NYHA class III and IV heart failure despite therapy with diuretics and an ACE inhibitor. Patients with myocardial infarction within 8 weeks, and premenopausal women were excluded.
Follow-up	Clinical evaluation and exercise test at baseline and after an average of 86 days for the placebo and 87 days for the xamoterol.
Treatment regimen	Xamoterol 200 mg X2/d or placebo.
Additional therapy	Any drug that influenced the ß-adrenoreceptors was not permitted. Digitalis was allowed.

Results	There was no significant change in body weight at the end of the protocol for either group. Except for heart rate (79 vs 83 bpm, $p<0.01$) there was no difference in clinical signs between the groups. Visual analogue scale (11% vs 0%, $p<0.02$) and Likert scale (8% vs 2%, $p=0.02$) indicated that breathlessness improved with xamoterol. However, there was no difference in either the symptoms of fatigue, or exercise duration or total work done. Xamoterol did not affect the number of ventricular premature beats after exercise and had no proarrhythmogenic activity. More patients in the xamoterol group withdrew from the study (19% vs 12%). On intention to treat analysis 9.2% of the xamoterol and 3.7% of the placebo died within 100 days (hazard ratio 2.54, 95% CI 1.04-6.18, $p=0.02$). Death due to progression of heart failure occurred in 1.2% and 4.8% of the placebo and xamoterol groups, while sudden death in 1.8% and 3.7%, respectively.
Conclusions	Xamoterol therapy resulted in excess of mortality and was not associated with objective measures of improvement of exercise capacity. The study was terminated prematurely by the safety committee.

PROMISE

Prospective Randomized Milrinone Survival Evaluation Trial

Title	Effect of milrinone on mortality in severe chronic heart failure.
Authors	Packer M, Carver JR, Rodeheffer RJ, et al.
Reference	N Engl J Med 1991;325:1468–1475.
Disease	Congestive heart failure.
Purpose	To investigate the effects of milrinone on survival of patients with severe chronic heart failure.
Design	Randomized, double blind, placebo controlled, multicenter.
Patients	1088 patients with chronic heart failure NYHA class III–IV, with left ventricular ejection fraction ≤0.35. Patients who received ß-blockers, calcium channel blockers, disopyramide, flecainide, encainide, dopamine, or dobutamine were excluded.
Follow-up	1 day to 20 months (median 6.1 months).
Treatment regimen	Milrinone 10 mg X4/d or placebo PO.
Additional therapy	All patients received digoxin, diuretics, and ACE inhibitors. Nitrates, hydralazine, prazosin, and other vasodilators were permitted.

Results	Mortality was 30% in the milrinone and 24% in the placebo group. Milrinone was associated with a 28% increase in total mortality (95% CI 1-61%, p=0.038), and with 34% increase in cardiovascular mortality (95% CI 6-69%, p=0.016). The adverse effect of milrinone was more pronounced in patients with NYHA class IV (53% increase in mortality, 95% CI 13-107%, p=0.006) than in patients with class III (3% increase, 95% CI -28% to 48%, p=0.86). Milrinone did not have a beneficial effect on survival of any subgroup. Patients treated with milrinone had more hospitalization (44% vs 39%, p=0.041) and more serious adverse cardiovascular reactions, including hypotension (11.4% vs 6.5%, p=0.006) and syncope (8.0% vs 3.8%, p=0.002).
Conclusions	Long term therapy with milrinone increased the mortality and morbidity of patients with severe heart failure.

SOLVD-Treatment Study

Studies of Left Ventricular Dysfunction

Title	a. Studies of left ventricular dysfunction (SOLVD): rationale, design, and methods. 2 trials that evaluate the effect of enalapril in patients with reduced ejection fraction. b. Effect of enalapril on survival in patients with reduced left ventricular ejection fractions and congestive heart failure.
Authors	The SOLVD Investigators.
Reference	a. Am J Cardiol 1990;66:315–322. b. N Engl J Med 1991;325:293–302.
Disease	Congestive heart failure, left ventricular dysfunction.
Purpose	To investigate whether enalapril therapy will reduce mortality and morbidity in patients with chronic heart failure and left ventricular ejection fraction ≤0.35.
Design	Randomized, double blind, placebo controlled, multicenter.
Patients	2569 Patients, age 21–80, with chronic heart failure and left ventricular ejection fraction ≤0.35. Patients with active angina pectoris requiring surgery, unstable angina, myocardial infarction within 1 month, renal failure, or pulmonary disease were excluded. Patients already on ACE inhibitor therapy were excluded. Only patients that could tolerate enalapril 2.5 mg X2/d for 2–7 days were included.
Follow-up	22–55 months (average 41.4 months).
Treatment regimen	Enalapril (2.5 or 5mg X2/d initially, with gradual increase to 10 mg X2/d) or placebo.
Additional therapy	No restriction, except for other ACE inhibitors.

SOLVD-Treatment Study

Studies of Left Ventricular Dysfunction

(continued)

Results	39.7% of the placebo and 35.2% of the enalapril patients died (risk reduction 16%, 95% CI 5–26%, p=0.0036). Cardiovascular deaths occurred in 35.9% and 31.1%, respectively (risk reduction 18% (6–28%), p<0.002). The major difference was in death due to progressive heart failure (19.5% vs 16.3%, risk reduction 22% (6–35%), p=0.0045). 57.3% and 47.7% of the placebo and enalapril patients died or were hospitalized due to heart failure (risk reduction 26% (18–34%), p<0.0001). After 1 year there were 31.2% such events in the placebo and 20.4% in the enalapril (risk reduction 40% (30–48%)). 74% of the placebo and 69% of the enalapril patients were hospitalized at least once (p=0.006), 63% and 57% of the patients were hospitalized for primarily cardiovascular reasons (p<0.001).
Conclusions	Enalapril added to conventional therapy significantly reduced mortality and hospitalizations in patients with chronic heart failure due to systolic dysfunction.

SOLVD (retrospective analysis)

Studies Of Left Ventricular Dysfunction

Title	Racial differences in the outcome of left ventricular dysfunction.
Authors	Dries DL, Exner DV, Gersch BJ et al.
Reference	N Engl J Med 1999; 340:609-616.
Disease	Congestive heart failure.
Purpose	To determine if there were differences in congestive heart failure and outcomes by race in the SOLVD trials (both asymptomatic LV dysfunction and symptomatic LV dysfunction).
Design	As per SOLVD trials.
Patients	4228 patients in prevention trial (asymptomatic LV dysfunction) and 2569 in treatment trial (symptomatic LV dysfunction). Both studies evaluated efficacy of enalapril.
Follow-up	Mean follow-up 34 months in prevention trial, 32 months in treatment trial.
Treatment regimen	Treatment study: Enalapril (2.5 or 5 mg twice a day) with gradual increase to 10 mg twice a day vs placebo. Prevention study: Enalapril 2.5 mg twice a day with gradual increase to 10 mg twice a day vs placebo.

SOLVD (retrospective analysis)

Studies Of Left Ventricular Dysfunction

(continued)

Results	Black patients had higher diastolic blood pressure, serum creatinine concentrations; black patients were younger than white patients and had a higher prevalence of diabetes, prior stroke, and LV dysfunction due to nonischemic etiology. In the treatment study 42% of blacks and 36% of whites died; in the prevention trial 22% of blacks vs 14% of whites died. Mortality rates were 8.1 per 100 person years for blacks and 5.1 per 100 person years for whites in the prevention trial; and 16.7 vs 13.4 in the treatment trial, respectively. Deaths due to pump failure and hospitalization for heart failure were more common in blacks.
Conclusions	Black patients with congestive heart failure are at greater risk of death and for worsening heart failure than are white patients receiving similar therapy. The authors postulated that there could be physiologic differences in renin/angiotensin systems and neuroendocrine systems that explain the differences. Also ACE inhibitors may be less effective in halting disease progression in blacks vs whites.

SOLVD-Prevention Study

Studies Of Left Ventricular Dysfunction

Title	a. Studies of left ventricular dysfunction (SOLVD): Rationale, design, and methods. 2 trials that evaluate the effect of enalapril in patients with reduced ejection fraction. b. Effect of enalapril on mortality and the development of heart failure in asymptomatic patients with reduced left ventricular ejection fractions.
Authors	The SOLVD Investigators.
Reference	a. Am J Cardiol 1990;66:315-322. b. N Engl J Med 1992;327:685-691.
Disease	Congestive heart failure, left ventricular dysfunction.
Purpose	To investigate whether enalapril therapy will reduce mortality and morbidity in asymptomatic patients with left ventricular dysfunction.
Design	Randomized, double blind, placebo controlled, multicenter.
Patients	4228 patients, age 21-80, with left ventricular ejection fraction ≤0.35, who did not receive therapy for heart failure. However, diuretic therapy for hypertension and digoxin for atrial fibrillation were permitted.
Follow-up	Clinical follow-up for an average of 37.4 months (range 14.6-62.0 months).
Treatment regimen	Enalapril (2.5 mg X2/d initially, with gradual increase to 10 mg X2/d) or placebo.
Additional therapy	No restriction, except for other ACE inhibitors.

SOLVD-Prevention Study

Studies Of Left Ventricular Dysfunction

(continued)

Results	Total mortality was 15.8% and 14.8% in the placebo and enalapril groups (reduction of risk 8%, 95% CI -8% to 21%, p=0.30). The difference was entirely due to a reduction in cardiovascular death (14.1% vs 12.6%, respectively, risk reduction 12%, 95% CI -3% to 26%, p=0.12). Heart failure developed in 30.2% vs 20.7% of the placebo and enalapril patients (risk reduction 37%, 95% CI 28% to 44%, p<0.001). The median length of time to development of heart failure was 8.3 vs 22.3 months, respectively. Hospitalization due to heart failure occurred in 12.9% vs 8.7%, respectively (p<0.001). The median length of time to the first hospitalization for heart failure was 13.2 vs 27.8 months, respectively.
Conclusions	Enalapril therapy delayed the development of heart failure and reduced the rate of related hospitalizations among patients with asymptomatic left ventricular dysfunction. There was also a trend toward decreased cardiovascular mortality in the enalapril group.

V-HeFT II

Vasodilator-Heart Failure Trial II

Title	A comparison of enalapril with hydralazine-isosorbide dinitrate in the treatment of chronic congestive heart failure.
Authors	Cohn JN, Johnson G, Zeische S, et al.
Reference	N Engl J Med 1991;325:303–310.
Disease	Congestive heart failure.
Purpose	To compare the effects of hydralazine-isosorbide dinitrate and enalapril in the treatment of congestive heart failure.
Design	Randomized, double blind, multicenter.
Patients	804 men, age 18–75 years, with chronic congestive heart failure (cardiothoracic ratio ≥0.55 on chest radiography, LV internal diameter at diastole >2.7 cm/m² body surface area on echocardiography, or LVEF <0.45 on radionuclide scan) and reduced exercise tolerance. Patients with active angina were excluded.
Follow-up	0.5–5.7 years (mean 2.5 years).
Treatment regimen	1. Enalapril 10 mg X2/d. 2. Hydralazine 75 mg X4/d and isosorbide dinitrate 40 mg X4/d.
Additional therapy	Digoxin and diuretics.

V-HeFT II

Vasodilator-Heart Failure Trial II

(continued)

Results

2 year mortality was lower in the enalapril arm (18%) than the hydralazine arm (25%, $p=0.016$) which was attributed to a reduction of sudden death, especially in patients with NYHA class I or II. The reduction in mortality with enalapril was 33.6%, 28.2%, 14.0%, and 10.3% after 1, 2, 3, and 4 years. Body oxygen consumption at peak exercise was increased after 13 weeks and after 6 months only in the hydralazine-isosorbide dinitrate group ($p<0.05$). However, after 1 year, oxygen consumption began to decline in both groups. Left ventricular ejection fraction increased more during the first 13 weeks in the hydralazine-isosorbide dinitrate group (0.033 vs 0.021, $p<0.03$). However, after 3 years there was no difference between the groups. An increase in the incidence of cough and symptomatic hypotension was noted in the enalapril group and of headache in the hydralazine-isosorbide dinitrate group.

Conclusions

While enalapril improved survival better than hydralazine-isosorbide dinitrate, the improvement of left ventricular ejection fraction and exercise capacity was greater with hydralazine-isosorbide dinitrate. A combination of these drugs may enhance their efficacy.

V-HeFT III

Vasodilator-Heart Failure Trial III

Title	Effect of the calcium antagonist felodipine as supplementary vasodilator therapy in patients with chronic heart failure treated with enalapril.
Author	Cohn JN, Ziesche S, Smith R, et al.
Reference	Circulation 1997;96:856-863.
Disease	Chronic heart failure.
Purpose	1. To determine whether addition of the calcium channel blocker felodipine extended release (ER) to enalapril could improve short term symptoms and exercise capacity over 3 months. 2. To determine with felodipine (ER) could slow the progression of heart failure and improve long term morbidity and mortality.
Design	Randomized, double blind, multicenter.
Patients	450 male patients with chronic heart failure, average age 63-64.
Follow-up	Average 18 months (range 3-39 months).
Treatment regimen	97% of patients were on enalapril, 89% on diuretics. Patients were randomized to felodipine ER (5 mg bid) or placebo.

V-HeFT III

Vasodilator-Heart Failure Trial III

(continued)

Results	There was no difference in long term mortality in the felodipine (13.8%) vs placebo group (12.8%). At 3 months felodipine increased ejection fraction (+2.1%) compared to placebo (-0.1%, p=0.001), but did not improve exercise tolerance, quality of life, or frequency of hospitalizations. There was a trend toward better exercise tolerance and quality of life in the second year of treatment. At 27 months exercise times were significantly better with felodipine than placebo (p=0.01). At 12 months there was no significant difference in ejection fraction between the 2 groups. Edema was more common with felodipine.
Conclusions	Felodipine resulted in a trend toward better exercise tolerance and less depression of quality of life in the second year of treatment. It was well tolerated in heart failure patients but not effective in reducing mortality or improving ejection fraction long term.

MDC

Metoprolol in Dilated Cardiomyopathy

Title	Beneficial effects of metoprolol in idiopathic dilated cardiomyopathy.
Authors	Waagstein F, Bristow MR, Swedberg K, et al.
Reference	Lancet 1993;342:1441-1446.
Disease	Congestive heart failure, dilated cardiomyopathy.
Purpose	To evaluate the effect of metoprolol therapy upon survival and morbidity in patients with dilated cardiomyopathy.
Design	Randomized, double blind, placebo controlled, multicenter.
Patients	383 patients, 16-75 years old, with dilated cardiomyopathy (ejection fraction <0.40). Patients treated with ß-blockers, calcium channel blockers, inotropic drugs (except digoxin), or high doses of tricyclic antidepressant drugs were excluded. Patients with significant coronary artery disease, active myocarditis, chronic obstructive lung disease, insulin dependent diabetes, and alcoholism were not included. Only patients that could tolerate metoprolol 5 mg X2/d for 2-7 days were included.
Follow-up	Clinical follow-up for 12-18 months. Exercise test, right heart catheterization, and radionuclide ventriculography at baseline, 6 and 12 months.
Treatment regimen	Placebo or metoprolol. The target dose was 100-150 mg/d for 12-18 months.
Additional therapy	Digitalis, diuretics, ACE inhibitors, and nitrates were permitted.

Results

The primary end point of death or need for cardiac transplantation was reached by 20.1% of the placebo and 12.9% of the metoprolol group (34% risk reduction, 95% CI -6-62%, p=0.058). 10.1% vs 1.0% of the placebo and metoprolol patients needed cardiac transplantation (p=0.0001). However, there was no difference in mortality alone (10.0% vs 11.9%, respectively). Mean ejection fraction was similar at baseline (0.22±0.09 vs 0.22±0.08). However, ejection fraction increased more in the metoprolol group after 6 months (0.26±0.11 vs 0.32±0.13, p<0.0001 and after 12 months (0.28±0.12 vs 0.34±0.14, p<0.0001. The improvement in ejection fraction was independent of the use of other medications and on the initial ejection fraction. Quality of life improved more in the metoprolol group (p=0.01). Exercise time at 12 months was significantly longer (p=0.046) in the metoprolol group. Heart rate and pulmonary wedge pressure decreased significantly more in the metoprolol than in the placebo group, whereas systolic pressure, stroke volume, and stroke work index increased more with metoprolol.

Conclusions

Metoprolol reduced clinical deterioration, improved symptoms and cardiac function, and was well tolerated. However, mortality was not reduced.

FACET

Flosequinan-ACE Inhibitor Trial

Title	Can further benefit be achieved by adding flosequinan to patients with congestive heart failure who remain symptomatic on diuretic, digoxin, and an ACE inhibitor? Results of the Flosequinan-ACE Inhibitor Trial (FACET).
Authors	Massie BM, Berk MR, Brozena SC, et al.
Reference	Circulation 1993;88:492-501.
Disease	Congestive heart failure.
Purpose	To evaluate whether the addition of flosequinan to ACE inhibitors, diuretics and digoxin will improve exercise tolerance and quality of life of patients with congestive heart failure.
Design	Randomized, double blind, placebo controlled, multicenter.
Patients	322 patients, ≥18 years old, with congestive heart failure ≥12 weeks, left ventricular ejection fraction ≤35%, and were able to exercise to an end point of dyspnea or fatigue. All patients were on ACE inhibitor and diuretic therapy for ≥12 weeks.
Follow-up	Clinical follow-up, 24 h ECG monitoring, and repeated exercise test for 16 weeks.
Treatment regimen	Placebo, flosequinan 100 mg X1/d, or flosequinan 75 mg X2/d. If the heart rate increased by ≥15 bpm, the dose was reduced to 75 mg X1/d or 50 mg X2/d.

FACET

Flosequinan-ACE Inhibitor Trial

(continued)

Additional therapy	Calcium channel blockers, ß- or α-blockers, long acting nitrates, disopyramide or other class Ic antiarrhythmic agents, theophylline, bronchodilators, or other investigational drugs were not permitted.
Results	After 16 weeks, exercise time increased by 64 seconds in the 100 mg/d flosequinan group compared with only 5 seconds in the placebo group ($p<0.05$), whereas the higher dose did not reach statistical significant improvement. Flosequinan 100 mg/d resulted in improvement of the Minnesota Living With Heart Failure Questionnaire (LWHF) score compared with placebo. Both flosequinan doses were associated with improvement of the physical score, whereas the 75 mg X2/d was associated with worsening of the emotional component. NYHA class was improved in 22.0% and worsened in 14.7% of the placebo group, while the corresponding rates for flosequinan 100 mg/d were 30.9% and 16.4%, and for flosequinan 75 mg X2/d 39.3% and 15.7%, respectively. There was no significant difference in mortality, hospitalization for all causes, hospitalization for heart failure, or withdrawal for worsening of heart failure among the groups. There was no increase in ventricular arrhythmias with flosequinan.
Conclusions	Flosequinan resulted in symptomatic benefit when added to ACE inhibitor and diuretic therapy for heart failure. However, in another study, the same dose resulted in an adverse effect on survival.

REFLECT

Randomized Evaluation of Flosequinan on Exercise Tolerance

Title	Double blind, placebo controlled study of the efficacy of flosequinan in patients with chronic heart failure.
Authors	Packer M, Narahara KA, Elkayam U, et al.
Reference	J Am Coll Cardiol 1993;22:65-72.
Disease	Congestive heart failure.
Purpose	To evaluate the effects of flosequinan on symptoms and exercise capacity in patients with chronic heart failure who remained symptomatic despite therapy with digitalis and diuretics.
Design	Randomized, double blind, placebo controlled, multicenter.
Patients	193 patients, ≥18 years old, with dyspnea or fatigue on exertion (NYHA II or III), left ventricular ejection fraction ≤40% and cardiothoracic ratio ≥50%. All patients were symptomatic despite therapy with digitalis and diuretics for ≥2 months. Patients with hypotension, angina, pulmonary renal or hepatic disease, claudication, or myocardial infarction within 3 months were excluded.
Follow-up	12 weeks of clinical follow-up and repeated exercise test and radionuclide ventriculography.
Treatment regimen	Flosequinan 100 mg/d or placebo in addition to diuretic agent and digoxin. If the dose was not tolerated, a dose of 75 mg/d was permitted.
Additional therapy	Use of other vasodilators was not permitted. Use of antiarrhythmic agents, except ß-blockers, was permitted.

REFLECT

Randomized Evaluation of Flosequinan on Exercise Tolerance

(continued)

Results	After 12 weeks, maximal exercise time increased by 96 seconds in the flosequinan vs 47 seconds in the placebo group ($p=0.22$). Maximal oxygen consumption increased by 1.7 vs 0.6 mL/kg/min, respectively ($p=0.05$). By 12 weeks, 55% of the flosequinan vs 36% of the placebo treated patients improved their heart failure symptoms ($p=0.018$), while 10% vs 19% had worsening heart failure ($p=0.07$). Flosequinan did not change the functional class, cardiothoracic ratio, or ejection fraction. 7 vs 2 deaths occurred in the flosequinan and placebo groups, respectively ($p>0.10$).
Conclusions	Flosequinan therapy resulted in symptomatic improvement and an increase in exercise time. However, the effect on survival remains to be determined.

GESICA

Grupo de Estudio de la Sobrevida en la Insuficiencia Cardiaca en Argentina

Title	Randomized trial of low dose amiodarone in severe congestive heart failure.
Authors	Doval HC, Nul DR, Grancelli HO, et al.
Reference	Lancet 1994;344:493–498.
Disease	Congestive heart failure, arrhythmia.
Purpose	To evaluate the effect of low dose amiodarone on survival of patients with severe heart failure.
Design	Randomized, multicenter.
Patients	516 patients with severe heart failure NYHA class II–IV with evidence of cardiac enlargement or reduced ejection fraction ≤0.35. Patients with thyroid dysfunction, concomitant serious disease, valvular heart disease, hypertrophic or restrictive cardiomyopathy, angina pectoris, or history of sustained ventricular arrhythmias were excluded.
Follow-up	2 years.
Treatment regimen	Amiodarone 600 mg/d for 14 d and then 300 mg/d for 2 years.
Additional therapy	Low sodium diet, diuretics, digitalis, and vasodilators. Antiarrhythmic agents were not permitted.

GESICA

Grupo de Estudio de la Sobrevida en la Insuficiencia Cardiaca en Argentina (continued)

Results	Mortality was 41.4% in the control and 33.5% in the amiodarone group (risk reduction 28%, 95% CI 4–45%, p=0.024). Both sudden death and death due to progressive heart failure were reduced. Fewer patients in the amiodarone group died or were hospitalized due to worsening of heart failure (45.8% vs 58.2%, RR 31%, 95% CI 13–46%, p=0.0024). The beneficial effect was evident in all subgroups examined and was independent of the presence of nonsustained ventricular tachycardia. Side effects were reported in 6.1% of the amiodarone group and lead to drug withdrawal in 4.6%.
Conclusions	Low dose amiodarone is a safe and effective treatment for reduction of mortality and morbidity in patients with severe heart failure.

CIBIS

The Cardiac Insufficiency Bisoprolol Study

Title	A randomized trial of ß-blockade in heart failure. The Cardiac Insufficiency Bisoprolol Study (CIBIS).
Authors	CIBIS Investigators and Committees.
Reference	Circulation 1994;90:1765–1773.
Disease	Congestive heart failure.
Purpose	To assess the effects of bisoprolol therapy on mortality in patients with heart failure.
Design	Randomized, double blind, placebo controlled, multicenter.
Patients	641 patients, 18–75 years of age, with chronic heart failure (NYHA class III or IV) treated with diuretics and vasodilators, and left ventricular ejection fraction <40%. Patients with heart failure due to hypertrophic or restrictive cardiomyopathy, or due to mitral or aortic valve disease, or within 3 months of myocardial infarction were excluded. Patients awaiting for coronary artery bypass grafting or cardiac transplantation were not included.
Follow-up	Mean follow-up 1.9±0.1 years.
Treatment regimen	Placebo or bisoprolol. Initial dose was 1.25 mg/d with gradual increase to 5 mg/d.
Additional therapy	Diuretics and a vasodilator therapy. Digitalis and amiodarone were permitted. ß-blockers or mimetic agents and phosphodiesterase inhibitors were prohibited. Only calcium channel blockers of the dihydropyridine type were allowed.

CIBIS

The Cardiac Insufficiency Bisoprolol Study

(continued)

Results	Bisoprolol was well tolerated. Premature withdrawal from treatment occurred in 25.5% of the placebo and 23.4% of the bisoprolol group (p=NS). Bisoprolol did not significantly reduce mortality (20.9% vs 16.6% in the placebo and bisoprolol group, RR 0.80, 95% CI 0.56–1.15, p=0.22). No significant difference was found in sudden death rate (5.3% vs 4.7%, respectively), death due to documented ventricular tachycardia, or fibrillation (2.2% vs 1.3%). However, bisoprolol improved the functional status of the patients. Hospitalization for cardiac decompensation occurred in 28.0% vs 19.1% (p<0.01), and improvement by >1 NYHA class was noted in 15.0% vs 21.3%, respectively (p<0.03).
Conclusions	ß-blockers conferred functional improvement in patients with severe heart failure. However, there was no improvement in survival.

CIBIS-II

The Cardiac Insufficiency Bisoprolol Study II

Title	The cardiac insufficiency study II (CIBIS-II): A randomized trial.
Authors	CIBIS-II Investigators and Committees.
Reference	Lancet 1999;353:9-13.
Disease	Congestive heart failure.
Purpose	To assess the efficacy of bisoprolol, a $ß_1$ selective blocker in decreasing mortality in chronic heart failure.
Design	Randomized, double blind, placebo controlled, multicenter.
Patients	2647 patients with congestive heart failure, 18–80 years old, with LVEF ≤35%, NYHA class III or IV. Clinical condition had to be stable for at least 6 weeks before enrollment. Patients with uncontrolled hypertension, myocardial infarction or unstable angina in the previous 3 months, revascularization within 6 months, previous or scheduled heart transplant, heart block, hypotension, renal failure, reversible obstructive lung disease, or therapy with ß-blockers were excluded.
Follow-up	An average of 1.3 years.
Treatment regimen	Bisoprolol 1.25 mg/d or placebo. The dose was increased gradually up to 10 mg/d if tolerated. There was no run in period.

Additional therapy	Patients had to receive diuretics and a vasodilator (mainly ACE inhibitors). The use of digoxin was optional. Other ß-blockers, calcium antagonists, antiarrhythmic agents (except amiodarone), and inotropic agents (except digitalis) were not permitted.
Results	The trial was terminated prematurely because all cause mortality was significantly less in the bisoprolol treated patients. Mortality was 11.8% in the bisoprolol group vs 17.3% in the placebo group ($p<0.0001$; hazard ratio 0.66; 95% CI 0.54 to 0.81). Cardiovascular mortality was 12% in the placebo and 9% in the bisoprolol group (hazard ratio 0.71; 95% CI 0.56 to 0.90; $p=0.0049$). Readmissions to hospital occurred less often in the bisoprolol group (33% vs 39%; hazard ratio 0.80; 95% CI 0.71 to 0.91; $p=0.0006$). The combined end point of cardiovascular death and admission to hospital for cardiovascular reason occurred less often in the bisoprolol group (29% vs 35%; hazard ratio 0.79; 95% CI 0.69 to 0.90; $p=0.0004$). Permanent treatment withdrawal occurred in the same rate (15%) in both groups. Subgroup analysis revealed that bisoprolol was effective in reducing mortality among patients with ischemic heart disease, idiopathic cardiomyopathy, and in patients with valvular or hypertensive etiology. Similarly, bisoprolol was effective both among patients with NYHA class III and IV. 43% of the patients reached the target bisoprolol dose of 10 mg/d, 12% received 7.5 mg/d, and 13% received 5.0 mg/d.
Conclusions	Bisoprolol therapy was well tolerated and reduced mortality and hospitalization rates in patients with stable congestive heart failure.

Title	Long term evaluation of treatment for chronic heart failure: A 1 year comparative trial of flosequinan and captopril.
Authors	Cowley AJ, McEntegart DJ, Hampton JR, et al.
Reference	Cardiovasc Drugs Ther 1994;8:829–836.
Disease	Congestive heart failure.
Purpose	To compare the efficacy of flosequinan and captopril in patients with moderate to severe heart failure who remained symptomatic despite optimal diuretic therapy.
Design	Randomized, double blind, multicenter.
Patients	209 patients with moderate to severe heart failure (NYHA class III–IV) despite ≥80 mg frusemide/d or an equivalent diuretic, and a cardiothoracic ratio >50% on a standard chest x-ray. Patients treated with vasodilators were excluded.
Follow-up	12 months of clinical follow-up and either repeated exercise test or corridor walk test.
Treatment regimen	Flosequinan (50 mg/d for 2 weeks and then 100 mg/d for 2 weeks and 150 mg/d thereafter) or captopril 12.5 mg X3/d for 2 weeks, 25 mg X3/d for additional 2 weeks and then, 50 mg X3/d.
Additional therapy	Other vasodilators were not permitted.

Results	64% of the flosequinan vs 40% of the captopril groups failed to complete the study due to death or withdrawal ($p<0.001$). There was no statistically significant difference in mortality (18.6% in the flosequinan vs 14.0% in the captopril groups, 38% increase risk of death with flosequinan, 95% CI -30% to 172%, $p=0.29$). Worsening of heart failure occurred in 12.7% vs 10.3%, respectively. There were more adverse effects in the flosequinan treated patients. Both medications had similar effects on treadmill exercise test. The mean increase in exercise time at 52 weeks was 117 vs 156 seconds in the flosequinan and captopril groups ($p=0.57$). The increase in corridor walk distance was 40 vs 62 meters, respectively ($p=0.015$).
Conclusions	Flosequinan had comparable long term efficacy to captopril. However, it is associated with a higher incidence of adverse events.

Carvedilol in Congestive Heart Failure Due to Ischemic Heart Disease

Title	a. Effects of carvedilol, a vasodilator ß-blocker, in patients with congestive heart failure due to ischemic heart disease. b. Randomized, placebo controlled trial of carvedilol in patients with congestive heart failure due to ischaemic heart disease.
Authors	a. Australia-New Zealand Heart Failure Research Collaborative Group.
Reference	a. Circulation 1995;92:212-218. b. Lancet 1997;349:375-380.
Disease	Congestive heart failure.
Purpose	To evaluate the effects of carvedilol on symptoms, exercise performance, and left ventricular function in patients with heart failure due to coronary artery disease.
Design	Randomized, double blind, placebo controlled, multicenter.
Patients	415 patients, with chronic stable heart failure NYHA class II or III due to ischemic heart disease, left ventricular ejection fraction of <45%. Patients with systolic blood pressure <90 mm Hg, heart rate of <50/min, heart block, coronary event or procedure within 4 weeks, primary myocardial or valvular disease, insulin dependent diabetes, chronic obstructive airway disease, renal impairment, current therapy with verapamil, ß-blockers, or agonists were excluded.
Follow-up	a. Clinical follow-up for 6 months and repeated exercise test, radionuclide ventriculography, and echocardiography at 6 months have been reported. b. Left ventricular radionuclide ventriculography, echocardiography, treadmill exercise duration, and clinical follow-up at baseline, 6 and 12 months. Average follow-up of 19 months.
Treatment regimen	2-3 weeks of open label carvedilol, started at 3.125 mgX2/d and increased to 6.25 mgX2/d. Patients who could tolerate the dose were randomized to placebo or carvedilol with gradual increments of the dose towards 25 mgX2/d.
Additional therapy	Patients were treated with conventional therapy including ACE inhibitors, diuretics, and digoxin.

Results

a. A total of 30 patients in the carvedilol vs 13 in the placebo group withdrew from the study (p=0.01), but no single cause accounted for the difference. After 6 months, left ventricular ejection fraction increased by 5.2% in the carvedilol group compared with placebo (95% CI 3.7%-6.8%, p<0.0001). Left ventricular end diastolic diameter did not change from baseline to 6 months of follow-up in the placebo group (68.1 vs 68.3 mm, respectively), whereas it decreased in the carvedilol group (69.5 mm at baseline vs 68.3 mm at 6 months, p=0.048 for the difference between the groups). Left ventricular end systolic diameter did not change in the placebo group (56.1 vs 56.1 mm, respectively) whereas it decreased in the carvedilol group (57.3 mm at baseline vs 55.0 mm at follow-up, p=0.0005 for the difference between the groups). There was no change in exercise time between the groups after 6 months (mean difference -22 seconds, 95% CI -59–15 seconds). There was no difference in 6 min walk distance between the groups (mean difference -6 meter, 95% CI -18–6 meter). The severity of symptoms was unchanged in 67% of the of the placebo vs 65% of the carvedilol treated patients. However, 28% of the placebo vs 23% of the carvedilol patients were improved according to NYHA classification, while 5% vs 12% were worsened (p=0.05). The same trend was present using the Specific Activity Scale (p=0.02).
b. By the end of the follow-up, the numbers of withdrawals from the 2 groups were comparable (41 vs 30 in the carvedilol and placebo groups, respectively, p>0.1). After 12 months, left ventricular ejection fraction increased from 28.4% at baseline to 33.5% among the carvedilol assigned patients, whereas left ventricular ejection fraction did not change much in the placebo treated group. Therefore, at 12 months, left ventricular ejection fraction was 5.3% higher in the carvedilol than placebo group (p<0.0001). After 12 months, left ventricular end-diastolic and end systolic dimensions were 1.7 mm (p=0.06) and 3.2 mm (p=0.001) smaller in the carvedilol compared with the placebo group. There was no clear differences between the groups in 6 min walk distance, treadmill exercise duration, NYHA class, or Specific Activity Scale. After 19 months, there was no difference between the groups in the incidence of worsening of heart failure (82 vs 75 of the carvedilol and placebo groups; relative risk 1.12; 95% CI 0.82–1.53) and mortality (20 vs 26, respectively; relative risk 0.76; 95% CI 0.42–1.36; p>0.1). However, the rate of death or hospitalization was lower in the carvedilol group (104 vs 131; relative risk 0.74; 95% CI 0.57–0.95; p=0.02).

Carvedilol in Congestive Heart Failure Due to Ischemic Heart Disease

(continued)

Conclusion	a. In patients with heart failure due to coronary artery disease, 6 month therapy with carvedilol improved left ventricular function, but symptoms were slightly worsened. b. 12 months of carvedilol therapy resulted in improvement in left ventricular ejection fraction and a decrease in end systolic and end diastolic dimensions. There was an overall reduction in the combined end point of death or hospitalization. However, there was no effect on mortality, exercise performance, symptoms, or episodes of worsening of heart failure.

Amiodarone in Patients With Congestive Heart Failure and Asymptomatic Ventricular Arrhythmia

Title	a. Amiodarone in patients with congestive heart failure and asymptomatic ventricular arrhythmia. b. Effect of amiodarone on clinical status and left ventricular function in patients with congestive heart failure.
Authors	a. Singh SN, Fletcher RD, Fisher SG, et al. b. Massie BM, Fisher SG, Deedwania PC, et al.
Reference	a. N Engl J Med 1995;333:77-82. b. Circulation 1996;93:2128-2134.
Disease	Congestive heart failure, arrhythmia.
Purpose	To evaluate the efficacy of amiodarone to reduce mortality in patients with heart failure and asymptomatic ventricular arrhythmias.
Design	Randomized, double blind, placebo controlled, multicenter.
Patients	674 patients with congestive heart failure, left ventricular ejection fraction of ≤0.40, and ≥10 PVCs/h, unaccompanied by symptoms.
Follow-up	Clinical follow-up and repeated 24 h ambulatory ECG monitoring for >1 year (median follow-up 45 months, range 0-54 months).
Treatment regimen	Placebo or amiodarone 800 mg/d for 14 days, then 400 mg/d for 50 weeks, and then 300 mg/d until the end of the study.
Additional treatment	All patients received vasodilator therapy. Digoxin and diuretics were permitted.

Amiodarone in Patients With Congestive Heart Failure and Asymptomatic Ventricular Arrhythmia

(continued)

Results	During follow-up 39% of the amiodarone vs 42% of the placebo patients died (p=NS). The overall actuarial survival at 2 years was 69.4% vs 70.8%, respectively (p=0.6). At 2 years the rate of sudden death was 15% vs 19% in amiodarone and placebo (p=0.43). Amiodarone had no effect on mortality among patients with ischemic heart disease. However, there was a trend toward less mortality with amiodarone therapy among the 193 patients with nonischemic heart disease (p=0.07). Survival without cardiac death or hospitalization for heart failure was significantly reduced in amiodarone treated patients with nonischemic heart disease (relative risk 0.56 (95% CI 0.36-0.87); p=0.01), but not in patients with ischemic heart disease (relative risk 0.95 (0.73-1.24); p=0.69). Amiodarone was effective in suppressing ventricular arrhythmias. While left ventricular ejection fraction was comparable at baseline (24.9±8.3% in the amiodarone vs 25.7±8.2% in the placebo), ejection fraction was significantly improved in the amiodarone group (at 24 months 35.4±11.5% vs 29.8±12.2, p<0.001). However, this increase in ejection fraction was not associated with greater clinical improvement, less diuretic requirements, or fewer hospitalization for heart failure.
Conclusions	Although amiodarone therapy suppressed ventricular tachyarrhythmias and improved left ventricular function, it was not associated with improved outcome, except for reduction of cardiac mortality and hospitalization for heart failure among patients with nonischemic cardiomyopathy.

MEXIS

Metoprolol and Xamoterol Infarction Study

Title	a. Effects of ß-receptor antagonists in patients with clinical evidence of heart failure after myocardial infarction: double blind comparison of metoprolol and xamoterol. b. Effects of ß-receptor antagonists on left ventricular function in patients with clinical evidence of heart failure after myocardial infarction.A double blind comparison of metoprolol and xamoterol. Echocardiographic results from the metoprolol and xamoterol infarction study (MEXIS).
Authors	a. Persson H, Rythe'n-Alder E, Melcher A, et al. b. Persson H, Eriksson SV, Erhardt L.
Reference	a. Br Heart J 1995;74:140-148. b. Eur Heart J 1996;17:741-749.
Disease	Congestive heart failure.
Purpose	To compare the effects of xamoterol and metoprolol on exercise time in patients with mild to moderate heart failure after myocardial infarction.
Design	Randomized, double blind, single center.
Patients	210 patients, age 40-80 years, with evidence of heart failure at any time during the 5-7 days after myocardial infarction. Patients with NYHA class IV, hypertrophic cardiomyopathy, aortic stenosis, pulmonary disease, or unstable angina were excluded.
Follow-up	12 months of clinical follow-up and repeated exercise test and echocardiography.
Treatment regimen	Metoprolol 50 mgX2/d or xamoterol 100 mgX2/d for 1 day, and then the dose was doubled.The lowest dose allowed was 50 mg/d metoprolol and 100 mg/d xamoterol.

Metoprolol and Xamoterol Infarction Study (continued)

Additional therapy	Diuretics, digitalis, nitrates, and ACE inhibitors were allowed. Calcium channel blockers were not permitted.
Results	a. Exercise time increased at 3 months by 22% in the metoprolol and 29% in the xamoterol groups (p=NS). Improvements in quality of life, clinical signs of heart failure, and NYHA class were seen in both groups over 1 year. Breathlessness improved only with xamoterol (p=0.003 and p=0.046 vs metoprolol after 3 and 6 months, however, there was no difference at 12 months). 18 vs 22 patients of the metoprolol and xamoterol groups withdrew from the study during 1 year. 5 and 6 patients of the metoprolol and xamoterol patients died. b. In the xamoterol treated patients, there was an increase in E-point septal separation from 12.2 mm at baseline to 13.2 mm after 12 months, whereas in the metoprolol group it decreased from 12.4 mm to 11.1 mm (p<0.005). Fractional shortening decreased in the xamoterol group (from 26.0% to 25.0%) and increased in the metoprolol group (from 25.8% to 26.9%) (p<0.05). There were no significant differences between the groups concerning left ventricular end systolic and end diastolic dimensions.
Conclusions	a. The efficacy of xamoterol and metoprolol in improving exercise tolerance, quality of life, and signs of heart failure were comparable. b. In contrast to metoprolol, xamoterol therapy was associated with impairment of left ventricualr systolic function in patients with heart failure after myocardial infarction.

Carvedilol Heart Failure Study

Title	The effect of carvedilol on morbidity and mortality in patients with chronic heart failure.
Authors	Packer M, Bristow MR, Cohn JN, et al.
Reference	N Engl J Med 1996;334:1349–1355.
Disease	Congestive heart failure.
Purpose	To evaluate the effects of carvedilol, a nonselective ß-blocker that also blocks α_1-receptors and has antioxidant properties, on survival and hospitalization of patients with chronic heart failure.
Design	Randomized, double blind, placebo controlled, multicenter.
Patients	1094 patients with symptomatic heart failure for ≥3 months and left ventricular ejection fraction ≤0.35, despite ≥2 months of treatment with diuretics and an ACE inhibitor. Patients with primary valvular heart disease, active myocarditis, ventricular tachycardia or advanced heart block not controlled by antiarrhythmic intervention, or a pacemaker were excluded. Patients with systolic blood pressure >160 or <85 mm Hg, heart rate <68 bpm, major cardiovascular event or surgery within 3 months, comorbidity that could affect survival or limit exercise capacity, or patients treated with ß-blocker, calcium channel antagonist, or class IC or III antiarrhythmics were not included.
Follow-up	6 months (12 months for the group with mild heart failure).

(continued)

Treatment regimen	During the open label phase, all patients received carvedilol 6.25 mgX2/d for 2 weeks. Patients who tolerated the drug were randomized on the basis of their baseline exercise capacity to 1 of 4 treatment protocols. Within each of the 4 protocols patients with mild, moderate, or severe heart failure were randomized to either carvedilol 12.5–50 mgX2/d or placebo.
Additional therapy	Treatment with digoxin, hydralazine, or nitrate were permitted.
Results	Of the 1197 patients that had entered the open label phase, 5.6% failed to complete the period due to adverse effects. Another 3.0% violated the protocol. 1094 patients were randomized to the double blind stage. The overall mortality was 7.8% in the placebo and 3.2% in the carvedilol group (65% reduction of risk, 95% CI 39–80%; $p<0.001$). Death from progressive heart failure was 3.3% in the placebo vs 0.7% in the carvedilol group. Sudden death occurred in 3.8% vs 1.7% of the placebo and carvedilol groups. The reduction in mortality was similar regardless of age, sex, the cause of heart failure, ejection fraction, exercise tolerance, systolic blood pressure, or heart rate. During the follow-up 19.6% vs 14.1% of the placebo and carvedilol groups were hospitalized at least once for cardiovascular causes (27% reduction of risk, 95% CI 3–45%; $p=0.036$). The combined end point of hospitalization for cardiovascular causes or death was reduced by 38% (24.6% vs 15.8% in the placebo and carvedilol group; 95% CI 18–53%, $p<0.001$).
Conclusions	Carvedilol reduces the risk of death and the risk of hospitalization for cardiovascular causes in patients with heart failure who are receiving treatment with digoxin, diuretics, and ACE inhibitor.

MOCHA

Multicenter Oral Carvedilol Heart failure Assessment

Title	Carvedilol produces dose related improvements in left ventricular function and survival in subjects with chronic heart failure.
Authors	Bristow MR, Gilbert EM, Abraham WT, et al.
Reference	Circulation 1996;94:2807-2816.
Disease	Congestive heart failure.
Purpose	To asses the dose response characteristics of carvedilol in patients with chronic heart failure.
Design	Randomized, double blind, placebo controlled, dose response evaluation, multicenter.
Patients	345 patients, aged 18 to 85 years, with left ventricular ejection fraction ≤0.35 and symptoms of stable heart failure for ≥3 months. All patients had to be treated with diuretics and ACE inhibitor for ≥1 month before entry. Patients had to be able to walk 150 to 450 m on the 6 min walk test. Patients with heart rate <68 bpm, uncorrected valvular disease, hypertrophic cardiomyopathy, uncontrolled ventricular tachycardia, sick sinus syndrome, advanced AV block, symptomatic peripheral vascular disease, severe concomitant disease, a stroke or myocardial infarction within 3 months, hypertension, or hypotension were excluded. A PTCA, CABG, or transplantation could not be planned or be likely for the 6 months after entry. Only patients that completed a 2 to 4 week challenge phase of open label carvedilol 6.25 mgX2/d were included.
Follow-up	6 months.

MOCHA

Multicenter Oral Carvedilol Heart failure Assessment (continued)

Treatment regimen	Randomization to: 1. Placebo; 2. Carvedilol 6.25 mgX2/d; 3. Carvedilol 12.5 mgX2/d; or 4. Carvedilol 25 mgX2/d.
Additional therapy	Diuretic therapy was mandatory. ACE inhibitors were recommended. Digoxin, hydralazine, and nitrates were permitted, if they had been started ≥2 months before entry. Calcium channel blockers, flosequinan, α- or ß-blockers, antiarrhythmic agents, and monoamine oxidase inhibitors were not permitted.
Results	92% of subjects tolerated the open label challenge period. Carvedilol therapy was not associated with an improvement in either the 6 min corridor walk test or the 9 min self-powered treadmill test. Similarly, there was no difference in the Minnesota Living With Heart Failure Questionnaire scores among the groups. However, carvedilol therapy resulted in a dose related increase in left ventricular ejection fraction (by 5, 6, and 8% ejection fraction units in the low, medium, and high dose carvedilol, compared with only 2 units in the placebo group; $p<0.001$ for the linear dose response). Carvedilol improved ejection fraction both in patients with ischemic and with nonischemic cardiomyopathy. Carvedilol therapy was associated with lower cardiovascular hospitalization rate (mean number of hospitalization per patient 0.36, 0.14, 0.15, and 0.13, for the placebo, lower, medium and high carvedilol dose, respectively; $p=0.003$ for linear trend). Moreover, carvedilol reduced mortality (from 15.5% in the placebo group to 6.0% ($p<0.05$), 6.7% ($p=0.07$), and 1.1% ($p<0.001$) in the low, medium and high carvedilol dose; $p<0.001$ for the linear trend). The reduction in mortality occurred both in patients with ischemic and nonischemic cardiomyopathy. When the 3 carvedilol groups were combined, mortality risk was 73% lower than in the placebo group (relative risk 0.272; 95% CI 0.124 to 0.597; $p<0.001$).
Conclusions	In subjects with mild to moderate heart failure due to systolic dysfunction and who can tolerate carvedilol therapy, carvedilol treatment resulted in dose related improvement in LV function and reduction in mortality and hospitalization rates.

Title	Carvedilol inhibits clinical progression in patients with mild symptoms of heart failure.
Authors	Colucci WS, Packer M, Bristow MR, et al.
Reference	Circulation 1996;94:2800–2806.
Disease	Congestive heart failure.
Purpose	To evaluate the effect of carvedilol in patients with mildly symptomatic heart failure.
Design	Randomized, double blind, placebo controlled, dose response evaluation, multicenter.
Patients	366 patients, 18–85 years old, with chronic stable symptomatic heart failure despite treatment with diuretics and an ACE inhibitor, and left ventricular ejection fraction ≤0.35. Patients with primary valvular disease; hypertrophic cardiomyopathy; symptomatic ventricular arrhythmias; myocardial infarction, unstable angina or CABG within 3 months; likelihood for revascularization or transplantation within 12 months; sick sinus syndrome or high degree AV block; hypotension or hypertension; or serious concomitant disease were excluded. Only patients who were able to walk 450–550 m on a 6 min walk test and tolerated a carvedilol 6.25 mgX2/d during a 2 week challenge open label phase were included in this protocol.
Follow-up	12 months of maintenance phase.

(continued)

Treatment regimen	Randomization in a 2:1 ratio to carvedilol (n=232) or placebo (n=134). There was an initial 2-6 week double blind up-titration phase, beginning at 12.5 mgX2/d (maximum 25 mgX2/d for patients <85 kg; 50 mgX2/d for heavier patients).
Additional therapy	Diuretics and an angiotesnin converting enzyme inhibitor. Digoxin, hydralazine, and nitrates were allowed. Antiarrhythmic drugs, calcium channel blockers, α or ß-blockers, flosequinan, and monoamine oxidase inhibitors were prohibited.
Results	Clinical progression of heart failure (defined as death due to heart failure, hospitalization for heart failure, or the need for a sustained increase in heart failure medications) occurred in 21% of the placebo group and in 11% of the carvedilol group (relative risk 0.52; 95% CI 0.32 to 0.85; p=0.008). This favorable effect was not influenced by gender, age, race, etiology of heart failure, or baseline left ventricular ejection fraction. 4.0% vs 0.9% of the placebo and carvedilol treated patients died (risk ratio 0.231; 95% CI 0.045 to 1.174; p=0.048). NYHA functional class improved in 12% of the carvedilol treated patients vs 9% of the placebo-treated patients, whereas it worsened in 4% vs 15%, respectively (p=0.003). During the study more carvedilol than placebo treated patients stated that their symptoms improved (75% vs 60%; p=0.013). Similarly, the physician global assessment rated improvement in 69% vs 47% of the patients, respectively (p=0.001). However, there was no difference in the quality of life scores and the distance walked in 9 min treadmill test between the groups. At follow-up, the mean increase in left ventricular ejection fraction was larger in the carvedilol (0.10) than in the placebo (0.03) patients (p<0.001). The drug was well tolerated.
Conclusions	In patients with mildly symptomatic stable heart failure due to systolic dysfunction and who could tolerate carvedilol treatment, carvedilol reduced clinical progression of heart failure and mortality.

PRECISE

Prospective Randomized Evaluation of Carvedilol on Symptoms and Exercise

Title	Double blind, placebo controlled study of the effects of carvedilol in patients with moderate to severe heart failure. The Precise Trial.
Authors	Packer M, Colucci WS, Sackner-Bernstein JD, et al.
Reference	Circulation 1996;94:2793–2799.
Disease	Congestive heart failure.
Purpose	To evaluate the effect of carvedilol in patients with moderate to severe heart failure.
Design	Randomized, double blind, placebo controlled, dose response evaluation, multicenter.
Patients	278 patients, with chronic stable symptomatic heart failure despite treatment with diuretics and an ACE inhibitor for ≥2 months, and left ventricular ejection fraction ≤0.35. Patients with primary valvular disease; active myocarditis; restrictive or hypertrophic cardiomyopathy; symptomatic ventricular arrhythmias; myocardial infarction, unstable angina or CABG within 3 months; angina that limits exercise capacity; sick sinus syndrome or high degree AV block; hypotension or hypertension; stroke; peripheral vascular or pulmonary disease; or serious concomitant disease were excluded. Patients receiving antiarrhythmic drugs, calcium channel blockers, or α- or ß-blockers or agonists, were not included. Only patients who were able to walk 150–450 m on a 6 min walk test and tolerated carvedilol 6.25 mgX2/d during a 2 week challenge open label phase were included in this protocol.
Follow-up	Maintenance phase of 6 months.

PRECISE

Prospective Randomized Evaluation of Carvedilol on Symptoms and Exercise

(continued)

Treatment regimen	Randomization to placebo or carvedilol 12.5 mgX2/d.The dose was increased gradually to 25 mgX2/d (50 mgX2/d for patients >85 kg)
Additional therapy	Diuretics and an ACE inhibitor. Digoxin, hydralazine, and nitrates were allowed. Antiarrhythmic drugs, calcium channel blockers, α- or ß-blockers, or agonists were prohibited.
Results	Of the 301 patients entering the open label phase, 23 (8%) did not complete it (17 patients due to adverse effects). By intention-to-treat analysis, the 6 min walk distance increased by 9 meters in the carvedilol and decreased by 3 meters in the placebo group (p=0.048). There was no difference between the groups on the 9 min treadmill test and in quality of life scores. Carvedilol was associated with greater improvement in NYHA class (p=0.014). Whereas the proportion of patients with NYHA class III or IV remains unchanged in the placebo group (from 58% to 51%), it decreased in the carvedilol treated patients (from 64% to 41%). A deterioration in NYHA class was observed in 3% of the carvedilol group vs 15% of the placebo group (p=0.001). Global assessment of disease severity by the patients and by the physicians revealed greater improvement with carvedilol than placebo. Left ventricular ejection fraction increased by 0.08 and 0.03 U with carvedilol and placebo therapy (p<0.001). 16.5% of the carvedilol treated patients vs 25.5% of the placebo group had a cardiovascular hospitalization (p=0.06), and 4.5% vs 7.6% died (p=0.26). Death or cardiovascular hospitalization occurred in 19.6% of the carvedilol group vs 31.0% of the placebo group (p=0.029). The effects of carvedilol were similar in patients with ischemic or nonischemic cardiomyopathy.
Conclusions	In patients with moderate to severe stable heart failure due to systolic dysfunction who are treated with diuretics, ACE inhibitors and digoxin, and can tolerate carvedilol treatment, carvedilol produces clinical benefits.

DiDi

Diltiazem in Dilated Cardiomyopathy

Title	Diltiazem improves cardiac function and exercise capacity in patients with idiopathic dilated cardiomyopathy. Results of the diltiazem in dilated cardiomyopathy trial.
Authors	Figulla HR, Gietzen F, Zeymer U, et al.
Reference	Circulation 1996;94:346-352.
Disease	Dilated cardiomyopathy.
Purpose	To evaluate whether diltiazem in addition to conventional therapy improves survival, hemodynamics, and well-being in patients with idiopathic dilated cardiomyopathy.
Design	Randomized, double blind, placebo controlled, multicenter.
Patients	186 patients, 18-70 years old, with idiopathic dilated cardiomyopathy (LVEF<0.50). Patients with hypertension, 2nd or 3rd degree AV block, valvular or congenital heart disease, coronary artery disease, active myocarditis, insulin dependent diabetes, or systemic disease were excluded. Patients with previous treatment with any calcium antagonist or ß-blocker for >3 months were not included.
Follow-up	Coronary angiography with left heart catheterization, pulmonary artery catheterization at rest and during supine ergometry, 24 h ambulatory ECG monitoring, echocardiography, radionuclide ventriculography, endomyocardial biopsy, plasma norepinephrine and ergorespirometry at baseline. Patients were followed every 6 months for 2 years.
Treatment regimen	Placebo or diltiazem started at 30 mgX3/d. Target dose was 90 mgX3/d or 60 mgX3/d (for patients weighing ≤50 kg).

DiDi

Diltiazem in Dilated Cardiomyopathy (continued)

Additional therapy	Any other calcium antagonist or ß-blocker was prohibited. ACE inhibitors, digitalis, diuretics, and nitrates were prescribed as needed.
Results	33 patients dropped out of the study (13 receiving placebo and 20 receiving diltiazem). 24 month survival was 80.6% for the placebo vs 83.3% for the diltiazem group ($p=0.78$). Of the 153 patients that finished the protocol, 27 died or had a listing for heart transplantation (16 in the placebo and 11 in the diltiazem). The transplant listing-free survival was 85% for diltiazem vs 80% for the placebo ($p=0.44$). After 2 years, only the diltiazem group had an increase in cardiac index at rest (0.37±1.40 vs 0.33±1.14 L/min in the placebo, $p=0.011$), cardiac index at workload (0.57±1.52 vs 0.33±1.81 L/min, $p=0.017$), stroke volume index (8±24 vs 3±18 mL/m^2, $p=0.003$), and stroke work index (15±31 vs 5±20 g • min • m^{-2}, $p=0.000$), and decreased pulmonary artery pressure under workload (-5.2±12.2 vs -3.4±10.9 mm Hg, $p=0.007$). Diltiazem increased exercise capacity (180±450 vs 60±325 W • min, $p=0.002$), and subjective well being ($p= 0.01$). Adverse effects were minor and evenly distributed in both groups.
Conclusions	Diltiazem improves cardiac function, exercise capacity, and subjective status in patients with idiopathic dilated cardiomyopathy without deleterious effects on transplant listing free survival.

PRAISE

Prospective Randomized Amlodipine Survival Evaluation trial

Title	Effect of amlodipine on morbidity and mortality in severe chronic heart failure.
Authors	Packer M, O'Connor CM, Ghali JK, et al.
Reference	N Engl J Med 1996;335:1107–1114.
Disease	Congestive heart failure.
Purpose	To evaluate the long term effect of amlodipine, a calcium channel blocker, on mortality and morbidity in patients with advanced congestive heart failure.
Design	Randomized, double blind, placebo controlled, multicenter.
Patients	1153 patients with congestive heart failure (NYHA class IIIB or IV) and left ventricular ejection fraction <0.30, despite therapy with digoxin, diuretics, and an ACE inhibitor. Patients with uncorrected primary valvular disease, active myocarditis, constrictive pericarditis, history of cardiac arrest or who had sustained ventricular fibrillation or tachycardia within the previous year, unstable angina or acute myocardial infarction within the previous month, cardiac revascularization or stroke within 3 months, severe concomitant disease, hypotension or hypertension, or serum creatinine >3.0 mg/dL were excluded.
Follow-up	6 to 33 months (median 13.8 months).
Treatment regimen	Randomization to amlodipine or placebo. The initial dose of amlodipine was 5 mg X1/d for two weeks and than increased to 10 mg/d.
Additional therapy	Diuretics, digoxin, and an ACE inhibitor. Nitrates were permitted, but other vasodilators, ß-blockers, calcium channel blockers, and, class IC antiarrhythmic agents were prohibited.

Results	Of the patients with ischemic heart disease, 370 were assigned to placebo and 362 to amlodipine. Of the patients with nonischemic cardiomyopathy, 212 were assigned to placebo and 209 patients to amlodipine. A primary end point of the study (mortality from all causes or cardiovascular morbidity, defined as hospitalization for ≥24 h for pulmonary edema, severe hypoperfusion, acute myocardial infarction, or ventricular tachycardia/fibrillation) was reached by 39% of the amlodipine treated patients and in 42% of the placebo group. Amlodipine therapy was associated with insignificant risk reduction of primary end points (9%; 95% CI 24% reduction to 10% increase; p=0.31). 33% vs 38% of the amlodipine and control groups died, respectively (16% risk reduction; 95% CI 31% reduction to 2% increase; p=0.07). Among patients with ischemic etiology, amlodipine therapy did not affect mortality or the combined end point of mortality and cardiovascular morbidity. 45% of the patients in both groups had a fatal or non fatal event, and 40% of the patients in both groups died. However, in patients with nonischemic cardiomyopathy amlodipine was associated with better outcome. Primary end point was reached by 36.8% of the placebo, but in only 27.8% of the amlodipine group (31% risk reduction; 95% CI 2% to 51% reduction; p=0.04). Mortality was 34.9% vs 21.5% in the placebo and amlodipine group, respectively (46% risk reduction; 95% CI 21% to 63% reduction; p<0.001). Subgroup analysis revealed that amlodipine therapy was not associated with adverse effects in any of the subgroups. A favorable effect on survival was found only in patients without a history of angina. Total adverse effects that mandated discontinuation of double blind therapy was comparable between the groups. However, peripheral edema (27% vs 18%, p<0.001) and pulmonary edema (15% vs 10%, p=0.01) occurred more frequently in the amlodipine group, while uncontrolled hypertension (2% vs <1%, p=0.03) and symptomatic cardiac ischemia (31% vs 25% among patients with ischemic heart disease, p=0.07) was more frequent in the placebo than amlodipine group. The frequencies of myocardial infarction, arrhythmias, and worsening of heart failure were similar.
Conclusions	Amlodipine was not associated with increased mortality and morbidity among patients with severe congestive heart failure. Amlodipine was associated with better outcome in patients with nonischemic cardiomyopathy, whereas in patients with ischemic heart disease there was no difference in outcome.

PICO

Pimobendan in Congestive Heart Failure

Title	Effect of pimobendan on exercise capacity in patients with heart failure: Main results from the Pimobendan In Congestive Heart Failure (PICO) trial.
Authors	The Pimobendan in Congestive Heart Failure (PICO) Investigators.
Reference	Heart 1996;76:223-231.
Disease	Congestive heart failure.
Purpose	To assess the effects of pimobendan, a positive inotropic agent, on exercise capacity in patients with congestive heart failure.
Design	Randomized, double blind, placebo controlled, multicenter.
Patients	317 patients, ≥18 years old, with stable chronic heart failure (NYHA class II-III), and left ventricular ejection fraction of ≤0.45. Patients with stenotic, obstructive, or infectious cardiac disease, exercise capacity limited by angina, on waiting list for transplantation, acute myocardial infarction, coronary revascularization, episodes of syncope or cardiac arrest within 3 months, AICD implantation, or severe concomitant disease were excluded. Patients in whom a first testing dose of pimobendan caused significant intolerance were excluded.
Follow-up	24 weeks of therapy with repeated exercise tests (efficacy phase). Clinical follow-up for a mean of 11 months.
Treatment regimen	Randomized to placebo or pimobendan 1.25 or 2.5 mg twice a day.

PICO

Pimobendan in Congestive Heart Failure (continued)

Additional therapy	An ACE inhibitor and a diuretic were mandatory. Digitalis, nitrates, and molsidomine were permitted. Other inotropic agents, phosphodiesterase inhibitors, ibopamine, antiarrhythmic agents (except amiodarone), ß-blockers, calcium antagonists, and other vasodilators were prohibited.
Results	Exercise duration on bicycle ergometry of the 2.5 mg/d pimobendan treated patients was 13, 27, and 29 sec longer than that of the placebo treated patients, after 4, 12, and 24 weeks of therapy, respectively (p=0.03), and in the 5 mg/d treated patients it was 19, 17, and 28 sec longer than that of the placebo group (p=0.05). After 24 weeks of therapy there was no difference in the percent of patients still alive and able to exercise to at least the baseline level (63% of the pimobendan group vs 59% of the placebo group; p=0.5). Pimobendan did not affect oxygen consumption or quality of life (assessed by questionnaire). 4% of the placebo vs 10% of the pimobendan treated patients did not worsen or die and were in better NYHA class at least once during follow-up than at baseline (p=0.06). Double blind therapy was stopped or reduced more often in the pimobendan than placebo treated group (p=0.04). All cause mortality after a mean of 11 months of follow-up was lower in the placebo group (10.8 per 100 person years) than in the pimobendan treated patients (21.3 and 17.4 per 100 person years in the 2.5 mg/d and 5 mg/d groups) (Hazard ratio of the pimobendan 2.5 mg/d 2.0; 95% CI 0.9 to 4.1; and that of the 5.0 mg/d 1.6; 95% CI 0.7 to 3.4). When both pimobendan groups were combined, the hazard ratio of death was 1.8 (95% CI 0.9-3.5) times higher than in the placebo group.
Conclusions	Pimobendan therapy in patients with congestive heart failure and left ventricular ejection fraction ≤0.45 was associated with an increase in exercise capacity. However, there was a trend towards an increased mortality in the treated patients.

DIG

The Digitalis Investigation Group study

Title	The effect of digoxin on mortality and morbidity in patients with heart failure.
Authors	The Digitalis Investigation Group.
Reference	N Engl J Med 1997;336:525-533.
Disease	Congestive heart failure.
Purpose	To assess the effects of digoxin on morbidity and mortality in patients with heart failure and normal sinus rhythm.
Design	Randomized, double blind, placebo controlled, multicenter.
Patients	6800 patients with left ventricular ejection fraction of ≤0.45 and 988 patients with left ventricular ejection fraction of >0.45. All patients had heart failure and were in sinus rhythm.
Follow-up	The mean duration of follow-up was 37 months (28 to 58 months).
Treatment regimen	Digoxin or placebo.
Additional therapy	ACE inhibitors were encouraged. If patients remained symptomatic despite efforts to optimize other forms of therapy, open label digoxin therapy was allowed and the study drug was discontinued.

DIG

The Digitalis Investigation Group study (continued)

Results

In patients with ejection fraction ≤0.45, the mortality was similar (34.8% with digoxin and 35.1% with placebo, risk ratio 0.99; 95% CI 0.91-1.07, p=0.80). Cardiovascular mortality was similar (29.9% vs 29.5% in the digoxin and placebo group, respectively). There was a trend toward lower mortality ascribed to worsening of heart failure among the digoxin treated patients (11.6% vs 13.2%; risk ratio 0.88; 95% CI 0.77-1.01; p=0.06). Hospitalization rate due to cardiovascular reasons was lower in the digoxin treated group (49.9% vs 54.4%, risk ratio 0.87; 95% CI 0.81-0.93; p<0.001). Hospitalization rate due to worsening of heart failure was lower in the digoxin group (26.8% vs 34.7%, respectively; risk ratio 0.72; 95% CI 0.66-0.79; p<0.001). There was no significant difference between the 2 groups in hospitalization rate for ventricular arrhythmia or cardiac arrest (4.2% vs 4.3%). In all, 64.3% of the digoxin and 67.1% of the placebo group were hospitalized (risk ratio 0.92; 95% CI 0.87-0.98; p=0.006). There was no difference in hospitalization rate for myocardial infarction or unstable angina and for noncardiovascular reasons. At 1 year, 85.6% and 82.9% of the digoxin and placebo treated patients were taking the study medication. At the final study visit, 70.8% of the surviving digoxin-treated patients were taking study medication and an additional 10.3% received open label digoxin. In the placebo-group, 67.9% of the patients that were alive were taking placebo and 15.6% received open label digoxin. In the cohort of patients with left ventricular ejection fraction >0.45, mortality was 23.4% in both groups. The combined end point of death or hospitalization for worsening of heart failure occurred less in the digoxin treated patients (risk ratio 0.82; 95% CI 0.63-1.07).

Conclusions

Digoxin therapy in patients with heart failure and left ventricular ejection fraction ≤0.45 was associated with lower rates of overall hospitalization and hospitalization due worsening of heart failure. There was no difference in mortality and occurrence of myocardial ischemia or arrhythmia between the digoxin and placebo groups.

ELITE

Evaluation of Losartan In The Elderly

Title	Randomized trial of losartan vs captopril in patients ≥65 with heart failure (Evaluation of Losartan in the Elderly study, ELITE).
Authors	Pitt B, Martinez FA, Meurers GG, et al.
Reference	Lancet 1997;349:747-752.
Disease	Congestive heart failure.
Purpose	To compare the efficacy and safety of losartan (a specific angiotensin II receptor blocker) and captopril (an ACE inhibitor) in the treatment of elderly patients with heart failure.
Patients	722 patients, ≥65 years old, with symptomatic heart failure (NYHA class II-IV), left ventricular ejection fraction ≤0.40, and no history of prior ACE inhibitor therapy. Patients with systolic blood pressure <90 mm Hg or diastolic blood pressure >95 mm Hg, significant obstructive valvular heart disease, symptomatic arrhythmias, pericarditis or myocarditis, PTCA within 72h, CABG within 2 weeks, ICD within 2 weeks, likelihood for cardiac surgery during the study period, acute myocardial infarction within 72 h, unstable angina within 3 months, stable angina, stroke or transient ischemic attack within 3 months, concomitant severe disease, creatinine ≥2.5 mg/dL, anemia, leukopenia, and electrolyte disturbances were excluded.
Follow-up	48 weeks.
Treatment regimen	A 2 week placebo run in phase, and then randomization to captopril (6.25-50 mg X3/d) plus placebo losartan, or placebo captopril plus losartan (12.5-50 mg X1/d).

ELITE

Evaluation of Losartan In The Elderly (continued)

Additional therapy	Treatment with all other cardiovascular medications (except open label ACE inhibitors) was permitted.
Results	352 patients were randomized to losartan and 370 to captopril. Persisting increases in serum creatinine (≥0.3 mg/dL) occurred in 10.5% in each group (risk reduction 2%; 95% CI -51% to 36%; p=0.63). Death and/or admissions for heart failure occurred in 9.4% in the losartan group vs 13.2% in the captopril group (risk reduction 32%; 95% CI -4% to 55%; p=0.075). Mortality was 4.8% in the losartan group vs 8.7% in the captopril group (risk reduction 46%; 95% CI 5% to 69%; p=0.035). Sudden death occurred in 1.4% vs 3.8%, respectively (risk reduction 64%; 95% CI 3% to 86%). The cumulative survival curves separated early and remained separated throughout the study. 22.2% of the losartan group vs 29.7% of the captopril group were admitted to the hospital for any reason (risk reduction 26%; 95% CI 5% to 43%; p=0.014). However, there was no difference in admission for heart failure (5.7% in each group; p=0.89). NYHA class improved in both treatment groups. The percentage of patients in NYHA class I or II was increased from 66% at baseline to 80% at the end of the study in the losartan group, and from 64%–81% in the captopril group. 18.5% of the losartan group vs 30% of the captopril group discontinued the study medication or died (p≤0.001). 12.2% vs 20.8% of the patients, respectively, discontinued the study medication because of adverse effects (p≤0.002). Cough leading to discontinuation of therapy was reported in 0 vs 3.8%, respectively. Persistent (≥0.5 mmol/L) increases in serum potassium was observed in 18.8% of the losartan group vs 22.7% of the captopril group (p=0.069).
Conclusions	Losartan therapy was associated with lower mortality and hospitalization rate than captopril therapy in elderly patients with symptomatic heart failure. Losartan was better tolerated than captopril.

ELITE II

Evaluation of Losartan In The Elderly II

Title	1.Effect of losartan compared with captopril on mortality in patients with symptomatic heart failure: rationale, design, and baseline characteristics of patients in the losartan heart failure survival study—ELITE II. 2. Effect of losartan compared with captopril on mortality in patients with symptomatic heart failure: randomized trial—the Losartan Heart Failure Survival Study ELITE II.
Authors	Pitt B, Poole-Wilson PA, Segal R, et al.
Reference	1.J Card Fail 1999;5:146-154. 2. Lancet 2000;355:1582-1587.
Disease	Congestive heart failure.
Purpose	To verify whether losartan is better than captopril in reducing mortality in patients with heart failure.
Design	Randomized, double blind, multicenter.
Patients	3152 patients, >60 years old, with congestive heart failure (NYHA Class II-IV), LVEF ≤40%, who were not on ACE inhibitor or angiotensin II antagonist therapy, or were exposed to such therapy for ≤7 days. Patients with intolerance to the study drugs, systolic blood pressure <90 mm Hg, diastolic blood pressure >95 mm Hg, stenotic valvular disease, active pericarditis or myocarditis, AICD, recent PCI within a week prior to randomization, acute coronary syndrome or acute myocardial infarction within 2 weeks prior to enrollment, recent CABG, CVA or TIA within 6 weeks prior to enrollment, renal artery stenosis, renal failure, or hematuria were excluded.
Follow-up	Median follow-up 1.5 years.

ELITE II

Evaluation of Losartan In The Elderly II

(continued)

Treatment regimen	After a run-in of 1–28 days of single blind placebo phase, patients were randomized to losartan (initial dose 12.5 mg/d; dose was increased gradually up to 50 mg/d) + captopril-matched placebo (n=1578), or to captopril (initial dose 12.5 mg tid; dose was increased gradually up to 50 mg tid) + losartan matched placebo (n=1574).
Results	All cause mortality was 17.7% in the losartan group vs 15.9% in the captopril group (Hazard ratio [HR] 1.13; 95.7% CI 0.95–1.35; p=0.16).The estimated average annual mortality rate was 11.7% and 10.4%, respectively. Sudden death or resuscitated cardiac arrest occurred in 9.0% in the losartan group vs 7.3% in the captopril group (HR 1.25; 95.7% CI 0.98–1.60; p=0.08). Sudden death occurred in 8.2% vs 6.4%, respectively (HR 1.30; 95.7% CI 1.00–1.69). Overall, 41.8% of the losartan group vs 40.5% of the captopril group were hospitalized (HR 1.04; 95.7% CI 0.94–1.16; p=0.45). Hospitalization for heart failure occurred in 17.1% vs 18.6%, respectively (HR 0.92; 95.7% CI 0.78–1.08; p=0.32). More patients in the captopril group than in the losartan group discontinued study medication because of adverse effects (14.7% vs 9.7%; p<0.001). Cough caused discontinuation of study medication in 2.7% of the captopril treated patients vs 0.3% of the losartan treated patients.
Conclusions	Losartan was not superior to captopril in reducing mortality in patients >60 years old with congestive heart failure. However, losartan was better tolerated than captopril.

NETWORK

Clinical Outcome With Enalapril in Symptomatic Chronic Heart Failure

Title	a. The NETWORK study: Rationale, design, and methods of a trial evaluating the dose of enalapril in patients with heart failure. b. Clinical outcome with enalapril in symptomatic chronic heart failure: A dose comparison.
Authors	a. Long C, on behalf of the Steering Committee of the Network Study. b. The NETWORK investigators
Reference	a. Br J Clin Res 1995;6:179–189. b. Eur Heart J 1998;19:481–489.
Disease	Congestive heart failure.
Purpose	To study the relationship between enalapril dose and the incidence of mortality, heart failure related hospitalizations and progression of disease in patients with symptomatic heart failure.
Design	Randomized, double blind, parallel group, multicenter.
Patients	1532 patients, aged 18–85 years, with symptomatic heart failure (NYHA class II–IV). Patients with significant valvular disease, unstable angina, recent myocardial infarction, uncontrolled hypertension, hypotension, severe pulmonary disease, hypokalemia, renal failure, previous ACE inhibitor therapy, or contraindications to ACE inhibition were excluded.
Follow-up	6 months.

NETWORK

Clinical Outcome With Enalapril in Symptomatic Chronic Heart Failure

(continued)

Treatment regimen	Randomization to enalapril 2.5 mg bid (group I), 5 mg bid (group II) and 10 mg bid (group III).
Results	99.8%, 95.9%, and 84.7% reached the target dose level in group I, II and III, respectively. Less patients in group III were on study drug at the end of 24 weeks follow-up period (73%) than in group II (81%) or group I (81%). There was no relationship between enalapril dose and clinical event rates. The primary end point (death, heart failure related hospitalizations, and progression of heart failure) occurred in 12.3%, 12.9% and 14.7% of group I, II and III, respectively. Worsening of heart failure in 7.7%, 7.8% and 7.8%, respectively; hospitalization due to heart failure in 5.1%, 5.5% and 7.0%, respectively; and death in 4.2%, 3.3% and 2.9%, respectively. The percentages of patients with improvement in NYHA class were 34%, 33% and 31%, respectively. Deterioration by 1 NYHA grade occurred in 5.3%, 4.9% and 2.7%.
Conclusions	Increasing the enalapril dose from 2.5 mg bid to 10 mg bid did not result in better clinical outcome in patients with heart failure.

PRIME II

The Second Prospective Randomized Study of Ibopamine on Mortality and Efficacy

Title	Randomized study of effect of ibopamine on survival in patients with advanced severe heart failure.
Authors	Hampton, JR, van Veldhuisen DJ, Kleber FX, et al.
Reference	Lancet 1997;349:971-977.
Disease	Congestive heart failure.
Purpose	To investigate the efficacy of ibopamine, an agonist of dopaminergic DA-1 and DA-2 receptors that causes peripheral and renal vasodilatation, on survival in patients with advanced heart failure.
Design	Randomized, placebo controlled, multicenter.
Patients	1906 patients, aged 18–80 years, with advanced severe heart failure (NYHA class III or IV), despite therapy with ACE inhibitor, diuretics, digoxin or other vasodilators. Patients with obstructive valve disease, obstructive or restrictive cardiomyopathy, any potential transient cause of heart failure, myocardial infarction within 3 months, unstable angina, uncontrolled arrhythmias, current need for intravenous inotropic agents, pregnancy or lactation, intolerance to dopamine or dobutamine, and concomitant therapy with agents that interact with ibopamine were excluded.
Follow-up	An average of 363 days in the placebo group and 347 days in the ibopamine group.
Treatment regimen	Oral ibopamine 100 mg tid or placebo for >6 months.

Results	The study was terminated prematurely by the safety committee due to a significantly higher mortality rate among the ibopamine treated patients than among the placebo treated group. The interim analysis revealed that 24.3% of the ibopamine vs 20.3% of the placebo group died (relative risk 1.26; 95% CI 1.04 to 1.53; p=0.017). Kaplan-Meier survival curve revealed that survival was similar in both groups for the first 3 months of therapy, and then diverged. Sudden death tended to be more common in the ibopamine group (29.8% of all fatality cases) than in the placebo group (23.8%). However, death due to progression of heart failure was comparable (47.0% vs 45.6%, respectively). In contrast, death due to acute myocardial infarction tended to occur less in the ibopamine group (6.5%) than in the placebo group (10.9%). Admission to the hospital was comparable (46% vs 44% in the ibopamine and placebo groups, respectively; relative risk 1.13; 95% CI 0.99 to 1.29). The patients' self assessment scores of symptoms in the 2 groups were similar. There was no difference between the groups in the distribution between the NYHA classes. In multivariate analysis, only the use of antiarrhythmic drugs at baseline was independently associated with increased fatality with ibopamine therapy.
Conclusions	Ibopamine therapy increased mortality without improvement in NYHA class or the patients' self assessment scores among patients with advanced congestive heart failure. Antiarrhythmic therapy was the only independent predictor of adverse outcome with ibopamine treatment.

Randomized, controlled trial of long term moderate exercise training in chronic heart failure. Effects of functional capacity, quality of life, and clinical outcome.

Title	Randomized, controlled trial of long term moderate exercise training in chronic heart failure. Effects of functional capacity, quality of life, and clinical outcome.
Authors	Belardinelli R, Georgiou D, Cianci G, et al.
Reference	Circulation 1999; 99:1173–1182.
Disease	Congestive heart failure.
Purpose	To determine whether long term moderate exercise training in CHF patients improves functional capacity, quality of life, and outcome.
Design	Control, randomized, prospective.
Patients	99 patients with stable CHF, average age 59 years; 88 men; 11 women. Patients had to have clinical heart failure with LV EF ≤40% and sinus rhythm.
Follow-up	14 months.
Treatment regimen	Patients were randomized to 2 groups: exercise (n=50) and control (n=49). Initial exercise consisted of exercise 3 times a week for 8 weeks at 60% of peak VO_2; followed by a second phase, a 12 month maintenance program with same intensity of exercise but for 2 sessions per week. Sessions lasted about an hour with a warm up phase followed by 40 minutes of cycling.
Additional therapy	Standard anti CHF medicines.

Randomized, controlled trial of long term moderate exercise training in chronic heart failure. Effects of functional capacity, quality of life, and clinical outcome.

(continued)

Results	Peak VO_2 and thallium scores improved at 2 months (18% and 24%, respectively; p<0.001). These parameters did not change further after 1 year. 75% of exercise trained vs 2% of untrained patients with ischemic heart disease had an improvement in thallium uptake (p<0.001). Patients did not experience significant cardiovascular events during the training session; some had supraventricular arrhythmias and ventricular premature beats during exercise. Quality of life questionnaires showed improved scores in the trained patients after 2 months that remained stable during the subsequent 12 months. Improvements in score paralleled the improvements in peak VO_2 in trained patients (r=0.80; p<0.001). Mortality was lower in trained patients (n=9) vs those without training (RR=0.37; 95% CI = 0.17–0.84; p=0.01). Hospitalization for heart failure was lower in trained (n=5) than untrained patients (n=14; RR=0.29; 95% CI 0.11–0.88, p=0.02).
Conclusions	Moderate exercise training in patients with heart failure improved functional capacity, quality of life, and improved outcome.

A dose dependent increase in mortality with vesnarinone among patients with severe heart failure

Title	A dose dependent increase in mortality with vesnarinone among patients with severe heart failure.
Authors	Cohn JN, Goldstein SO, Greenberg BH, et al.
Reference	N Engl J Med 1998; 339:1810–1816.
Disease	Congestive heart failure.
Purpose	To determine the effect of daily vesnarinone at doses of 30 mg or 60 mg vs placebo on mortality and morbidity of heart failure patients.
Design	Randomized, double blind, multicenter.
Patients	3833 patients with NYHA class III or IV heart failure and LV ejection fraction of ≤30%.
Follow-up	Mean of 286 days.
Treatment regimen	Following a 2 week stabilization phase during which baseline medicines and clinical status were stable, patients were randomized to placebo, 30 mg, or 60 mg of vesnarinone per day.
Additional therapy	Conventional heart failure therapy: diuretics, digitalis, vasodilators, ACE inhibitors.

A dose dependent increase in mortality with vesnarinone among patients with severe heart failure

(continued)

Results	Fewer patients in the placebo group died (242 deaths; 18.9%) compared to patients on the 60 mg dose of vesnarinone (292; 22.9%). Time to death was shorter in the 60 mg vesnarinone group vs the placebo group (p=0.02). There were 268 deaths (21%) in the 30 mg group. The increase in mortality in vesnarinone treated patients was due to an increase in sudden cardiac death (presumably arrhythmias) and the number of deaths due to worsening heart failure was similar among the 3 groups. At 8 and 16 weeks quality of life was reported to be better at the 60 mg dose vs placebo. Mortality results and quality of life with the 30 mg showed similar trends to 60 mg group but did not reach statistical significance vs placebo.
Conclusions	Vesnarinone caused a dose dependent increase in mortality in patients with severe heart failure despite the fact that it improved short term quality of life.

Metoprolol in idiopathic dilated cardiomyopathy

Title	Long term survival effect of metoprolol in dilated cardiomyopathy.
Authors	Di Lenarda A, De Maria R, Gavazzi A, et al.
Reference	Heart 1998;79:337-344.
Disease	Congestive heart failure, idiopathic dilated cardiomyopathy.
Purpose	To assess the effects of long term metoprolol administration in patients with idiopathic dilated cardiomyopathy.
Design	Multicenter registry, nonrandomized.
Patients	586 patients with idiopathic dilated cardiomyopathy. Patients with >50% luminal diameter coronary artery stenosis, active myocarditis, or other specific cardiac muscle disease identified by endomyocardial biopsy, and those with a left ventricular ejection fraction ≥50% were excluded.
Follow-up	Mean 52±32 months.
Treatment regimen	175 patients with left ventricular ejection fraction <40%, or a history of symptomatic congestive heart failure were treated with metoprolol (5 mg bid for 2-7 days, followed by slow upgrade titration up to 50 mg tid or achieving a resting heart rate of 60 bpm.
Additional therapy	ACE inhibitors, digitalis, and diuretics.

(continued)

Results	The average daily dose of metoprolol was 117±46 mg (range 20–200 mg). Only 5% of patients discontinued metoprolol during the 7 years of follow-up. 7 year survival was higher in the 175 patients treated with metoprolol (81%) than in the other 411 patients without metoprolol (60%; $p<0.001$). Similarly, transplant free survival was better in the metoprolol group (69% vs 49%; $p<0.001$). Using Cox multivariate model, it was demonstrated that metoprolol was independently associated with reduced all-cause mortality rate (odds ratio 0.49; 95% CI 0.31–0.79; $p=0.002$), and death or transplantation rate (0.66; 0.47–0.95; $p=0.01$).
Conclusions	Long term metoprolol treatment, added to conventional therapy for congestive heart failure, reduces all cause mortality and the need for transplantation in patients with idiopathic dilated cardiomyopathy.

Title	Study on propionyl-L-carnitine in chronic heart failure.
Authors	The Investigators of the Study on Propionyl-L-Carnitine in Chronic Heart Failure.
Reference	Eur Heart J 1999;19:70–76.
Disease	Congestive heart failure.
Purpose	To assess the effect of propionyl-L-carnitine on exercise capacity in patients with mild to moderate congestive heart failure treated with diuretics and ACE inhibitors.
Design	Randomized, double blind, placebo controlled, parallel, multicenter.
Patients	537 patients with chronic heart failure (≥2 months duration), NYHA class II or III, LVEF ≤40%, maximum exercise duration on a bicycle exercise test 3–12 min, and stable treatment with ACE inhibitors and diuretics for ≥20 days. A maximal bicycle exercise test was performed at the screening visit and repeated twice during the 14 day run in single blind period. Only patients whose maximum exercise duration variability between the tests was ≤10% were finally included.
Follow-up	6 months.
Treatment regimen	Propionyl-L-carnitine or placebo 1 g bid.

Additional therapy	All patients received diuretics and ACE inhibitors.
Results	There were 271 and 266 patients in the propionyl-L-carnitine and placebo group, respectively. 353 patients competed the protocol (188 and 165 patients, respectively in the propionyl-L-carnitine and placebo group). Propionyl-L-carnitine was not associated with prolongation of exercise duration, both in an intention-to-treat analysis and analysis of the 353 patients who completed the protocol. There were no differences between the groups on the rates of negative outcomes (increases in treatment for heart failure, death and hospitalization) (21.4% in the propionyl-L-carnitine and 17.3% in the placebo group, p=0.289). Adverse events occurred in similar rates in the two groups (p=0.882). Subgroup analysis revealed that among patients with baseline maximum exercise duration of ≤480 s, propionyl-L-carnitine was associated with more prolongation of exercise time at follow-up (11±92 vs 4±83 seconds; p=0.38 in the intention to treat analysis, and 28±83 vs 16±81 seconds; p=0.08 among patients who completed the trial). Among patients with baseline LVEF ≤30%, propionyl-L-carnitine was associated with 17±109 seconds decrease in exercise time, whereas in the placebo group exercise time increased by 6±87 seconds (p=0.06). In contrast, among patients with baseline LVEF 30–40%, exercise time increased in the propionyl-L carnitine group by 33±89 seconds and decreased by 7±95 seconds in the placebo group (p<0.01).
Conclusions	Propionyl-L-carnitine therapy was safe, but was not associated with prolongation of exercise time. Propionyl-L-carnitine may increase exercise capacity in patients with preserved left ventricular systolic function.

Dose related beneficial long term hemodynamic and clinical efficacy of irbesartan in heart failure

Title	Dose related beneficial long term hemodynamic and clinical efficacy of irbesartan in heart failure.
Authors	Havranek EP, Thomas I, Smith WB, et al.
Reference	J Am Coll Cardiol 1999; 33:1174-1181.
Disease	Congestive heart failure.
Purpose	To assess the effects of the angiotensin II AT_1 receptor antagonist irbesartan on acute and long term hemodynamics.
Design	Randomized, double blind, multicenter, dose ranging study.
Patients	218 patients with NYHA class II-IV heart failure, LV ejection fraction of ≤40%, pulmonary capillary wedge pressure (PCWP) ≥14 mm Hg; cardiac index ≤3.0 L/min/m².
Follow-up	12 weeks.
Treatment regimen	Irbesartan 12.5 mg, 37.5 mg, 75 mg, or 150 mg acutely and then once daily for 12 weeks; placebo acutely then one of 4 doses of irbesartan over 12 weeks.
Additional therapy	ACE-I were discontinued ≥4 days before baseline hemodynamic measures.

Dose related beneficial long term hemodynamic and clinical efficacy of irbesartan in heart failure

(continued)

Results	Primary end point was change in PCWP from baseline to 12 weeks. Irbesartan showed a dose related decrease in PCWP over 12 weeks with an average decrease of 5.9±0.9 mm Hg at the 75 mg dose and a decrease of 5.3±0.9 mm Hg at the 150 mg dose. Irbesartan decreased mean systemic arterial pressure. It did not cause reflex tachycardia or increase plasma norepinephrine levels. There was a nonsignificant trend toward increase in left ventricular ejection fraction as a function of irbesartan dose. 5, 6, 2, 1 patients discontinued drug due to worsening heart failure at the 12.5 mg, 37.5, 75, and 150 mg dose, respectively. 13.9% of patients receiving either 12.5 mg or 37.5 mg of irbesartan vs 5.5% of patients receiving either 75 or 150 mg of irbesartan experienced death, discontinuation of study medicine for worsening heart failure, or hospitalization for worsening heart failure (p=0.04).
Conclusions	75 and 150 mg once daily doses of irbesartan resulted in sustained hemodynamic benefit and decreased worsening of heart failure.

High vs low dose ACE inhibition in chronic heart failure. A double blind, placebo controlled study of imidapril.

Title	High vs low dose ACE inhibition in chronic heart failure. A double blind, placebo controlled study of imidapril.
Authors	Van Veldhuisen DJ, Genth-Zotz S, Brouwer J, et al.
Reference	J Am Coll Cardiol 1998; 32:1811–1818.
Disease	Congestive heart failure.
Purpose	To determine the effects of high vs low dose of ACE inhibition on clinical and neurohumoral response in heart failure patients.
Design	Randomized, double blind, placebo controlled, multicenter.
Patients	244 patients with NYHA Class II–III CHF stable on digoxin and diuretics.
Follow-up	12 weeks.
Treatment regimen	2 week placebo run in phase, then double blind phase of 12 weeks in which patients were randomized and titrated to 2.5 mg, 5 mg, 10 mg of imidapril or placebo.

High vs low dose ACE inhibition in chronic heart failure. A double blind, placebo controlled study of imidapril.

(continued)

Results	3 of 182 patients developed progressive CHF in the imidapril group vs 6/26 in the placebo group, ($p<0.05$). At 12 weeks exercise time (bicycle ergometer) increased 45±82 sec with the 10 mg dose ($p=0.018$ vs placebo) but changes with the 5 and 2.5 mg doses of imidapril were not significantly different compared to placebo. There was a dose related increase in physical work capacity. At baseline, plasma atrial natriuretic (ANP) and brain natriuretic peptide (BNP) levels were increased. There was a dose dependent reduction of these with imidapril. Plasma ACE inhibition was suppressed to a similar level with all 3 doses.
Conclusions	High dose ACE inhibition with imidapril was better than low dose for improving exercise capacity and depressing ANP and BNP in patients with chronic CHF.

DIAMOND-CHF

Danish Investigations of Arrhythmia and Mortality On Dofetilide in Congestive Heart Failure

Title	Dofetilide in patients with congestive heart failure and left ventricular dysfunction.
Authors	Torp-Pedersen C, Moller M, Bloch-Thomsen PE, et al.
Reference	N Engl J Med 1999;341:857-865.
Disease	Congestive heart failure, atrial fibrillation.
Purpose	To determine whether dofetilide, a novel class III antiarrhythmic drug, alters survival or morbidity in patients with decreased LV function and congestive heart failure.
Design	Randomized, double blind, multicenter.
Patients	1518 patients with severe left ventricular dysfunction and symptomatic congestive heart failure.
Follow-up	18 months.
Treatment regimen	Therapy was begun in-hospital with 3 days of dose adjustment and cardiac monitoring. 756 patients received placebo and 762 received dofetilide. Initially 500 μg of dofetilide twice-a-day to patients without atrial fibrillation, and 250 μg twice-a-day to patients with atrial fibrillation. Later in the study dose was based on creatinine clearance: those with a creatinine clearance of 40-<60 mL per minute received 250 μg twice-a-day; those with a clearance of 20-<40 mL per minute received 250 μg once-a-day. Additional changes if there was prolongation of QT interval.

DIAMOND-CHF

Danish Investigations of Arrhythmia and Mortality On Dofetilide in Congestive Heart Failure

(continued)

Additional therapy	Other usual therapy for congestive heart failure.
Results	Primary end point was death from any cause. There was no difference in incidence of death between groups (41% in the dofetilide group and 42% in the placebo group). Dofetilide decreased the risk of hospitalization for worsened congestive heart failure (RR=6.75; 95% CI=0.63-0.89) and at one month restored sinus rhythm in 22 of 190 patients with atrial fibrillation at baseline (12%) vs only 3 of 201 patients (1%) that were given placebo. Dofetilide was more effective than placebo in maintaining sinus rhythm once it had been restored. Torsade de pointes occurred in 25 patients receiving dofetilide (3.3%) vs none in the placebo group. While overall rates of adverse events and discontinuation of therapy did not differ significantly between dofetilide and placebo, prolongation of the corrected QT interval was a more common reason for discontinuation in the dofetilide (n=14) vs placebo patients (n=3). Increase in the corrected QT interval peaked within the first 2 days of treatment.
Conclusions	In patients with congestive heart failure and reduced LV function dofetilide did not affect mortality. Dofetilide did convert atrial fibrillation to sinus rhythm better than placebo, maintained sinus rhythm better than placebo, and decreased hospitalizations for worsening congestive heart failure.

RALES

Randomized Aldactone Evaluation Study Investigators

Title	The effect of spironolactone on morbidity and mortality in patients with severe heart failure.
Authors	Pitt B, Zannad F, Remme WJ, et al.
Reference	N Engl J Med 1999;341:709–717.
Disease	Congestive heart failure.
Purpose	To determine whether spironolactone would decrease the risk of death in patients with severe heart failure due to systolic dysfunction who were also receiving standard therapy including an ACE inhibitor.
Design	Randomized, double blind, placebo controlled, multicenter.
Patients	822 patients with NYHA Class III–IV heart failure at time of enrollment who were receiving ACE inhibitor (if tolerated), loop diuretic, and had an LV ejection fraction of no more than 35%.
Follow-up	Mean of 24 months.
Treatment regimen	25 mg spironolactone orally once daily vs placebo. Patents were excluded if serum creatinine was >2.5 mg/dL and if serum potassium was >5.0 mmol/L.
Additional therapy	Digitalis and vasodilators were allowed as well as ACE inhibitors; potassium sparing diuretics were not allowed. Potassium supplements not recommended unless hypokalemia present.

RALES

Randomized Aldactone Evaluation Study Investigators

(continued)

Results	The primary end point was death from all causes. 841 patients assigned to placebo and 822 to spironolactone. 200 patients in placebo and 214 in spironolactone discontinued therapy for lack of response, adverse events, or other reasons. The study was stopped early because interim analysis showed a lower death rate among spironolactone treated patients. 386 patients died in the placebo group (46%) vs 284 in the spironolactone group (35%; RR=0.70; 95% CI=0.60-0.82; p<0.001). The 30% decrease in death among treated patients was due to a lower rate of death from progressive heart failure and sudden cardiac death. There was a 30% reduction in risk of hospitalization for cardiac causes in the spironolactone group (RR=0.70; 95% CI=0.59-0.82, p<0.001). There was a significant improvement in NYHA Functional Class among patients who received spironolactone. The median creatinine concentration in the spironolactone patients increased by 0.05-0.10 mg/dL, median potassium concentration increased by 0.30 mmol/L. The incidence of serious hyperkalemia was 1% in the placebo group and 2% in the spironolactone group (n=NS). Gynecomastia was more common in the spironolactone group (10%) vs the placebo group (1%; p<0.001).
Conclusions	The aldosterone receptor blocker spironolactone, in addition to standard therapy, reduced morbidity and mortality in patients with severe heart failure.

ATLAS

Assessment of Treatment with Lisinopril and Survival

Title	Comparative efects of low and high doses of the ACE inhibitor, lisinopril, on morbidity and mortality in chronic heart failure.
Authors	Packer M, Poole-Wilson PA, Armstrong PW, et al.
Reference	Circulation 1999;100:2312–2318.
Disease	Chronic congestive heart failure.
Purpose	To compare the efficacy and safety of low and high doses of ACE inhibitor on the risk of death and hospitalization in patients with congestive heart failure.
Design	Randomized, double blind, multicenter.
Patients	3164 patients with NYHA Class II–IV and LVEF ≤30%. Patients with an acute coronary ischemic event, revascularization procedure within the preceding 2 months, a history of sustained ventricular tachycardia, intolerance to ACE inhibitors, serum creatinine >2.5 mg/dL, or severe noncardiac disease were excluded.
Follow-up	39–58 months (median 45.7).
Treatment regimen	All patients received open label lisinopril for 4 weeks. Only patients who could tolerate 12.5–15 mg/d for ≥2 weeks were further randomized to either low dose (2.5–5.0 mg/d) or high dose (32.5–35 mg/d) lisinopril.

Results	Of the 3793 patients who entered the open label phase, 176 patients experienced adverse effects or had laboratory abnormalities that prevented their randomization to the double blind phase. 1596 patients were included in the low dose group and 1568 in the high dose group. Target doses were achieved in 92.7% and 91.3% of the patients in the low dose and high dose groups, respectively. During follow-up 30.6% and 27.2% of the patients in the low and high dose groups stopped taking the study medications. Open label ACE inhibitors were initiated in 22.1% and 18.3% of the patients, respectively. The high dose group had an insignificant 8% lower risk of total mortality (42.5% vs 44.9%; p=0.128) and a 10% lower risk of cardiovascular mortality (37.2% vs 40.2%; p=0.073) than the low dose group. The combined end point of all cause mortality and hospitalization was significantly 12% lower in the high dose group (79.7% vs 83.8%; p=0.002). The high dose group had 13% fewer hospitalizations for any cause (3819 vs 4397; p=0.021), 16% fewer hospitalization for a cardiovascular cause (2456 vs 2923; p=0.05), and 24% fewer hospitalization for heart failure (1199 vs 1576; p=0.002). During follow-up 18.0% of the low dose vs 17.0% of the high dose group had to stop the study medication due to side effects.
Conclusions	High dose lisinopril was more effective than low dose lisinopril therapy for patients with heart failure. Patients with heart failure should receive the high doses found effective in randomized studies, unless high doses cannot be tolerated.

RESOLVD

Randomized Evaluation of Strategies for Left Ventricular Dysfunction

Title	Comparison of candesartan, enalapril, and their combination in congestive heart failure. RESOLVD Pilot Study.
Authors	McKelvie RS, Yusuf S, Pericak D, et al.
Reference	Circulation 1999;100:1056–1064.
Disease	Congestive heart failure.
Purpose	To determine the effects of the angiotensin II antagonist candesartan alone, enalapril alone, and their combination on various parameters of congestive heart failure.
Design	Randomized, double blind, parallel, placebo controlled, multicenter.
Patients	768 patients with NYHA Functional Class II–IV with ejection fraction <0.40 and 6 minute walk distance <500 m.
Follow-up	43 weeks.
Treatment regimen	Candesartan (4, 8, or 16 mg daily) vs enalapril 10 mg twice-a-day, vs combination of candesartan at either 4 or 8 mg daily plus enalapril 10 mg twice-a-day.
Additional therapy	After 19 weeks, patients were eligible for randomization to metoprolol vs placebo. No interactions occurred across outcomes between use of metoprolol and the other groups.

RESOLVD

Randomized Evaluation of Strategies for Left Ventricular Dysfunction

(continued)

Results

Primary end points included change in 6 minute walking distance, ejection fraction, ventricular volumes, neurohormone levels, quality of life, NYHA Functional Class at 17 or 18 weeks and 43 weeks. There were no differences in walking distance, functional class, or quality of life among the groups. There was a nonsignificant increase in ejection fraction assessed by radionuclide angiography in the combination group (0.025±0.004) compared with the candesartan (0.015±0.004) or enalapril group (0.015±0.005). Combination of candesartan and enalapril had less increase ($p<0.01$) in end diastolic volume (8±4 mL), than with candesartan alone (27±4 mL) or enalapril alone 23±7 mL). Also the increase in end systolic volumes increased less ($p<0.01$) with combination therapy (1±4 mL), than with candesartan alone (18±3 mL) or enalapril alone (14±6 mL). Blood pressure decreased more with combination therapy (-6/-4 mm Hg) than with either therapy alone. Combination therapy decreased aldosterone levels at 17 but not 43 weeks compared to candesartan or enalapril alone. Combination therapy was also associated with a greater decrease in brain natriuretic peptide. Death, hospitalization for heart failure, and any hospitalizations did not differ among the groups. Death occurred in 8.7% with combination therapy, 6.1% in candesartan, and 3.7% in enalapril alone groups (p=NS). Heart failure hospitalizations occurred in 9.3%, 13.1%, and 6.4% in combination, candesartan, and enalapril groups respectively ($p=0.09$).

Conclusions

Both candesartan and enalapril were effective, safe, and tolerable for treating heart failure. Combination of candesartan and enalapril reduced left ventricular dilation greater than either agent alone.

RESOLVD (Metoprolol Study)

Randomized Evaluation of Strategies for Left Ventricular Dysfunction

Title	Effects of metoprolol CR in patients with ischemic and dilated cardiomyopathy. The RESOLVD Pilot Study.
Authors	The RESOLVD Investigators.
Reference	Circulation 2000;101:378–384.
Disease	Congestive heart failure.
Purpose	To determine the effects of controlled release metoprolol on clinical status, LV volumes and function, and neurohumoral activation in patients with congestive heart failure.
Design	Randomized, double blind 3 x 2 partial factorial design, 2 stage randomization.
Patients	426 eligible patients from Stage 1 (see RESOLVD: candesartan vs enalapril). NYHA Class II–IV, 6 minute walk distance of <500 m, LVEF of <40%, had to tolerate 12.5 mg metoprolol once daily for 1 week.
Follow-up	From randomization into Stage II (metoprolol vs placebo) until end of this study was 24 weeks.
Treatment regimen	Metoprolol CR (25 mg) once daily or placebo.
Additional therapy	As per RESOLVD: candesartan, enalapril, or both.

RESOLVD (Metoprolol Study)

Randomized Evaluation of Strategies for Left Ventricular Dysfunction

(continued)

Results

Metoprolol CR attenuated an increase in LV end diastolic volumes (+6±61 mL metoprolol vs +23±65 mL placebo, p=0.01). Metoprolol also attenuated an increase in LV end systolic volumes (-2±51 mL metoprolol vs +19±55 mL in placebo, p<0.001). LV ejection fraction increased by 2.4% in metoprolol patients vs -0.05% in the placebo group (p=0.001). 6 minute walk distance, NYHA, and quality of life were not changed by metoprolol. Metoprolol was associated with fewer deaths (3.4%) vs placebo (8.1%) but no difference in number of patients with composite end point of death or any hospitalization. Greater decreases in angiotensin II and renin occurred with metoprolol; but it increased N-terminal natriuretic and brain natriuretic peptide.

Conclusions

Metoprolol CR improved LV function, reduced LV dilation, and resulted in fewer deaths in heart failure patients who were already on an ACE inhibitor, angiotensin II receptor antagonist, or both.

STRETCH

Symptom, Tolerability, Response to Exercise Trial of Candesartan Cilexetil in Heart Failure

Title	Improvement in exercise tolerance and symptoms of congestive heart failure during treatment with candesartan cilexetil.
Authors	Riegger GAJ, Bouzo H, Petr P, et al.
Reference	Circulation 1999;100:2224–2230.
Disease	Congestive heart failure.
Purpose	To determine the effect of the angiotensin II type 1 receptor antagonist, candesartan, on exercise tolerance and symptoms in patients with congestive heart failure.
Design	Prospective, randomized, double blind, placebo controlled, multicenter, parallel group.
Patients	844 patients with congestive heart failure; NYHA Class II or III; ejection fraction of 30%–45%.
Follow-up	12 weeks.
Treatment regimen	Candesartan 4, 8, or 16 mg orally once-a-day or matching placebo.
Additional therapy	Diuretics, long acting nitrates, cardiac glycosides. Patients were not on ACE inhibitors during the trial.

Results	Primary efficacy data was total exercise time assessed by bicycle ergometry. Other measures were NYHA Functional Class, signs and symptoms of congestive heart failure, and cardiothoracic ratio on chest x-ray. Candesartan cilexetil 16 mg resulted in significantly greater exercise time (47.2 seconds) compared to placebo (30.8 seconds, $p = 0.046$), and there was a dose related improvement in exercise time (39.7 seconds at 4 mg and 45.8 sec at 8 mg). Dyspnea Fatigue Index scores were improved on candesartan compared with placebo and there was a trend toward improved NYHA Class. There was a small but significant decrease in cardiothoracic ratio. Candesartan was associated with an increase in plasma renin activity and angiotensin II levels and a decrease in aldosterone levels. The drug was well tolerated.
Conclusions	In patients with mild to moderate congestive heart failure, candesartan improved exercise tolerance times, symptoms and signs of congestive heart failure, and cardiothoracic ratio.

MERIT-HF

Metoprolol CR/XL Randomised Intervention Trial in Congestive Heart Failure

Title	a. Effect of metoprolol CR/XL in chronic heart failure: Metoprolol CR/XL randomized intervention trial in congestive heart failure (MERIT-HF). b. Effects of controlled release metoprolol on total mortality, hospitalization, and well being in patients with heart failure. The metoprolol CR/XL randomized intervention trial in congestive heart failure (MERIT-HF).
Authors	a. MERIT-HF Study Group b. Hjalmarson A, Goldstein S, Fagerberg B, et al.
Reference	a. Lancet 1999;353:2001-2007. b. JAMA 2000;283:1295-1302.
Disease	Congestive heart failure.
Purpose	To assess the effects of metoprolol CR/XL on mortality, hospitalization, quality of life, and symptoms in patients with congestive heart failure.
Design	Randomized, double blind, placebo controlled, multicenter.

MERIT-HF

Metoprolol CR/XL Randomised Intervention Trial in Congestive Heart Failure

(continued)

Patients	3991 patients, aged 40–80 years, with LVEF ≤0.40 and stable chronic congestive heart failure (NYHA Class II–IV) despite optimal standard therapy (diuretics and an ACE inhibitor or hydralazine, long acting nitrate, or an angiotensin II receptor antagonist). Patients with acute coronary syndromes within 28 days before enrollment, indication or contraindication for ß-blockers or drugs with ß-blocking activity, heart failure secondary to systemic disease or alcohol abuse were excluded. Patients scheduled for or who had cardiomyoplasty, heart transplantation or AICD and patients scheduled for or who underwent within 4 months prior enrollment CABG or PTCA were not included. Other exclusion criteria were atrioventricular block, resting heart rate <68/minute, hypotension (<100 mm Hg), other serious disease, use of amiodarone within 6 months before enrollment, and use of calcium antagonists.
Follow-up	Mean 1 year.
Treatment regimen	Randomization to metoprolol controlled release/ extended release (CR/XL) (n=1990) or placebo (n=2001). The initial dose was 12.5 mg or 25 mg/d. Every 2 weeks, the dose was doubled until the target dose of 200 mg/d was achieved.
Additional therapy	Diuretics, ACE inhibitors (or hydralazine and nitrates or angiotensin II blockers in case of intolerance) and digoxin.

MERIT-HF

Metoprolol CR/XL Randomised Intervention Trial in Congestive Heart Failure

(continued)

Results

a. Study drug was permanently stopped before the end of the study in 13.9% of the metoprolol assigned patients and in 15.3% of the placebo group. The mean daily dose of the study drug at the end of the study was 159 mg in the metoprolol group (with 64% receiving the target dose of 200 mg/d) and 179 mg in the placebo group (with 82% receiving the target dose). The study was terminated early by the international steering committee. Total mortality was 7.2% per patient year of follow-up in the metoprolol group vs 11.0% per patient year in placebo group (relative risk [RR] 0.66; 95% CI 0.53–0.81; p=0.00009). There were 128 cardiovascular deaths in the metoprolol group vs 203 in the placebo (RR 0.62; 95% CI 0.50–0.78; p=0.00003). Sudden death occurred less in the metoprolol group (79 vs 132; RR 0.59; 95% CI 0.45–0.78; p=0.0002). Death due to worsening of heart failure occurred in 30 patients in the metoprolol group vs 58 patients in the placebo group (RR 0.51; 95% CI 0.33–0.79; p=0.0023).

b. The combined end point of total mortality or all cause hospitalization occurred in 641 patients of the metoprolol group vs 767 patients in the placebo group (19% risk reduction; 95% CI 1–27; p<0.01). Total mortality or hospitalization due to worsening heart failure occurred in 311 vs 439 patients, respectively (31% risk reduction; 95% CI 20–40; p<0.001), and cardiac death or nonfatal acute myocardial infarction occurred in 139 vs 225 patients (39% risk reduction; 95% CI 25–51; p<0.001). 581 (29.1%) patients of the metoprolol vs 668 (33.3%) patients of the placebo group were hospitalized (p=0.004). Days in hospital were 10,172 in the metoprolol vs 12,262 in the placebo group (p=0.004). 394 patients (19.8%) of the metoprolol vs 494 patients (24.7%) of the placebo group were hospitalized due to cardiovascular causes (p<0.001), and 200 (10.0%) vs 294 (14.7%), respectively were hospitalized due to worsening of heart failure (p<0.001). Improvement in the NYHA Class was noted in 28.6% of the metoprolol group vs 25.8% of the placebo group, and deterioration in 6.0% vs 7.5%, respectively

	(p=0.003). There was an improvement in the McMaster Overall Treatment Evaluation score, as assessed by the patients, in the metoprolol group compared with the placebo group (p=0.009).
Conclusions	a. Metoprolol controlled release/ extended release once daily, added to standard therapy, was well tolerated, safe, and reduced mortality in patients with mild to severe stable chronic congestive heart failure secondary to left ventricular systolic dysfunction of ischemic or on-ischemic etiology. b. Metoprolol CR/XR reduced the need for hospitalization, improved NYHA Functional Class, and had beneficial effects on patients well being.

7. Lipid Lowering Studies

POSCH

Program On the Surgical Control of the Hyperlipidemias

Title	Effect of partial ileal bypass surgery on mortality and morbidity from coronary heart disease in patients with hypercholesterolemia. Report of the Program on the Surgical Control of the Hyperlipidemias (POSCH).
Authors	Buchwald H, Varco RL, Matts JP, et al.
Reference	N Engl J Med 1990;323:946-955.
Disease	Hyperlipidemia, coronary artery disease.
Purpose	To evaluate whether cholesterol lowering induced by the partial ileal bypass operation would reduce mortality or morbidity due to coronary heart disease.
Design	Randomized, open label.
Patients	838 patients, 30-64 years of age, 6-60 months after a single myocardial infarction with total plasma cholesterol >5.69 mmol/l or LDL cholesterol >3.62 mmol/l. Patients with hypertension, diabetes mellitus, or obesity were excluded.
Follow-up	7-14.8 years (mean 9.7 years).
Treatment regimen	Partial ileal bypass of either the distal 200 cm or 1/3 of the small intestine, whichever was greater.
Additional therapy	American Heart Association Phase II diet. Hypocholesterolemic medications were discontinued.

Program On the Surgical Control of the Hyperlipidemias

(continued)

Results	5 years after randomization the surgical group had lower total plasma cholesterol (4.71±0.91 vs 6.14±0.89 mmol/l; $p<0.0001$) and LDL cholesterol (2.68±0.78 vs 4.30±0.89 mmol/l; $p<0.0001$); while HDL cholesterol was higher (1.08±0.26 vs 1.04±0.25 mmol/l; $p=0.02$). There was a trend towards lower overall mortality and mortality due to coronary artery disease in the surgical group, however, without statistical significance. The combined end point of cardiovascular death or nonfatal myocardial infarction was 35% lower in the surgical group (82 vs 125 events; $p<0.001$). The surgical group had less disease progression on follow-up angiograms ($p<0.001$ at 5 and 7 years). During follow-up, 52 and 137 patients of the surgical and control groups underwent coronary artery bypass grafting surgery ($p<0.0001$), while 15 and 33 of the surgical and control group patients underwent angioplasty ($p=0.005$).
Conclusions	Partial ileal bypass surgery induced a sustained reduction in plasma cholesterol levels and reduced the morbidity due to coronary artery disease.

FATS

Familial Atherosclerosis Treatment Study

Title	Regression of coronary artery disease as a result of intensive lipid lowering therapy in men with high levels of apolipoprotein B.
Authors	Brown G, Alberts JJ, Fisher LD, et al.
Reference	N Engl J Med 1990;323:1289–1298.
Disease	Hyperlipidemia, coronary artery disease.
Purpose	To assess the effect of intensive lipid lowering therapy on coronary atherosclerosis among high risk men.
Design	Randomized, double blind, placebo (or colestipol) controlled, multicenter.
Patients	146 men, ≤62 years of age, with plasma levels of apolipoprotein ß ≥125 mg/dL, documented coronary artery disease (≥1 lesion of ≥50% stenosis, or ≥3 lesions of ≥30% stenosis), and a positive family history of vascular disease.
Follow-up	Clinical evaluation, plasma lipid levels, and coronary angiography at baseline and at 30 months.
Treatment regimen	1. Lovastatin 20 mg X2/d, and colestipol 10gX3/d. 2. Niacin 1gX4/d, and colestipol 10gX3/d. 3. Placebo or colestipol (if LDL cholesterol exceeded the 90th percentile for age).
Additional therapy	American Heart Association Phase I and II diet.

FATS

Familial Atherosclerosis Treatment Study

(continued)

Results	The levels of LDL and HDL cholesterol changed only slightly in the control group (mean change -7% and +5%, respectively). However they were improved with the lovastatin+colestipol (-46% and +15%) or niacin+colestipol (-32% and +43%) arms. In the control group 46% of the patients had definite lesion progression, while 11% had regression. Progression was observed in only 21% and 25% of the lovastatin+ colestipol and niacin+colestipol patients, while regression was observed in 32% and 39%, respectively (p for trend=0.005). Multivariate regression analysis revealed that reduction in the apolipoprotein ß levels, and in systolic blood pressure, and an increase in HDL cholesterol were associated with regression of coronary lesions. Death, myocardial infarction, or revascularization due to worsening symptoms occurred in 10 of the 52 patients with conventional therapy, as compared to 3 of 46 and 2 of 48 of the lovastatin+colestipol and niacin+colestipol treated patients (p=0.01). Overall, intensive lipid lowering therapy reduces the incidence of clinical events by 73% (95% CI 23-90%).
Conclusions	In men with coronary artery disease who are at high risk, intensive lipid lowering therapy reduced the frequency of progression and increases regression of atherosclerotic coronary lesions, and reduced the incidence of cardiovascular events.

EXCEL

Expanded Clinical Evaluation of Lovastatin

Title	a. Expanded Clinical Evaluation of Lovastatin (EXCEL) study: Design and patient characteristics of a double blind, placebo controlled study in patients with moderate hypercholesterolemia. b. Expanded Clinical Evaluation of Lovastatin (EXCEL) study results. I. Efficacy in modifying plasma lipoproteins and adverse event profile in 8245 patients with moderate hypercholesterolemia. c. Expanded Clinical Evaluation of Lovastatin (EXCEL) study results: III. Efficacy in modifying lipoproteins and implications for managing patients with moderate hypercholesterolemia. d. Expanded Clinical Evaluation of Lovastatin (EXCEL) study results: IV. Additional perspectives on the tolerability of lovastatin.
Authors	a–c. Bradford RH, Shear CL, Chremos AN, et al. d. Dujovne CA, Chermos AN, Pool JL, et al.
Reference	a. Am J Cardiol 1990;66:44B–55B. b. Arch Intern Med 1991;151:43–49. c. Am J Med 1991;91(suppl 1B):18S–24S. d. Am J Med 1991;91(suppl 1B):25S–30S.
Disease	Hypercholesterolemia.
Purpose	To evaluate dose response relation of lovastatin in lipid/lipoprotein modifying efficacy and of drug related adverse effects in patients with moderate hypercholesterolemia.
Design	Randomized, double blind, multicenter.

EXCEL

Expanded Clinical Evaluation of Lovastatin

(continued)

Patients	8245 patients, age 18–70 years, with primary type II hyperlipidemia (fasting total plasma cholesterol 6.21–7.76 mmol/l, LDL cholesterol ≥4.14 mmol/l, and triglyceride <3.95 mmol/l). Patients with diabetes mellitus requiring medications, secondary hypercholesterolemia, and premenopausal women were excluded.
Follow-up	48 weeks.
Treatment regimen	One of the following regimens for 48 weeks: 1. lovastatin 20 mg X1/d; 2. lovastatin 40 mg X1/d; 3. lovastatin 20mg X2/d; 4. lovastatin 40mg X2/d; and 5. placebo.
Additional therapy	American Heart Association phase I diet.
Results	Lovastatin therapy resulted in a sustained, dose related decrease of total cholesterol (-17%, -22%, -24%, and -29% for groups 1–4, while it increased by +0.7% in the placebo group, p<0.001 for dose trend), of LDL cholesterol (-24%, -30%, -34%, and -40% for groups 1–4, while it increased by +0.4% in the placebo group, p<0.001 for dose trend), and of triglyceride (-10%, -14%, -16%, and -19%, respectively, while in the placebo it increased by 3.6%, p<0.001 for dose trend). HDL cholesterol increased by 6.6%, 7.2%, 8.6%, and 9.5%, respectively, while in the placebo it increased in only 2.0%. (p<0.001 for dose trend). Patients withdrawal due to adverse effects occurred in 6% of the placebo and 7–9% of the lovastatin groups. Increases in serum transaminase occurred in 0.1%, 0.1%, 0.9%, 0.9%, and 1.5% of groups 1–5, p<0.001 for trend). Myopathy was rare.
Conclusions	Lovastatin is a safe and highly effective and well tolerated therapy for hypercholesterolemia.

MAAS

Multicentre Anti-Atheroma Study

Title	Effect of simvastatin on coronary atheroma: The Multicentre Anti-Atheroma Study (MAAS).
Authors	MAAS Investigators.
Reference	Lancet 1994;344:633-638.
Disease	Coronary artery disease.
Purpose	To evaluate the effects of simvastatin on coronary atheroma in patients with moderate hypercholesterolemia and coronary artery disease.
Design	Randomized, double blind, placebo controlled, multicenter.
Patients	381 patients, age 30-67 years, with documented coronary artery disease, serum cholesterol 5.5-8.0 mmol/l and triglyceride <4.0 mmol/l. Patients with unstable angina or myocardial infarction within 6 weeks, angioplasty or surgery within 3 months, treated diabetes mellitus, or patients with congestive heart failure or ejection fraction <30% were excluded.
Follow-up	Clinical follow-up for 4 years. Coronary angiography before therapy was started and after 2 and 4 years.
Treatment regimen	Simvastatin 20 mg/d or placebo.
Additional therapy	Lipid lowering diet.

MAAS

Multicentre Anti-Atheroma Study

(continued)

Results	Patients receiving simvastatin had 23% reduction of serum cholesterol, 31% reduction of LDL cholesterol, and a 9% increase in HDL cholesterol compared with placebo after 4 years. 345 patients had repeated angiograms after 4 years. Mean luminal diameter was reduced by 0.08±0.26 mm vs 0.02±0.23 mm in the placebo and simvastatin groups (treatment effect 0.06, 95% CI 0.02–0.10), and minimal luminal diameter was reduced by 0.13±0.27 mm vs 0.04±0.25 mm (treatment effect 0.08, 95% CI 0.03–0.14) (combined p=0.006). Diameter stenosis was increased by 3.6±9.0% vs 1.0±7.9%, respectively (treatment effect -2.6%, 95% CI -4.4% to -0.8%). The beneficial effect of simvastatin was observed regardless of the initial diameter stenosis. Angiographic progression occurred in 32.3% vs 23.0% of the placebo and simvastatin groups, and regression in 12.0% vs 18.6%, respectively (combined p=0.02). New lesions developed in 3.7% vs 2.0% of the segments studied, respectively. There was no difference in clinical outcome. However, more patients in the placebo than simvastatin group (34 vs 23 patients) underwent coronary revascularization.
Conclusions	Simvastatin 20 mg/d reduced hyperlipidemia and slowed the progression of diffuse and focal coronary artery disease.

4S

Scandinavian Simvastatin Survival Study

Title	a. Randomized trial of cholesterol lowering in 4444 patients with coronary heart disease: The Scandinavian Simvastatin Survival Study (4S). b. Baseline serum cholesterol and treatment effect in the Scandinavian Simvastatin Survival Study (4S). c. Reducing the risk of coronary events: evidence from the Scandinavian Simvastatin Survival Study (4S). d. Cholesterol lowering therapy in women and elderly patients with myocardial infarction or angina pectoris. Findings from the Scandinavian Simvastatin Survival Trial (4S). e. Cost effectiveness of simvastatin treatment to lower cholesterol levels in patients with coronary heart disease. f. Lipoprotein changes and reduction in the incidence of major coronary heart disease events in the Scandinavian Simvastatin Survival Study (4S). g. Effect of simvastatin on ischemic signs and symptoms in the Scandinavian Simvastatin Survival Study (4S).
Authors	a + b. Scandinavian Simvastatin Survival Study Group. c. Kjekshus J, Pedersen TR, for the Scandinavian Simvastatin Survival Study Group d. Miettinen TA, Pyorala K, Olsson AG, et al. e. Johannesson M, Jonsson B, Kjekshus J, et al. f. Pederson TR, Olsson AG, Faergeman O, et al. g. Pedersen TR, Kjekshus J, Pyorala K, et al.
Reference	a. Lancet 1994;344:1383-1389. b. Lancet 1995;345:1274-1275. c. Am J Cardiol 1995;76:64C-68C. d. Circulation 1997; 96:4211-4218. e. N Engl J Med 1997; 336:332-336. f. Circulation 1998;97:1453-1460. g. Am J Cardiol 1998; 81:333-335.
Disease	Coronary artery disease, hyperlipidemia.

Purpose	To assess the effect of simvastatin therapy on mortality and morbidity of patients with coronary artery disease and serum cholesterol 5.5-8.0 mmol/L. e. To determine the cost effectiveness of lowering cholesterol in relationship to age, sex, and the cholesterol level from the 4S study. f. To determine which baseline lipoproteins are predictive of coronary events. To determine which changes in lipoproteins accounted for the reduction in coronary events in the 4S. g. To determine effect of lipid intervention with simvastatin on noncoronary ischemic symptoms and signs over 5.4 years.
Design	Randomized, double blind, placebo controlled, multicenter. e. As per 4S trial. Estimation of cost per year of life gained with simvastatin therapy.
Patients	4444 patients, aged 35-70 years, with a history of angina pectoris or myocardial infarction, and serum cholesterol 5.5-8.0 mmol/L, (213-209 mg per deciliter) and serum triglyceride ≤2.5 mmol/L. Premenopausal women and patients with secondary hypercholesterolemia were excluded. Patients with myocardial infarction within 6 months, congestive heart failure, planned coronary artery surgery, or angioplasty were not included.
Follow-up	Clinical follow-up for 4.9-6.3 years (median 5.4 years). e. 5 years. f. 5.4 years.

Treatment regimen	Simvastatin 20 mg/d or placebo. If serum cholesterol did not reach the target range of 3.0–5.2 mmol/L by simvastatin 20 mg/d, the dose was increased to 40 mg/d, or decreased to 10 mg/d. f. Placebo vs simvastatin 20 mg/day with titration to 40 mg. Target serum total cholesterol 116–201 mg/dL.
Additional therapy	Dietary advice.
Results	Lipid concentrations changed only little in the placebo group, whereas simvastatin resulted in -25%, -35%, +8%, and -10% change from baseline of total, LDL, and HDL cholesterol, and triglycerides. After 1 year, 72% of the simvastatin group had achieved total cholesterol <5.2 mmol/L. During the follow-up mortality was 12% in the placebo and 8% in the simvastatin group (RR 0.70, 95% CI 0.58–0.85, p=0.0003). The Kaplan-Meier 6 year probability of survival was 87.7% in the placebo vs 91.3% in the simvastatin group. Coronary mortality was 8.5% vs 5.0%, respectively (RR 0.58, 95% CI 0.46–0.73). There was no difference in noncardiovascular death. 28% of the placebo and 19% of the simvastatin group had 1 or more major coronary events (coronary death, myocardial infarction, or resuscitated cardiac arrest (RR 0.66, 95% CI 0.59–0.75, p<0.00001). The relative risk of having any coronary event in the simvastatin group was 0.73 (95% CI 0.66–0.80, p<0.00001). Simvastatin also reduced the risk of undergoing coronary artery bypass surgery or angioplasty (RR 0.63, 95% CI 0.54–0.74, p<0.00001). The overall rates of adverse effects were not different between the groups. Simvastatin significantly reduced the risk of major coronary events in all quartiles of baseline total, HDL, and LDL cholesterol, by a similar amount in each quartile. d. A recent post hoc analysis showed that patients ≥65 years of age who received simvastatin had a reduced relative risk (RR) for clinical events. The RRs (95% confidence intervals) were 0.66 (0.40–0.90) for all cause mortality; 0.57 (0.39–0.83) for coronary heart disease mortality; and 0.66 (0.52–0.84) for major coronary

events. The RR was also reduced for any atherosclerotic-related events and revascularization procedures. In women the RRs were 1.16 (0.68–1.99), 0.86 (0.42–1.74), and 0.66 (0.48–0.91) for all cause mortality, coronary heart disease mortality, and major coronary events. Any atherosclerotic related event and revascularization procedures also were reduced in women on simvastatin.
e. The cost of each year of life gained ranged from $3,800 for 70 year old men with cholesterol levels of 309 mg/dL to $27,400 for 35 year old women with 213 mg/dL. With indirect costs included, the costs ranged from youngest patients exhibiting a savings in money while 70 year old women with 213 cholesterol levels cost $13,300 per year of life gained.
f. Simvastatin reduced cholesterol by 25% and LDL cholesterol by 34%. Three fourths of patients on simvastatin had reduction of LDL cholesterol by 30%; a quarter had reduction by > 45%. Reduction in coronary events on simvastatin correlated with on-treatment levels and changes in total, LDL cholesterol, and apolipoprotein B. There was less of a correlation with triglyceride levels. Each 1% reduction in LDL cholesterol reduced coronary risk by 1.7%. There was no evidence for any % reduction or on-treatment threshold below which further reduction of LDL cholesterol did not have benefit.
g. Risk of claudication, bruits, and angina were decreased by simvastatin. The risk of new or worsening carotid bruits was significantly decreased. Fatal plus nonfatal cerebral events (stroke or transient ischemic attacks) was reduced by 28% with simvastatin. New or worsening intermittent claudication was decreased by 38% with the statin; new or worsening angina was decreased by 26%.

Conclusions	Long term therapy with simvastatin is safe and effective in improvement of survival and reduction of the rate of coronary events. d. Simvastatin produced similar reductions in relative risk for major coronary events in women vs men and in elderly vs younger patients. e. In patients with coronary artery disease, simvastatin is cost effective. f. The beneficial effect of simvastatin on major coronary events was dependent upon the magnitude of reduction in LDL cholesterol, without a threshold below which reduction was no longer beneficial. g. Cholesterol lowering with simvastatin 20–40 mg/day retards progression of atherosclerosis throughout the vascular system.

4S Update

Scandinavian Simvastatin Survival Study

Title	Extended follow-up of patients on 4S shows increased survival benefit of simvastatin therapy.
Authors	Pedersen TR, Wilhelmsen L, Faegerman O, et al.
Reference	Presentation at the November 1998 American Heart Association Scientific Sessions, Dallas, Texas.
Disease	Hyperlipidemia, coronary artery disease.
Purpose	To assess whether the benefit of reduction in cardiac outcomes from lipid lowering remained 2 years after the original 5.4 year study completed.
Design	As per 4S.
Patients	4444 patients (aged 35–70 years) were in original 4S trial. Mean baseline LDL was 188 mg/dL and mean total cholesterol at baseline was 261 mg/dL.
Follow-up	Median 7.4 years.
Treatment regimen	As per 4S. Then at the conclusion of the study, further therapy was left to the discretion of the physician.
Results	The 30% decrease in risk of death reported in the original study was maintained during 2 year follow up; that is out to 7–8 years. Over the 5.4 study period plus 2 year follow-up, 15.8% assigned to placebo group had died vs 11.5 of patients assigned to simvastatin.
Conclusions	Benefit of cholesterol lowering with simvistatin was maintained long term.

4S (Substudy)

Scandinavian Simvistatin Survival Study

Title	Reduced coronary events in simvistatin treated patients with coronary heart disease and diabetes or impaired fasting glucose levels. Subgroup analysis in the Scandinavian Simvistatin Survival Study.
Authors	Haffner SM, Alexander CM, Cook TJ, et al.
Reference	Ann Intern Med 1999;59:2661-2667.
Disease	Coronary heart disease, hyperlipidemia, diabetes mellitus.
Purpose	To determine the effect of simvistatin on coronary events in patients with coronary heart disease and diabetes or impaired fasting glucose levels.
Design	As per 4S.
Patients	678 patients had plasma glucose levels ≥110 mg/dL but less than 126 mg/dL which is diagnostic for impaired fasting glucose; 281 patients had plasma glucose ≥126 mg/dL but did not have a previous clinical history of diabetes; and 202 had clinical histories of diabetes (total of 483 patients with diabetes as defined by 1997 American Diabetes Association criteria). 3237 patients had normal fasting glucose.
Follow-up	5.4 years.
Treatment regimen	As per 4S.
Additional therapy	As per 4S.

Results	Incidence of coronary events increased in the placebo group by baseline glucose status. Impaired fasting glucose group had a relative risk of 1.15; in diabetics with elevated fasting glucose but no prior history this was 1.19; in diabetics with a history the relative risk was increased to 1.83. The relative risk of having increased coronary heart events in the combined diabetic groups vs those with a normal fasting blood sugar was increased at 1.44 (95% CI=1.14–1.82). Diabetic patients treated with simvistatin had decreased number of major coronary events compared to the placebo group (RR=0.58 ; p=0.001) as well as revascularization procedures (RR=0.52; p=0.005). There was a nonsignificant trend toward a reduction in total and coronary mortality in diabetic patients that received simvistatin vs placebo. Simvistatin also decreased the incidence of major coronary events (RR=0.62; p=0.003), revascularizations (RR=0.57; p=0.009), and total (RR=0.57; p=0.02) and coronary (RR=0.45; p=0.007) mortality in patients with impaired fasting glucose but not overt diabetes.
Conclusions	Cholesterol lowering with simvistatin decreased coronary events and revascularizations in patients with diabetes (as defined by 1997 American Diabetes Association) and decreased the incidence of coronary events, revascularization, and mortality in patients with impaired fasting glucose levels.

PLAC I and II

Pravastatin Limitation of Atherosclerosis in the Coronary Arteries

Title	a. Design and recruitment in the United States of a multicenter quantitative angiographic trial of pravastatin to limit atherosclerosis in the coronary arteries (PLAC I). b. Pravastatin, lipids, and atherosclerosis in the carotid arteries (PLAC-II). c. Reduction in coronary events during treatment with pravastatin.
Authors	a. Pitt B, Ellis SG, Mancini GBJ, et al. b. Crouse JR III, Byington RP, Bond MG, et al. c. Furberg CD, Pitt B, Byington RP, et al.
Reference	a. Am J Cardiol 1993;72:31-35. b. Am J Cardiol 1995;75:455-459. c. Am J Cardiol 1995;76:60C-63C.
Disease	Hyperlipidemia.
Purpose	To assess the effects of pravastatin on progression and regression of coronary artery disease in patients with moderate hypercholesterolemia.
Design	Randomized, double blind, placebo controlled, multicenter.
Patients	559 patients (PLAC I: 408 patients, age ≤75 years, with documented ≥1 stenosis ≥50% in a major epicardial coronary artery, LDL cholesterol 130-189 mg/dL, and triglycerides ≤350 mg/dL. Patients with secondary hyperlipidemia, diabetes mellitus, congestive heart failure, and other serious concomitant diseases were excluded. PLAC II: 151 patients with coronary artery disease and extracranial carotid lesion. Same criteria as above.
Follow-up	Clinical follow-up for 3 years. Coronary angiography at baseline and after 36 months (PLAC I).

PLAC I and II

Pravastatin Limitation of Atherosclerosis in the Coronary Arteries (continued)

Treatment regimen	Pravastatin 40 mg X1/d or placebo for 3 years in PLAC-I, 20–40 mg/d in PLAC-II.
Additional therapy	Patients whose LDL cholesterol remained ≥190 mg/dL received cholestyramine, and then 5–10 mg open label pravastatin or placebo. If these measures failed, the patient was withdrawn from the study.
Results	The incidence of coronary events was 4.0%/year in the placebo vs 1.8%/year in the pravastatin patients (55% risk reduction, 95% CI 19–79%, p=0.014). A similar effect was seen in patients <65 years and ≥65 years of age. 11 patients vs 7 patients in the placebo and pravastatin groups died (40% risk reduction, 95% CI -65% to 85%, p=0.31). Nonfatal myocardial infarction occurred in 24 patients of the placebo vs 9 of the pravastatin group (67% risk reduction, 95% CI 32%–88%, p=0.006). The angiographic results have not been published yet.
Conclusions	Pravastatin therapy was associated with reduction of clinical events in coronary patients with mild to moderate hyperlipidemia.

WOSCOPS

Prevention of Coronary Heart Disease With Pravastatin in Men With Hypercholesterolemia: The West Of Scotland Coronary Prevention Study

Title	a. Prevention of coronary heart disease with pravastatin in men with hypercholesterolemia. b. Influence of pravastatin and plasma lipids on clinical events in the West of Scotland Coronary Prevention Study (WOSCOPS).
Authors	a. Shepherd J, Cobbe SM, Ford I, et al. b. West of Scotland Coronary Prevention Study Group.
Reference	a. N Engl J Med 1995;333:1301-1307. b. Circulation 1998; 97:1440-1445.
Disease	Hypercholesterolemia, coronary artery disease.
Purpose	a. To assess whether pravastatin therapy reduces the incidence of acute myocardial infarction and mortality from coronary heart disease in hypercholesterolemic men without a history of prior myocardial infarction. b. To determine the extent to which reduction of LDL influenced coronary heart disease risk reduction in the WOSCOPS.
Design	a. Randomized, double blind, placebo controlled, multicenter. b. Relationship between baseline lipid levels and rates of cardiovascular events; relationships between on-treatment lipid concentrations and risk reduction in patients taking pravastatin were examined by Cox regression models and division of cohorts into quintiles.

WOSCOPS

Prevention of Coronary Heart Disease With Pravastatin in Men With Hypercholesterolemia: The West Of Scotland Coronary Prevention Study (continued)

Patients	6595 men, 45-64 years of age, with fasting LDL cholesterol >252 mg per deciliter before diet and >155 mg per deciliter after 4 weeks of diet. None of the patients had a history of prior myocardial infarction. 78% of the patients were ex- or current smokers and 5% had angina pectoris.
Follow-up	a. The average follow-up was 4.9 years (32,216 subject years of follow-up). b. 5 years.
Treatment regimen	Pravastatin (40 mg/d) or placebo.
Results	a. Compared to baseline values pravastatin reduced plasma total cholesterol levels by 20% and LDL cholesterol by 26%, whereas no such changes were observed in the placebo treated group. Pravastatin reduced coronary events by 31% (95% CI 17-43%; p<0.001). There were 174 (5.5%) and 248 (7.9%) coronary events in the pravastatin and control group, respectively. Pravastatin reduced the risk for nonfatal infarction by 31% (4.6% vs 6.5%; p<0.001; 95% CI 15-45%), and the risk for death from all cardiovascular causes by 32% (1.6 vs 2.3%; p=0.033; 95% CI 3-53%). There was no increase in mortality from noncardiovascular causes. b. Baseline LDL cholesterol was only a weak predictor of cardiac risk in both treated and untreated groups. The reduction in risk of a cardiac event by pravastatin was similar across all quintiles of baseline LDL levels. Baseline HDL showed a strong negative association with cardiovascular event rate, but reduction in risk with pravastatin was similar for all quintiles of HDL elevation. The fall in LDL level in the pravastatin group did not correlate with the reduction in risk of a cardiac event on multivariate regression. The maximum benefit of about a 45% risk reduction was

observed in the middle quintile of LDL reduction, representing a 24% fall in LDL. Further decreases in LDL, up to 39%, did not result in further reduction in coronary heart disease risk reduction. When event rates between placebo and pravastatin treated subjects with the same LDL cholesterol level were compared, there was evidence for an LDL independent treatment benefit of pravastatin that remains to be determined.

Conclusions

a. Primary prevention in moderately hypercholesterolemic men with 5 years Pravastatin therapy reduced the incidence of myocardial infarction and death from cardiovascular causes. No excess of noncardiovascular death was observed.

b. A fall in LDL cholesterol of 24% was sufficient to produce full benefit in patients taking pravastatin. Further reduction was not associated with further reduction in coronary heart disease risk.

WOSCOPS (Substudy)

West Of Scotland Coronary Prevention Study

Title	The effects of pravastatin on hospital admission in hypercholesterolemic middle aged men.
Authors	West Of Scotland Coronary Prevention Study Group.
Reference	J Am Coll Cardiol 1999; 33:909–915.
Disease	Hypercholesterolemia.
Purpose	To determine the effect of lipid lowering with pravastatin on hospital admissions in the WOSCOPS.
Design	As per WOSCOPS.
Patients	As per WOSCOPS.
Follow-up	Mean of 4.9 years.
Treatment regimen	As per WOSCOPS.
Results	Overall 2198 (33%) of the 6595 men were admitted to the hospital. There were 4333 admissions and 28% were related to cardiac disease. The number of men requiring hospitalization for cardiovascular causes was reduced by 21% (95% CI = 9–31, p = 0.008) in the pravastatin group compared to placebo. Hospital admissions for cardiac causes per 1000 subject years was decreased by 10.8% (95% CI = 4–17; p = 0.0013) in the pravastatin group compared to the placebo group. Hospitalizations for compliant patients was reduced to a greater extent than in non-compliant patients.

WOSCOPS (Substudy)

West Of Scotland Coronary Prevention Study

(continued)

Conclusions	Pravastatin decreased hospital admissions for cardiovascular disease in middle aged men with hypercholesterolemia.

REGRESS

The Regression Growth Evaluation Statin Study

Title	a. Effects of lipid lowering by pravastatin on progression and regression of coronary artery disease in symptomatic men with normal to moderately elevated serum cholesterol levels.The regression Growth Evaluation Statin Study (REGRESS). b. Reduction of transient myocardial ischemia with pravastatin in addition to the conventional treatment in patients with angina pectoris.
Authors	a. Jukema JW, Bruschke AVG, van Boven AJ, et al. b. van Boven AJ, Jukema JW, Zwinderman AH, et al.
Reference	a. Circulation 1995;91:2528-2540. b. Circulation 1996;94:1503-1505.
Disease	Hyperlipidemia, coronary artery disease.
Purpose	To evaluate whether 2 years of statin therapy will affect the progression of coronary artery disease and clinical outcome of patients with coronary artery disease who have normal to moderately elevated plasma cholesterol levels.
Design	Randomized, double blind, placebo controlled, multicenter.
Patients	a. 885 men with serum cholesterol 4-8 mmol/L and ≥1 coronary lesion with ≥50% of luminal narrowing. b. 768 men with stable angina pectoris, with serum cholesterol 4-8 mmol/L and ≥1 coronary lesion with ≥50% of luminal narrowing.
Follow-up	a. Clinical evaluation and repeated angiography after 2 years. b. Ambulatory holter ECG monitoring before randomization, and after intervention (in patients that underwent CABG or PTCA) or after 2 years (in patients treated medically).

REGRESS

The Regression Growth Evaluation Statin Study

(continued)

Treatment regimen	Pravastatin 40 mg/d or placebo.
Additional therapy	Dietary advice. Cholestyramine for patients with cholesterol >8.0 mmol/L on repeated assessments. Routine antianginal therapy.
Results	a. 778 (88%) had an evaluable final coronary angiography. Mean segment diameter decreased 0.10 mm and 0.06 mm in the placebo and pravastatin groups (mean difference 0.04 mm, 95% CI 0.01-0.07 mm, p=0.19). The median minimum obstruction diameter decreased 0.09 and 0.03 mm, respectively (difference of the medians 0.06 mm, 95% CI 0.02-0.08 mm, p=0.001). After 2 years 89% of the pravastatin and 81% of the placebo treated patients were without new cardiovascular events (p=0.002). b. In the pravastatin-assigned patients, transient myocardial ischemia was detected at baseline in 28% and after treatment in 19%. In the placebo treated patients it was found in 20% at baseline and 23% at follow-up (odds ratio 0.62; 95% CI 0.41 to 0.93; p=0.021). The number of ischemic episodes per ambulatory ECG monitoring was reduced at follow-up by 0.53±0.25 episodes in the placebo group and by 1.23±0.25 episodes in the pravastatin group (p=0.047). Ischemic burden (the product of duration of ischemia in minutes multiplied by ST segment depression in mm) decreased from 41±5 to 22±5 mm • min in the pravastatin treated patients (p=0.0058), and from 34±6 to 26±4 mm • min in the placebo group (p=0.24). After adjustment for other independent risk factors, the effect of pravastatin on reduction of ischemia remained significant (odds ratio 0.45; 95% CI 0.22 to 0.91; p=0.026).
Conclusions	a. 2 years of pravastatin therapy, in men with coronary artery disease and normal to moderately elevated cholesterol levels, resulted in less progression of coronary atherosclerosis and fewer new cardiovascular events. b. Pravastatin ameliorated transient myocardial ischemia in patients with coronary artery disease and optimal antianginal therapy.

REGRESS (Substudy)

Regression Growth Evaluation Statin Study

Title	B-mode ultrasound assessment of pravastatin treatment effect on carotid and femoral walls and its correlations with coronary arteriographic findings. A report of the Regression Growth Evaluation Statin Study (REGRESS).
Authors	deGroot F, Jukema JW, Montauban AD, et al.
Reference	J Am Coll Cardiol. 1998; 31:1561-1567.
Disease	Atherosclerosis.
Purpose	To determine the effects of pravastatin on carotid and femoral artery walls.
Design	As per REGRESS. Imaging of carotid and femoral arteries by B-mode ultrasound at baseline, 6, 12, 18, and 24 months.
Patients	255 patients that were part of REGRESS.
Follow-up	24 months (ultrasound findings).
Treatment regimen	As per REGRESS.
Results	Baseline IMT (intimal thickness) was 0.86±0.33 mm. IMT decreased 0.05±0.20 (SEM) mm in patients receiving pravastatin; IMT was unchanged in the placebo group (p=0.0085 pravastatin vs placebo). Maximal IMT was 1.07±0.43 mm and decreased 0.05±0.22 mm with pravastatin but increased by 0.01±0.21 mm in the placebo patients. There was a correlation between baseline IMT and mean coronary artery segment diameter (r=-0.32, p=0.001).

REGRESS (Substudy)

Regression Growth Evaluation Statin Study (continued)

Conclusions	Pravastatin decreased intimal medial thickening of carotid and femoral arteries.

CARE

Cholesterol And Recurrent Events

Title	a. The effect of pravastatin on coronary events after myocardial infarction in patients with average cholesterol levels. b. Relationship between plasma LDL concentrations during treatment with pravastatin and recurrent coronary events in the cholesterol and recurrent events trial. c. Reduction of stroke incidence following myocardial infarction with pravastatin: the CARE study.
Authors	a. Sacks FM, Pfeffer MA, Moye LA, et al. b. Sacks FM, Moye LA, Davis BR, et al. c. Plehn JF, et al.
Reference	a. 1. Am J Cardiol 1991;68:1436-1446. 2. Am J Cardiol 1995;75:621-623. 3. Am J Cardiol 1995;76:98C-106C. 4. N Engl J Med 1996;335:1001-1009. b. Circulation 1998; 97:1446-1452. c. Presentation at the American Heart Association's 23rd International Joint Conference on Stroke and Cerebral Circulation. February 5-7, 1998, Orlando, Florida.
Disease	a. Coronary artery disease, myocardial infarction. b. Myocardial infarction, hypercholesterolemia.
Purpose	a. To evaluate the effectiveness of lowering blood cholesterol levels with pravastatin in patients after myocardial infarction and its effect on subsequent cardiac events. b. To determine the relationship between the LDL concentration during therapy, absolute reduction in LDL, and percent reduction in LDL and outcome. c. To analyze the effect of lipid lowering with pravastatin on the risk of stroke and transient ischemic attacks in the CARE trial.
Design	Randomized, double blind, placebo controlled, multicenter.

Patients	4159 patients, 21–75 years old, who have experienced myocardial infarction 3–20 months before randomization, had plasma total cholesterol <240 mg/dL, LDL cholesterol 115–174 mg/dL, triglycerides <350 mg/dL, fasting glucose levels ≤ 220 mg/dL, left ventricular ejection fraction ≥25%, and no symptomatic congestive heart failure.
Follow-up	Median follow-up 5 years (4-6.2 years).
Treatment regimen	Pravastatin 40 mg/d or placebo. For patients with LDL cholesterol >175 mg/dL at follow-up, dietary counseling, and then cholestyramine.
Results	a. Pravastatin therapy lowered the mean LDL cholesterol of 139 mg/dL by 32% and maintained mean levels of 98 mg/dL. During follow-up LDL cholesterol was 28% lower, total cholesterol was 20% lower, HDL 5% higher, and triglycerides level 14% lower in the pravastatin than placebo group (p<0.001 for all comparisons). Primary end points (death from coronary artery disease or nonfatal myocardial infarction) occurred in 13.2% vs 10.2% in the placebo and pravastatin group, respectively (risk reduction 24%; 95% CI 9-36%; p=0.003). Cardiovascular death occurred in 5.7% in the placebo vs 4.6% in the pravastatin group (risk reduction 20%; 95% CI -5-39%; p=0.10), and non fatal myocardial infarction occurred in 8.3% vs 6.5%, respectively (risk reduction 23%; 95% CI 4-39%; p=0.02). However, total mortality was comparable (9.4% vs 8.6% in the placebo and pravastatin group, respectively; 9% risk reduction; 95% CI -12-26%; p=0.37). There was no difference in mortality from noncardiovascular causes. The risk of myocardial infarction was 25% lower in the pravastatin group (7.5% vs 10.0%; 95% CI 8-39%; p=0.006). The rate of coronary artery bypass surgery or PTCA was lower in the pravastatin group (14.1% vs 18.8%; risk reduction 27%; 95% CI 15-37%; p<0.001). The pravastatin group had also a 31% lower incidence of stroke (2.6% vs 3.8%; 95% CI 3-52%; p=0.03). There was also a trend toward less unstablangina in the pravastatin group (15.2% vs 17.3%; risk reduction 13%; 95% CI -1-25%; p=0.07). The effect of pravastatin was greater among women then among men (46% vs 20% risk reduction for women and men respectively).

Patients with baseline LDL cholesterol >150 mg/dL had a 35% reduction in major coronary events, as compared with a 26% reduction in those with baseline LDL cholesterol of 125-150 mg/dL, and a 3% increase in those with baseline levels < 125 mg/dL (p=0.03 for the interaction between baseline LDL cholesterol level and risk reduction). The overall incidence of fatal or nonfatal cancer was comparable (161 in the placebo vs 172 in the pravastatin group). However, breast cancer occurred in 1 patient in the placebo and in 12 in the pravastatin group (p=0.002). Of the 12 cases in the pravastatin group, 3 occurred in patients who had previously had breast cancer. There was no other significant differences between the groups in the occurrence of other types of cancer.
b. Coronary death or recurrent MI were reduced by 24% with pravastatin. Coronary event rate declined as LDL was reduced from 174 to about 125 mg/dL; however, no further decline occurred in the LDL range of 71-125 mg/dL. LDL concentration achieved during follow-up was a significant but nonlinear predictor of coronary event rate; the extent of LDL reduction as absolute amount or percentage of LDL reduction was not a significant predictor of event rate. Triglycerides but not HDL weakly but significantly were associated with coronary event rate.
c. The stroke incidence was 3.7% in placebo patients and 2.5% in patients on pravastatin. Stroke or transient ischemic attack occurred in 6% of patients on placebo and 4.4% of patients on pravastatin. Thus, pravastatin decreased strokes by 32%; it decreased either strokes or transient ischemic attacks by 27% over 5 years. Unlike the CARE findings for reduced risk of myocardial infarction, (whereby lowering LDL below 125 mg/dL did not further reduce myocardial infarction), the investigators did not observe a threshold effect of LDL's below 125 mg/dL for stroke. Patients with LDL's above 150 had a 44% lower rate of strokes; those between 125-150, a 28% lower stroke rate; and under 125, a 25% reduction in stroke rate with pravastatin.

CARE

Cholesterol And Recurrent Events

(continued)

Conclusions	a. Pravastatin therapy lowered cardiac mortality, the need for revascularization, and occurrence of stroke in both men and women with coronary artery disease, plasma total cholesterol of <240 mg per deciliter and plasma LDL cholesterol >125 mg per deciliter. In this study, no reduction in event rate was found in patients with LDL cholesterol <125 mg per deciliter. There was no reduction in overall mortality. b. Reduction of LDL down to a concentration of about 125 mg/dL was associated with a reduction in coronary events. Further reduction to <125 mg/dL with therapy was not associated with additional benefit. c. In the population of patients in the CARE study, pravastatin reduced the rates of stroke and stroke or transient ischemic attacks.

CARE (Substudy)

Cholesterol And Recurrent Events Study

Title	Reduction of stroke incidence after myocardial infarction with pravastatin.
Authors	Plehn JF, Davis BR, Sacks FM, et al.
Reference	Circulation 1999; 99:216-223.
Disease	Stroke, hypercholesterolemia, post myocardial infarction.
Purpose	To determine whether cholesterol lowering with pravastatin in the CARE study reduced the incidence of cerebrovascular events.
Design	As per CARE trial.
Patients	As per CARE trial.
Follow-up	As per CARE trial.
Treatment regimen	As per CARE trial.
Results	76 strokes occurred in the placebo group and 52 occurred in the pravastatin group; 124 strokes or TIAs (transient ischemic attacks) occurred in the placebo group and 92 in the pravastatin group. There was a 32% reduction (95% CI, 4%-52%, p=0.03) in stroke and 27% reduction in strokes or TIAs (95% CI; 4%-44%; p=0.02). A reduction in stroke with pravastatin was present after adjusting for a number of variables. The occurrence of hemorrhagic stroke was 2 in pravastatin patients and 6 in placebo patients.

Conclusions	In patients post myocardial infarction with average cholesterol levels, pravastatin reduced the incidence of stroke or TIA.

CARE (Substudy)

Cholesterol And Recurrent Events

Title	Cardiovascular events and their reduction with pravastatin in diabetic and glucose intolerant myocardial infarction survivors with average cholesterol levels. Subgroup analyses in the Cholesterol and Recurrent Events (CARE) trial.
Authors	Goldberg RB, Melliec MJ, Sacks FM, et al.
Reference	Circulation 1998; 98:2513-2519.
Disease	Diabetic patients with coronary artery disease and average cholesterol levels as part of the CARE trial.
Purpose	To determine whether pravastatin prevented recurrent cardiovascular events in diabetic patients.
Design	As per CARE.
Patients	586 patients in the CARE trial with diabetes.
Follow-up	5 years.
Treatment regimen	As per CARE.

Results	Mean baseline lipid levels in the diabetic subgroup of CARE was 136 mg/dL for LDL, 206 mg/dL for total cholesterol, 38 mg/dL for HDL, and 164 mg/dL for triglycerides and these values were similar for the nondiabetic group. Pravastatin reduced LDL cholesterol by 27% in the diabetic and 28% in the nondiabetic group. In patients randomized to placebo, diabetes was associated with a higher rate of coronary events than nondiabetic patients (37% vs 25%). Pravastatin induced a 25% reduction in coronary events (coronary heart disease death, nonfatal myocardial infarction, CABG and PTCA) p=0.05; it reduced the risk for revascularization procedures by 32% (p=0.04). Because of a greater coronary event rate in the diabetic group, pravastatin resulted in a greater absolute risk reduction in diabetic vs nondiabetic group (8.1% vs 5.2%). Nondiabetic patients with abnormal fasting glucose levels had higher rates of coronary events than patients with normal fasting glucose levels, and again pravastatin was protective.
Conclusions	Both diabetic and nondiabetic patients with elevated fasting glucose levels are at risk for recurrent coronary events post infarction; pravastatin can reduce these events.

CARE (Substudy)

Cholesterol And Recurrent Events

Title	Inflammation, pravastatin, and the risk of coronary events after myocardial infarction in patients with average cholesterol levels.
Authors	Ridker PM, Rifai N, Pfeffer MA, et al.
Reference	Circulation 1998;98:839-844.
Disease	Myocardial infarction.
Purpose	To determine whether inflammation plays a role in recurrent events following myocardial infarction.
Design	Nested case: control substudy of CARE trial.
Patients	391 patients in CARE trial who developed recurrent nonfatal MI or fatal coronary event (cases), and comparison to equal number of controls that were age and sex matched but remained free of recurrent cardiac event (controls).
Follow-up	As per CARE.
Treatment regimen	As per CARE.

CARE (Substudy)

Cholesterol And Recurrent Events

(continued)

Results	C-reactive protein (CRP) and serum amyloid A (SAA), markers of inflammation, were highest among cases vs controls. Patients with highest quintiles had a relative risk of recurrent events that was 75% higher than patients in the lowest quintile, (p=0.02). Highest risk of recurrent events occurred in the placebo patients with elevations of both CRP and SAA. Assessment of stratified analyses revealed that while the association between inflammation and the risk of recurrent events was increased in patients randomized to placebo (RR=2.11, p=0.048), this association was not significant in patients randomized to pravastatin (RR=1.29, p=0.5).
Conclusions	Inflammation assessed by elevations of C-reactive protein and serum amyloid following myocardial infarction is associated with recurrent cardiac events; pravastatin may reduce this risk.

CARE (Substudy)

Cholesterol And Recurrent Events

Title	Effect of pravastatin on cardiovascular events in older patients with myocardial infarction and cholesterol levels in the average range.
Authors	Lewis SJ, Moye LA, Sacks FM, et al.
Reference	Ann Intern Med 1998; 129:681-689.
Disease	Hypercholesterolemia.
Purpose	To determine whether lipid lowering with pravastatin decreases recurrent cardiovascular events in patients 65 years and older.
Design	As per CARE.
Patients	Subset of patients from the CARE Trial who were 65-75 years old. 1283 post MI patients. Total cholesterol level had to be <240 mg/dL and LDL cholesterol of 115-174 μg/dL.
Follow-up	5 years.
Treatment regimen	As per CARE.

CARE (Substudy)

Cholesterol And Recurrent Events

(continued)

Results	At 5 years major coronary events (coronary death, nonfatal MI, PTCA or CABG) were reduced in the pravastatin group from 28.1% in placebo patients to 19.7% in pravastatin patients (relative risk reduction = 32%; p<0.001). Death from coronary artery disease was reduced from 10.3% in placebo patients to 5.8% in the pravastatin group (relative risk reduction = 45%; p=0.004). Stroke was reduced from 7.3% in placebo patients to 4.5% in the pravastatin group (relative risk reduction = 40%; p=0.03).
Conclusions	In older post myocardial infarction patient with average cholesterol levels, pravastatin decreased the rate of major coronary heart disease events and stroke.

CARE (Substudy)

Cholesterol And Recurrent Events

Title	Influence of baseline lipids on effectiveness of pravastatin in the CARE trial.
Authors	Pfeffer MA, Sacks FM, Moyé LA, et al.
Reference	J Am Coll Cardiol 1999; 33:125-130.
Disease	Hypercholesterolemia, postmyocardial infarction.
Purpose	To determine effect of baseline lipid levels on cardiac events and effect of lipid lowering with pravastatin.
Design	As per CARE.
Patients	As per CARE.
Follow-up	As per CARE.
Treatment regimen	As per CARE.

CARE (Substudy)

Cholesterol And Recurrent Events

(continued)

Results	The time to a primary end point (coronary artery death or nonfatal MI) or to secondary end points including revascularization as assessed as a function of baseline lipid values. Within the range of cholesterol levels in the CARE patients (159-239 mg/dL) baseline cholesterol level did not influence risk of a coronary event even in the placebo group.A higher baseline LDL (in Care Trial LDL's ranged from 115-174 mg/dL) was associated with greater coronary event rates. For placebo patients each 25 mg/dL increment in LDL was associated with a 28% increase in risk of primary events. For patients receiving pravastatin, a 25 mg/dL increase in baseline LDL was not associated with an increased risk of coronary death. This differential influence of baseline LDL's in placebo vs pravastatin resulted in convergence of event rates at lower LDL's (≤ 126 mg/dL).There was an inverse relationship between HDL cholesterol and coronary events in both treatment groups (10 mg/dL lower baseline HDL was associated with 10% increase in primary end points).
Conclusions	Baseline LDL cholesterol levels influences risk of coronary events in the placebo group; pravastatin's effect on reducing cardiac events was more dramatic at higher LDL levels.

CARE (Substudy)

Cholesterol And Recurrent Events

Title	Effect of pravastatin on cardiovascular events in women after myocardial infarction. The Cholesterol And Recurrent Events (CARE) Trial.
Authors	Lewis SJ, Sacks FM, Mitchell JS, et al.
Reference	J Am Coll Cardiol 1998; 32:140-146.
Disease	Post myocardial infarction, hypercholesterolemia.
Purpose	To determine effect of the lipid lowering agent pravastatin on recurrent cardiovascular events in women post MI.
Design	As per CARE.
Patients	576 postmenopausal women, with total cholesterol <240 mg/dL and LDL cholesterol of 115-174 mg/dL, between 3 and 20 months after MI.
Follow-up	5 years.
Treatment regimen	As per CARE.

CARE (Substudy)

Cholesterol And Recurrent Events

(continued)

Result	Pravastatin resulted in a 43% risk reduction for the primary end point (death from coronary heart disease or nonfatal MI; p =0.035), 46% reduction for combined coronary events (p=0.001); and a 56% reduction in stroke (p=0.07). Women who received pravastatin also exhibited lower rates of need for revascularization over the study period (48% reduction in need for PTCA, p=0.025; 40% reduction in CABG, p=0.14). The magnitude of reduction of coronary events in women was actually greater than men in the CARE trial. Pravastatin reduced cholesterol and LDL to a similar degree in men and women. Total cholesterol was reduced by 19%-20%, and LDL cholesterol by 28%; HDL increased by 4%-5%.
Conclusions	Pravastatin reduced cardiovascular events in women with myocardial infarcts who had average cholesterol levels.

CARE (Substudy)

Cholesterol And Recurrent Events

Title	Long term effects of pravastatin on plasma concentration of C-reactive protein.
Authors	Ridker PM, Rifai N, Pfeffer MA, et al.
Reference	Circulation 1999;100:230-235.
Disease	Post myocardial infarction patients with total cholesterol <240 mg/dL and LDL cholesterol between 115-175 mg/dL.
Purpose	To determine whether long term therapy with pravastatin reduces the levels of the inflammatory marker, C-reactive protein.
Design	As per CARE.
Patients	472 randomly selected participants in CARE in whom C-reactive protein was measured at baseline and at 5 years and who had remained free of recurrent vascular events during follow-up.
Follow-up	5 years.
Treatment regimen	As per CARE.
Additional therapy	As per CARE.

CARE (Substudy)

Cholesterol And Recurrent Events

(continued)

Results	While C-reactive protein levels increased over time in placebo patients (median change = +4.2%; p=0.2 and mean change =+0.07 µg/dL; p=0.04), they decreased in pravastatin patients (median change =-17.4%; p=0.004 and mean change =-0.07 mg/dL; p=0.002). Median, mean, and absolute change in C-reactive protein were significantly lower in the pravastatin group at 5 years (-21.6%; p=0.007; -37.8%, p=0.002; and -0.137 µg/dL; p=0.003, respectively). The changes in C-reactive protein over time did not correlate with change in LDL cholesterol among pravastatin or placebo treated patients. There was also a lack of a correlation between change in C-reactive protein and changes in total cholesterol or HDL levels. Pravastatin reduced C-reactive protein levels at all LDL change increments.
Conclusions	In post myocardial infarction patients, C-reactive protein levels tended to increase over 5 years in patients receiving standard therapy plus placebo; pravastatin decreased C-reactive protein levels independent of the degree of lipid improvement.

Title	Comparison of 1 year efficacy and safety of atorvastatin vs lovastatin in primary hypercholesterolemia.
Authors	Davidson M, McKenney J, Stein E, et al.
Reference	Am J Cardiol 1997;79:1475–1481.
Disease	Hyperlipidemia.
Purpose	To compare the efficacy and safety of 2 3-hydroxy-3-methylglutaryl coenzyme A reductase inhibitors, atorvastatin and lovastatin, in patients with hypercholesterolemia.
Design	Randomized, double blind, placebo controlled, multicenter.
Patients	1049 patients (58% men), 18–80 years old, with LDL cholesterol ≥3.75 mmol/L and triglycerides <4.52 mmol/L and a body mass index ≤32 kg/m^2. Patients with renal or hepatic disease, insulin dependent diabetes mellitus, uncontrolled type II diabetes mellitus, unstable medical conditions, elevated creatine kinase levels, <80% compliance with study medications during the placebo run in phase were excluded. Patients on immunosuppressive agents, drugs known to affect lipid levels, or medications known to be associated with rhabdomyolysis were not included.
Follow-up	1 year.
Treatment regimen	Randomization to 4 groups: 1. atorvastatin 10 mg/d for 52 weeks; 2. lovastatin 20 mg/d for 52 weeks; 3. placebo for 16 weeks followed by atorvastatin for 36 weeks; and 4. placebo for 16 weeks followed by lovastatin for 36 weeks. In patients who had not reached their LDL cholesterol goal after 22 weeks of therapy, the medication dose was doubled.

(continued)

Additional therapy	NCEP step 1 diet.
Results	Throughout the study compliance was >93%. At the end of the 52 week treatment, 12% of patients had withdrawn from the study. LDL cholesterol level at week 16 increased by 1.0±1.0% compared to the baseline in the placebo group. In contrast, it was reduced by 27±0.8% with lovastatin and by 36.0±0.5% with atorvastatin (p=0.0001 vs placebo and vs lovastatin). HDL cholesterol at week 16 increased by 1.0±1.0% in the placebo group, by 7.0±0.9% in the lovastatin group (p<0.05 vs placebo), and by 7.0±0.5% in the atorvastatin group (p<0.05 vs placebo). Triglycerides increased by 4.0±2.3% in the placebo group, decreased by 19.0±0.6% in the lovastatin group, and decreased by 27.0±0.4% in the atorvastatin group (p<0.05 vs placebo and vs lovastatin). Apolipoprotein B increased by 3.0±1.0% in the placebo group, decreased by 20.0±0.8% in the lovastatin group, and decreased by 28.0±0.5% in the atorvastatin group (p<0.05 vs placebo and vs lovastatin). At week 16, 74% of the atorvastatin group vs 55% of the lovastatin group and 7% of the placebo group reached NCEP target. At week 52, 27% of the atorvastatin group and 49% of the lovastatin group needed to double their medication dose based on response to therapy and risk status. At the end of follow-up 78% of the atorvastatin group vs only 63% of the lovastatin group reached NCEP target. Among patients with coronary artery disease, target LDL cholesterol levels were achieved by 37% of the atorvastatin group vs only 11% of the lovastatin group. By week 52, LDL cholesterol was reduced by 29.0±0.7% and 37.0±0.5% in the lovastatin and atorvastatin groups respectively (p<0.05), HDL cholesterol was increased by 7.0±0.9% and 7.0±0.5%, triglycerides were reduced by 8.0±2.0% and 16.0±1.3% (p<0.05), and apolipoprotein B was reduced by 22.0±0.7% and 30.0±0.4%, respectively. Adverse effects occurred in similar rates with both medications (20% with atorvastatin and 21% with lovastatin). Serious adverse effects occurred in 8% vs 7% of the atorvastatin and lovastatin groups, respectively.
Conclusions	Atorvastatin was better than lovastatin in reducing LDL cholesterol, apolipoprotein B, and triglycerides and had a similar safety profile as lovastatin.

CCAIT

The Canadian Coronary Atherosclerosis Intervention Trial

Title	Effects of monotherapy with an HMG-CoA reductase inhibitor on the progression of coronary atherosclerosis as assessed by serial quantitative arteriography. The Canadian Coronary Atherosclerosis Intervention Trial.
Authors	Waters D, Higginson L, Gladstone P, et al.
Reference	Circulation 1994;89:959-968.
Disease	Coronary artery disease, hypercholestolemia.
Purpose	To evaluate whether lovastatin (a HMG-CoA reductase inhibitor) therapy will affect coronary atherosclerosis as assessed by serial quantitative coronary angiography.
Design	Randomized, double blind, placebo controlled, multicenter.
Patients	331 patients (81% men), 27-70 years old, with angiographically proven diffuse coronary artery disease, total serum cholesterol 220-300 mg/dL, and serum triglycerides ≤500 mg/dL. Women with childbearing potential, and patients with previous coronary artery bypass surgery; previous coronary angioplasty within 6 months; ejection fraction <40%; left main coronary artery stenosis>50%; 3 vessel disease with proximal LAD stenosis >70%; coexisting severe illness; myocardial infarction or unstable angina within 6 weeks prior to randomization; concurrent use of lipid lowering drugs, corticosteroids, anticoagulants, cimetidine, or cyclosporine; liver function disturbances; or renal failure were excluded.
Follow-up	Clinical follow-up for 24 months. Coronary angiography at baseline and 24 months.
Treatment regimen	Randomization to lovastatin 20 mg/d (n=165) or placebo (n=166). The dose was increased to 40 mg/d in patients whose LDL cholesterol was >130 mg/dL despite 4 weeks of therapy. If LDL cholesterol was still >130 mg/dL, the dose was increased to 80 mg/d.

CCAIT

The Canadian Coronary Atherosclerosis Intervention Trial (continued)

Additional therapy	AHA phase I diet. Aspirin 325 mg on alternate days. Revascularization (CABG or PTCA) was not permitted during the 24 month study period.
Results	The mean lovastatin dose was 36 mg/d. The target LDL cholesterol ≤130 mg/dL was achieved by 69% of the lovastatin and 10% of the placebo treated patients. Total cholesterol reduced by 21±11% (p<0.001), LDL cholesterol reduced by 29±11% (p<0.001), HDL cholesterol increased by 7.3±19% (p<0.001), and apolipoprotein B decreased by 21±12% (p<0.001) in the lovastatin assigned patients. Angina class improved by ≥1 grade in 50 lovastatin and 43 placebo patients, and worsened by ≥1 grade in 23 lovastatin and 27 placebo patients (p=0.087). There was a trend towards less coronary events in the lovastatin group (14 vs 18 patients had ≥1 event) that was not statistically significant. A second coronary angiography was obtained in 299 patients (90%). Coronary change score (defined as the per patient mean of the minimum lumen diameter changes (follow-up minus baseline angiogram) for all lesions measured, excluding those with <25% stenosis on both films) worsened by 0.09±0.16 mm in the placebo group and by 0.05±0.13 mm in the lovastatin group (p=0.01). Mean percent diameter stenosis increased by 2.89±5.59% in the placebo group and by 1.66±4.5% in the lovastatin group (p=0.039). Progression ≥ a decrease in minimum lumen diameter of ≥1 lesion by ≥0.4 mm) with no regression at other coronary segments was observed in 33% of the lovastatin vs 50% of the placebo group (p=0.003). 6.8% vs 9.4% of the lesions in the lovastatin and placebo treated patients progressed, respectively (p=0.017). ≥15% diameter stenosis progression was noted in 5.9% and 9.6% of the lesions in the lovastatin and placebo treated patients, respectively (p=0.008). Progression to a new total occlusion was noticed in 1.6% of the lovastatin group vs 1.9% of the placebo group. New coronary lesions were detected in 16% of the lovastatin vs 32% of the placebo group (p=0.001). Lovastatin was equally effective in men and women.
Conclusions	Lovastatin slowed the progression of coronary atherosclerotic lesions and inhibited the formation of new coronary stenotic lesions.

CIS

The Multicenter Coronary Intervention Study

Title	The effect of simvastatin on progression of coronary artery disease. The multicenter Coronary Intervention Study (CIS).
Authors	Bestehorn HP, Rensing UFE, Roskamm H, et al.
Reference	Eur Heart J 1997;18:226–234.
Disease	Coronary artery disease, hyperlipidemia.
Purpose	To assess the effects of 40 mg/d simvastatin therapy on progression of coronary artery disease in young male patients with coronary artery disease and hyperlipidemia.
Design	Randomized, double blind, placebo controlled, multicenter.
Patients	254 men, aged 30–55 years, with total plasma cholesterol 207–350 mg/dL and total triglycerides <330 mg/dL, and known coronary artery disease by angiography. Patients with hypertension, diabetes, LVEF <30%, myocardial infarction within 4 weeks, PTCA within 4 months, CABG in the past, or scheduled for coronary interventions were excluded.
Follow-up	Coronary angiography at baseline and at follow-up (up to 4 years, an average of 2.3 years).
Treatment regimen	Simvastatin 20 mg/d or placebo. After 6 weeks if LDL cholesterol >90 mg/dL, the simvastatin dose was increased to 40 mg/d.

The Multicenter Coronary Intervention Study

(continued)

Additional therapy	Lipid lowering diet. An ion-exchange resin was added after 12 weeks if LDL cholesterol was ≥120 mg/dL or ≥250 mg/dL in the simvastatin and placebo groups, respectively.
Results	129 patients were randomized to simvastatin and 125 to placebo. Follow-up angiogram was performed in 205 patients. Mean simvastatin daily dose was 34.5 mg. Simvastatin therapy resulted in 35% reduction of LDL cholesterol compared with placebo (p=0.0000). Coronary artery disease progressed slower in the simvastatin group. The mean global change score (visual evaluation by the method of Blankenhorn, a 7 point scale from -3 (strong regression) to +3 (strong progression)) was +0.20±0.08 in the simvastatin and +0.58±0.10 in the placebo group (p=0.02). 34.6% of the simvastatin and 53.5% of the placebo treated patients had progression. Minimum lumen diameter decreased by 0.02±0.014 mm in the simvastatin vs 0.10±0.02 mm in the placebo group (p=0.002). In patients receiving simvastatin, there was a significant correlation between LDL cholesterol levels during therapy and the per patient mean loss of minimum lumen diameter (r=0.29; p=0.003). There was no difference between the groups in the incidence of serious cardiac events.
Conclusions	Simvastatin therapy, 40 mg/d for an average of 2.3 years, reduced serum cholesterol and slowed the progression of coronary artery disease in young men with hypercholesterolemia and known coronary artery disease.

The CURVES Study

Comparative Dose Efficacy of Atorvastatin, Simvastatin, Pravastatin, Lovastatin, and Fluvastatin

Title	Comparative dose efficacy study of atorvastatin vs simvastatin, pravastatin, lovastatin, and fluvastatin in patients with hypercholesterolemia (The CURVES Study).
Authors	Jones P, Kafonek S, Laurora I, et al.
Reference	Am J Cardiol 1998;81:582–587.
Disease	Hyperlipidemia.
Purpose	To assess comparative dose efficacy of 5 different 3-hydroxy-3-methylglutaryl coenzyme A reductase inhibitors in hypercholesterolemic patients during 8 weeks of therapy.
Design	Randomized, open label, parallel group, multicenter.
Patients	534 patients, 18–80 years old, with plasma LDL cholesterol ≥160 mg/dL and triglyceride ≤400 mg/dL. Patients with hypothyroidism, nephrotic syndrome, insulin dependent or uncontrolled diabetes, hepatic dysfunction, elevated levels of creatine kinase, body mass index >32 kg/m^2, uncontrolled hypertension, myocardial infarction, coronary revascularization, or severe or unstable angina within the preceding 3 months, or hypersensitivity to hypolipemic medications were not included.
Follow-up	8 weeks.
Treatment regimen	Atrovastatin 10, 20, 40, or 80 mg/d; simvastatin 10, 20, pravastatin 10, 20 and 40 mg/d; lovastatin 20, 40 or 80 mg/d; and fluvastatin 20 or 40 mg/d.

The CURVES Study

Comparative Dose Efficacy of Atorvastatin, Simvastatin, Pravastatin, Lovastatin, and Fluvastatin

(continued)

Addtional therapy	Medications known to affect clinical laboratory parameters, anticoagulants, immunosuppressive agents, steroids, and lipid lowering agents were prohibited.
Results	518 patients completed the study. The intention to treat analysis included 522 patients (59% men). Atorvastatin, pravastatin and simvastatin 10 mg/d produced 38%, 19%, and 28% reduction in LDL cholesterol ($p \leq 0.02$ for atorvastatin vs pravastatin and vs simvastatin). Total cholesterol was reduced by 28%, 13%, and 21%, respectively ($p \leq 0.02$ for atorvastatin vs pravastatin and vs simvastatin), and HDL cholesterol was increased by 5.5%, 9.9%, and 6.8%, respectively (p=NS). Atorvastatin, pravastatin, simvastatin, fluvastatin, and lovastatin 20 mg/d caused reduction of 46%, 24%, 35%, 17%, and 29% in LDL cholesterol ($p \leq 0.05$ for atorvastatin against each of the other 4 agents); 35%, 18%, 26%, 13%, and 21% reduction in total cholesterol levels ($p \leq 0.02$ for atorvastatin vs each of the other 4 agents); and an increase of 5.1%, 3.0%, 5.2%, 0.9%, and 7.3% in HDL cholesterol (p=NS). Atorvastatin, pravastatin, simvastatin, fluvastatin, and lovastatin 40 mg/d caused reduction of 51%, 34%, 41%, 23%, and 31% in LDL cholesterol ($p \leq 0.05$ for atorvastatin against each of the other 4 agents); 40%, 24%, 30%, 19%, and 23% reduction in total cholesterol levels ($p \leq 0.02$ for atorvastatin vs each of the other 4 agents); and an increase of 4.8%, 6.2%, 9.6%, -3.0% and 4.6% in HDL cholesterol ($p \leq 0.05$ for simvastatin vs atorvastatin). Atorvastatin and lovastatin 80 mg/d produced 54% and 48% decrease in LDL cholesterol, 42% and 36% in total cholesterol, and -0.1% and 8.0% increase in HDL cholesterol. Atorvastatin 10 mg/d was more effective in reducing LDL cholesterol levels than simvastatin 10mg/d; pravastatin 10 and 20 mg/d; lovastatin 20 and 40 mg/d; and fluvastatin 20 and 40 mg/d ($p \leq 0.02$). Atorvastatin 20 mg/d resulted in greater reduction in LDL cholesterol than simvastatin 10, 20, and 40 mg/d; pravastatin 10, 20, and 40 mg/d; lovastatin 20 and 40 mg/d; and fluvastatin 20 and 40 mg/d ($p \leq 0.01$). The effect on triglycerides was comparable among the groups, except for atorvastatin 40 mg/d which produced greater (32%; $p \leq 0.05$) decrease in levels. The effect of atorvastatin on HDL cholesterol was comparable to that of the other

	agents, except that simvastatin 40 mg/d produced the greatest increase in levels. Adverse event rates were comparable among the groups. There were no cases of persistent elevations in serum transaminases or creatine kinase, or reports of myopathy.
Conclusions	Atorvastatin at a dose of 10, 20, and 40 mg/d produced a significantly greater reduction in LDL cholesterol levels. All 5 agents were safe and well tolerated.

LCAS

Lipoprotein and Coronary Atherosclerosis Study

Title	Effects of fluvastatin on coronary atherosclerosis in patients with mild to moderate cholesterol elevations: Lipoprotein and Coronary Atherosclerosis Study (LCAS).
Authors	Herd JA, Ballantyne CM, Farmer JA, et al.
Reference	Am J Cardiol 1997;80:278-286.
Disease	Coronary artery disease.
Purpose	To assess whether therapy with fluvastatin, a 3-hydroxy-3-methylglutaryl coenzyme A reductase inhibitor, would induce regression or slow the progression of coronary atherosclerosis in patients with coronary artery disease and mild to moderate hypercholesterolemia.
Design	Randomized, double blind, placebo controlled, single center.
Patients	429 patients (19% women), 35-75 years old, with angiographically proven coronary artery disease with 30%-75% diameter stenosis, LDL cholesterol levels 115-190 mg/dL despite diet, and triglycerides ≤300 mg/dL. Patients with prior angioplasty or myocardial infarction within 6 months, >50% left main coronary artery stenosis, prior CABG, uncontrolled hypertension, diabetes mellitus, or treatment with other hypolipemic agents were excluded.
Follow-up	Coronary angiography at baseline and after 130 weeks.
Treatment regimen	Randomization to fluvastatin 20 mg bid or placebo.

Lipoprotein and Coronary Atherosclerosis Study (continued)

Additional therapy	NCEP Step I diet. Open label cholestyramine, up to 12 g/d was given as adjunctive therapy to patients whose mean LDL levels before randomization remained ≥160 mg/dL.
Results	In 340 patients, both the baseline and follow-up angiograms were evaluable. By the end of follow-up total cholesterol levels decreased by 13.5±13.1% in the fluvastatin group and increased by 0.3±12.5% in the placebo group (p<0.0001). LDL cholesterol decreased by 22.5±17.6% and 2.2±17.1%, respectively (p<0.0001), HDL cholesterol increased by 8.7±15.2% and 3.9±15.4%, respectively (p=0.0054), and triglyceride levels decreased by 0.1±40.3% and increased by 9.5±42.1%, respectively (p=0.0297). In the fluvastatin + cholestyramine total cholesterol decreased by 18.3±12.4%, LDL cholesterol decreased by 27.9±16.9%, HDL increased by 8.0±14.9%, and triglyceride decreased by 0.3±29.2%. Final minus baseline minimal lumen diameter of qualifying lesions within each patient, adjusted for age and gender demonstrated less progression in the fluvastatin treated patients (with or without cholestyramine)(-0.028±0.021 mm) compared with the placebo treated patients (with or without cholestyramine) (-0.100±0.022 mm; p=0.005). Minimal lumen diameter decreased by 0.024 mm in the fluvastatin alone group and by 0.094 mm in the placebo alone group (p<0.02). Diameter stenosis increased by 0.6±0.7% in the fluvastatin group and by 2.8±0.8% in the placebo group (p=0.0137). Among the 84 patients with baseline LDL cholesterol <130 mg/dL, fluvastatin-treated patients had 0.021±0.040 mm increase in the minimal lumen diameter, indicating regression, whereas the placebo treated patients had a decrease of 0.062±0.040 mm in minimal lumen diameter (p=0.083). Progression was detected in 28.7% of the fluvastatin groups (with or without cholestyramine) vs 39.1% of the placebo groups (with or without cholestyramine), regression in 14.6% vs 8.3%, and mixed change or no response in 56.7% vs 52.7%, respectively (p=0.0198 for the difference in distribution between the 2 groups). New lesions appeared in 13% of the fluvastatin groups vs 22% of the placebo groups (p=0.03). Clinical event rates were lower with fluvastatin (14.5%) than with placebo (19.1%)(p=NS). Fewer fluvastatin treated patients underwent myocardial revascularization (10.7% vs 13.5%; p=NS).

Conclusions	Fluvastatin therapy in patients with coronary artery disease and mild to moderate hypercholesterolemia reduced the rate of progression of coronary atherosclerotic lesions.

LCAS (Substudy)

Lipoprotein and Coronary Atherosclerosis Study

Title	Influence of low HDL on progression of coronary artery disease and response to fluvastatin therapy.
Authors	Ballantyne CM, Herd A, Ferlic LL, et al.
Reference	Circulation 1999;99:736-743.
Disease	Hypercholesterolemia.
Purpose	To determine the effects of fluvastatin therapy on the angiographic progression of coronary artery disease in patients with low vs higher HDL C as part of LCAS.
Design	As per LCAS.
Patients	339 patients with biochemical and angiographic data. 68 had baseline HDL C <35 mg/dL with a mean of 31.7±2.2 mg/dL vs patients with baseline HDL ≥35 mg/dL at a mean of 47.4±11.2 mg/dL. Patients had to have evidence of CAD. LDL's were 115-190 mg/dL.
Follow-up	Quantitative coronary angiography at 2.5 years.
Treatment regimen	As per LCAS.

LCAS (Substudy)

Lipoprotein and Coronary Atherosclerosis Study

(continued)

Results	Patients with low LDL were more likely to be male and have increased triglyceride. Placebo patients with low HDL had more progression of coronary artery disease on quantitative angiography than placebo patients with higher HDL. In patients with low HDL fluvastatin significantly reduced angiographic progression measured as minimum lumen diameter (0.065±0.036 mm in fluvastatin group vs 0.274±0.045 mm in the placebo group, p=0.0004). In patients with higher HDL C the minimum lumen diameter was (0.036±0.021 mm vs 0.083±0.019 mm, p=0.09). Fluvastatin's effect was therefore greater in patients with low HDL vs those with high HDL. Fluvastatin's major effect on lipids in both high and low HDL groups was to lower LDL C and apoB-100. In patients with low HDL event free survival was improved with fluvastatin (p=0.002). Clinical events (PTCA, CABG, definite or probable MI, unstable angina requiring hospitalization, death) occurred in 8 out of 25 placebo patients and 2 of 43 fluvastatin patients.
Conclusions	Fluvastatin's major benefit is to decrease LDL C but patients with baseline low HDL have the greatest angiographic and clinical benefit.

PREDICT

Prevention of Restenosis by Elisor After Transluminal Coronary Angioplasty

Title	Effect of pravastatin on angiographic restenosis after coronary balloon angioplasty.
Authors	Bertrand ME, McFadden EP, Fruchart J-C, et al.
Reference	J Am Coll Cardiol 1997;30:863-869.
Disease	Coronary artery disease, restenosis.
Purpose	To assess the efficacy of pravastatin, a HMG coenzyme A reductase inhibitor, to prevent restenosis after coronary balloon angioplasty.
Design	Randomized, double blind, placebo controlled, multicenter.
Patients	695 patients, 25-75 years old, with LVEF >40%, total cholesterol levels 200-310 mg/dL and triglyceride levels <500 mg/dL who had undergone successful uncomplicated PTCA of one or more coronary artery lesions. Patients with a recent myocardial infarction (<15 d) and patients who had undergone previous PTCA or CABG of the target vessel were excluded. Randomization within 24 h of the PTCA.
Follow-up	Clinical follow-up, repeated blood lipid measurement and coronary angiography at 6 months.
Treatment regimen	Randomization to pravastatin 40 mg/d or placebo.
Additional therapy	All patients received aspirin 100 mg/d. Fish oil and other lipid lowering agents, corticosteroids, or immunosuppressive drugs were prohibited.

PREDICT

Prevention of Restenosis by Elisor After Transluminal Coronary Angioplasty (continued)

Results

347 patients were randomized to pravastatin and 348 patients to placebo. 625 (90%) patients had angiographic follow-up. At baseline, the average total cholesterol levels was 231±36 mg/dL in the placebo group and 228±38 mg/dL in the pravastatin group (p=0.42). The average LDL cholesterol was 157±29 mg/dL and 155±32 mg/dL, respectively (p=0.3). After 6 months of therapy total cholesterol decreased to 195±37 mg/dL in the pravastatin group, but remained the same (239±40 mg/dL) in the placebo group (p=0.0001), and LDL cholesterol decreased to 119±31 mg/dL in the pravastatin group but did not change (159±33 mg/dL) in the placebo group (p=0.0001). HDL cholesterol levels after 6 months were 52±13 mg/d in the pravastatin group and 49±14 mg/dL in the placebo group (p=0.01). Apolipoprotein A1 at 6 months was higher in the pravastatin group (150±27 mg/dL) than in the placebo group (144±28 mg/dL)(p=0.003). At baseline average minimal lumen diameter (MLD) was similar in the 2 groups. At follow-up angiography MLD was 1.54±0.66 mm in the pravastatin group and 1.47±0.62 mm in the placebo group (p=0.21). The late loss in MLD was comparable between the pravastatin group (0.46±0.58 mm) and the placebo group (0.48±0.56 mm)(p=0.54), as was the net gain (0.71±0.62 mm and 0.62±0.59 mm, respectively; p=0.07). Percent stenosis before and immediately after PTCA was comparable between the groups. At follow-up angiography mean restenosis severity was 48.4±20% in the pravastatin and 49.7±20% in the placebo group (p=0.44). Restenosis (>50%) occurred in 39.2% of the pravastatin group vs 43.8% of the placebo group (p=0.26). Target vessel revascularization was performed in 19% of the pravastatin vs 21.6% of the placebo group during follow-up. There was no relationship between late loss in MLD and the magnitude of change in lipid blood levels with pravastatin.

Conclusions

Pravastatin 40 mg/d, started within 24 h of successful elective PTCA did not reduce restenosis after 6 months of therapy.

POST-CABG TRIAL

The Post Coronary Artery Bypass Graft Trial

Title	The effect of aggressive lowering of low density lipoprotein cholesterol levels and low dose anticoagulation on obstructive changes in saphenous vein coronary artery bypass grafts.
Author	The Post Coronary Artery Bypass Graft Trial Investigators.
Reference	N Engl J Med 1997;336:153–162.
Disease	Coronary artery disease.
Purpose	To determine whether aggressive lowering of low density lipoprotein (LDL) cholesterol levels or low dose anticoagulation would delay progression of atherosclerosis in saphenous vein coronary artery bypass grafts.
Design	A 2 x 2 factorial design to test if aggressive lowering of LDL (with a goal of 60–85 mg per deciliter) is more effective than moderate lowering (with a goal of 130–140 mg per deciliter) in delaying progression of atherosclerosis in grafts; and low dose anticoagulation as compared to placebo, in reducing obstruction of bypass grafts.
Patients	1351 patients who had undergone bypass surgery 1-11 years prior to baseline with LDL cholesterols of 130–175 mg per deciliter and at least 1 patent vein graft observed on coronary angiographic study.
Follow-up	4.3 years.

Treatment regimen	For aggressive lipid lowering, lovastatin was given at 40 mg per day vs 2.5 mg per day in moderate treatment group. Doses were adjusted to reach target LDL cholesterol levels of less that 85 mg per deciliter in aggressive treatment group and target of less than 140 in moderate treatment group. Cholestyramine at 8 g per day was added if needed. Warfarin or placebo started at 1 mg and then increased by 1 mg up to 4mg and adjusted to an INR of 1.8 to < 2.
Results	The percentage of grafts with progression of atherosclerosis was 27% for patients with aggressive LDL cholesterol lowering and 39% for those who received moderate treatment (p=0.001). There was no difference in angiographic findings on patients receiving warfarin vs placebo. 6.5% of patients with aggressive lipid therapy vs 9.2% with moderate therapy required additional revascularization procedures over 4 years (p=0.03).
Conclusions	Aggressive lowering of LDL cholesterol to <100 mg per deciliter reduced progression of atherosclerosis in saphenous vein coronary artery bypass grafts. Low dose warfarin was ineffective.

Simvastatin reduced graft vessel disease and mortality after heart transplantation. A 4 year randomized trial.

Title	Simvastatin reduced graft vessel disease and mortality after heart transplantation. A 4 year randomized trial.
Author	Wenke K, Meiser B, Thiery J, et al.
Reference	Circulation 1997; 96:1398–1402.
Disease	Accelerated graft vessel disease (GVD) in heart transplant patients.
Purpose	To determine the effects of long term antihypercholesterolemic therapy with diet and simvastatin on cholesterol levels, survival, and graft rejection.
Design	Prospective, randomized.
Patients	72 consecutive patients with heart transplant.
Follow-up	4 years.
Treatment regimen	35 patients treated with a low cholesterol diet and simvastatin and 37 with diet alone. All patients received azathioprine. Dose of simvastatin adjusted to a maximum of 20 mg/day. Target LDL cholesterol level of 110–120 mg/dL.

Simvastatin reduced graft vessel disease and mortality after heart transplantation. A 4 year randomized trial.

(continued)

Results	During therapy, mean cholesterol level was lower in the simvastatin group (198±18 mg/dL) than the control group (228±19 mg/dL, p=0.03). LDL cholesterol levels were also reduced by simvastatin (115±14 vs 156±17 mg/dL, p=0.002). After 4 years, survival rate was higher in the simvastatin group (88.6%) vs the control group (70.3%, p=0.05). Severe graft rejection as a cause of death occurred in 1 patient in the simvastatin group and 5 in the control group. At 4 years coronary angiographic signs of GVD were 16.6% in treated vs 42.3% in controls. Intravascular ultrasound in a subgroup of patients showed less intimal thickening in patients with LDL cholesterol levels of <110 mg/dL.
Conclusions	Simvastatin plus diet in heart transplant patients was more effective than diet in reducing cholesterol, LDL cholesterol, and GVD; and improving survival rate.

AFCAPS/TexCAPS

The Air Force Texas Coronary Atherosclerosis Prevention Study

Title	a. Design and rationale of the airforce/Texas coronary atherosclerosis prevention study (AFCAPS/TexCAPS) b. Primary prevention of acute coronary events with lovastatin in men and women with average cholesterol levels. Results of AFCAPS/TexCAPS.
Author	a. Downs JR, Beere PA, Whitney E, et al. b. Downs JR, Clearfield M, Whitney E, et al.
Reference	a. Am J Cardiol 1997;80:287-293. b. JAMA 1998;279:1615-1622.
Disease	Coronary artery disease.
Purpose	To investigate whether lovastatin therapy, in addition to a lipid lowering diet, will be associated with reduction in major coronary events in patients with normal to mildly elevated cholesterol levels and no evidence of atherosclerotic cardiovascular disease.
Design	Randomized, double blind, placebo controlled, 2 centers.
Patients	5608 men (age 45-73 years) and 997 women (age 55-73 years), with serum total cholesterol 180-264 mg/dL, LDL cholesterol 130-190 mg/dL, HDL cholesterol ≤45 mg/dL for men and ≤47 mg/dL for women, and triglycerides ≤400 mg/dL. Patients with prior history of cardiovascular disease, secondary forms of hyperlipidemia, nephrotic syndrome, insulin dependent or uncontrolled diabetes mellitus, or uncontrolled hypertension were excluded.
Follow-up	An average of 5.2 years (0.1-7.2 years).
Treatment regimen	Randomization placebo or lovastatin 20 mg/d, titrated to 40 mg/d in patients who had LDL cholesterol >110 mg/dL.

AFCAPS/TexCAPS

The Air Force Texas Coronary Atherosclerosis Prevention Study

(continued)

Additional therapy	AHA step 1 diet for all patients.
Results	The study was terminated early after the second interim analysis due to a finding of statistically significant benefit for lovastatin therapy. Study drug regimens were maintained until the termination of the study by 71% of the patients assigned to lovastatin and by 63% if the patients assigned to placebo. Lovastatin theapy was associated with 25% decrease in LDL cholesterol levels (p<0.001), 18% decrease in triglyceride levels (p<0.001), and 6% increase in HDL levels (p<0.001). Changes in the lipid profile among the placebo treated patients were small and insignificant. Lovastatin was equally effective in men and women. the primary end point (myocardial infarction, unstalbe angina, or sudden cardiac death) was reached by 10.9% of the placebo group vs 6.8% of the lovastatin group (relative risk 0.63; 95% CI 0.50–0.79; p<0.001). 9.3% of the placebo vs 6.2% of the lovastatin assigned patients needed revascularization (relative risk 0.67; 95% CI 0.52–0.85; p=0.001). 5.6% of the placebo vs only 33% of the lovastatin group had myocardial infarction (relative risk 0.60; 95% CI 0.43–0.83; p=0.002). Unstable angina occurred in 5.1% of the placebo vs 3.5% of the lovastatin group 9relative risk 0.68; 95% CI 0.49–0.95; p=0.02). Life-table plots demonstrated that treatment benefit began in the first year of treatment and continued throughout the study period. The effect of lovastatin therapy on the relative risk of first acute major coronary events was 46% in women vs 37% in men (p=NS). The overal mortality (4.4 vs 4.6 per 1000 patient years) and the incidence of cancer (15.6 vs 15.1 per 1000 patient years) were comparable in the placebo and lovastatin groups. Lovastatin was well tolerated. Adverse events leading to discontinuation of the study medication occurred in 13.6% of the lovastatin group vs 13.8% in the placebo group.

AFCAPS/TexCAPS

The Air Force Texas Coronary Atherosclerosis Prevention Study (continued)

Conclusion	Lovastatin therapy for an average of 5.2 years reduced the risk for the first acute major coronary event in men and women without prior history of coronary artery disease and with average triglyceride and LDL cholesterol levels and low HDL cholesterol levels.

LOCAT

Lopid Coronary Angiographic Trial

Title	Association between lipoproteins and the progression of coronary and vein graft atherosclerosis in a controlled trial with gemfibrozil in men with low baseline levels of HDL cholesterol.
Authors	Syvanne M, Nieminen MS, Frick H, et al.
Reference	Circulation 1998; 98:1993-1999.
Disease	Lipid abnormality; specifically low HDL.
Purpose	To determine angiographic coronary artery disease progression in men with low HDL levels who then underwent therapy with gemfibrozil or placebo.
Design	Randomized, placebo controlled.
Patients	395 men who had undergone CABG and had HDL ≤42.5 mg/dL, LDL ≤174 mg/dL, and serum TG ≤354 mg/dL were randomized to placebo vs gemfibrozil. 372 completed the study with suitable angiograms.
Follow-up	2 years.
Treatment regimen	1200 mg/day of gemfibrozil or placebo.

Results

Median decrease in triglyceride levels was 40%; serum cholesterol was reduced by 9%; LDL by 6%. HDL_2 cholesterol was increased by 5% and HLD_3 cholesterol was increased by 9%. In placebo patients, 95 patients showed progression only, 31 had mixed response, 40 had no change, and 21 had regression only. In the gemfibrozil group 61 patients had progression, 40 a mixed response; 57 no change; 27 regression only (χ^2 p=0.007). 126 placebo and 101 gemfibrozil had any progression and 61 and 84 patients had no progression. Total serum cholesterol, TG, and cholesterol in IDL (intermediate density lipoprotein) and LDL correlated with risk of global progression (native plus graphs). Only HDL_3 exhibited protection against atherosclerotic progression, especially in native coronary lesions. VLDL was most predictive of new vein graft lesions, as was IDL.

Conclusions

The triglyceride rich lipoproteins, especially IDL, were predictors of angiographic progression, as well as elevated LDL. Of the HDL subtractions only HDL_3 was protective.

LIPID

Long term Intervention with Pravastatin in Ischemic Disease

Title	Prevention of cardiovascular events and death with pravastatin in patients with coronary heart disease and a broad range of initial cholesterol levels.
Authors	The long term Intervention with Pravastatin in Ischemic Disease (LIPID) Study Group.
Reference	N Engl J Med 1998;339:1349-1357.
Disease	Coronary artery disease.
Purpose	To evaluate the effects of cholesterol lowering therapy with pravastatin, a 3-hydroxy-3-methylglutaryl-coenzyme A reductase, on coronary heart disease mortality among patients with a history of myocardial infarction or unstable angina and a wide range of baseline cholesterol levels.
Design	Randomized, double blind, placebo controlled, multicenter.
Patients	9014 patients, 31-75 years old, with a history of acute myocardial infarction or unstable angina within 3-36 months prior to enrollment. Patients had to have baseline plasma total cholesterol levels of 155 to 271 mg/dL and a fasting triglyceride levels of <445 mg/dL. Patients with a clinically significant medical or surgical event within the 3 months preceding the study were not included. Patients with heart failure, renal failure, hepatic disease or current use of any cholesterol lowering agents were excluded.
Follow-up	A mean of 6.1 years.

Treatment regimen	An 8 week single blind placebo run in phase with dietary advise for low fat diet. Thereafter, patients were randomized to either pravastatin 40 mg/d or placebo.
Additional therapy	Low fat diet (<30% of the total energy intake).
Results	After one year, 3 years, and at the end of the study, 6%, 11%, and 19% of the pravastatin assigned patients stopped their study medications, whereas 3%, 9%, and 24% of the placebo assigned patients began open label cholesterol-lowering therapy. Total plasma cholesterol fell by 39 mg/dL in the pravastatin assigned group. The reduction in total cholesterol levels was 18% greater in the pravastatin than placebo assigned group (p<0.001). The decrease in plasma LDL cholesterol was 25% greater in the pravastatin group. Total mortality was 11.0% in the pravastatin group vs 14.1% in the placebo group (reduction in risk 22%; 95% CI 13 to 31%; p<0.001). Mortality from coronary heart disease was 6.4% in the pravastatin group vs 8.3% in the placebo group (reduction in risk 24%; 95% CI 12 to 35%; p<0.001). Cardiovascular mortality was 7.3% and 9.6% in the pravastatin and placebo groups, respectively (reduction in risk 25%; 95% CI 13 to 35%; p<0.001). Death from trauma, suicide or cancer occurred less often in the pravastatin group (p=NS). Myocardial infarction occurred in 7.4% vs 10.3%, respectively (reduction in risk 29%; 95% CI 18 to 38%; p<0.001). Less patients in the pravastatin group needed CABG (9.2% vs 11.6%; reduction in risk 22%; 95% CI 11 to 31%; p<0.001), or PTCA (4.7% vs 5.6%; reduction in risk 19%; 95% CI 3 to 33%; p=0.024). Pravastatin was associated with less hospitalization for unstable angina (22.3% vs 24.6%; p=0.005) and less strokes (3.7% vs 4.5%; p=0.048). Among patients with prior myocardial infarction, coronary heart disease mortality was 23% lower (p=0.004) and total mortality was 21% lower (p=0.002) in the pravastatin group. Among the subgroup of patients with unstable angina, coronary heart disease mortality was 26% lower (p=0.036) and total mortality 26% lower (p=0.004) in the

pravastatin group. Subgroup analysis revealed that pravastatin was effective in patients with high (≥251 mg/dL), medium (213-250 mg/dL), and low (<213 mg/dL) baseline total cholesterol levels. However, the reduction in risk among patients with LDL cholesterol <136 mg/dL was not significant (16%; 95% CI -4 to 32%). Pravastatin therapy was safe. There was no increase in the incidence of newly diagnosed primary cancers, including breast cancer. Increase in serum alanine aminotransferase >3 times the upper limit of normal occurred in 2.1% of the pravastatin vs 1.9% of the placebo group (p=0.41). There was no increase in the incidence of myopathy or elevation of serum creatine kinase levels. Adverse effects, ultimately attributed to the study medication occurred in 3.2% of the pravastatin vs 2.7% of the placebo group (p=0.16).

Conclusions

Secondary prevention therapy with pravastatin was associated with reduced all cause mortality and mortality from coronary heart disease in patients with a history of myocardial infarction or unstable angina who had a broad range of initial plasma cholesterol levels.

Effects of diet and exercise in men and postmenopausal women with low levels of HDL cholesterol and high levels of LDL cholesterol

Title	Effects of diet and exercise in men and postmenopausal women with low levels of HDL cholesterol and high levels of LDL cholesterol.
Authors	Stefanick ML, Mackey S, Sheehan M, et al.
Reference	N Engl J Med. 1998; 339:12–20.
Disease	Hypercholesterolemia.
Purpose	To determine the effects of exercise and diet alone and together on plasma lipoproteins.
Design	Randomized, controlled study.
Patients	180 postmenopausal women (ages 45–64 years) and 197 men (ages 30–64 years) who had plasma HDL cholesterol levels below 60 mg per dL for women and 45 for men and plasma LDL greater than 125 mg per dL but below 210 for women and greater than 125 but below 190 for men.
Follow-up	1 year.
Treatment regimen	Patients were randomly assigned to NCEP (National Cholesterol Education Program) Step 2 diet, aerobic exercise, diet plus exercise, or to a control group (no intervention).

Effects of diet and exercise in men and postmenopausal women with low levels of HDL cholesterol and high levels of LDL cholesterol

(continued)

Results	For both women and men, weight loss occurred: in the diet group or diet plus exercise group, compared to exercise group or controls. For women: LDL cholesterol baseline was 161 mg/dL. It decreased by -2.5±16.6 mg/dL in the control group; -5.6±19.4 in the exercise group; -7.3±18.9 in the diet group; and -14.5±22.2 in the diet plus exercise group. Only the diet plus exercise group vs control was significant. Baseline HDL was 47 mg/dL and did not significantly change in any of the treatment groups. For men: Baseline LDL was 156 mg/dL. It decreased by -4.6±21.1 in the control group; -3.6±18.8 in the exercise group; -10.8±18.8 in the diet group; and -20.0±17.3 in the LDL group. Diet plus exercise was significantly lower than control or exercise alone. Baseline HDL was 35.8 mg/dL and did not significantly change. For both men and women, changes in LDL cholesterol were not significant in the diet group compared with the control group.
Conclusions	NCEP Step 2 diet alone was ineffective in lowering LDL cholesterol in men and women with high risk lipid profiles. However, when diet was combined with aerobic exercise, LDL was lowered.

BECAIT

Bezafibrate Coronary Atherosclerosis Intervention Trial (BECAIT)

Title	Treatment effects on serum lipoprotein lipids, apolipoproteins and low density lipoprotein in particle size and relationship of lipoprotein variables to progression of coronary artery disease in the Bezafibrate Coronary Atherosclerosis Intervention Trial (BECAIT).
Authors	Ruotolo G, Ericsson C-G, Tettamanti C, et al.
Reference	J Am Coll Cardiol 1998; 32:1648–1656.
Disease	Male survivors of a first MI under 45 years of age with cholesterol of at least 5.2 mmol/L and triglyceride of at least 1.6 mmol/L, respectively.
Purpose	To determine the mechanism whereby bezafibrate delayed progression of coronary disease in BECAIT trial.
Design	Double blind, placebo controlled, randomized angiographic trial.
Patients	81 patients from the original BECAIT study (Ericsson et al. Lancet 1996; 347:849–853) who had a baseline and at least one post treatment angiogram.
Follow-up	5 years.
Treatment regimen	Bezafibrate (200 mg 3 times a day) or placebo.

BECAIT

Bezafibrate Coronary Atherosclerosis Intervention Trial (BECAIT)

(continued)

Results	Bezafibrate decreased VLDL cholesterol by 53%, decreased triglyceride by 46% and apolipoprotein B by 9%. It increased HDL3 by 9% and shifted LDL subclass toward a larger particle size. As described in the original report, bezafibrate retarded the progression of focal CAD assessed by angiography. HDL3 cholesterol and plasma apo B concentration during the study were independent predictors of the changes in mean minimum lumen diameter and percent stenosis.
Conclusions	Bezafibrate retarded the progression of focal coronary atherosclerosis and this effect could be attributed at least in part to an increase in HDL3 cholesterol and a decrease in apo B containing lipoproteins.

Simvastatin 80 mg/d

Title	Efficacy and safety of simvastatin 80 mg/day in hypercholesterolemic patients.
Authors	Stein EA, Davidson MH, Dobs AS, et al.
Reference	Am J Cardiol 1998;82:311–316.
Disease	Hyperlipidemia.
Purpose	To assess the safety and efficacy of simvastatin 80 mg/d.
Design	Randomized, double blind, parallel group, multicenter.
Patients	521 patients, 21–70 years old, with hypercholesterolemia (for patients with coronary heart disease, LDL cholesterol ≥130 mg/dL; for patients without coronary artery disease but with ≥2 risk factors, LDL cholesterol ≥160 mg/dL; and for patients without coronary heart disease and <2 risk factors, LDL cholesterol ≥190 mg/dL). All patients had to have a triglycerides level ≤350 mg/dL. Patients with uncontrolled hypertension, severe obesity, uncontrolled type I diabetes, type II diabetes, revascularization or myocardial infarction within the preceding 3 months, serum creatinine >1.8 mg/dL, or elevation of serum hepatic enzyme or creatine kinase were excluded. Patients receiving anticoagulants, systemic antifungal agents, and immunosuppressant agents were not included.
Follow-up	24 weeks.
Treatment regimen	A 4 week placebo run in period. Then, randomization to simvastatin 40 mg/d (n=207) or 80 mg/d (n=314) for 24 weeks.

(continued)

Additional therapy	Other lipid lowering drugs were not permitted.
Results	487 patients (94%) completed the study. 6.3% and 6.7% of the simvastatin 40 mg and 80 mg groups discontinued therapy permanently. Total cholesterol decreased by 29% (95% CI 30.1% to 27.3%) compared to baseline in the simvastatin 40 mg/d, and by 35% (36.2% to 34.0%) in the simvastatin 80 mg/d ($p<0.001$ for the difference between the groups). LDL cholesterol was reduced by 38% (40.1% to 36.2%) in the simvastatin 40 mg/d and by 46% (47.3% to 44.6%) in the simvastatin 80 mg/d group ($p<0.001$). HDL cholesterol was increased (6.0% and 6.1%, respectively; $p=0.849$) and VLDL cholesterol decreased (31% and 36%; $p=0.676$) were reduced by similar rates. Simvastatin 80 mg/d reduced the triglycerides levels more than the simvastatin 40 mg/d (25%; 27.7% to 21.7%) vs 17% (21.4% to 12.6%; $p=0.002$). 68% of the simvastatin 40 mg/d group reached their LDL cholesterol target levels vs 82% of the simvastatin 80 mg/d. Among patients with coronary artery disease (target LDL cholesterol ≤100 mg/dL) 30% and 69% of the simvastatin 40 mg/d and 80 mg/d patients, respectively, reached their target levels. None of the patients experienced serious adverse effect. Drug related adverse effects were noted in 16% and 18% of the 40 mg/d and 80 mg/d groups. Myopathy was diagnosed in 0 and 0.6% of the patients, respectively. Myalgia was reported in 1.4% and 1.6% of the patients, respectively. ≥X3 increase in liver transaminases was noted in 1.4% and 1.9% of the patients, respectively.
Conclusions	Simvastatin 80 mg/d is safe and effective in reducing LDL cholesterol levels. Simvastatin 80 mg/d can be used to reach NCEP target cholesterol levels in the majority of the patients.

VA-HIT

Veterans Affairs High Density Lipoprotein Cholesterol Intervention Trial Study Group

Title	Gemfibrozil for the Secondary Prevention of coronary heart disease in men with low levels of high density lipoprotein cholesterol.
Authors	Rubins HB, Robins SJ, Collins D, et al.
Reference	N Engl J Med 1999;341:410–418.
Disease	Patients with low levels of high density lipoprotein (HDL) levels, coronary artery disease.
Purpose	To determine whether increasing HDL with gemfibrozil would improve outcome in men with coronary artery disease, an HDL of ≤40 mg/dL and an LDL cholesterol of ≤140 mg/dL.
Design	Randomized, double blind, matching placebo, mutlicenter.
Patients	2531 men with coronary artery disease (history of myocardial infarction, angina with objective evidence of ischemia, coronary revascularization, coronary stenosis >50% by angiography) and lipid parameters described above.
Follow-up	5.1 years.
Treatment regimen	Slow release gemfibrozil at 1200 mg once daily vs placebo.
Additional therapy	American Heart Association Step 1 diet.

Results	Primary end point was combined incidence of nonfatal myocardial infarction or death from coronary artery disease. Primary event developed in 275/1267 patients in the placebo group (21.7%) vs 219/1264 patients in the gemfibrozil group (17.3%) with an overall reduction in risk of 4.4%, and decrease in RR=22%; 95% CI=7%-35%; p=0.006. There was a 22% decrease in death from coronary artery disease (p=0.07) and 23% decrease in nonfatal myocardial infarction (p=0.02). The benefits did not become apparent until about 2 years of randomization. Gemfibrozil treatment resulted in a 24% relative risk reduction in the combined outcomes of death from coronary heart disease, nonfatal myocardial infarction, or confirmed stroke (95% CI=11%-36%; p<0.001). Gemfibrozil also reduced the incidence of transient ischemic attacks and need for carotid endarterectomy. At 1 year, mean HDL cholesterol was 6% higher and triglycerides were 31% lower, with no change in LDL cholesterol, in the gemfibrozil group.
Conclusions	In men with coronary artery disease, whose main lipid abnormality was low HDL cholesterol, gemfibrozil, which increased HDL cholesterol and lowered triglycerides, reduced the risk of major cardiovascular events.

Title	Efficacy and safety of cerivastatin, 0.2 mg and 0.4 mg, in patients with primary hypercholesterolemia: A multinational, randomised, double blind study.
Authors	Ose L, Luurila O, Eriksson J, et al.
Reference	Curr Med Res Opin 1999;15:228-240.
Disease	Hyperlipidemia.
Purpose	To compare the efficacy and safety of cerivastatin 0.2 mg/d and 0.4 mg/d in patients with primary hypercholesterolemia.
Design	Randomized, double blind, parallel group, multicenter.
Patients	494 patients, 18-75 years old, with primary hypercholesterolemia (LDL cholesterol ≥160 mg/dL or ≥130 mg/dL and either a history of coronary heart disease or ≥2 cardiovascular risk factors). All patients had triglyceride levels ≤350 mg/dL. Patients with obesity, diabetes mellitus, other endocrine disorders, clinically significant ophthalmic abnormalities, a history of hepatic disease, renal failure or malignancy, alcohol abuse, a history of myocardial infarction, unstable angina, stroke, transient ischemic attack or uncontrolled hypertension were excluded.
Follow-up	24 weeks.
Treatment regimen	After a 6 week placebo run-in phase patients were randomized in a 2:1 ratio to cerivastatin 0.4 mg/d (n=332) or 0.2 mg/d (n=162).

(continued)

Additional therapy	Treatment with hypoglycemic agents, corticosteroids, androgens, erythromycin, oral anticoagulants, immunosuppressants, and other lipid lowering agents was not permitted.
Results	By intention to treat analysis, LDL cholesterol was lowered by 37.9±0.7% with cerivastatin 0.4 mg/d and by 30.3±1.0% by cerivastatin 0.2 mg/d ($p<0.0001$). Maximal treatment effect was noticed after 4 weeks of therapy and sustained for the 24 weeks of the study. 97% and 94% of the patients in the cerivastatin 0.4 and 0.2 mg/d, respectively, had ≥15% decrease in their LDL cholesterol. Total cholesterol decreased by 25.6±0.5% and 20.6±0.7% with cerivastatin 0.4 and 0.2 mg/d ($p<0.0001$). There were no statistically significant differences between the groups in the change in HDL cholesterol and in serum triglycerides. With per protocol analysis, cerivastatin was more effective in women than men in lowering LDL cholesterol. Adverse effects were noted in 65.5% of the patients in the cerivastatin 0.4 mg/d vs 60.5% in the cerivastatin 0.2 mg/d, 21.4% and 19.8% were probably or possibly related to the drug. Minor increase (≤3 X ULN) in creatine kinase levels was noted in 19.9% and 14.8% of the patients in the cerivastatin 0.4 and 0.2 mg/d, respectively, and >3 X ULN elevation in creatine kinase occurred in 2.7% and 0%, respectively. Minor ALT elevations (≤3 X ULN) were noted in 18.7% and 13.6%, respectively, whereas >3 X ULN elevations occurred in 0.3% and 0%, respectively. Overall, 2.4% and 3.1% of the patients in the cerivastatin 0.4 and 0.2 mg/d, respectively, withdrew from the study due to adverse effects.
Conclusions	Cerivastatin was safe and effective in lowering LDL cholesterol levels in a dose dependent manner.

Extended release niacin vs gemfibrozil for the treatment of low levels of high density lipoprotein cholesterol

Title	Extended release niacin vs gemfibrozil for the treatment of low levels of high density lipoprotein cholesterol.
Authors	Guyton JR, Blazing MA, Hagar J, et al.
Reference	Arch Intern Med 2000;160:1177-1184.
Disease	Lipid abnormality: low HDL cholesterol.
Purpose	To compare the effect of extended release niacin (Niaspan) vs gemfibrozil on high density lipoprotein cholesterol (HDL-C) in patients with baseline low levels of HDL-C.
Design	Randomized, double blind, placebo controlled, multicenter.
Patients	173 patients with an HDL-C level of ≤40 mg/dL, LDL ≤160 mg/dL, or <130 mg/dL with atherosclerotic disease, and a triglyceride level of ≤400 mg/dL.
Follow-up	16 weeks after an initial titration phase.
Treatment regimen	Gemfibrozil 600 mg or its placebo given twice daily. Niaspan or its placebo given once at bedtime (after low fat snack). Niaspan was titrated during an initial 3 week titration phase from 375 mg daily up to 1000 mg for 4 weeks; 1500 mg for 4 weeks; and 2000 mg for 8 weeks.
Additional therapy	Aspirin a half hour before bedtime study medication.

Extended release niacin vs gemfibrozil for the treatment of low levels of high density lipoprotein cholesterol

(continued)

Results	72 patients assigned to Niaspan completed the protocol; 68 assigned to gemfibrozil completed the study. Niaspan raised HDL-C level by 21% at the 1500 mg dose and 26% at the 2000 mg dose which was >13.3% increase achieved with gemfibrozil ($p=0.01$; $p<0.001$). Niaspan at 1500 and 2000 mg raised apolipoprotein A-1 level by 9% and 11%, respectively, vs 4% with gemfibrozil ($p=0.02$; $p=0.001$). Niaspan reduced lipoprotein (a) by -7% and -20% while gemfibrozil did not affect it. Niaspan had no adverse effects on LDL (2% and 0%); gemfibrozil was associated with a 9% increase in LDL. Triglycerides were decreased by gemfibrozil (-40%) to a greater extent than Niaspan 1000 mg (-16%; $p<0.001$); or Niaspan 2000 mg (-29%, $p=0.02$). Niaspan tended to decrease fibrinogen levels while gemfibrozil tended to increase fibrinogen levels.
Conclusions	At higher doses extended release niacin increased HDL to a greater extent than gemfibrozil. Niaspan also decreased lipoprotein (a), and lowered fibrinogen levels compared to gemfibrozil. Gemfibrozil reduced triglyceride levels to a greater extent than Niaspan.

LISA

Lescol in Severe Atherosclerosis Trial

Title	The effect of fluvastatin on cardiac events in patients with symptomatic coronary artery disease during one year of treatment.
Authors	Riegger G, Abletshauser C, Ludwig M, et al.
Reference	Atherosclerosis 1999;144:263-270.
Disease	Hypercholesterolemia, coronary artery disease.
Purpose	To determine whether aggressive therapy with fluvastatin reduces cardiac events within one year in patients with hyperlipidemia and symptomatic coronary artery disease.
Design	Randomized, placebo controlled, multicenter.
Patients	365 patients with symptomatic coronary artery disease and hypercholesterolemia. LDL cholesterol had to be >160 mg/dL.
Follow-up	1 year.
Treatment regimen	Fluvastatin (40 mg daily; increased to twice daily if LDL cholesterol did not decrease more than 30%) vs placebo.
Additional therapy	Antianginal drugs including nitrates, calcium blockers, ß-blockers, aspirin.

Results	Primary outcome was major cardiac events (fatal MI, sudden death, nonfatal MI, CABG, unstable angina pectoris). Ten major cardiac events occurred in patients on placebo vs 3 in fluvastatin patients. Fluvastatin also demonstrated a trend towards less angina; fluvastatin improved exercise tolerance. Fluvastatin caused a 17% decrease in total cholesterol, a 27% decrease in LDL cholesterol, and a 25% decrease in triglycerides (in patients whose triglycerides were >227 mg/dL). The drug was well tolerated.
Conclusions	Although overall event rates were low over 1 year, fluvastatin was associated with less cardiac events, less angina, and better exercise tolerance.

8. Arrhythmia

CAST

Cardiac Arrhythmia Suppression Trial

Title	a. Preliminary report: Effect of encainide and flecainide on mortality in a randomized trial of arrhythmia suppression after myocardial infarction. b. Mortality and morbidity in patients receiving encainide, flecainide, or placebo. The Cardiac Arrhythmia Suppression Trial. c. Events in the Cardiac Arrhythmia Suppression Trial (CAST): Mortality in the entire population enrolled. d. Events in the Cardiac Arrhythmia Suppression Trial (CAST): Mortality in patients surviving open label titration but not randomized to double blind therapy. e. Association between ease of suppression of ventricular arrhythmia and survival.
Authors	a. The CAST Investigators. b. Echt DS, Leibson PR, Mitchell LB, et al. c. Epstein AE, Bigger JT Jr, Wyse DG, et al. d. Wyse DG, Hallstrom A, McBride R, et al. e. Goldstein S, Brooks MM, Ledingham R, et al.
Reference	a. N Engl J Med 1989;321:406-412. b. N Engl J Med 1991;324:781-788. c. J Am Coll Cardiol 1991;18:14-19. d. J Am Coll Cardiol 1991;18:20-28. e. Circulation 1995;91:79-83.
Disease	Ventricular arrhythmia, coronary artery disease.
Purpose	To evaluate whether suppression of asymptomatic or mildly symptomatic ventricular arrhythmias in patients after myocardial infarction would reduce mortality from arrhythmia.
Design	Randomized, open label (titration phase), double blind (main phase), placebo controlled, multicenter.

CAST

Cardiac Arrhythmia Suppression Trial (continued)

Patients	2309 patients, 6 days to 2 years after myocardial infarction, with ≥6 PVCs per h, and left ventricular ejection fraction of ≤0.55 for patients with infarction within 90 days and ≤0.40 for patients with infarction 90 days to 2 years before randomization. Patients with ventricular arrhythmias that caused severe symptoms (such as presyncope or syncope) were excluded.
Follow-up	An average of 9.7 months.
Treatment regimen	An open label titration phase (average 15 days), during which up to 3 drugs (encainide, flecainide and moricizine) at 2 oral doses were tested. This phase was terminated as soon as suppression of ≥80% of the PVCs and ≥90% suppression of nonsustained ventricular tachycardia was detected by 24 h ambulatory ECG monitoring 4–10 days after each dose was begun. Flecainide was not used in patients with ejection fraction <0.30. In patients with ejection fraction ≥0.30, moricizine was used as a second drug. Patients whose arrhythmia worsened or who were intolerant were not included in the main phase. In the main phase patients were randomized to receive either the active drug that had suppressed the arrhythmia or placebo.

CAST

Cardiac Arrhythmia Suppression Trial (continued)

Results	1727 patients (75%) had initial suppression of their arrhythmia and were included in the main phase. 1498 patients were assigned to flecainide, encainide, or placebo. After an average of 10 months total mortality was 7.7% in the encainide/flecainide groups vs 3.0% in the placebo (relative risk 2.5, 95% CI 1.6–4.5). The relative risks for death from any cause for encainide and flecainide considered separately were not different (2.7 vs 2.2 compared to placebo). Death from arrhythmia was more common in the encainide/flecainide groups (4.5%) than placebo (1.2%, relative risk 3.6, 95% CI 1.7–8.5, p=0.0004). The relative risk for encainide was 3.4 and for flecainide 4.4, compared with placebo. The relative risk for death or cardiac arrest with resuscitation was 2.38 (95% CI 1.59–3.57). Subgroup analyses revealed that in every subgroup tested, flecainide and encainide were associated with increased total mortality and arrhythmic death. The mortality in the placebo-treated patients was lower than expected. This was probably due to selection bias including only patients whose arrhythmias were suppressable in the titration phase. Nonrandomized patients had more extensive coronary disease and experienced higher mortality and arrhythmic events than the randomized placebo group.
Conclusions	Encainide and flecainide were associated with increased death rate due to arrhythmia and acute myocardial infarction complicated by shock in patients after acute myocardial infarction with asymptomatic ventricular arrhythmias, even though these drugs were effective in suppression of the arrhythmia.

BASIS

Basel Antiarrhythmic Study of Infarct Survival

Title	a. Effect of antiarrhythmic therapy on mortality in survivors of myocardial infarction with asymptomatic complex ventricular arrhythmias: Basel Antiarrhythmic Study of Infarct Survival (BASIS). b. Long term benefit of 1 year amiodarone treatment for persistent complex ventricular arrhythmias after myocardial infarction.
Authors	a. Burkart F, Pfisterer M, Kiowski W, et al. b. Pfisterer ME, Kiowski W, Brunner H, et al.
Reference	a. J Am Coll Cardiol 1990;16:1711-1718. b. Circulation 1993;87:309-311.
Disease	Arrhythmia, acute myocardial infarction.
Purpose	To evaluate the effects of prophylactic antiarrhythmic treatment in survivors of myocardial infarction with persisting asymptomatic complex arrhythmias.
Design	Randomized, 3 centers.
Patients	312 patients, <71 years old, who survived acute myocardial infarction and had asymptomatic complex ventricular ectopic activity on a 24 h ECG recording 24 h after discontinuation of all antiarrhythmic medications.
Follow-up	a. Clinical evaluation and 24 h ECG monitoring at baseline and after 3, 6, and 12 months. b. 55-125 months (mean 72 months).

BASIS

Basel Antiarrhythmic Study of Infarct Survival

(continued)

Treatment regimen	Patients were randomized to either: 1. Individualized antiarrhythmic drugs guided by continuous ECG monitoring (quinidine and mexiletine as first line drugs and ajmaline, disopyramide, flecainide, propafenone, or sotalol as second line drugs). If none of these drugs suppressed the arrhythmias, amiodarone was given. 2. Low dose amiodarone. 1g/d for 5 days followed by 200 mg/d. If symptomatic arrhythmias developed, the therapy was changed and the patients were considered to be treatment deviators.Treatment was continued for 1 year. 3. Control without prophylactic antiarrhythmic drug. If symptoms occurred, antiarrhythmic medications were given, and they were considered as treatment deviators.
Additional therapy	No limitations on other nonantiarrhythmic medications.
Results	a. During 1 year follow-up, 10%, 5.1%, and 13.2% of groups 1, 2, and 3 died (61% reduction of mortality by amiodarone vs control; $p=0.048$).After exclusion of noncardiac mortality, amiodarone was still associated with 55% reduction of mortality. Sudden death or sustained ventricular tachycardia or fibrillation occurred in 5.1% of the amiodarone and 16.7% of the control group ($p<0.01$).The effect of individualized therapy (group 1) was less marked (40% reduction, p=NS). b.The probability of death after 84 months (Kaplan Meier) was 30% for amiodarone and 45% for control patients ($p=0.03$). However, this was entirely due to the first year amiodarone effect. A similar effect was observed regarding cardiac death ($p=0.047$).
Conclusions	Low dose amiodarone decreased mortality during the first year after acute myocardial infarction in asymptomatic patients with persistent complex ventricular arrhythmias. The beneficial effect of amiodarone lasted several years after discontinuation of amiodarone.

CASCADE

Cardiac Arrest in Seattle: Conventional vs Amiodarone Drug Evaluation

Title	a. Cardiac Arrest in Seattle: Conventional vs Amiodarone Drug Evaluation (the CASCADE study). b. the CASCADE study: Randomized antiarrhythmic drug therapy in survivors of cardiac arrest in Seattle.
Authors	a. The CASCADE Investigators. b. Greene HL, for the CASCADE Investigators.
Reference	a. Am J Cardiol 1991;67:578-584. b. Am J Cardiol 1993;72:70F-74F.
Disease	Ventricular fibrillation.
Purpose	To evaluate the efficacy of empiric amiodarone therapy and electrophysiologic testing and ambulatory ECG monitoring guided drug therapy in survivors of out-of-hospital ventricular fibrillation.
Design	Randomized, open label, multicenter.
Patients	228 patients who survived an episode of out-of-hospital ventricular fibrillation that was not associated with Q wave infarction. Only patients who were considered high risk for recurrence were included.
Follow-up	Up to 6 years.
Treatment regimen	Amiodarone or electrophysiologic testing and ambulatory ECG monitoring guided conventional drug therapy.
Additional therapy	Approximately 50% of all patients received an implanted defibrillator (since 1988).

CASCADE

Cardiac Arrest in Seattle: Conventional vs Amiodarone Drug Evaluation (continued)

Results	Of the 115 patients randomized to conventional therapy 33 received quinidine, 26 procainamide, 12 received flecainide, and 17 combination therapy. 82% and 69% of the amiodarone and conventional therapy groups were free from either cardiac death, resuscitated VF, or syncopal shocks from implanted defibrillator after 2 years. The corresponding numbers for 4 and 6 years are 66% vs 52% and 53% vs 40%, in the amiodarone and conventional therapy groups, respectively (p=0.007). 83% vs 78%, 65% vs 62%, and 58% vs 37% of the patients were still alive after 2, 4, and 6 years. 105 patients had automatic implantable defibrillators. 38% of the amiodarone and 60% of the conventional therapy experienced shock from the defibrillator (p=0.032). However, 29% of the amiodarone and only 17% of the conventional therapy group stopped their medications. Possible pulmonary toxicity was diagnosed in 6% of the patients over 12 months and 10% over 3 years. Thyroid dysfunction was relatively common (22.1%) in the amiodarone group.
Conclusions	Although amiodarone was associated with mild reduction of mortality, overall mortality remained high, and side effects were common.

CAST-2

Cardiac Arrhythmia Suppression Trial-2

Title	a. The Cardiac Arrhythmia Supression Trial: first CAST, then CAST-II. b. Effect of the antiarrhythmic agent moricizine on survival after myocardial infarction.
Authors	a. Greene HL, Roden DM, Katz RJ, et al. b. The Cardiac Arrhythmia Suppression Trial II investigators.
Reference	a. J Am Coll Cardiol 1992;19:894-898. b. N Engl J Med 1992;327:227-233.
Disease	Ventricular arrhythmia, coronary artery disease.
Purpose	To evaluate whether suppression of asymptomatic or mildly symptomatic ventricular premature depolarizations by moricizine would decrease mortality in patients after myocardial infarction.
Design	Randomized, double blind, placebo controlled, multicenter.
Patients	Patients, 6-90 days after myocardial infarction, with ≥6 PVCs per h, and left ventricular ejection fraction of ≤0.40. Patients with ventricular arrhythmias that caused severe symptoms (such as presyncope or syncope), or runs ≥30 seconds at a rate of ≥120 bpm were excluded. 1325 patients (10 patients were included in CAST-I) were included in the short term trial and 1374 patients (536 patients were included in CAST-I) in the long term trial.
Follow-up	Short term protocol: 2 weeks. Long term protocol: a mean of 18 months.

Treatment regimen	Short term protocol: moricizine 200 mg X3/d for 14 days vs placebo or no therapy. Long term protocol: titration phase of moricizine started with 200 mg X3/d and increased to 250 mg X3/d and then to 300 mg X3/d until arrhythmia was suppressed or adverse effects occurred. Only patients in whom suppression of ≥80% of the PVCs and ≥90% suppression of nonsustained ventricular tachycardia was detected by 24 h ambulatory ECG monitoring were entered into the long term protocol.
Results	CAST-II was stopped early because moricizine therapy was associated with excess mortality in the first 14 day phase. The rate of death or resuscitated cardiac arrest was 2.6% (17 of 665 patients) of the moricizine group vs 0.5% (3 of 660 patients) of the no therapy group (adjusted $p<0.01$, relative risk 5.6, 95% CI 1.7–19.1). Other adverse effects such as recurrent myocardial infarction, new or worsened heart failure, and proarrhythmia tended to be higher in the moricizine group. Arrhythmia suppression was achieved in 1155 patients (87.2%) who were included in the long term phase. During a mean follow-up of 18 months 8.4% of the moricizine vs 7.3% of the placebo treated group died or had cardiac arrests due to arrhythmias ($p=0.4$). The 2 year survival rate was 81.7% in the moricizine vs 85.6% in the placebo. Nonfatal adverse effects were more common with moricizine ($p=0.03$).
Conclusions	Moricizine was effective in suppression of asymptomatic or mildly symptomatic ventricular arrhythmias in patients after myocardial infarction. However, therapy with moricizine was associated with increased mortality in the short protocol and no beneficial effect in the long term protocol.

ESVEM

The Electrophysiologic Study vs Electrocardiographic Monitoring

Title	a. The ESVEM Trial: Electrophysiologic Study vs Electrocardiographic Monitoring for selection of antiarrhythmic therapy of ventricular tachyarrhythmias. b. Determinants of predicted efficacy of antiarrhythmic drugs in the electrophysiologic study vs electrocardiographic monitoring trial. c. A comparison of electrophysiologic testing with holter monitoring to predict antiarrhythmic drug efficacy for ventricular tachyarrhythmias. d. A comparison of 7 antiarrhythmic drugs in patients with ventricular tachyarrhythmias. e. Cost of initial therapy in the electrophysiological study vs ECG monitoring trial (ESVEM). f. Significance and incidence of concordance of drug efficacy predictions by holter monitoring and electrophysiological study in the ESVEM Trial.
Authors	a +b. The ESVEM Investigators. c +d. Mason JW, for the ESVEM Investigators. e. Omioigui NA, Marcus FI, Mason JW, et al. f. Reiter MJ, Mann DE, Reiffel JE, et al.
Reference	a. Circulation 1989;79:1354-1360. b. Circulation 1993;87:323-329. c. N Engl J Med 1993;329:445-451. d. N Engl J Med 1993;329:452-458. e. Circulation 1995;91:1070-1076. f. Circulation 1995;91:1988-1995.
Disease	Ventricular tachyarrhythmias.
Purpose	To compare the efficacy and accuracy of electrophysiologic study (EPS) vs ambulatory electrocardiographic holter monitoring (HM) for prediction of antiarrhythmic drug efficacy in patients with aborted sudden death or sustained ventricular tachyarrhythmias.
Design	Randomized, open label, multicenter.

ESVEM

The Electrophysiologic Study vs Electrocardiographic Monitoring (continued)

Patients	486 patients who had been resuscitated from sudden death, or had documented sustained ventricular tachycardia or unmonitored syncope (with subsequent EPS demonstration inducible sustained monomorphic ventricular tachycardia) were screened. Only patients with ≥10 PVCs/h during 48 h HM and reproducibly inducible sustained ventricular tachyarrhythmias at EPS were included.
Follow-up	6.2 years.
Treatment regimen	Patients were randomized to serial drug evaluation by HM and exercise test or by EPS. Patients underwent testing of up to 6 drugs until one or none was predicted to be effective: imipramine, mexiletine, procainamide, quinidine, sotalol, pirmenol, and propafenone. Drugs were tested in random order. Patients were discharged from the hospital with a predicted effective drug. Subjects in whom no drug was effective were withdrawn from the study.
Results	Efficacy predictions were achieved in 45% of the EPS and 77% in the HM arms ($p<0.001$). Ejection fraction of <0.25 and presence of coronary artery disease were negative correlates ($p<0.10$) of drug efficacy prediction in the EPS arm. In the HM arm, only ejection fraction correlated with efficacy, although with only marginal significance ($p=0.11$). A multivariate model selected assessment by HM and higher ejection fraction as independent predictors ($p<0.05$) of drug efficacy. The drug evaluation process required an actuarial median time of 25 days in the EPS vs 10 days in the HM arms ($p<0.0001$). There was no significant difference between the EPS and HM arms in the actuarial probabilities of either death or recurrence of arrhythmia. Patients randomized to EPS had higher mean charge for evaluation ($42,002 vs $29,970, $p=0.0015$) and more drug trials (3.0 vs 2.1, $p=0.0001$). In the EPS group, the percentage of patients who had predictions of drug efficacy was higher with sotalol (35%) than with any other drugs (26%–10%, $p<0.001$). There was no significant difference among the drugs in the HM group. The least adverse effects was noted with sotalol (16% vs 23%–43% with the other drugs). The patients that received sotalol

had the lowest actuarial probability of recurrence of ventricular arrhythmia (RR 0.43, 95% CI 0.29-0.62, $p<0.001$), death from any cause (RR 0.50, 95% CI 0.30-0.80, $p=0.004$), cardiac death (RR 0.50, 95% CI 0.28-0.90, $p=0.02$), or arrhythmic death (RR 0.50, 95% CI 0.26-0.96, $p=0.04$). At the time of the first drug trial in the EPS group, HM and EPS were concordant in predicting efficacy in 23% and in predicting inefficiency in 23%. In 54% of the patients there was discordance between HP and EPS. At the time EPS predicted efficacy, 68 of the 100 patients also had suppression of arrhythmias in HM. Rates of arrhythmia recurrence or mortality were similar among patients with suppression of arrhythmias on both HM and EPS, compared with those who had suppression on EPS alone. There was no significant difference in outcome between the patients with suppression on both HM and EPS and those with suppression on the HM arm.

Conclusions

Drug efficacy predictions are achieved more frequently and faster with HM than EPS strategy. However, there was no significant difference in the success of drug therapy as selected by either EPS or HM. Sotalol was more effective than the other 6 drugs in preventing death and recurrence of ventricular arrhythmia, and was associated with less adverse effects than the other medications. There is frequent discordance in prediction of drug efficacy between HM and EPS. However, suppression of ventricular arrhythmias on both tests did not predict better outcome.

MADIT

The Multicenter Automatic Defibrillator Implantation Trial

Title	Improved survival with an implanted defibrillator in patients with coronary disease at high risk for ventricular arrhythmia.
Authors	Moss AJ, Hall WJ, Cannom DS, et al.
Reference	N Engl J Med 1996;335:1933-1940.
Disease	Coronary artery disease, arrhythmia.
Purpose	To assess whether prophylactic implantation of cardioverter defibrillator, as compared with conventional medical therapy, would decrease mortality in patients with prior myocardial infarction, low ejection fraction, and episodes of asymptomatic unsustained ventricular tachycardia.
Design	Randomized, multicenter.
Patients	196 patients of either sex, 25-80 years old, with myocardial infarction >3 weeks before entry, documented episode of asymptomatic, nonsustained ventricular tachycardia (3-30 ventricular ectopic beats at a rate >120 per min), and left ventricular ejection fraction ≤0.35. Patients in NYHA class IV, indication for revascularization, previous cardiac arrest or symptomatic ventricular tachycardia, CABG within 2 months or PTCA within 3 months, advanced cerebrovascular disease, and serious noncardiac medical condition were not included. Eligible patients underwent electrophysiologic study, and only patients with reproducibly induced ventricular tachycardia or fibrillation that was not suppressed by procainamide or an equivalent drug were included.
Follow-up	Average follow-up 27 months (range <1 month to 61 months).

MADIT

The Multicenter Automatic Defibrillator Implantation Trial

(continued)

Treatment regimen	Within 30 days after the electrophysiologic study, patients were randomized to implantation of defibrillator or conventional medical therapy. The choice of medical therapy, including whether to use antiarrhythmic agents, was made by the patient's physician. The first 98 patients were randomized to medical therapy (n=53) or transthoracic defibrillator (n=45), and the last 98 patients to medical therapy (n=48) or nonthoracotomy defibrillator implantation with transvenous leads (n=50).
Results	The baseline characteristics of the defibrillator and medical therapy groups were similar. 11 patients in the medical therapy group received a defibrillator during the follow-up period and 5 patients assigned to defibrillator never received a defibrillator. There were no operative deaths. There were 15 deaths in the defibrillator group and 39 deaths in the medical therapy group (hazard ratio 0.46; 95% CI 0.26–0.82; p=0.009). There were 11 deaths from cardiac causes in the defibrillator group vs 27 in the medical therapy group. Both defibrillator types, with transthoracic and with intravenous leads were equally effective (ratio of the hazard ratios 0.86; p=0.78). There was no evidence that ß-blockers, amiodarone, or other antiarrhythmic drugs had an influence on the hazard ratio. However, the power of the analysis for the drug interactions with hazard ratio is limited, due to small number of treated patients.
Conclusions	In patients with prior myocardial infarction, reduced left ventricular ejection fraction, and asymptomatic nonsustained ventricular tachycardia, who had reproducible sustained ventricular arrhythmia during electrophysiologic study that was not suppressible by intravenous antiarrhythmic drug, prophylactic implantation of defibrillator improved survival as compared with conventional medical therapy.

MADIT (Substudy)

Multicenter Automatic Defibrillator Implantation Trial

Title	The cost effectiveness of automatic implantable cardiac defibrillators: Results from MADIT.
Authors	Mushlin AI, Hall J, Zwanziger J, et al.
Reference	Circulation 1998; 97:2129-2135.
Disease	Asymptomatic, nonsustained, ventricular tachycardia.
Purpose	To determine the economic consequences of automatic defibrillator implantation.
Results	Mean survival for patients receiving a defibrillator over 4 years was 3.66 vs 2.80 in patients receiving conventional therapy. Accumulated net costs (including hospitalization, physician visits, medicines, laboratory tests, procedures, cost of defibrillators) was \$97,560 for the defibrillator group vs \$75,980 for medication alone group. The incremental cost effectiveness ratio was \$27,000 per life saved with older devices and \$23,000 for transvenous defibrillators.
Conclusions	Implanted cardiac defibrillators are cost effective in selected patients who are at high risk for lethal ventricular arrhythmias.

AVID

Antiarrhythmics Vs Implantable Defibrillators

Title	A comparison of antiarrhythmic drug therapy with implantable defibrillators in patients resuscitated from near fatal ventricular arrhythmias.
Author	The Antiarrhythmics vs Implantable Defibrillator (AVID) investigators.
Reference	N Engl J Med 1997;337:1576–1583.
Disease	Ventricular fibrillation (VF), sustained ventricular tachycardia (VT).
Purpose	To determine survival of initial therapy of an implantable defibrillator vs amiodarone or sotalol in patients who were resuscitated from near fatal VF; or patients with symptomatic, sustained, and hemodynamically compromising VT.
Design	Randomized, multicenter, VT patients had to have sustained VT with syncope or an ejection fraction <0.40 and symptoms suggesting severe hemodynamic compromise (near syncope, heart failure, angina).
Patients	1016 patients; mean age 65 years; 79% male. 455 had VF; 561 had VT.
Follow-up	3 years plus.
Treatment regimen	Implantable cardioverter defibrillator vs antiarrhythmic drug treatment (most took amiodarone followed by sotalol).

Results	There were fewer deaths among patients assigned to the implantable defibrillator (80) than antiarrhythmic drug group (122). Death rates at 18.2 months were 15.8% in the defibrillator group vs 24% in the antiarrhythmic group. There was a decrease in death rate at 1, 2, and 3 years of 39, 27, 31%, respectively, in patients receiving the device vs drug; hence patients receiving the defibrillator had a better survival throughout the course of the study (p<0.02). Automatic pacing or shocks were more common among patients who entered the study with VT compared to those that entered with VF.
Conclusions	For survivors of VF or sustained, severely symptomatic VT, the implantable cardioverter defibrillator is superior to antiarrhythmic drugs regarding survival.

AVID (ß-blocker Substudy)

Antiarrhythmics Vs Implantable Defibrillators

Title	ß-blocker use and survival in patients with ventricular fibrillation or symptomatic ventricular tachycardia:The AVID Trial.
Authors	Exner DV, Reiffel JA, Epstein AE, et al.
Reference	J Am Coll Cardiol 1999;34:325-333.
Disease	Ventricular fibrillation, ventricular tachycardia.
Purpose	To determine whether ß-blockers alone or in combination with other specific antiarrhythmics improve survival in patients with VT/VF.
Design	As per AVID.
Patients	Determination of survival of 1016 randomized and 2101 eligible but nonrandomized patients with VF or symptomatic VT in the AVID trial.
Follow-up	As per AVID
Treatment regimen	As per AVID.
Additional therapy	As per AVID.

AVID (ß-blocker Substudy)

Antiarrhythmics Vs Implantable Defibrillators

(continued)

Results	There were 817 (28%) patients discharged from hospital on ß-blockers. Patients discharged from hospital on ß-blockers had fewer symptoms of heart failure and were less likely to be on a diuretic or ACE inhibitor. Metoprolol and atenolol were the two most commonly used ß-blockers. ß-blocker therapy was associated with improved survival in patients that did not receive amiodarone or an implantable defibrillator (RR=0.36; 95% CI=0.21-0.64; p=0.0004). However, ß-blocker use at hospital discharge was not associated with improved survival in randomized amiodarone treated (RR=0.88; 95% CI=0.48-1.61; p=NS) or defibrillator patients (RR=0.69; 95% CI=0.39-1.24; p=0.22). ß-blocker also was not associated with survival in eligible, nonrandomized patients that received amiodarone or defibrillator alone. Following adjustment, ß-blockers were unrelated to survival in randomized and nonrandomized patients receiving amiodarone or defibrillator alone. ß-blocker was independently associated with better survival in eligible, nonrandomized patients who were not treated with specific antiarrhythmic therapy (adjusted RR=0.47; 95% CI=0.25-0.88; p=0.018).
Conclusions	ß-blockers improved survival in patients with lethal ventricular arrhythmias who were not treated with amiodarone or implantable defibrillators, but did not have a protective effect on patients already receiving these specific forms of antiarrhythmic therapy.

CABG-PATCH

Coronary Artery Bypass Graft (CABG) Patch

Title	Prophylactic use of implanted cardiac defibrillators in patients at high risk for ventricular arrhythmias after coronary artery bypass graft surgery.
Author	Bigger JT, for the CABG patch trial investigators.
Reference	N Engl J Med 1997;337:1569–1575.
Disease	Sudden death by sustained ventricular tachyarrhythmias in patients with coronary artery disease, left ventricular dysfunction, and abnormalities on signal averaged electrocardiograms.
Purpose	To determine the effect of prophylactic implantation of cardioverter defibrillators at the time of coronary artery bypass surgery on survival in patients with coronary artery disease, left ventricular dysfunction, and abnormalities in signal averaged electrocardiograms.
Design	Randomized, multicenter.
Patients	1422 eligible, 1055 enrolled; 900 randomized (446, device; 454, no device). Patients had to be less than 80 (average ages were 64 and 63 in treated and untreated groups, respectively); had to have a left ventricular ejection fraction of <0.36; and had to have abnormalities on signal averaged electrocardiogram.
Follow-up	Average follow-up was 32±16 months.
Treatment regimen	Implantable cardioverter defibrillator or no device therapy at time of CABG. Trial prohibited use of antiarrhythmic drugs for asymptomatic ventricular arrhythmias.

CABG-PATCH

Coronary Artery Bypass Graft (CABG) Patch (continued)

Results	At 32 months there were 101 deaths in the defibrillator group and 95 in the control group. There were 71 deaths due to cardiac causes in the defibrillator group and 72 in the control group (p=NS).
Conclusions	Survival was not improved by prophylactic implantation of automatic cardioverter defibrillator at the time of CABG in high risk patients.

CABG Patch (Substudy)

Coronary Artery Bypass Graft (CABG) Patch

Title	Mechanisms of death in the CABG Patch Trial. A randomized trial of implantable cardiac defibrillator prophylaxis in patients at high risk of death after coronary artery bypass graft surgery.
Authors	Bigger JT, Whang W, Rottman JN, et al.
Reference	Circulation 1999; 99:1416–1421.
Disease	Ventricular arrhythmias.
Purpose	To determine whether ICD therapy significantly reduced arrhythmic death rate in the CABG Patch Trial.
Design	As per CABG patch trial.
Patients	198 (22%) of the 900 randomized patients who died during average follow-up of 32 months.
Follow-up	As per CABG patch.
Treatment regimen	As per CABG patch.
Results	79 (82%) of 96 deaths in the control group and 76 (75%) of 102 deaths in ICD group were due to cardiac causes. At 42 months, cumulative arrhythmic mortality was 6.9% in control group vs 4.0% in the ICD group (p=0.057). There was no difference in cumulative nonarrhythmic cardiac mortality at 42 months (12.4% in controls, 13.0% in ICD group, p=NS).
Conclusions	ICD therapy reduced arrhythmic death by 45% but had no effect on nonarrhythmic death. Since most (71%) of deaths in CABG Patch Trial were nonarrhythmic, total mortality was not reduced significantly in this trial.

D,l-Sotalol in Patients with Ventricular Tachycardia and in Survivors of Cardiac Arrest

Title	Efficacy and safety of d,l-Sotalol in patients with ventricular tachycardia and in survivors of cardiac arrest.
Authors	Haverkamp W, Martinez-Rubio A, Hief C, et al.
Reference	J Am Coll Cardiol 1997;30:487–495.
Disease	Ventricular tachycardia, ventricular fibrillation.
Purpose	To evaluate the safety and efficacy of d,l-sotalol in patients with ventricular tachycardia or ventricular fibrillation undergoing programmed ventricular stimulation.
Patients	396 patients, 56±14 years old, with inducible sustained ventricular tachycardia, ventricular fibrillation, or aborted sudden cardiac death who underwent programmed electrophysiologic ventricular stimulation. Patients within 48 h of acute myocardial infarction, unresponsive congestive heart failure, asthma or chronic obstructive pulmonary disease, previous adverse reaction to ß-blockers, renal failure, and the need for concomitant medications that prolong the QT interval were excluded.
Follow-up	Mean follow-up 34±18 months.
Treatment regimen	d,l-sotalol 80 mg bid for 48 h. Dosage was increased gradually up to 480 mg/d. Programmed ventricular stimulation was repeated after reaching the target dose. If ventricular tachyarrhythmia was not suppressed, the dose was increased, if tolerated, up to 640 mg/d and programmed ventricular stimulation was repeated. Patients with noninducible or more difficult to induce arrhythmia were discharged with d,l-sotalol.

Results	d,l-sotalol at an average dose of 465±90 mg/d suppressed inducible ventricular tachyarrhythmia in 151 patients (38.1%). In additional 76 patients (19.2%) induction of arrhythmia became more difficult. Side effects demanding discontinuation of d,l-sotalol during the short term treatment phase occurred in 28 patients (7.1%). Proarrhythmic effects were detected in 10 patients (2.5%) and Torsade de pointes ventricular tachycardia occurred in 7 patients (1.8%). Only 210 patients (53%) were discharged receiving d,l-sotalol. During the follow-up period, symptomatic ventricular arrhythmia occurred in 41 patients (19.5%). Actuarial rates for patients free of arrhythmic event were 89% at 1 year and 77% at 3 years. Actuarial total survival rates were 94% at 1 year and 86% at 3 years. Actuarial sudden death rates at one year were 8% and at 3 years 11% for patients with coronary artery disease and 6% and 25% for patients with dilated cardiomyopathy. Ventricular tachyarrhythmia suppression during programmed stimulation by d,l-sotalol was an independent predictor of arrhythmia recurrence. However, noninducible ventricular arrhythmia did not predict freedom from sudden death.
Conclusions	Oral d,l-sotalol is safe and effective in suppression of ventricular tachyarrhythmias. However, sudden cardiac death occurred in a considerable proportion of patients despite d,l-sotalol therapy, and electrophysiologic studies did not discriminate between patients who developed sudden cardiac death during therapy.

Preoperative amiodarone as prophylaxis against atrial fibrillation after heart surgery

Title	Preoperative amiodarone as prophylaxis against atrial fibrillation after heart surgery.
Author	Daoud EG, Strickberger A, Man KC.
Reference	N Engl J Med 1997; 337:1785-1791.
Disease	Atrial fibrillation.
Purpose	To determine the effectiveness of preoperative amiodarone as prophylaxis against atrial fibrillation following cardiac surgery.
Design	Double blind, randomized study.
Patients	124 patients scheduled for cardiac surgery, average ages 57-61 years.
Follow-up	~ 7 days post hospital discharge.
Treatment regimen	64 patients received amiodarone; and 60 received placebo for a minimum of 7 days prior to surgery. Amiodarone was given as 600 mg per day x 7 days, then 200 mg per day until hospital discharge.
Results	Atrial fibrillation occurred in 25% of patients in the amiodarone group and 53% of patients in the placebo group following surgery (p=0.003). Duration of hospitalization was shorter in the amiodarone patients (6.5±2.6 days) compared to placebo patients (7.9±4.3 days, p=0.04). Hospitalization costs were lower in the amiodarone group.

Preoperative amiodarone as prophylaxis against atrial fibrillation after heart surgery

(continued)

Conclusions	Administration of oral amiodarone prior to cardiac surgery reduces the incidence of postoperative atrial fibrillation and duration and cost of hospitalization.

THEOPACE

Theophylline vs Pacemaker on the symptoms and complications of sick sinus syndrome

Title	Effects of Permanent Pacemaker and Oral Theophylline in Sick Sinus Syndrome. The THEOPACE Study: A randomized controlled trial.
Author	Alboni P, Menozzi C, Brignole M, et al.
Reference	Circulation 1997; 96:260-266.
Disease	Sick sinus syndrome (arrhythmias).
Purpose	To determine the effects of oral theophylline vs permanent pacing on the symptoms and complications of sick sinus syndrome.
Design	Randomized, controlled, prospective trial.
Patients	170 patients with symptomatic sick sinus syndrome.
Follow-up	48 months.
Treatment regimen	No treatment (35 patients); oral theophylline (n=36) or dual chamber rate responsive pacemaker therapy (n=36).
Results	Frequency of syncope was lower in the pacemaker (6%) compared to control group (23%, p=0.02) and tended to be lower than in the group receiving theophylline (17%, p=0.07). Development of clinical heart failure was lower in the pacemaker (3%) and theophylline groups (3%) compared to no treatment (17%, p=0.05). The frequency of sustained paroxysmal tachycardias, permanent atrial fibrillation, and thromboembolic events did not show any difference among the 3 groups.

Theophylline vs Pacemaker on the symptoms and complications of sick sinus syndrome

(continued)

Conclusions	In patients with symptomatic sick sinus syndrome, the frequency of syncope was lowered with pacemaker therapy. Both pacemaker therapy and theophylline reduce heart failure.

SWORD

Survival With ORal D-sotalol

Title	a. The SWORD trial. Survival with oral d-sotalol in patients with left ventricular dysfunction after myocardial infarction: Rationale, design, and methods. b. Effect of d-sotalol on mortality in patients with left ventricular dysfunction after recent and remote myocardial infarction. c. Mortality in the Survival with ORAL D-Sotalol (SWORD) Trial: Why did patients die?
Authors	Waldo AL, Camm AJ, deRuyter H, et al. c. Pratt CM, Camm AJC, Cooper W, et al.
Reference	a. Am J Cardiol 1995;75:1023-1027. b. Lancet 1996;348:7-12. c. Am J Cardiol 1998;81:869-876.
Disease	Congestive heart failure.
Purpose	To evaluate the effectiveness of d-sotalol, an antiarrhythmic agent with a pure potassium channel blocking effect, and to reduce mortality in patients with previous myocardial infarction and left ventricular dysfunction.
Design	Randomized, double blind, placebo controlled, multicenter.
Patients	3121 patients, age ≥18 years, with left ventricular ejection fraction of ≤40% and a recent (6-42 days) or a remote (>42 days) myocardial infarction and class II-III heart failure. Patients with unstable angina, class IV heart failure, history of life threatening arrhythmia unrelated to a myocardial infarction, sick sinus syndrome or high-grade atrioventricular block, recent (<14 days) coronary angioplasty or coronary artery bypass surgery, electrolyte abnormalities, prolonged QT, renal failure, or concomitant use of antiarrhythmic drugs were excluded.
Follow-up	Mean follow-up 148 days.

SWORD

Survival With ORal D-sotalol
(continued)

Treatment regimen	Randomization to oral d-sotalol 100 mg X2/d or placebo for 1 week. If the dose was tolerated and QTc <520 msec, the dose was increased to 200 mg X2/d. If QTc was >560 msec, the dose was reduced.
Additional therapy	ß-blockers, calcium channel blockers, digoxin, diuretics, nitrates, and ACE inhibitors were permitted.
Results	The trial was stopped prematurely after 3121 patients had been enrolled because of excess in mortality in the d-sotalol group. All causes mortality was 5.0% vs 3.1% in the d-sotalol and placebo group, respectively (relative risk (RR) 1.65; 95% CI 1.15–2.36; p=0.006), cardiac mortality was 4.7% vs 2.9%, respectively (RR 1.65; 95% CI 1.14–2.39; p=0.008), and presumed arrhythmic deaths 3.6% vs 2.0% (RR 1.77; 95% CI 1.15–2.74; p=0.008). Rates of non-fatal cardiac events were similar between the groups. The adverse effect associated with d-sotalol therapy was greater in patients with left ventricular ejection fraction of 31%–40% than in those with ≤30% (RR 4.0 vs 1.2; p=0.007). c. The mortality associated with d-sotalol was greatest in patients with remote myocardial infarction and LV ejection fractions of 31%–40%. Comparable placebo patients in this group had a very low mortality. Most variables associated with torsades de pointes were not predictive of d-sotalol risk of death, except female gender.
Conclusions	D-sotalol therapy in patients after myocardial infarction and a reduced left ventricular ejection fraction were associated with increased total and cardiac mortality, which was presumed primarily to be due to arrhythmic deaths.

CHF-STAT (Substudy)

Congestive Heart Failure Survival Trial of Antiarrhythmic Therapy

Title	Spontaneous conversion and maintenance of sinus rhythm by amiodarone in patients with heart failure and atrial fibrillation. Observations from the Veterans Affairs Congestive Heart Failure Survival Trial of Antiarrhythmic Therapy (CHF-STAT).
Authors	Deedwania PC, Singh BN, Ellenbogen K, et al.
Reference	Circulation 1998; 98: 2574-2579.
Disease	Congestive heart failure, atrial fibrillation.
Purpose	To determine the effects of amiodarone vs placebo on conversion to and maintenance of sinus rhythm in patients with dilated cardiomyopathy and baseline atrial fibrillation.
Design	As per CHF-STAT.
Patients	103 patients with baseline atrial fibrillation who were in the CHF-STAT study.
Follow-up	4-5 years.
Treatment regimen	Amiodarone 800 mg daily for the first 2 weeks, 400 mg daily for the next 50 weeks, and 300 mg daily for the remainder of the study.

CHF-STAT (Substudy)

Congestive Heart Failure Survival Trial of Antiarrhythmic Therapy

(continued)

Results	Amiodarone reduced the mean ventricular response by 20% at 2 week measurement (p=0.001); by 18% at 6 months (p=0.001) and by 16% at 12 months (p=0.006). Maximal ventricular rates were also reduced by amiodarone. A greater number of patients in the amiodarone group converted to normal sinus rhythm (16 of 51 patients) vs placebo (4 of 52, χ^2 = 12.88, p=0.005). Amiodarone decreased the development of new onset atrial fibrillation in patients who were in sinus rhythm at the time of randomization. Amiodarone patients who converted to sinus rhythm and who were maintained in sinus rhythm demonstrated lower mortality compared to patients on amiodarone that did not convert and stay in sinus rhythm (p=0.04).
Conclusions	In patients with CHF and atrial fibrillation amiodarone reduced ventricular rates, was more successful in spontaneously converting patients to sinus rhythm than placebo, with improved survival in patients who did successfully convert on the drug.

The European Epinephrine Study Group

Title	A comparison of repeated high doses and repeated standard doses of epinephrine for cardiac arrest outside the hospital.
Authors	Gueugniaud P-Y, Mols P, Goldstein P, et al.
Reference	N Engl J Med 1998;339:1595-1601.
Disease	Ventricular fibrillation, cardiac arrest.
Purpose	To compare the efficacy of repeated standard doses vs high doses of epinephrine in patients with out-of-hospital cardiac arrest.
Design	Prospective, double blind, randomized, multicenter.
Patients	3327 patients, 18 years old, who had cardiac arrest outside the hospital, if they remained in ventricular fibrillation despite 3 countershocks or if they had asystole or pulseless electrical activity. Patients with traumatic cardiac arrest were excluded. Patients with obvious signs of irreversible cardiac arrest or those who had received epinephrine before randomization were not included.
Follow-up	1 year.
Treatment regimen	Randomization to up to 15 high (5 mg) or standard (1 mg) doses of epinephrine at 3 min intervals.
Additional therapy	Resuscitation according to standard American Heart Association and European Resuscitation Council guidelines.

(continued)

Results	Patients in the high dose group had a higher rate of return of spontaneous circulation (40.4% vs 36.4%; p=0.02), and a higher rate of admission alive to the hospital (26.5% vs 23.6%; p=0.05). However, the rate of discharge alive from the hospital was similar (2.3% in the high dose vs 2.8% in the standard dose group; p=0.34). Patients who were successfully resuscitated had comparable neurologic outcomes in the high dose and standard dose group. Long term survival was comparable between groups. Subgroup analysis revealed that the rates of achieving spontaneous circulation was higher in the high dose group among patients with: 1) witnessed cardiac arrest (45.1% vs 40.1%; p=0.009); 2) witnessed arrest with suspected cardiac causes in which a bystander administered the first resuscitation (50.9% vs 42.4%; p=0.15); and asystole as a primary rhythm (36.9% vs 32.2%; p=0.01). When the initial rhythm was ventricular fibrillation, there was no advantage to the high dose.
Conclusions	Long term survival after out-of-hospital cardiac arrest was comparable when standard dose or high dose epinephrine was administered, although high dose was associated with better immediate survival (return of spontaneous circulation and arrival alive to the hospital), especially in patients with asystole.

Title	Superiority of ibutilide (a new class III agent) over DL-sotalol in converting atrial flutter and atrial fibrillation.
Authors	Vos MA, Golitsyn SR, Stangl K, et al.
Reference	Heart 1998; 79: 568–575.
Disease	Atrial flutter, atrial fibrillation.
Purpose	To compare the efficacy and safety of ibutilide and DL-sotalol in terminating recent onset, sustained atrial flutter or fibrillation in hemodynamically stable patients.
Design	Randomized, double blind, multicenter.
Patients	319 patients, >18 years old (mean age 60 years), with recent onset (3 hours to 45 days) sustained atrial flutter or fibrillation. Patients should have been hemodynamically stable, with serum potassium ≥4 mEq/l, ventricular rate >60 bpm, and QT_c ≤440 ms. Patients with thyrotoxicosis, unstable angina, bronchospasm, myocardial infarction or heart surgery within 30 days, known sinus node dysfunction or advanced AV block, bundle branch block, Wolff-Parkinson-White syndrome and torsade de pointes were excluded. Patients treated with verapamil, diltiazem, or drugs that prolong the QT interval were not included. Treatment with class I or III antiarrhythmic drugs and ß-blockers was discontinued for ≥5 half lives before enrollment. 70% of the patients were men and 48% had heart disease.
Follow-up	31 hours of continuous ECG and Holter monitoring. Telephone contact at 72 hours.

Treatment regimen	Randomization to ibutilide 1 mg, ibutilide 2 mg, or DL-sotalol 1.5 mg/kg. Drugs were administered as a single 10 min IV infusion.
Results	11 patients were excluded because of having arrhythmia for >45 days (n=9) and incorrect dose of study medication (n=2). 99 patients received 1 mg ibutilide, 106 patients received 2 mg ibutilide, and 103 patients received DL-sotalol. Among patients with atrial flutter, ibutilide 1 mg was succesful in 56% of 16 patients, ibutilide 2 mg in 70% of 20 patients, and DL-sotalol in only 19% of 21 patients. Among patients with atrial fibrillation, ibutilide 1 mg was succesful in 20% of 83 patients, ibutilide 2 mg in 44% of 86 patients, and DL-sotalol in 11% of 82 patients. Ibutilide 2 mg was more effective than DL-sotalol both in converting atrial flutter ($p<0.05$) and in atrial fibrillation ($p<0.05$). The mean time to termination of arrhythmia was 19±15 min with ibutilide 1 mg, 13±7 min with ibutilide 2 mg, and 25±17 min with DL-sotalol ($p=0.0017$). Ibutilide 2 mg was succesful in terminating atrial fibrillation of more than 30 days duration in 48% of cases. Concomitant use of digoxin or nifedipine and prolongation of the QT_c interval were not predictive of termination of arrhythmia. Ventricular premature beats were detected in 6%, 9%, and 2% of patients receiving ibutilide 1 mg, ibutilide 2 mg, and DL-sotalol, respectively ($p=0.065$). Two patients (0.9%) receiving ibutilide 2 mg developed polymorphic ventricular tachycardia. Nonsustained ventricular tachycardia was detected in 4.9%, 7.3%, and 3.7% of the ibutilide 1 mg, ibutilide 2 mg, and DL-sotalol groups. Bradycardia (6.5%) and hypotension (3.7%) were more prevalent with DL-sotalol than with ibutilide.
Conclusions	Ibutilide is more effective than DL-sotalol in terminating persistent atrial flutter and fibrillation. Ibutilide is relatively safe and can be used under monitored conditions for termination of atrial flutter and fibrillation.

OPALS

Ontario Prehospital Advanced Life Support

Title	Improve out-of-hospital cardiac arrest survival through the inexpensive optimization of an existing defibrillation program. OPALS Study Phase II.
Authors	Stiell IG, Wells GA, Field BJ, et al.
Reference	JAMA 1999; 281:1175–1181.
Disease	Cardiac arrest.
Purpose	To determine the effect of a rapid defibrillation program in a large multicenter emergency medical service on out-of-hospital cardiac arrest survival.
Design	Controlled trial.
Patients	4690 patients in Phase I (before implementation) and 1641 in Phase 2 (after implementation of rapid defibrillation program) who developed out-of-hospital cardiac arrest and for whom resuscitation was attempted.
Follow-up	Up to 1 year.
Treatment regimen	Compound implementation of "an inexpensive system optimization approach to rapid defibrillation (defined as arriving at the scene with a defibrillator within 8 minutes of receiving the call in 90% of cases) in an existing multicenter ambulance based BLSD EMS system." Rapid defibrillation was achieved by: defibrillation by fire fighters, decrease in dispatch intervals, improved efficiency in deployment of ambulances.

OPALS

Ontario Prehospital Advanced Life Support

(continued)

Results	The percent of cases meeting the 8 minute response time improved with initiation of the rapid defibrillation protocol, from 76.7% in Phase I to 92.5% in Phase II ($p<0.001$). Survival to hospital discharge improved from 3.9% to 5.2%, $p = 0.03$, or a 33% relative improvement. This represents an additional 21 lives saved each year in the study (about 1 life per 120,000 residents). Estimated costs were U.S. $46,900 per life saved for establishing the program and U.S. $2400 per life saved annually to maintain the program.
Conclusions	A multifaceted system optimization approach to rapid defibrillation improved survival after cardiac arrest.

VPS

Vasovagal Pacemaker Study

Title	The North American Vasovagal Pacemaker Study (VPS). A randomized trial of permanent cardiac pacing for the prevention of vasovagal syncope.
Authors	Connolly SJ, Sheldon R, Roberts R, et al.
Reference	J Am Coll Cardiol 1999; 33:16–20.
Disease	Vasovagal syncope.
Purpose	To determine whether pacemaker therapy could decrease incidence of syncope.
Design	Randomized, multicenter.
Patients	54 patients with ≥6 lifetime episodes of syncope and a tilt table test with syncope or presyncope and relative bradycardia.
Follow-up	15 months.
Treatment regimen	Patients were randomized to a dual chamber pacemaker or no pacemaker. A minimum pacing rate of 60 bpm was programmed for all patients; in addition the pacemaker was programmed to detect a drop in heart rate of 5 to 15 bpm and if this persisted provide a pacing response of 100 bpm.

Results	Patients had a baseline mean of 35 prior lifetime episodes of syncope (in those without a pacemaker) and 14 in those with a history of a pacemaker. Pacemaker therapy resulted in a significant reduction in post randomization risk of syncope (relative risk reduction 85.4%, 95% CI = 59.7% -94.7%; 2p=0.000022). 70% of no pacemaker patients developed post randomization syncope vs 22% of pacemaker patients. The mean time interval between randomization to syncope was 54 days in untreated patients and 112 in pacemaker treated patients. Presyncope was reported in 74% of untreated and 63% of pacemaker-treated patients (p=NS).
Conclusions	In patients with histories of recurrent vasovagal syncope, dual chamber pacing with a rate drop response function reduced the incidence of recurrent syncope.

Prevention of implantable defibrillator or shocks by treatment with sotalol

Title	Prevention of implantable defibrillator or shocks by treatment with sotalol.
Authors	Pacifico A, Hohnloser SH, Williams JH, et al.
Reference	N Engl J Med 1999;340:1855–1862.
Disease	Sudden cardiac death, ventricular tachyarrhythmias.
Purpose	To assess the efficacy and safety of sotalol, an agent with Class III antiarrhythmic and ß-blocking properties for prevention of appropriate and inappropriate shocks delivered to patients who had implantable cardioverter defibrillators.
Design	Double blind, placebo controlled, parallel group, randomized, multicenter.
Patients	302 patients with histories of life threatening ventricular arrhythmias who had received an implantable cardioverter defibrillator within 3 months of enrollment, and had undergone successful defibrillation at the time of implantation.
Follow-up	12 months.
Treatment regimen	Patients were randomized to placebo (n=151) or 160–320 mg of sotalol per day (n=151); patients were stratified by LV ejection fraction (≤0.30 or >0.30).
Additional therapy	Treatment with ß-blockers, calcium blockers, and digoxin was allowed; other antiarrhythmic drugs were not allowed.

Prevention of implantable defibrillator or shocks by treatment with sotalol

(continued)

Results	Overall, 4 patients in the sotalol group died (2 of heart failure; 2 of noncardiac cause); 7 patients in the placebo group died (3 were cardiac). The primary end point was death from any cause or delivery of a first shock. End points were also analyzed regarding whether the first shock was appropriate (those delivered for ventricular tachycardia or fibrillation being deemed appropriate; those delivered for supraventricular arrhythmias or other events were deemed inappropriate). A secondary end point was frequency of shocks due to any cause. Treatment with sotalol resulted in a lower risk of death from any cause or delivery of a first shock for any reason (reduction in risk=48%; $p<0.001$); lower risk of death from any cause or delivery of a first appropriate shock (reduction in risk=44%; $p=0.007$). Sotalol also resulted in a lower rate of death from any cause or delivery of a first inappropriate shock (reduction in risk=64%; $p=0.004$). The mean of frequency of delivered shocks from any cause was reduced in the sotalol group (1.43 per year) vs the placebo group (3.89 per year). In the sotalol group, reduction in risk of death or delivery of first shock did not differ between those with higher vs lower ejection fractions.
Conclusions	Sotalol was safe and effective in decreasing the risk of death or delivery of a first shock in patients with implantable defibrillators.

Facilitating transthoracic cardioversion of atrial fibrillation with ibutilide pretreatment

Title	Facilitating transthoracic cardioversion of atrial fibrillation with ibutilide pretreatment.
Authors	Oral H, Souza JJ, Michand GF, et al.
Reference	N Engl J Med 1999;340:1849-1854.
Disease	Atrial fibrillation.
Purpose	To determine the effect of ibutilide on energy requirements for atrial defibrillation; to assess the ability of ibutilide to cardiovert patients with atrial fibrillation who are resistant to electrical transthoracic cardioversion.
Design	Randomized, single center study.
Patients	100 patients referred for cardioversion for atrial fibrillation of at least 6 hours duration.
Follow-up	6 months.
Treatment regimen	50 patients randomized to electrical transthoracic cardioversion with no ibutilide pretreatment; 50 assigned to undergo transthoracic cardioversion with ibutilide pretreatment. Ibutilide given as 1 mg infused over a 10 minute period. Cardioversion was performed with a step up protocol of 50, 100, 200, 300, and 360 J.
Additional therapy	Patients on antiarrhythmic drug therapy at the time of cardioversion, continued on drug therapy after restoration of sinus rhythm. Anticoagulant therapy for 1 month post cardioversion in patients in atrial fibrillation for >48 hours.

Facilitating transthoracic cardioversion of atrial fibrillation with ibutilide pretreatment

(continued)

Results	Cardioversion was successful in 36 (72%) of patients randomized to transthoracic cardioversion with no ibutilide. Of 50 patients in the ibutilide group, 10 (20%) cardioverted chemically. In the 40 remaining patients (80%), all cardioverted following transthoracic cardioversion. Overall efficacy of transthoracic electrical cardioversion was higher with ibutilide (100%) vs without the drug pretreatment (72%, p<0.001). Ibutilide pretreatment reduced the mean energy needed for defibrillation (166±80 J with ibutilide vs 228±93 J without ibutilide, p<0.001). Mean corrected QT interval was increased by ibutilide (482±49 msec vs 432±37 msec, p<0.001). In 2 of 64 patients that received ibutilide, both of whom had LV ejection fraction of ≤0.20, sustained polymorphic ventricular tachycardia occurred. There was no difference in the rate of freedom from recurrent atrial fibrillation at 6 months between the groups (57% in the no ibutilide group vs 64% who received ibutilide, p=NS).
Conclusions	Pretreatment with ibutilide enhanced the efficacy of transthoracic electrical cardioversion for patients with atrial fibrillation. Ibutilide should be avoided in patients with very low left ventricular ejection fractions.

French Active Compression-Decompression Cardiopulmonary Resuscitation Study

Title	A comparison of standard cardiopulmonary resuscitation and active compression-decompression resuscitation for out-of-hospital cardiac arrest.
Authors	Plaisance P, Lurie KG, Vicaut E, et al.
Reference	N Engl J Med 1999;341:569-575.
Disease	Cardiac arrest.
Purpose	To evaluate the 1 year survival of patients undergoing active compression-decompression method of cardiopulmonary resuscitation.
Design	Randomized, multicenter.
Patients	750 patients who had cardiac arrest out-of-hospital; >80% had asystole.
Follow-up	1 year.
Treatment regimen	Active compression-decompression resuscitation consisted of a hand held suction device. Active chest wall decompression reduces intrathoracic pressure, increasing venous blood return. Standard cardiopulmonary resuscitation (CPR, n=377); or active compression-decompression CPR (n=373), depending upon whether the arrest occurred on an even or odd day of the month.
Additional therapy	Advanced life support, including epinephrine.

French Active Compression-Decompression Cardiopulmonary Resuscitation Study

(continued)

Results	The primary end point was 1 year survival; the secondary end point was survival to hospital discharge without neurologic impairment and neurologic outcome. One year survival rate was 5% in the active compression-decompression CPR group vs 2% in the standard CPR group (p=0.03). Rate of hospital discharge without neurologic impairment was 6% in the active compression-decompression CPR group vs 2% in the standard CPR group (p=0.01). In 12 of 17 survivors who had received active compression-decompression CPR, neurologic status at 1 year had returned to baseline vs 3 of 7 survivors that received the standard CPR (p=NS). 9 of 17 one year survivors in the active compression-decompression CPR group and 2 of 7 in the standard CPR group had either asystole or cardiac electrical activity but no pulse. All of the survivors in both groups had a witnessed cardiac arrest.
Conclusions	CPR using an active compression-decompression technique during advanced life support improved one year survival in patients with out-of-hospital cardiac arrest.

MUSTT

Multicenter Unsustained Tachycardia Trial Investigation

Title	A randomized study of the prevention of sudden death in patients with coronary artery disease.
Authors	Buxton AE, Lee KL, Fisher JD, et al.
Reference	N Engl J Med 1999;341:1882-1890.
Disease	Sudden death, coronary artery disease.
Purpose	To determine whether electrophysiologically guided antiarrhythmic therapy would decrease sudden cardiac death in patients with coronary heart disease, LV ejection fraction of ≤40%, and asymptomatic, unsustained ventricular tachycardia (VT).
Design	Multicenter, randomized.
Patients	704 patients with coronary artery disease, LV ejection fraction of ≤40%, asymptomatic unsustained VT who had inducible sustained VT on electrophysiologic testing.
Follow-up	5 years.
Treatment regimen	Antiarrhythmic therapy guided by results of electrophysiologic testing or no antiarrhythmic therapy. Drugs were assigned randomly with the exception of amiodarone (amiodarone could be given if 2 tests had failed). Implantable defibrillator could be given after one unsuccessful drug test.
Additional therapy	ACE inhibitors, ß-blockers in some patients.

MUSTT

Multicenter Unsustained Tachycardia Trial Investigation

(continued)

Results	Of 704 patients who were randomized 351 were assigned to electrophysiologically guided therapy and 353 to no antiarrhythmic therapy.The primary end point of cardiac arrest or death from arrhythmia was reached in 25% of patients receiving electrophysiologically guided therapy vs 32% of patients assigned to no antiarrhythmic therapy (RR=0.73; 95% CI=0.53-0.99) representing a 27% reduction in risk (p=0.04). 5 year estimates of overall mortality were 42% and 48% in treated vs nontreated group (RR=0.80; 95% CI=0.64-1.01; p=0.06). Treatment with implantable defibrillators was associated with a lower risk of cardiac arrest or death from arrhythmias than patients discharged without defibrillators (RR=0.24; 95% CI=0.13-0.45; p<0.001). Rate of cardiac arrest or death from arrhythmia nor overall mortality rate was lower among patients assigned to electrophysiologically guided therapy and treated with antiarrhythmic drugs compared to patients in the untreated group that did not receive antiarrhythmic drugs.
Conclusions	While electrophysiologically guided therapy with subsequent therapy with implantable defibrillators reduced the risk of cardiac arrest or death from arrhythmias in high risk patients, antiarrhythmic drugs alone were not successful.

CTAF

Canadian Trial of Atrial Fibrillation

Title	Amiodarone to prevent recurrence of atrial fibrillation.
Authors	Roy D, Talajic M, Dorion P, et al.
Reference	N Engl J Med 2000;342:913–920.
Disease	Atrial fibrillation.
Purpose	To compare low dose amiodarone to sotalol or propafenone for the prevention of recurrence of atrial fibrillation.
Design	Prospective, nonblinded, randomized, multicenter.
Patients	403 patients who had at least one episode of symptomatic atrial fibrillation within the previous 6 months. One episode had to have lasted at least 10 minutes and be confirmed by ECG.
Follow-up	16 months.
Treatment regimen	Amiodarone (10 mg/kg daily for 14 days; then 300 mg per day for 4 weeks; then 200 mg daily). Sotalol at doses varying by age, creatinine concentration, and weight; propafenone dose based on age and weight.
Additional therapy	For atrial fibrillation lasting >48 hours, anticoagulant therapy. Electrical cardioversion if necessary (recommended if atrial fibrillation persisted after 14 days of loading doses of amiodarone and after 4 days of treatment with sotalol or propafenone).

CTAF

Canadian Trial of Atrial Fibrillation

(continued)

Results

Primary end point was length of time to first ECG documented recurrence of atrial fibrillation. 71 (35%) of 201 patients assigned to amiodarone vs 127 (63%) of 202 patients assigned to sotalol or propafenone had recurrent atrial fibrillation ($p<0.001$). Median time for recurrence of atrial fibrillation in the sotalol or propafenone group was 98 days but was >468 days in the amiodarone group. The probability of staying in sinus rhythm for 1 year without recurrence of atrial fibrillation was 69% in amiodarone patients and 39% in the sotalol or propafenone group (39%; $p<0.001$). Drug therapy was discontinued due to adverse events in 18% of patients on amiodarone and 11% of those on sotalol or propafenone ($p=0.06$).

Conclusions

Amiodarone was more effective than sotalol or propafenone for preventing recurrent episodes of atrial fibrillation.

CIDS

Canadian Implantable Defibrillator Study

Title	A randomized trial of the implantable cardioverter defibrillator against amiodarone.
Authors	Connolly SJ, Gent M, Roberts RS, et al.
Reference	Circulation 2000;101:1297–1302.
Disease	Ventricular fibrillation, ventricular tachycardia.
Purpose	To compare the efficacy of the implantable cardioverter defibrillator (ICD) to amiodarone for preventing death in patients with previous life threatening sustained ventricular arrhythmia.
Design	Randomized, multicenter.
Patients	659 patients with resuscitated ventricular fibrillation, ventricular tachycardia, or unmonitored syncope.
Follow-up	5 years.
Treatment regimen	ICD vs amiodarone starting at ≥1200 mg/day for at least 1 week and then ≥300 mg/day. Could be lowered to 200 mg/day if side effects developed.
Additional therapy	ß-blocker, sotalol, digoxin, Class I antiarrhythmics. Note: There was imbalance in use of other antiarrhythmics between the 2 groups. Sotalol and other ß-blockers more commonly used in the ICD group.

Results	Primary end point was all cause mortality. All cause mortality occurred in 10.2% per year of amiodarone patients vs 8.3% per year of ICD patients (19.7% relative risk reduction for ICD therapy; 95% CI=-7.7%-40.0%; p=0.142). Hence, this reduction in risk of all cause mortality with ICDs over amiodarone did not achieve statistical significance. Also there was a nonsignificant decrease in arrhythmic death from ICDs from 4.5% with amiodarone to 3.0% per year for ICDs (relative risk reduction =32.8%; 95% CI=-7.2%-57.8%; p=0.094). 1.9% per year of amiodarone patients experienced pulmonary infiltrate.
Conclusions	There were nonsignificant trends toward reductions in all cause mortality and arrhythmic death in patients receiving ICDs vs amiodarone.

TRACE (Atrial fibrillation Substudy)

Trandolapril Cardiac Evaluation Study

Title	Trandolapril reduces the incidence of atrial fibrillation after acute myocardial infarction in patients with left ventricular dysfunction.
Authors	Pedersen OD, Bagger H, Kober L, et al.
Reference	Circulation 1999;100:376-380.
Disease	Atrial fibrillation.
Purpose	To determine whether the ACE inhibitor trandolapril could reduce the incidence of atrial fibrillation in patients with left ventricular dysfunction following acute myocardial infarction.
Design	Randomized, double blind , placebo controlled, multicenter study.
Patients	Of 1749 patients who had been entered into the original TRACE study, 1577 had sinus rhythm at randomization. Impaired LV function by echocardiography with randomization between 3-7 days after onset of acute myocardial infarction.
Follow-up	4 years.
Treatment regimen	790 patients randomized to trandolapril; 787 to placebo. Trandolapril initially given as 1 mg/day, then increased to 2 mg/day before hospital discharge. At about 4 weeks after myocardial infarction dose was increased to 4 mg/day. Dose adjustment if necessary.
Additional therapy	As per physician.

TRACE (Atrial fibrillation Substudy)

Trandolapril Cardiac Evaluation Study

(continued)

Results	During the follow-up period, 42 (5.3%) patients developed atrial fibrillation in the placebo group vs 22 (2.8%) in the trandolapril group ($p<0.05$). After adjusting for a number of baseline characteristics, trandolapril significantly decreased the risk of developing atrial fibrillation (RR=0.45; 95% CI=0.26–0.76; $p<0.01$). Factors associated with development of atrial fibrillation included severe congestive heart failure at baseline, LV function, male sex, digitalis use at baseline, age, and systolic blood pressure. There was a nonsignificant trend toward higher mortality in patients that developed atrial fibrillation (RR=1.2; 95% CI=0.73–2.06; p=NS).
Conclusions	Trandolapril decreased the incidence of atrial fibrillation in post MI patients with LV dysfunction.

ARCH

The Amiodarone Reduction in Coronary Heart Trial

Title	Intravenous amiodarone for the prevention of atrial fibrillation after open heart surgery: The ARCH Trial.
Authors	Guarnieri T, Nolan S, Gottlieb SO, et al.
Reference	J Am Coll Cardiol 1999;34:343–347.
Disease	Atrial fibrillation.
Purpose	To determine whether low dose IV amiodarone would prevent atrial fibrillation and shorten hospital stay in patients undergoing cardiac surgery.
Design	Randomized, double blind, placebo controlled, single center.
Patients	300 patients undergoing standard open heart surgery with no evidence of preoperative atrial fibrillation.
Follow-up	1 month.
Treatment regimen	Amiodarone IV 1 g over 24 hours for a total of 48 hours (2 g total) or placebo infusion.
Additional therapy	About 50% of both groups were taking ß-blockers before surgery.

Results	Primary end points were postoperative atrial fibrillation and length of stay in hospital. Atrial fibrillation occurred in 67 of 142 (47%) placebo patients and in 56 of 158 (35%) amiodarone patients (p=0.01). There was no difference in length of hospital stay in the placebo group (8.2±6.2 days) vs the amiodarone group (7.6±5.9 days). No deaths occurred in the amiodarone group; 2 in the placebo group. Drug effect appeared to occur during the first few days of treatment.
Conclusions	Low dose IV amiodarone was effective in decreasing the frequency of atrial fibrillation following cardiac surgery.

Oral d,l sotalol reduces the incidence of postoperative atrial fibrillation in coronary artery bypass surgery patients: A randomized, double blind, placebo controlled study

Title	Oral d,l sotalol reduces the incidence of postoperative atrial fibrillation in coronary artery bypass surgery patients: A randomized, double blind, placebo controlled study.
Authors	Gomes JA, Ip J, Santoni-Rugiu F, et al.
Reference	J Am Coll Cardiol 1999;34:334-339.
Disease	Atrial fibrillation.
Purpose	To determine the efficacy of preoperative and postoperative oral d,l sotalol in preventing the occurrence of postoperative atrial fibrillation.
Design	Randomized, double blind, placebo controlled, 2 center study.
Patients	85 patients (73 to undergo CABG; 12 CABG plus valvular surgery). Ejection fraction had to be ≥28% and no clinical evidence of heart failure.
Follow-up	Hospital stay (~7-8 days).
Treatment regimen	Placebo (n=45) or sotalol (n=40; mean dose=190±43 mg/day) given 24-48 hours prior to surgery and continued for up to 4 days postoperatively. Sotalol was given as 80 mg orally twice daily and advanced to a dose of 120 mg orally twice daily if there was no bradycardia, CHF or QTc >500 msec. Study medicine was stopped if QTc was >500 msec, or if significant bradycardia with hypotension occurred.

Oral d,l sotalol reduces the incidence of postoperative atrial fibrillation in coronary artery bypass surgery patients: A randomized, double blind, placebo controlled study

(continued)

Additional therapy	Dose of ß-blockers was halfed in those patients on ≥200 mg/day of metoprolol or its equivalent.
Results	The end point was occurrence of atrial fibrillation lasting ≥30 minutes or for any length of time requiring intervention secondary to symptoms of atrial fibrillation. 38% of patients in the placebo group developed atrial fibrillation vs 12.5% in the sotalol group (p=0.008). Drug was withdrawn for clinically significant bradycardia/hypotension in none of the placebo group and 5% of the sotalol patients (p=0.2). No patients that received sotalol developed torsade de pointes or sustained ventrical arrhythmias. QTc was prolonged on sotalol (458±38 msec) vs before sotalol (419±29 msec; p=0.0001). There was one death in the placebo group and none in the sotalol group. There was a nonsignificant trend toward shorter length of stay in the sotalol group (7 vs 8 days).
Conclusions	Sotalol reduced the frequency of postoperative atrial fibrillation in patients undergoing CABG who did not have heart failure or significant LV dysfunction.

Efficacy and safety of ibutilide fumarate for the conversion of atrial arrhythmias after cardiac surgery

Title	Efficacy and safety of ibutilide fumarate for the conversion of atrial arrhythmias after cardiac surgery.
Authors	VanderLugt JT, Mattioni T, Denker S, et al.
Reference	Circulation 1999;100:369-375.
Disease	Atrial fibrillation, atrial flutter.
Purpose	To assess the efficacy and safety of ibutilide fumarate for rapid conversion of atrial fibrillation and flutter shortly after cardiac surgery.
Design	Randomized, double blind, placebo controlled, dose response, multicenter.
Patients	302 patients, ≥18 years old, <300 lbs body weight, hemodynamically stable, with atrial fibrillation (n=201) or flutter (n=101), 1 hour to 3 days in duration that had occurred 1-7 days after cardiac surgery. All patients were in normal sinus rhythm at the time of surgery with a corrected QT ≤440 ms. Patients with a history of torsade de pointes arrhythmia, a heart rate <60 bpm, myocardial infarction within 30 days, thyrotoxicosis, severe liver impairment, an electrolyte abnormality, recent treatment with antiarrhythmic agents or vasopressor drugs, and those who had been exposed to ibutilide were excluded.
Follow-up	72 hours.

Efficacy and safety of ibutilide fumarate for the conversion of atrial arrhythmias after cardiac surgery

(continued)

Treatment regimen	Patients were randomized to intravenous infusion of placebo or 0.25, 0.5, or 1.0 mg of ibutilide fumarate over 10 minutes. If the arrhythmia did not terminate within 10 minutes, an identical second dose was administered. The infusion was stopped after the arrhythmia terminated or if there was a fall in systolic blood pressure (<90 mm Hg), an increase in QTc (>600 ms), or the development of ventricular arrhythmia.
Additional therapy	Other antiarrhythmic agents were not permitted within 4 hours after study drug failure and within 24 hours in cases who converted to sinus rhythm. Electrical cardioversion was permitted >90 min after treatment failure or in patients with recurrence of atrial arrhythmia after successful cardioversion by the study drug.
Results	The conversion to sinus rates within 90 minutes was 15% with placebo and 40%, 47%, and 57% with ibutilide 0.25 mg, 0.5 mg, and 1.0 mg, respectively (p=0.0001). The conversion rates were 20%, 28%, 42%, and 44% with placebo and 0.25, 0.5, and 1.0 mg ibutilide, respectively for patients with atrial fibrillation (p=0.0055) and 4%, 56%, 61%, and 78%, respectively, for patients with atrial flutter (p=0.0001). Mean time to cardioversion was 36 minutes for the 0.25 mg dose, 33 minutes for the 0.5 mg dose and 23 minutes for the 1.0 mg dose. Of the 104 patients successfully converted to sinus rhythm with ibutilide, 63% remained in sinus rhythm for 24 hours. 8 out of the 13 patients (62%) who converted spontaneously with placebo remained in sinus rhythm for 24 hours. Ibutilide 0.5 and 1.0 mg caused prolongation of the QTc. Ventricular arrhythmia was noted in 8.3% of the 218 patients randomized to ibutilide vs 1.2% of the 84 patients randomized to placebo. Nonsustained monomorphic ventricular tachycardia was noted in 3.2% and 0, respectively, nonsustained polymorphic ventricular tachycardia in 1.4% and 1.2%, respectively, and sustained polymorphic ventricular tachycardia in 0.9% and 0%, of the patients, respectively. There were no deaths, strokes, or myocardial infarctions.

Conclusions	Ibutilide was safe and effective, when used in a carefully supervised clinical setting, for cardioversion of atrial fibrillation, and especially atrial flutter, in patients after a recent cardiac surgery.

Amiodarone Early After Acute Myocardial Infarction

Title	Morbidity and mortality following early administration of amiodarone in acute myocardial infarction.
Authors	Elizari MV, Martinez JM, Belziti C, et al.
Reference	Eur Heart J 2000;21:198–205.
Disease	Acute myocardial infarction.
Purpose	To evaluate the effects of amiodarone on mortality and morbidity in the first few hours after acute myocardial infarction.
Design	Randomized, double blind, placebo controlled, multicenter.
Patients	1073 patients within 24 hours of onset of an acute myocardial infarction. Patients with systolic blood pressure <100 mm Hg, heart rate <60 bpm, atrioventricular block, intraventricular block, long QT, severe heart failure, ventricular or supraventricular arrhythmia, significant liver disease, or amiodarone treatment within the last 3 months were excluded.
Follow-up	180 days.

Treatment regimen	Randomization to either placebo (n=531) or amiodarone (n=542). Study drug was initiated within the first 24 hours of onset of symptoms, and in those receiving thrombolytic therapy, amiodarone was administered immediately after the thrombolytic drug. Patients received amiodarone IV for 48 hours for a total dose of 2700 mg. Oral amiodarone 600 mg bid was initiated immediately and continued for 4 days. From day 5 to day 90 patients received placebo or amiodarone 400 mg/d, and then 200 mg/d for the next 90 days. After the first 516 patients were analyzed, the Safety and Monitoring Board suggested changing the IV amiodarone dose to 1200 mg over 48 hours and the oral amiodarone to 800 mg/d for 2 days, 400 mg/d from day 3 to day 90, and then 200 mg/d for the next 90 days.
Additional therapy	Reperfusion therapy by either thrombolytic drugs or PCI was permitted. Aspirin, nitrates, ß-blockers, digitalis, diuretics, calcium channel blockers, and ACE inhibitors were permitted.

Results	The study was terminated early by the Safety and Monitoring Board, because amiodarone did not have an effect on 30 day survival. A total of 270 patients received high dose amiodarone and 246 received placebo. Total mortality was 16.3% with amiodarone vs 10.2% with placebo (odds ratio [OR] 1.72; 95% CI 0.99–3.01; p=0.04). Cardiac mortality was 9.6% vs 7.7%, respectively (OR 1.27; 95% CI 0.66–2.47; p=0.40), and noncardiac mortality was 6.7% vs 2.4% (OR 2.86; 95% CI 1.05–8.19; p=0.02). More patients in the amiodarone group were hospitalized (32.6% vs 23.2%; p=0.01). However, fewer patients in the amiodarone group had postinfarction angina (19.6% vs 30.9%; p=0.003). Amiodarone did not reduce the incidence of non-fatal arrhythmic events (9.6% vs 10.6%; p=0.70). Hypotension was detected more often in the amiodarone group (11.5% vs 4.9%). A total of 272 patients received the lower dose of amiodarone and 285 patients received the placebo. Total mortality was 6.6% in the amiodarone group vs 9.5% in the placebo group (p=0.20). Cardiac mortality was 3.3% vs 6.0% (p=0.10), and noncardiac mortality was 3.3% vs 3.5% (p=0.80). Fewer patients in the amiodarone group had postinfarction angina (19.1% vs 29.8%; OR 0.56; 95% CI 0.37–0.84; p=0.004). There was no difference in readmission rate (25.7% vs 27.4%; p=0.60). Hypotension occurred in 4.0% of the amiodarone vs 4.6% in the control group.
Conclusions	Early administration of high dose amiodarone was associated with increased mortality, especially noncardiac mortality. Low dose amiodarone did not significantly affect mortality. Early administration of low dose amiodarone in acute myocardial infarction may be used only to treat life threatening arrhythmia.

CTOPP

Canadian Trial of Physiologic Pacing

Title	Effects of physiologic pacing vs ventricular pacing on the risk of stroke and death due to cardiovascular causes.
Authors	Connolly SJ, Kerr CR, Gent M, et al, for the Canadian Trial of Physiologic Pacing Investigators.
Reference	N Engl J Med 2000;342:1385–1391.
Disease	Symptomatic bradycardia.
Purpose	To determine whether there is a benefit of physiologic (dual chamber or atrial) pacing compared to single chamber (ventricular) pacing in patients with symptomatic bradycardia.
Design	Randomized, multicenter.
Patients	2568 patients scheduled for initial implantation of a pacemaker to correct symptomatic bradycardia and did not have chronic atrial fibrillation.
Follow-up	3 years.
Treatment regimen	1474 patients were assigned to ventricular pacing and 1094 to physiologic pacing.
Additional therapy	Anticoagulant, antiplatelet drugs; 11.5 and 12.6% on antiarrhythmic drugs in ventricular pacing and physiologic pacing groups, respectively.

CTOPP

Canadian Trial of Physiologic Pacing

(continued)

Results	Primary outcome was occurrence of either stroke or death due to cardiovascular cause. Secondary outcome events were death from any cause, documented atrial fibrillation lasting more than 15 minutes, and admission to the hospital for congestive heart failure. Annual rate of stroke or death due to cardiovascular causes was 5.5% in the ventricular pacing group vs 4.9% in the physiologic pacing group (p=NS). Annual rate of atrial fibrillation was 6.6% in the ventricular pacing group vs 5.3% in the physiologic pacing group (p=0.05). This benefit was not apparent until 2 years after pacemaker implantation. Annual rate of death was 6.6% for ventricular pacing and 6.3% for physiologic pacing (p=NS); rate for hospitalization for congestive heart failure was 3.5% for ventricular pacing and 3.1% for physiologic pacing (p=NS). Annual rate of stroke was 1.1% in ventricular pacing and 1.0% in physiologic pacing group. Perioperative complications were more common in the physiologic pacing (9.0%) vs ventricular pacing (3.8%) groups; p<0.001.
Conclusions	Physiologic pacing was no better than ventricular pacing in preventing rate of stroke or death due to cardiovascular cause.

Effective prevention of atrial fibrillation by continuous atrial overdrive pacing after coronary artery bypass surgery

Title	Effective prevention of atrial fibrillation by continuous atrial overdrive pacing after coronary artery bypass surgery.
Authors	Blommaert D, Gonzalez M, Mucumbitsi J, et al.
Reference	J Am Coll Cardiol 2000;35:1411-1415.
Disease	Atrial fibrillation—after coronary artery bypass grafting.
Purpose	To determine the efficacy of an algorithm with continuous atrial dynamic overdrive pacing to prevent or reduce atrial fibrillation post CABG.
Design	Randomized, consecutive patients.
Patients	96 consecutive patients undergoing CABG for severe, symptomatic coronary artery disease. Patients had to be in sinus rhythm without antiarrhythmic drugs and stable on second day following surgery.
Follow-up	Inhospital.
Treatment regimen	Two sets of epicardial wire electrodes placed on the right ventricle and high right atrium in all patients. External pacemaker was connected to the atrial wires for 24 hours continuous atrial pacing with a lower rate of 80 bpm in an AAI pacing mode. The algorithm for dynamic overdrive was programmed to allow pacing above the patient's own rate. Patients were randomized to atrial stimulation vs no stimulation.
Additional therapy	If necessary, atrial fibrillation was treated with antiarrhythmic drugs, usually an infusion of amiodarone.

Effective prevention of atrial fibrillation by continuous atrial overdrive pacing after coronary artery bypass surgery

(continued)

Results	Primary end point was occurrence on 24 hour Holter ECG of an episode of atrial fibrillation when sustained for at least 15 minutes. 5 of 48 (10%) of patients in the paced group developed atrial fibrillation vs 13 of 48 (27%) in the control, nonpaced group. Duration of atrial fibrillation was 120 minutes (median) in paced and 378 minutes in nonpaced group. Mean heart rates were greater in the paced groups at 93±11 bpm vs unpaced groups at 87±11 bpm, as expected.A multivariate analysis revealed that atrial fibrillation increased with age. Atrial fibrillation decreased with a better left ventricular ejection fraction in patients undergoing atrial pacing.Atrial pacing was more effective when left ventricular ejection fraction was >50%.
Conclusions	Continuous atrial pacing with an alogrithm for dynamic overdrive decreases atrial fibrillation after coronary artery bypass surgery.

Atrial pacing for the prevention of atrial fibrillation after cardiovascular surgery

Title	Atrial pacing for the prevention of atrial fibrillation after cardiovascular surgery.
Authors	Greenberg MD, Katz NM, Iuliano S, et al.
Reference	J Am Coll Cardiol 2000;34:1416–1422.
Disease	Atrial fibrillation (postoperative).
Purpose	To assess the efficacy of atrial pacing for prevention of atrial fibrillation after cardiovascular surgery.
Design	Randomized, single center.
Patients	154 patients undergoing cardiac surgery (CABG: 88.3%; aortic valve replacement: 4.5%; both: 7.1%). Right and left atrial epicardial pacing electrodes placed at time of surgery.
Follow-up	Inhospital.
Treatment regimen	Patients randomly assigned to no postoperative pacing: right atrial pacing, left atrial pacing, or bi-atrial pacing. Pacing rate varied from 100–110 bpm depending on the native heart rate.
Additional therapy	Postoperative ß-blockers were started in all patients without contraindications.

Atrial pacing for the prevention of atrial fibrillation after cardiovascular surgery

(continued)

Results	Primary end point was atrial fibrillation lasting longer than 1 hour in duration or causing hemodynamic compromise requiring electrical or chemical cardioversion. Patients assigned to one of the 3 pacing strategies had a lower incidence of postoperative atrial fibrillation (17%) compared to patients that were not assigned to pacing (37.5%; $p<0.005$). The incidence of atrial fibrillation was 8% with right atrial pacing, 20% with left atrial pacing, and 26% with bi-atrial pacing vs patients that did not receive pacing (37.5%; $p=0.002$ for right atrial vs no pacing; p=NS for other pacing groups individually vs no pacing). Length of hospital stay was reduced by 22% in patients who received pacing (6.1±2.3 days) vs those that did not (7.8±3.7 days, $p=0.003$).
Conclusions	Postoperative atrial pacing in the setting of postoperative ß-blockade significantly decreased the incidence of atrial fibrillation and length of hospital stay. Right atrial pacing appeared to be the most beneficial but additional studies are needed to assess the most effective site for pacing.

Cardiopulmonary resuscitation by chest compression alone or with mouth to mouth ventilation

Title	Cardiopulmonary resuscitation by chest compression alone or with mouth to mouth ventilation.
Authors	Hallstrom A, Cobb L, Johnson E, Copass M.
Reference	N Engl J Med 2000;342:1546-1553.
Disease	Cardiac arrest.
Purpose	To compare cardiopulmonary resuscitation (CPR) with chest compression alone vs CPR with chest compression plus mouth to mouth ventilation.
Design	Randomized. Emergency medical services personnel blinded as much as possible.
Patients	520 patients with witnessed cardiac arrest.
Follow-up	Hospital discharge. Also follow up of all survivors (enrollment began in 1992 and ended in 1998).
Treatment regimen	Dispatcher instructed bystander CPR with chest compression alone vs dispatcher instructed chest compression plus mouth to mouth ventilation.

Cardiopulmonary resuscitation by chest compression alone or with mouth to mouth ventilation

(continued)

Results	64 patients survived to hospital discharge. 29/278 (10.4%) survived in the group receiving chest compression plus mouth to mouth ventilation vs 35/240 (14.6%) of patients who received chest compression only (p=0.18). 95/279 (34.1%) survived to hospital admission in the chest compression plus mouth to mouth ventilation group vs 97/241 (40.2%) in the chest compression alone group (p=0.15). Telephone instructions from dispatcher to bystander were completely delivered to 62% of episodes assigned to chest compression plus mouth to mouth ventilation vs 81% of episodes assigned to only chest compression (p=0.005).
Conclusions	Hospitalization and survival to hospital discharge were similar among cardiac arrest victims who received bystander CPR with chest compression alone or with chest compression plus mouth to mouth ventilation.

ARREST

Amiodarone in Out-of-Hospital Resuscitation of Refractory Sustained Ventricular Tachyarrhythmias

Title	Amiodarone for resuscitation after out-of-hospital cardiac arrest due to ventricular fibrillation.
Authors	Kudenchuk PJ, Cobb LA, Copass MK, et al.
Reference	N Engl J Med 1999;341:871-878.
Disease	Cardiac arrest.
Purpose	To determine the effect of IV amiodarone in patients with out-of-hospital cardiac arrest with ventricular fibrillation or tachycardia who were refractory to precordial shocks.
Design	Randomized, double blind, placebo controlled.
Patients	504 patients who had out-of-hospital cardiac arrest with ventricular fibrillation or pulseless ventricular tachycardia and could not be resuscitated after receiving ≥3 defibrillator shocks.
Follow-up	Hospital discharge.
Treatment regimen	300 mg IV amiodarone (n=246) or placebo (n=258) administered by paramedics on the scene of the cardiac arrest.
Additional therapy	1 mg epinephrine IV.

Amiodarone in Out-of-Hospital Resuscitation of Refractory Sustained Ventricular Tachyarrhythmias

(continued)

Results	Primary end point was survival through admission to hospital with a spontaneously perfusing rhythm. 44% of the amiodarone group vs 34% of the placebo group survived to be admitted to the hospital (p=0.03). The adjusted odds ratio for survival to admission in amiodarone treated patients vs placebo patients was 1.6 (95% CI=1.1-2.4; p=0.02) and the benefit of amiodarone was observed across subsets of patients. Patients with ventricular fibrillation were more likely to survive to hospital admission (44%) than patients with initial rhythm of asystole or pulseless electrical activity (14%; p<0.001). Patients with transient return of spontaneous circulation before receiving amiodarone or placebo were more likely to survive to be admitted vs those who remained pulseless before getting study drug. Hypotension was more common with amiodarone (59%) vs placebo (48%; p=0.04); bradycardia was more common with amiodarone (41%) compared to placebo (25%; p=0.004). The percentage of patients discharged alive was 13.4% in the amiodarone group and 13.2% in the placebo group; the study was not powered to detect statistically significant differences in survival till hospital discharge between groups.
Conclusions	Amiodarone resulted in a higher rate of survival to hospital admission in patients with out-of-hospital cardiac arrest and refractory ventricular arrhythmias.

9. Anticoagulation for Atrial Fibrillation

AFASAK

Aspirin vs Warfarin in Atrial Fibrillation

Title	Placebo controlled, randomized trial of warfarin and aspirin for prevention of thromboembolic complications in chronic atrial fibrillation. The Copenhagen AFASAK study.
Authors	Petersen P, Boysen G, Godtfredsen J, et al.
Reference	Lancet 1989;I:175-179.
Disease	Atrial fibrillation.
Purpose	To evaluate the effects of low dose aspirin and warfarin anticoagulation on the incidence of thromboembolic events in patients with chronic nonrheumatic atrial fibrillation.
Design	Randomized, open label (warfarin vs no warfarin), double blind in the group of no warfarin (aspirin vs placebo), 2 centers.
Patients	1007 patients, ≥18 years old with chronic atrial fibrillation. Patients with previous anticoagulation therapy >6 months, cerebrovascular event within 1 month, severe hypertension, alcoholism, valve replacement, rheumatic heart disease, or with contraindication to aspirin or warfarin were excluded.
Follow-up	2 years.
Treatment regimen	Warfarin (open label), target INR was 2.8-4.2. Aspirin 75 mg/d or placebo.

AFASAK

Aspirin vs Warfarin in Atrial Fibrillation

(continued)

Results	Patients on warfarin were within INR 2.8–4.2 for 42% of the time. 26% of the time the INR was <2.4. Thromboembolic complications occurred in 1.5% of the warfarin, 6.0% in the aspirin, and 6.3% of the control group ($p<0.05$).The yearly incidence of thromboembolic events was 2.0% on warfarin and 5.5% on either aspirin or placebo. Vascular death occurred in 0.9%, 3.6%, and 4.5% of the warfarin, aspirin and placebo groups ($p<0.02$). 6.3% of the warfarin patients had nonfatal bleeding, while only 0.6% and 0 of the aspirin and placebo patients had bleeding.
Conclusions	Chronic anticoagulation with warfarin, but not with low dose aspirin, reduced vascular mortality and thromboembolic complications in patients with chronic nonrheumatic atrial fibrillation.

AFASAK 2 (Substudy)

Second Copenhagen Atrial Fibrillation, Aspirin and Anticoagulation

Title	Bleeding during warfarin and aspirin therapy in patients with atrial fibrillation.
Authors	Gulløv AL, Koefold BG, Petersen P.
Reference	Arch Intern Med. 1999;159:1322–1328.
Disease	Atrial fibrillation.
Purpose	To determine the rate of bleeding as part of the AFASAK 2 study. Both major and minor bleeding was assessed.
Design	As Per AFASAK 2.
Patients	670 patients in AFASAK 2 study.
Follow-up	~3.5 years.
Treatment regimen	Patients were randomized to: 1) warfarin sodium 1.25 mg/day; 2) warfarin sodium, 1.25 mg/day plus aspirin, 300 mg/day; 3) aspirin 300 mg/day; or 4) adjusted dose warfarin therapy to obtain an INR of 2.0–3.0 U.

AFASAK 2 (Substudy)

Second Copenhagen Atrial Fibrillation, Aspirin and Anticoagulation

(continued)

Results	Major bleeding was defined as fatal life threatening or potentially life threatening. Minor bleeding was non-threatening including overt or occult gastrointestinal bleeding, hemoptysis, gross hematuria, nose bleeding, bruising, symptomatic anemia due to bleeding, chronic bleeding. Median age was 77 years—range of 67–89 years. 19.2% (130 of 677 randomized patients) experienced any bleeding. 13 major (1 woman and 12 men) and 139 minor bleeding events occurred. 4 patients had intracranial bleeds; 2 of these were fatal. The annual rate of major bleeding was 0.8% for mini dose warfarin, 0.3% for warfarin plus aspirin, 1.4% for aspirin, and 1.1% for adjusted dose warfarin (p=0.20). Following 3 years of therapy, cumulate rate of bleeding was 24.7% in patients on mini dose warfarin, 24.4% on warfarin plus aspirin, 30.0% on aspirin, and 41.1% on adjusted dose warfarin (p=0.003 for adjusted dose warfarin vs the other groups). Independent risk factors for bleeding included adjusted dose warfarin therapy and prior myocardial infarction. Risk for bleeding increased with higher INR values.
Conclusions	Incidence of major bleeding was low in patients on adjusted dose warfarin. This finding plus a lack of influence of age on risk of bleeding suggests that even elderly patients with atrial fibrillation can tolerate adjusted dose warfarin to an INR of 2–3.

SPAF

Stroke Prevention in Atrial Fibrillation

Title	a. Preliminary report of the stroke prevention in atrial fibrillation study. b. Stroke prevention in atrial fibrillation study. Final results.
Authors	SPAF Investigators.
Reference	a. N Engl J Med 1990;322:863-868. b. Circulation 1991;84:527-539.
Disease	Atrial fibrillation.
Purpose	To determine the efficacy of warfarin and aspirin for primary prevention of ischemic stroke and systemic embolism in patients with nonrheumatic atrial fibrillation.
Design	Randomized, open label (warfarin), double blind (aspirin vs placebo), multicenter.
Patients	1330 patients with chronic or paroxysmal atrial fibrillation, without prosthetic heart valve or rheumatic mitral stenosis. Patients with congestive heart failure were excluded. 627 patients were eligible to receive warfarin (group 1) and 703 patients were not eligible (group 2).
Follow-up	a. An average of 1.13 years. b. An average of 1.3 years.
Treatment regimen	Group 1. warfarin vs aspirin 325 mg/d or placebo. Target INR for warfarin 2.0-4.5. Group 2. aspirin 325 mg/d vs placebo.

Results	a. The overall primary events (ischemic stroke and embolism) rate was 1.6% per year in the patients who received either aspirin or warfarin, and 8.3% per year in the placebo treated patients in group 1 (risk reduction 81%, 95% CI 56-91%, p<0.00005). Total primary end points occurred in 3.2% and 6.3% of the aspirin and placebo treated patients (group 1+2)(risk reduction 49% (15-69%), p=0.014). On the basis of these results, the placebo arm was discontinued by the safety committee. b. Warfarin reduced the risk of primary events by 67% (2.3% vs 7.4% per year, 95% CI 27-85%, p=0.01). Aspirin reduced the risk of primary events by 42% (3.6% vs 6.3%, 95% CI 9-63%, p=0.02). Primary events or death were reduced by 58% (95% CI 20-78%, p=0.01) by warfarin and 32% (95% CI 7-50%, p=0.02) by aspirin. The risk of significant bleeding was 1.5%, 1.4%, and 1.6% per year in the warfarin, aspirin, and placebo, respectively.
Conclusions	Aspirin and warfarin are both effective in prevention of ischemic stroke and systemic embolism in patients with nonrheumatic atrial fibrillation.

BAATAF

Boston Area Anticoagulation Trial for Atrial Fibrillation

Title	The effect of low dose warfarin on the risk of stroke in patients with nonrheumatic atrial fibrillation.
Authors	The Boston Area Anticoagulation Trial for Atrial Fibrillation Investigators.
Reference	N Engl J Med 1990;323:1505-1511.
Disease	Atrial fibrillation.
Purpose	To assess the efficacy of low dose warfarin therapy in preventing stroke in patients with nonrheumatic atrial fibrillation.
Design	Randomized, open label, multicenter.
Patients	420 patients with chronic or paroxysmal atrial fibrillation without mitral stenosis. Patients with left ventricular thrombus, aneurysm, prosthetic heart valve, severe heart failure, transient ischemic attack or stroke within 6 months, or clear indication or contraindications to anticoagulant therapy were excluded.
Follow-up	Clinical follow-up up to 4.5 years (mean 2.2 years).
Treatment regimen	Warfarin (target range for prothrombin-time ratio 1.2-1.5X control value [INR 1.5-2.7]) or no treatment.
Additional therapy	Aspirin therapy was not allowed in the anticoagulation group. Aspirin was permitted in the control group.

Results	Prothrombin time in the warfarin group was in the target range 83% of the time. Only 10% of the patients discontinued warfarin permanently.There were 2 strokes in the warfarin and 13 in the control groups (p=0.0022);(incidence of 0.41%/year vs 2.98%/year (incidence ratio 0.14, 95% CI 0.04-0.49. 2 and 1 patients in the warfarin and control group had major bleeding.There was no statistical significant difference in the occurrence of minor bleeding.Total mortality was 11 and 26 patients in the warfarin and control patients (RR 0.38, 95% CI 0.17-0.82, p=0.005).The same trend was seen for cardiac and noncardiac mortality. Patients with paroxysmal and chronic atrial fibrillation had similar risk of stroke.
Conclusions	Long term low dose warfarin therapy was associated with reduced mortality and prevention of stroke in patients with atrial fibrillation not associated with mitral stenosis.

CAFA

Canadian Atrial Fibrillation Anticoagulation

Title	Canadian Atrial Fibrillation Anticoagulation (CAFA) study.
Authors	Connolly SJ, Laupacis A, Gent M, et al.
Reference	J Am Coll Cardiol 1991;18:349-355.
Disease	Atrial fibrillation.
Purpose	To assess the efficacy and safety of warfarin therapy for nonrheumatic atrial fibrillation.
Design	Randomized, double blind, placebo controlled, multicenter.
Patients	378 patients, ≥19 years of age, with paroxysmal recurrent or chronic atrial fibrillation, without mitral stenosis or mitral or aortic prosthetic valves. Patients with clear indications or contraindications to anticoagulation therapy, stroke or transient ischemic attack within 1 year, myocardial infarction within 1 month, uncontrolled hypertension, or antiplatelet therapy were excluded.
Follow-up	Clinical follow-up for up to 2.75 years (mean 15.2 months).
Treatment regimen	Warfarin or placebo. Target INR for warfarin was 2-3.
Additional therapy	Aspirin or antiplatelet therapy was not advised.

Results	Early permanent discontinuation of the therapy, not due to primary outcome event, occurred in 26.2% of the warfarin and 22.5% of the placebo group. The estimated percent of days during which the INR was 2–3 was 43.7%. The ratio was below the target in 39.6% of the days. The annual rate of major bleeding was 0.5% in the placebo and 2.5% in the warfarin group. Minor bleeding occurred in 9.4% and 16% of the patients, respectively. The annual rate of ischemic nonlacunar stroke, systemic embolization, or intracranial or fatal hemorrhage was 3.5% and 5.2% in the warfarin and placebo groups (risk reduction 37%, 95% CI -63.5%–75.5%, p=0.17).
Conclusions	Chronic anticoagulation therapy is relatively safe and effective therapy for reducing the risks of stroke and death in patients with nonrheumatic atrial fibrillation. This study was stopped prematurely due to the results of the AFASAK and SPAF studies.

SPINAF

Stroke Prevention in Nonrheumatic Atrial Fibrillation

Title	Warfarin in the prevention of stroke associated with nonrheumatic atrial fibrillation.
Authors	Ezekowitz MD, Bridgers SL, James KE, et al.
Reference	N Engl J Med 1992;327:1406–1412.
Disease	Atrial fibrillation.
Purpose	To evaluate whether low intensity anticoagulation will reduce the risk of stroke among patients with nonrheumatic atrial fibrillation.
Design	Randomized, double blind, placebo controlled, multicenter.
Patients	525 males, no age limitation, with atrial fibrillation and no echocardiographic evidence of rheumatic heart disease.
Follow-up	Up to 3 years (an average of 1.7 years).
Treatment regimen	Sodium warfarin or placebo. Target INR 1.4–2.8.
Additional therapy	Aspirin and other anti-inflammatory drugs were not permitted.

Results	Patients assigned to warfarin had their INR within the target range 56% of the time. Among patients with no previous stroke, cerebral infarction occurred at a rate of 4.3% per year in the placebo vs 0.9% per year in the warfarin group (risk reduction of 0.79, 95% CI 0.52-0.90, p=0.001). The annual event rate among the 228 patients over 70 years of age was 4.8% vs 0.9%, respectively (risk reduction 0.79, 95% CI 0.34-0.93, p=0.02). Only 1 nonfatal cerebral hemorrhage occurred in a patient that received warfarin. Major hemorrhages occurred in 0.9% vs 1.3% in the placebo and warfarin no previous stroke groups (risk reduction -0.53, 95% CI -4.22-0.55, p=0.54). Mortality of patients without prior stroke was 5.0% in the placebo vs 3.3% in the warfarin group (risk reduction 0.31, 95% CI -0.29-0.63, p=0.19). In patients with prior stroke, cerebral infarction occurred in 4 of the 25 patients in the placebo and in 2 of the 21 patients in the warfarin group (risk reduction 0.40, 95% CI -1.66-0.87, p=0.63).
Conclusions	Low intensity anticoagulation with warfarin reduced the rate of cerebral infarction in patients with nonrheumatic atrial fibrillation, without association with excess risk of bleeding.

EAFT

The European Atrial Fibrillation Trial

Title	a. Secondary prevention in nonrheumatic atrial fibrillation after transient ischaemic attack or minor stroke. b. Optimal oral anticoagulant therapy in patients with nonrheumatic atrial fibrillation and recent cerebral ischemia.
Authors	The European Atrial Fibrillation Trial Study Group.
Reference	a. Lancet 1993;342:1255–1262. b. N Engl J Med 1995;333:5–10.
Disease	Atrial fibrillation.
Purpose	a. To evaluate the effectiveness of oral anticoagulant therapy and oral aspirin for secondary prevention in patients with nonrheumatic atrial fibrillation and recent transient ischemic attack or minor ischemic stroke. b. To determine the optimal intensity of anticoagulation for secondary prevention in patients with nonrheumatic atrial fibrillation and recent transient ischemic attack or minor ischemic stroke.
Design	Randomized, open label (oral anticoagulant), double blind (aspirin vs placebo), multicenter.
Patients	a. Group 1: 669 patients, >25 years old, with chronic or paroxysmal nonrheumatic atrial fibrillation and recent (<3 months) minor ischemic stroke or transient ischemic attack randomized to anticoagulant, aspirin or placebo. Group 2: 338 patients with the same clinical characteristics but with contraindication to oral anticoagulants randomized to aspirin or placebo. b. 214 patients with nonrheumatic atrial fibrillation and a recent episode of minor cerebral ischemia who received anticoagulant therapy.
Follow-up	Mean follow-up 2.3 years.

EAFT

The European Atrial Fibrillation Trial (continued)

Treatment regimen	1. Oral anticoagulant (open label). 2. Aspirin 300 mg/d or placebo (double blind).
Results	a. Group 1. The annual rate of events (vascular death, stroke, myocardial infarction, and embolism) was 8% in patients assigned to anticoagulants and 17% in the placebo treated (Hazard ratio 0.53, 95% CI 0.36–0.79). The risk of stroke was reduced from 12%–4% per year (hazard ratio 0.34, 95% CI 0.20–0.57). Group 1+2: The annual incidence of outcome events was 15% in the aspirin vs 19% in the placebo (hazard ratio 0.83, 95% CI 0.65–1.05). The hazard ratio for stroke of aspirin vs placebo was 0.86 (95% CI 0.64–1.15). Anticoagulation was better than aspirin (hazard ratio 0.60, 95% CI 0.41–0.87; p=0.008). b. The optimal anticoagulation that results in the lower rate of bleeding and ischemic episodes was of INR 2.0–3.9. Most major bleedings occurred when INR was ≥5.0.
Conclusions	a. Oral anticoagulant is a safe and effective therapy for secondary prevention. Aspirin is less effective than anticoagulants. b. The target value for INR should be 3.0. Values <2.0 and >5.0 should be avoided.

SPAF-2

Stroke in Atrial Fibrillation II Study

Authors	Stroke Prevention in Atrial Fibrillation Investigators.
Title	Warfarin vs aspirin for prevention of thromboembolism in atrial fibrillation: Stroke prevention in atrial fibrillation II study.
Reference	Lancet 1994;343:687-691.
Disease	Atrial fibrillation.
Purpose	To compare the efficacy of aspirin and warfarin for prevention of stroke and systemic embolism in patients with nonrheumatic atrial fibrillation.
Design	Randomized, multicenter.
Follow-up	Mean 2.3 years.
Treatment regimen	Warfarin (target prothrombin time ratio 1.3-1.8; INR 2.0-4.5) or aspirin 325 mg/d.
Patients	1100 patients (715 patients ≤75 years old and 385 patients >75 years old) with atrial fibrillation in the previous 12 months. Patients with prosthetic valves, mitral stenosis, or indication or contraindications to aspirin or warfarin were excluded. Patients <60 years old with lone atrial fibrillation and those with ischemic stroke or transient ischemic attack within 2 years were excluded.

SPAF-2

Stroke in Atrial Fibrillation II Study

(continued)

Results

In patients ≤75 years old primary events (ischemic stroke or systemic embolism) occurred at a rate of 1.3% per year in the warfarin group vs 1.9% in the aspirin group (RR 0.67, 95% CI 0.34–1.3, p=0.24). The absolute rate of primary events in low risk younger patients (without hypertension, heart failure, or previous thromboembolism) was 0.5% on aspirin vs 1.0% on warfarin. Among older patients, the primary event rate was 3.6% per year with warfarin vs 4.8% with aspirin (RR 0.73, 95% CI 0.37–1.5, p=0.39). There was no statistically significant difference in mortality, or occurrence of all strokes with residual deficit between the aspirin and warfarin treated patients in both the ≤75 and >75 years old cohorts. In patients ≤75 years old rates of major hemorrhage were 0.9% per year with aspirin vs 1.7% per year with warfarin (p=0.17). For older patients the rates were 1.6% vs 4.2%, respectively (p=0.04).

Conclusions

Warfarin may be more effective than aspirin for prevention of ischemic stroke or systemic embolism in patients with nonrheumatic atrial fibrillation. However, the absolute reduction in total stroke rate is small. Younger patients without risk factors had a low rate of stroke when treated with aspirin. The risk was higher for older patients, irrespective of which agent was used.

Optimal Oral Anticoagulant Therapy in Patients With Mechanical Heart Valves

Title	Optimal oral anticoagulant therapy in patients with mechanical heart valves.
Authors	Cannegieter SC, Rosendaal FR, Wintzen AR, et al.
Reference	N Engl J Med 1995;333:11-17.
Disease	Mechanical heart valves.
Purpose	To determine the optimal intensity of anticoagulation in patients with mechanical heart valves.
Design	Events that occurred during a period of endocarditis were excluded.
Patients	1608 patients with mechanical valves.
Follow-up	Up to 6 years (6475 patient years).
Treatment regimen	Phenprocoumon or acenocoumarol.
Results	The optimal intensity of anticoagulant therapy is that associated with the lowest incidence of both thromboembolic and bleeding events. This level has been achieved with an INR values of 2.5-4.9. At this level of INR the incidence of all adverse events was 2 per 100 patient years (95% CI 1.0-3.8). The incidence rose sharply to 7.5 per 100 patient year when INR was 2.0-2.4 (95% CI 3.6-12.6), and to 4.8 per 100 patient year (95% CI 2.6-7.7) when the INR rose to 5.0-5.5. When INR was ≥6.5, the incidence was 75 per 100 patient year (95% CI 54-101).
Conclusions	The intensity of anticoagulation for patients with prosthetic mechanical valves is optimal when the INR is 2.5-4.9. A target INR of 3.0-4.0 is recommended.

SPAF III

Stroke Prevention in Atrial Fibrillation III

Title	Adjusted dose warfarin vs low intensity, fixed dose warfarin plus aspirin for high risk patients with atrial fibrillation: Stroke Prevention in Atrial Fibrillation III randomized clinical trial.
Authors	Stroke Prevention in Atrial Fibrillation Investigators.
Reference	Lancet 1996;348:633-638.
Disease	Atrial fibrillation.
Purpose	To compare the efficacy of low intensity fixed dose warfarin plus aspirin with conventional adjusted dose warfarin in patients with atrial fibrillation at high risk of stroke.
Design	Randomized, multicenter.
Patients	1044 patients with atrial fibrillation. In addition, patients had to have at least 1 of the following 4 risk factors: 1. Recent congestive heart failure or left ventricular systolic dysfunction, 2. Systolic blood pressure >160 mm Hg, 3. Prior ischemic stroke, transient ischemic attack or systemic embolism >30 days prior to entry, or 4. Being a women >75 years old. Patients with prosthetic heart valves, mitral stenosis, recent pulmonary embolism, other conditions that needed anticoagulation therapy, contraindication to aspirin or warfarin, or regular use of nonsteroidal antiinflammatory drugs were excluded.
Follow-up	The trial was terminated prematurely after a mean follow-up of 1.1 years (range 0 to 2.5 years).

SPAF III

Stroke Prevention in Atrial Fibrillation III

(continued)

Treatment regimen	Randomization to either the combination therapy (warfarin 0.5–3.0 mg/d to raise INR to 1.2–1.5 on 2 successive measurements and aspirin 325 mg/d) or adjusted dose warfarin (target INR 2.0–3.0).
Results	Withdrawal of assigned therapy unrelated to primary or secondary events occurred at a rate of 8.2% per year in the combination therapy group and 5.6% in the adjusted dose group (p=0.13).The mean INR was 1.3 vs 2.4 in the combination therapy and adjusted dose groups . During the study period, 54% of the INRs in the combination therapy treated patients were 1.2–1.5 and 34% were <1.2. Among patients treated with adjusted dose warfarin, 61% of the INRs were within the therapeutic range 2.0–3.0, 25% were below this range. Ischemic stroke and systemic embolism occurred at a rate of 7.9% per year vs 1.9% per year in the combination therapy and adjusted dose group, respectively (absolute rate difference 6.0%; 95% CI 3.4 % to 8.6%; p<0.0001).The annual rates of disabling or fatal stroke (5.6% vs 1.7%; p=0.0007) and of stroke, systemic embolism, or vascular death (11.8% vs 6.4%; p=0.002) were higher in the combination therapy group. By analysis restricted to patients taking assigned therapy, the relative risk reduction by adjusted dose vs combination therapy was 77% for stroke or systemic embolism (p<0.0001) and 48% for stroke, systemic embolism, or vascular death (p=0.002). Rates of major bleeding were comparable (2.4% per year vs 2.1% per year in the combination therapy and adjusted dose group, respectively).
Conclusions	The efficacy of low intensity fixed dose warfarin plus aspirin in preventing stroke, systemic embolism or vascular death in patients with atrial fibrillation at high risk for thromboembolism is inferior to the conventional adjusted dose warfarin therapy.

SPAF III-Substudy

Stroke Prevention in Atrial Fibrillation III Study

(continued)

Title	Patients with nonvalvular atrial fibrillation at low risk of stroke during treatment with aspirin.
Authors	The SPAF III writing committee for the Stroke Prevention in Atrial Fibrillation Investigators.
Reference	JAMA 1998; 279:1273–1277.
Disease	Nonvalvular atrial fibrillation.
Purpose	To validate a risk stratification scheme for identifying atrial fibrillation patients at low risk of stroke when given aspirin.
Design	Prospective cohort study.
Patients	"Low risk" atrial fibrillation defined as nonvalvular atrial fibrillation in which there is no recent CHF or LV shortening of 25% or less, no previous thromboembolism, no systolic BP >160 mm Hg, or female sex older than 75 years.
Follow-up	2 years.
Treatment regimen	Aspirin 325 mg/day.

SPAF III-Substudy

Stroke Prevention in Atrial Fibrillation III Study (continued)

Results	892 patients; mean age 67; 78% were men. The rate of primary events - ischemic stroke and systemic embolism was 2.2% per year, ischemic stroke 2.0% per year, and disabling stroke was 8.8% per year. Patients with hypertension had a higher rate of primary events vs patients with no history of hypertension (3.6% per year vs 1.1%; p<0.001). Age was also a predictor of primary events. Rate of disabling ischemic stroke was low in patients with (1.4% per year) and without hypertension (0.5% per year). Rate of major bleeding on aspirin was 0.5% per year. For comparison the rate of stroke in these patients on aspirin approximated the rate for the general population in the age range of patients in the study (1% per year); while atrial fibrillation with 1 or more of the 4 thromboembolic risk factors in the SPAF study had much higher rates of stroke (8% per years), even with treatment with aspirin, in combination with low dose warfarin.
Conclusions	Patients with atrial fibrillation that have low rates of ischemic stroke during therapy with aspirin can be identified.

Title	Effectiveness of fixed minidose warfarin in the prevention of thromboembolism and vascular death in nonrheumatic atrial fibrillation.
Authors	Pengo V, Zasso A, Barbero F, et al.
Reference	Am J Cardiol 1998;82:433–437.
Disease	Atrial fibrillation.
Purpose	To compare the effectiveness and safety of a fixed minidose of warfarin and standard adjusted dose warfarin in patients with nonrheumatic atrial fibrillation.
Design	Randomized, open label, multicenter.
Patients	303 patients, >60 years old, with chronic (≥2 weeks) atrial fibrillation. Patients with systolic blood pressure >180 mm Hg, chronic renal or liver failure, life expectancy of <12 months, psychiatric disorder, major bleeding within 6 months, heart failure, recent antiplatelet drug, recent myocardial infarction, previous cerebral ischemia, planned cardioversion, dilated cardiomyopathy, mitral valve disease, or intracardiac thrombus were excluded.
Follow-up	Planned 2 years (mean follow-up 14.5 months).
Treatment regimen	Randomization to a fixed minidose of warfarin (1.25 mg/d) (n=150) or adjusted dose warfarin (target INR 2.0–3.0) (n=153).

Results	24 patients in the minidose and 23 patients in the fixed dose withdrew from the study due to causes unrelated to primary or secondary end points. The rate of cumulative primary events (ischemic stroke, peripheral or visceral embolism, cerebral bleeding, fatal bleeding, and vascular death) was 11.1%/year in the minidose group vs 6.1%/year in the adjusted dose group ($p=0.29$). Ischemic stroke occurred at a rate of 3.7%/year in the minidose group vs 0 in the adjusted dose group ($p=0.025$). Major bleeding occurred in 1%/year vs 2.6%/year in the minidose and adjusted dose group, respectively ($p=0.19$). Most hemorrhages occurred at INRs >3.0, whereas most thromboembolic events occurred at INRs <1.2.
Conclusions	Although there was no difference in the primary end point event rate between the fixed minidose and the adjusted dose warfarin, fixed minidose warfarin was associated with a significantly greater risk for ischemic stroke. It is suggested that the fixed minidose regimen is not protective against thromboembolism in patients with nonrheumatic atrial fibrillation.

10. Deep Vein Thrombosis/ Pulmonary Embolism

A clinical trial of vena caval filters in the prevention of pulmonary embolism in patients with proximal deep vein thrombosis

Title	A clinical trial of vena caval filters in the prevention of pulmonary embolism in patients with proximal deep vein thrombosis.
Author	Decousus H, Leizorovicz A, Parent F, et al.
Reference	N Engl J Med 1998; 338:409–415.
Disease	Deep vein thrombosis, pulmonary embolism.
Purpose	To determine the efficacy and risks of prophylactic placement of vena caval filters in addition to anticoagulant therapy in patients with deep vein thrombosis at high risk for pulmonary embolism.
Design	Randomized, multicenter.
Patients	400 patients with proximal deep vein thrombosis at risk for pulmonary embolism randomized to vena caval filter (200 patients) vs no filter (200 patients) and low molecular weight heparin (enoxaparin, 195 patients) vs unfractionated heparin (205 patients).
Follow-up	12 days and 2 years.
Treatment regimen	Unfractionated heparin 5000 IU bolus followed by a continuous infusion of 500 IU/kg per day for 8–12 days with aPTT at 1.5–2.5 controls or subcutaneous enoxaparin 1 mg every 12 h for 8–12 days. Permanent vena caval filters vs no vena caval filters, warfarin, or acenocourmarol was started on day 4 and continued for 3 months.

A clinical trial of vena caval filters in the prevention of pulmonary embolism in patients with proximal deep vein thrombosis

(continued)

Results	At day 12 1.1% of patients who received filters had pulmonary embolism vs 4.8% of those not receiving filters (odds ratio 0.22, 95% CI =0.05–0.90). At 2 years 20.8% of filter group vs 11.6% of no filter group had recurrent deep vein thrombosis (odds ratio 1.87; 95% CI = 1.10–3.20) There was no significant difference in mortality between groups. At 2 years symptomatic pulmonary embolism occurred in 6 patients in the filter group and 12 in the no filter group (p = 0.16).At day 12, 3 (1.6%) patients receiving low molecular weight heparin had pulmonary embolism vs 8 patients receiving unfractionated heparin (4.2%, odds ratio .38; 95% CI = 0.10–1.38).
Conclusions	An initial benefit of vena caval filters for prevention of pulmonary embolism was offset by an excess of recurrent deep vein thrombosis with no improvement in mortality. Low molecular weight heparin was as effective and safe as unfractionated heparin for prevention of pulmonary embolism.

DURAC II

Duration of Anticoagulation Trial Study

Title	The duration of oral anticoagulant therapy after a second episode of venous thromboembolism.
Author	Schulman S, Granqvist S, Holmstrom M, et al.
Reference	N Engl J Med 1997;336:393-398.
Disease	Second episode of venous thromboembolism.
Purpose	To determine the optimal duration of oral anticoagulation therapy after a second episode of venous thromboembolism.
Design	Randomized, open label trial, multicenter.
Patients	227 patients with second episode of venous thromboembolism (diagnoses included venography for deep vein thrombosis; angiography or combination of chest x-ray and ventilation perfusion lung scan for pulmonary embolism).
Follow-up	4 years.
Treatment regimen	Initial therapy was unfractionated or low molecular weight heparin given IV or S.C. for at least 5 days. Oral anticoagulation with warfarin sodium or dicumarol started at same time as heparin in order to achieve an INR of 2.0-2.85. 111 patients were randomized to 6 months of anticoagulation therapy and 116 were assigned to indefinite anticoagulation.

DURAC II

Duration of Anticoagulation Trial Study

(continued)

Results	At 4 years there were 23 (20.7%) recurrences of venous thromboembolism in the group assigned to 6 months of therapy and 3 (2.6%) in the group assigned to continuing therapy. Relative risk of thromboembolic recurrence in 6 month vs indefinite group was 8.0 (95% CI = 2.5–25.9). There were 3 major hemorrhages in the 6 month group (2.7%) and 10 in the indefinite treatment group (8.6%). There were no significant differences in mortality between the groups.
Conclusions	Indefinite oral anticoagulation following a second episode of venous thromboembolism was associated with a lower recurrence of venous thromboembolism compared to only 6 months of therapy. However major hemorrhage tended to be higher when anticoagulation was continued indefinitely.

Low molecular weight heparin in the treatment of patients with venous thromboembolism

Title	Low molecular weight heparin in the treatment of patients with venous thromboembolism.
Author	The Columbus Investigators.
Reference	N Engl J Med 1997;337:657-662.
Disease	Venous thromboembolism.
Purpose	To determine whether fixed dose, subcutaneous, low molecular weight heparin and adjusted dose, IV, unfractionated heparin infusion have equivalent efficacy in patients with symptomatic venous thromboembolism.
Design	Randomized, open label, multicenter.
Patients	1021 patients with acute symptomatic deep vein thrombosis, pulmonary embolism, or both. Diagnosis had to be documented by ultrasonography or venography, lung scanning, or pulmonary angiography.
Follow-up	12 weeks.
Treatment regimen	Reviparin sodium (low molecular weight heparin) given subcutaneously at various fixed doses by range of weight: 6300 U x2/d for patients > 60 kg; 4200 U x2/d for patients 46-60 kg; and 3500 U x2/d for patients 35-45 kg. Unfractionated heparin was given as IV bolus 5000 IU, followed by infusion of 1250 IU per hour and adjusted as needed. Study drug was continued for at least 5 days. Oral anticoagulant was started in the first or second day and continued for 12 weeks.

Low molecular weight heparin in the treatment of patients with venous thromboembolism

(continued)

Results	510 patients assigned to low molecular weight heparin reviparin and 511 patients to unfractionated heparin. 5.3% of patients receiving reviparin had recurrent thromboembolic events vs 4.9% of patients receiving unfractionated heparin. Major bleeding occurred in 3.1% of reviparin and 2.3% of unfractionated heparin group. Mortality rates were similar in the 2 groups at 7.1 and 7.6%, respectively.
Conclusions	Fixed dose, subcutaneous, low molecular weight heparin was as effective and safe as infusion of unfractionated heparin in patients with venous thromboembolism with or without pulmonary embolus.

THESEE

Tinzaparin ou Heparine Standard: Evaluations dans 1' Embolic Pulmonaire

Title	A comparison of low molecular weight heparin with unfractionated heparin for acute pulmonary embolism.
Author	Simonneau G, Sors H, Charbonnier B, et al.
Reference	N Engl J Med 1997; 337:663-669.
Disease	Pulmonary embolism.
Purpose	To determine whether low molecular weight heparin (tinzaparin) is safe and effective in treating acute pulmonary embolism.
Design	Randomized, multicenter.
Patients	612 patients with symptomatic pulmonary embolism not requiring thrombolytic therapy or embolectomy. Objective evidence of pulmonary embolism required by lung scanning of if lung scanning was indeterminant evidence of deep vein thrombosis was confirmed by venography or ultrasonography.
Follow-up	90 days.
Treatment regimen	175 IU/kg of tinzaparin, a low molecular weight heparin, given subcutaneously once daily or unfractionated heparin, given as an initial bolus of 50 IU/kg, followed by a continues IV infusion at an initial rate of 500 IU per kg/day, with adjustments based on aPTT. Oral anticoagulants begun within 1-3 days and continued for 3 months.

Tinzaparin ou Heparine Standard: Evaluations dans 1' Embolic Pulmonaire

(continued)

Results	Primary end point was combined outcome event of death, symptomatic recurrent thromboembolism, or major bleeding assessed on day 8 and 90. At day 8, 9 of 308 (2.9%) in the unfractionated heparin group reached at least 1 endpoint vs 9 of 304 (3.0%) assigned to low molecular weight heparin. At day 90 7.1% and 5.9% had reached 1 endpoint, respectively. Risk of major bleeding was similar between the 2 groups. In patients receiving follow-up lung scan the percentage of scintigraphically detectable vascular obstruction was similar in the 2 groups.
Conclusions	In patients with symptomatic pulmonary embolism, initial subcutaneous therapy with low molecular weight heparin was as effective and safe as IV infusions of unfractionated heparin.

A comparison of three months of anticoagulation with extended anticoagulation for a first episode of idiopathic venous thromboembolism

Title	A comparison of three months of anticoagulation with extended anticoagulation for a first episode of idiopathic venous thromboembolism.
Authors	Kearon C, Gent M, Hirsh J, et al.
Reference	N Engl J Med 1999; 340:901-907.
Disease	Venous thromboembolism.
Purpose	To determine whether anticoagulation beyond 3 months is beneficial in patients with a first episode of idiopathic venous thromboembolism.
Design	Randomized, double blind, multicenter.
Patients	162 patients with a first episode of idiopathic venous thromboembolism (confirmed, symptomatic, proximal deep vein or pulmonary embolism) in absence of major thrombogenic risk factor.
Follow-up	Average of 10 months.
Treatment regimen	After initial heparin therapy and 3 months of oral anticoagulation therapy, patients were randomized to warfarin (INR of 2.0–3.0) or placebo, planned for 24 months.
Results	The trial was terminated early after an average of 10 months of enrollment. 17 of 83 (27.4% per patient year) assigned to placebo had a recurrent episode of venous thromboembolism vs 1 of 79 assigned to warfarin (1.3 % per patient year, $p<0.001$). Nonfatal major bleeding occurred in 3 warfarin patients vs none in the placebo group.

A comparison of three months of anticoagulation with extended anticoagulation for a first episode of idiopathic venous thromboembolism

(continued)

Conclusions	Anticoagulation for longer than 3 months is indicated in patients with a first episode of idiopathic venous thromboembolism.

Enoxaparin plus compression stockings compared with compression stockings alone in the prevention of venous thromboembolism after elective neurosurgery

Title	Enoxaparin plus compression stockings compared with compression stockings alone in the prevention of venous thromboembolism after elective neurosurgery.
Authors	Agnelli G, Piovella F, Buoncristiani P, et al.
Reference	N Engl J Med 1998; 339:80-85.
Disease	Venous thromboembolism.
Purpose	To determine efficacy and safety of enoxaparin plus compression stockings for preventing venous thromboembolism in patients undergoing elective neurosurgery.
Design	Randomized, double blind multicenter, placebo controlled.
Patients	307 patients aged 18 or older scheduled for elective cranial or spinal surgery.
Follow-up	About 8 days.
Treatment regimen	Enoxaparin 40 mg per day, subcutaneously, or placebo given within 24 hours after surgery and then daily for about 8 days. Thigh length compression stockings for all patients until discharge.

Enoxaparin plus compression stockings compared with compression stockings alone in the prevention of venous thromboembolism after elective neurosurgery

(continued)

Results	84 (85%) of patients had venographic study adequate for analysis. 32% of patients receiving placebo and 17% receiving enoxaparin developed deep vein thrombosis (p=0.0004). Rates of proximal deep vein thrombosis were 13% vs 5% in placebo vs enoxaparin groups, respectively (p=0.04). 2 placebo patients died of autopsy confirmed pulmonary embolism. Three percent of patients in each group developed major bleeding (4 patients in the placebo group; 3 patients in the enoxaparin group).
Conclusions	Enoxaparin plus compressive stockings was more effective than stockings alone for prevention of venous thromboembolism in patients having elective neurosurgery.

MEDENOX

Prophylaxis in Medical Patients with Enoxaparin Study

Title	A comparison of enoxaparin with placebo for the prevention of venous thromboembolism in acutely ill medical patients.
Authors	Samama MM, Cohen AT, Darmon J-Y, et al.
Reference	N Engl J Med 1999;341:793-800.
Disease	Patients at risk for venous thromboembolism.
Purpose	To determine the frequency of deep vein thrombosis and pulmonary embolism in hospitalized medical patients and to determine safety and efficacy of regimens of low molecular weight heparin for their prevention.
Design	Randomized, multicenter.
Patients	1102 hospitalized patients over 40 years of age not immobilized for more than 3 days with risk factors for venous thromboembolism—congestive heart failure, acute respiratory failure, infection, acute rheumatic disorder, acute arthritis, acute inflammatory bowel disease, as well as other risk factors.
Follow-up	83-110 days.
Treatment regimen	Placebo, 20 mg of enoxaparin, or 40 mg of enoxaparin subcutaneously once-a-day for 6-14 days.
Additional therapy	Other standard therapy—elastic bandages, support stockings, physiotherapy as per usual practice.

MEDENOX

Prophylaxis in Medical Patients with Enoxaparin Study

(continued)

Results	The primary outcome was venous thromboembolism (defined as deep vein thrombosis, pulmonary embolism, or both) between days 1-14. Secondary outcome was venous thromboembolism between days 1-10. Diagnosis was made by venography, venous ultrasonography, high probability lung scanning, pulmonary angiography, helical computed tomography, or at autopsy. Primary outcome could be determined in 866 patients. Incidence of venous thromboembolism was lower in the 40 mg enoxaparin group (5.5%; 16 of 291 patients) vs placebo group (14.9%; 43 of 288 patients; RR=0.37; 97.6% CI=0.22-0.63, p<0.001). The 20 mg enoxaprin had a rate of 15.0% that was not statistically different than the placebo group. The benefit observed in the 40 mg group persisted at 3 months. There was no difference in mortality among groups. Adverse events did not differ among groups.
Conclusions	Prophylaxis with 40 mg of enoxaparin subcutaneously per day reduces risk of thromboembolism in patients hospitalized with acute medical illness.

11. Coronary Artery Disease, Atherosclerosis, Prevention of Progression

INTACT

International Nifedipine Trial on Antiatherosclerotic Therapy

Title	Retardation of angiographic progression of coronary artery disease by nifedipine. Results of the International Nifedipine Trial on Antiatherosclerotic Therapy (INTACT).
Authors	Lichtlen PR, Hugenholtz PG, Rafflenbeul W, et al.
Reference	Lancet 1990;335:1109-1113.
Disease	Coronary artery disease.
Purpose	To evaluate the effects of 3 years of nifedipine therapy on progression of coronary artery disease and formation of new lesions.
Design	Randomized, double blind, placebo controlled, multicenter.
Patients	348 patients, <65 years old, with mild or single vessel coronary artery disease. Patients with multivessel disease, ejection fraction <40%, mandatory therapy with calcium channel blockers, or prior therapy with calcium channel blockers >6 months were excluded.
Follow-up	Clinical follow-up and repeated angiography after 36 months.
Treatment regimen	Placebo or nifedipine 5 mg X3/d , with gradual increments to 20 mg X4/d.
Additional therapy	Oral nitrates, ß-blockers, aspirin, anticoagulants, and lipid lowering drugs were permitted.

INTACT

International Nifedipine Trial on Antiatherosclerotic Therapy

(continued)

Results	There were 16 side effects in the placebo and 55 in the nifedipine group (p=0.003), and 44 vs 52 critical cardiac events (p=0.60). Cardiac mortality was 0.8% vs 2.4%, in the placebo and nifedipine groups, respectively. On the repeated angiography, ≥20% progression of stenosis in pre-existing lesions was found in 9% vs 12%, respectively, while regression of ≥20% was found in 4% and 3%, respectively. 87% vs 85% of the lesions remained unchanged (p=NS). However, new lesions in previously angiographic normal sites were found more in the placebo than nifedipine treated patients (0.82 vs 0.59 new lesions per patient, 28% reduction, p=0.034). In contrast, the mean degree of stenosis did not differ between the groups.
Conclusions	Nifedipine was associated with mild reduction of the formation of new angiographic coronary lesions. However, nifedipine was associated with more side effects and a trend towards more critical cardiac events and death.

SCRIP

The Stanford Coronary Risk Intervention Project

Title	a. Effects of intensive multiple risk factor reduction on coronary atherosclerosis and clinical cardiac events in men and women with coronary artery disease. The Stanford Coronary Risk Intervention Project (SCRIP). b. Development of new coronary atherosclerotic lesions during a 4 year multifactor risk reduction program: the Stanford Coronary Risk Intervention Project (SCRIP).
Authors	a. Haskell WL, Alderman EL, Fair JM, et al. b. Quinn TG, Alderman EL, McMillan A, et al.
Reference	a. Circulation 1994;89:975-990. b. J Am Coll Cardiol 1994;24:900-908.
Disease	Coronary artery disease.
Purpose	To determine whether an intensive multifactor risk reduction program over 4 years would reduce the rate of progression of atherosclerosis.
Design	Randomized, 4 centers.
Patients	300 patients, age <75 years, with coronary artery disease (≥1 major coronary artery with 5-69% luminal stenosis that was unaffected by revascularization procedures). Patients with heart failure, pulmonary, or peripheral vascular disease were excluded.
Follow-up	4 years clinical follow-up. Coronary angiography at baseline and after 4 years.

SCRIP

The Stanford Coronary Risk Intervention Project

(continued)

Treatment regimen	Usual care by the patients' own physician or individualized, multifactor, risk reduction program including low fat low cholesterol diet, exercise, weight loss, smoking cessation, and medications for altering lipid profile. A major goal was to decrease LDL cholesterol to <110 mg/dl and triglyceride to <100 mg/dL and to increase HDL cholesterol to >55 mg/dL.
Results	274 patients (91.3%) completed a follow-up angiogram and 246 (82%) had comparative measurements of segments with visible disease at baseline and follow-up. Intensive risk reduction resulted in highly significant improvements in various risk factors, including the lipid profile, body weight, and exercise capacity, compared with the usual care group. No change was observed in lipoprotein (a). The change in minimal luminal diameter between the 4 years and baseline angiograms was -0.024±0.066 mm/y in the risk reduction group vs -0.045±0.073 mm/y in the usual care ($p<0.02$). Mortality rates were similar. However, there were 25 hospitalizations in the risk reduction vs 44 in the usual care group (RR 0.61, 95% CI 0.4–0.9, $p=0.05$). There were 7.6% segments with new lesions in the usual care group vs 4.7% in the risk reduction group ($p=0.05$). New lesions were detected in 31% vs 23%, respectively ($p=0.16$). The mean number of new lesions/patient was 0.47 vs 0.30, respectively ($p=0.06$).
Conclusions	Intensive risk reduction reduced the rate of progression of luminal narrowing in coronary arteries of patients with atherosclerosis and reduced the hospitalization rate for clinical cardiac causes.

CAPRIE

Clopidogrel vs Aspirin in Patients at Risk of Ischemic Events

Title	A randomized, blinded, trial of clopidogrel vs aspirin in patients at risk of ischaemic events (CAPRIE).
Authors	CAPRIE Steering Committee.
Reference	Lancet 1996;348:1329-1339.
Disease	Atherosclerotic cardiovascular disease.
Purpose	To compare the effect of clopidogrel, a new thienopyridine derivative that inhibits platelet aggregation induced by adenosine diphosphate, and aspirin in reducing the risk of ischemic stroke, myocardial infarction, or cardiovascular death in patients with atherosclerotic cardiovascular disease.
Design	Randomized, blind, multicenter.
Patients	19,185 patients with recent ischemic stroke (≤6 months), recent myocardial infarction (≤35 days), or symptomatic atherosclerotic peripheral arterial disease.
Follow-up	Average follow-up of 1.9 years (1-3 years).
Treatment regimen	Clopidogrel 75 mg X1/d or aspirin 325 mg X1/d.
Additional therapy	Use of anticoagulation or antiplatelet drugs was prohibited.

CAPRIE

Clopidogrel vs Aspirin in Patients at Risk of Ischemic Events (continued)

Results

21.1% vs 21.3% of the aspirin and clopidogrel-treated groups discontinued the drug early for reasons other than the occurrence of an outcome event. The rate of adverse effects was similar: rash (0.10% vs 0.26%, respectively), diarrhea (0.11% vs 0.23%), intracranial hemorrhage (0.47% vs 0.33%), and gastrointestinal hemorrhage (0.72% vs 0.52%). Neutropenia occurred in 0.10% of the clopidogrel vs 0.17% of the aspirin group, respectively. By intention to treat analysis, the clopidogrel treated patients had an annual 5.32% risk of ischemic stroke, myocardial infarction, or vascular death compared with 5.83% among the aspirin treated patients (relative risk reduction of 8.7%; 95% CI 0.3–16.5; p=0.043). For patients with stroke as the inclusion criterion, the average annual event rate was 7.15% vs 7.71 with clopidegrel and aspirin, respectively (relative risk reduction of 7.3% in favor of clopidogrel; p=0.26). For patients with myocardial infarction, annual event rates were 5.03% vs 4.84%, respectively (relative risk increase of 3.7%; p=0.66), whereas for patients with peripheral arterial disease, the annual event rates were 3.71% vs 4.86%, respectively (a relative risk reduction of 23.8%; 95% CI 8.9 to 36.2%; p=0.0028).

Conclusions

Long term clopidogrel therapy was more effective than aspirin in reducing the combined risk of ischemic stroke, myocardial infarction, or vascular death, especially in patients with peripheral arterial disease. Clopidogrel is as safe as medium dose aspirin and is probably safer than ticlopidine.

The Physician's Health Study (The Beta Carotene Component)

Title	Lack of effect of long term supplementation with ß-carotene on the incidence of malignant neoplasms and cardiovascular disease.
Authors	Hennekens CH, Buring JE, Manson JE, et al.
Reference	N Engl J Med 1996;334:1145-1149.
Disease	Coronary artery disease.
Purpose	To evaluate the long term effect of ß-carotene supplementation on mortality and morbidity.
Design	Randomized, double blind, placebo controlled, multicenter.
Patients	22,071 US male physicians, 40-84 years old at entry, with no history of cancer, myocardial infarction, stroke, or transient cerebral ischemia.
Follow-up	An average of 12 years (11.6-14.2 years).
Treatment regimen	Randomization to 1 of 4 groups: 1. Aspirin 325 mg on alternate days + ß–carotene 50 mg on alternate days; 2. Aspirin + ß–carotene placebo; 3. Aspirin placebo + ß–carotene; 4. Both placebo.

The Physician's Health Study (The Beta Carotene Component)

(continued)

Results	The randomized aspirin component of the study was terminated early in 1988 because there was a statistically significant 44% reduction in the risk of first myocardial infarction with aspirin ($p<0.001$). The ß–carotene component continued as planned. By the end of 11 years of follow-up, 80% of the participants were still taking the drug medication, 78% of the study drugs were still being taken by the ß–carotene patients, whereas 6% of the placebo group were taking supplemental ß–carotene. There were no early or late differences in overall mortality, the incidence of malignancy or cardiovascular disease between the groups. Myocardial infarction occurred in 468 vs 489 patients in the ß–carotene and placebo groups, respectively ($p=0.50$), stroke in 367 vs 382 patients ($p=0.60$), death from cardiovascular disease in 338 vs 313 patients ($p=0.28$), and the number of any of the major cardiovascular endpoints 967 vs 972 patients ($p=0.90$). There were no major side effects associated with ß–carotene supplementation.
Conclusions	Supplementation with ß–carotene for 12 years was not associated with either benefit or harm concerning mortality, incidence of malignancy, or cardiovascular morbidity.

CARET

The Beta Carotene and Retinol Efficacy Trial

Title	Effects of a combination of ß-carotene and vitamin A on lung cancer and cardiovascular disease.
Authors	Omenn GS, Goodman GE, Thornquist MD, et al.
Reference	N Engl J Med 1996;334:1150–1155.
Disease	Cardiovascular disease.
Purpose	To assess the efficacy of ß-carotene and retinol (Vitamin A) supplementation to reduce incidence of cancer and mortality rate from cancer and cardiovascular disease.
Design	Randomized, double blind, placebo controlled, multicenter.
Patients	18,314 men and women, 45–74 years of age, who were smokers, former smokers, or workers exposed to asbestos.
Follow-up	Mean length of follow-up, 4.0 years.
Treatment regimen	Patients were randomized to a combination of 30 mg/d ß-carotene and retinyl palmitate 25,000 IU/d, or placebo.
Additional therapy	Supplemental intake of vitamin A was restricted to <5500 IU/d. ß-carotene supplementation was prohibited.

Results	The ß-carotene retinol treated patients had higher incidence of lung cancer than the placebo group (5.92 vs 4.62 cases/1000 person year; a relative risk 1.28; 95% CI 1.04-1.57; p=0.02). Total mortality was 14.45 vs 11.91 deaths per 1000 person year, respectively; relative risk 1.17; 95% CI 1.03-1.33; p=0.02). The ß-carotene retinol group had a relative risk of cardiovascular mortality of 1.26 (95% CI 0.99-1.61). On the basis of these findings, the randomized trial was terminated prematurely.
Conclusions	Supplementation of ß-carotene and retinol for an average of 4 years in high risk patients (smokers and workers exposed to asbestos) had no benefit on the incidence of cancer and on mortality from cardiovascular causes and cancer. Supplementation of ß-carotene and retinol may have had an adverse effect on the incidence of lung cancer and mortality.

Title	Dietary antioxidant vitamins and death from coronary heart disease in postmenopausal women.
Authors	Kushi LH, Folsom AR, Prineas RJ, et al.
Reference	N Engl J Med 1996;334:1156-1162.
Disease	Coronary artery disease.
Purpose	To asses whether dietary intake of antioxidants is related to mortality from coronary artery disease.
Design	Prospective cohort study.
Patients	34,386 postmenopausal women, 55-69 years of age.
Follow-up	7 years.
Treatment regimen	The study evaluated the intake of vitamins A, E, and C from diet and supplements.
Results	In analyses adjusted for age and dietary calorie intake, an inverse correlation was found between vitamin E consumption and cardiovascular mortality. This association was especially significant in the subgroup of women who did not consume vitamin supplements (n=21,809; relative risks from lowest to highest quintile of vitamin E intake, 1.0, 0.68, 0.71, 0.42, and 0.42; p for trend=0.008). After adjustment for confounding variables, this association remained significant (relative risks 1.0, 0.70, 0.76, 0.32, and 0.38; p for trend=0.004). Multivariate analysis suggested no association between supplemental vitamin E intake and risk of death from coronary artery disease. Intake of vitamins A and C was not associated with the risk of mortality from coronary heart disease.

Conclusions	In postmenopausal women the intake of vitamin E from food, but not from supplements, is inversely associated with mortality rate from coronary heart disease. This may suggest that vitamin E consumed in food is a marker for other dietary factors associated with the risk of coronary heart disease. By contrast, intake of vitamins A and C, either from diet or from supplements, was not associated with lower mortality from coronary disease.

CHAOS

Cambridge Heart Antioxidant Study

Title	Randomized controlled trial of vitamin E in patients with coronary disease: Cambridge Heart Antioxidant Study (CHAOS).
Authors	Stephens NG, Parsons A, Schofield PM, et al.
Reference	Lancet 1996;347:781-786.
Disease	Coronary artery disease.
Purpose	To determine whether treatment with high dose α-tocopherol (Vitamin E) would reduce the incidence of myocardial infarction and cardiovascular death in patients with ischemic heart disease.
Design	Randomized, double blind, placebo controlled, single center.
Patients	2002 patients with angiographically proven coronary artery disease. Patients with prior use of vitamin supplements containing vitamin E were excluded.
Follow-up	Median follow-up 510 days (range 3 to 981 days).
Treatment regimen	α-tocopherol (Vitamin E) 400 or 800 IU/d or placebo.

CHAOS

Cambridge Heart Antioxidant Study

(continued)

Results	Plasma α-tocopherol levels were increased in the actively treated group (from baseline mean 34.2–51.1 μmol/L with 400 IU/d and to 64.5 μmol/L in the 800 IU/d), but remained the same in the placebo group (32.4 μmol/L). Treatment with α-tocopherol did not affect serum cholesterol. α-tocopherol therapy significantly reduced the risk of cardiovascular death and myocardial infarction. Nonfatal myocardial infarction occurred in 1.4% vs 4.2% of the α-tocopherol and placebo group, respectively (relative risk (RR) 0.23; 95% CI 0.11–0.47; $p<0.001$). However, cardiovascular mortality was similar (2.6% vs 2.4%, respectively; RR 1.18; 95% CI 0.62–2.27; $p=0.61$). Treatment was well tolerated. All cause mortality was 3.5% vs 2.7% ($p=0.31$). Only 0.55% of the patients discontinued therapy because of side effects. There was no significant difference between the placebo and α-tocopherol groups in occurrence of side effects.
Conclusions	α-tocopherol therapy in patients with coronary artery disease reduced the rate of nonfatal myocardial infarction. However, there was no effect on total or cardiovascular mortality.

Effect of vitamin E and ß-carotene on the incidence of primary nonfatal myocardial infarction and fatal coronary heart disease

Title	Effect of vitamin E and ß-carotene on the incidence of primary nonfatal myocardial infarction and fatal coronary heart disease.
Author	Virtamo J, Rapola JM, Ripatti S, et al.
Reference	Arch Intern Med 1998; 158:668-675.
Disease	Prevention of coronary events. Coronary artery disease, myocardial infarction.
Purpose	To determine the primary preventive effect of vitamin E (alpha tocopherol) and ß-carotene supplements on the development of major coronary events in the α-tocopherol, ß-carotene cancer prevention study.
Design	Randomized, double blind, placebo controlled trial.
Patients	Male smokers, ages 50-69, (N=27,271) with no history of myocardial infarction.
Follow-up	5-8 years; median 61 years.
Treatment regimen	Patients were randomized to receive vitamin E (50 mg), beta carotene (20 mg), both agents, or placebo.

Effect of vitamin E and ß-carotene on the incidence of primary nonfatal myocardial infarction and fatal coronary heart disease

(continued)

Results	The incidence of the primary major coronary events endpoint (nonfatal myocardial infarction or fatal coronary heart disease) was decreased 4% (95% CI = -12% to 4%) among patients receiving Vitamin E and increased by 1% (95% CI = -7% to 10%) among patients on beta carotene. Vitamin E decreased the incidence of fatal coronary heart disease by 8% (95% CI = -19% to 5%); ß-carotene had no effect on this endpoint. Neither agent influenced the incidence of nonfatal myocardial infarction.
Conclusions	Small doses of vitamin E have only marginal effects on the incidence of fatal coronary heart disease in male smokers and have no influence on nonfatal myocardial infarction. ß-carotene supplements had no effect on coronary events.

Thrombosis Prevention Trial

Title	Thrombosis Prevention Trial: Randomized trial of low intensity oral anticoagulation with warfarin and low dose aspirin in the primary prevention of ischaemic heart disease in men at increased risk.
Authors	The Medical Research Council's General Practice Research Framework.
Reference	Lancet 1998;351:233-241.
Disease	Coronary artery disease.
Purpose	To assess the effects of low dose aspirin, low dose warfarin, and their combination in the primary prevention of coronary artery disease.
Design	Randomized, double blind, placebo controlled, multicenter.
Patients	5499 men, aged 45-69 years, at high risk of coronary artery disease.
Follow-up	Up to 8-10 years.
Treatment regimen	Randomization to: 1. active warfarin and placebo aspirin (n=1268); 2. active warfarin and active aspirin (n=1277); 3. placebo warfarin and active aspirin (n=1268); and 4. placebo warfarin and placebo aspirin (n=1272). The initial dose of warfarin was 2.5 mg/d. The dose was adjusted to achieve INR 1.5.

Results	With a mean dose of 4.1 mg/d (range 0.5–12.5 mg), the mean INR of the patients treated with active warfarin was 1.47 (INR 1.41–1.54). Warfarin (with or without aspirin) reduced ischemic heart disease events by 21% (95% CI 4–35%; p=0.02). Warfarin therapy resulted in a reduction of coronary mortality and fatal myocardial infarction by 39% (95% CI 15–57%;p=0.003), and all causes mortality by 17% (95% CI 1–30%; p=0.04). Stroke occurred in 3.1 per 1000 person years of the active warfarin groups vs 2.7 in the placebo-warfarin groups (% proportional reduction -15%; 95% CI -68–22%). Aspirin therapy (with or without warfarin) resulted in a decrease in all ischemic heart disease events by 20% (95% CI 1–35%; p=0.04). However, aspirin reduced mainly nonfatal events (by 32%; 95% CI 12–48%; p=0.004). Aspirin therapy was associated with increased risk for fatal ischemic heart disease events (% proportional reduction -12% (95% CI -63– 22%). All causes mortality was 13.0 per 1000 person years in the aspirin treated patients vs 12.2 in the no-aspirin groups (% proportional reduction -6%; 95% CI -28–12%). Aspirin therapy resulted in increased risk of hemorrhagic stroke (0.6 per 1000 person years vs 0.1; p=0.01). Total ischemic heart disease events were 13.3 per 1000 person years in the placebo-aspirin and placebo warfarin group vs only 8.7 in the active aspirin and active warfarin group (proportional reduction by 34%; 95% CI 11–51%; p=0.006). Total ischemic heart disease events per 1000 person years was 10.3 in the warfarin alone group and 10.2 in the aspirin alone group (the difference vs the placebo aspirin and placebo warfarin group was not significant). Fatal ischemic heart disease event rate was 3.0 per 1000 person years in the aspirin and warfarin group; 2.4 in the warfarin alone group; 4.4 in the aspirin alone group; and 4.2 in the placebo aspirin and placebo warfarin group. All causes mortality rates were 12.4, 11.4, 13.6, and 13.1 per 1000 person years, respectively.
Conclusions	Aspirin reduces mainly nonfatal ischemic heart disease events, whereas warfarin reduces mainly fatal events. Combined therapy with low dose warfarin and aspirin was more effective in reducing all ischemic heart disease events, mainly due to a reduction of nonfatal events, as compared to warfarin alone. However, all causes mortality with warfarin alone tended to be lower than with the combination therapy.

Lyon Diet Heart Study

Title	Mediterranean diet, traditional risk factors, and the rate of cardiovascular complications after myocardial infarction. Final report of the Lyon Diet Heart Study.
Authors	DeLorgeril M, Salen P, Martin J-L, et al.
Reference	Circulation 1999; 99:779–785.
Disease	Coronary artery disease.
Purpose	To determine whether a Mediterranean diet vs a prudent Western diet decreases the recurrence of cardiac events after a first acute myocardial infarction.
Design	Randomized, single blind.
Patients	Consecutive patients who survived a first acute myocardial infarction, <70 years of age, were randomized between March 1988 and March 1992. 1383 and 1467 person year follow up mortality in control vs experimental groups.
Follow-up	Average 46 months per patient.
Treatment regimen	Mediterranean diet vs prudent Western diet. (Mediterranean diet is high in α-linolenic acid-rich foods, high intake of fresh fruits, vegetables, legumes, cereals, and B vitamins).

(continued)

Results	Patients on the Mediterranean diet had a reduction in the composite end point of cardiac death and nonfatal myocardial infarction at 14 events vs 44 in the prudent Western diet (p=0.0001).They also had a reduction in the first composite end point plus unstable angina, stroke, heart failure, pulmonary or peripheral embolism (27 vs 90; p=0.0001); they also had a reduction in the 2 composite end points above plus minor events requiring hospitalization (95 vs 180; p=0.0002). Total cholesterol, systolic blood pressure, and leukocyte count were associated with increased cardiac risk; female sex and aspirin were associated with reduced risk.
Conclusions	The Mediterranean diet was protective after a first myocardial infarction.

HERS

Heart and Estrogen/Progestin Replacement Study

Title	Randomized trial of estrogen plus progestin for secondary prevention of coronary heart disease on postmenopausal women.
Authors	Hulley S, Grady D, Bush T, et al.
Reference	JAMA 1998; 280:605-613.
Disease	Coronary artery disease.
Purpose	To determine if hormone therapy (estrogen plus progestin) improves coronary events in postmenopausal women with known coronary artery disease.
Design	Randomized, blinded, placebo controlled, multicenter.
Patients	2763 postmenopausal women younger than 80 with known CAD who have not had hysterectomies. CAD defined as MI, CABG, PTCA, angiographic evidence of at least a 50% occlusion of one or more coronary arteries. Average age was 66.7 years.
Follow-up	4.1 years.
Treatment regimen	0.625 mg of conjugated estrogens plus 2.5 mg of medroxyprogesterone acetate in one tablet daily (n=1380) vs placebo (1383).

Results	There was no difference in primary outcome (nonfatal MI or coronary heart disease death) between the women receiving hormone therapy (172) and the women receiving placebo (176). Patients receiving hormone therapy had an 11% lower LDL cholesterol and 10% higher HDL ($p<0.001$). There was a trend for more coronary artery disease events to occur during the first year in the hormone group compared to the placebo group; with fewer in the hormone group during years 4 and 5. There were no significant differences between groups for secondary cardiovascular outcomes (coronary revascularization, unstable angina, CHF, resuscitated cardiac arrest, stroke, transient ischemic attack, peripheral artery disease). Venous thromboembolism and gallbladder disease were more common in the hormone group than in the placebo group.
Conclusions	Oral conjugated estrogen plus medroxyprogesterone did not reduce the overall rate of coronary heart disease events in postmenopausal women with coronary artery disease over an average follow-up of 4.1 years.

ACADEMIC

The Azithromycin in Coronary Artery Disease: Elimination of Myocardial Infection with Chlamydia (ACADEMIC) Study

Title	Randomized secondary prevention trial of azithromycin in patients with coronary artery disease and serological evidence for Chlamydia pneumoniae infection.
Authors	Anderson JL, Muhlestein JG, Carlquist J, et al.
Reference	Circulation 1999; 99:1540–1547.
Disease	Coronary artery disease.
Purpose	To determine whether the antibiotic azithromycin could reduce coronary events in patients with coronary artery disease and positive antichlamydial antibody titers.
Design	Randomized, double blind, placebo controlled.
Patients	302 patients with coronary artery disease (previous MI, CABG, or by coronary angiography) and seropositive to C pneumoniae (IgG titers ≥1:16). Average age 64; 89% of patients were male.
Follow-up	2 years.
Treatment regimen	Azithromycin 500 mg/day for 3 days and then 500 mg/week for 3 months vs placebo.

The Azithromycin in Coronary Artery Disease: Elimination of Myocardial Infection with Chlamydia (ACADEMIC) Study

(continued)

Results	Azithromycin reduced a global score for 4 inflammatory markers at 6 (p=0.011) but not at 3 months (C-reactive protein, interleukin-1, interleukin-6, and tumor necrosis factor α); it also reduced a mean global change in score. Azithromycin did not change antibody titers. Cardiovascular events (cardiovascular death, resuscitated cardiac arrest, nonfatal MI or stroke, unstable angina, unplanned coronary interventions) were similar in the azithromycin group (n=9) and placebo group (n=7) at 2 years. Azithromycin reduced clinical infections over the 3 month period that patients were on therapy.
Conclusions	Azithromycin did not reduce number of cardiovascular events in patients with known coronary artery disease. It did decrease the global tests of inflammatory markers.

ATBC

Alpha Tocopherol and ß-carotene in angina pectoris

Title	Effects of alpha tocopherol and ß-carotene supplements on symptoms, progression, and prognosis of angina pectoris.
Authors	Rapola JM, Virtamo J, Ripatti S, et al.
Reference	a. Ann Epidemiol 1994;4:1-10. b. Heart 1998;79:454-458.
Disease	Angina pectoris, coronary artery disease.
Purpose	To assess the effects of long term ß-carotene and α-tocopherol administration on the incidence of major coronary events and the progression and recurrence of angina pectoris.
Design	Randomized, placebo controlled, multicenter.
Patients	1795 male smokers, 50-69 years old, with stable angina pectoris. Patients with malignancy, severe angina, renal insufficiency, liver disease, use of anticoagulants or vitamin A, E, or ß-carotene, excluded.
Follow-up	Median 4 years.
Treatment regimen	Randomization in a 2X2 design to alpha tocopherol 50 mg/day or placebo, and to ß-carotene 20 mg/day or placebo.

Alpha Tocopherol and ß-carotene in angina pectoris (continued)

Results	There was no significant beneficial effect of either alpha tocopherol (odds ratio 1.06; 95% CI 0.85 to 1.33), ß-carotene (1.06; 0.84–1.33), or both supplements (1.02; 0.82–1.27) compared with placebo on the incidence of recurrent angina. There were no significant differences in the rates of progression to severe angina pectoris during a median follow-up of 3 years among the 4 groups. The incidence of major coronary events, non fatal myocardial infarction, and coronary mortality was comparable among the 4 groups. The relative risk for major coronary events during a median follow-up of 5.5 years with alpha tocopherol compared with placebo was 0.95 (95% CI 0.68–1.33). The relative risk with ß-carotene and α tocopherol + ß-carotene was 1.08 (0.78–1.50) and 0.86 (0.61–1.20), respectively.
Conclusions	α-tocopherol and ß-carotene did not have a beneficial effect in male patients with angina pectoris who smoked.

The effect of dietary ω-3 fatty acids on coronary atherosclerosis: A randomized, double blind, placebo controlled trial

Title	The effect of dietary ω-3 fatty acids on coronary atherosclerosis: A randomized, double blind, placebo controlled trial.
Authors	Von Schacky C, Angerer P, Kothny W, et al.
Reference	Ann Intern Med 1999; 130:554-562.
Disease	Coronary artery disease.
Purpose	To determine the effect ω-3 fatty acids on the course of coronary atherosclerosis.
Design	Randomized, double blind, placebo controlled trial.
Patients	233 patients with known coronary artery disease.
Follow-up	2 years.
Treatment regimen	55% eicosapentaenoic and decohexaenoic acid vs placebo with fatty acid composition resembling average European diet.

The effect of dietary ω-3 fatty acids on coronary atherosclerosis: A randomized, double blind, placebo controlled trial

(continued)

Results	The primary end point was coronary angiographic analysis before and after 2 years of therapy. There was less progression and more regression in the fish oil group vs the placebo group. In the placebo group, of 48 coronary segments, 36 showed mild progression, 5 showed moderate progression, and 7 showed mild regression. In the fish oil group, of 55 coronary segments, 35 showed mild progression, 4 showed moderate progression, 14 showed mild progression, and 2 moderate regression ($p=0.041$). There was a nonsignificant trend toward less loss in minimal luminal diameter in the fish oil group (0.38±0.8 mm) vs the placebo group (0.45±0.8 mm). Clinical cardiovascular events including MI and stroke occurred in 7 patients in the placebo group and 2 in the fish oil group (p=NS).
Conclusions	Dietary ω-3 fatty acid supplements modestly decreases the course of coronary atherosclerosis.

AVERT

Atorvastatin Vs Revasularization Treatment

Title	Aggressive lipid lowering therapy compared with angioplasty in stable coronary artery disease.
Authors	Pitt B, Waters D, Brown WV, et al.
Reference	N Engl J Med 1999;341:70-76.
Disease	Coronary artery disease, hyperlipidemia.
Purpose	To determine the effect of aggressive lipid lowering vs percutaneous coronary revascularization for decreasing the incidence of ischemic events in patients with coronary artery disease and stable angina.
Design	Open label, randomized, multicenter study.
Patients	341 patients with stable coronary artery disease with stenosis of ≥50% of at least one coronary artery who had been recommended for treatment for angioplasty. Low density lipoprotein (LDL) cholesterol of at least 115 mg/dL, serum triglyceride of no more than 500 mg/dL. Patients either were asymptomatic or had mild to moderate angina and relatively normal LV function.
Follow-up	18 months.
Treatment regimen	Atorvastatin 80 mg once daily (n=164) or percutaneous revascularization procedure (angioplasty) plus usual care which could induce lipid lowering as per the physician (n=177).

AVERT

Atorvastatin Vs Revasularization Treatment

(continued)

Additional therapy	Atorvastatin group could not be on other lipid lowering drugs. Patients randomized to angioplasty could receive lipid lowering drugs as per usual care.
Results	The end point of ischemic events was defined as at least one of the following: death from cardiac disease, resuscitation after cardiac arrest, nonfatal myocardial infarction, cerebrovascular accident, coronary bypass surgery, angioplasty, and worsening angina with hospitalization. 22 (13%) of patients on high dose atorvastatin, vs 37 (21%) of patients who received angioplasty plus usual care developed ischemic events. This 36% lower incidence of ischemic events achieved a p value of 0.048 (this was not statistically significant following adjustment for interim analysis). Serum LDL was reduced by 46% to 77 mg/dL in the atorvastatin group vs the angioplasty plus usual care group that had a serum LDL reduced by 18% to a mean of 119 mg/dL ($p<0.05$). The decrease in ischemic events in the atorvastatin group was primarily secondary to a smaller number of revascularization procedures in that group (12%) compared to the angioplasty group (16%), a decrease in worsening angina with objective evidence of myocardial ischemia resulting in hospitalizations (6.7% vs 14.1% in atorvastatin vs angioplasty groups, respectively). Atorvastatin treatment was associated with a longer time to first ischemic event compared to the angioplasty ($p=0.03$). The incidence of adverse events was similar in the 2 groups.
Conclusions	In patients with stable coronary artery disease, aggressive lipid lowering was associated with a trend toward reduced need for further revascularization procedures compared to patients treated with angioplasty and usual care.

HOPE (Ramipril Study)

The Heart Outcomes Prevention Evaluation Study

Title	Effects of an ACE inhibitor, ramipril, on cardiovascular events in high risk patients.
Authors	The Heart Outcomes Prevention Evaluation Study Investigators.
Reference	N Engl J Med 2000;342:145–153.
Disease	Patients at high risk for cardiovascular events; coronary artery disease.
Purpose	To determine whether ramipril could reduce the incidence of myocardial infarction, stroke, or death from cardiovascular causes in patients at high risk for cardiovascular events without heart failure or LV dysfunction.
Design	Double blind, multicenter, two-by-two factorial design evaluating ramipril and vitamin E (vitamin E results given elsewhere).
Patients	9297 high risk patients, men and women at least 55 years old with "history of coronary artery disease, stroke, peripheral vascular disease, or diabetes plus at least one other cardiovascular risk factor." Patients could not have heart failure or LV ejection fraction <40%.
Follow-up	5 years.
Treatment regimen	Ramipril 10 mg once-a-day orally vs matched placebo.
Additional therapy	There was also a randomization to 400 IU of vitamin E vs placebo.

HOPE (Ramipril Study)

The Heart Outcomes Prevention Evaluation Study

(continued)

Results	The primary outcome was the composite of myocardial infarction, stroke, or death from cardiovascular causes. 826 (17.8%) patients in the placebo group achieved the primary end point vs 651 (14.0%) in the ramipril group. (RR=0.78; 95% CI=0.70–0.86; p<0.001). Ramipril significantly reduced death from cardiovascular causes, myocardial infarction, stroke, and death from any cause (10.4% vs 12.2%; RR=0.84, p=0.005). Ramipril decreased the need for revascularization procedures (16.0% vs 18.3%; RR=0.85; p=0.002), cardiac arrest, heart failure and complications of diabetes. Blood pressure at the start of the study was 139/79 mm Hg in both groups. At the end of the study, blood pressure was 136/76 mm Hg in the ramipril group and 139/77 mm Hg in the placebo group. Ramipril did not alter the hospitalizations for unstable angina. The benefit of ramipril on the composite end point was observed within one year after randomization.
Conclusions	Ramipril reduced death, myocardial infarction, and stroke in high risk patients without heart failure or LV dysfunction.

MICRO-HOPE

The MIcroalbuminuria, Cardiovascular and Renal Outcomes Heart Outcomes Prevention Evaluation

Title	Effect of ramipril on cardiovascular and microvascular outcomes in people with diabetes mellitus: Results of the HOPE study and MICRO-HOPE substudy.
Authors	Heart Outcomes Prevention Evaluation (HOPE) Study Investigators.
Reference	Lancet 2000;355:253-259.
Disease	Cardiovascular disease, atherosclerosis, diabetes mellitus.
Purpose	To assess the effects of ramipril, an ACE inhibitor on the risk of overt nephropathy in patients with diabetes mellitus.
Design	Randomized, two-by-two factorial, placebo controlled, multicenter.
Patients	3577 patients, ≥55 years old, with diabetes mellitus and a history of cardiovascular disease or at least one other cardiovascular risk factor (hypercholesterolemia, low HDL, hypertension, known microalbuminuria, or current smoking). Patients with overt proteinuria, diabetic nephropathy, other severe renal disease, hyperkalemia, congestive heart failure, LVEF <40%, uncontrolled hypertension, recent myocardial infarction or stroke, or use of or hypersensitivity to ACE inhibitors or vitamin E were excluded.
Follow-up	4.5 years.

MICRO-HOPE

The MIcroalbuminuria, Cardiovascular and Renal Outcomes Heart Outcomes Prevention Evaluation

(continued)

Treatment regimen

All patients completed a run-in phase, during which they received ramipril 2.5 mg/d for 7–10 days, followed by matching placebo for 10–14 days. Patients were randomized to ramipril 10 mg X1/d or matching placebo and to vitamin E 400 IU/d or matching placebo.

Results

The HOPE study was stopped prematurely after 4.5 years by the data safety and monitoring board because of consistent benefit of ramipril. At the end of the study, 65% of the surviving participants assigned to ramipril and 66% of those assigned to placebo were taking their study medications, whereas 12% and 15%, respectively, were taking open label ACE inhibitors. The primary end point of cardiovascular death, myocardial infarction, or stroke occurred in 15.3% of the ramipril group vs 19.8% of the placebo group (relative risk reduction [RRR] 25%; 95% CI 12%–36%; p=0.0004). Cardiovascular mortality was 6.2% in the ramipril group vs 9.7% in the placebo group (RRR 37%; 95% CI 21%–51%; p=0.0001). Myocardial infarction occurred in 10.2% and 12.9% of the ramipril vs placebo groups, respectively (RRR 22%; 95% CI 6%–36%; p=0.01), whereas stroke occurred in 4.2% vs 6.1% (RRR 33%; 95% CI 10%–50%; p=0.0074). Total mortality was lower in the ramipril group (10.8% vs 14.0%; RRR 24%; 95% CI 8%–37%; p=0.004). Less patients in the ramipril group developed overt nephropathy (6.5% vs 8.4%; RRR 24%; 95% CI 3%–40%; p=0.027). Ramipril reduced the rate of heart failure (11.0% vs 13.3%; p=0.019), transient ischemic attack (4.4% vs 5.9%; p=0.04), worsening angina (20.1% vs 22.4%; p=0.057), and the combined end point of over nephropathy, need for laser therapy or dialysis (15.1% vs 17.6%; p=0.036). Ramipril benefit was noted in the subset of patients with and without a history of cardiovascular events, those with and without hypertension, and those with or without microalbuminuria. Ramipril was effective both in patients with type 1 and type 2 diabetes and irrespective of the current medications for diabetes. After adjustment for the changes in systolic (2.4 mm Hg) and

	diastolic (1.0 mm Hg) blood pressure between the groups, ramipril was still associated with lower risk of the combined primary end point by 25% (95% CI 12%–36%; p=0.0004).
Conclusions	Ramipril was effective in reducing the risk of cardiovascular events, overt nephropathy, and death in patients with diabetes mellitus and an additional ≥ cardiovascular risk factor or cardiovascular disease. The effect on cardiovascular mortality and morbidity was greater than that can be ascribed to the mild reduction in systolic and diastolic blood pressure by ramipril.

HOPE (Vitamin E Study)

The Heart Outcomes Prevention Evaluation Study

Title	Vitamin E supplementation and cardiovascular events in high risk patients.
Authors	The Heart Outcomes Prevention Evaluation Study Investigators.
Reference	N Engl J Med 2000;342:154-160.
Disease	Patients at high risk for cardiovascular events; coronary artery disease.
Purpose	To determine whether a high dose of vitamin E (400 IU per day) reduced the composite of myocardial infarction, stroke, and death from cardiovascular causes.
Design	Double blind, multicenter, randomized trial within a two-by-two factorial design evaluating ramipril and vitamin E (ramipril data presented elsewhere).
Patients	9541 patients ≥55 years at high risk of cardiovascular events as they had known cardiovascular disease or diabetes plus at least one other risk factor (see ramipril limb of study for more details).
Follow-up	4.5 years.
Treatment regimen	Patients were randomly assigned to placebo (n=4780) or 400 IU of vitamin E (n=4761) from natural sources.
Additional therapy	Also randomized to ramipril vs placebo (see ramipril study).

HOPE (Vitamin E Study)

The Heart Outcomes Prevention Evaluation Study

(continued)

Results	The primary outcome measure was the composite end point of myocardial infarction, stroke, and death from cardiovascular causes. Primary outcome was reached in 15.5% of patients on placebo and 16.2% on vitamin E (p=NS). There were no significant differences in numbers of death due to cardiovascular cause, myocardial infarction, or stroke. There were no significant differences between groups in the secondary outcomes of unstable angina, congestive heart failure, new onset angina, worsening angina, claudication, hospitalization for heart failure, or complications of diabetes.
Conclusions	Vitamin E did not affect cardiovascular outcomes in patients at high risk of cardiovascular events.

APRES

The ACE inhibition Post revascularization study

Title	The ACE inhibition post revascularization study (APRES).
Authors	Kjøller-Hansen L, Steffensen R, Grande P.
Reference	J Am Coll Cardiol 2000;35:881-888.
Disease	Angina pectoris, coronary artery disease.
Purpose	To determine whether the ACE inhibitor ramipril could reduce the incidence of cardiac events following invasive revascularization in patients with asymptomatic LV dysfunction.
Design	Randomized, double blind, placebo controlled, single center study.
Patients	159 patients with chronic stable angina, LVEF of 0.30-0.50, and no clinical congestive heart failure referred for invasive revascularization with CABG or PTCA.
Follow-up	Median of 33 months.
Treatment regimen	If patients tolerated a test dose of 2.5 mg ramipril they were randomized to 5 mg ramipril daily vs placebo.
Additional therapy	As per physician.

The ACE inhibition Post revascularization study (continued)

Results	The composite end point of cardiac death, acute myocardial infarction, or clinical heart failure occurred in 18 of 79 placebo patients and 8 of 80 ramipril patients (RR=5%; 95% CI=7-80; p=0.031). The composite end point of cardiac death, acute myocardial infarction, clinical heart failure, or recurrent angina pectoris occurred in 41 of 79 placebo patients and 36 of 80 ramipril patients (p=NS). 2 patients (2.5%) died in the ramipril group and 8 patients (10%) died in the placebo group (p=0.053). Findings were consistent across various subgroups with regard to LVEF above or below 0.40 and whether CABG or PTCA was performed. Ramipril was well tolerated.
Conclusions	Long term ramipril therapy reduced the composite end point of cardiac death, acute myocardial infarction, or clinical heart failure in patients with angina and asymptomatic moderate LV dysfunction who underwent revascularization.

Physicians' Health Study

(Post trial aspirin substudy)

Title	Self selected post trial aspirin use and subsequent cardiovascular disease and mortality in the physicians' health study.
Authors	Cook NR, Hebert PR, Manson J, et al.
Reference	Arch Intern Med 2000;160:921-928.
Disease	Coronary artery disease.
Purpose	To examine post trial data from the Physicians' Health Study assessing the relationship of self selection of aspirin to subsequent morbidity and mortality following termination of the formal aspirin limb of the study.
Design	The original Physicians' Health Study was a randomized, double blind, placebo controlled, 2 x 2 factorial trial of aspirin and ß-carotene in male physicians. It began in 1982 and the aspirin component was terminated early (in 1988). This study examines data on participants after the formal aspirin limb was terminated.
Patients	18,496 male physicians with no previous history of cardiovascular disease.
Follow-up	Post trial use of aspirin at 7 years.
Treatment regimen	325 mg of aspirin (Bufferin) with placebo on alternate days vs placebo, vs ß-carotene (50 mg), vs both drugs.

Physicians' Health Study

(Post trial aspirin substudy)

(continued)

Results 5 year data during the randomized phase of this study have previously been reported (N Engl J Med 1989;321:129–135) and showed a 44% reduction in first myocardial infarctions in those participants assigned to aspirin ($p<0.00001$); there was a nonsignificant 22% increase in stroke. At 7 years following end of the aspirin limb 86.6% requested active aspirin. 59.5% of participants reported self selected aspirin for at least 180 days per year and 20.8% for 0–13 days per year. Self selected post trial use of aspirin was more common in those that had been randomized to receive aspirin during the trial. Selection of aspirin was more common in patients with family histories of myocardial infarction, hypertension, elevated cholesterol, body mass index, alcohol use, and use of vitamin E supplements. The adjusted relative risk of having a myocardial infarction was lower in patients who took aspirin ≥180 days/year vs 0–13 days/year (RR=0.72; 95% CI=0.55–0.95; $p=0.02$); total death was also lower in this group (RR=0.64; 95% CI=0.54–0.77; $p\leq0.001$). Cardiovascular death was also reduced (RR=0.65; CI 0.47–0.89; $p=0.03$). Stroke was not affected by aspirin ≥180 days/year (RR=1.02; 95% CI=0.74–1.39; p=NS).

Conclusions Post trial data showed reduction in myocardial infarction and cardiovascular and total death with more frequent (≥180 days/year) aspirin but did not show an increase in stroke as suggested by the initial randomized study. More large scale trials are needed to assess the effects of aspirin on primary prevention of stroke and cardiovascular related death.

QUIET

Quinapril Ischemic Event Trial (Angiographic Study)

Title	ACE inhibition as antiatherosclerotic therapy: No answer yet.
Authors	Cashin-Hemphill L, Holmvang G, Chan RC, et al.
Reference	Am J Cardiol 1999;83:43–47.
Disease	Coronary artery disease.
Purpose	To determine the effect of long term treatment with quinapril in coronary artery disease patients who had normal LV function and normal blood pressure, and normal cholesterol, on cardiac events and the progression of coronary atherosclerosis.
Design	Double blind, placebo controlled, randomized, multicenter.
Patients	1750 patients with normal LV function undergoing successful coronary angioplasty or atherectomy. Exclusion criteria included LDL cholesterol >165 mg/d, systolic BP >160 mm Hg, diastolic BP >100 mm Hg, LVEF <40%, and others. Quantitative coronary angiographic analysis reported in 477 patients.
Follow-up	3 years.
Treatment regimen	Quinapril (20 mg) or placebo once daily for 3 years.

QUIET

Quinapril Ischemic Event Trial (Angiographic Study)

(continued)

Results

Quantitative coronary angiography showed similar findings at baseline. At 3 years 111 of 234 (47%) of quinapril patients and 119 of 243 (49%) of placebo patients had progression of atherosclerosis (p=NS). Mean change in minimum lumen diameter index was -0.18±0.03 mm in quinapril patients and -0.21±0.03 mm in placebo patients (p=NS). 50 (22%) patients in the quinapril group developed new stenoses vs 44(19%) in the placebo group. Percent diameter stenosis index was +3.5±1.0 with quinapril and +5.1±1.0 with placebo (p=NS). Quinapril apparently did not reduce clinical end points (time to first cardiac event defined as cardiac death, resuscitated cardiac arrest, nonfatal MI, revascularization, hospitalization for angina pectoris). Discussion reviews some of the limitations of this study including dose and an increase in LDL cholesterol in both groups.

Conclusions

Quinapril had a neutral effect on quantitative coronary angiographic parameters of progression and nonprogression.

12. Valvular Heart Disease

Low molecular weight heparin after mechanical heart valve replacement

Title	Low molecular weight heparin after mechanical heart valve replacement.
Authors	Montalescot G, Polle V, Collet JP, et al.
Reference	Circulation 2000; 101:1083–1086.
Disease	Valvular heart disease. Mechanical heart valve replacement.
Purpose	To compare consecutive patients with mechanical heart valve replacement who received low molecular weight heparin (LMWH) to a similar series who received unfractionated heparin.
Design	Comparative, nonrandomized.
Patients	208 consecutive patients undergoing single or double heart valve replacement with mechanical valves.
Follow-up	Inhospital.
Treatment regimen	Subcutaneous unfractionated heparin (3 injections per day at 500 IU/kg/day adjusting activated partial thromboplastin time (APTT) to 1.5–2.5 times control. LMWH -72% received enoxaparin at 100 anti-Xa IU/kg (1 mg/kg) subcutaneously every 12 hours. Other patients received nadroparin at 87 anti-Xa IU/kg at 12 hour intervals. Over first part of study 106 patients received unfractionated heparin (UH); over the second phase similar patients received LMWH. Oral anticoagulation was also begun at the same time. The heparins were given until oral anticoagulation was effective.

Low molecular weight heparin after mechanical heart valve replacement

(continued)

Results	End points included effectiveness of anticoagulation and inhospital events. Mean duration of therapy with UH was 13.6 days and with LMWH was 14.1 days (p=NS). On day 2 of treatment anti-Xa activity had reached the range of efficacy (0.5–1 IU/mL) in 87% of LMWH patients. Only 9% of UH patients attained a therapeutic APTT level (1.5–2.5 times control) by this time (p<0.0001). On the final day of treatment, all LMWH patients had achieved anti-Xa activity >0.5 IU/mL; 19% were above 1 IU/mL level. At this time 27% of patients in the UH group reached an APPT >1.5 times control; however, 62% were over-anticoagulated (level of APPT >2.5 times control). One patient in the UH group had 2 successive transient ischemic strokes after aortic valve replacement. Two episodes of major bleeding occurred in each group.
Conclusions	Anticoagulation with LMWH appeared feasible and effective compared with UH anticoagulation following mechanical heart valve replacement. Randomized studies are warranted.

Early and long term (one year) effects of the association of aspirin and oral anticoagulant on thrombi and morbidity after replacement of the mitral valve with the St. Jude medical prosthesis

Title	Early and long term (one year) effects of the association of aspirin and oral anticoagulant on thrombi and morbidity after replacement of the mitral valve with the St. Jude medical prosthesis.
Authors	Laffort P, Roudaut R, Roques X, et al.
Reference	J Am Coll Cardiol 2000;35:739-746.
Disease	Mitral valve disease; mitral valve replacement.
Purpose	To assess low dose aspirin therapy with standard oral anticoagulants vs standard oral anticoagulation alone in decreasing strands, thrombi (assessed by transesophageal echocardiography) and thromboembolic events after mechanical mitral valve replacement.
Design	Randomized, controlled.
Patients	229 patients with mechanical mitral valve replacement.
Follow-up	1 year.
Treatment regimen	Patients were randomized to oral anticoagulation alone to maintain international normalized ratio (INR) between 2.5-3.5 (n=120) or oral anticoagulation plus 200 mg or aspirin per day (aspirin group; n=109).
Additional therapy	Anti-ulcer treatment. Mechanical mitral valve replacement was the St. Jude mechanical prosthesis.

Early and long term (one year) effects of the association of aspirin and oral anticoagulant on thrombi and morbidity after replacement of the mitral valve with the St. Jude medical prosthesis

(continued)

Results	Primary composite was death, major thromboembolic event, or major hemorrhage at one year. On day 9 postop on transesophageal echocardiography there was a decreased incidence of thrombi in the aspirin group (4.8%) vs the oral anticoagulation alone group (13.1%, p=0.03), but the incidence of strands was similar between the 2 groups. At 5 months strands were present in 58.6% in the aspirin group and 63.6% in the oral anticoagulation group alone. Thrombi were less frequent than in the early postoperative phase. There was a trend toward a lower incidence of thrombi in the aspirin group (4.5%) vs the oral anticoagulation alone group (8%, p=NS). At one year mortality was 9% in the aspirin group and 4% in the oral anticoagulation alone group. Total thromboembolic events occurred in 9% of the aspirin group and 25% of the oral anticoagulation alone group (p=0.004). Gastrointestional bleeding was more common in the aspirin group (7%) vs the oral anticoagulation alone group (0%). The composite primary end point was 29% in the aspirin and 16% in the oral anticoagulation alone group (p=NS). Valve related events occurred in 36% of both groups. Thromboembolic events occurred in 30% of patients with early thrombus on echo vs 13.6% of patients without early thrombus (1.3%, p=NS, p=0.0003).
Conclusions	In patients with mitral valve replacement with the St. Jude mechanical prosthesis combining aspirin with oral anticoagulation decreased thrombi and thromboembolic events but not overall morbidity due to an increase in hemorrhagic complications.

13. Preliminary Reports

During the last years numerous studies have been conducted on various cardiovascular subjects. In the previous chapters we described some of the major studies that have already been completed and published in the medical literature. Nevertheless, preliminary results have been published as abstracts or presented at major medical meetings; some of these trials are ongoing.

In this chapter we shall review some of these preliminary reports.

a. Acute Myocardial Infarction

GRAMI TRIAL

Coronary stents improved hospital results during coronary angioplasty in acute myocardial infarction: Preliminary results of a randomized controlled study (GRAMI Trial)

Reference	J Am Coll Cardiol 1997; 29 (Suppl A); 221A.
Disease	Acute myocardial infarction.
Purpose	To determine if GRII (Cook Inc) stents can improve outcome in patients undergoing angioplasty during acute myocardial infarction.
Design	Randomized.
Patients	Preliminary report of 65 patients randomized to primary PTCA (n=25) vs stent (n=40) for acute myocardial infarction. Patients underwent angiography predischarge. No difference in age, sex, previous MI, Killip class.
Follow-up	In-hospital, ongoing.
Treatment	Primary PTCA vs stent. Stent patients received IV heparin for 48 h, aspirin, ticlopidine.
Remarks	Technical failure or death occurred in 24% of PTCA patients and 0% of stent patients. Authors conclude that stents as a primary therapy of myocardial infarction improved this composite end point.

AMI

The Argatroban in Myocardial Infarction Trial

Reference	J Am Coll Cardiol 1997;30:1-7.
Disease	Acute myocardial infarction.
Purpose	To assess the effect of adding argatroban, a direct thrombin inhibitor, to streptokinase thrombolysis in patients with acute myocardial infarction.
Design	Randomized, double blind, placebo controlled, multicenter, phase II.
Patients	910 patients with acute myocardial infarction.
Treatment regimen	Intravenous streptokinase. Randomization to low or high dose argatroban or placebo.
Remarks	Death, shock, congestive heart failure, or recurrent myocardial infarction at 30 days occurred in 16.1% of the placebo group, in 19.9% of the low dose argatroban group, and in 18.8% of the high dose argatroban group (p=NS). The individual components of the composite end point occurred in similar rates among the 3 groups. In patients treated ≤3 h of onset of symptoms, the high dose argatroban was associated with a significant risk reduction. Argatroban was not associated with increased major bleeding rate. The safety profile of argatroban was good.

GIK

Glucose-Insulin-Potassium Pilot Trial

Reference	Clin Cardiol 1997;20:1031.
Disease	Acute myocardial infarction.
Purpose	To assess the efficacy of adding glucose-insulin-potassium (GIK) solution to standard therapy in patients with acute myocardial infarction (treated with or without thrombolytic therapy).
Design	Randomized, multicenter.
Patients	407 patients with suspected acute myocardial infarction presented within 24 h of symptom onset.
Treatment regimen	Randomization to: 1. high dose GIK (25% glucose 500 mL, 25 IU insulin and 40 mEq KCL at a 1.5 mg/kg/h infusion over 24 h); 2. low dose GIK (10% glucose 500 ml, 10 IU insulin and 20 mEq KCL at a 1.0 mg/kg/h infusion over 24 h; 3. control.
Remarks	Data were presented at the XIX congress of the European Society of Cardiology, Stockholm, Sweden, 1997. 252 (60%) of the patients received reperfusion therapy. GIK infusion was associated with lower rate of electromechanical dissociation (1.5%) than the control group (5.8%)(p=0.0161). There was a nonsignificant trend toward fewer events (death, severe heart failure, severe arrhythmias) with GIK compared with control. Among patients who received reperfusion therapy, GIK infusion was associated with a 66% reduction in mortality (5.2% vs 15.2%; p=0.008). GIK infusion was well tolerated and side effects were few and minor. GIK infusion is feasible and safe and is beneficial in patients undergoing reperfusion therapy.

ADMIRAL

Abciximab Before Direct Angioplasty and Stenting in Myocardial Infarction Regarding Acute and Long Term Follow-up

Title	Abciximab Before Direct Angioplasty and Stenting in Myocardial Infarction Regarding Acute and Long Term Follow-up.
Authors	Montalescot G, et al.
Reference	Presented at the March 1999, American College of Cardiology 48th Annual Scientific Sessions, New Orleans.
Disease	Coronary artery disease.
Purpose	Determine effectiveness of abciximab therapy with placebo for myocardial infarct patients undergoing angioplasty or stenting.
Design	Randomized, double blind, placebo controlled, multicenter.
Patients	300 patients with acute MI.
Follow-up	30 days.
Treatment regimen	0.25 mg/kg bolus of abciximab followed by 12 hour infusion (0.125 μg/kg every minute) vs placebo as adjunct to PTCA or stenting for acute MI.
Additional therapy	Ticlopidine (stents), aspirin, heparin.

ADMIRAL

Abciximab Before Direct Angioplasty and Stenting in Myocardial Infarction Regarding Acute and Long Term Follow-up (continued)

Results	At 30 days the end points of death, recurrent MI, or need for urgent revascularization was <11% in the abciximab group vs 20% in placebo patients. This represented a 47% reduced risk in the abciximab group. By angiography TIMI grade 3 was achieved in 21% of the abciximab patients vs 10% in the placebo group. There was no difference in major hemorrhage between groups.
Conclusions	Abciximab was advantageous in acute myocardial infarction patients undergoing PTCA or stenting.

BIRD

Bolus vs Infusion Rescupase Development

Reference	Eur Heart J 1999;20:7–10.
Disease	Acute myocardial infarction.
Purpose	To compare the efficacy of saruplase (a single chain urokinase like plasminogen activator), given as a single bolus of 80 mg to saruplase administered as 20 mg bolus followed by 60 mg infusion over 1 hour in acute myocardial infarction.
Design	Randomized, double blind, multicenter.
Patients	2410 patients with acute myocardial infarction with ST segment elevation, presenting <6 hours of onset of symptoms.
Follow-up	30 days.
Results	Results were presented at the 20th Congress of the European Society of Cardiology, Aug 1998 by F. Bar. 30 day mortality was comparable (5.9% and 6.0% in the 80 mg bolus vs the 20 mg bolus and 60 mg infusion group; p=0.86). Recurrent myocardial infarction occurred in 6.5% of the bolus group vs 5.0% of the bolus + infusion group (p=0.10). Intracranial hemorrhage occurred in 0.7% of the patients in both groups.
Conclusions	Both saruplase regimens were equal regarding mortality and complications.

APLAUD

Anti Platelet Useful Dose Trial

Reference	Am Heart J 1999;137:555-574.
Disease	Atherosclerosis.
Purpose	To define an effective and safe dose of lotrafiban (an oral GP IIb/IIIa antagonist) in patients with either cardiovascular or cerebrovascular disease.
Design	Randomized, placebo controlled, multicenter.
Patients	444 patients with recent myocardial infarction or unstable angina (62%), or recent ischemic stroke or transient ischemic attack (38%).
Treatment regimen	Randomization to lotrafiban (5 mg, 20 mg, 50 mg, or 100 mg bid) or a placebo for 12 weeks. All patients received oral aspirin.
Follow-up	12 weeks.
Results	Preliminary results were presented at the 71st American Heart Association meeting by R.A. Harrington, et al, November, 1998. The 100 mg bid dose was discontinued prematurely because of high bleeding rate. Minor bleeding occurred in 34.7% of the placebo, 35.8% of the 5 mg bid, 53.6% of the 20 mg bid, 61.8% of the 50 mg bid, and 69.7% of the 100 mg bid group. Major bleeding occurred in 2.1% of the placebo and in 0.9%, 3.1%, 2.9%, and 11.8% in the 5, 20, 50, and 100 mg bid groups. Lotrafiban was associated with bruising, epistaxis, gingival bleeding, and gastrointestinal bleeding. Thrombocytopenia (<100,000 10^9/L) occurred in 1.4% of the lotrafiban and 1.1% of the placebo group. There was a trend towards reduction in clinical events with lotrafiban compared with placebo (10.0% vs 13.8%; p=0.29).

Conclusions	The reported rate of thrombocytopenia is comparable to those with other GP IIb/IIIa inhibitors. The 20 mg bid and 50 mg bid doses appear to be safe. Further studies should assess the efficacy and safety of these doses in a large phase III trial.

InTIME 2

Intravenous nPA for Treatment of Infarcting Myocardium Early 2

Reference	Presented at the 48th Annual Scientific Session of the American College of Cardiology, March 1999.
Disease	Acute myocardial infarction.
Purpose	To compare the safety and efficacy of lanoteplase (nPA) and tPA in patients with acute myocardial infarction.
Design	Randomized, double blind, multicenter.
Patients	15,078 patients, >18 years old (median age 61.1 years), 75% men, with acute myocardial infarction.
Treatment regimen	Randomization to nPA 1250 KU/Kg (n=10051) or front loaded tPA (n=5027).
Follow-up	180 days.

InTIME 2

Intravenous nPA for Treatment of Infarcting Myocardium Early 2

(continued)

Results	Preliminary data presented by Neuhaus K-L. The median time from onset of symptoms to therapy was 3.1 hours. 42% of the patients had anterior wall myocardial infarction. 24 hour mortality was 2.39% in the nPA vs 2.49% in the tPA group. 30 day mortality was 6.60% in the nPA vs 6.77% in the tPA group. Death due to intracranial bleeding occurred in 0.66% of the nPA vs 0.40% in the tPA group (p=0.051). Stroke occurred in 1.89% and 1.52% of the nPA and tPA groups (p=0.103). Intracranial hemorrhage occurred in 1.13% of the nPA vs 0.62% of the tPA group (p=0.003). Ischemic stroke occurred in 0.53% and 0.62%, respectively (p=0.49). Major nonintracranial bleeding occurred at a similar rate (0.6% in both groups, but minor bleeding was more common in the nPA group (19.6% vs 14.7%; p=0.000). More patients in the nPA group needed urgent revascularization. 180 day mortality was comparable between the groups.
Conclusions	Mortality was comparable between tPA and nPA. Lanoteplase was associated with slightly higher risk of intracranial bleeding and minor bleeding.

OPTIMAAL

The Optimal Therapy in Myocardial Infarction with the Angiotensin II Antagonist Losartan

Title	Comparison of the effects of losartan and captopril on mortality in patients after acute myocardial infarction: The OPTIMAAL trial design.
Authors	Dickstein K, Kjekshus J, for the OPTIMAAL Study Group.
Reference	Am J Cardiol 1999;83:477-481.
Disease	Acute myocardial infarction.
Purpose	To evaluate whether losartan will be more effective than captopril in reducing all cause mortality in high risk patients after myocardial infarction.
Design	Randomized, double blind, placebo controlled, multicenter.
Patients	5000 patients, ≥50 years old, with definite myocardial infarction, within 10 days after the onset of symptoms, with signs or symptoms of heart failure during the acute phase, will be included. Only clinically stable patients will be included. Patients with systolic blood pressure <100 mm Hg at the time of randomization, patients already receiving ACE inhibitors or angiotensin II antagonists, and patients with hemodynamically significant arrhythmia or valvular disease will be excluded.
Follow-up	≥6 months.
Treatment regimen	Randomization within 10 days of onset of symptoms to captopril (6.25 mg titrated up to 50 mg tid) or losartan (12.5 mg titrated up to 50 mg/d).

OPTIMAAL

The Optimal Therapy in Myocardial Infarction with the Angiotensin II Antagonist Losartan

(continued)

Additional therapy	All patients will receive standard therapy (ß-blockers, thrombolysis, aspirin, nitrates, etc).
Results	The first patient was enrolled in February 1998. The trial is planned to be completed in the year 2000.

BRAVO

Blockade of the GP IIB/IIIA Receptor to Avoid Vascular Occlusion

Disease	Coronary artery disease, atherosclerosis.
Purpose	To assess the effects of lotrafiban, an oral GP IIb/IIIa blocker, combined with aspirin in patients with cardiovascular or cerebrovascular disease.
Design	Randomized, placebo controlled, double blind, multicenter.
Patients	Approximately 9200 patients with acute myocardial infarction, unstable angina, transient ischemic attack, ischemic stroke, or double bed vascular disease will be recruited.
Treatment regimen	Randomization to placebo or lotrafiban 30 mg or 50 mg bid. All patients will receive aspirin 75–325 mg/d.
Follow-up	6 months–2 years.
Results	Not available yet.

PENTALYSE Study

Pentasaccharide, as an Adjunct to Fibrinolysis in ST-Elevation Acute Myocardial Infarction

Reference	Presented at the 49th American College of Cardiology Meetings, Anaheim, CA, March 2000.
Disease	Acute myocardial infarction.
Purpose	To assess the safety, tolerability and efficacy of SR9010A/ORG31540, a synthetic pentasaccharide that selectively inhibits factor Xa in addition to rt-PA and aspirin in patients with ST elevation acute myocardial infarction.
Patients	333 patients, 21-75 years old, with ST elevation acute myocardial infarction, ≤6 hours of onset of symptoms. Patients with prior CABG, recent stent implantation, cardiogenic shock or pulmonary edema, high bleeding risk, renal failure and concomitant therapy with unfractionated heparin or oral anticoagulants were excluded.
Follow-up	Coronary angiography at 90 minutes and at day 6. Clinical follow-up for 30 days.
Treatment regimen	All patients received aspirin and rt-PA 100 mg over 90 minutes and then randomized to 1of 3 doses of synthetic pentasaccharide (SP) for 5±1 days or to IV unfractionated heparin for 48-72 hours. SP was given subcutaneously at a dose of 4 mg (n=84), 8 mg (n=80), or 12 mg (n=83).

PENTALYSE Study

Pentasaccharide, as an Adjunct to Fibrinolysis in ST-Elevation Acute Myocardial Infarction

(continued)

Results	Preliminary data were presented by PK Coussement at the 49th American College of Cardiology meeting, Anaheim, CA, in March 2000. 321 patients underwent coronary angiography at 90 minutes and 250 at day 6. At 90 minutes, TIMI grade flow 3 was achieved in 68% of the heparin group vs 64% in the SP group (p=0.595). At day 6, TIMI grade flow 3 was seen in 79% in the heparin group vs in 88% in the SP groups (p=0.177). TIMI frame counts were significantly lower in the SP treated patients at day 6. The combined incidence of intracranial hemorrhage and transfusions occurred in 7.1% of the heparin group vs 6.3% of the SP group (p=0.8). 7.1% of the heparin group vs 5.9% of the SP groups needed transfusions. 30 day mortality was 1.2% with heparin and 2.5% with SP. Less patients in the SP groups (38.6%) than the heparin group (51.2%) underwent urgent revascularization within 30 days (p=0.054).
Comments	A synthetic pentasaccharide (a direct factor Xa inhibitor), added to rt-PA in patients with ST elevation acute myocardial infarction, was safe and was associated with similar rates of complete reperfusion (TIMI grade flow 3) at 90 minutes when compared with unfractionated heparin. There was no dose related effect on early patency. There was a trend toward less reocclusion and need for urgent revascularization with the synthetic pentasaccharide.

HART-II

Low Molecular Weight Heparin and Unfractionated Heparin Adjunctive to t-PA Thrombolysis and Aspirin

Reference	Presented at the 49th American College of Cardiology Meetings, Anaheim, CA, March 2000.
Disease	Acute myocardial infarction.
Purpose	To compare the efficacy and safety of unfractionated heparin to enoxaparin as an adjunct to thrombolytic therapy with t-PA and aspirin.
Design	Randomized, open label.
Patients	400 patients, >18 years old, with ST elevation acute myocardial infarction, within 12 hours of onset of symptoms and without contraindications to enoxaparin or to thrombolytic therapy.
Follow-up	Coronary angiography at 90 minutes and after 5–7 days.
Treatment regimen	All patients received aspirin and t-PA 100 mg and then were randomized to unfractionated heparin (UFH, 5000 U bolus, followed by 15 U/kg/h for up to 72 hours) or to enoxaparin (30 mg IV followed by subcutaneous injections of 1 mg/kg bid started 15 minutes after the initial IV dose and continued for up to 72 hours).

HART-II

Low Molecular Weight Heparin and Unfractionated Heparin Adjunctive to t-PA Thrombolysis and Aspirin

(continued)

Results	Preliminary data were presented by A Ross at the 49th American College of Cardiology meeting, Anaheim, CA, in March 2000. Infarct related artery patency (TIMI grade flow 2–3) at 90 minutes was 80.1% with enoxaparin vs 75.1% with UFH, whereas TIMI grade flow 3 at 90 minutes was achieved by 52.9% in the enoxaparin vs 47.6% in the UFH group. Reocclusion within 7 days occurred in 9.8% and 5.9% of the patients in the UFH and enoxaparin groups who had TIMI grade flow 2–3 at 90 minutes. Intracranial hemorrhage occurred in 1% in each group. Major bleeding occurred in 3.0% in the UFH group vs 3.6% in the enoxaparin group, and 7.1% vs 5.6%, respectively, needed ≥2 U blood transfusions. ≥3 g/dL decrease in hemoglobin concentration was noted in 10.7% in the UFH group vs 12.8% in the enoxaparin group. 30 day mortality was 5.0% in both groups and 3.0% of the UFH and 4.0% of the enoxaparin treated patients needed urgent percutaneous coronary interventions during hospitalization.
Comments	Enoxaparin was safe and associated with a trend toward better patency of the infarct related artery and less reocclusion.

ALKK

Arbeitsgemeinschaft Leitender Kardiologischer Krankenhausarzte

Reference	Presented at the 49th American College of Cardiology Meetings, Anaheim, CA, March 2000.
Disease	Acute myocardial infarction.
Purpose	To compare the effect of medical therapy and routine PTCA on outcome of asymptomatic patients with single vessel disease who survived an acute myocardial infarction.
Design	Randomized, open label, multicenter.
Patients	300 patients with a recent myocardial infarction (1-6 weeks before enrollment) and no or only mild angina (CCS class 1-2), single vessel disease, and coronary anatomy compatible with PTCA of the infarct related artery. Patients with left main coronary artery disease or with indication for cardiac surgery were excluded.
Follow-up	One year in all patients and up to 66 months in 208 patients (69%).
Treatment regimen	After coronary angiography, patients were randomized to medical therapy without PTCA (n=151) or to PTCA (n=149).

Results	Preliminary data were presented by K-L Neuhaus at the 49th American College of Cardiology meeting, Anaheim, CA, in March 2000. More patients in the PTCA group underwent thrombolytic therapy for their myocardial infarction (63% vs 50%; p=0.03). The median time from myocardial infarction to randomization was 21 days in the PTCA group and 22 days in the medical therapy group. Mean stenosis of the infarct related artery was 88±10% in the PTCA group and 88±11% in the medical therapy group. 29% and 28% of the patients had total occlusion of the infarct related artery. Concurrent medications were similar in the two groups, with >75% of the patients receiving ß-blockers. Eleven patients, assigned to PTCA did not undergo PTCA. PTCA was successful in 119/138 (86.2%) of the patients. 17.4% of the patients who underwent PTCA received stents. One year event free survival was 90% in the PTCA group vs 82% in the medical therapy group (p=0.066). Death occurred in 1% and 4% of the PTCA and medical therapy group, respectively (p=NS), reinfarction in 4% and 6%, respectively (p=NS). 8% of the PTCA group vs 29% of the medical therapy group underwent (re)PTCA (p=0.03), and 1% and 4% underwent CABG (p=NS). At extended follow-up of up to 66 months, event free survival was 76% in the PTCA group vs 67% in the medical group (p=0.1), death rate was 5.3% vs 10.7% (p=NS), recurrent nonfatal myocardial infarction occurred in 8% and 7% (p=NS), and 13% and 19% of the patients underwent (re)PTCA (p=NS). Fewer patients in the PTCA group were using nitrates (38% vs 67%; p=0.001).
Comments	At one year and the extended follow-up there was a non-statistically significant trend toward improved event free survival in the PTCA arm among stable patients with single vessel coronary artery disease after myocardial infarction.

ENRICHD

ENhancing Recovery In Coronary Heart Disease

Reference	Am Heart J 2000;139:1-9.
Disease	Acute myocardial infarction, coronary heart disease.
Purpose	To assess the effects of a psychosocial intervention targeting depression and/or low social support on survival and reinfarction among patients after acute myocardial infarction who are at high risk for recurrent cardiac events.
Design	Randomized, multicenter.
Patients	The study will enroll 3000 patients within 28 days of an acute myocardial infarction with depression or low social support.
Treatment regimen	Randomization to psychosocial intervention group or a usual care group.
Follow-up	Minimum 18 months (1.5-4.5 years).
Results	Not yet available.
Conclusions	Not yet available.

MAGIC

MAGnesium In Coronaries

Reference	Am Heart J 2000;139:10–14.
Disease	Acute myocardial infarction.
Purpose	To study whether early administration of IV magnesium sulfate before reperfusion therapy in high risk patients with acute ST elevation myocardial infarction will reduce 30 day mortality.
Design	Randomized, double blind, placebo controlled, multicenter.
Patients	The study will enroll 10,400 patients, ≥65 years old, with ST elevation acute myocardial infarction or new left bundle branch block, within 6 hours of onset of symptoms. In stratum I, patients must be candidates for reperfusion therapy (thrombolysis or primary PCI). Patients who are not candidates for reperfusion therapy will be included in stratum II. Patients with persistent hypotension, bradycardia, advanced heart block or renal failure will be excluded.
Treatment regimen	Randomization to IV magnesium sulfate or placebo. Magnesium sulfate will be administered intravenously as a 2.0 g bolus over 15 minutes, followed by a 17.0 g over 24 hours.
Follow-up	30 days.
Results	Not yet available.
Conclusions	Not yet available.

GUSTO IV AMI

Global Utilization of Strategies To Open Occluded Coronary Arteries IV, Acute Myocardial Infarction

Disease	ST elevation acute myocardial infarction.
Purpose	To compare the efficacy of reteplase alone and reteplase and abciximab in patients with ST elevation acute myocardial infarction.
Design	Randomized, open label, multicenter.
Patients	16,600 patients, ≥18 years old, ≤120 kg body weight, with ST elevation acute myocardial infarction or new LBBB with symptoms suggesting acute myocardial infarction, within 6 hours of onset of symptoms and without contraindication to thrombolytic therapy.
Treatment regimen	Randomization to reteplase 10 U + 10 U, 30 minutes apart, or to reteplase 5 U + 5 U, 30 minutes apart and abciximab (0.25 mg/kg bolus and 0.125 μg/kg/minutes infusion for 12 hours). All patients receive aspirin and heparin.
Follow-up	30 days.
Results	Not yet available.
Conclusions	Not yet available.

VALIANT

VALsartan In Acute myocardial Infarction

Disease	Acute myocardial infarction.
Purpose	To assess the effects of valsartan on mortality and morbidity in patients with LV dysfunction or heart failure after acute myocardial infarction.
Design	Randomized, multicenter.
Patients	14,500 patients post myocardial infarction with congestive heart failure or left ventricular systolic dysfunction.
Treatment regimen	Randomization to valsartan alone, captopril alone, or their combination.
Follow-up	4 years.
Results	Not yet available.
Conclusions	Not yet available.

CHAMP

Combination Hemotherapy and Mortality Prevention

Title	Combination Hemotherapy and Mortality Prevention.
Authors	Fiore L, Ezcekowitz M, et al.
Reference	Presented at the 72nd Scientific Sessions of the American Heart Association in Atlanta, GA, in 1999.
Disease	Acute myocardial infarction.
Purpose	To determine whether aspirin plus warfarin would improve long term survival over aspirin alone in patients with acute myocardial infarction.
Design	Randomized, multicenter, Veterans Affairs Cooperative Study.
Patients	5059 patients who survived an initial acute myocardial infarction. Mean age was 62.
Follow-up	Median follow-up was 2.7 years; range 1-5 years.
Treatment regimen	Within 14 days of acute myocardial infarction, patients were assigned to aspirin alone (162 mg daily; n=2537) or aspirin 81 mg daily plus warfarin titrated to INR of 1.5-2.0 (n=2522).

CHAMP

Combination Hemotherapy and Mortality Prevention

(continued)

Results	Primary end point of all cause mortality was similar between the 2 groups at 438 (17%) deaths in the aspirin alone group vs 444 (18%) deaths in the aspirin plus warfarin group. There were no significant differences in nonfatal myocardial infarction or nonfatal strokes between groups. Major gastrointestinal bleeding was more frequent in the combination group. The risk of bleeding increased with age and patients >70 years old were at highest risk.
Conclusions	Adding warfarin to aspirin for post myocardial infarction therapy had no advantage over aspirin alone.

CADILLAC

Controlled Abciximab and Device Investigation to Lower Late Angioplasty Complications

Title	Controlled Abciximab and Device Investigation to Lower Late Angioplasty Complications.
Authors	Stone G, et al.
Reference	Presented at the 72nd Scientific Sessions of the American Heart Association in Atlanta, GA, in 1999.
Disease	Acute myocardial infarction.
Purpose	To determine whether outcomes of primary PTCA or primary stenting for acute myocardial infarction could be improved by adding glycoprotein IIb/IIIa blocker.
Design	Multicenter, randomized.
Patients	2081 patients with acute myocardial infarction. Patients could not have received a prior stent to the infarct vessel. Infarct related vessel had to be amenable to successful stent delivery. Interim data on 1961 patients were presented at this meeting.
Follow-up	Patients to be followed for up to at least one year (data pending).
Treatment regimen	Patients were randomized to: 1) primary PTCA; 2) PTCA + abciximab; 3) primary stenting; 4) primary stenting + abciximab.
Additional therapy	Aspirin, ticlopidine, heparin, IV ß-blockers.

CADILLAC

Controlled Abciximab and Device Investigation to Lower Late Angioplasty Complications

(continued)

Results	Primary outcome was composite of death, myocardial infarction, stroke, or ischemic target vessel revascularization at 6 months. Overall hospital mortality did not differ among the 4 arms (1–1.6%). Disabling strokes occurred in 0.4% of patients and did not differ among treatments. Reinfarction tended to be higher in the 2 arms not receiving abciximab (0.6% with PTCA vs 0% with PTCA plus abciximab; 0.8% with stent vs 0.2% with stent plus abciximab). Target vessel revascularization was 2.3% in patients receiving PTCA vs 0.2% in patients receiving PTCA plus abciximab. Target vessel revascularization was 0.2% in patients receiving stents plus abciximab vs 0.8% in patients receiving stents only (although this difference was not statistically significant). Recurrent ischemia was decreased by abciximab: 1.4% in patients treated with PTCA plus abciximab vs 4.9% with PTCA alone; 1.2% who received stents plus abciximab vs 3.9% of patients that received stents alone.
Conclusions	Abciximab lowered rate of recurrent ischemia in patients undergoing stenting or PTCA for acute myocardial infarction.

ERASE Chest-Pain

Emergency Room Assessment of Sestamibi for Evaluating Chest Pain

Title	Emergency Room Assessment of Sestamibi for Evaluating Chest Pain.
Authors	Udelson J, et al.
Reference	Presented at the 72nd Scientific Sessions of the American Heart Association in Atlanta, GA, in 1999.
Disease	Chest pain. Acute coronary syndromes.
Purpose	To determine whether perfusion imaging in the emergency department evaluation of chest pain could improve diagnosis and also decrease unnecessary hospitalizations in patients presenting with chest pain.
Design	Randomized.
Patients	2456 patients with symptoms of acute cardiac ischemia and normal or nondiagnostic ECGs presenting to emergency department.
Follow-up	Inhospital.
Treatment regimen	Patients randomized to usual care strategy (n=1246) or to sestamibi perfusion imaging (n=1210).

ERASE Chest-Pain

Emergency Room Assessment of Sestamibi for Evaluating Chest Pain

(continued)

Results	13-14% of patients in each group had acute cardiac ischemia (2% acute myocardial infarction, 11-12% unstable angina) diagnosed by ECG, enzymes, and stress testing with imaging. In patients without acute cardiac ischemia 42% of patients that received sestamibi scans were hospitalized; 52% in the usual care group were hospitalized. Thus, there was a 14% decrease in total hospitalizations with cost savings in patients who had received sestamibi scans. There was no difference in appropriate hospitalization admission rates between the 2 groups of patients who later were shown to have a true diagnosis of acute cardiac ischemia.
Conclusions	Sestamibi perfusion imaging as part of the emergency department work up of chest pain safely reduced the number of unnecessary admissions.

SPEED (Interim Results)

Strategies for Patency Enhancement in the Emergency Department

Title	Strategies for Patency Enhancement in the Emergency Department.
Authors	Topol E,et al.
Reference	Presented at the 1999 European Society of Cardiology Meeting; Internal Medicine World Report, December 1999.
Disease	Acute myocardial infarction.
Purpose	To determine optimal dosing of reteplase (r-PA)—1 of 5 doses to administer in combination with abciximab. To compare angiographic patency of abciximab plus half dose reteplase with full dose reteplase in patients with acute myocardial infarction.
Design	Randomized, open controlled, dose ranging, and then confirmation phase.
Patients	528 patients with acute ST elevation myocardial infarction.
Treatment regimen	Dose finding part: abciximab alone, or abciximab plus 1 of 5 doses of reteplase. In confirmation phase: abciximab plus half dose reteplase (5 U + 5 U as separate boluses; given 30 minutes apart) vs full dose reteplase alone (10 U + 10 U as separate boluses). Angiography done as soon as possible after treatment.
Additional therapy	Variable doses of heparin.

SPEED (Interim Results)

Strategies for Patency Enhancement in the Emergency Department

(continued)

Results	During dose finding part of study, 60–90 minute TIMI 3 flow ranged 55%–62% with abcixmab plus reteplase; the best dose of reteplase to give plus abciximab was 5 U reteplase + 5 U reteplase, given 30 minutes apart. Only 27% of abcixmab alone achieved TIMI 3 vs 62% of abcixmab + reteplase 5 U + 5 U group (p=0.001). In the 200 patient confirmation phase, that compared reteplase 5 U + 5 U plus abciximab vs 10 U + 10 U boluses of reteplase, TIMI 3 flow was 54% in the 5 U + 5 U reteplase + abciximab vs 47% in the 10 U + 10 U reteplase alone group. There was also a trend favoring 60 U/kg heparin. The combination of death, MI, urgent revascularization was reduced in patients receiving combination of abciximab plus 5 U + 5 U reteplase (6.1%) vs reteplase alone (11.0%). There was an increase in percentage of patients who achieved TIMI 3 flow at the time of percutaneous intervention with combination therapy. The incidence of major bleeding did not differ between groups.
Conclusions	Combined abciximab plus low dose reteplase resulted in excellent coronary angiographic patency.

HALT-MI

Hu23F2G anti Adhesion to Limit cytoToxic injury Following AMI

Title	Hu23F2G anti adhesion to limit cytotoxic injury following AMI.
Authors	Faxon D,et al.
Reference	Presented at the Scientific Sessions of the American Heart Association in Atlanta, GA, in 1999.
Disease	Acute myocardial infarction.
Purpose	To test the efficacy of the monoclonal antibody HU23F2G (which blocks neutrophil adhesion) on myocardial infarct size in patients with acute MI.
Design	Randomized, double blinded, multicenter,
Patients	637 patients with acute myocardial infarct and TIMI 0-1.
Follow-up	30 days.
Treatment regimen	HU23F2G 0.3mg/kg bolus, 1 mg/kg bolus, or placebo.
Additional therapy	After receiving drug, patients had PTCA, stenting, or other devices abciximab could be used.

HALT-MI

Hu23F2G anti Adhesion to Limit cytoToxic injury Following AMI

(continued)

Results	As assessed by nuclear imaging, HU23F2G did not significantly decrease myocardial infarct size. 30 day mortality was 0.8% in low dose; 1.4% high dose; and 3.3% in placebo, although this was not significantly different among groups. Reinfarction rates did not differ among groups. There was a trend toward more urinary tract infections in the treated group.
Conclusions	Inhibition of neutrophil adhesion with the monoclonal antibody HU23F2G did not reduce acute myocardial infarct size.

13. Preliminary Reports

b. Unstable Angina, Non Q Wave Myocardial Infarction

GUSTO IV Unstable Angina

Global Utilization of Strategies To Open Occluded Coronary Arteries IV, Unstable Angina

Disease	Unstable angina.
Purpose	To assess the effects of abciximab infusion on the composite end point of 30 day death and myocardial infarction in patients with acute coronary syndromes without ST elevation.
Design	Randomized, double blind, placebo controlled, multicenter, phase III.
Patients	~7800 patients, ≥21 years old, with anginal syndrome at rest, ≤24 h of the last episode, associated with ST segment depression and/or positive troponin T/I test. Patients who receive thrombolytic therapy, have ST segment elevation, or are scheduled for coronary revascularization within 30 days of enrollment will be excluded.
Follow-up	6 months.
Treatment regimen	Randomization to: 1) Abciximab bolus + infusion for 48 h; 2) Abciximab bolus + infusion for 24 h and placebo infusion for additional 24 h; 3) Placebo bolus + placebo infusion for 48 h.
Remarks	Results are not available yet.

OPUS-TIMI 16

Orbofiban in Patients with Unstable Coronary Syndromes, Thrombolysis in Myocardial Infarction

Title	Orbofiban in Patients with Unstable Coronary Syndromes.
Authors	Cannon C, et al.
Reference	Presentation at the 48th Annual Scientific Session of the American College of Cardiology, New Orleans, March 7-10, 1999.
Disease	Unstable coronary syndromes.
Purpose	To determine the efficacy of the oral antiplatelet glycoprotein IIb/IIIa inhibitor, orbofiban in patients with unstable coronary syndromes.
Design	Randomized, placebo controlled, multicenter.
Patients	More than 10,000 patients with unstable coronary syndromes.
Follow-up	Up to 300 days as of this report.
Treatment regimen	Patients were randomized to placebo vs orbofiban 50 mg orally twice a day or orbofiban 50 mg for 30 days followed by 30 mg twice a day.

OPUS-TIMI 16

Orbofiban in Patients with Unstable Coronary Syndromes, Thrombolysis in Myocardial Infarction

(continued)

Results	The study was stopped early when there was an increased mortality in one of the orbofiban groups. At 30 days the mortality rate was 2.3% in the orbofiban 50/30 group, 1.6% in the orbofiban 50/50 group and 1.4% in the patients that received placebo. There was a decreased rate of urgent revascularization associated with orbofiban. At 300 day follow-up preliminary analysis continued to demonstrate an increase in mortality in the orbofiban treated groups and an increased rate of major severe bleeding.
Conclusions	Oral GP IIb/IIIa antagonism with orbofiban was associated with more deaths, more severe bleeding but less urgent revascularization.

Nadoparin in Unstable Angina and Non Q wave Myocardial Infarction

Reference	Eur Heart J 1999;20:7–10.
Disease	Unstable angina, non Q wave myocardial infarction.
Purpose	To assess the efficacy of nadoparin, a low molecular weight heparin, in acute coronary syndromes.
Design	Randomized, multicenter.
Patients	3468 patients with unstable angina or non Q wave acute myocardial infarction.
Treatment regimen	Randomization to: 1) subcutaneous nadoparin 87 U/kg bid for 6 days; 2) subcutaneous nadoparin 87 U/kg bid for 14 days; or IV unfractionated heparin for 6 days.
Follow-up	3 months.
Results	Results were presented at the 20th Congress of the European Society of Cardiology, Aug 1998 by A. Leizorovicz. The primary end point (cardiovascular mortality, myocardial infarction, refractory angina, or recurrent angina) was similar among the groups at 6 days, 14 days, and 3 months. Major bleeding occurred at comparable rates between the intravenous heparin group and the 6 day nadoparin group, however, the risk of major bleeding increased in the 14 day nadoparin group.
Conclusions	Nadoparin was comparable to intravenous heparin in patients with acute coronary syndromes. Prolonged (14 days) nadoparin use was associated with increased risk for bleeding with no additional benefit on mortality and morbidity.

PARAGON B

The Platelet IIb/IIIa Antagonist for the Reduction of Acute Coronary Syndrome Events in a Global Organization Network

Reference	Presented at the 49th American College of Cardiology Meetings, Anaheim, CA, March 2000.
Disease	Acute coronary syndrome.
Purpose	To assess the effect of renal based lamifiban dosing on clinical outcomes in patients with acute coronary syndromes.
Design	Randomized, double blind, placebo controlled, multicenter.
Patients	5225 patients with non ST elevation acute coronary syndrome, within 12 hours of onset of symptoms.
Follow-up	30 days and up to 6 months.
Treatment regimen	All patients received aspirin and heparin (unfractionated or low molecular weight). Randomization to placebo (n=2597) or to lamifiban (n=2628). Lamifiban was administered as a 500 μg bolus followed by an IV infusion for 72 hours at a rate of 1.0 -2.0 μg/minutes (the dose was adjusted to renal function).

PARAGON B

The Platelet IIb/IIIa Antagonist for the Reduction of Acute Coronary Syndrome Events in a Global Organization Network

(continued)

Remarks

Preliminary data were presented by R Harrington at the 49th American College of Cardiology meeting, Anaheim, CA, in March 2000. The primary end point of death, myocardial infarction or urgent revascularization at 30 days was achieved by 12.8% of the placebo vs 11.8% of the lamifiban group (p=0.329). Death or myocardial infarction at 30 days occurred in 11.5% of the placebo vs 10.6% in the lamifiban group (p=0.320). Death occurred in 3.3% vs 2.9%, respectively (p=0.487). The survival curves up to 6 months were comparable between the groups. The cumulative rate of death or myocardial infarction at 180 days was 15.5% in the placebo group vs 14.4% in the lamifiban group. Nonhemorrhagic stroke occurred in 0.6% vs 1.1%, respectively (p=NS). Bleeding occurred more often in the lamifiban group (14.0% vs 11.5%; p=0.002). However, there was no difference in the rate of major bleeding (0.9% of the placebo group vs 1.3% of the lamifiban group). Thrombocytopenia was detected in 0.5% of the placebo group vs 0.7% of the lamifiban group. There was no excess bleeding risk among patients receiving lamifiban who underwent CABG. Subgroup analysis revealed that lamifiban was beneficial among patients undergoing early percutaneous coronary interventions (death, myocardial infarction, or urgent revascularization at 30 days; 11.6% vs 18.5%), and among patients with positive troponin test (11% vs 19%; p=0.018). Among troponin negative patients lamifiban was not beneficial.

Comments

Overall, dose adjusted lamifiban did not reduce 30 day event rates in patients with non ST elevation acute coronary syndromes. Lamifiban increased the risk of bleeding, but not the rates of major bleeding or intracranial bleeding. Among patients subjected to early percutaneous interventions and among those with positive troponin test, lamifiban was effective in reducing event rates at 30 days.

SYMPHONY 2

Sibrafiban vs Aspirin to Yield Maximum Protection from Ischemic Heart Events Post Acute Coronary Syndromes

Reference	Presented at the 49th American College of Cardiology Meetings, Anaheim, CA, March 2000.
Disease	Acute coronary syndrome.
Purpose	To study the safety and efficacy of combined low dose aspirin and low dose sibrafiban, an oral glycoprotein IIb/IIIa inhibitor, compared with aspirin alone and high dose sibrafiban alone in patients with an acute coronary syndrome.
Design	Randomized, double blind, placebo controlled, multicenter.
Patients	6671 stable patients within 7 days of an acute coronary syndrome, without ongoing ischemia or heart failure. Patients at high risk of bleeding, Thrombocytopenia or anemia, serum creatinine >1.5 mg/dL, and central nervous system pathology were excluded.
Follow-up	90 days.
Treatment regimen	Randomization to aspirin 80 mg bid alone (n=2231), high dose (3-6 mg bid, depending on serum creatinine and body weight) sibrafiban alone (n=2174), or low dose (3-4.5 mg bid) sibrafiban+ aspirin (n=2232).

SYMPHONY 2

Sibrafiban vs Aspirin to Yield Maximum Protection from Ischemic Heart Events Post Acute Coronary Syndromes

(continued)

Results

Preliminary data were presented by K Newby at the 49th American College of Cardiology meeting, Anaheim, CA, in March 2000. The trial was terminated prematurely by Roche Laboratories after the results of SYMPHONY 1 trial were published. The primary end point of death, myocardial infarction, or severe recurrent ischemia occurred in 9.3% in the aspirin group, 9.2% in the aspirin+sibrafiban group and in 10.5% in the sibrafiban group. Death or myocardial infarction occurred in 6.1% in the aspirin group, 6.8% in the aspirin+ sibrafiban group, and in 8.6% in the sibrafiban alone group ($p<0.05$ vs aspirin). Mortality was higher in the sibrafiban alone group (2.4%) than in the aspirin (1.3%) or aspirin+ sibrafiban group (1.7%) ($p<0.05$). Similarly, myocardial infarction occurred more often in the sibrafiban alone group (6.9%) than in the aspirin alone group (5.3%) or the combination group (5.3%) ($p<0.05$). More patients in the sibrafiban group suffered reversible ischemia (7.5%) than in the aspirin alone (5.9%) or in the combination group (6.3%) ($p<0.05$). Patients in the aspirin alone group had less rehospitalization (21.5%) than in the sibrafiban alone (25.8%) or combination group (25.1%) ($p<0.05$ vs aspirin). There were no differences in stroke or coronary revascularization among the three groups. Among patients who underwent stent implantation, those in the sibrafiban alone group had more stent thrombosis (6.4%) than in the aspirin alone (4.0%) or in the combination group (3.9%). (Patients in the aspirin group received ticlopidine after stent implantation whereas the patients in the other 2 groups did not). Bleeding occurred less often in the aspirin group (11.7%) than in the sibrafiban alone group (22.0%) or the combination group (21.0%). 6.3% of the patients in the combination group and 5.0% in the sibrafiban alone group, as compared to only 3.3% in the aspirin alone group needed blood transfusion. Thrombocytopenia was detected in 2.0% in the aspirin alone, 1.9% in the sibrafiban alone and 1.7% in the combination group.

SYMPHONY 2

Sibrafiban vs Aspirin to Yield Maximum Protection from Ischemic Heart Events Post Acute Coronary Syndromes

(continued)

Comments	The combination of low dose sibrafiban and aspirin did not improve 90 day clinical outcomes relative to aspirin alone. Moreover, the combination therapy was associated with significantly more bleeding events than aspirin alone. High dose sibrafiban was associated with an increased risk of death and myocardial infarction in both SYMPHONY trials.

ESSENCE (Substudy)

Efficacy and Safety of Subcutaneous Enoxaparin in Non Q Wave Coronary Events

Title	Efficacy and Safety of Subcutaneous Enoxaparin in Non Q Wave Coronary Events.
Authors	Cohen M, et al.
Reference	Presented at the 72nd Scientific Sessions of the American Heart Association in Atlanta, GA, in 1999.
Disease	Myocardial Infarction.
Purpose	To determine the outcomes of patients in the ESSENCE trial who developed Q wave myocardial infarction.
Design	As per ESSENCE.
Patients	252 patients who were determined to have developed Q wave myocardial infarction in the ESSENCE trial.
Follow-up	1 year.
Treatment regimen	Enoxaparin (1 mg/kg every 12 hours) plus aspirin vs unfractionated heparin (adjusted to activated partial thromboplastin time) plus aspirin.
Results	Among patients who had initially developed Q wave myocardial infarctions enoxapin group had lower rate of death, myocardial infarction, or urgent revascularization (27%) vs the group that received unfractionated heparin (29%). There was no significant difference between groups in development of major bleeding but patients in the enoxaparin group had an increase in minor bleeding.

ESSENCE (Substudy)

Efficacy and Safety of Subcutaneous Enoxaparin in Non Q Wave Coronary Events

(continued)

Conclusions	Enoxaparin benefited patients who had developed Q wave myocardial infarction in the original ESSENCE study.

13. Preliminary Reports

c. Hypertension

LIFE STUDY

Losartan Intervention for Endpoint Reduction in Hypertension

Disease	Hypertension.
Purpose	To compare the effects of losartan and atenolol on cardiovascular mortality and morbidity in patients with hypertension.
Design	Randomized, triple blind, controlled.
Patients	8300 patients, aged 55–88 years, with hypertension and ECG documented LVH. Patients with prior myocardial infarction, heart failure, or stroke will be excluded.
Follow-up	4 years or more.
Treatment regimen	2 week placebo initiation period. Active therapy for 4 years. Randomization to losartan + placebo or placebo + atenolol in daily 50 mg doses. Hydrochlorothiazide and additional agents may be added to provide blood pressure control.

PRESERVE

Prospective Randomized Enalapril Study Evaluating Regression of Ventricular Enlargement

Reference	Am J Cardiol 1996;78:61-65.
Disease	Hypertension.
Purpose	To compare the efficacy of enalapril and nifedipine GITs to reduce left ventricular mass and to normalize the Doppler echocardiographic ratio of early to late mitral inflow flow velocities in hypertensive patients.
Design	Randomized, double blind, parallel group, multicenter.
Patients	480 patients, ≥50 years old, with ≥140 mm Hg systolic blood pressure if on anti-hypertensive therapy, or ≥150 systolic blood pressure if unmedicated, and/or ≥90 mm Hg diastolic blood pressure, and echocardiographic LV mass >116 g/m^2 in men and >104 g/m^2 in women. Patients with left ventricular ejection fraction <0.40 or evidence of severe valvular heart disease or coexisting cardiomyopathy will be excluded.
Follow-up	1 year with clinical follow-up and repeated echocardiogram at baseline, 6 and 12 months.
Treatment regimen	Enalapril 10-20 mg/d or nifedipine GITs 30-60 mg/d. In cases where maximum dose is reached and further blood pressure control is needed, hydrochlorothiazide 25 mg, and then atenolol 25 mg will be added.

AASK

African American Study of Kidney Disease

Reference	Journal of Controlled Clinical Trials, August 1996.
Disease	Hypertension, hypertensive nephrosclerosis.
Purpose	Evaluate the efficacy of different antihypertensive treatment regimens and different levels of blood pressure control in slowing the progression of renal artery disease in African American hypertensive patients with chronic renal insufficiency.
Design	Prospective, blinded, randomized, controlled study.
Patients	~ 1000 African American patients with hypertension and established renal insufficiency.
Follow-up	~ 5 years.
Treatment regimen	Amlodipine, ramipril, and metoprolol XL with 2 levels of blood pressure control on progression of hypertensive nephrosclerosis. One group will have goal mean arterial pressure (MAP) ≤92 mm Hg and the other group will have a MAP between 102–107 mm Hg. BP will also be treated to <160/90 mm Hg in all participants. There will be 3 drug regimens, each initiated by a different agent.
Remarks	End points include measurement of GFR (glomerular filtration rate) and end stage renal disease. The study is expected to be completed in 2001.

ABCD-2V

Appropriate Blood Pressure Control in Diabetes-Part 2 with Valsartan

Disease	Type 2 diabetes mellitus.
Purpose	To evaluate effects of intensive vs moderate blood pressure control on diabetic nephropathy in both hypertensive and normotensive patients with type 2 diabetes mellitus.
Design	Randomized, prospective, parallel group trial.
Patients	500 patients.
Follow-up	5 years.
Treatment regimen	Patients are divided into hypertensive and normotensive cohorts and randomized to intensive or moderate blood pressure control groups. Valsartan is the primary antihypertensive agent.
Results	Study began in 1998 and will conclude in 2003. Secondary end points include cardiovascular morbidity and mortality, diabetic retinopathy, and diabetic neuropathy.

ASCOT

Anglo-Scandinavian Cardiac Outcomes Trial

Authors	Dahlof B, et al.
Reference	Am J Hypertens 1998;11:9A–10A.
Disease	Hypertension.
Purpose	To compare the effects of atenolol based with amlodipine based therapy in hypertensive patients on the prevention of coronary heart disease and vascular events. To compare the effects of atorvastatin vs placebo in patients with a total cholesterol of <6.6 mmol/L on coronary and vascular events.
Design	Randomized, factorial study. The antihypertensive limb will be prospective, randomized, open blinded end points. The lipid lowering limb will be double blind, randomized.
Patients	18,000 patients, males or females, ages 40–79 years. Blood pressure must be ≥160/100 mm Hg at baseline untreated or ≥140/90 mm Hg treated. Patients must have at least 3 prespecified cardiovascular risk factors.
Follow-up	About 5 years.
Treatment regimen	1. In the hypertension limb: Patients randomized to ß-blocker (atenolol)±diuretic or calcium channel blocker (amlodipine)±ACE inhibitor. Doxazosin GITS (gastrointestinal therapeutic system) will be added to each limb if required. Target blood pressure reduction will be <140/90 mm Hg. 2. In the lipid lowering limb: Patients will be randomized to atorvastatin vs placebo.

ASCOT

Anglo-Scandinavian Cardiac Outcomes Trial

(continued)

Results — Primary end points will include nonfatal MI and fatal coronary heart disease. Secondary end points will include all cause mortality, stroke, heart failure, and all cardiovascular events. No results are available as yet.

VALUE

Valsartan Antihypertensive Long term Use Evaluation

Reference	Blood Press. 1998;7:176-83.
Disease	Hypertension.
Purpose	To compare the effects of amlodipine and valsartan on mortality and morbidity in hypertensive patients at high risk.
Design	Randomized, double blind, multicenter.
Patients	14,400 patients, ≥50 years old with hypertension and coronary artery disease or with risk factors for coronary artery disease.
Treatment regimen	Randomization to valsartan 80-160 mg/d, amlodipine 5-10 mg/d.
Follow-up	4 years.
Results	Not yet available.
Conclusions	Not yet available.

High Blood Pressure Care in Young Urban Black Men

Title	High Blood Pressure Care in Young Urban Black Men.
Authors	Hill MN,et al.
Reference	72nd Scientific Sessions of the American Heart Association in Atlanta, GA, in 1999.
Disease	Hypertension.
Purpose	To determine whether intensive strategy (multidisciplinary team of physician, nurse practitioner, community health worker, home visits, provision of transportation, social services referral) vs less intensive strategy (referred to source of care in the community) resulted in superior blood pressure control.
Design	Randomized, community based studies.
Patients	309 inner city African American men.
Follow-up	24 months.
Treatment regimen	Losartan (50/100 mg) with or without hydrochlorothiazide (12.5/25 mg) or other medicines if these were not tolerated. Antihypertensive medicines were provided for free.

High Blood Pressure Care in Young Urban Black Men

(continued)

Results	At 24 months, 39% had controlled blood pressure vs only 19% at baseline. Improvement in blood pressure control from baseline was significant in both groups at 12 and 24 months. For the intensive strategy mean systolic and diastolic blood pressures (in mm Hg) were 149.5/101.1 at baseline, 138.3/90.8 at 12 months, and 142.3/86.8 at 24 months. For the less intensively treated group mean blood pressure at baseline was 151.2/103.4, at 12 months it was 141.9/94.9, and at 24 months it was 143.2/90.0. Thus, blood pressure lowering was greater in the intensive therapy group.
Conclusions	A multidisciplinary program that includes community members and staff, with regular follow-up, can facilitate blood pressure lowering in a high risk group.

CONVINCE

Controlled Onset Verapamil INvestigation of Cardiovascular End points (CONVINCE) Trial

Title	Rationale and Design for the Controlled ONset Verapamil INvestigation of Cardiovascular End points (CONVICE) Trial.
Authors	Black HR, Elliott WJ, Neaton JD, et al.
Reference	Controll Clin Trials 1998;19:370-390.
Disease	Hypertension.
Purpose	To compare incidence of fatal or nonfatal myocardial infarction, fatal or nonfatal stroke, or cardiovascular disease related deaths in two antihypertensive protocols.
Design	Randomized, prospective, double blind, parallel group, controlled, multicenter.
Patients	To include 15,000 patients with hypertension, at least 55 years of age, with established second risk factor for cardiovascular disease.
Follow-up	5 years.

CONVINCE

Controlled Onset Verapamil INvestigation of Cardiovascular Endpoints (CONVINCE) Trial

(continued)

Treatment regimen	Controlled onset extended release (COER) verapamil (with major antihypertensive effect at 6–12 hours after administration): 180 mg daily as initial treatment vs standard of care arm consisting of hydrochlorothiazide (12.5 mg/day) or atenolol (50 mg/day) as initial therapy. If blood pressure does not reach goal of <140/<90 mm Hg initial doses are doubled. If BP still not controlled, hydrochlorothiazide is added to COER verapamil or the standard of care choice not initially selected is added to the standard care arm. The next step if blood pressure still is not controlled is addition of an ACE inhibitor. Patients take 2 sets of tablets daily, one in the morning and one in the evening.
Results	Study to be completed in the third quarter of 2002.

ABC ARII Blocker Trial

Association of Black Cardiologists Angiotensin Receptor II Blocker Trial

Title	Blood pressure control in African Americans: Is there a drug of choice?
Authors	Jamerson KA.
Reference	Symposium presented at the American Society of Hypertension Fourteenth Scientific Meeting, New York, May 1999.
Disease	Hypertension.
Purpose	To determine whether an angiotensin II receptor blocker effectively reduces blood pressure in black hypertensives.
Design	Randomized, placebo controlled, multicenter.
Patients	304 African Americans with hypertension.
Follow-up	12 weeks.
Treatment regimen	Candesartan 16 mg/day (n=156) vs placebo (n=148). At the end of 4 weeks dosage was doubled if diastolic blood pressure greater than 90 mm Hg. After 8 weeks hydrochlorothiazide added if diastolic pressure still greater than 90 mm Hg.

ABC ARII Blocker Trial

Association of Black Cardiologists Angiotensin Receptor II Blocker Trial

(continued)

Results	At 8 weeks diastolic blood pressure fell by 5.1 mm Hg with candesartan vs 2.7 mm Hg with placebo. About 61% had full or partial response to candesartan vs 41% of patients who received placebo. At 12 weeks, including combination with hydrochlorothiazide if needed, decrease in diastolic blood pressure from baseline was 7.5 mm Hg with candesartan and 5.2 mm Hg for placebo. At study end only 27.2% of patients on candesartan required the addition of hydrochlorothiazide vs half of the patients on placebo. Efficacy was somewhat less in blacks compared to previous reports of this agent in whites.
Conclusions	Candesartan was effective in 61% of African American hypertensive patients.

13. Preliminary Reports

d. Congestive Heart Failure

OPTIME-CHF

Outcomes of a Prospective Trial of IV Milrinone for Exacerbations of Chronic Heart Failure

Reference	Presented at the 49th American College of Cardiology Meetings, Anaheim, CA, March 2000.
Disease	Congestive heart failure
Purpose	To assess the efficacy of IV milrinone, in addition to medical therapy, in reducing hospitalizations for cardiovascular events within 60 days among patients hospitalized with an exacerbation of heart failure, but not requiring inotropic support or vasopressor therapy.
Design	Randomized, double blind, placebo controlled, multicenter.
Patients	949 patients, >18 years old, hospitalized for acute exacerbation of chronic congestive heart failure, with LVEF <40%. Patients requiring inotropic or vasopressor support, having active myocardial ischemia, or ischemia within 3 month prior to enrollment, systolic blood pressure <80 mm Hg or >150 mm Hg, sustained ventricular arrhythmia, atrial fibrillation with ventricular rate >110 bpm, and severe renal failure were excluded.
Follow-up	60 days.
Treatment regimen	Randomization within 48 h of admission to IV milrinone (n=477) 0.5 μg/kg/minutes without a loading dose, or placebo (n=472) for 48 hours.

OPTIME-CHF

Outcomes of a Prospective Trial of IV Milrinone for Exacerbations of Chronic Heart Failure

(continued)

Results

Preliminary data were presented by M Gheorghiade at the 49th American College of Cardiology meeting, Anaheim, CA, in March 2000. The mean age of the patients was 66 years and 65 years in the placebo and milrinone groups, 68% and 64% were males. The etiology of heart failure was ischemic in 51% of the patients and non-ischemic in 49% of the patients in both groups. Mean LVEF was 23% in both groups. The length of hospitalization was comparable between the placebo and milrinone groups (median 7.0 and 6.0 days; mean 12.5 and 12.3 days; $p=0.714$). Heart failure score was comparable between the groups at baseline, day 3 and at discharge. The percentage of patients achieving target ACE inhibitor dose at 48 hours and at discharge was similar. The milrinone group had more complications (12.6% vs 2.1%; $p<0.001$). Myocardial infarction occurred in 1.5% in the milrinone group vs 0.4% in the placebo group ($p=0.178$). Treatment failure or worsening of congestive heart failure occurred in 7.9% in the milrinone group vs 6.6% in the placebo group ($p=0.536$). Treatment related new atrial fibrillation occurred in 4.6% in the milrinone group vs 1.5% in the placebo group ($p=0.004$). Sustained hypotension was detected in 10.7% in the milrinone group vs 3.2% in the placebo group ($p<0.001$). In hospital mortality was 3.8% in the milrinone group vs 2.3% in the placebo group ($p=0.194$), whereas 60 day mortality was 10.3% and 8.9%, respectively. Subgroup analysis showed an insignificant trend in favor of milrinone in patients with nonischemic etiology of heart failure and in patients with hyponatremia at baseline.

Comments

Patients who are hospitalized because of exacerbation of chronic congestive heart failure but do not need inotropic or vasopressor support do not benefit from milrinone infusion. Patients with nonischemic cardiomyopathy and those with low sodium levels may benefit from milrinone infusion.

PRAISE-2

Prospective Randomized Amlodipine Survival Evaluation

Reference	Presented at the 49th American College of Cardiology Meetings, Anaheim, CA, March 2000.
Disease	Congestive heart failure
Purpose	To determine the effects of amlodipine on mortality in patients with severe heart failure of nonischemic etiology.
Design	Randomized, double blind, placebo controlled, multicenter.
Patients	1652 patients with chronic congestive heart failure due to nonischemic cardiomyopathy, LVEF <30%, NYHA Class IIIB or IV, despite therapy with diuretics, an ACE inhibitor and digoxin. Patients receiving calcium channel blockers, ß-blockers, or cardiodepressant antiarrhythmic drugs were excluded.
Follow-up	48 months.
Treatment regimen	Randomization to placebo (n=826) or amlodipine (n=826). Amlodipine was started at a dose of 5 mg/d and after 2 weeks the dose was increased to 10 mg/d.

Results Preliminary data were presented by M Packer at the 49th American College of Cardiology meeting, Anaheim, CA, in March 2000. Mean age was 58.5 years in the placebo group and 59.0 years in the amlodipine group. 66.5% and 66.2% of the patients, respectively were males. Mean LVEF was 21% in both groups and 80.8% and 79.9% of the patients, respectively, were in NYHA Class III. All cause mortality was 31.7% in the placebo and 33.7% in the amlodipine group (hazard ratio 1.09; 95% CI 0.92–1.29; p=0.32). Similarly, there was no difference in cardiac mortality between the groups. Subgroup analysis did not show a difference among the various subgroups of the study population (gender, age group, NYHA Class, LVEF). All cause mortality in the combined population of PRAISE-1 and PRAISE-2 studies was 34% in the placebo group vs 33.4% in the amlodipine group (hazard ratio 0.98; 95% CI 0.87–1.12; p=0.81).

Comments Long term treatment with amlodipine in addition to standard therapy with diuretics, digoxin, and ACE inhibitors did not affect mortality in patients with severe congestive heart failure of nonischemic etiology.

WASH

Warfarin/Aspirin Study of Heart Failure

Reference	Clin Cardiol 1999;22:753-756.
Disease	Heart failure.
Purpose	To compare the efficacy of aspirin, warfarin or no antithrombotic therapy in patients with congestive heart failure.
Design	Randomized, open label, blinded end point evaluation, multicenter.
Patients	279 patients with congestive heart failure (mostly NYHA Class II) and left ventricular dysfunction.
Treatment regimen	Randomization to aspirin 300 mg/d, warfarin (target INR 2.5), or no antithrombotic therapy.
Follow-up	A mean of 27 months.

Results	Preliminary results were presented at the 21st Congress of the European Society of Cardiology, Barcelona, Spain, by JGF Cleland. The primary end point of death, myocardial infarction, and stroke occurred in 26% in the warfarin group, 32% in the aspirin group, and 27% in the control group (p=NS). Mortality was 30%, 25%, and 21%, respectively. Acute myocardial infarction occurred in 3, 8, and 9 patients, respectively and stroke in 0, 2% and 2%, respectively. Death or cardiovascular hospitalization occurred in 16%, 23%, and 31% in the warfarin, aspirin, and control group, respectively. There were 5 vascular events in the warfarin group, 12 in the aspirin group, and 17 in the control group (p=0.041). The warfarin group had 200 fewer hospitalization days than the aspirin group. This could be attributed to more hospitalization for cardiovascular reasons (p=0.007) and heart failure (p=0.014) in the aspirin than the warfarin group. Scores of angina and breathlessness, NYHA Class, and the occurrence of atrial fibrillation were comparable among the groups. Serious adverse events were highest for aspirin and lowest for warfarin.
Conclusions	Among patients with congestive heart failure predominantly due to coronary artery disease, aspirin did not reduce morbidity, whereas warfarin reduced morbidity and hospitalization time and was associated with fewer serious adverse events.

LIDO

Levosimendan Infusion vs Dobutamine in Severe Congestive Heart Failure

Reference	Presented at the 21st Congress of the European Society of Cardiology, Barcelona, Spain, 1999.
Disease	Congestive heart failure.
Purpose	To compare the effects of levosimendan (a calcium sentisizer that adheres to troponin C and causes vasodilatation and increases contractility) to dobutamine in patients with severe heart failure.
Design	Randomized, double blind, multicenter.
Patients	203 patients with LVEF<35%, cardiac index <2.5 L/M^2/minutes, mean pulmonary capillary wedge pressure >15 mm Hg and severe heart failure despite oral medical therapy or acute heart failure.
Treatment regimen	Randomization to 24 hours infusion of either dobutamine (5 μg/kg/minutes; n=100) or levosimendan (24 μg/kg bolus followed by 0.1 μg/kg/minutes; n=103). Study drug infusion rate was increased if cardiac index was not improved.
Follow-up	180 days.

LIDO

Levosimendan Infusion vs Dobutamine in Severe Congestive Heart Failure

(continued)

Results	Preliminary results were presented at the 21st Congress of the European Society of Cardiology, Barcelona, Spain. 28% of the levosimendan group vs only 18% of the dobutamine group reached the primary efficacy end point of ≥30% increase in cardiac index and ≥25 mm Hg decrease in pulmonary capillary wedge pressure compared to baseline (p=0.022). Cardiac index increased by 31% with dobutamine and by 34% with levosimendan. Pulmonary capillary wedge pressure decreased by 16 mm Hg and 29 mm Hg in the dobutamine and levosimendan groups, respectively (p=0.001). 31-day mortality was 17.0% with dobutamine and 7.8% with levosimendan (p=0.42). Death or worsening of heart failure at 31 days occurred in 20% and 9.7%, respectively (p=0.037). 6 month mortality was lower in the levosimendan than in the dobutamine group (relative risk 0.57; 95% CI 0.34–0.95; p=0.029). Levosimendan was better tolerated than dobutamine.
Conclusions	Levosimendan was associated with lower mortality and worsening of heart failure at 31 days and lower mortality at 6 months than dobutamine. Levosimendan was associated with greater hemodynamic improvement than dobutamine.

COPERNICUS

CarvedilOL ProspEctive RaNdomIzed Cumulative Survival Trial

Disease	Congestive heart failure.
Purpose	To assess the effects of carvedilol on mortality in patients with severe chronic congestive heart failure.
Design	Randomized, double blind, placebo controlled, multicenter.
Patients	2200 patients, >18 years old, with chronic congestive heart failure.
Treatment regimen	Randomization to placebo or carvedilol (initial dose 3.125 mg bid. Dose increased gradually to 25 mg bid).
Follow-up	1.25-3.75 years.
Results	The study has been terminated recently because carvedilol showed a significant reduction of mortality. No details have yet been published.

MOXON

SR MOXonidine for CONgestive Heart Failure

Reference	Presented at the 21st Congress of the European Society of Cardiology, Barcelona, Spain, 1999.
Disease	Congestive heart failure.
Purpose	To evaluate the effects of slow release moxonidine (a drug that lowers plasma cathecholamine levels) in patients with congestive heart failure NYHA Class II-IV.
Design	Randomized, double blind, placebo controlled, multicenter.
Patients	1860 patients with congestive heart failure, NYHA Class II-IV.
Treatment regimen	Randomization to placebo or SR moxonidine (titrated from 0.25 mg bid to 1.5 mg bid).
Results	Preliminary results were presented at the 21st Congress of the European Society of Cardiology, Barcelona, Spain, by JN Cohn. The study was stopped early by the Data and Safety Monitoring Board because of higher mortality in the moxonidine arm. There were 53 deaths in the moxonidine group vs only 29 in the placebo group. The excess mortality in the moxonidine group was related to sudden death and was found at all doses of the drug. Acute myocardial infarction occurred in 17 patients in the moxonidine group vs 6 in the placebo group. More patients in the moxonidine group were hospitalized (72 vs 57 patients). Moxonidine reduced plasma norepinephrine levels.
Conclusions	SR moxonidine was associated with increased mortality in patients with congestive heart failure.

VAL-HeFT

The Valsartan Heart Failure Trial

Reference	J Card Fail 1999;5:155–160.
Disease	Congestive heart failure.
Purpose	To assess the efficacy of valsartan in patients with heart failure.
Design	Randomized, double blind, placebo controlled, multicenter.
Patients	5005 patients with NYHA Class II–IV congestive heart failure.
Treatment regimen	Randomization to placebo or valsartan.
Follow-up	Until 906 deaths have been recorded.
Results	Not yet available.
Conclusions	Not yet available.

IMAC

Intervention with Myocarditis and Acute Cardiomyopathy with IV Immunoglobulin

Title	Intervention in Myocarditis and Acute Cardiomyopathy with IV Immunoglobulin.
Reference	Presented at the 1999 Heart Failure Society of America Meetings.
Disease	Adult cardiomyopathy, heart failure.
Purpose	To determine the effect of immunotherapy on left ventricular function in patients with new onset cardiomyopathy.
Design	Randomized, placebo controlled.
Patients	61 patients with new onset cardiomyopathy. Patients had ejection fractions <40% at baseline.
Follow-up	2 years.
Treatment regimen	2 gm/kg IV IgG followed by 1 gm/kg of IV IgG on 2 sequential days vs placebo infusions.
Results	There was an increase in ejection fraction (mean increase over 15 ejection fraction units) in both groups. At 2 years, event free survival was 88%. There was no difference in event free survival between groups.
Conclusions	IV immunoglobulin did not improve clinical outcome or ejection fraction in patients with new onset cardiomyopathy. Both untreated and treated patients demonstrated overall improvements in left ventricular ejection fraction.

BEST

Beta blocker Evaluation of Survival Trial

Title	Beta blocker Evaluation of Survival Trial.
Authors	Eichhorn EJ, Domanshi M, et al.
Reference	Presented at the 72nd Scientific Sessions of the American Heart Association in Atlanta, GA, in 1999.
Disease	Congestive heart failure.
Purpose	To determine whether adding ß-blocker to standard therapy for heart failure can decrease mortality in patients with NYHA Classes III and IV CHF.
Design	Randomized, placebo controlled, multicenter.
Patients	2708 patients. 92% had Class III CHF; 8% were in Class IV CHF. Patients had LVEF <35% and were on ACE inhibitors.
Follow-up	Study terminated early. At least 12 months.
Treatment regimen	Bucindolol (initial dose of 3 mg twice a day titrated over 6–8 weeks to target of 50 mg twice a day for patients <75 kg and 100 mg twice a day for patients ≥75 kg, as tolerated) vs placebo.

Results	Primary end point was all cause mortality. There was a nonsignificant trend toward reduced death (by 10%) among patients receiving bucindolol (30.2%) vs placebo (33%; p=0.109). Cardiovascular death was reduced by 12.5% with bucindolol and patient hospitalization for congestive heart failure was decreased by 16.5%. Individual components of cardiovascular death (sudden death, heart failure death, death secondary to pump failure, death due to myocardial infarction) did not differ between groups. Black patients and patients with Class IV heart failure did not benefit from bucindolol. Nonblack patients with Class III heart failure had a trend toward better survival.
Conclusions	Bucindolol did not significantly impact all cause mortality rates in patients with severe heart failure.

IMPRESS

Inhibition of MetalloProteinase BMS-186716, Omipatrilat, in a Randomized Exercise and Symptom Study with Heart Failure

Title	Vasopeptidase inhibitor or angiotensin converting enzyme in heart failure? Results of the IMPRESS Trial.
Authors	Rouleau JL, Pfeffer MA, Stewart DJ, et al.
Reference	Presented at the American Heart Association, 72nd Scientific Session, Atlanta, GA, 1999.
Disease	Congestive heart failure.
Purpose	To test the vasopeptidase inhibitor, omapatrilat vs lisinopril in heart failure patients. Vasopeptidase inhibitors are a new class of drugs that inhibits both neural endopeptidases and ACE.
Design	Double blind, randomized, multicenter.
Patients	573 heart failure patients.
Follow-up	24 weeks.
Treatment regimen	Omapatrilat 40 mg vs lisinopril 20 mg.

IMPRESS

Inhibition of MetalloProteinase BMS-186716, Omipatrilat, in a Randomized Exercise and Symptom Study with Heart Failure

(continued)

Results	The primary end point of exercise tolerance improved in both groups. Omapatrilat was more effective than lisinopril in lowering the risk of combined end point of hospitalization, death, or discontinuation of therapy due to worsening heart failure. 45% fewer omapatrilat treated patients experienced this combined end point. About 35% more patients with severe heart failure treated with omapatrilat demonstrated improved clinical status. Marked elevations of creatinine and blood urea nitrogen were less common with omapatrilat. Both treatments were well tolerated.
Conclusions	Omapatrilat is a promising new drug for treating heart failure. Larger scale studies are underway to examine the long term effects of this agent vs ACE inhibitors.

13. Preliminary Reports

e. Prevention of Progression of Coronary Artery Disease

BANFF

Brachial Artery ultrasound Normalization of Forearm Flow

Title	A comparative study of 4 antihypertensive agents on endothelial function agents on endothelial function in patients with coronary disease. (Brachial Artery Ultrasound Normalization of Forearm Flow).
Author	Anderson TJ, et al.
Reference	47th Scientific Session of the American College of Cardiology, Atlanta, Georgia 1998.
Disease	Coronary artery disease.
Purpose	To compare the chronic effects of 4 antihypertensives on brachial artery flow mediated vasodilation in patients with documented coronary artery disease.
Design	Partial block, cross over design trial, and randomized in 1 of 4 different, open label drug sequences. High resolution ultrasound to compare flow mediated vasodilator and nitroglycerin dilation before and after 8 weeks of study drug.
Patients	80 patients with coronary artery disease.
Preliminary results	Of quinapril, enalapril, losartan, and amlodipine, only quinapril improved flow mediated dilatation.

PREVENT

Prospective Randomized Evaluation of the Vascular Effects of Norvasc Trial

Reference	1. Clin Cardiol 1999;22:47-49. 2. Circulation 1999;99:2486-2491. 3. Am J Hypertens 1999;12:42A. 4. J Am Coll Cardiol 1999;33:314A.
Disease	Coronary artery disease.
Purpose	To assess whether amlodipine will reduce the progression of new atherosclerotic lesions in the coronaries as measured by quantitative coronary angiography and secondarily in the carotids by B mode ultrasonography, and to examine the effect of amlodipine on the 3 year occurrence of cardiovascular events and procedures.
Design	Randomized, double blind, placebo controlled, multicenter.
Patients	825 patients with predefined angiographic evidence of CAD.
Follow-up	3 years. Patients underwent coronary angiography at the beginning and end of the trial (46% of patients had PTCA at time of entry). A subset of patients underwent B mode carotid artery ultrasound examination at baseline and at 6 month intervals.
Treatment regimen	Amlodipine up to 10 mg/d or placebo. Patients were treated for CAD as deemed necessary.

PREVENT

Prospective Randomized Evaluation of the Vascular Effects of Norvasc Trial

(continued)

Results Preliminary results were presented at the 71 st American Heart Association meeting, November, 1998, by C. Furberg. At the end of 3 years there was a significant progression in carotid wall thickness assessed by B mode ultrasonography (+0.0121 mm/year) in the placebo group and a trend toward regression in the amlodipine group (-0.0024 mm/year). Amlodipine did not alter quantitative coronary angiography. Nonfatal vascular events (hospitalization for congestive heart failure or unstable angina) were reduced by 35% (p=0.02, 95%CI=0.47-0.91) and the need for revascularization (CABG and PTCA) was reduced by 46% (p=0.001, 95% CI=0.39-0.77) in the amlodipine group. Major vascular events, including fatal/nonfatal MI, fatal/nonfatal stroke, and other vascular events were not significantly reduced by amlodipine (hazard ratio of 0.82, 95% CI=0.47-1.42, p=NS). A composite end point of all of the end points described above (composite cardiovascular morbidity and mortality) was reduced by 31% in the amlodipine group (p=0.01, 95% CI=0.52-0.92).

Conclusions In patients with known coronary artery disease, amlodipine demonstrated a significant trend toward regression in carotid wall thickness vs placebo but no effect on quantitative coronary angiography. Amlodipine reduced hospitalizations for congestive heart failure and unstable angina and reduced the need for revascularization.

SCAT

The Simvastatin/Enalapril Coronary Atherosclerosis Trial

Reference	Presented at the 48th Annual Scientific Session of the American College of Cardiology, March 1999.
Disease	Coronary artery disease.
Purpose	To evaluate the effect of simvastatin and enalapril on progression and regression of coronary atherosclerosis.
Design	Randomized, placebo controlled, multicenter.
Patients	460 patients, mean age 61±9 years, 89% men, with coronary artery disease and normal serum cholesterol levels.
Treatment regimen	Randomization to simvastatin + enalapril (S+E) (n=112); simvastatin + placebo (S) (n=118); placebo + enalapril (E) (n=117); and placebo + placebo (P) (n=113). The simvastatin dose was up to 40 mg/d, and the enalapril dose was up to 10 mg bid.
Follow-up	Mean follow-up 48 months.

SCAT

The Simvastatin/Enalapril Coronary Atherosclerosis Trial

(continued)

Results	10% of the patients had diabetes, 54% had angina pectoris, 70% had previous myocardial infarction, and 35% had hypertension. The combination of enalapril and simvastatin was safe. There were no differences in total mortality, myocardial infarction rate, and stroke rate among the groups. Repeated angiography revealed that in the simvastatin-treated patients there was less decrease in vessel diameter than in the placebo treated patients (p=0.006). Simvastatin slowed the progression of atherosclerosis, whereas enalapril had no effect on progression of atherosclerosis. Progression occurred in 3.7% of the lesions in the placebo group and in 1.6% of the lesions in the simvastatin group (p=0.0004). There was no difference in the percentage of lesions that progressed between the enalapril and placebo treated patients. The simvastatin-treated patients had less revascularization than the placebo treated patients did.
Conclusions	Long term simvastatin therapy slowed the rate of progression of atherosclerosis in patients with normal cholesterol levels. Enalapril had no effect on the progression of atherosclerosis.

QUO VADIS

Effects of Quinapril On Vascular ACE and Determinants of Ischemia

Reference	Circulation 1999;99:2486–2491.
Disease	Coronary artery disease, CABG.
Purpose	To assess the effects of long term quinapril (an ACE inhibitor) in patients before and after CABG.
Design	Randomized, placebo controlled, multicenter.
Patients	149 patients undergoing elective CABG.
Treatment regimen	Randomization 27±1 days before CABG to placebo or quinapril 40 mg/d. Study medication was continued for 1 year.
Follow-up	Exercise testing at baseline and after 1 year. 48 hours Holter monitoring at 1 year.
Results	Preliminary results concerning 30 day outcome were presented at the 71st American Heart Association meeting, November, 1998, by W van Gilst. The quinapril group had an insignificant longer exercise time at 1 year compared with the placebo. The frequencies of ischemic ST changes with exercise were comparable in the two groups. Clinical ischemic events occurred in 4% of the quinapril vs 18% of the placebo group (odds ratio 0.2; 95% CI 0.04–0.96; p=0.03). There was an insignificant trend toward less ischemic ST segment changes on Holter monitoring in the quinapril group.
Conclusions	Quinapril, started 3 weeks before elective CABG and continued for 1 year was associated with a decrease in ischemic events, but was ineffective in prolongation of exercise time or amelioration of the ischemic response to exercise.

CAMELOT

Comparison of Amlodipine vs Enalapril to Limit Occurrences of Thrombosis

NORMALISE

Norvasc for Regression of Manifest Atherosclerotic Lesions by Intravascular Sonagraphic Evaluation

Disease	Coronary artery disease.
Purpose	To evaluate the effectiveness of amlodipine vs enalapril or placebo in preventing clinical events in a population of patients with known coronary artery disease. To determine the correlation between blood pressure and the incidence of clinical events in a population of patients with known coronary artery disease.
Design	Multicenter, randomized, double blind, placebo controlled trial. This includes a substudy entitled Norvasc for Regression of Manifest Atherosclerotic Lesions by Intravascular Sonographic Evaluation (NORMALISE).
Patients	3000 patients. 2,250 randomized patients without intravascular ultrasound (IVUS); 750 randomized patients with IVUS. Patients will be male or female, 30-75 years, in whom coronary angiography is clinically indicated. There must be at least one segment of a native coronary artery that has >20% decrease in lumen diameter by angiography. Patients must have stable coronary artery disease.
Follow-up	24 months.

CAMELOT

Comparison of Amlodipine vs Enalapril to Limit Occurrences of Thrombosis

NORMALISE

Norvasc for Regression of Manifest Atherosclerotic Lesions by Intravascular Sonagraphic Evaluation

(continued)

Treatment regimen	Patients will be randomized to amlodipine 5–10 mg, enalapril 10–20 mg, or placebo daily. Patients will be followed over 24 months for the occurrence of cardiovascular events. Primary end points will be the combined incidence of major adverse cardiovascular events that occur in patients treated with amlodipine versus enalapril vs placebo. The major adverse cardiovascular events include: cardiovascular death, nonfatal myocardial infarction, resuscitated cardiac arrest, need for coronary revascularization, hospitalization for angina pectoris, hospitalization for congestive heart failure, stroke or transient ischemic attacks, new diagnosis of peripheral vascular disease or admission for a procedure to treat peripheral vascular disease. Secondary end points–death from any cause, the influence of amlodipine on requirements for revascularization in vessels that have undergone stent placement. The primary end point for the NORMALISE Substudy is the percent change (end of treatment minus baseline) in total plaque area for all slices of anatomically comparable segments of the target coronary artery.
Results	The study is ongoing at this point; results not yet available.

ERA

Estrogen Replacement and Atherosclerosis trial

Reference	Presented at the 49th American College of Cardiology Meetings, Anaheim, CA, March 2000.
Disease	Atherosclerosis, coronary artery disease, postmenopausal women
Purpose	To assess the effects of estrogen replacement therapy on progression of atherosclerosis in postmenopausal women with coronary artery disease.
Design	Randomized, double blind, placebo controlled, multicenter.
Patients	309 postmenopausal women, 55–80 years old (mean 65.8 years), with ≥30% coronary artery stenosis in ≥1 coronary artery, LDL cholesterol 100–250 mg/dL.
Follow-up	Coronary angiography at baseline and after 3.2 years.
Treatment regimen	Randomization to estrogen alone (conjugated equine estrogen 0.625 mg/d; n=100), estrogen + progesterone (medroxyprogesterone acetate 2.5 mg/d; n=104), or placebo (n=105).

Results

D Herrington presented preliminary results at the 49th American College of Cardiology meeting, Anaheim, CA, in March 2000. At follow-up, LDL cholesterol decreased by 10% in the estrogen group, 17% in the estrogen + progesterone group, and by only 2% in the placebo group. HDL cholesterol increased by 12% in the estrogen group, 17% in the estrogen + progesterone group and by only 6% in the placebo group. Triglycerides increased by 6% and 10% in the estrogen and estrogen + progesterone group, whereas there was only a negligible rise in the placebo group. Mean minimum luminal diameter at follow-up was 1.872 mm in the placebo group, 1.865 mm in the estrogen group (p=NS, compared with placebo), and 1.839 mm in the estrogen + progesterone group (p=NS, compared to placebo). There was no difference among the three groups in progression of coronary artery disease, or in the development of new coronary lesions. Mortality related to coronary heart disease was 3% in the placebo group, 4% in the estrogen group and 2% in the estrogen + progesterone group (p=0.65). Myocardial infarction occurred in 7%, 6% and 6%, respectively (p=1.0), and total mortality was 6%, 8%, and 3%, respectively (p=0.28). A subgroup analysis looking only at the women who complied with treatment showed no differences among the three groups.

Conclusions

Estrogen alone or with combination with progesterone did not prevent disease progression in post menopausal women with coronary artery disease.

ISAR

Intracoronary Stenting and Antibiotic Regimen

Reference	Presented at the 49th American College of Cardiology Meetings, Anaheim, CA, March 2000.
Disease	Coronary artery disease
Purpose	To assess whether antibiotic treatment with roxithromycin will affect restenosis and clinical outcomes after intracoronary stent implantation.
Design	Randomized, double blind, placebo controlled.
Patients	1000 patients (mean age 65 years) undergoing successful stent implantation. Patients with contraindications to roxithromycin or a need for antibiotic therapy were excluded.
Follow-up	One year clinical follow-up, repeated coronary angiography at 6 months.
Treatment regimen	Immediately after successful stent implantation patients were randomized to roxithromycin 300 mg/d or placebo. Treatment was continued for 28 days.
Results	Preliminary data were presented by F-J Newmann at the 49th American College of Cardiology meeting, Anaheim, CA, in March 2000. Compliance was >90% in both groups. >80% of the patients underwent angiographic follow-up. Restenosis occurred in 31.5% in the roxithromycin vs 29.3% in the placebo group (p=NS). Target vessel revascularization occurred in 21% in the roxithromycin vs 18.9% in the placebo (p=NS). The rates of major adverse cardiac events at 30 days were comparable (3.2% vs 2.8% in the roxithromycin and placebo group, respectively). Survival at 8 months was comparable.

ISAR

Intracoronary Stenting and Antibiotic Regimen

(continued)

Comments	Roxithromycin 300 mg/d for 4 weeks did not affect early and late angiographic results and clinical outcomes after coronary artery stenting.

SECURE

Study to Evaluate Carotid Ultrasound Changes in Patients Treated with Ramipril and Vitamin E

Title	Results of the study to Evaluate Carotid Ultrasound Changes in Patients Treated with Ramipril and Vitamin E.
Authors	Lonn EM,et al.
Reference	Presented at Annual Scientific Sessions of the American Heart Association in Atlanta, GA, in 1999.
Disease	Atherosclerosis.
Purpose	To determine the effects of ramipril and vitamin E on atherosclerosis progression, assessed by ultrasound of the carotid artery.
Design	Randomized, placebo controlled, double blind. A substudy of HOPE trial.
Patients	Over 700 patients.
Treatment regimen	Low dose ramipril (2.5 mg); high dose ramipril (10 mg); placebo. In vitamin E arm patients received 400 IU vitamin E vs placebo.
Results	The composite end point of myocardial infarction, stroke, or death tended towards being lower with ramipril. Ramipril decreased the progression of carotid atherosclerosis measured as intimal-medial thickness by ultrasound. Mean maximal intimal-medial thickness slope over time was 0.014 mm for 10 mg ramipril vs 0.022 mm for placebo (p=0.028). Vitamin E had no effect on progression of carotid intimal medial thickness over time.

SECURE

Study to Evaluate Carotid Ultrasound Changes in Patients Treated with Ramipril and Vitamin E

(continued)

Conclusions	Similar to the HOPE trial, ramipril but not vitamin E reduced cardiovascular events. Ramipril also prevented progress of carotid atherosclerosis.

MARISA

Monotherapy Assessment of Ranolazine in Stable Angina.

Title	Monotherapy Assessment of Ranolazine in Stable Angina.
Authors	Pepine CJ, Parker JO, et al.
Reference	Cardiology Today 1999;September:5.
Disease	Angina pectoris, coronary artery disease.
Purpose	To determine whether ranolazine, a partial fatty acid oxidation inhibitor, could increase treadmill exercise time in patients with chronic, stable, angina pectoris.
Design	Randomized, double blind, placebo controlled.
Patients	175 patients with stable angina pectoris, not on other anti-anginal drugs.
Follow-up	Acute.
Treatment regimen	Ranolazine 500 mg, 1000 mg, and 1500 mg twice daily.
Results	Ranolazine significantly increased exercise duration. Exercise duration at peak (4 hours after dosing) in placebo was 504 seconds vs 532, 555, and 561 seconds in the 500 mg, 1000 mg, and 1500 mg groups, respectively ($p<0.001$ for each). Exercise duration at trough was also greater in the treated group. Exercise time to onset of angina and exercise time to 1 mm ST segment depression on the ECG were also increased with ranolazine at all 3 doses compared to placebo. In earlier studies it was shown that ranolazine had these benefits without decreasing heart rate or blood pressure. Heart rate and blood pressure analysis for this study are underway.

Conclusions	Ranolazine, a partial fatty acid oxidation inhibitor, significantly improved exercise duration in patients with stable angina pectoris.

13. Preliminary Reports

f. Arrhythmia

ALIVE

The Azimilide Post-Infarct Survival Evaluation

Reference	Am J Cardiol 1998;81:35D–39D.
Disease	Arrhythmia.
Purpose	To assess the effects of azimilide dihydrochloride, a novel type of antiarrhythmic agent that blocks both the rapid (I_{Kr}) and slow (I_{Ks}) components of the delayed rectifier K+ currents, on survival of patients after myocardial infarction who are at high risk for sudden cardiac death.
Design	Randomized, double blind, placebo controlled, multicenter.
Patients	Will enroll 5900 patients, 18–75 years old, who had a recent (within 6–21 days) acute myocardial infarction, with left ventricular ejection fraction 15–35%, and a low heart rate variability. Patients with a history of torsade de pointes; ventricular tachycardia; decompensated congestive heart failure at the time of enrollment or chronic NYHA class IV; unstable angina; syncope or aborted sudden death after the qualifying myocardial infarction; severe valvular disease; AV block or bradycardia; scheduled for revascularization; AICD; long QTc; stroke; Wolff-Parkinson-White syndrome; concomitant severe illness; renal or hepatic failure; uncontrolled hypertension; prior amiodarone therapy; on current antiarrhythmic therapy or are alcohol or drug abusers will be excluded.
Follow-up	1 year.
Treatment regimen	Randomization to: 1. azimilide 75 mg/d; 2. azimilide 100 mg/d; and 3. placebo.
Remarks	Results are not available yet.

EMERALD

European and Australian Multicenter Evaluative Research on Atrial Fibrillation Dofetilide

Reference	Circulation 1999;99:2486-2491.
Disease	Atrial fibrillation.
Purpose	To evaluate the efficacy of dofetilide, a class III antiarrhythmic agent, in converting atrial fibrillation and maintaining sinus rhythm.
Design	Randomized, placebo controlled, 2 phase study.
Patients	Patients with atrial fibrillation or flutter.
Treatment regimen	Phase 1: randomization to placebo, sotalol 80 mg bid, or dofetilide 125, 250 or 500 μg bid for 72 hours. Phase 2. Patients who revert to sinus rhythm by drugs or after cardioversion in phase 1 continued with their study medications for up to 2 years.
Follow-up	Phase 1: 1 week. Phase 2: 2 years.
Results	Preliminary results concerning 30-day outcome were presented at the 71st American Heart Association meeting, November, 1998, by R A Greenbaum. Phase 1: 6% of the dofetilide 125 μg bid, 11% of the dofetilide 250 μg bid, 29% of the dofetilide 500 μg bid, and 5% of the sotalol group reverted to sinus. Most of the remaining patients were DC cardioverted to sinus. Phase 2: After one year, 79% of the placebo, 34% of the dofetilide 500 μg bid, 48% of the dofetilide 250 μg bid, and 60% of the dofetilide 125 μg bid had recurrence of atrial fibrillation. There were 3 episodes of torsade de pointes and one episode of out-of-hospital sudden cardiac death in the dofetilide 500 μg bid group.

Conclusions	Dofetilide is efficient in converting patients with atrial fibrillation to sinus and maintaining sinus rhythm. However, at high doses there may be a proarrhythmic effect in some patients.

BLOSS

ß-Blockers Length of Stay

Reference	Presented at the 49th American College of Cardiology Meetings, Anaheim, CA, March 2000.
Disease	Atrial fibrillation, cardiac surgery.
Purpose	To evaluate whether prophylactic metoprolol therapy will reduce the incidence of atrial fibrillation and will be associated with shortened hospitalization period in patients after cardiac surgery.
Design	Randomized, single center.
Patients	1306 patients scheduled for elective cardiac surgery, without contraindications to beta blockers and without chronic atrial fibrillation. Patients with heart rate <50 bpm, cardiac index <2.3, bronchospasm and need for inotropic support after surgery were not included.
Follow-up	Hospital stay.
Treatment regimen	Within 12 hours after heart surgery patients were randomized to metoprolol or placebo. Metoprolol dose was 50 mg X 2-3/d (as long as cardiac index was >2.7). Therapy was continued until discharge or for 14 days.

BLOSS

ß-Blockers Length of Stay

(continued)

Results

SJ Connolly presented preliminary results at the 49th American College of Cardiology meeting, Anaheim, CA, in March 2000. Of the 3114 patients that underwent cardiac surgery, 1490 met the inclusion criteria, 1306 patients consented. 306 patients were further excluded and 1000 were included, 500 patients in each group. Atrial fibrillation was noted in 39% in the placebo group vs 31% in the metoprolol group (20% reduction; p=0.0098). However, duration of hospitalization in ICU was not shortened by metoprolol (34±24 hours in the placebo group vs 39±54 hours in the metoprolol group; p=0.10). Similarly, there was no difference in total hospitalization length (152±61 hours vs 155±90 hours, respectively; p=0.79). Stroke occurred in 0.6% in the placebo group and in 1.6% in the metoprolol group, myocardial infarction in 1% vs 2%, and ventricular tachycardia or fibrillation in 1.4% vs 0.4%, respectively. Multivariate regression analysis showed that age (odds ratio 2.18; 95% CI 1.86–2.55; p<0.0001), a prior history of atrial fibrillation (odds ratio 7.23; p<0.0001), type of surgery (odds ratio 1.88; p=0.0028) and metoprolol (odds ratio 0.61; 95% CI 0.46–0.81; p<0.0006) were independent predictors of postoperative atrial fibrillation.

Conclusions

Prophylactic therapy with metoprolol reduced the risk of postoperative atrial fibrillation in patients undergoing elective cardiac surgery. However, metoprolol was not associated with shortening of hospitalization length.

ACUTE 1

Assessment of Cardioversion Using Transesophageal Echocardiography

Reference	Presented at the 49th American College of Cardiology Meetings, Anaheim, CA, March 2000.
Disease	Atrial fibrillation.
Purpose	To compare the strategy of transesophageal echocardiography (TEE) guided with short term anticoagulation to conventional 3 week anticoagulation prior to cardioversion of atrial fibrillation.
Design	Randomized, open label.
Patients	1222 patients, >18 years old (mean age 65 years), with atrial fibrillation/flutter for >48 hours who are eligible for cardioversion. Patients with >7 days anticoagulation; hemodynamic instability and contraindications to TEE or anticoagulation were excluded.
Follow-up	8 weeks.
Treatment regimen	Randomization to the conventional strategy (3 weeks of oral anticoagulation prior to cardioversion; n=603) or to TEE guided strategy (n=619). In the TEE guided arm patients received immediate anticoagulation, underwent TEE, and if no left atrial thrombus was detected, underwent cardioversion. All patients received oral anticoagulation for 4 weeks after cardioversion.

Assessment of Cardioversion Using Transesophageal Echocardiography

(continued)

Results

Preliminary data were presented by A Klein at the 49th American College of Cardiology meeting, Anaheim, CA, in March 2000. The study was terminated prematurely by the Data and Safety Monitoring Board. Among the 619 patients assigned to the TEE guided strategy, 68 patients did not undergo TEE, mainly due to spontaneous conversion to sinus (n=31). 551 patients underwent TEE. In 71 patients a thrombus was detected and in an additional 31 patients spontaneous conversion occurred. Cardioversion was performed in 427 patients and was successful in conversion to sinus rhythm in 344 patients. Of the 603 patients assigned to the conventional strategy, 124 had spontaneous conversion to sinus rhythm, the INR was not therapeutic in 24, and 24 patients were lost to follow-up. A total of 367 patients underwent cardioversion, which was successful in 293 patients. The primary end point of stroke, TIA or peripheral embolism occurred in 0.5% in the conventional strategy vs 0.81% in the TEE guided strategy (p=0.501). Bleeding occurred more often in the conventional strategy group (5.5% vs 3.1%; p=0.025). Major bleedings occurred in 1.5% in the conventional strategy vs 0.81% in the TEE guided strategy (p=0.261), whereas minor bleedings occurred in 4% and 2.3% (p=0.084). Total mortality was 1% vs 2.42% in the conventional strategy and TEE guided strategy group (p=0.055), and cardiac mortality was 0.66% vs 1.29% (p=0.265). At 8 weeks 50.4% in the conventional strategy vs 52.7% in the TEE guided strategy were in sinus rhythm (p=0.431).

Comments

The TEE guided strategy allows for early cardioversion but did not reduce the risk of embolic events, or caused improvement in immediate or 8 week functional capacity or sinus rhythm. However, the TEE guided strategy was associated with lower risk of bleeding. TEE guided strategy can be used safely to perform early cardioversion in patients with atrial fibrillation.

ASAP

Azimilide Supraventricular Arrhythmia Program

Title	Azimilide Supraventricular Arrhythmia Program.
Authors	Pritchett ELC, et al.
Reference	Presented at the 72nd Scientific Sessions of the American Heart Association in Atlanta, GA, in 1999.
Disease	Atrial fibrillation, atrial flutter, paroxysmal supraventricular tachycardia.
Purpose	To determine the efficacy of azimilide to keep patients with the above atrial arrhythmias in sinus rhythm.
Design	Randomized, placebo controlled.
Patients	462 patients, mean age 63, with atrial fibrillation-flutter (n=402) or paroxysmal supraventricular tachycardia (n=60) who were in sinus rhythm at time first dose of drug given.
Follow-up	Time to first ECG documented symptomatic recurrence of atrial arrhythmia.
Treatment regimen	Azimilide (125 mg daily) or placebo.
Results	Primary outcome was first ECG documented episode of symptomatic recurrence of atrial fibrillation, flutter, or paroxysmal supraventricular tachycardia. Median time to end point was about 38 days with azimilide vs 27 days with placebo which was not statistically significantly different.

Conclusions	Unlike previous studies, azimilide did not significantly lengthen the atrial arrhythmia free period.

13. Preliminary Reports

g. Interventional Cardiology

ASCENT

ACS Multilink Clinical Equivalence Trial

Reference	Clin Cardiol 1997;20:1030–1031.
Disease	Coronary artery disease.
Purpose	To compare the ACS Multilink stent with Palmaz-Schatz stent.
Design	Randomized.
Patients	1040 patients with de novo coronary artery lesions. 538 patients were assigned to repeated angiography at 6 months.
Follow-up	6 months.
Treatment regimen	Randomization to 15 mm ACS or Palmaz-Schatz stents.
Remarks	Preliminary data were presented at the XIX congress of the European Society of Cardiology, Stockholm, Sweden, 1997. Successful stent delivery was obtained in 95.8% of the Palmaz-Schatz assigned patients and in 97.5% of the ACS assigned group. Immediately post procedure residual stenosis was 8% in the ACS vs 10% in the Palmaz-Schatz group. There was a trend towards less major events (death, myocardial infarction, or target vessel revascularization) at 30 days in the ACS group (4.4% vs 6.5%). #0-day mortality was 0 in the ACS vs 1.2% in the Palmaz-Schatz group. Restenosis rates were comparable. Cumulative rates at 6 months of target vessel failure or need for revascularization were comparable (16.5% vs 18.3%, respectively). Mortality was higher in the Palmaz-Schatz group (3.1% vs 1.5%). The data shows that the ACS stent is equivalent or superior to the Palmaz-Schatz stent in treatment of de novo coronary lesions.

REST

Stent Implantation and Restenosis Study

Reference	Clin Cardiol 1997;20:1030–1031.
Disease	Coronary artery disease, restenosis.
Purpose	To compare stenting vs conventional PTCA for restenosis after PTCA.
Design	Randomized.
Patients	400 patients with restenosis after initially successful PTCA.
Follow-up	Coronary angiography at baseline and after 6 months. Clinical follow-up for 6 months.
Treatment regimen	PTCA with or without 15 mm Palmaz-Schatz stent implantation. Intravenous heparin during procedure and aspirin and coumadin for 3 months for the patients who underwent stent implantation. The PTCA assigned group received aspirin 100 mg/d.

REST

Stent Implantation and Restenosis Study

(continued)

Remarks

Data were presented at the XIX congress of the European Society of Cardiology, Stockholm, Sweden, 1997. Procedure was technically successful in 98.9% of the stent group vs only 93.2% of the PTCA alone group. Of the PTCA assigned group, 12 patients crossed over to bailout stenting. Mortality was similar (2 patients in each group). Q wave myocardial infarction occurred more frequently in the stent group (2.8%) than in the PTCA group (0.6%)(p=NS). Thrombotic complications (3.9% vs 0) and bleeding (6.3% vs 1.4%) were more prevalent in the stent group. Hospitalization was longer in the stent group. Post procedure minimum lumen diameter was larger for the stent group (3.02 mm) than the PTCA group (2.23 mm). Minimum lumen diameter at 6 months was 2.23 mm in the stent group vs 1.85 mm for the PTCA group (p=0.01). Restenosis at 6 months occurred in 18% of the stent group vs 32% of the PTCA group. 10% of the stent group vs 24% of the PTCA group underwent repeated revascularization procedures. The anticoagulation regimen was associated with increased risk of bleeding and thrombotic events. Stenting restenotic coronary lesions was associated with better technical success, larger post procedure and 6 months minimum lumen diameter, less restenosis, and less need for revascularization.

OPUS

Optimal angioplasty and primary stenting

Title	Optimal angioplasty and primary stenting.
Reference	Presented at the American College of Cardiology Scientific Sessions, March 1999, New Orleans.
Disease	Coronary artery disease.
Purpose	To determine the effects of primary stenting vs PTCA with provisional stenting in patients with coronary artery disease.
Design	Randomized, multicenter.
Patients	479 patients with coronary artery disease and lesions <20 mm.
Follow-up	6 months.
Treatment regimen	Primary stenting vs PTCA with provisional stenting.
Results	Post procedure residual stenosis was less in the primary stent group (1%) vs the PTCA group (9%). Of patients initially randomized to PTCA, 37% crossed over into the stent group. At 6 months the composite end point of death, MI, and target revascularization was 4% in the primary stent group vs 14.9% in the PTCA group ($p<0.003$).
Conclusions	Primary stenting was superior to PTCA in this group of patients.

CLASSICS

Clopidogrel Aspirin Stent Interventional Cooperative Study

Title	Clopidogrel Aspirin Stent Interventional Cooperative Study.
Authors	Bertrand ME, et al.
Reference	Presented at the American College of Cardiology 48th Annual Scientific Sessions. March 7-10, New Orleans, 1999.
Disease	Coronary artery disease.
Purpose	To compare clopidogrel/aspirin vs ticlopidine/aspirin in patients undergoing intracoronary stent procedures.
Design	Randomized, multicenter.
Patients	Patients undergoing coronary stenting.
Treatment regimen	Loading dose of clopidogrel (300 mg) and then clopidogrel (75 mg once daily) from days 2-28 (n=345); clopidogrel 75 mg daily for 28 days (n=375); or ticlopidine (250 mg daily) for 28 days.
Additional therapy	Daily aspirin.
Results	There was a decrease in rate of adverse events in the clopidogrel group (4.56%) vs ticlopidine group (9.12%). Discontinuations of ticlopidine included gastrointestinal side effects, rash, allergic reactions. The composite end point of death, MI target revascularization was 0.9% in the ticlopidine group and 1.2% in the clopidogrel group (with loading) and 1.5% in the clopidogrel group without loading (p=NS).

Clopidogrel Aspirin Stent Interventional Cooperative Study

(continued)

Conclusions	Clopidogrel plus aspirin were associated with lower adverse events rates compared to ticlopidine plus aspirin.

TRAPIST

Trapidil for in-stent restenosis

Reference	1. Eur Heart J 1999;20:7–10. 2. Am Heart J 1999;137:555–574.
Disease	Coronary artery disease, restenosis.
Purpose	To assess the efficacy of trapidil, an inhibitor of cell proliferation induced by platelet derived growth factor (PDGF) in cell culture, to prevent in-stent restenosis.
Design	Randomized, placebo controlled, multicenter.
Patients	312 patients with single lesion de-novo lesions in native coronary arteries suitable for stent implantation. 75% of the patients were men, 45% had previous myocardial infarction, 25% had previous revascularization, 57% had stable angina, and 35% had unstable angina.
Follow-up	6 months.
Treatment regimen	Trapidil 200 mg tid, or placebo.
Results	Results were presented at the 20th Congress of the European Society of Cardiology, Aug 1998 by P. Serruys. Drug safety was good. At follow-up the mean diameter stenosis was 43% in the trapidil group vs 40% in the placebo group, and the mean lumen diameter was 1.63 mm vs 1.74 mm in the trapidil and placebo group. In-stent restenosis occurred in 31% of the trapidil group vs 24% in the placebo group. Intracoronary ultrasound study at 6 months did not show differences between the 2 groups.
Conclusions	Trapidil did not prevent restenosis in patients who underwent intracoronary stent implantation.

NICOLE study

Nisoldipine in coronary artery disease in Leuven

Reference	Eur Heart J 1999;20:7-10.
Disease	Coronary artery disease, restenosis.
Purpose	To investigate whether nisoldipine, a dihydropyridine calcium antagonist, will prevent restenosis after PTCA.
Design	Randomized, placebo controlled, multicenter.
Patients	646 patients who underwent PTCA.
Treatment regimen	Nisoldipine 40 mg/d or placebo.
Results	Results were presented at the 20th Congress of the European Society of Cardiology, Aug 1998 by J. Dens. Angiographic restenosis was observed in 55% of the placebo assigned patients and in 49% of the nisoldipine group (p=NS). Quantitative coronary angiographic analysis did not reveal differences between the groups.
Conclusions	Nisoldipine did not prevent restenosis following PTCA.

OPTICUS

Optimization With Intracoronary Ultrasound to Reduce Stent Restenosis

Reference	Am Heart J 1999;137:555–574.
Disease	Coronary artery disease, stent, restenosis.
Purpose	To assess whether intracoronary ultrasound (IVUS) guided stenting will reduce the rates of restenosis compared with angiographic guided stenting.
Design	Randomized, multicenter.
Patients	550 patients with stable or unstable angina, lesion length of ≤25 mm that was able to be covered with ≤2 stents, and reference vessel diameter of ≥2.5 mm. Patients with Braunwald angina class 3A to 3C, significant left main stenosis, bifrucational lesions, or a >60° bend were excluded.
Treatment regimen	Randomization to IVUS guided or angiographic guided stenting. All patients received aspirin and ticlopidine for 4 weeks. Either Palmaz-Schatz or NIR stents were used.

OPTICUS

Optimization With Intracoronary Ultrasound to Reduce Stent Restenosis

(continued)

Results	Preliminary results were presented at the 71st American Heart Association meeting, by H. Mudra November, 1998. Only 69% of the IVUS assigned patients underwent predilatation IVUS, and in only 59% of these patients IVUS was used for balloon sizing. The restenosis rate was 22.8% in the angiographic guided group and 24.5% in the IVUS-guided group. The lumen loss index was 0.54 in both groups. The 30 day cardiac event rate was 3.6% in the IVUS group vs 6.5% in the no IVUS group (p=NS). Re-PTCA was performed less often in the IVUS group (p<0.05). Overall, survival curves for freedom from target-vessel failure overlapped. However, when patients with IVUS optimal results were compared with patients who underwent angiographic guided stenting, the event free survival was better with IVUS guidance.
Conclusions	IVUS did not reduce the rates of restenosis after stent deployment. However, IVUS guided stenting was used in less than 2/3 of the IVUS assigned patients.

PACIFIC trial

Potential Angina Class Improvement From Intramyocardial Channels

Reference	Am Heart J 1999;137:555–574. Presentation at both the 71st American Heart Association, November, 1998, Dallas and presentation at the 48th Annual Scientific Session of the American College of Cardiology, March 1999, New Orleans.
Authors	Oesterle S, Sanborn T, et al.
Disease	Coronary artery disease, angina.
Purpose	To assess the efficacy of percutaneous myocardial revascularization (PMR) in patients with angina.
Design	Randomized, open label.
Patients	The first 75 patients were considered the rolling phase, during which the physicians were trained to use the device. Thereafter, 245 patients with stable angina despite medical therapy were randomized to PMR + medical therapy or to medical therapy alone. Patients should have been in Canadian Cardiovascular Society class 3–4, to have positive dipyridamole-thallium study, LVEF >30%, and not to be candidates for PTCA or CABG.
Treatment regimen	PMR was performed with the Cardiogenesis system, with a holmium: yttrium-aluminum-garnet laser.
Follow-up	12 months.

PACIFIC trial

Potential Angina Class Improvement From Intramyocardial Channels

(continued)

Results

Preliminary results were presented at the 71st American Heart Association meeting, November, 1998. Mean age of the patients was 60 years, 79% were men. In the PMR group, exercise time increased from 444 seconds at baseline to 538 seconds at 6 months, whereas in the medical therapy alone group exercise test did not change. ≥66% of the PMR patients experienced ≥2 Canadian Cardiovascular Society class improvement. After 3 months, ~75% of the PMR group were in Canadian Cardiovascular Society class 1 to 2. Mortality was 4% in the roll in phase and 7% in the randomized trial with no difference between the groups. There was no in-hospital mortality and there was only one patient with perforation requiring pericardiocentesis. There were 3 episodes of transient bradycardia, one patient needed permanent pacemaker, and one patient experienced ventricular tachycardia.

Update at the March 1999 American College of Cardiology Meeting described 221 randomized patients. Two-thirds of the PMR patients had improvement of anginal class to Class 1 or 2. Only 6% in the control group showed improvement in anginal class. At 6 months exercise tolerance was improved by 45% in the PMR group vs 5% in the control group.

Conclusions

PMR improved anginal symptoms and exercise tolerance. The preliminary results show that the procedure is safe.

VeGAS-2

Vein Graft Angiojet Study-2

Reference	Am Heart J 1999;137:555-574.
Disease	Coronary artery disease
Purpose	To compare intracoronary urokinase and mechanical thrombectomy for intracoronary thrombus.
Design	Randomized, multicenter.
Patients	349 patients with angiographically visible thrombus in a coronary artery >2.5 mm diameter. Patients with unstable angina or recent myocardial infarction were excluded.
Treatment regimen	Randomization to thrombectomy by AngioJet device or intracoronary urokinase (250 kU over 30 min, followed by 20-240 kU/h for 6-30 hours). All patients received aspirin and IV heparin.
Follow-up	30 days.

VeGAS-2

Vein Graft Angiojet Study-2

(continued)

Results	Preliminary results were presented at the 71st American Heart Association meeting by Ramee SR, et al, November, 1998. The trial was stopped prematurely because of a difference in safety, and slow enrollment. About 54% of patients had saphenous vein graft lesions. Procedural success was 72.7% with urokinase vs 86.3% with AngioJet ($p<0.05$). Device success was 75.8% with urokinase vs 87.4% with AngioJet ($p<0.05$). There were slightly more in-hospital adverse cardiac events (32.5% vs 13.9%), bleeding complications (11.8% vs 5.0%), and vascular complications (17.8% vs 4.4%) in the urokinase treated patients. The rates of the primary safety end point (30 day mortality, emergency CABG, myocardial infarction, or repeated target revascularization) occurred in similar rates in the AngioJet and urokinase groups.
Conclusions	AngioJet thrombectomy for thrombotic coronary lesions resulted in better procedural success rate, lower rates of major adverse cardiac events, less bleeding and vascular complications than intracoronary infusion of urokinase.

RRR

Reopro Readministration Registry

Reference	Am Heart J 1999;137:555-574.
Disease	Coronary artery disease.
Purpose	To evaluate the safety of readministration of abciximab (Reopro).
Design	Registry, multicenter.
Patients	576 patients that received ≥2 doses of abciximab at least 6 days apart.
Treatment regimen	Abciximab (Reopro).
Results	Preliminary results were presented at the 71st American Heart Association meeting by J.E.Tcheng, et al. November, 1998. 455 patients (91%) received 2 doses of abciximab, 35 patients (7%) received 3 doses, and 10 patients (2%) >3 doses. Angiographic success was 97.2% and did not differ in patients with multiple administrations of abciximab. There were no reports of mortality, allergic reactions, intracranial or retroperitoneal bleedings. Thrombocytopenia (<100,000 10^9/L) occurred in 4.4% of the patients, severe thrombocytopenia (<20,000 10^9/L) occurred in 2.2% of the patients. 20.2% of the patients developed new human antichimeric antibodies with readministration of abciximab. However, these antibodies do not appear to be associated with adverse outcome.
Conclusions	Readministration of abciximab appears to be safe. The agent does not seem to lose its efficacy with readministration. However, readministration of abciximab is associated with a moderate risk of thrombocytopenia that seems to be higher than the reported incidence in patients with first administration.

GUARDIAN

Guard During Ischemia Against Necrosis

Reference	Clin Cardiol 1999;22:369-372.
Disease	Coronary artery disease.
Purpose	To assess the efficacy of Cariporide, a Na+/H+ exchange inhibitor, in patients with acute ischemic syndromes and in patients scheduled for high risk PTCA or CABG.
Design	Randomized, placebo controlled, multicenter.
Patients	11,590 patients, mean age 64 years, 70% men, with acute coronary syndromes or candidates for high risk percutaneous trans-catheter interventions or CABG.
Treatment regimen	Randomization to IV placebo (n=2910) or to cariporide 20 mg tid (n=2909), cariporide 80 mg tid (n=2888), cariporide 120 mg tid (n=2883) for 2-7 days.
Follow-up	180 days.
Results	Preliminary results concerning 30 day outcome were presented at the 48th American College of Cardiology meeting, March, 1999, by P. Theroux. 36 day mortality was 13.4% in the placebo group, 13.5% in the cariporide 20 mg, 14.1% in the cariporide 80 mg, and 11.1% in the cariporide 120 mg group (p=NS). For the subgroup of patients referred for CABG, death or myocardial infarction occurred in 16.7% of the placebo group, 18.1% of the cariporide 20 mg, 18.2% of the cariporide 80 mg, and 12.8% of the cariporide 120 mg group (p=0.03 vs placebo).

GUARDIAN

Guard During Ischemia Against Necrosis

(continued)

Conclusions	Cariporide was ineffective in patients with unstable angina and in those scheduled for high risk percutaneous trancatheter interventions. Cariporide may reduce mortality and morbidity in patients scheduled for high risk CABG.

VIVA

Vascular Endothelial Growth Factor in Ischemia for Vascular Angiogenesis

Reference	Clin Cardiol 1999;22:369-372.
Disease	Angina pectoris.
Purpose	To assess the effects of VEGF (vascular endothelial growth factor) on exercise performance and angina in patients with angina pectoris unsuitable for revascularization.
Design	Randomized, placebo controlled, phase II.
Patients	178 patients with angina pectoris and abnormal nuclear perfusion stress test, who were unsuitable for revascularization.
Treatment regimen	Randomization to placebo or VEGF in low or high dose. Infusion was given intracoronary (placebo or VEGF 17 or 50 ng/kg/min) for 20 min, followed by 4 hours of IV infusion on day 3, 6, and 9.
Follow-up	120 days with repeated exercise tests.
Results	Preliminary results concerning 30 day outcome were presented at the 48th American College of Cardiology meeting, March, 1999, by TD Henry. At 60 days, exercise time improved in all three groups (43 seconds in the placebo, 26 seconds in the low-dose, and 32 seconds in the high dose VEGF group; p=NS). Similarly, angina improved by the same extent in all three groups. There were no differences in exercise time or anginal class among the groups. The VEGF was safe.
Conclusions	At 60 days, VEGF infusion did not improve exercise time or ameliorate the severity of angina compared to placebo.

BE SMART

BEStent in Small ARTeries

Reference	Presented at the 49th American College of Cardiology Meetings, Anaheim, CA, March 2000.
Disease	Coronary artery disease
Purpose	To assess whether stenting small coronary arteries will reduce restenosis rate.
Design	Randomized, open label.
Patients	381 patients, 30–80 years old, with symptomatic angina and with coronary artery disease, >50% diameter stenosis of de novo lesions in ≥1 native coronary arteries with <3.0 mm reference diameter, and lesion length 36–80 mm. Patients in whom >3 mm or a 2.75 mm compliant balloon was used for stent delivery were excluded. Patients with acute myocardial infarction, ostial or bifurcation lesions, left ventricular dysfunction and contraindication to ticlopidine were not included.
Follow-up	6 months.
Treatment regimen	All patients received heparin 80 u/kg before PTCA, and aspirin 100 mg/d and ticlopidine 500 mg/d for 1 month. Patients were randomized to PTCA alone or PTCA + Bestent. Stent was delivered on a 2.0–2.75 mm noncompliant balloon.

BE SMART

BEStent in Small ARTeries

(continued)

Results	Preliminary data were presented by R Koning at the 49th American College of Cardiology meeting, Anaheim, CA, in March 2000. The mean reference diameter in both groups before PTCA was 2.2 mm. Minimal luminal diameter after the procedure was larger in the stent group (2.08 mm) than in the PTCA group (1.72 mm; p=0.0001). Procedural success rate was 98.4% in the PTCA and 98.9% in the stent group. 24% of the PTCA assigned patients were crossed over to stenting, whereas 3% of the stent group underwent PTCA alone. In hospital complication rate was comparable between the groups. Occlusion of the target lesion during the initial hospitalization occurred in 1.6% in the PTCA group vs 1.0% in the stent group (p=NS). Myocardial infarction occurred in 4.8% in the PTCA group vs 3.6% in the stent group (p=NS). Six month restenosis rate was 48.5% in the PTCA group vs 22.7% in the stent group (relative risk 0.48; 95% CI 0.33-0.70; p<0.0001). Four patients in the PTCA group vs 1 in the stent group died during the first 6 months (p=NS). Myocardial infarction occurred in 2 vs 1 patient in the PTCA and stent group, respectively (p=NS). However, fewer patients in the stent group (13%) than in the PTCA group (25%) underwent target lesion revascularization (p=0.016).
Conclusions	Stenting of small coronary arteries is feasible, safe and was associated with better angiographic results and less restenosis at 6 months.

LONG WRIST

The Washington Radiation for In-Stent Restenosis Trial for Long Lesions

Reference	Presented at the 49th American College of Cardiology Meetings, Anaheim, CA, March 2000.
Disease	Coronary artery disease, in-stent restenosis.
Purpose	To analyze the efficacy and safety of brachytherapy with gamma radiation for diffuse long in-stent restenosis coronary lesions.
Design	Randomized, placebo controlled.
Patients	120 patients, 30–80 years old (mean 62 years), with a stent implanted in a native coronary artery, with diffuse in-stent restenosis and symptomatic angina. In the present study only patients with an arterial reference diameter of 3.0–5.0 mm, lesion length 36–80 mm and successful dilatation of the lesion by standard balloon angioplasty, rotational atherectomy, laser ablation, or restenting of the lesion were included. Patients with recent myocardial infarction (<72 hours), LVEF <20%, and prior irradiation of the chest or mediastinum were excluded.
Follow-up	6 months.
Treatment regimen	After successful PCI, a monorail closed end lumen catheter mounted on a guidewire was inserted over the lesion. The catheter contained varying length ribbons of Ir-192 radioactive seeds or placebo. The radiation doses delivered were 15 Gy at 2.4 mm from the center in vessels >4.0 mm and 14–15 Gy at 2 mm from the center of the source in vessels ≤4.0 mm.

The Washington Radiation for In-Stent Restenosis Trial for Long Lesions

(continued)

Results	Preliminary data were presented by R Waxman at the 49th American College of Cardiology meeting, Anaheim, CA, in March 2000. Of 60 patients randomized to placebo, 29 patients crossed over to irradiation. Before randomization, 68.3% of the Ir-192 and 66.7% of the placebo underwent rotational atherectomy, 18.3% and 18.3% underwent laser ablation, 10% and 11.7% underwent stent implantation alone, 1.7% and 3.3% underwent balloon angioplasty alone, and 71.7% and 58.3% had additional stent implantation (p=0.13). 6 month in-stent restenosis was 32% in the Ir-192 group vs 71% in the placebo group (p=0.0002). In-lesion restenosis occurred in 46% in the Ir-192 group vs 78% in the placebo group (p=0.001). Minimal luminal diameter at 6 months was 1.4 mm in the Ir-192 and 1.01 mm in the placebo group (p=0.0008). Late luminal diameter loss in the stent was 0.65 mm in the Ir-192 group and 1 mm in the placebo group (p=0.03). Late loss in the lesion was 0.6 mm in the Ir-192 group vs 0.85 mm in the placebo group (p=0.05). The "edge effect" was detected more often in the Ir-192 group (13.1%) than in the placebo group (6.6%; p=NS). Death occurred in 4.6% of the Ir-192 group vs 6.1% of the placebo group (p=1.0), Q wave myocardial infarction in 8.3% vs 0% (p=0.06). 26.7% of the Ir-192 group vs 55.0% of the placebo group underwent repeated PTCA (p=0.001), whereas 30% vs 60%, respectively, underwent target lesion revascularization (p=0.001) and 33.3% vs 60.7% underwent target vessel revascularization (p=0.003). Major adverse cardiac events occurred in 38.3% in the Ir-192 group vs 61.7% in the placebo group (p=0.01). Subacute thrombosis occurred more often in the Ir-192 group (4.6% vs 1.7%). Moreover, late thrombotic events (between 30 days and 6 months) occurred more often in the Ir-192 group (11.7% vs 5%). Late total reocclusion rate was 15% in the Ir-192 group and 6.7% in the placebo group.

LONG WRIST

The Washington Radiation for In-Stent Restenosis Trial for Long Lesions

(continued)

Comments	Intracoronary gamma radiation for diffuse long in-stent restenosis was associated with reduced rate of restenosis at 6 months, less rates of target vessel and target lesion revascularization and major adverse cardiac events, but with an increased risk of subacute and late thrombotic occlusions.

ESPRIT

Enhanced Suppression of the Platelet IIb/IIIa Receptor with Integrilin Therapy

Reference	Presented at the 49th American College of Cardiology Meetings, Anaheim, CA, March 2000.
Disease	Coronary artery disease, stent.
Purpose	To evaluate the safety and efficacy of eptifibatide, a glycoprotein IIb/IIIa inhibitor in elective intracoronary stent implantation.
Design	Randomized, double blind, placebo controlled, multicenter.
Patients	2064 patients (mean age 62±11 years) undergoing elective percutaneous coronary intervention (PCI) with stenting of a native coronary artery. Patients with acute myocardial infarction, unstable angina and current or planned use of GP IIb/IIIa inhibitors were excluded.
Follow-up	One year.
Treatment regimen	All patients received aspirin and a thienopyridine, started before procedure, and bolus heparin 60 U/kg just before procedure. Patients were randomized to placebo (n=1024) or eptifibatide (n=1040), started immediately before PCI. Eptifibatide was administered as two 180 μg/kg boluses, 10 minutes apart and a 2 μg/kg/minutes infusion for 18-24 hours.

Results

Preliminary data concerning outcome at 48 hours were presented by J Tcheng at the 49th American College of Cardiology meeting, Anaheim, CA, in March 2000. The study was terminated early by the Data and Safety Monitoring Committee. 98.6% of the eptifibatide group and 99.1% of the placebo group underwent PCI, and 94.8% and 97.4% received stents. Median duration of Integrilin infusion was 18 hours. The primary end point of death, myocardial infarction, urgent target vessel revascularization, or bailout GP IIb/IIIa use within the first 48 hours occurred in 6.6% of the eptifibatide group vs 10.5% of the placebo group (37% risk reduction; p=0.0015). Death, myocardial infarction or urgent target vessel revascularization occurred in 6.0% vs 9.3% (35% risk reduction; p=0.0045). Death and myocardial infarction occurred in 5.4% vs 9.2% (40% risk reduction; p=0.0013). Death and large myocardial infarction (CK MB >5X upper limit of normal) occurred in 3.4% vs 5.1% (33% risk reduction; p=0.053). Myocardial infarction occurred in 5.4% vs 9.0% (40% risk reduction; p=0.0015). 48 hour mortality was 0.1% vs 0.2% (50% risk reduction; p=NS). Subgroup analysis showed that eptifibatide was beneficial in patients who received stents, in patients with diabetes (42% relative risk reduction; p=NS), women (56% relative risk reduction; p=0.001), and in all range of ACT. Major bleeding was detected in 1.4% in the eptifibatide group vs 0.4% in the placebo group, minor bleeding in 2.8% vs 1.8% . Most of the bleeding events were related to the groin access site. Intracranial hemorrhage occurred in 0.2% in the eptifibatide group vs 0.1% in the placebo group. Thrombocytopenia occurred in 0.2% vs 0%, respectively, and 1.4% and 1.0% of the patients, respectively needed blood transfusion.

Comments

Eptifibatide infusion was associated with a significant reduction of risk of major adverse cardiac events within 48 hours after elective intracoronary stent implantation. Eptifibatide was associated with a slight excess of bleeding, mostly related to the groin access site.

ARTS

Arterial Revascularization Therapy Study

Reference	1. Semin Interv Cardiol 1999;4:209–219. 2. Clin Cardiol 1999;22:47–49. 3. Circulation 1999;99:2486–2491. 4. Clin Cardiol 1999;22:753–756.
Disease	Coronary artery disease.
Purpose	To compare coronary stenting with CABG in patients with multivessel coronary artery disease eligible for either procedure.
Design	Randomized, multicenter.
Patients	1205 patients (average age 61 years) with multivessel coronary artery disease, suitable for both CABG and PTCA.
Treatment regimen	Randomization to CABG or stenting (Cordis Palmaz-Schatz CROWN or CrossFlex).
Follow-up	1 year.

Results	Preliminary results concerning 30 day outcome were presented at the 71st American Heart Association meeting, November, 1998, and 1 year outcome at the 21st Congress of the European Society of Cardiology, Barcelona, Spain, by PW Serruys. The average time to treatment was 27 days for CABG and 11 days for stenting. The average procedure time was 4 hours and 1.5 hours, respectively. The average hospitalization for the CABG patients was 11.3 days and for the stent patients 3.4 days. In both groups an average of 2.7 lesions were treated. According to randomization treatment was successful in 96% of the CABG and in 97% of the stent groups. 19 patients (2.2%), assigned to stent, crossed over to CABG and 21 patients, assigned to CABG, crossed over to stenting. Combined end point of death, disabling stroke, or acute myocardial infarction occurred in 6.0% of the CABG vs 5.0% of the stent group at 30 days. The primary end point (death, stroke, myocardial infarction, or revascularization) at 30 days occurred in 8.7% of the stent group vs 6.8% of the CABG group (p=NS). After one year, the stent assigned patients underwent more re-interventions (4.7% CABG, 12.2% repeated PTCA) than the CABG assigned patients (0.5% CABG, 3.0% PTCA). 87.8% of the CABG patients vs 73.7% of the stent patients were event free at one year. The initial procedure was more expensive with CABG ($11,300) than with stenting ($6800). However, total follow-up costs were lower for the CABG ($3054) than for stenting ($4435). Overall, the total costs were $3100 higher for CABG than for stenting.
Conclusions	There were no significant differences between the groups in the primary end point. Patients in the stent arm needed more revascularization. However, the rehabilitation time was shorter.

Beta Intracoronary Irradiation for the Prevention of Restenosis

Reference	Clin Cardiol 1999;22:753-756.
Disease	Coronary artery disease.
Purpose	To assess the effect of 9, 12, 15, and 18 Gy of intracoronary ß irradiation on the prevention of restenosis after PTCA.
Design	Randomized.
Patients	180 patients, ≥50 years old, with angina pectoris or silent angina and a single de novo lesion <15 mm long and a reference vessel diameter of 2.5-4.0 mm.
Treatment regimen	Randomization to intracoronary ß irradiation using 9, 12, 15, or 18 Gy. Stents were used only after irradiation in cases with sub-optimal initial results with PTCA (28% of the patients).
Follow-up	Repeated coronary angiography at 6 months.

Beta Intracoronary Irradiation for the Prevention of Restenosis

(continued)

Results	Preliminary results were presented at the 21st Congress of the European Society of Cardiology, Barcelona, Spain, by V Verin. 154 patients underwent follow-up angiography. Among patients receiving the 18 Gy dose mean minimal luminal diameter was 2.09 mm compared to those who received the 9 Gy dose (1.68 mm). Restenosis occurred in 8.3% in the high dose (18 Gy) irradiation vs 27.6% in the low dose (9 Gy) irradiation. Late luminal diameter loss was higher in the 9 Gy group (0.35 mm) than in the 18 Gy group (0.09 mm). Among the 116 patients who underwent balloon angioplasty and irradiation without stent implantation, minimal luminal diameter was 2.14 mm vs 1.67 mm in the 18 Gy and 9 Gy groups, respectively, and late luminal diameter loss was -0.03 mm vs 0.33 mm, respectively. Major cardiac events were comparable among the groups; six patients in the 9 Gy group vs only 3 patients in the other 3 groups.
Conclusions	ß-irradiation was safe and reduced restenosis after PTCA.

BAAS

Balloon Angioplasty and Anticoagulation Study

Reference	Presented at the 21st Congress of the European Society of Cardiology, Barcelona, Spain, 1999.
Disease	Coronary artery disease, PTCA.
Purpose	To compare the efficacy of aspirin alone to a combination of aspirin and warfarin before PTCA.
Design	Randomized, open label, multicenter.
Patients	1058 patients, mean age 60 years, undergoing PTCA
Treatment regimen	Randomization to aspirin alone or aspirin + Coumadin.
Follow-up	One year.

Balloon Angioplasty and Anticoagulation Study (continued)

Results	Preliminary results were presented at the 21st Congress of the European Society of Cardiology, Barcelona, Spain, by JM Ten Berg. The warfarin + aspirin group had lower rate of acute myocardial infarction (2.6% vs 4.0%). Acute re-intervention by PTCA was less often needed in the warfarin + aspirin group (2.5% vs 4.4%). 0.6% of the patients in both groups underwent urgent CABG within the first 30 days. Less patients in the warfarin + aspirin group underwent target lesion revascularization (10.6% vs 14.3%). The combined cardiovascular end point was reached by 6.4% of the patients in the aspirin group vs 3.4% of the patients in the warfarin + aspirin group within 30 days (relative risk 0.53). The combined end point was reached by 15.1% vs 11.6% of the patients after one year, respectively (p=NS). One year event free survival was 86% in the warfarin + aspirin group vs 80% in the aspirin group (relative risk=0.71). There were 7 major bleedings during hospitalization in the warfarin + aspirin group vs only one in the aspirin group. There were 10 pseudoaneurysms in the warfarin + aspirin group vs 4 in the aspirin group.
Conclusions	The combination of warfarin and aspirin was associated with lower incidence of myocardial infarction and need for revascularization than aspirin alone in patients undergoing PTCA.

PRESTO

Prevention of REStenosis with Tranilast and its Outcomes

Reference	Am Heart J 2000;139:23-31.
Disease	Coronary artery disease, PCI.
Purpose	To assess the effects of tranilast, a drug that interferes with proliferation and migration of vascular medial smooth muscle cells, on the composite clinical event rate and on restenosis after percutaneous coronary intervention (PCI).
Design	Randomized, placebo controlled, multicenter.
Patients	The study will enroll 11,500 patients, >18 years old, undergoing successful elective or emergency PCI. Patients using oral anticoagulants, phenytoin or investigational drugs, and patients with non Q wave myocardial infarction within 48 hours before enrollment, PCI in the previous 3 months, chronic liver disease, renal impairment, gout, anemia, severe concomitant disease and a history of contrast media induced nephrotoxicity will be excluded.
Treatment regimen	Randomization to 1 of 5 treatment groups: 1) 3 months placebo bid; 2) 3 months tranilast 300 mg bid; 3) 3 months tranilast 450 mg bid; 4) 1 month tranilast 300 mg bid and then placebo bid for 2 months; or 5) 1 month tranilast 450 mg bid and then placebo bid for 2 months. All noninvestigational PCI (directional atherectomy, rotational atherectomy, laser ablation, and stents) are permitted.
Follow-up	9 months. A subgroup of the patients will undergo coronary angiography at 9 months.
Results	Not yet available.
Conclusions	Not yet available.

BENESTENT (Update)

Belgium Netherlands Stent

Title	Belgium Netherlands Stent.
Reference	Presented at the 1999 TCT Symposium.
Diseas	Coronary artery disease.
Purpose	To compare Palmaz-Schatz (Cordis) stent implantation and ultrasound directed stent placement with balloon angioplasty in patients with stable angina.
Design	Randomized, multicenter.
Patients	800 patients with stable angina pectoris and single de novo lesion amenable to percutaneous intervention.
Treatment regimen	Palmaz-Schatz (Cordis) stent with ultrasound directed stent placement vs percutaneous transluminal coronary angioplasty.
Results	Ultrasound directed stenting resulted in better acute stent dimensions and did not increase complications. The incidence of target lesion resvascularization at 12 months was 8.4% in stent with ultrasound group vs 12.4% with angioplasty group.
Conclusions	Elective stenting with ultrasound guidance is safe and effective.

GAMMA-1

Intracoronary Gamma radiation for in-stent restenosis

Title	Intracoronary gamma radiation to reduce in-stent restenosis: The multicenter gamma-1 randomized clinical trial.
Authors	Leon MB, Teirstein PS, Lansky AJ, et al.
Reference	Presented at the American College of Cardiology Interventional Symposium, March 1999, New Orleans, LA.
Disease	Coronary artery disease.
Purpose	To determine the effect of gamma radiation, using source ribbons containing 192-Ir radioactive seeds, in patients with in-stent restenosis of native coronary arteries.
Design	Placebo, controlled, multicenter.
Patients	252 patients with in-stent restenosis of native coronaries.
Follow-up	Data presented at 6 months.
Treatment regimen	In-stent stenosis was treated with PTCA, atheroablation, and/or additional stents. Then either 192-Ir seeds or placebo seeds were delivered into the stented segment. Dosimetry calculations based on intravascular ultrasound measurements. Mean dwell time was just over 20 minutes.
Additional therapy	Ticlopidine and aspirin.

GAMMA-1

Intracoronary Gamma radiation for in-stent restenosis

(continued)

Results	Diameter stenosis was 6% for 192 Ir and 9% for patients receiving placebo. Quantitative coronary angiography revealed that radiation reduced restenosis compared to placebo (by 58%) as well as in-stent restenosis (by 43%). In-hospital clinical events were infrequent in both groups (3.4% for placebo and 1.5% for 192-Ir). There were 3 in-hospital stent closures in the placebo patients, but none in the radiated patients.
Conclusions	Intracoronary gamma radiation reduced in-stent restenosis.

START (ß-radiation)

SR-90 Treatment of Angiographic Restenosis Trial

Title	Late clinical and angiographic outcomes after use of Sr/Y ß radiation for the treatment of in-stent restenosis: Results from the START trial.
Authors	Popma JJ, et al.
Reference	Presented at the American College of Cardiology Scientific Sessions, Anaheim, CA, March, 2000.
Disease	Coronary artery disease.
Purpose	To determine efficacy and safety of brachytherapy with strontium-90 ß irradiation in patients with in-stent restenosis.
Design	Randomized.
Patients	476 patients with single lesion/single vessel disease in a native coronary artery with in-stent restenosis of >50% in which target lesions could be treated with a 20 mm angioplasty balloon.
Follow-up	8 months.
Treatment regimen	Strontium - 90 ß radiation vs placebo. Treatment durations were 3–5 minutes.
Additional therapy	Ticlopidine or clopidogrel.

START (ß-radiation)

SR-90 Treatment of Angiographic Restenosis Trial

(continued)

Results	Procedural success of stenting was 97% for both groups with an average length of stented segment of 22 mm. The primary end point was target vessel revascularization at 8 months which occurred in 16% of patients receiving ß radiation and 24% of the control group, which was a significant difference. There was a significantly lower rate of restenosis in the radiation group (24.1%) vs the placebo group (46%). The radiation group demonstrated a 31% reduction in major adverse cardiac events. There was no difference in mortality between the radiation group (1.2%) vs the placebo group (0.4%). There was no occurrence of delayed thrombosis with brachytherapy.
Conclusions	ß radiation in the management of in-stent restenosis decreases the need for target vessel revascularization and reduces the rate of major adverse cardiac events.

13. Preliminary Reports

h. Lipid Lowering Studies

MIRACL

Myocardial Ischemia Reduction With Aggressive Cholesterol Lowering

Reference	Am J Cardiol 1998;81:578-581.
Disease	Non Q wave myocardial infarction, unstable angina, hypercholesterolemia.
Purpose	To assess whether early intensive reduction in serum total and LDL cholesterol will reduce subsequent recurrent ischemia in patients presenting with unstable angina or non Q wave myocardial infarction.
Design	Randomized, double blind, placebo controlled, multicenter.
Patients	2100 patients, ≥18 years old, with unstable angina or non Q wave myocardial infarction. Patients are randomized 24 96 h after admission. Patients with serum total cholesterol >270 mg/dL; those who are scheduled for coronary intervention during the index hospitalization; CABG within 3 months; PTCA within 6 months; Q wave myocardial infarction within 4 weeks; left bundle branch block; life threatening arrhythmias; severe heart failure; hepatic dysfunction or renal failure requiring dialysis; uncontrolled diabetes; concurrent therapy with lipid altering drugs, immunosuppressive agents, erythromycin, or azole antifungals; pregnancy or lactation are excluded.
Follow-up	16 weeks.
Treatment regimen	Randomization to atorvastatin 80 mg/d or placebo.
Remarks	Results are not available yet.

BIP

Bezafibrate Infarction Prevention Study

Reference	Eur Heart J 1999;20:7–10.
Disease	Coronary artery disease.
Purpose	To assess the effects of bezafibrate on the incidence of coronary events in patients with coronary artery disease.
Design	Randomized, placebo controlled, multicenter.
Patients	3122 patients with ischemic heart disease and total cholesterol levels between 180–250 mg/dL, triglycerides levels ≤300 mg/dL, and HDL cholesterol ≤45 mg/dL.
Follow-up	Mean 6.2 years.
Treatment regimen	Randomization to bezafibrate 400 mg/d or placebo.
Results	Results were presented at the 20th Congress of the European Society of Cardiology, Aug 1998, by E. Kaplinski. Compared with placebo, the bezafibrate group had an increase in HDL cholesterol by 12%, a decrease in triglycerides by 22%, a decrease in fibrinogen by 9%, a decrease in total cholesterol by 4%, and a decrease in LDL cholesterol by 5%. The primary end point (myocardial infarction and sudden cardiac death) was not different between the 2 groups. Post hoc analysis showed that bezafibrate reduced the occurrence of the primary end point by 40% (p=0.03) only in patients with triglycerides ≥200 mg/dL.
Conclusions	Bezafibrate was not effective in reducing mortality and morbidity in low risk patients with ischemic heart disease.

GISSI Prevention trial-pravastatin arm

Reference	Eur Heart J 1999;20:7-10.
Disease	Coronary artery disease
Purpose	To assess whether low dose pravastatin will reduce mortality and morbidity in patients with recent (<6 months) myocardial infarction and total cholesterol 200-250 mg/dL.
Design	Randomized, open label, multicenter.
Patients	4280 patients with recent (<6 months) myocardial infarction and serum total cholesterol 200-250 mg/dL.
Follow-up	Mean 22 months.
Treatment regimen	Randomization to pravastatin 20 mg/d or no pravastatin.
Results	Results were presented at the 20th Congress of the European Society of Cardiology, Aug 1998 by R. Marchioli. The trial was stopped prematurely after publication of the results of the CARE trial. Pravastatin was associated with 13% decrease in total cholesterol, 19% decrease in LDL cholesterol, 8% decrease in triglycerides, and 4% increase in HDL cholesterol. The primary end point (death, stroke, and myocardial infarction) occurred in 5.4% of the pravastatin group vs in 6.0% of the control group (relative risk 0.91; 95% CI 0.71-1.17; p=0.45). 3.9% of the controls and 3.2% of the pravastatin group died (relative risk 0.84; 95% CI 0.61-1.15; p=0.27).
Conclusions	Low dose (20 mg/d) pravastatin therapy over 22 months was not associated with reduced mortality and morbidity in patients with recent myocardial infarction and serum cholesterol 200-250 mg.

Reference	Eur Heart J 1999;20:725-741.
Disease	Coronary artery disease.
Purpose	To investigate the effects of cholesterol lowering therapy and of antioxidant vitamin supplementation on mortality and morbidity of patients at high risk of coronary artery disease.
Design	Randomized, 2X2 factorial, placebo controlled, multicenter.
Patients	20,536 patients, 40-80 years old with an increase risk of coronary heart disease.
Treatment regimen	Randomization in a 2X2 factorial design to simvastatin 40 mg/d or placebo and to antioxidant vitamins (600 mg vitamin E, 250 mg vitamin C and 20 mg ß-carotene/d) or placebo.
Follow-up	>5 years.
Results	During an average follow-up of 25 months (range 13-47 months) side effects were comparable among the 4 groups. Compliance after 30 months was 81%. Simvastatin reduced total cholesterol by 1.5-1.6 mmol/L and LDL cholesterol by 1.1-1.2 mmol/L.
Conclusions	The estimated annual rate of all cause mortality is 2.2%, cancer 1.4%, stroke 1.3%, and myocardial infarction or fatal coronary heart disease 2.4%.

4D Study

Determination of cardiovascular end points in NIDDM dialysis patients

Title	Determination of cardiovascular end points in NIDDM (noninsulin dependent diabetes mellitus) patients.
Reference	Kidney International 1999;56(suppl 71):222-226.
Disease	NIDDM endstage renal disease.
Purpose	To assess whether treatment with atorvastatin will reduce cardiovascular mortality and nonfatal myocardial infarction.
Design	Randomized, double blind, placebo controlled, multicenter.
Patients	1200 patients, aged 18-80 years, diabetes type 2, enrollment within 24 months after start of chronic hemodialysis, LDL cholesterol 80-190 mg/dL. Patients with a cardiovascular event within 3 months, excluded.
Follow-up	4 years.
Treatment regimen	Atorvastatin 20 mg daily vs placebo.
Results	Results pending.

TNT

Treating to New Targets

Disease	Coronary artery disease.
Purpose	To assess whether aggressive lowering LDL cholesterol levels to 75 mg/dL with atorvastatin 80 mg/d is associated with additional benefit over the currently recommended level of 100 mg/dL.
Design	Randomized, double blind, multicenter.
Patients	Will recruit 8600 patients, 35–75 years old, with major coronary event in the previous 5 years and LDL cholesterol 130–250 mg/dL, and triglyceride <600 mg/dL.
Treatment regimen	Patients will be recruited to an 8 weeks open label run-in phase of atorvastatin 10 mg/dL. Those who achieve LDL cholesterol <130 mg/dL will be randomized to atorvastatin 10 mg/d or 80 mg/d.
Follow-up	5 years.
Results	Not yet available.
Conclusions	Not yet available.

IDEAL

Incremental Decrease in End points through Aggressive Lipid lowering

Disease	Coronary artery disease.
Purpose	To evaluate the effects on coronary heart disease mortality and morbidity of aggressive lipid lowering regimen with atorvastatin vs a conventional lipid lowering regimen with simvastatin.
Design	Randomized, parallel groups, PROBE, multicenter.
Patients	Will recruit 7600 patients, <78 years old, with current or prior myocardial infarction.
Treatment regimen	Randomization to atorvastatin 80 mg/d or to simvastatin 20–40 mg/d.
Follow-up	5.5 years or 1880 events.
Results	Not yet available.
Conclusions	Not yet available.

ALLIANCE

Aggressive Lipid Lowering Initiation Abates New Cardiac Events

Disease	Coronary artery disease.
Purpose	To compare the effects of aggressive lipid lowering regimen with atorvastatin vs conventional care in patients after myocardial infarction.
Design	Randomized, open label, multicenter.
Patients	2443 patients, 18–75 years old, with a history of coronary artery disease and LDL cholesterol 130–250 mg/dL.
Treatment regimen	Randomization to usual care or to atorvastatin 10–80 mg/d.
Follow-up	4 years.
Results	Not yet available.
Conclusions	Not yet available.

SPARCL

Stroke Prevention by Aggressive Reduction in Cholesterol Levels

Disease	Stroke/TIA.
Purpose	To assess whether aggressive lipid lowering strategy with atorvastatin will reduce the incidence of stroke in patients without coronary heart disease.
Design	Randomized, double blind, placebo controlled, multicenter.
Patients	Will recruit 4200 patients, ≥18 years old, with a stroke or TIA within 1-6 months prior to enrollment and LDL cholesterol 100-190 mg/dL. Patients with a history of coronary artery disease and/or prior endarterectomy in the preceding month will be excluded.
Treatment regimen	Randomization to placebo or atorvastatin 80 mg/d.
Follow-up	5 years.
Results	Not yet available.
Conclusions	Not yet available.

CARDS

Collaborative Atorvastatin Diabetes Study

Disease	Diabetes mellitus type 2.
Purpose	To assess whether aggressive lipid lowering strategy with atorvastatin will reduce ischemic events in patients with type 2 diabetes mellitus.
Design	Randomized, double blind, placebo controlled, multicenter.
Patients	Will recruit 1820 patients, 40–75 years old, with type 2 diabetes mellitus, no prior myocardial infarction, LDL cholesterol ≤160 mg/dL and triglyceride ≤600 mg/dL, and ≥1 of the following risk factors: retinopathy, albuminuria, current smoking, or hypertension.
Treatment regimen	Randomization to atorvastatin 10 mg/d or to placebo.
Follow-up	4 years.
Results	Not yet available.
Conclusions	Not yet available.

ASPEN

Atorvastatin Study for the Prevention of coronary heart disease End point in Noninsulin dependent diabetes mellitus patients

Disease	Diabetes mellitus type 2.
Purpose	To assess whether aggressive lipid lowering strategy with atorvastatin will reduce ischemic events in patients with type 2 diabetes mellitus.
Design	Randomized, double blind, placebo controlled, multicenter.
Patients	Will recruit 2250 patients with type 2 diabetes mellitus and either: 1) no prior myocardial infarction, LDL cholesterol ≤160 mg/dL, and triglyceride ≤600 mg/dL; or 2) prior myocardial infarction and LDL cholesterol ≤140 mg/dL and triglyceride ≤600 mg/dL.
Treatment regimen	Randomization to atorvastatin 10 mg/d or to placebo.
Follow-up	4 years.
Results	Not yet available.
Conclusions	Not yet available.

REVERSAL

REVERSal of Atherosclerosis with Lipitor

Disease	Atherosclerosis, coronary artery disease.
Purpose	To evaluate whether aggressive lipid lowering with atorvastatin will result in regression of coronary artery disease.
Design	Randomized, double blind, multicenter.
Patients	600 patients, 30–75 years old, with a history of coronary artery disease.
Treatment regimen	Randomization to pravastatin 40 mg/d or atorvastatin 80 mg/d.
Follow-up	Intravascular ultrasound at baseline and after18 months.
Results	Not yet available.
Conclusions	Not yet available.

BELLES

Beyond Endorsed Lipid Levels Evaluation Study

Disease	Coronary artery disease.
Purpose	To assess whether aggressive lipid lowering with atorvastatin produces regression of coronary atherosclerosis beyond that shown with conventional lipid lowering strategy in postmenopausal women.
Design	Randomized, double blind, multicenter.
Patients	600 post menopausal women.
Treatment regimen	Randomization to atorvastatin 80 mg/d or to pravastatin 40 mg/d.
Follow-up	Electron beam computerized tomography (EBCT) at baseline and after 12 months.
Results	Not yet available.
Conclusions	Not yet available.

13. Preliminary Reports

i. Valvular Heart Disease

The VA randomized Trial of Valvular Heart Disease Outcomes 15 Years After Valve Replacement With a Mechanical Vs Bioprosthetic Valve

Reference	Presented at the 49th American College of Cardiology Meetings, Anaheim, CA, March 2000. J Am Coll Cardiol 2000;36:323-324.
Disease	Valvular heart disease.
Purpose	To compare the long term results of bioprosthetic (Hancock porcine heterograft) valves and mechanical (Bjork-Shiley spherical disc) valves.
Design	Randomized, multicenter.
Patients	575 patients with valvular heart disease who were randomized to a mechanical or bioprosthetic valves in either the aortic position (n=394) or the mitral position (n=181).
Follow-up	15 years.

The VA randomized Trial of Valvular Heart Disease Outcomes 15 Years After Valve Replacement With a Mechanical Vs Bioprosthetic Valve

(continued)

Results

Preliminary data were presented by SH Rahimtoola at the 49th American College of Cardiology meeting, Anaheim, CA, in March 2000. Complete follow-up was available in 97% of the patients. Among patients who underwent mitral valve replacement, 15-year mortality was comparable between those who had received bioprosthetic valve (79%) or mechanical valve (81%). Among patients who underwent aortic valve replacement, mortality was 66% in those who had received mechanical valves vs 79% in patients with bioprosthetic valves ($p=0.02$). The difference favoring mechanical valves in the aortic position was apparent only after the first 10 years of follow-up. Rate of primary valve failure was increased with bioprosthesis; 0% for mechanical valves and 23% for bioprosthetic valves for aortic valve replacement ($p=0.0001$); 5% for mechanical valves and 44% for bioprosthetic valves for mitral valve replacement ($p=0.0002$). After 15 years bioprosthetic valve failure was detected in >40% of the mitral valves vs only 23% of the aortic valves. Age was a major determinant of bioprosthetic aortic valve failure, with failure in 26% in the patients <65 years old and 9% in the patients ≥65 years old. There were no significant differences between bioprosthetic and mechanical valves for valve thrombosis, endocarditis, systemic embolism, or any valve related complication. Bleeding complications were more common in patients randomised to mechanical valves.

Comments

Mechanical valves in the aortic position were associated with lower mortality and nearly no primary valve failure. The differences in outcome became apparent only 10 years after valve replacement. Primary valve failure is frequent with bioprosthetic valves after 15 years. Patients younger than 65 years have a higher rate of primary valve failure with bioprosthetic valves, especially in the aortic position, than patients >65 years.

INDEX

A

B

C

D

E

F

G

H

I

P

Q

R

S

U

V

W

X

Send for your copies now!

Send to:
Le Jacq Communications, Inc.,
777 West Putnam Avenue,
Greenwich, CT, 06830

Phone 203-531-0450
FAX 203-531-0533

Also available on www.amazon.com
www.borders.com
www.barnesandnoble.com

- ❑ The Beta Virus
  Price $9.00
- ❑ Mind Cure
  Price $12.00
- ❑ The Guide to Cardiology
  Third Edition
  Price $68.00

- ❑ Check enclosed (publisher pays shipping)
- ❑ Bill me (add $5.00 shipping charge)

Name______________________________

Organization______________________________

Address______________________________

City______________________ State__________ Zip__________

NOTES

NOTES

(continued)

NOTES

(continued)

NOTES

(continued)

NOTES

(continued)

NOTES

(continued)

NOTES

(continued)